NORMAL FAMILY PROCESSES

Second Edition

THE GUILFORD FAMILY THERAPY SERIES
Alan S. Gurman, *Series Editor*

Recent volumes

NORMAL FAMILY PROCESSES

SECOND EDITION

EDITED BY
Froma Walsh

FOREWORD BY
Lyman C. Wynne

THE GUILFORD PRESS
New York/London

*To the ordinary and extraordinary families
everywhere, from whom we have so much to learn about
normal family processes.*

*And to my own family,
whose love and vitality, even in the midst
of adversity, have inspired this work.*

© 1993 The Guilford Press
A Division of Guilford Publications, Inc.
72 Spring Street, New York, NY 10012

Printed in the United States of America

This book is printed on acid-free paper.

Last digit is print number: 9 8 7 6 5 4 3 2

Library of Congress Cataloging-in-Publication Data
Normal family processes/edited by Froma Walsh.—2nd ed.
     p. cm.—(The Guilford family therapy series)
   Includes bibliographical references and index.
   ISBN 0–89862–090–2
   1. Family—Research. 2. Family assessment. I. Walsh, Froma.
II. Series.
   [DNLM: 1. Family Therapy. 2. Family. WM 430.5.F2 N842 1993]
HQ728.N83   1993
306.85—dc20
DNLM/DLC
for Library of Congress   93-1577
                                    CIP

CONTRIBUTORS

Carol Anderson, PhD, University of Pittsburgh, Department of Psychiatry, University of Pittsburgh Medical Center, Pittsburgh, Pennsylvania

Sherry Anderson, MSW, Family Connections, Three Rivers Adoption Council, Pittsburgh, Pennsylvania

W. Robert Beavers, MD, Department of Psychiatry, University of Texas Southwestern Medical Center, Dallas, Texas

Duane Bishop, MD, Department of Psychiatry and Human Behavior, Brown University, Providence, Rhode Island

Nancy Boyd-Franklin, PhD, Rutgers University, Graduate School of Applied and Professional Psychology, New Brunswick, New Jersey

Danielle A. Bussell, PhD, Center for Family Research, George Washington University, Washington, DC

Betty Carter, MSW, Family Institute of Westchester, Westchester, New York

Barbara Ellman, MSW, Private Practice, Houston, Texas

Nathan B. Epstein, MD, Department of Psychiatry and Human Behavior, Brown University, Providence, Rhode Island

Robert B. Hampson, PhD, Department of Psychology, Southern Methodist University, Dallas, Texas

Ann Hartman, DSW, Smith College School for Social Work, Northampton, Massachusetts

Marsha Heiman, Family Institute of New Jersey, Metuchen, New Jersey

E. Mavis Hetherington, PhD, Department of Psychology, University of Virginia, Charlottesville, Virginia

Diane Hughes, PhD, Department of Psychology, New York University, New York, New York

Gabor Keitner, PhD, Department of Psychiatry and Human Behavior, Brown University, Providence, Rhode Island

Joan Laird, MS, Smith College School for Social Work, Northampton, Massachusetts

Tracy C. Law, MA, Department of Psychology, University of Virginia, Charlottesville, Virginia

Monica McGoldrick, MSW, Family Institute of New Jersey, Metuchen, New Jersey

Ivan Miller, PhD, Department of Psychiatry and Human Behavior, Brown University, Providence, Rhode Island

Thomas G. O'Connor, MA, Department of Psychology, University of Virginia, Charlottesville, Virginia

David H. Olson, PhD, University of Minnesota, St. Paul, Minnesota

Maria Piantanida, PhD, Quality Learning Systems, Pittsurgh, Pennsylvania

Chaya S. Piotrkowski, PhD, NCJW Center for the Child, New York, New York

David Reiss, MD, Center for Family Research, George Washington University, Washington, DC

John S. Rolland, MD, Department of Psychiatry and Center for Family Health, University of Chicago, Chicago, Illinois

Christine Ryan, PhD, Department of Psychiatry and Human Behavior, Brown University, Providence, Rhode Island

Morris Taggart, PhD, Private Practice, Houston, Texas

Emily B. Visher, PhD, California School of Professional Psychology, Alameda, California

John S. Visher, MD, Department of Psychiatry, Stanford University School of Medicine, Stanford, California

Froma Walsh, PhD, School of Social Service Administration, Department of Psychiatry, and Center for Family Health, The University of Chicago, Chicago, Illinois

Lyman C. Wynne, MD, PhD, Department of Psychiatry, University of Rochester School of Medicine and Dentistry, Rochester, New York

FOREWORD

The second edition of *Normal Family Processes* marks a transition point in the developmental history of the field of family therapy. In 1982, the first edition proclaimed that the field was emerging from the cocoon of preoccupied concern with dysfunction. While the evidence in that volume showed that the field was struggling valiantly to spread its wings, we are now presented with a more complete transformation. This volume provides a new level of clinically relevant and conceptually clear exposition about normal family processes than has heretofore been available.

The difficulty in thinking about "normality" that has afflicted psychology and psychiatry of the individual is exponentially compounded in the family field by the tremendous diversity of family forms and relevant contexts. Froma Walsh's comprehensive overview surveys and elucidates the scope of these issues. Subsequent chapters then do not constitute a fruitless effort to cover all conceivable aspects of family diversity. Instead, and more sensibly, certain key family forms and contexts are discussed in detail that should be sufficient to give readers a template for their own observations and formulations.

I expect that this volume will go a long way toward resolving the ambivalence that family clinicians have persistently harbored about "normality." My own attitudes about this topic were shaped—but not resolved—by a series of discussions with Carl Whitaker beginning about 1968. We both had been observing some "normal" families with schizophrenic members and some seemingly more "deviant" families that appeared to have a positive potential for growth. Further complicating these observations was our notion that to be "normal," you have to be a little crazy.

Subsequently, our "qualitative research" on normal, healthy families only confirmed our ambivalence and confusion about the topic. During a visit with me at NIMH in October, 1969, we planned that Carl would interview and I would observe a normal family in order to help us learn something more about this mysterious species. Unfortunately, we were unable to find such a family, so Carl interviewed the Wynnes instead. This was illuminating, at least for the Wynnes, and led us to pursue the topic by suggesting that the American Psychiatric Association sponsor a program, eventually scheduled for May, 1971, in which a pair of families would be interviewed, one disturbed and one normal. We were hoping to find what Froma Walsh would call a family with optimal functioning, but did not know what to look for, and so we settled for a "nonclinical" family—one in which no one had seen a mental health professional. We eventually located such a family, with two parents and seven kids from age 4 to 16, unscathed by contact with the mental health system.

What was most fascinating at the time of Carl's interview in front of a panel of eminent family therapists and an audience of 1,500 was the profound, generalized disbelief in the reality of what everyone observed. One member of the audience felt that the normal family was headed for mediocrity because they were so normal; several viewers were convinced that family therapy would reveal that under the "shared family denial" deep-seated, even explosive, problems were lurking. The father, especially, was regarded as needing treatment because he was "pathologically anxious," in that he viewed the future with some uncertainty (Anti-Vietnam war demonstrators were parading nearby in downtown Washington). Carl summarized his view by saying that this was a baseball team in which all the players knew their positions and all played the game with zest and vigor. In contrast to the placidity of the audience and panel when they observed the "disturbed" family, the "normal" family threw these professionals into an uproar, as if they were seeing an alien, highly threatening, entirely unfamiliar phenomenon.

Carl and I were urged by the assembled professionals to find some way of providing therapy for this family. We did not do this, but we did ask the family if we could maintain contact with them to see how they coped with life during the subsequent years. None of the audience's dire predictions were confirmed, even as the family dealt with the developmental crisis of "launching" older offspring out of the home. We continued to see the family as "deviant" but not dysfunctional—that is, as abnormally healthy in more complex and interesting ways. I learned from them some ideas about family living that to this day I share with families who need to be, and want to be, in family therapy. My brush with "normality" was lastingly illuminating.

One of the important implications of the present volume is that recognition of the diversity of relational problems and solutions calls for far greater flexibility and adaptability on the part of family clinicians than has been generally appreciated. Froma Walsh discusses how our goals in family therapy are closely linked to our concepts of "normality," and that these concepts vary significantly from one model of family therapy to the next. Clarifying and making explicit which of the multiple meanings of normality we are using can help family clinicians be more relevant and effective with a greater variety of families in diverse contexts. In addition, both qualitative and quantitative family therapy researchers need to study, in a more thoughtful and thorough way, normal family processes in families both in treatment and not in treatment. Family therapists also would do well to attend more closely to the findings of our colleagues in family sociology, cultural anthropology, and even behavioral genetics. However, there can be no substitute for direct, personal observations and experience with families and relationships in all of their rich diversity. This volume points the way for such observations and is a landmark contribution that will deepen the understanding and challenge the preconceptions of family clinicians and researchers alike.

Lyman C. Wynne
Rochester, New York

PREFACE

The first edition of *Normal Family Processes*, published in 1982, was hailed as a landmark volume in clinical literature. It was the first text to examine normality from a family systems orientation, presenting pioneering research and conceptual developments. With clinical theory, training, and practice focused almost exclusively on family deficits and conflicts, I remarked in the overview chapter of the first edition—only half jokingly—that a normal family might be defined as one that had not yet been clinically assessed. The volume provided fresh perspectives on "non-clinical" families, laying the groundwork for identifying normative stresses and attributes of healthy families, based on newly emerging theory and research on normal family functioning. The book proved to be enormously influential in rebalancing the skewed clinical perspective that had tended to overpathologize families. It was widely adopted as a textbook in family studies programs and in the training of mental health professionals, especially family therapists.

In the decade since the publication of the first edition, we have made considerable progress in conceptualization of family normality and in developing useful frameworks for the assessment of family functioning. The field of family therapy has brought greater attention to the recognition and promotion of family strengths, and we have moved a healthy distance beyond the simplistic quest to discover a singular, universal model for family normality and health. We are grappling with the complexities inherent in defining normality, and we are attending to the diversity of family forms, life challenges, and values in our society. The second edition of *Normal Family Processes* presents these important developments by researchers and scholars on family functioning who are at the forefront of knowledge building and clinical training.

It has become both more challenging and more imperative to examine assumptions about family normality and to expand our knowledge base in order to foster healthy family functioning. Some might wish to adopt a position of neutrality on questions of normality, yet we cannot escape the influence of powerful social constructions of normality in clinical practice, research, and social policy, as well as in the beliefs and concerns of families about their own health or dysfunction. The tremendous social changes of recent decades and the increasing family diversity heighten uncertainty for families about how to survive and thrive in a rapidly changing world. More than ever, we need to increase our knowledge and understanding of normal family processes.

The overview chapter by the editor advances our conceptualization of normal family processes, clarifying different perspectives on the definition of family normality, examining myths of "the normal family" and changing family norms in sociohistorical perspective, and surveying clinical views of normal family functioning and dysfunction that underlie major approaches to family therapy. The challenges ahead for clinical training, practice, and research are addressed.

In Part II, leading family process researchers, W. Robert Beavers, David Olson, Nathan Epstein, and their colleagues, present their widely influential systems-based models for assessment of family functioning. Each identifies major dimensions and key components found to distinguish well-functioning families in their investigations of a wide range of nonclinical families. Danielle Bussell and David Reiss expand our ability to examine the interaction of biological and psychosocial variables for individual and family functioning.

Parts III and IV address the diverse patterns of family functioning relative to varying family structural forms, sociocultural contexts, and developmental challenges. Family policy as well as family assessment and intervention have lagged behind emerging realities of contemporary family life by maintaining a single standard of "the normal family," fitting a mythical ideal of the so-called "traditional" middle-class, intact, nuclear family, circa the 1950s. Clinicians, and families themselves, too often set unrealistic and inappropriate aims to meet this standard that only reinforce a sense of failure and deficiency. As these chapters demonstrate, families vary in their configurations and they confront different sets of environmental and developmental challenges that require diverse adaptational strategies. Family patterns that are "functional" for mastering one set of challenges—be it adolescence, remarriage, or illness in a family member—may be quite different from those patterns that prove functional for other conditions.

In Part III, leading authorities examine family functioning relative to the variety of family forms that are increasingly prevalent and visible in the "normal" spectrum in our changing society. Chaya Piotrkowski and Diane Hughes address dual-earner families (the new "norm"). Mavis Hetherington and her colleagues examine the challenges for post-divorce families from her extensive longitudinal research. Emily and John Visher, leading authorities on stepparenting, provide insight and guidelines concerning the issues facing remarriage families. Carol Anderson and her colleagues identify the normative challenges in families by adoption, families who have received insufficient attention in earlier considerations of normal families. Joan Laird provides a critically important analysis of the myths and realities of gay and lesbian families, who have been the most stigmatized of all "non-traditional" families in American society.

Part IV examines family diversity in relation to sociocultural and developmental challenges. Monica McGoldrick presents a broad cross-cultural perspective of ethnicity and normality. Nancy Boyd-Franklin examines the impact of social class and racism for poor African-American families. Barbara Ellman and Morris Taggart provide a valuable perspective on changing gender norms for women and men in families. Monica McGoldrick, Marsha Heiman, and Betty Carter present the family life cycle framework, highlighting normative stages, transitional stresses, and family tasks for successful life cycle passage. John Rolland applies this developmental systems perspective to the issues confronting normal families challenged by adversity in illness and disability. In the concluding chapter, Ann Hartman directs our attention to the family impact of recent social policy and the critical challenges to suppport and strengthen families.

Contributors to this volume, as in the first edition, have been selected because of their significant contributions to clinical theory and research on normal family processes. About half of the authors contributed to the first volume and have continued to expand our knowledge about well-functioning families; others have been included who have more recently advanced the frontier of theory building and research in important and neglected areas of consideration.

This volume, like the first edition, is designed to serve as a basic textbook in the training of family therapists, social workers, psychologists, psychiatrists, and a range of health and mental health care professionals and social scientists concerned with the understanding and promotion of healthy family functioning. It will be invaluable as a sourcebook for family researchers and practitioners to compare and apply leading models of assessment of family functioning, to develop their own new concepts, assessment tools, and intervention strategies, and to inform family policy and program development.

Clinical training and practice can be particularly enriched by the perspectives and knowledge we are gaining in the study of normal family processes. A normative orientation heightens appreciation for each family's strengths and potential resources as they confront life challenges. As we become more aware of our own values and beliefs about normality, we become better attuned to support and empower the families who seek our help. Increased knowledge about what works in well-functioning families can guide clinical interventions and programs to promote family strengths, build resiliency, and facilitate successful adaptation to life challenges.

Three sets of questions frame discussion throughout the book:

1. How do socially constructed beliefs and assumptions about family normality influence clinical theory, practice, research, and social policy?
2. What are the "normal" (i.e. expectable, typical) family processes relative to various social conditions and life challenges?
3. What are the critical processes for "healthy" (i.e. optimal) family functioning? How do these processes covary with different family forms, values, and contexts? What family patterns and mediating variables distinguish well-functioning from dysfunctional families in adapting to their particular sets of challenges?

The complexity and diversity of normal family processes preclude any simple or definitive answers to these questions, which are intended to guide us toward still better questions and more useful knowledge. We have much to learn from normal families. The contributions in this volume all reflect the sense of excitement and potential in expanding our understanding of key processes in family wellbeing.

CONTENTS

PART I

Overview

CHAPTER 1

CONCEPTUALIZATION OF NORMAL FAMILY PROCESSES

Froma Walsh

> All happy families are alike; every unhappy family is
> unhappy in its own way.   —*Leo Tolstoy*
>
> All happy families are more or less dissimilar; all
> unhappy ones are more or less alike. —*Vladimir Nabokov*
>
> The ache for home lives in all of us, the safe place
> where we can go and not be questioned.
>   —*Maya Angelou*

THE FIRST EDITION OF THIS volume posed the question, "What is a normal family?" Over the past decade, attempts to define family normality have become both more complicated and more important. The tumultous social changes of recent years have altered the familiar landscape of "normal" family life, leading to concern about the demise of the family. Yet, in the midst of turmoil and uncertainty, we "ache for home" more than ever, forging new and varied family connections, seeking caring and commited relationships for our well-being and future survival. These efforts are made more difficult by concerns of families about their own normality and confusion in the construction of new models for healthy family functioning.

Clinicians and family scholars have been further humbled in addressing normality by our increasing awareness that all views of normality are socially constructed, influenced by our own world view and by the larger culture. As we approach questions of family normality in the 1990s, the observer, the family, and the social context all continue to shift and evolve, and we have become less certain about what we thought we knew and valued in the past. Thus, our current conceptualizations of normal family processes must take into account the changing views of changing families in a changing world.

These developments make it all the more imperative to examine the explicit and implicit assumptions about family normality that are embedded in our cultural and clinical belief systems. This overview chapter seeks to advance our understanding of normal family processes by examining conceptualizations of family normality and their impact for the understanding and treatment of family dysfunction. First, we address the problems in defining a "normal" family by clarifying four major perspectives on family normality, drawing on conceptual contributions from the clinical field and the social sciences. Next, the myths and realities of typical family patterns and ideal models of the family are examined from a sociohistorical perspective to more fully understand our legacy of cultural norms and to appreciate the diversity and challenges of contemporary families. Then, we survey conceptual stances toward family normality and dysfunction that underlie major approaches to family therapy, reviewing the most influential founding models and noting more recent developments. Finally, we consider the challenges ahead for clinical training, practice, and research.

DEFINING FAMILY NORMALITY

The very definition of family normality has been problematic. The term "normal" is used to refer to quite different concepts, depending on one's frame of reference, which are strongly influenced by the subjective position of the observer and by the cultural surround. The label may hold quite different meanings to a clinician, to a researcher, or to a family concerned about its own normality. Our cultural belief systems, our personal experiences, and our professional orientations all influence our perspectives on normality. Our language confounds matters when we use such terms as "healthy," "typical," and "functional" interchangeably with the label "normal." Clearer distinctions among terms and concepts are needed (Walsh 1989a).

In an overview of theoretical and clinical concepts of mental health in the clinical and social science literature, Offer and Sabshin (1966, 1974) were struck by the varied definitions of a "normal" person. They synthesized those views into four major perspectives on normality:

1. *Normality as Health,* from a medico-psychiatric model, is based on the criterion of absence of pathology. Persons who are asymptomatic, manifesting no disturbances, are considered normal and healthy.

2. *Normality as Average,* an approach common in sociological and behavioral studies, uses the statistical norm, or average, to identify typical patterns or traits.

3. *Normality as Utopia,* an approach embodied in psychoanalytic and humanistic theories, conceives of normality as ideal or optimal functioning, or as "self-actualization" of potential.

4. *Normality as Process* attends to individual developmental processes over the life course in the context of transactional systems dependent on an interaction of biopsychosocial variables. This fourth perspective, based on General System Theory (Bertalanffy, 1968; Grinker, 1967), was thought, by Offer and Sabshin, to be most fruitful and allowing for unique coping styles and multiple adaptational routes.

Perspectives on Family Normality

When we shift our focus from the individual to the family unit, we confront similar problems in defining what is normal. To clarify our constructs, four perspectives on family normality were distinguished in the first edition of this volume (Walsh, 1982). Families can be considered normal in terms of: asymptomatic functioning, average functioning, optimal functioning, and transactional processes.

Normal Families as Asymptomatic

From this common clinical perspective grounded in the medical model, a family is regarded as normal—and healthy—if there are no symptoms of disorder in any family member. The judgment of normality is based on negative criteria: the absence of pathology.

One limitation of this perspective is its deficit-based skew and inattention to positive attributes of family well-being. Healthy family functioning involves more than the absence of problems and can be found in the midst of problems. As Minuchin (1974) has emphasized, no families are problem-free. Since most families have occasional problems, the presence of a problem should not automatically be viewed as an indication of family pathology. Similarly, freedom from symptoms is rare: research has found that 75% of all people are "symptomatic" (physical or psychological distress) at any given time, yet most don't seek treatment, but define it as part of normal life (Kleinman, 1988).

Another problem lies in the common assumption that an individual disorder is invariably a symptom of family dysfunction. It is erroneous to presume that all individual problems are necessarily symptomatic of—and caused by—a dysfunctional family. Likewise, it is erroneous to assume that a healthy individual has come from a healthy family. Wolin's Challenge Model (Wolin & Wolin, 1993) grew out of his study of highly resilient individuals who mastered the adversities of growing up in seriously troubled families.

There is no simple one-to-one correlation between individual and family health or dysfunction (Walsh & Olson, 1989). One black single parent was praised for her parenting when her son graduated with honors from college. "What does it mean about our family, then, that my other son is in prison?" she asked. We must be cautious not to reflexly tie the fate of any individual family member to family health or dysfunction.

Another complication arises when researchers define therapy as the marker for family health or dysfunction, comparing clinical and nonclinical families as disturbed and normal samples (Riskin & Faunce, 1972). We cannot equate therapy versus nontherapy with assumptions of family pathology versus health. Simply because a family (or any individual member) is not in treatment, we can not presume healthy functioning, nor even that it is a typical family. "Nonclinical" families are a heterogeneous group (Riskin, 1982), comprising a variety of configurations and spanning the entire range of functioning. What is defined as a problem and whether help is sought vary with different family and cultural norms. A dysfunctional family may not seek therapy or may attempt to handle problems in other ways, as through kin support or religion. Conversely, request or referral for therapy can not be presumptive of a dysfunctional family. As mental health professionals are the first to avow, seeking help can be a sign of health.

Normal Families as Average

A family is viewed as normal from this perspective if it is *typical*, or fits a pattern that is common and expectable in ordinary families. The concept has been widely used by social scientists with statistical measures of frequency or central tendency. In the normal distribution (or bell-shaped curve), the middle range on a continuum is taken as normal and both extremes as deviant. Thus, by definition, families deviating from the norm are abnormal. Unfortunately, the negative connotations of deviance lead to pathologizing difference. We should keep in mind that by the definition of "average," an optimally functioning family would be as "abnormal" (i.e., as atypical) as a severely dysfunctional family.

From this perspective, the concept of health is distinct from that of normality as average. Patterns of interaction that are common may be destructive, such as violence. Moreover, as noted above, since average families have occasional problems, the presence of a problem does not in itself imply family abnormality or pathology. This perspective thus disengages the concepts of health, normality, and absence of symptoms.

Normal Families as Optimal

This approach to normality seeks to define a *healthy* family in terms of optimal functioning or ideal traits. Optimally, a well-functioning family is seen as successful in accomplishing family tasks and promoting the growth and well-being of individual members. Clinicians must be cautious about standards of optimal family functioning derived from clinical theory and largely based on inference and extrapolation from disturbed cases. More recent empirically based models provide a more solid base for assessment of optimal family functioning. (See Part II, this volume.)

We need to be aware of the pervasiveness of cultural ideals in defining family normality and health. Social norms of the ideal family are culturally constructed values that prescribe how families ought to be (Bott, 1957). A certain range of conduct is deemed permissible and particular family forms and traits are considered desirable according to prevailing standards in the dominant society. Ideals may vary in particular ethnic communities. We must also keep in mind that patterns that may be optimal for the functioning of a particular family may not fit the standard deemed ideal.

Normal Family Processes

A systems orientation offers an overarching perspective on family normality for considering both average and optimal functioning in terms of basic *processes* characteristic of human systems. The transactional view is distinguished by its attention to processes *over time*, in contrast to the above perspectives, that have generally sought to identify fixed traits of a so-called "normal family," thought of as a static, timeless entity or viewed cross-sectionally, at a single point in time. Normal functioning is conceptualized according to organizational principles governing interaction (Bateson, 1979; Watzlawick, Beavin, & Jackson, 1967; Minuchin, 1974). Such processes involve the integration and maintenance of the family unit and its ability to carry out essential tasks for the growth and well-being of its members, such as the nurturance and protection of offspring and care of the aged.

Families develop their own internal norms, expressed through relationship rules, both implicit and explicit (Jackson, 1965). They organize family interaction and serve to maintain a stable, yet flexible, system by prescribing and limiting members' behavior. Family norms provide expectations about roles, actions, and consequences that guide family life. A family tends to interact in repetitive sequences, so that family operations are governed by a relatively small set of patterned and predictable rules (Metcoff & Whitaker, 1982). Family belief systems, or family paradigms, are shared values and assumptions that provide meaning and serve to organize experience in the social world (Constantine, 1986; Reiss, 1981; Rolland, 1988). Cultural and religious values exert leverage on family relationships by enforcing or affirming family norms (Spiegel, 1971; McGoldrick, Pearce, & Giordano, 1982; see McGoldrick, Chapter 11, this volume).

A biopsychosocial systems orientation takes into account the multiple, recursive influences in individual and family functioning. From an ecosystemic perspective (Bronfenbrenner, 1979; Keeney & Sprenkle, 1982; Schwartzman, 1982), each family's capabilities and unique coping style must be considered in relation to the attributes and needs of individual members and to the larger social systems in which the family is embedded. Successful family functioning is dependent on the *fit*, or compatibility, between the family, its individual members, and other social systems. Symptoms of dysfunction must be viewed in context: They may be generated by internal stressors, such as the strain of coping with a member's illness (Walsh & Anderson, 1988; Rolland, Chapter 15, this volume), or triggered by external stressors, such as job pressures (see Piotrkowski & Hughes, Chapter 6, this volume) or financial strain and racism (see Boyd-Franklin, Chapter 12, this volume).

A family life cycle framework considers normal processes in the multigenerational system as it moves forward over time (Carter & McGoldrick, 1980, 1989; see McGoldrick, Heiman, & Carter, Chapter 14, this volume). Normal family development is conceptualized in terms of adaptational processes that involve mastery of life-stage tasks and transitional stress (Duvall, 1977; Hill & Rogers, 1964; McCubbin et al., 1980; Solomon, 1973; Wynne, 1988). The concept of normal as average can be used systemically to describe typical, expectable transactional processes over the course of the family life cycle. What is normal, in terms of optimal family functioning, will vary with different developmental demands and structural configurations. For example, high cohesion, (a centripetal system pattern), is both expectable and optimal in families with small children, but becomes less typical and potentially dysfunctional in adolescence, when preferences for more separateness (a centrifugal pattern) become more adaptive (Combrinck-Graham, 1985; see also Olson, Chapter 3, this volume).

Certain stressors are considered normative, that is, common and predictable, accompanying the particular challenges of family life cycle phases and major transitions (Rapaport, 1962). It is, thus, normal and not necessarily indicative of family pathology for disruption and distress to be experienced with the birth of the first child, at launching, or in divorce and remarriage (see Hetherington, Chapter 7; McGoldrick, Heiman, & Carter, Chapter 14, this volume). Nonnormative stressors that are uncommon or unexpected tend to be more traumatic for families (Neugarten, 1968), as in the untimely death of a child (Walsh & McGoldrick, 1991) or in the devastation of a hurricane or earthquake (Figley, 1989). How the family, as a functional unit, responds is as critical for adaptation as the stress event itself (Walsh & McGoldrick, 1991). A number of adaptational routes are possible, with healthier families thought to use a larger variety of coping techniques, more effective problem-solving strategies, and more flexibility in dealing with internal and external life events. More recent work has sought to better understand the key elements in family resilience and mastery (Walsh, in press[a]).

In sum, the integration of systems and developmental perspectives form an overarching framework for considering normality. The definition of average and optimal family processes is contingent on both social and developmental contexts. What is normal—either typical or optimal—varies with different internal and external demands posing challenges for both continuity and change over the course of the family life cycle (Falicov, 1988a). This systems paradigm provides a common foundation throughout the field of family therapy and for the family process research and conceptual work by contributors to the present volume.

Functional and Dysfunctional

The concept of "functional" is frequently used to define family normality. Functional essentially means workable. It refers to a judgment about the utility of a family pattern in achieving family goals. In addition to the instrumental criteria in judging a family functional (i.e., the family unit remains intact; it solves its problems), we have more recently given greater attention to the sense of well-being and connectedness among family members. Any judgment of functional (or dysfunctional) is contingent on each family's aims—involving their own beliefs about normality and health—as well as situational and life-stage challenges, economic circumstances, and cultural imperatives.

The term dysfunctional, likewise, is a descriptive one, referring to family patterns that are unworkable and associated with symptoms of distress—regardless of the origin of the problem. However, the term has taken on connotations of serious family disturbance and causal attributions that tend to overpathologize families and blame them for individual and social problems. Popular self-help and recovery movements currently abound for survivors, or so-called Adult Children of Dysfunctional Families (Kaminer, 1992). It must be kept in mind that individual problems are not invariably caused by family pathology. Caution is urged in use of the label "dysfunctional family", distinguishing those families with serious transactional disorders, abuse, and neglect, from most families who are struggling with ordinary problems in living. It is preferable, and less stigmatizing, to identify particular family *patterns*, or processes, as dysfunctional, rather than to label the family.

In identifying a family pattern as functional, we need to ask: functional to what end and for whom. As family therapists well know, a pattern that may be functional at one system level, or for a subsystem, may be dysfunctional for another. As a classic example, interactional rules that serve a function in stabilizing a fragile marriage may have dysfunctional consequences for a child.

Maintaining family functioning may take a toll on an individual member who is overburdened, such as a single parent lacking adequate financial and social support, or in parentification, if the developmental needs of a child are sacrificed for the functioning of the family unit. We need to reexamine our expectations for a well-functioning family if it comes at the expense of the well-being of any member or part of the system.

Every assessment of family functioning must evaluate the resources available to the family and the impact of other systems. For instance, social policies and workplace practices deemed necessary for a healthy economy and functional work system have in many ways been dysfunctional for families (see Piotrkowski & Hughes, Chapter 6, this volume). Traditional breadwinner role demands have kept fathers peripheral to family life and homemaker-mothers disproportionately overburdened. Two-earner and single-parent households experience tremendous role strain with the pressures of multiple, often conflicting job and childcare demands and the lack of supportive resources. Many parents manage to keep their families and children functional only at a high cost to their marriage and personal well-being. Clinical and social interventions need to address not only intrafamilial realignments but also the family interface with other systems and resources.

BEYOND THE MYTHS OF THE NORMAL FAMILY: A SOCIOHISTORICAL PERSPECTIVE

The very definition of "family" has been called into question as human relationships have so greatly reconfigured in recent decades. Yet controversy and change in the definition of the family have a long and continuous history. In the current cultural climate of uncertainty about the future of the family, some have sought to discover (or recover) "the normal family" and to catalogue its attributes, as if it were a distinct (or near-extinct) species. Anxiety over the fate of the family has focused heightened scrutiny on supposed deficits in families who deviate from idealized normal family images of the past.

Concern over family crisis is not unique to our times. Throughout American history, the family has been regarded as the linchpin of the social order (Hareven, 1982). Yet every generation has expressed doubts about the stability and continuity of the family and has thought it was witnessing the breakdown of the "traditional family." Gordon (1988) writes: "For at least 150 years, there have been periods of fear that 'the family'—meaning a popular image of what families were supposed to be like, by no means a correct recollection of any actual 'traditional family'—was in decline; and these fears have tended to escalate in periods of social stress" (p. 17).

While Western societies have been changing dramatically in recent decades, cherished myths of the traditional family have persisted, lagging behind emerging social realities and yet exerting a powerful influence. Current perceptions of family demise are supported by commonly held myths about family life in the past. Two eras of family life have become idealized in our "normal family" folklore: the intact extended family of the distant past and the modern nuclear family of the recent past.

Just as story-telling has served in every age and culture to transmit family norms, television has become the prime medium for transmitting family folklore in contemporary society, both shaping and reflecting the values and beliefs of the dominant culture. Today's parents—as well as clinicians, researchers, and public-policy makers—were socialized by the television families of their childhood. Such series as "The Waltons" and "Little House on the Prairie" transported viewers back to the distant past, to a simpler time of large families, "homespun" values, and multigenerational connectedness. Family life portrayed in such shows as "Father Knows Best," "Ozzie and Harriet," and "Leave It to Beaver" exemplified the more recent "tradition" of the middle-class nuclear family, self-contained within the boundaries of their white picket fence, with bread-winner father in charge and a supportive, homemaker mother. As Hareven (1982) has noted, the lasting popularity of such images expresses longing not only for a romanticized notion of the family, but also for a simpler, happier, more secure life in the world around them. Although television families of the 1990s show much greater diversity, as in the option of unwed single parenting for Murphy Brown, they also reflect more uncertainty and spark much more controversy about the direction in which families are headed.

Just as a family looks to its multigenerational past to shed light on its present dilemmas and chart its future course, a sociohistorical lens offers a valuable perspective on the current challenges and future directions of families in contemporary society. As Stacey (1990) has observed, "Rare are the generations, or even the sociologists, who perceive the historical idiosyncrasies of the normal cultural arrangements of their time." It is useful to examine some influential myths of "the normal family" and the historical record of actual experiences of normal family life.

The Myth of the Traditional Family of the Distant Past

The idealized image of the intact, multigenerational family household of the distant past distorts their actual diversity and instability. Recent research has dispelled the myth of multigenerational family solidarity (Hareven, 1982). Most households did not include grandparents or other extended family members. In fact, there has never been an era when three generations typically lived together, as adults and their parents, although interdependent, have always preferred to live separately (Cohler & Geyer, 1982).

In nostalgia for the "intact" family of the past, we have not realized the frequent disruption in family life by early death (Walsh & McGoldrick, 1991). With the high mortality rate, most families experienced the death of a young child. With the average life expectancy in the mid-40s, parental death commonly disrupted the family unit before children were launched and led to stepfamilies and to child placements with extended family, foster care, or orphanages. Thus, the chances of not growing up in an intact family were much greater in the past. As Skolnick (1991) observes, although this fact does not diminish the stresses of divorce today, it does help to correct the tendency to contrast "the terrible Present with an idealized Past."

Another widely held myth is that family patterns in the past were more orderly and stable than with today's complex and varied family structure and roles. In fact, family transitions were more complicated, diverse, and unpredictable as a result of the many life uncertainties, particularly unplanned pregnancies and sudden, early mortality. Families now have greater control over the options and timing of family events, in part because of advances in medical technology and birth control. Increased life expectancy has brought the prospect for more longlasting marital and intergenerational relations, with four- and five-generation families increasingly common. Ironically, the current high divorce rate in part is due to the fact that couples can now expect to live another 20 to 40 years after launching children.

Unlike our sentimental view of family life in olden days, the premodern family was essentially a corporate entity in which individual well-being was subordinated to the collective functioning of the economic, social, and political unit. The family patriarch held authority over the women and children in the family, controlling all major decisions and resources. Relationships between husbands and wives, parents and children, and among other kin were based on assumptions of mutual obligations and exchange of services, support, and assistance, especially in times of crisis. Sentiment was important, but secondary to family needs and survival strategies. Marriage and parenthood were partnerships governed by family economic and social needs. Authoritarian parenting was the rule, to break the will and "save the soul" of offspring (a norm more recently called into question by concerns about family violence).

In addition to childrearing, preindustrial families functioned as a workshop, school, church, and asylum. Most work took place in the household, with children considered economic assets and members of the work force. Although families had many more children in the past, women invested relatively less time in mothering because of their other contributions to the shared family economy and the active participation in childrearing by fathers, older children, and extended family members who lived nearby. The integration of family and work life allowed for intensive sharing of labor between husbands and wives and between parents and children, with less segregation along sex and age lines. Permeable boundaries between family and community furthered social support in times of need and maintained regulation of proper family conduct.

Family households were quite diverse, commonly including nonkin boarders, such as apprentices, orphaned or delinquent youth, or frail elderly. Young adults from other communities or other countries often lived in the households of widows or older people whose children had left home. This practice provided surrogate families and facilitated adaptation of new immigrants as well as income and companionship for widows and older people, enabling them to continue to head their own households and not be isolated. Interestingly, the current proliferation of diverse family arrangements and nonkin networks, although termed "nontraditional forms," actually continues this tradition. When two single parents combine households and resources, we can see a similar resilience that strengthens family stability. Such flexibility was lost in the era of the modern nuclear family.

The Myth of the Modern Nuclear Family as Ideal and Essential

The concept of the "modern" family refers to a historically specific form and conception of family life that arose with industrialization in the 19th century and peaked in the post-World War II era. Americans who came of age in the 1950s "were encouraged to absorb a particularly distorted impression of the normalcy and timelessness of the modern American family system" (Stacey, 1990, p. 9). This model was the intact nuclear household unit composed of a male breadwinner, his full-time homemaker wife, and their dependent children. Many mistake this model for an ancient, essential, and now endangered institution when it was actually peculiar to its times. Current social analysts (Skolnick & Skolnick, 1992) view the postwar decade as an aberrant historical period, largely a delayed reaction to the traumas of the Great Depression and World War II. Fueled by the country's strong postwar economy and government benefits, families prospered and bought homes in the suburbs. Three-fifths of American households conformed to the vision of modern nuclear family domesticity. The 1950s reversed the century's steady decline in the birth rate, and couples married at an earlier age and in greater numbers than at any other time before or since.

In earlier times, the family had fulfilled a broad array of functions intertwined with the larger community, and relationships were valued for a wide array of contributions to the collective family unit. The nuclear family household become a rigid, closed system and lost extended kin and community connections and major sources of resilience and adaptability (Anderson, 1982). As Hareven (1982) emphasizes, what was lost was not some great extended family of the past, but the flexibility of the family that enabled households to expand or reconfigure when necessary and to take people in to live in surrogate family settings rather than in isolation.

Industrialization and urbanization brought a redefinition of family roles and functions. Family work and "productive" paid work became competitive and segregated into separate gendered spheres of home and workplace (Bernard, 1982). A cult of domesticity arose, glorifying the home as a retreat from the outside world (Lasch, 1977). Women were assigned the role as custodian of the hearth, nurturer of the young, and caretaker of the old. As sentiment replaced economic partnership, love and companionship became the ideal purposes of marriages, yet set unrealistic expectations for emotional fulfillment and romantic love. A new concept of childhood also emerged, viewing children as dependents needing nurture and protection through adolescence (Aries, 1962). Women were expected to model ideal traits of tenderness, sweetness, affection, and a comforting demeanor. The glorification of full-time motherhood served both to enshrine the family as a domestic retreat and to support child-centered family life. Yet, women's unpaid domestic work was demeaned and rendered invisible as women and children became economically dependent on the earnings of male breadwinners. Further, the work ethic and systematized schedules diminished men's involvement with their families.

The changes in family life were gradual and varied. Ethnic and working-class families continued to function as collective economic units, and only in the national prosperity of the 1950s did they achieve the dream of the modern family. When financial necessity brought many working-class women into the workforce, their wages were considered supplemental earnings, and they remained bound to fulfill their primary family obligations. Women's work outside the home became viewed as demeaning, with lower status and pay than men's jobs. The idealization of the family as a refuge requiring women's full-time responsibility for the well-being of all members furthered the myth that outside work by mothers was harmful, both compromising for their husbands' esteem as breadwinners and dangerous for their children's healthy development.

Although the modern family experience is far more complicated than its image, historians do agree it is no golden age of ideal family happiness to return to. The model was challenged by the gap between the dominant cultural ideology and the discordant life experience for so many families. Yet, because of the postwar baby boom, the beliefs and behaviors of the '50s became disproportionately significant for the next decades as the media, the market, and social and political institutions followed those trends. The first generation of childhood television viewers grew up immersed in models of this family ideology. Thus, this particular period in American family history set the terms for the waves of rebellion against, and nostalgia for, the passing modern family and gender order (Stacey, 1990).

Contemporary Families in the Postmodern Era: The Myth That One Norm Fits All

The present postmodern era does not hail a new model of family life, or the next stage in an orderly progression of family history, but, rather, coexisting sets of evolving family cultures. Sociologists refer to such diverse reshaping of contemporary family life as "the postmodern family," since no singular family structure or ideology has arisen to supplant the modern family (Skolnick, 1991). With the political and economic upheavals of the past two decades, the family landscape has been altered by a host of factors, most notably the feminist movement, economic insecurity, working mothers, and two-earner households, and by rising rates of divorce, single-parent households, remarriage, and cohabitation. Marriage and birth rates, along with the standard of living, have declined (Glick, 1992).

In the '90s, the dual-earner family has replaced the breadwinner/home-maker model as the statistical norm, a trend likely to continue (see Piotrkowski & Hughes, Chapter 6, this volume). In two-thirds of all two-parent households, both parents hold jobs. By choice and necessity, most mothers are currently in the workforce—over 70% of mothers of school-aged children and nearly 60% of mothers of preschool children (1990 U.S. Census data). Divorce rates, after climbing rapidly, have leveled off at around 50%. Single-parent and remarriage families have become increasingly com-mon. Over one-third of children can be expected to live in a single-parent household at some point in their development (see Hetherington, Law, & O'Conner, Chapter 7, this volume). Following divorce, about 75% of men and 65% of women go on to remarry. By the year 2000, remarried families are predicted to become the predominant family form—the most normal, in the sense of typical (Cherlin & Furstenberg, 1988; see Visher & Visher, Chapter 8, this volume). Families formed through adoption have also been on the rise, for single parents as well as for couples (see Anderson, Piantanida, & Anderson, Chapter 9, this volume). The social movement for gay and les-bian rights has led to advocacy for the normalization of a homosexual orienta-tion and of families of choice (Weston, 1991; see Laird, Chapter 10, this volume).

Much anxiety has been expressed over this growing array of family forms and options (Macklin, 1980), particular the increase in divorce, unmarried couples living together, individuals choosing to become single parents, and homosexual partners and parents. Some concerns are well founded, particularly in the sharp rise of unwed teen parenting. Today, one in four babies is born to an unwed parent. One in four adolescent girls become pregnant; over half of those births and over 90% of births to black teenagers are nonmarital. Studies have documented the high risk of "children having children" for long-term poverty, poor quality parenting, and a cluster of health and psychosocial problems (Brooks-Gunn & Chase-Lansdale, 1993; Chase-Lansdale & Brooks-Gunn, 1991).

However, a major source of anxiety is rooted in the tensions between the idealized expectations in our culture and the actual experience of con-temporary family life. Nostalgia for a lost family tradition that never existed has distorted our perceptions and fueled the myth that any deviation from the idealized normal family is inherently pathological.

The backlash to these changes began in the late 1970s, as many sought to restore the old family and gender order in a "culture of nostalgia" that ushered in the Reagan era. The social sciences, the field of mental health, and public policy all upheld the modern family model as ideal. As Skolnick observes, Americans as a nation spent most of the 1980s backing into the future (1991). Heated debates over changing family life polarized discourse. Some have viewed changing family forms as symptomatic of the demise of the family. Such concern reflects the decline in this modern two-parent breadwinner/homemaker model of the normal family, which represents an increasingly narrow segment of American families, fewer than 8% of all households. Other analysts have contended that it was the rigid adherence to this particular family form that has crumbled (Bane, 1976; Bohannen, 1985). They assert that the modern family structure was inflex-ible, closed to kin and community resources, and inequitable in gendered role definitions, with rigid conformity-oriented family patterns stifling growth, intimacy, and creativity. Yet, despite the ever-widening gap with social realities, the image of the modern nuclear family has persisted as the kind of family so many still think we should all have.

Debates about the future of the family have touched a vulnerable core of anxiety and uncertainty about contemporary life in the postmodern era (Bellah, Madsen, Sullivan, Swidler, & Tipton, 1985; Gergen, 1991). Families are struggling with actual and symbolic losses as they alter family arrange-ments and as their world is changing around them. The many discontinuities and the loss of the familiar for the unknown generate an uncomfortable tension (Bateson, 1989). There is a widespread sense of disruption and con-fusion about the very structure and meaning of family relationships, about what is normal (typical and expectable) in family life and how to construct healthy (optimally functioning) families.

Myths of the ideal family, out of touch with the real-life challenges and diversity of families in the 1990s, compound the sense of loss, deficiency, and failure for families in transition. Experimenting with new family arrange-ments, many families find themselves in unfamiliar territory, lacking a map or compass to guide their passage. When they compare themselves to myths of the normal family, they judge themselves—as do many others—as deficient even when that standard doesn't fit their situation. In reifying a single family type as ideal and essential, all other "nontraditional families" tend to be lumped together and judged as pathological. Even the term "alternative family forms" frames unconventional family arrangements as deviant from the implicit standard and stigmatizes the differences.

For example, the myth that an intact nuclear family is inherently healthier than all others leads to the presumption that divorce is inevitably damaging and that single-parent and remarriage families are deficient. Such attitudes, supported by clinical cases of dysfunction (Wallerstein & Blakeslee, 1989), are not borne out by an accumulating body of research on nonclinical families, which finds a wide range of functioning among "nonintact" fami-lies (see Hetherington, Law, & O'Conner, Chapter 7, this volume; Ahrons & Rogers, 1989; Furstenberg & Cherlin, 1991; Furstenberg & Spanier, 1987; Walsh, 1991). Longitudinal studies have found that about a third of divorced parents and their children function remarkably well over time, a third man-age moderately well, and a third do poorly. Those who assail the destruc-tive consequences of divorce fail to weigh in the harmful legacies of staying in an abusive or deadened family situation—where children, in comparison, are found to fare worse than most children after divorce. The critical differ-ence between well-functioning and dysfunctional families is found not in their form but, rather, in the quality of their relatonships and their adaptive processes.

It is inappropriate, as well, to compare divorce to an idealized image of an intact family: If the family were actually so ideal, divorce would be unlikely. Further, families in the past never did live up to the fairy tale image of "happily ever after." Marriages were commonly disrupted by early widowhood, separation, and desertion, and, with the social unacceptability of divorce, incompatible couples lived under the same roof in conflict or maintained separate lives. It could be argued that today many people care enough about the quality of family life to go through the painful and costly process of divorce, endure the difficulties of single parenthood, and, in most cases, move on to attempt a more satisfying remarriage. However, the attempt by remarried families to conform to the idealized image of the intact family only complicates adaptation.

Notions of deviance have been most destructive to gay and lesbian individuals and their families. As the courts have begun to expand the legal definition of the family to extend protection to gay couples, conservative coalitions have blocked implementation on "domestic partner" ordinances granting legal status to unmarried heterosexual and homosexual couples. In a recent ruling in one landmark case supporting gay rights, the judge concluded: "It is the totality of the relationship, as evidenced by the dedication, caring, and self-sacrifice of the parties which should, in the final analysis, control the definition of family" (Stacey, 1990, p. 4).

Although many families today are confused and troubled, many others are showing remarkable resilience and flexibility. Despite family instability and a larger context of economic and social uncertainties, most people are committed to forming and being part of a family. The change has come in the definition of family that has broadened to encompass a wide spectrum of relationship options. If we see this transition as an opportunity to experiment with new approaches to family life, to enlarge the repertoire of family patterns, our families and society can experience new growth and transformation to greater individual and family well-being. Although attempts to forge new family arrangements are often met with tremendous institutional resistance, potentially viable models for families of the future are emerging through the creative strategies and resilience of ordinary families.

In *Brave New Families*, an ethnographic study of working-class families in a central California community, Stacey (1990) found that men and women have been creatively reworking American family life during the recent decades of postindustrial economic upheaval. The traditional image of family life, revolving around a blue-collar male breadwinner and his homemaker wife (epitomized by the television images of "The Honeymooners" and of Archie Bunker) has been superseded by a wide range of family arrangements no longer rigidly defined by blood ties and traditional gender roles. In what Stacey calls "recombinant family life," people have drawn on a diverse array of resources, fashioning them into new gender and kinship strategies to cope with new challenges, burdens, and opportunities. She found men and women sharing housework and childcare, unmarried women choosing to have children on their own, strong extended family connections sustained across serial marriages, and long-time close friends claiming kinship. She also found same-sex couples exchanging marital vows and sharing childrearing commitments as gay and lesbian individuals more openly seek intimacy, community, and spirituality outside mainstream institutional forms. Stacey was particularly impressed by women's creative initiatives in reshaping the experience of divorce from an irreparable schism and loss of economic and social resources, into a viable kinship network incorporating new and former mates, their multiple sets of children, stepkin, and friends into households collaborating to survive and flourish.

Some social changes are a continuation of long-term trends, whereas others are discontinuous. Many different kinship forms have actually been in existence all along but were less visible, such as homosexual relationships. Although today's families are undergoing some important changes, we lose sight of the fact that families have always been changing, just as they have struggled to maintain important continuities. Moreover, we must look beyond the boundary of the household in considering significant family relationships, particularly with the increase of single-parent and remarriage families as well as of individuals living on their own. As anthropologists have shown, the family is a locus not of residence but of meaning and relationship. Thus, the question for the future is not whether "the family" will survive at all, but how our heirs will be arranging their significant relationships (Chilman, Nunally, & Cox, 1988).

In fact, recent ethnographic studies dispell the myth that certain family patterns are universal, finding considerable diversity in family forms and childrearing practices across cultures throughout the world. What is most striking is that whatever family patterns are prevalent in a particular culture, and however ideosyncratic they may be, each society regards its own practices as the normal and natural way to raise children (Braverman, 1989).

In short, there is no longer a single culturally dominant family pattern to which the majority of Americans conform and to which most aspire as an ideal. While some regard this as the demise of the family, others see, instead, that families are becoming "unstuck" from futile attempts to conform to a model that was neither ideal in its time nor relevant to contemporary life challenges. Any monolithic concept of the family as a timeless entity built into biology and society (Skolnick, 1991) imposes mythical homogeneity on the diverse ways in which people organize their intimate relationships, distorting and devaluing the rich variety of kinship patterns. In place of that mold, we are crafting multiple family and household arrangements that are inhabited uneasily and reconstituted in response to changing circumstances. Choice is a major element: Rather than strict adherence to a particular form with rigidly defined roles and interactional rules, individuals are entering partnerships or assuming sole leadership of families, involving extended family and friendship networks in new and different ways and experimenting with a variety of arrangements. Rather than reliance on narrow biological definitions of the family, we need to recall the effectiveness of surrogate family ties of the past in coping with migration, economic uncertainties, and family disruptions. What we are witnessing is not a fragmentation of traditional family patterns but, rather, the reemergence of a pluralism in family ways. Such diversity was normal—that is, typical—in families of the past, and it was healthy in enabling resilience.

We need to move beyond the myth that one type of family is the paragon of virtue to be emulated by all families and that all others are inherently deficient. In perpetuating this myth, and the need to conform, family *form* has been confused with family *substance*. As researchers and clinicians are finding, different structural arrangements are potentially workable—none is inherently healthy or pathological. It is not family form, but rather family processes—the quality of family relationships—that make the difference.

The Myth of the Proper Gender Order

The myth of "proper gender roles" has until very recently held sway in the social sciences since Talcott Parsons (Parsons & Bales, 1955) formulated the most influential conceptualization of the modern American family, based on his observations of white, middle-class suburban families in the 1950s (Boss, 1989). In his view, the nuclear family structure provided for a healthy complementarity in the division of roles into male "instrumental" leadership and female "socioemotional" support. The view of normal as average was confounded with normal as healthy, in making a theoretical leap from the description of typical family patterns to the prescription of that "norm" as ideal and as a universal standard essential for healthy family functioning and the proper development of offspring. Leading authorities in the fields of psychiatry and child development adhered to this model of the family and further held that any deviation was pathological. Lidz, for example, contended that the failure of a family to uphold "proper" heterosexual gender roles—particularly in the "skew" of a more dominant ("domineering") mother—was one of the basic family structural deficits contributing to schizophrenia in offspring (Lidz, 1963; Lidz, Fleck, & Cornelison, 1965).

The breadwinner/homemaker model was highly adaptive to the demands of the industrial economy of the times. But what was functional at the societal level was not functional for the family unit and for individual members. "Momism" glorified the joys of motherhood, yet women's domestic role was demeaned and mothers were blamed for any and all child and family problems. Fathers were exalted as head of household, and yet they were marginal to family life. One critic wrote:

> each suburban family is somehow a broken home, consisting of a father who appears as an overnight guest, [and] a put-upon housewife with too much to do. (Skolnick, 1991, p. 60)

Typical patterns in traditional families—the subordination of wives to their husbands and the peripheral position of fathers demanded by the workplace—was, in retrospect, not healthy for the functioning of the family or the well-being of its members. More recently, we have come to realize that keeping the family "functional" proved dysfunctional for women in families, and the role expectation for wives and mothers to maintain the idealized traditional family came at great personal cost. The disproportionate responsibility for maintaining the household and the well-being of husband, children, and elders, while sacrificing their own needs and identities, proved detrimental to their physical and mental health (McGoldrick, Anderson, & Walsh, 1989).

In viewing recent changes in the family as part of a historical continuum, the changing status of women emerges as the major ongoing dynamic from the end of the Victorian era to the present. Historians have noted that the first wave of feminism came in reaction to the exploitive and stultifying effects of the modern family model, with its separate and unequal spheres for men and women. The loss of community further isolated suburban women behind the white picket fence. The modern nuclear family with "proper" gender roles was an outmoded Victorian model that only temporarily reversed long-term trends toward more women in the workplace, falling birth rates, and a rising incidence of divorce. As birth control and the legalization of abortion offered reproductive choice and family planning, the first wave of feminism turned to the work sphere, where women sought the personal growth and status denied them in the traditional homemaker role. Television models such as Mary Tyler Moore portrayed an idealization of the workplace as the primary realm of fulfillment. Marriage and children didn't exist in that world.

The "Superwoman syndrome" began to emerge as women sought to "have it all," combining jobs and childrearing, but found they were adding on a "second shift" (Hochschild, 1989), since most men have not made reciprocal changes toward greater sharing of family responsibilities (see Piotrkowski & Hughes, Chapter 6, this volume). Several studies have found that employed women continue to carry upwards of 80% of household and childcare obligations. Accordingly, the second wave of the women's movement has made family politics central in efforts to redefine and rebalance gendered role relations so that men and women can both seek personal fulfillment, be gainfully employed, and share in the responsibilities and joys of family life (McGoldrick et al., 1989). Further, the myth that family life is women's work has denied men their full partnership in parenting (Edelman, 1992).

Debates about gender roles and relations lie at the core of today's deeply polarized discourse on American family life (Hare-Mustin, 1986). In the context of societal upheaval, many men and women became susceptible to conservative "profamily" appeals and an antifeminist backlash (Faludi, 1991) that would solve the problems of the family and society by restoring the "proper" gender order: for working mothers to return to their traditional homemaking roles and for men to reassert their position as head of every household.

Instead, most families are struggling toward greater sharing and equitablity of power and responsibilities in work and home spheres (Walsh, 1989b). Increasingly, men and women are seeking to base family relations on a personal and shared vision of a more complete life, rather than being defined and constrained by traditional gender-based norms (see Ellman & Taggart, Chapter 13, this volume). In the context of tremendous institutional resistance, this will be a continuing challenge in the decade ahead.

Cultural and Class Diversity:
The Myth of the Melting Pot

The myth of the melting pot belies the tremendous cultural diversity that has always characterized American society (Spiegel, 1971; see McGoldrick, Chapter 11, this volume). Despite some homogenization of American culture, there have been longstanding differences and tensions between family patterns in the dominant culture and those of black and other ethnic families. The influx of new immigrants has kept introducing new cultural variety in family patterns. As the general population is aging, high birthrates in African-American and recent immigrant families from Latin America and Asia have led to new projections of a significant increase in the proportion of people of color in the society over the coming decades, predicted to be over one-third of the population by the year 2000, and one-half soon after.

Social norms, traditions, and life challenges vary considerably among ethnic groups. We need to avoid the error of mislabeling as pathological those patterns that are different from the norms—either typical or ideal—in the dominant culture, when such patterns may be typical, desirable, and functional in that family's ethnic community. The rich cultural diversity in the United States poses a challenge for clinicians, as well as social scientists, to become more knowledgeable and appreciative of different cultural norms.

A dilemma is posed for families in transition between two cultures, such as immigrant families, whose processes may have been functional in their country of origin, but do not enable them to adapt in their new culture (Sluzki, 1979; Falicov, in press; Landau-Stanton, 1985). Such families may become caught between two social worlds, with tugs in incompatible directions. Here especially, we must assess the fit, or adaptability of individuals, couples, families, and their sociocultural context in any evaluation of health or dysfunction.

Historians and social scientists have too often generalized for the entire society on the basis of white, middle-class experience (Mintz & Kellogg, 1988). Despite the dominant ideology, poor and working-class families have continued to adhere to a collective view of the family. Extended kin networks in African-American and other ethnic families have been misinterpreted by some as "family disorganization" because they did not conform to the norm of the nuclear family household. We need to recognize the strength and resilience enabled by these traditional resources of kinship and religion, particularly in poor, single-parent families (Burton, 1990; Chase-Lansdale & Brooks-Gunn, 1991). Such values and flexibility have been especially vital for surviving the ravages of poverty, racism, and inner city violence (Edelman, 1992; see Boyd Franklin, Chapter 12, this volume).

The myth of the melting pot has led to intolerance for cultural diversity and blindness to racism and disparity between socioeconomic classes. Over the past decade, the middle class has been shrinking as the gap has widened between the rich and poor, and between whites and minorities (Ehrenreich, 1989). Increasingly, families have required two incomes to support even a modest standard of living. As the postindustrial economy has shifted from production to services and computer-based technology, middle- and working-class families have been hardest hit. Declining economic conditions and job dislocation have had a devastating impact on family stability and well-being, fueling family conflict and violence, marital dissolution, and the increase in poor, single-parent households. Social and economic disenfranchisement have contributed to the rise in unwed teenage parenting (Burton, 1990; Brooks-Gunn & Chase-Lansdale, 1993). In 1990, 56% of black families were headed by a single mother, up from 17% in 1950, and the black unemployment rate was double that of whites (*The New York Times*, May 20, 1992). The failure of young, inner-city black men to marry and assume financial responsibility for children they have fathered has been directly linked to their lack of job opportunities and bleak future prospects, both largely due to racism (Wilson, 1987). The trauma of inner-city gang violence holds serious dysfunctional consequences for even the healthiest families and their children (Garborino, 1992).

Women's economic and social conditions have worsened disproportionately (McGoldrick et al., 1989). Gender inequities persist in the workplace, and the earnings gap between men and women, although improving somewhat over the past decade (due in part to the drop in male earnings) still leaves women currently earning 71 cents to each dollar earned by men. Increasing numbers of single and divorced women are rearing children alone with little or no support by fathers. Even full-time employment does not sustain some above the poverty line. In later life, too, women are more likely than men to lack economic security and family support. There is a growing recognition of economic differences and the impact of poverty and disempowerment on families, particularly on women, children, the elderly, and people of color.

There is no question that many families are in crisis today, yet this crisis reflects not merely problems *in* the family, but scarce resources and a pile-up of other social problems that impact on the family. There have been two interpretations of the locus of the problem—individual or societal—and, correspondingly, the locus of change needed to solve the problem. Those who define the problem as internal to the family blame those who have not upheld the "traditional" nuclear family form. Former Vice President Quayle, in his speech on cities and poverty immediately following the Los Angeles riots in the wake of the first jury verdict in the Rodney King trial, asserted:

> Right now the failure of our families is hurting America deeply. When families fail, society fails. The anarchy and lack of structure in our inner cities are testament to how quickly civilization falls apart when the family foundation cracks. (*The New York Times*, May 20, 1992)

Blaming families for urban poverty, decay, and violence ignores evidence that family change is often the *result* of societal upheaval, not the cause of it. Such linear framing of the problem fails to address the overwhelming social and economic forces that contribute to family breakdown.

We need to shift from moral debate over the form the family should take to a pragmatic approach that supports the family in its many manifestations. People need to feel they can exercise family options and that society will support those choices. Although virtually all industrialized countries have been experiencing recent social and economic changes, disruptions elsewhere have been cushioned by social policies intended to guard the well-being of children and families. Throughout Europe, family policy is part of general economic policy, providing a range of supports for children and families across income groups, not merely for the poor, and without stigma attached. In contrast, support for children and families in America has generally been based on the assumption that families are inadequate if they are not self-sufficient. We forget that the prosperity and government supports for education, jobs, and home ownership following World War II provided the foundation for the modern nuclear family so idealized.

We must beware of the myth of family self-reliance growing out of our culture's individualistic strain. The major problems of families today largely reflect the difficulties in adaptation to the social and economic upheavals of recent decades and the unresponsiveness of larger community and societal institutions. These pressures make it difficult, if not impossible, for families to sustain mutual support and control over their lives. For example, to meet the realities of dual-earner and single-parent families, such supports are needed as affordable childcare and flexible work schedules (which are provided in other developed nations). There is an urgent need in our society for responsive family policy (see Hartman, Chapter 16, this volume).

Today's family is a changing institution but not a dying one. Instead of indulging in "nostalgia and moral panic," Skolnick advises that we put our efforts into supporting and protecting the family as: "a place of enduring bonds and fragile relationships, of the deepest love and the most intractable conflicts, of the most intense passions and the routine tedium of everyday life. It is a shelter from the workings of a harsh economy, and it is battered by forces beyond its control" (Skolnick, 1991).

The question of family values has become prominent in public discourse on the family. Depending on perspective, this decade of family life will bring either more deterioration, unless a return to traditional values occurs, or it will bring continued creative change, troublesome only if social institutions keep facing backwards. Doherty (1991) recommends a both/and position: acknowledging the need for a transformation of values, yet more carefully considering what those values are. Some values maintain continuity with the past in terms of commitment and personal responsibility; others differ sharply in rejection of the male-dominated hierarchy, with its concomitant subordination, exploitation, and abuse of women.

The 1960s through the 1980s, which coincided with the young-adult phase of the baby-boom generation, was a period marked by individual pursuits, personal options, and the search for meaning in life through self-expression. With the 1990s, as the baby-boom cohort has settled down, there is currently a reassessment of norms and a renewed appreciation of the value of family connections, albeit in varied arrangements. From a long-range perspective, concerns over the diversity of life styles are overshadowed by more serious problems such as the aging of our population and the isolation of the elderly; the economic strain on families; and the cultural transmission of violence, sexism, and racism. Women and men are joining forces to press for creative strategies to rebalance work and family commitments. In defining individual and family well-being, quality-of-life issues are at the fore, including a desire for more community involvement, greater social justice, and a concern for the environment.

Our understanding of what constitutes the family has undergone radical change. The "normal" family can no longer be seen as a monolithic stereotypical entity. The norm of the modern nuclear family has given way to a multiplicity of family arrangements. All demand careful theoretical and therapeutic attention. Our task now is to create social and economic policies and clinical approaches to support the new family realities.

TRADITIONAL CLINICAL VIEWS OF THE FAMILY: THROUGH A LENS DARKLY

Assumptions about family normality, embedded in our cultural and professional belief systems, underlie all clinical theory and practice. We need to be aware of these constructions as they exert a powerful, and largely unexamined, influence in every family assessment and therapeutic intervention.

In the first edition of this volume, I remarked, only half-jokingly, that a normal family could be defined as one that has not yet been clinically assessed. Traditionally, the clinical field, grounded in medical and psychoanalytic paradigms, has held a pathology-based view of families. Attention has been focused on the diagnosis of negative family influences in the origin and development of individual disorders. Family assessment has been skewed toward identification of deficits and conflicts and has been inattentive to family strengths and resources. Indeed, throughout much of the clinical literature, families have been portrayed as noxious and destructive environments. Parents, particularly mothers, have been viewed harshly and blamed for problems in the lives of their offspring, as in the following family case analysis, published in a leading psychiatric journal:

> In this paper, it has been possible to examine minutely a specific family situation. The facts speak rather boldly for themselves. The mother and wife is a domineering, aggressive, and sadistic person with no redeeming good qualities. She crushes individual initiative and independent thinking in her husband, and prevents their inception in her children. The latter, particularly, are open to no counterbalancing, healthy social forces. (Gralnick, 1943, pp. 32–33)

Seeing "no redeeming good qualities" in parents, especially mothers has been pervasive in psychiatric theory and practice. Often such mother-blaming judgments have been formed without the therapist ever having had direct contact with the family, based on subjective impressions from interviews with the patient and deduced from theories of family pathology. Reference to counterbalancing "healthy social forces," as above, has tended to be vague and unspecified, but generally meant to counteract the mother's presumed detrimental influence.

The field of mental *health*, ironically, has neglected the definition of *health*. In the concentration on mental illness, family normality became equated with the absence of symptoms, a situation rarely if ever seen in the clinical setting. Clinical assumptions about normal families have been derived mainly from theory based on experience with dysfunctional cases. Normative (typical) family patterns have received scant attention. Positive attributes of healthy family functioning, where explicit in clinical theory, have tended to be largely speculative and utopian.

VIEWS OF NORMAL FAMILY PROCESSES IN MODELS OF FAMILY THERAPY

The family systems perspective advanced conceptualizations of the family from a linear view of family causality to the recognition of multiple, recursive influences that shape individual and family functioning. Still, in the early development of the field of family therapy, the focus was primarily on dysfunctional family processes presumed to be implicated in the ongoing *maintenance* of individual symptoms, if not in their origins (Hoffman, 1981). Beliefs and assumptions about family normality and the components of healthy functioning remained largely implicit. Over the past decade, there has been a welcome shift in attention and therapeutic aims toward greater recognition and enhancement of family strengths and resources, although these are not well defined.

Because of their critical influence in clinical practice, it is extremely important to examine the views of family normality and dysfunction underlying the major approaches to family therapy. The most influential founding models and more recent developments in the field will be surveyed, considering the four perspectives on family normality outlined above. Despite some differences among various approaches, all consider normal family functioning—whether in terms of average or optimal family patterns—from the overarching perspective of systemic processes. Although any generalizations in a rapidly evolving field must be made with caution, some basic premises about family normality, health, and dysfunction can be discerned in the various approaches. Two questions will frame discussion:

1. *Family Processes*: What are the explicit and implicit assumptions about normal—typical and optimal—family functioning and views of problem development and maintenance?
2. *Therapeutic Goals and Change Processes*: How do these beliefs about normality influence therapeutic objectives and intervention strategies?

As can be seen, various aspects of family functioning receive selective attention as they fit with different views of problem formation, therapeutic goals, and change processes.

Structural Model

Structural family therapy, as developed by Salvador Minuchin and his colleagues, has emphasized the importance of family organization for the functioning of the family unit and the well-being of its members. The model focuses on the patterning of transactions in which symptoms are embedded. Problems are viewed as an indication of imbalance in the family's organization.

Minuchin (1974) directly addressed the issue of normality, contending that a normal, or ordinary, family cannot be distinguished from an abnormal family by the absence of problems. He attacked the myth of "placid" normality—the prevailing idealized view of the normal family as nonstressful, living in constant harmony and cooperation, while coping with social input without upset. Such an image crumbles, argued Minuchin, whenever one looks at any family with ordinary problems.

Through interviews with effectively functioning families from different cultures, Minuchin illustrated the normal difficulties of family life that transcend cultural differences. He described an ordinary family as one in which "the couple has many problems of relating to one another, bringing up children, dealing with in-laws, and coping with the outside world. Like all nor-

mal families, they are constantly struggling with these problems and negotiating the compromises that make a life in common possible" (1974, p. 16).
Particular sensitivity has been shown by structural family therapists to the
barrage of external pressures and constraints on poor inner-city families that
contribute to problems in family organization (Minuchin, Montalvo, Gurney,
Rosman, & Schumer, 1967; Aponte, 1976; Montalvo, 1982). More recently,
Minuchin has directed his efforts to change in larger systems, such as court
and foster-care policies and practices that "dismember" and undermine the
functioning of poor families (Minuchin, 1992).

Assuming that problems are common to all families, Minuchin cautioned therapists not to base judgments of family normality or abnormality
on the presence or absence of problems. Instead, he proposed a conceptual
schema of family functioning to guide family assessment and therapy. This
structural model views the family as a social system, operating within specific social contexts. Three components are emphasized. First, the family
structure is that of an open sociocultural system in transformation. Second,
the family undergoes development over time, progressing through successive stages requiring reorganization. Third, the family adapts to changed
circumstances in ways that allow it to maintain continuity and to further
the psychosocial growth of its members. Symptoms are most commonly a
sign of a maladaptive reaction to changing environmental or developmental requirements.

Falicov (1988a), like Minuchin, has cautioned that therapists who concentrate on pathology and related family dynamics may not give sufficient
attention to processes of continuity and change in family adaptation. All families must respond to internal pressures with developmental transitions or
ideosyncratic problems, such as illness or disability, as well as extrafamilial
forces, such as job loss or racial discrimination. Each new situation stresses
the family and requires reorganization. Transitional processes of adaptation
carry a lack of differentiation and anxiety that may be misjudged or
mislabeled as pathological. Minuchin has therefore urged therapists to view
the family as a social system in transformation:

> With this orientation, many more families who enter therapy would be seen
> and treated as average families in transitional situations, suffering the pains of
> accommodation to new circumstances. The label of pathology would be
> reserved for families who in the face of stress increase the rigidity of their trans-
> actional patterns and boundaries, and avoid or resist any exploration of alter-
> natives. (1974, p. 60)

These distinctions lead to different therapeutic strategies:

> In average families, the therapist relies on the motivation of family resources
> as a pathway to transformation. In pathological families, the therapist needs to
> become an actor in the family drama, entering into transitional coalitions in
> order to skew the system and develop a different level of homeostasis. (p. 60)

In this model, the family structure is conceived as an invisible set of functional demands that organize family interaction. Transactional patterns defining relationships and regulating behavior are maintaned by two constraints: universal rules governing family organization, especially the power hierarchy; and mutual expectations in particular families—explicit or implicit contracts that persist out of habit, mutual accommodation, and functional effectiveness. Each system maintains itself according to preferred patterns, resisting change beyond a certain accustomed range. At the same time, a functional family must be able to adapt to changing developmental and environmental demands. (These requisites of stability and flexibility for family functioning are core dimensions in the research-based family system assessment models of Beavers & Hampson, Chapter 2 and Olson, Chapter 3, this volume.)

Family boundaries—the rules defining who participates how—function to protect the differentiation of the system. Minuchin has stressed that the *clarity* of boundaries is far more important than the particular family composition. The parental subsystem—whether two-parent or single-parent—must establish generational boundaries to maintain its own psychosocial territory and protection from interference by demands of children and extended family. A parental subsystem that includes a grandparent or a parental child can function well as long as lines of authority and responsibility are clearly drawn.

For effective family functioning, while boundaries must be clear and firm, the system must also be flexible enough for interchange between autonomy and interdependence. Both are necessary for promotion of psychosocial growth of members, for maintenance of the integrity of the system, and for continuity and restructuring in response to stress.

In evaluation of family functioning, proximity and hierarchy are two major structural variables (Wood, 1985). Proximity is akin to the concept of cohesion (see Olson, Chapter 3, this volume), and the systemic properties of centripetal and centrifugal tendency (see Beavers & Hampson, Chapter 2, this volume). It is conceived along a continuum, in terms of degree of connectedness, with most families falling within the wide normal range. Patterns of closeness and separateness are viewed as transactional styles or preferences for a type of interaction and not as qualitative differences between functional and dysfunctional families. Cultural norms vary widely; a highly cohesive family style may be both typical and functional in some ethnic groups (see McGoldrick, Chapter 11). Patterns may also vary with different requirements at various life cycle stages (see McGoldrick, Heiman, & Carter, Chapter 14, this volume), as when a family pulls together with young children and then shifts to greater separation and autonomy with adolescence and launching (Combrinck-Graham, 1985).

In practice, the terms "enmeshment" and "disengagement" have tended to be used too loosely, pathologizing patterns of high connectedness or separateness that may be normal in different contexts and functional in particular situations. In most cases, high and low cohesion are preferable terms except for families at dysfunctional extremes. Enmeshment, at one extreme, is characterized by diffuse boundaries, blurred differentiation, and pressure for togetherness that interfere with autonomy, privacy, and problem mastery. Such systems readily become overloaded, lack resources to adapt under stress, and show intolerence for separation at normal developmental transitions. At the other extreme of disengagement, rigid boundaries and distance block communication, relatedness, and the mutually protective functions of the family. These extremes of enmeshment and disengagement have been found to be prevalent in severely dysfunctional families (see Beavers & Hampson, Chapter 2; Olson, Chapter 3, this volume).

The spouse subsystem requires complementarity and mutual accommodation to implement vital tasks. In healthier families, spouses support the better characteristics and creative aspects of their partners. Yet at times, average couples may undermine partners in attempts to improve or rescue them. Minuchin cautions that such negative patterns do not necessarily imply malevolent motivation or serious pathology.

Structural family therapists have emphasized the importance of generational hierarchy in effective family functioning. A strong parental subsystem—whether two-parent or single-parent—is required to perform child-rearing tasks. As parenting has become an increasingly difficult process in today's complex, rapidly changing world, the unquestioned authority of the traditional patriarchal model has been replaced by a concept of flexible, rational authority. Minuchin notes that the ideal family is often described as a democracy: "But they mistakenly assume that a democracy is leaderless, or that a family is a society of peers" (Minnchin, 1974, p. 58). Rather, effective family functioning requires authority, the power to carry out essential functions. Accordingly, a primary structural objective in family therapy is to strengthen the parental subsystem and hierarchy.

Curiously, structural family therapists focused on the generational hierarchy and on forces in the social context but appeared blind to the gender hierarchy in families and sexism in the larger culture (Walsh & Scheinkman, 1989). Yet, the notion of requisite gender roles and power differential, although never explicit in family therapy theory, has nonetheless operated as an implicit assumption in structural formulations of family dysfunction and in therapeutic objectives. Patterns typical (normal) in the modern nuclear family—mother's centrality in the family and father's peripheral position—when seen clinically were linked causally to child symptoms. Therapy was commonly directed to "rebalance" the family by decreasing the mother's influence and involvement while reasserting the father's position of authority and leadership. Goldner (1988) has pointed out that since gender, as well as generation, is a basic structural axis in the family system, therapists must attend to gender differentials in power and status. The feminist critique has challenged Parsonian assumptions linking health with male dominance and with rigid, segregated gender roles and spheres of influence (Hare-Mustin, 1986). Consistent with this challenge, Beavers and his colleagues, examining the power dimension in family systems, have found that a power skew in *either* direction in the couple's relationship (one partner authoritarian and subordinating the other) was associated with more dysfunctional families, whereas healthy families demonstrated more equitable power sharing between spouses (see Beavers & Hampson, Chapter 2, this volume). Also of note is their finding that in many cases family functioning was accompanied by symptoms of distress in mothers, suggesting their disproportionate burden.

In summary, from a structural perspective, no family style is inherently normal or abnormal. Each family develops its own structure and preferences for certain transactional patterns. Whether those processes are functional or dysfunctional depends largely on the *fit* of a system's organization with its functional requirements in developmental and social contexts (Aponte & VanDeusen, 1981). Any style is potentially workable and may meet ordinary demands, although extreme togetherness (enmeshment) or distance (disengagement) are more likely to be dysfunctional. For optimal functioning, a strong generational hierarchy and clear lines of parental authority are considered essential. An equal sharing of power in the couple/parental unit is crucial for a healthy balance. The strength of the system requires clear yet flexible boundaries and subsystems for the ability to mobilize alternative patterns when stressed by internal or external change.

Strategic/Systemic Approaches

Among the most influential and innovative approaches in the field of family therapy have been the strategic approach of the MRI group in Palo Alto, the problem-solving approach by Haley and Madanes, and the systemic approach of the Milan team. More recent outgrowths have been the solution-focused and constructionist/narrative approaches. Strategic therapists, generally, have been more concerned with developing a theory of therapeutic change than a model of the family (Watzlawick et al., 1967). Haley (1976) has made a careful distinction between the two, believing that clinicians have been hampered by theory that attempts to explain human experience and pathology but does not lead to problem solution.

Strategic and systemic approaches view healthy families as highly flexible, using a large repertoire of behaviors to cope with problems. In contrast, a pathological family demonstrates a rigidity and a paucity of alternatives. Beyond this generalization, they deliberately avoid definitions of normality (Jackson, 1977), believing that each family must define what is normal or healthy for itself in its situation. A tolerance for differences and ideosyncracies of families is emphasized (Madanes, 1991). The symptom is seen as a communicative act that is part of a repetitious sequence of behaviors among family members. It appears when an individual is locked into a family pattern and cannot see a nonsymptomatic way of altering it. Therapy focuses on problem resolution by altering feedback loops that maintain symptoms. The therapeutic task is to formulate, or recast, the problem in solvable, behavioral terms. The responsibility of the therapist is limited to initiating change that will get a family "unstuck" from unworkable interactional patterns.

The MRI model (Weakland, Fisch, Watzlawick, & Bodin, 1974) centers on the issue of how families attempt to handle or resolve normal problems in living. Based on the assumption that all families confront problems, a misguided attempted solution may exacerbate the problem, or itself become a serious problem. Therapy focuses on how families *maintain* a problem by precisely the means they are using to handle it. The attempted solution thus becomes the problem requiring therapeutic change.

Haley saw descriptions of family interaction as a way of thinking for purposes of therapy where there is a disturbed child, but stressed that it would be an error to deduce from that a model for what normal families *should* be like. In research observations of over 200 normal—average—families, Haley found patterns so diverse that to talk about a "normal" family seemed to him naive:

> How to raise children properly, as a normal family should, remains a mystery that awaits observational longitudinal studies with large samples. Thinking about the organization of a family to plan therapy is another issue. As an analogy, if a child breaks a leg, one can set it straight and put it in a plaster cast. But one should not conclude from such therapy that the way to bring about the normal development of children's legs is to place them in plaster casts. (1976, p. 108)

Haley therefore selectively focused on key family variables involving power and organization that he considered relevant to therapeutic change. His problem-solving approach, developed with Madanes, combined an interactional view with basic structural principles (Haley, 1976; Madanes, 1991). Haley, like Minuchin, considered family functioning in the context of its current ecosystem, viewing individual symptoms and family crises as arising when families are unable to adjust to life-cycle transitions, such as launching in young adulthood (Haley, 1973, 1980). He also emphasized the importance of social organization and a clear generational hierarchy for effective family functioning. Depending on the culture and composition of a family, three or even four generations may be involved. A variety of arrangements can be functional if the family deals with hierarchical issues (i.e., authority, nuturance, and discipline) and establishes clear rules to govern the power and status differential. For Haley, it is a fundamental rule of social organization that a system becomes dysfunctional and members experience distress when the hierarchical arrangement is confused, particularly when covert coalitions are formed across family generations, as between parent and child against the other parent. The degree of disturbance increases with multiple triangles or malfunctioning hierarchies in which members are embedded. The therapeutic goal is to reduce presenting symptoms and change rigid repeating sequences by interrupting dysfunctional coalitions, encouraging parents to relate as peers in an executive capacity and to define a clearer hierarchy.

Implicitly, strategic and systemic therapists assume an asymptomatic perspective on family normality, equating the absence of symptoms with normality and health and limiting therapeutic responsibility to symptom reduction, freeing a family from unworkable patterns to define its own functional alternatives. They contend that most families do what they do because family members believe it is the right or best way to approach a problem or because it is the only tack they know how to take. The therapeutic task is to interrupt ways of handling the problem that do not work, that is patterns that are dysfunctional. It requires learning the language and conceptualization of each family in order to see the problem through its members' eyes, taking into account their values and expectations that determine their approach to handling the problem and their inability to change (Selvini Palazzoli, Boscolo, Cecchin, & Prata, 1978; Boscolo, Cecchin, Hoffman, & Penn, 1987).

Through such techniques as relabeling and reframing, a problem situation is strategically redefined in order to cast it in a new light and to shift a family's rigid view or response, alter a destructive or stigmatizing blaming or scapegoating process, and overcome impasses to change (Stanton, 1981). Similarly, circular questioning, positive connotation, and neutrality, emphasized in the Milan approach (Boscolo et al., 1987), are often used to contextualize symptoms, attribute benign intentions, and generate hope. Problems are commonly depathologized by viewing them as normative life-cycle complications, considering their adaptive functions for the family, and suggesting the helpful, albeit misguided, intentions of caring members trying to help one another. A problem presented as "inside" an individual, as a character trait, is redefined behaviorally in interactional context. A label of "hysteric" or a diagnosis of depression might be recast as a wife's futile attempt to get attention from her unresponsive husband. In a vicious cycle, the more she complains, the more he withdraws; the more he distances, the more upset she becomes. In such reformulation of a set, new solutions can become apparent (Watzlawick, Weakland, & Fisch, 1974).

Recent developments of solution-focused and narrative approaches (Anderson & Goolishian, 1988; deShazer, 1988; O'Hanlon & Weiner-Davis, 1989; White & Epston, 1990) are based in constructionist views of reality (Hoffman, 1990). Such approaches shift therapeutic attention from problems and the patterns that maintain them to solutions that have worked in the past in other situations or might work now and in the future. With this focal shift, less attention is given to questions concerning the nature of problems or how they arise, and more is directed to future possibilities (Penn, 1985). As in the MRI model, people are thought to be constrained by their narrow, pessimistic views of problems, which limit the range of alternatives for resolution. However, they oppose the view that problems serve ulterior functions, and they assume that clients really do want to change. The therapeutic relationship is less hierarchical than earlier strategic approaches, emphasizing respect for clients, and is oriented more toward recognizing and amplifying the positive strengths and resources that clients bring (Tomm, 1987). Therapeutic rituals are encouraged to facilitate both continuity and change (Imber-Black, Roberts, & Whiting, 1988).

Solution-focused approaches of deShazer (1988) and O'Hanlon (O'Hanlon & Weiner-Davis, 1989) avoid complex formulations of a situation when simple assumptions will lead more quickly to change. They believe complicated problems do not necessarily require complicated solutions. The risk here lies in not addressing the complex web of experience and reciprocal influences inherent in the social context of a problem.

The uses of narrative and "restorying" and White's technique of externalizing problems serve as means through language and perspective to reframe problem situations toward more empowering constructions that enable problem resolution. White and Epston (1990) define an external force, outside the family, that is responsible for wreaking havoc on their lives. The therapist's goal is to align with the child and family as partners who will, together, defeat this negative external force, leaving the family feeling successful and victorious and shifting from vicious cycle to virtuous cycle.

In the constructivist philosophy, multiple realities are accepted and valued pragmatically if useful (Watzlawick, 1984). A serious danger here lies in the assumption that all views presented are equally valid and that they are honest and accurate representations of the experience. Such assumptions become problematic where an individual or family distorts or denies experience and events, such as alcohol abuse, sexual abuse, or suicide.

The widely accepted principle of neutrality, intended to be respectful of each family's values and goals, has been challenged particularly in feminist critique for tacitly reinforcing the status quo of culturally sanctioned gender biases. Even redefined as curiosity without judgment (Cecchin, 1987), a neutral stance, combined with assumptions of circular causality, fails to address abuses of power, especially violence most often destructive to women and children (Walsh & Scheinkman, 1989). We cannot fully understand individual and family distress without considering how family and cultural views of normality—including ethnic, racial, class, and gender norms shape transactions. Further, a therapist cannot be neutral when it comes to issues of normality, since our own world view, including value assumptions about what is healthy or dysfunctional, influence the very questions we ask, our decisions to interrupt or encourage particular family patterns, and the therapeutic conversations we consider important.

Behavioral Approaches

Behavioral approaches to family therapy have developed chiefly from behavior modification and social-learning traditions in psychology. Like the models above, they emphasize the importance of family rules and communication processes, as well as a functional approach to outcome. In distinction, they focus more straightforwardly on the interactional behaviors and conditions under which social behavior is learned, influenced, and changed. Although giving little direct attention to the question of normality in families, behavioral approaches implicitly define a normal family in a functional sense with the assumption that all behavior is adaptive in terms of its functional relationship properties.

Families are conceptualized as critical learning contexts that are simultaneously created and responded to by members. According to social exchange principles, in well-functioning families, the exchange of benefits is far more frequent than the exercise of mutual coercion. Since family relationships involve behavioral exchange over a wide range of possibilities, there are many opportunities for rewarding exchanges likely to maintain the relationship. The importance of positive reward for desired behavior is stressed. In well-functioning families, not only is maladaptive behavior not reinforced, but also adaptive behavior is rewarded through attention, acknowledgment, and approval.

Adaptability, the capability of using diverse behaviors in different situations, is seen as a hallmark of well-functioning families (Weiss, 1978). Reciprocity is also important (Patterson, Reid, Jones, & Conger, 1975), with functional relationships characterized by long-term reciprocity and a trust that the give and take will be balanced out over time. Dysfunctional relationships tend to be more skewed, without mutual accommodation, or are more restricted to short-term tit-for-tat exchanges.

Relationship failure is explained by deficient reward exchanges, as when they shift from positive rewards to coercive control (Patterson et. al., 1975). Relationships may also become distressed by communication deficits, when there is a discrepancy between the intended communication and the impact of the message on the receiver. Symptoms or maladaptive behavior, regardless of origin, may be reinforced or rewarded by the family.

Treatment problems and goals are specified in concrete and observable behavioral terms, with the aim of educating and guiding family members in a straightforward way to learn more effective modes of dealing with each other (Barton & Alexander, 1981). Families may be helped to change the interpersonal consequences of behavior, or contingencies of reinforcement, for more positive acknowledgment and approval of desired behavior. Building communication skills—particularly clear, direct expression of feelings and opinions, negotiation, and problem-solving—is considered a key to promoting more functional family processes.

Several behaviorally oriented researchers of marital functioning have identified factors that predict the long-term success of a marital relationship (Holtzworth-Munroe & Jacobson, 1991). All involve the capacity for adaptability, flexibility, and change. Spouses must be able to evolve together and cope with the multitude of challenges and external forces in their lives. It is assumed that these competencies can be learned. There is increasing recognition of gender differences in relationship styles and preferences, for example, in women's greater valuing of closeness as a requisite for relationship satisfaction (Jacobson & Margolin, 1979).

A range of communication skills are seen as essential for marital satisfaction versus dissatisfaction and divorce. Gottman and Levenson (1992) describes a cascade of negative interactions that lead to marital failure. Similarly, Markman (1981) has found that the hallmark of marital satisfaction and best predictor of marital success is not the absence of conflict but conflict management: how differences, when they arise, are handled and resolved. His behavioral approach teaches ground rules for handling conflict. Among the tenets of effective problem solving are that: difficult issues must be controlled, partners may mutually call time out whenever needed, escalating conflicts need to be slowed down, arguments should be kept constructive, withdrawal should be avoided, and involvement maintained. Partners are coached to accomplish these aims. The approach empowers couples to fight for their marriage.

The assumptions by behavioral family therapists about the adaptive value of specific family behaviors are largely construed from observations of distressed couples and families. Although empirical support of their ideas and methods is considered essential, they acknowledge that the scant data on nondistressed families as yet provides little confirmation of these assumptions about optimally functioning families in the real world (Falloon, 1991).

Psychoeducational Approaches

Psychoeducational approaches to family intervention by Anderson (Anderson, Reiss, & Hogarty, 1986) and others (Goldstein & Kopeikin, 1981; Falloon, Boyd, & McGill, 1984; McFarlane, 1991) were developed to provide information, management guidelines, and social support to families in the treatment of schizophrenia. The model is based on the assumption that the patient has a core biological deficit and that environmental sources of stress interact negatively with that vulnerability to produce disturbed thinking and behavior.

The approach does much to correct the blaming, causal attributions experienced by so many families of the mentally ill (Hatfield & Lefley, 1987). In contrast to more traditional treatment approaches that presumed the family invariably to be a pathogenic influence on the patient, family members are engaged as valued and essential collaborators in the treatment process. Families are viewed as caregivers and vital resources in the long-term adaptation of the patient and for effective functioning in the community. The rationale for family intervention is based on the importance of support to the family, practical information, and problem-solving assistance through predictably stressful periods that can be anticipated in the future course of a serious and chronic mental illness.

Psychoeducational approaches are finding application in a wide range of problem situations faced by normal (i.e., average) families, including marital and family enrichment (Guerney, 1991), family caregiving with chronic physical illness (see Rolland, Chapter 15, this volume), and stressful family transitions, such as divorce and remarriage (Walsh, 1991). By identifying common challenges associated with stressful situations, family distress is reduced and normalized through refocus on mastery of adaptational tasks. Families are helped to develop and implement coping skills through direct teaching, coaching, and practice. They are helped to anticipate crises and plan how to handle future stress. Psychoeducationally oriented multifamily groups provide social support, sharing of problem-solving experiences, and reduction of stigma and isolation of families.

Psychoanalytic/Transgenerational Approaches

Growth-oriented transgenerational approaches to family therapy rooted in psychoanalytic traditions have bridged psychodynamic, object relations, self psychology, and family systems theories. Family interaction is conceptualized in terms of object relations, related internalizations, and processes of introjection, projection, and projective identification (Meissner, 1978; Skynner, 1976). Traditionally, psychoanalytic models, from Freud to attachment theory, have focused narrowly on the role of maternal influences in early childhood in determining normal or pathological individual development. Psychodynamically oriented family therapists have expanded attention to the ongoing dynamic processes of the family as a social unit over the course of individual and family development, including the importance of sibling relationships (Bank & Kahn, 1982).

The primary goal of a normal family is seen as promoting the development of well-differentiated and individuated identity in offspring. The parents, individually and through the marital and parental relationships they construct, are regarded as the architects of healthy or pathological family functioning, promoting attachment, separation, and individuation processes necessary for the healthy development of offspring. An optimally functioning family provides a "holding environment" for members, a context of security, trust, and nurturance to support individual maturation (Scharff & Scharff, 1987). The object relations model attends particularly to the quality and nature of emotional dynamics underlying bonding and differentiation. Attention to parenting has tended to retain much of the traditional analytic focus on early maternal influences, with a skewed concentration on deficiencies in contrast to a vague ideal postulated in the notion of the "good enough mother" (Walsh & Scheinkman, 1989).

From an intergenerational stance, the capacity to function as a spouse and as a parent is largely determined by each individual's family of origin experiences. The relative success or failure in accomplishing developmental

tasks is influenced strongly by residues of internalized objects and the organization of introjects contributing to identity integration. A functional marriage is described as a committed relationship, capable of intimacy, relatively
well-differentiated and unambivalent, with few irrational expectations,
motives, and fantasies projected onto the other, and with self-acceptance and
acceptance of the partner as "good enough" despite flaws and disappointments (Scharff & Scharff, 1987).

The interlocking of individual projection and introjection processes
forms a shared projection process based on complementarity of needs,
influencing mate choice as well as marital and parent–child relationship patterns (Boszormenyi-Nagy & Spark, 1973). Reciprocal relationship bargains
involve implicit agreements among family members to relate on the basis
of unfulfilled needs. In a functional family, each partner/parent is able to
take responsibility for his or her own pathological projections, can contain,
accept, or modify projections by the other, and can maintain trust and
empathy. Parents are aware and free enough from intrapsychic conflicts to
invest in parenting and be responsive to their children's developmental needs.
Over time, family interactions modify the images of spouses, parents, and
siblings, so that perceptions can mature without becoming frozen or distorted.

In dysfunctional families, a greater degree of unconscious unresolved
conflict or loss interferes with realistic appraisal of and response to other
family members (Paul & Paul, 1975). Accordingly, Framo (1970) has viewed
symptoms as resulting primarily from unconscious attempts by spouses/
parents to reenact, externalize, or master through current relationships the
intrapsychic conflicts originating in the family of origin. The symptomatic
member may serve as a scapegoat for family conflicts (Ackerman, 1958). The
loss of a significant relationship may disrupt the entire family system, with
emotional upheaval and unresolved grief expressed in symptoms by a family member or distress in other relationships (Paul & Grosser, 1991; Paul &
Paul, 1975). In some cases, symptoms may express an irrational role assignment, or projective transference distortion, which is reinforced by family
myths and ritualized into the family's structural pattern. For example, Stierlin
(1974) described the ways in which adolescent separation problems can result from intense centripetal or centrifugal family pressures (enmeshment
or disengagement) to either bind or expel members. (His clinical observations were consistent with the empirically based Beavers Systems Model,
[see Beavers & Hampson, Chapter 2, this volume] and the Circumplex Model
by Olson [see Olson, Chapter 3, this volume]).

Accordingly, assessment and treatment explore the connection of multigenerational family dynamics to resulting disturbances in current functioning and relationships. The therapist facilitates awareness of covert emotional
processes and encourages members to confront and deal directly with one
another, either in sessions or between, to work through unresolved conflicts

and losses, and to test out, update, and alter negative introjects from the past (Framo, 1991). The conjoint format serves to build empathy and mutuality, strengthening the marital and family unit.

The contextual approach of Boszormenyi-Nagy (1987) emphasizes the ethical dimension of healthy family relationships, examining the multigenerational legacies of parental accountability and filial loyalty that guide members over the course of the life cycle. Families are thought to be strengthened by actions toward trustworthiness, based on consideration of members' welfare interests for survival, growth, and relatedness. Trustworthiness functions to enhance autonomy in problem-solving. In well-functioning families, autonomy is encouraged by the family legacy, and members are not bound by any real or imagined "ledger" of unpaid debts. Autonomy is attained through efforts toward relational equitability. Whereas imbalances of fairness are seen as inevitable, flexibility and reciprocity over time are seen as crucial requisites. Ideally, the family life cycle is characterized by open negotiation of transitions and changing loyalty commitments, with awareness of legacy expectations. Dysfunction is thought to stem from covert but powerful unresolved issues of family-of-origin loyalty. Therapy aims toward the reconstruction and reunion of current extended family relationships through the resolution of grievances involving loyalty and legacy issues.

In sum, from a psychodynamic perspective, family processes and psychopathology are primarily conceptualized in terms of the interlocking of parental individual dynamics, multigenerational loyalties, conflicts, and losses, and transferences or unconscious role assignments from the past. More implicitly than explicitly, these approaches hold a model of optimal functioning toward which therapeutic growth is encouraged. The ideal, however, is not clearly articulated, and theory and therapy generally focus on the reduction of negative and unconscious dynamic processes in the family through insight, facilitation of more direct communication, and efforts toward relational equitability. Views of healthy family processes have been extrapolated from clinical theory based on dysfunctional cases. Between the pathological and the ideal, little is said about average, or ordinary families. The pathological bent is strong. With few exceptions, notably Boszormenyi-Nagy, intergenerational dynamics are usually presented as negative influences to be contained or resolved. More attention should be given to sources of strength and positive legacies from family of origin experience that contribute to healthy marital and family functioning and can be drawn upon in therapy.

Bowen Model

Bowen (1978; Kerr & Bowen, 1988) developed both a theory of the family emotional system and a method of therapy from observation of a wide range of families, viewing them on a continuum from the most impaired, to normal (i.e., average), to optimally functioning families. Bowen believed that psychiatry never adequately defined normality simply in terms of freedom from emotional symptoms or of behavior in the normal range. Instead, he accounted for the variability in functioning by the degree of anxiety and degree of differentiation in a family. The concept of differentiation of self is not directly tied to the presence or absence of symptoms. Even well-differentiated people can be stressed into dysfunction, but they tend to use a variety of coping mechanisms and to recover rapidly. When anxiety is low, most systems can appear normal, in the sense of being symptom-free. When anxiety increases and remains high, tensions develop in the relationship system, interfering with differentiation and resulting in symptoms of dysfunction.

The characteristic of differentiation of self, thought to be universal, is used to categorize all people on a continuum, according to the degree of fusion between emotional and intellectual functioning. At the low extreme, lives are dominated by automatic emotional processes and reactivity; people are easily stressed into dysfunction and have difficulty recovering. Toward the high end, intellectual functioning remains relatively autonomous under stress; individuals are more adaptable, flexible, and independent of surrounding emotionality, and they cope better with life stresses. The upper extreme is a theoretical ideal level of functioning that is rarely, if ever, attained. Most people fall in the moderate range, with variable intellectual and emotional balance. Their overt feelings are intense, and their relationship orientations make them reactive to others out of needs for closeness and approval. Human problems and neurotic-level symptoms are thought to erupt when the emotional system is unbalanced.

In the profile of "moderate to good differentiation of self," Bowen (1978) described marriage as a functioning partnership in which spouses can enjoy the full range of emotional intimacy without losing their autonomy. They can permit their children to develop autonomous selves without undue anxiety or attempts to mold offspring in their own images. Parents and children are each responsible for themselves and do not credit others for their successes or blame others for their failures. As situations require, they are able to function well alone or with others. Their lives are more orderly, they cope with a broad range of human situations, and they are relatively free of human problems.

Bowen believed that each family has its own average level of differentiation around which members fluctuate. Variation in individual and family levels is related to several factors:

1. The *nuclear family emotional system* is the pattern of emotional functioning between spouses and between parents and children, which replicates patterns of past generations. The level of functioning depends chiefly on the degree of differentiation of each spouse from the family of origin.

2. A *triangle*, a three-person configuration in an emotional system, is formed when a two-person system, overloaded and anxious under stress,

involves a vulnerable third person. If tension cannot be absorbed, a series of interlocking triangles may be formed, spreading to extended family and outsiders.

3. Through the *family projection process*, parental anxiety is focused on one or more children triangulated with parents. This process, present to some degree in all families, can range from minimally to severely impairing. When families use a combination of mechanisms to deal with stress, it is less likely to be disabling. In almost every family, one child is more triangled than others, with poorer life adjustment. The intensity and involvement of a particular child is dependent on many factors, such as the developmental timing of stress (McGoldrick & Walsh, 1991).

4. *Emotional cut-off* is an attempt at separation from the family through isolation, withdrawal, running away, or denying the importance of the parental family. Bowen maintained that the more viable emotional contact is sustained with families of origin, the more orderly and asymptomatic the life processes will tend to be.

Stresses on the family system, especially by death, tend to decrease differentiation and heighten reactivity (Bowen, 1978). Anxiety commonly results in triangulation or cutoffs of highly charged relationships. Underfunctioning, or symptoms, may be linked with and reinforced by overfunctioning in other parts of the system in a compensatory cycle. Improved functioning is believed to result when emotional reactivity no longer blocks intellectual processes.

Bowen has emphasized the importance of a healthy balance of intellectual and emotional functioning and of differentiation and togetherness. The model has been criticized for its implicit gender bias in defining this balance. Attributes of healthy functioning include: autonomous, being-for-self, intellectual, and goal-directed. The poorly differentiated person is described as: valuing relatedness, seeking love and approval, and being-for-others. A traditionally feminine orientation appears to be devalued and pathologized, whereas male norms of autonomy, reason, and achievement are set as the criteria for health, with little balance evident on the scale (Luepnitz, 1988). Although Bowen did tilt the balance of intellect and emotion toward cognitive control of feelings, it is a fused, reactive emotional position that is regarded as dysfunctional (Carter & McGoldrick Orfanidis, 1976; Herz, 1991). Those low in differentiation are dominated by their emotions, which override planful, intellectual modes of thought.

The emphasis on differentiation has been misunderstood by some to be concerned only with achieving separateness and autonomous functioning. Overdependency on others in relationships blocks the ability to pursue independent interests and achievements. At the same time, differentiation is promoted in order to achieve the goal of richer, deeper relationships, blocked when members are either too closely fused or reactively distanced or cut off. The Bowen model emphasizes a relationship orientation by maintaining connectedness and repairing relationship cut-offs. The central objective in Bowen therapy is the differentiation of self *in relation to others*. It involves being both separate and connected.

The Bowen model is growth-oriented, with a therapeutic mandate for exploration and change beyond symptom reduction toward increased differentiation of self. It is assumed that current marital or family problems or symptoms in a child will be resolved with the increased differentiation of the spouses/parents from each other and from their extended families. Accordingly, the goal of therapy is to assist both individuals to modify their relationships with their families of origin, achieving a higher level of differentiation and reduced anxiety in direct contact. The therapist assumes a role as consultant or coach, guiding each individual through carefully planned steps of intervention (Carter & McGoldrick Orfanidis, 1976).

The family evaluation process surveys the entire nuclear and extended family field. A genogram (McGoldrick & Gerson, 1985) and timeline diagram the network of relationships, important facts and nodal events (e.g., births, deaths, illnesses, ethnicity), and complex relationship information (e.g., alliances, conflicts, triangles, cut offs). An individual is coached to contact extended family members to clarify obscured information and to gain new perspectives on relationships and family members as persons. The process of differentiation is advanced by redeveloping personal relationships with key family members, repairing cut offs, detriangling from conflicts, and changing the part played in emotionally charged vicious cycles. The therapist encourages an "I-position," a clear statement asserting one's own thoughts and feelings. Detriangling and other methods are employed to open up rigid interactional patterns; humor is used to detoxify emotional situations. Follow-through is essential to handle the anxiety generated by the process and self-correcting attempts by the system that undermine change.

In sum, Bowen theory defines healthy/optimal functioning in terms of differentiation of self. Functioning is thought to be impaired by poorly differentiated relationship patterns characterized by high anxiety and emotional reactivity. Although the ideal is rarely attainable, it does serve as a model toward which therapeutic progress is directed.

Experiential Approaches

Experiential approaches to family therapy were developed by two leading pioneers in the field, Virginia Satir and Carl Whitaker. Their therapeutic approaches are highly intuitive and relatively atheoretical, yet both have held strong views on the essential elements of healthy family functioning.

Satir (1964, 1988), who blended a communication approach with a humanistic orientation, observed a consistent pattern in her experience with optimally functioning families—defined as untroubled, vital, and nurturing. The sense of self-worth in family members is high. Communication is direct, clear, specific, and honest. Family rules for members are flexible, human, appropriate, and alterable. The family linkage to society is open and hopeful. By contrast, in troubled families the sense of self-worth is low; communication is indirect, vague, and dishonest; rules are rigid, inhuman, non-negotiable, and everlasting; and social linkages are fearful, placating, and blaming. Regardless of the specific problem that leads a family into treatment, Satir believed it is crucial to change those key factors to relieve family pain and enhance family vitality.

Those four aspects of family life—self-worth, communication, rules, and link to society—were regarded by Satir as the basic forces operating in all families, whether an intact, one-parent, blended, or institutional family. She envisioned the even greater variety and complexity of families in the future, making these family ingredients for human growth all the more essential.

Whitaker, in his symbolic–experiential model, has distinguished the healthy, well-functioning family by a number of attributes (Whitaker & Keith, 1981; Metcoff & Whitaker, 1982). Foremost is the maintenance of an integrated whole, characterized by appropriate separation of parent–child generations and by flexibility in power distribution, rules, and role structure. Normal families maintain open systems with clear yet permeable boundaries, relating to the extended family and the outside world while maintaining the primacy of the nuclear family unit. They are able to demonstrate a wide range of levels of intimacy and separateness, with the ability for separateness required for high intimacy. The same counterbalancing linkage is seen between dependency and autonomy, and in the expression of positive and negative feelings. Whitaker stresses the importance of family humor and playfulness—or "as if" behavior—for creative fantasy and experimental process. Humor can diffuse tensions and metacommunicate about contentious issues and positions without direct confrontation. He believes that normal families are able to regress, temporarily, *en masse* for the sake of growth. However, he doesn't clarify the distinction from destructive regression in pathological cases.

The dimension of time is central in Whitaker's conception of health. Normal families have an evolutionary sense of time and of becoming, a continual process of growth and change, progressing through the life cycle and over several generations. Strong transgenerational connections are experienced, with internal images brought up to date and modified. Loyalty and mutual commitment (similar to Boszormenyi-Nagy's concept of merited trust) create a foundation of relational permanence, fostering a sense of group wholeness and buffering periods of stress and disorganization. Family rituals are valued, and a guiding mythology (akin to belief system) evolves over time. Family patterns are stable and yet modifiable as life changes are demanded. Whitaker believes that all families are essentially normal and only become abnormal in the process of pain caused by trying to be normal.

All families are seen to have normative stresses. The capacity for problem solving, or generating solutions, is a critical aspect of healthy functioning. A well-functioning family possesses the resources to solve its problems, drawing on past experience, family myths and stories, creative fantasy, input from support networks, new and untried solutions, and random trial and error. Tolerance for conflict allows for overt disagreement and acknowledgment of differences, with resolution through agreement, compromise, or new framing of the problem. Expectations are periodically reexamined and renegotiated. Negotiations do not necessarily proceed smoothly and may involve conflict, pain, and anger, but in a well-functioning family they are experienced as transient disruptions that do not result in long-term despair, perceptions of failure, or family dissolution.

For Whitaker, the marital relationship lays the foundation for a healthy family. A functional marriage is continuously balanced, or mutual, and reciprocal in terms of the partners' interest and emotional responsivity. Whitaker is the only family systems theorist to address sexuality and intimacy as critical components in marital functioning. Symbolic–experiential theory has emphasized the importance of role flexibility and balance to promote adult growth and development for both husband and wife, with gender inequality as one major contributor to dysfunctional marriages (Roberto, 1992).

Experiential approaches are aimed beyond symptom reduction to individual and family growth, attending to the shared affective experience and the totality of the family as an interactive, self-maintaining system (Napier & Whitaker, 1978). Regardless of awareness or intent, old pains are propagated and intensified by current interaction around them. To explain and change behavior, key elements in family process and their mutual influence are addressed. All are believed to be changeable and correctable.

These growth-oriented approaches promote fuller awareness and appreciation of oneself in relation to others through an intense, affective experience in open communication of feelings and differences. The therapist takes a phenomenological approach to assessment and treatment of the individual in the family interaction process, following and reflecting the immediate experience, and catalyzing exploration, experimentation, and spontaneity of members' responses to one another to stimulate genuine and nondefensive relating. Experiential exercises, such as family sculpting and role play facilitate this process.

Summary of Clinical Models

The family models surveyed reflect somewhat different, yet in many respects overlapping definitions of family normality. All approaches are firmly grounded in a family systems orientation, viewing normality in terms of ongoing transactional processes over time. At the same time, various family systems theorists and family therapy approaches differ in further elaboration of normality as "average" and normality as "healthy" (optimal functioning).

Table 1.1 summarizes the views of normal family functioning, dysfunction, and therapeutic goals embedded in major approaches to family therapy.

The brief, problem-solving approaches (structural, strategic-systemic, behavioral, and psychoeducational models) tend to view normality in functional terms; normal family processes are those that work without reinforcing symptoms in any member. The theoretical and clinical approaches tend to be cross-sectional and immediate in focus on altering current dysfunctional patterns in the most proximate interactional context. Clinicians who incorporate developmental, cultural, and feminist perspectives attend more broadly to family processes over time and to wider influences of health and dysfunction in the extended family and larger systems.

The growth-oriented transgenerational approaches, in particular, psychodynamic, Bowen, and experiential models, hold more explicit views of family normality in terms of emotional dynamics and optimal processes for family functioning and the healthy development of offspring. They give greater attention to historical influences in health and dysfunction and yet focus intervention on change in current family transactions. They share the view that healthy, or functional, family processes are characterized by completion of important developmental tasks, by acceptance and nurture of the attributes and needs of individual members through empathic relatedness, and by tolerance for differentiation, conflict, and adaptive change (Roberto, 1992). Although there is tacit recognition that optimal functioning is unattainable in most families, therapeutic goals nonetheless are directed beyond symptom reduction to growth toward those ideals.

Brief therapy approaches that focus too narrowly on problem solving in the immediate context may err in presuming that a family, once unblocked from a dysfunctional pattern, will be able to shift to and sustain healthier modes on their own. At the other extreme, growth-oriented approaches risk pushing families toward unrealistic and unreachable ideals of functioning. This can be especially dangerous when therapy becomes an endless quest for vaguely defined value-laden visions of family health reflecting the clinician's own belief system.

Conceptually, although the various family approaches differ in many ways in their definition of family normality and dysfunction, they are remarkably free in general from major contradiction or inconsistency. There is considerable overlap among clinical theorists in their views of the functioning of nonclinical or average families. Those who posit a model of healthy functioning are largely in agreement about the distinguishing features of optimally functioning families. Where differences among models do appear, they reflect more a conceptual focus, or selective emphasis on particular aspects of family functioning: on structural patterns, communication and problem-solving processes, relational dynamics, or meaning systems.

Components of family functioning posited in one domain of family functioning can be seen to have correlates in other domains. For example, the

TABLE 1.1. Major Approaches to Family Therapy: Normality, Dysfunction, and Therapeutic Goals

Model of family therapy	View of normal family functioning	View of dysfunction/symptoms	Goals of therapy
Problem-solving approaches			
Structural	1. Generational hierarchy with strong parental authority. 2. Boundaries and subsystems clear. 3. Flexibility of system for: a. Autonomy and interdependence. b. Continuity and adaptive restructuring to fit changing internal and external demands.	No families are problem-free. Symptoms result from current family structural imbalance: 1. Malfunctioning generational hierarchy, boundaries 2. Enmeshed or disengaged style. 3. Maladaptive reaction to changing demands (developmental, environmental).	Reorganize family structure: 1. Shift members relative positions to disrupt malfunctioning pattern and strengthen parental hierarchy. 2. Reinforce clear, flexible boundaries. 3. Mobilize more adaptive alternative patterns.
Strategic/ systemic	1. Flexibility. 2. Large behavioral repertoire for: a. Problem resolution. b. Life-cycle passage.	Symptom is a communicative act embedded in interaction pattern. Multiple origins of problems; symptoms maintained by: 1. Unsuccessful problem-solving attempts. 2. Impasse at life-cycle transition. 3. Rigid view; paucity of alternatives.	1. Resolve presenting problem; specific pragmatic objectives. 2. Interrupt rigid feedback cycle: change symptom-maintaining sequence to new outcome. 3. Shift perspective to enable more empowered position.
Behavioral	1. Adaptive behavior is rewarded; maladaptive behavior is not. 2. Exchange of benefits outweighs costs; reciprocity. 3. Communication and problem-solving ability. 4. Flexibility.	Maladaptive, symptomatic behavior reinforced by: 1. Family attention and reward. 2. Deficient exchanges (e.g., coercive, skewed). 3. Communication deficits.	Concrete, observable behavioral goals: 1. Change contingencies of social reinforcement. 2. Reward adaptive behavior, not maladaptive. 3. Communication, problem-solving skills training.
Psycho-educational	Successful coping and mastery of developmental challenges: 1. Caregiving in chronic illness. 2. Tasks and skills in couples' relationships and family life.	1. Stress/diathesis in biologically based disorders. 2. Normative and non-normative stresses (e.g. in couples' relationships, parenting, remarriage, adverse life events).	Information, coping skills, and social support for: 1. Family management of chronic illness. 2. Stress and stigma reduction. 3. Mastery of family adaptational challenges.
Transgenerational/ growth approaches			
Psychodynamic	1. Parental personalities and relationships well differentiated. 2. Relationship perceptions based on current realities, not projections from past. 3. Provide context of security, trust, nurturance for bonding and individuation.	Symptoms due to shared family projection process stemming from unresolved conflicts, loyalty issues, and losses in family of origin. a. Scapegoating. b. Unconscious role assignment.	1. Insight and resolution of family of origin conflicts and losses. 2. ↓Family projection processes. 3. Relationship reconstruction and reunion. 4. More empathic relating.
Bowen approach	1. Differentiation of self in relation to others 2. Intellectual/emotional balance.	Functioning impaired by relationships with family of origin: a. Poor differentiation (fusion). b. Anxiety (reactivity). c. Triangulation. d. Emotional cut-off.	1. Differentiation: separate and connected. 2. ↑Cognitive functioning. 3. ↓Emotional reactivity. 4. Modify relationships in family system: a. Detriangulation. b. Repair cut-offs.
Experiential	1. High self-worth. 2. Clear, honest communication. 3. Flexible, appropriate family rules and roles. 4. Open, hopeful social links. 5. Evolutionary growth, change. 6. Pleasureable, playful interaction.	Symptoms are nonverbal messages in reaction to current communication dysfunction in system.	1. Direct, clear communication through immediate shared experience. 2. Catalyze exploration, experimentation, spontaneity. 3. Genuine non defensive relating.

Bowen model emphasizes relationship patterns in the differentiation of self; this concept has structural and communicational correlates in such terms as clear differentiation of generations in the organizational hierarchy and in clarity of communication. Flexibility, or adaptability, is viewed across all models as critical to healthy family functioning.

PROGRESS AND CHALLENGES FOR FAMILY THERAPY: TRAINING, PRACTICE, AND RESEARCH

As a new generation of family therapists has come to the fore over the past decade, there has been increasing dialogue and integration of family therapy approaches (Lebow, 1984) and more multidimensional views of family functioning (Breunlin, Schwartz, & MacKune-Karrer, 1992; Nichols & Schwartz, 1991; Rolland & Walsh, 1993). It is useful to highlight a number of important developments over the past decade, noting progress and challenges ahead for family therapy training and practice, and for family process research.

Clinicians' Views of Family Normality and Health

With recent perspectives from constructivism and social constructionism (Hoffman, 1990), we have become more aware that clinicians—as well as researchers—co-construct the pathologies they "discover" in families. We also co-construct therapeutic goals tied to family and therapist beliefs about family health. Therapists cannot avoid normative thinking at some level (Atkinson & Heath, 1990; Keeney & Sprenkle, 1982). This makes it imperative for clinicians to be aware of their own assumptions about normality and cognizant of cultural norms.

Clinical sensitivity to normative (typical) family challenges and judgments about optimal family functioning reflect therapists' values and beliefs rooted in cultural, professional, and personal orientations. It is important for clinical training programs to explore how these basic premises about normal family functioning influence family assessment and intervention (Fisher & Sprenkle, 1978; Walsh, 1987).

In a survey of 184 family therapists in the Midwest, I found that judgments of criteria for healthy family functioning varied widely. Not surprisingly, the attributes rated most highly were those most valued in each clinician's particular practice model. Psychodynamically oriented clinicians listed such qualities as empathy, mutual trust, and absence of distorting projection processes. Bowen therapists emphasized differentiation. Structural family therapists regarded parental leadership and clear generational boundaries as most crucial to optimal family functioning. Behaviorally oriented therapists considered communication and problem-solving skills to be paramount. Most rated flexibility highly, a consistent value across models.

Beliefs about family normality from clinicians' own life experience also influence family evaluation and intervention goals. In the above survey, family therapists tended to rate as normal those interactional styles that were either similar to or opposite from their own family experience. Most interestingly, almost half of the clinicians perceived their own family of origin as not having been "normal." Yet, being "abnormal" held quite different meanings for respondents, much like the different perspectives on normality identified above. Some viewed their own families as very disturbed, or pathological. Others saw their families as abnormal in being *atypical,* not conforming to average families in their community, such as having a "working" mother or being a divorced family. Still others felt their families were deficient in not living up to the *ideal* "normal family," as portrayed in television images popular when they were growing up such as "Leave It to Beaver." Generally, family differences from either average or optimal norms were experienced as stigmatized deviance (bad or harmful) and as deficiencies in failing to measure up to a standard.

Clinicians' perceptions were also found to be influenced by the experience of having been in therapy themselves. Those who had received traditional psychodynamically oriented individual therapy tended to view their own families as more pathological—especially their mothers—and were more pessimistic about changing family patterns than those who had been in systems-oriented therapies, who were less blaming and more hopeful about change. Such experiences and perceptions profoundly influence clinical beliefs about the families we treat and the possibilities for change.

Training Experience with "Nonclinical" Families

The training of therapists profits immeasurably from exposure to non-clinical families. Clinicians tend to notice what they are trained to see. They are likely to be blind where training is lacking and to ascribe dysfunction where training is skewed toward pathology. In my own family therapy courses, I routinely assign an assessment interview with a non-clinical family, attending to the diversity of family perspectives and experiences relative to life-cycle phase, family form, gender position, and socioeconomic context (Walsh, 1987). Such contact and the discussion generated by the range of "normal" families encountered proves to be one of their most valuable learning experiences.

When clinical students are given this opportunity, several interesting responses typically occur. First, students voice concern that they don't know any "normal" families and wouldn't know how to recognize or find one. They puzzle and disagree over definitions of both "family" and "normality." The myth of a singular model of the normal family persists—even among bright and talented students. One African–American student worried that she couldn't do the assignment because all the inner-city families she knew weren't "normal"—they were single-parent families. Another student

wondered if a gay couple would "count." Such questions provide an opportunity to deconstruct stereotyped images, myths, and assumptions and
to construct new definitions encompassing a broad spectrum of family normality.

The assignment also brings to the fore pathologizing tendencies in clinical training. The problem focus of clinical interviewing leaves students anxious about what to talk about without a presenting problem. Some worry
that the "normal" family they interview may turn out to "really" be disturbed
as they "uncover" pathology, as they have indeed been trained to do. They
further worry that they might expose—or explode—underlying family tensions and damage the family. Many return from their interviews believing
they had been wrong in their first impression of the family as "normal"
because the family had revealed problems, conflicts, deficits, deviant life
styles, or skeletons in their closet.

In sharing their experiences, students begin to appreciate that all families are challenged in one way or another and have some problematic areas
of functioning. But since they are also guided to assess strengths and
resources, students become much more appreciative of family competencies and resilience and see that they can be found in quite diverse family
arrangements. As trainees discuss and compare their experiences, skewed
perceptions of family normality and pathology shift perceptibly. Multiple-
observer perspectives are enhanced by having students pair up to conduct
the interview. Students are encouraged to discuss their observations and assessments and to notice similarities and differences in experience of the family
related to their own gender, ethnic background, and current family life cycle
stage. An important byproduct of the experience is the discovery that each
clinician is part of the assessment system and influences what is observed,
the information that emerges, and the functional versus dysfunctional judgments ascribed to relational patterns. In expanding clinicians' perspectives
on normality, the experience also depathologizes their views of clinical families in distress.

A multimodal family assessment is highly recommended, including the
following: (1) interviews to gather different family member perspectives on
their shared history, experience, and worldview; and (2) direct observation
of family interaction on a structured task, such as planning an activity together, solving a problem, discussing a topic on which they disagree, or joint
story-telling. A family functioning assessment framework or rating scale, such
as those presented in Section II of this volume, can be used to describe and
evaluate specific aspects of family interaction, highlighting strengths and
resources as well as deficits and conflicts.

Errors in Pathologizing Normal Processes

In practice, clinicians risk making two types of errors in regard to questions
of normality (Walsh, 1983). The first is to mistakenly identify as pathological a pattern that is normal, or to misconstrue difference (deviance) as ab-

normal (pathological). Certain family processes may be typical and expect-able (normal as average) in particular family situations or under stressful circumstances. For instance, in cases of chronic mental or physical illness, family distress generated by the demands of coping with a member's dis-abling condition can be misdiagnosed as family pathology and presumed to have played a causal role in the development of the disorder. In fact, the family may be coping as well as could be realistically expected, given that patient's biological vulnerability and the family's depleted resources (Walsh & Anderson, 1988; see Rolland, Chapter 15, this volume).

In other cases, a clinician may confound family style variance with pathology. A pattern that differs from norms—either typical or ideal—is not necessarily dysfunctional. For example, the pathologizing label "enmeshed family" is too readily misapplied to families showing high cohesion. The value of autonomy and separateness versus togetherness varies widely. In the dominant American culture, the great weight on independence and self-reliance can lead to misdiagnosis of family pathology in ethnic groups whose norms vary and thus can lead to inappropriate therapeutic goals.

A common error is to type a family as "enmeshed," presuming pathol-ogy when high cohesion may be functional and even necessary in that family's life context, as when a family must pull together to meet a crisis. Laird (Chapter 10) raises precisely this concern in the tendency to label high connectedness in lesbian couples as "fusion," with its pathological implica-tions. Similarly, Zacks, Green, and Marrow (1988) found that on the Circumplex Model cohesion scale, lesbian couples scored in the high ex-treme, a pattern labeled enmeshment and widely considered dysfunctional. However, for the women in the relationship, this high cohesion was mutu-ally satisfying and functional in fortifying the relationship in a homophobic social context.

Such concerns should make us wary of any family typology that labels a family by a single trait or stylistic feature. Clinical assessments that reduce the richness of family interaction to a one-dimensional label, (e.g., "This is an Enmeshed Family") should be avoided. Such labels too often stereotype families, are reductionistic, and are too readily confounded with pathology. As Lewis, Beavers, Gossett, and Phillips (1974) observed in their pioneering study of a wide range of families, "no single thread" distinguishes healthy from dysfunctional families. Rather, we must consider the many strands that are intertwined in family functioning and assess families on multiple system dimensions and be aware that differences are not necessarily dysfunctional. (See Beavers & Hampson, Chapter 2, Olson, Chapter 3, and Epstein et al., Chapter 4, this volume, for leading multifaceted systems models of family functioning.)

Errors in Normalizing Dysfunction

The second type of error is to fail to recognize a dysfunctional family pat-tern by assuming it to be normal. Here, it is important for clinicians to be aware of their own value-laden assumptions and to be knowledgeable about research on family functioning. For example, the myth that healthy families are conflict-free (Walsh, 1983, 1992) may lead a therapist to collude in a couple's claims of perfect harmony. Conflict avoidance can be dysfunctional over time, heightening the risk for later marital dissatisfaction and divorce (Gottman & Levenson, 1992). Healthy relationships are distinguished not by the absence of conflict but by effective conflict management, requiring open disagreement with good communication skills for resolution.

Normalizing Family Distress

Ordinary nonclinical families in our society worry a good deal about their own normality (Walsh, 1983, 1992). In a culture that readily pathologizes families for any problem and touts the virtue in self-reliance, family members are likely to approach therapy feeling abnormal for having a problem and deficient for being unable to solve it on their own. Such feelings and beliefs are compounded by the overwhelming and confusing changes in family life, along with dwindling resources and a lack of relevant models for effective functioning. Further, referrals for family therapy are often based on the presumption that if an individual, especially a child, is showing a problem, the family must be the "real" problem and cause, or must need the problem to serve a function for them. Much of what clinicians label as family "resistance" in therapy stems from the fear of being judged abnormal or deficient and blamed for their problems. This "resistance" is too often taken as further evidence of their pathology.

It is crucial to appreciate the shaming and stigmatizing experience of families who have felt prejudged and blamed in contacts with mental health professionals, schools, or courts. Such families are likely to expect a therapist to judge them negatively and may mistake a silent neutral stance as confirmation of this view. Clinicians should explore each family's beliefs about its own normality or deficiency and the models and myths they hold as ideal. And we need to disengage assumptions of pathology from participation in therapy. Rather than presenting—or implying—family causality as the rationale for family therapy, we need to emphasize every family's importance as collaborators in problem resolution.

The aim of normalizing is to *depathologize* and *contextualize* family distress. It is not intended to reduce all problems and families to a common denominator and should not trivialize a family's experience and distress. We need to be careful neither to oversimplify the complexity of contemporary family life nor to err in normalizing truly destructive family patterns. Violence and sexual abuse should never be normalized, even though they have become all too common in families as in the larger society. Likewise, acceptance of diversity is not the same as "anything goes," when family processes are destructive to any family member. We are only beginning the most important dialogue in our field, examining the myth of therapeutic neutrality and sorting out serious ethical questions and therapeutic responsibility.

Cultural Diversity: Critical Challenges

Diverse Family Forms

There is growing recognition of the importance of larger socioeconomic and cultural influences in family well-being and dysfunction (e.g., Imber-Black, 1988; Mirkin, 1990). Yet, clinical theory and practice have not kept pace with the dramatic changes in family structure and options that have occurred. The ideal model of the middle-class, intact nuclear family, with traditional gender roles, often subtly, yet powerfully underlies therapist views of families and what should change (Walsh & Scheinkman, 1989) just as it influences a family's self-appraisal. We must make clear to families that we do not presume that varying family arrangements are inherently pathological or the likely cause of any presenting problems.

Our beliefs and language can pathologize or distort family relationships. The label "latchkey child" attributes maternal neglect when parents must work. The term "single-parent family" can blind us to the important role of a noncustodial parent (Walsh, 1991). A stepparent or adoptive parent relationship is viewed as inherently deficient when framed as not the "real" or "natural" parent (Visher & Visher, 1979, 1988). One judge denied a parental rights request by a lesbian woman who shared parenting for her partner's biological child on the grounds that it would be too confusing for a child to have two mothers. The same argument disenfranchises stepparents. Even when a child is functioning well, the knowledge that he or she is living in any family situation other than the standard too often sets expectations by teachers or counselors that there must be underlying or latent damage that, like a time bomb, will sooner or later explode (Wallerstein & Blakeslee, 1989). We need to be mindful that families in the distant past and in many other cultures have had multiple caregivers and that healthy family processes matter more than family form.

The wide spectrum of family arrangements should receive greater attention in clinical theory and training. Of particular value is knowledge about the normative expectable challenges and tasks accompanying various family transitions and configurations (Carter & McGoldrick, 1988; see McGoldrick, Heiman, & Carter, Chapter 14). Research on nonclinical families, particularly longitudinal process studies, holds enormous import for clinicians to identify and support adaptive processes (see Hetherington et al., Chapter 7). Further, our attention should not be limited to members who share a household but, rather, extend to significant relational networks: every individual is a member of a family, whether living under the same roof, within a community, or scattered at great distance. The myth of the isolated nuclear family, intact and self-sufficient within the boundary of the white picket fence, should not blind us to the intimate and powerful connections among family members living separately and even at great distance. We need to recognize the significance of families of choice, especially the intimate partnerships and friendship networks formed in gay and lesbian communities (Weston, 1991). The strength and support of such networks in times of adversity, as in the AIDS crisis (Walker, 1991; Landau-Stanton, 1993), holds a model of community that too many families in the dominant culture have lost.

Gender and Sexism

Feminist critique in family therapy (in particular, Goldner, 1985, 1988; Goodrich, Rampage, Ellman, & Halstead, 1988; Hare-Mustin, 1986; McGoldrick, Anderson, & Walsh, 1989; Walters, Carter, Papp, & Silverstein, 1988) has brought long overdue attention to the subordinated status of women in families and in the larger society and to gender biases in family theory and family therapy (Luepnitz, 1988; Taggart, 1985; Walsh & Scheinkman, 1989). A therapeutic stance of neutrality and the tenet of circular influence can be seen to tacitly reinforce cultural biases and to ignore the power differential that perpetuates violence and sexual abuse of vulnerable women and children. Therapists still tend to blame mothers for individual and family problems, pathologizing the traditional gender-role care-taking responsibility as enmeshment and overinvolvement, or the nontraditional working mothers' role as neglect. Although we have become more aware of these issues, we have yet to adequately deal with them in clinical training and practice (Wheeler, Avis, Miller, & Charney, 1989).

Concern for men's gendered role expectations and experiences is also coming to the fore (Meth & Passick, 1990; Pittman, 1993), exploring how the male model for rationality, competition, power, and instrumental success in the workplace has constrained family involvement, intimacy, and emotional expressiveness. Increased attention is needed to gender socialization and sexism in larger social systems and their reverberations for family relations. In particular, we need to rebalance the power differential between men and women, share more fully in parenting, and expand options for our children.

Culture, Race, and Class

Family therapists are becoming more attuned to cultural diversity. Many ethnic scholars and practitioners, notably in the work of McGoldrick and her colleagues (McGoldrick, Pearce, & Giordano, 1982; see McGoldrick, Chapter 11, this volume), Aponte (1976), Billingsley (1992); Falicov (1983; in press), Boyd-Franklin (1989; see Chapter 12, this volume), Landau-Stanton (1990), McAdoo (1985), Saba, Karrer & Hardy (1989) have enriched our understanding of different cultural norms and experiences and have alerted us not to pathologize differences that may indeed be functional—or necessary for survival. Yet we must give far greater attention to issues of poverty and racism.

Diverse Life-Cycle Challenges

Family therapy, concentrating in its early development on families with children and adolescents, needs to attend to the full and varied course of the life cycle, to the normative (typical) developmental phases and transitions (Cowen & Hetherington, 1991; see McGoldrick, Heiman, & Carter, Chapter 14, this volume) as well as the challenges that make every family unique. Some women and men become first-time parents at the age that others become grandparents. Adults who remain single or couples who remain childless have intimate relationships and significant kin and friendship bonds that clinicians should not ignore. New technologies enabling conception and others prolonging the dying process pose unprecedented family and clinical challenges. Family relationships in later life, a neglected area of clinical attention (Walsh, 1988), should become an arena of training priority as our society ages over coming decades, four and five generations become more common, and growing numbers of aging family members require caregiving.

Interactive Effects

Consideration of cultural diversity needs to be better integrated into our training and practice approaches, not marginalized as special issues (Falicov, 1988b), with attention to the *interactions* of sexism, racism, heterosexism, ageism, classism, handicapping conditions, and other forms of discrimination and prejudice. Further, as systems therapists, we have an affirmative responsibility to advocate for meaningful social change to benefit the families we treat. Goldner (1988) has voiced a concern shared by many that the emphasis of pragmatic family therapy approaches on "what works is best" can blind therapists to the social and cultural factors behind simplistic assumptions about the causes of human distress and the ease of solutions. A risk in a narrow focus on immediate intrafamilial problem situations is the failure to address larger issues, such as gender bias and racism, that permeate society. We have only begun the most important dialogue in our field to address serious ethical questions concerning our responses and responsibilities toward achieving gender equality and social justice.

From Deficit to Resource Model

The skewed perspective that long dominated the clinical field is being rebalanced as we shift our focus from limitations, deficits, and pathology to a competency-based, health-oriented paradigm, recognizing and amplifying family strengths and resources. This is a positive, future-oriented stance, shifting the emphasis of therapy from what went wrong to what can be done for enhanced functioning—imagining possible options appropriate to each family and reachable through shared, constructive efforts.

The very language of therapy can pathologize the family. We have become more sensitive to the blame, shame, and guilt implicit in labels of "schizophrenogenic mother" or "schizophrenic family," with their attributions of family causality. We must be more careful to avoid demeaning language and pejorative assumptions about dysfunctional family processes, such as "dirty games" played by "destructive" families with a seriously disturbed member (Selvini Palazzoli, 1986; Anderson, 1986). Clever but dehumanizing metaphors, as in *Fishing for Barracuda* (Bergman, 1985), present an image of therapy with dysfunctional families as a hazardous sport, in which the family can devour the therapist if not hooked and outmaneuvered. Clinical training posits an adversarial struggle when therapist skills are taught as powerful strategies to reduce family pathology and overcome family resistance. Implicit in such power-based approaches to therapy has been an asymmetrical relationship between the expert helper/healer as normal/ healthy, and the patient/family who is pathological/deficient.

We need to recognize that successful interventions rest as much on the resources of the family as on the resources of the therapist (Karpel, 1986). Social constructionist perspectives have heightened awareness that our therapeutic language and constructions need to become more respectful of families. Power-based, hierarchical models of family therapy are, likewise, being eschewed in favor of more egalitarian and collaborative approaches. Rather than viewing the therapist as expert and powerful, and the family as deficient, incompetent, and resistant, this orientation views the therapist in partnership with the family, building on existing or potential systemic strengths and resources. Similarly, Combrinck-Graham (1990) has argued against the tendency to focus on psychopathology and proposes instead that we search for competence and work within larger systems—empowering family, friends, and teachers—as a more powerful way to promote the well-being of children.

A family resource perspective is especially useful in work with multi-problem families (Walsh, in press[a]). Treatment that is overly problem-focused can grimly replicate the joyless experience of family life where problems are all-pervasive. Interventions aimed at enhancing positive interactions, supporting coping efforts, and building extrafamilial resources are more effective to reduce stress, enhance pride and competence, and promote more effective functioning. Considerable potential can be found in psycho-educational approaches, marital and family enrichment, and family consultation (Wynne, McDaniel, & Weber, 1986) to provide much needed information, skills, and support to families coping with serious and chronic disorders, as well as to those in more normative, transitional distress. Problem-solving communication skills training workshops are being designed to stabilize and strengthen families, such as divorce prevention programs for high-risk couples. Premarital inventories, such as Olson's Prepare (see Chapter 3), can predict later marital satisfaction or divorce and target specific strengths and problem areas. We need to expand such approaches in the development of community-based programs, offering natural settings for valuable family-focused prevention and early intervention services.

My own clinical approach and research have evolved toward a family resilience framework for understanding the strengths and vulnerabilities of families as they confront inevitable life challenges (Walsh, in press[a]). This involves a shift in perspective from family damage to family challenge. A challenge model of family resiliency corrects the tendency to think of family strengths and resources in a mythologized problem-free family. Instead, we need to understand how families can survive and regenerate even in the midst of overwhelming stress, adversity, or life-altering transition (Karpel, 1986). This approach has much in common with emerging approaches to understand individual resiliency (Cohler, 1987; Master & Garmezy, 1989; Rutter, 1987), and the concept of relational resilience (Jordan, 1992). In particular, Wolin's Challenge Model (Wolin & Wolin, 1993) has sought to identify the qualities of healthy individuals who showed resilience despite growing up in troubled families. Just as important, we need to direct research attention to healthy families who demonstrate resilience in response to adverse life challenges to identify the key transactional processes that enable mastery. It is important to understand the ingredients of family resilience: how it is possible for some families to emerge hardier from adversity—not in spite of, but actually strengthened through their experience.

Progress and Challenges for Family Research

A rebalancing of family research and funding priorities from psychopathology to health and prevention is crucial to move beyond the rhetoric of family strengths and resources to clearer delineation of the components of healthy family functioning and interventions to support them. Section II of this volume presents three pioneering models of family system functioning that have found wide application. Such models offer empirically based family assessment tools with potential utility for intervention planning and outcome evaluation. Clinicians can assess a family's current functioning on key system dimensions and target focal priorities for support or change toward more optimal levels (Walsh & Olson, 1989).

Family studies have become increasingly multidisciplinary (Berardo, 1991; Booth, 1991), yet the bridges between the social sciences and the clinical field need to be developed further for mutual exchange of perspectives and approaches to understanding family functioning (Walsh, in press[b]). As new concepts and methods are advanced, three areas of research challenge are important to note.

Stress, Coping, and Adaptation

Stress research in the social sciences has long held promise for understanding individual and family coping and adaptation (Boss, 1987). Two recent developments hold particular potential. The Family Adjustment and Adaptation Response (FAAR), a process model by McCubbin and Patterson (1983), evolved from earlier work grounded in Hill's (1949) pioneering ABCX Model (1949). The cognitive appraisal model of stress and coping, advanced by Lazarus and Folkman (1984) offers a multi-level, multi-process model for individual adaptation with many parallels yet to be fully explored at the family system level.

A family life challenge framework can usefully guide inquiry with families undergoing stressful transitions, crises, and hardship, distinguishing the critical family processes and mediating variables that buffer stress and enable the family unit and its members to adapt. We have much to learn from resilient families to inform our interventions with families in distress, such as families who are able to successfully navigate the disruptions and reorganizations in divorce and remarriage processes (see Hetherington et al., Chapter 7; Visher & Visher, Chapter 8, this volume), or families confronting challenges such as serious illness and loss (see Rolland, in press and Chapter 15, this volume; Walsh & McGoldrick, 1991).

Quantitative and Qualitative Methods

We are coming to value the contributions of both quantitative and qualitative methodologies. More quantitative family functioning research has focused on organizational and communication patterns that can be measured through observation, rating scales, and self-report questionnaires. Qualitative methods, currently coming into greater use, hold potential for exploring meanings, perceptions, and other subjectivities in and about families (Gilgun, Daly, & Handel, 1993; Moon, Dillon, & Sprenkle, 1990; Rosenblatt & Fischer, 1993). Both insider and outsider perspectives yield important information (Olson, 1977). Ethnographic methods and narrative accounts of experiences and their meanings for family members can be particularly valuable for understanding family development over time, as well as for understanding the formation and transformation of shared family belief systems that both shape and reflect family organizational patterns and communication processes. Postpositivist research, currently coming to the fore, does not reject empirical research and the pursuit of knowledge but, rather, emphasizes the contextual and self-referential nature of the research process and findings (Doherty, Boss, LaRossa, Schumm, & Steinmetz, 1993). Postpositivist approaches are finding application in phenomenologically based theories of the family and critical theories attending to sociocultural and political influences, particularly gender, race, and ethnicity.

Dilemmas of Diversity

Early research on family functioning centered on white, Protestant, middle-class, intact nuclear families, considered typical of the dominant culture in the United States and Canada, and, most often, in the life-cycle stage of adolescence. Over the past decade, our data base has been extended to other groups and through comparison studies (e.g., Kazak et al., 1989; Vega, 1990; Beavers & Hampson, 1990; Beavers & Hampson, Chapter 2, Olson, Chapter 3, this volume), but we have much to learn.

Many questions arise concerning the applicability to diverse families of questionnaire items and evaluation scales standardized on normative samples currently representing a narrow band on the spectrum. Families in other developmental stages, structural arrangements, or economic and cultural contexts still tended to be evaluated in comparison to that standard, with assessment instruments, categories, and norms that might not be relevant. The influences of cultural value biases and social desirability have been problematic in some family assessment schemas, such as the Family Environment Scale (FES) by Moos and Moos (1976, 1986). Do we pathologize families who differ from the norming standard? Are the constructs of health valid in different contexts? Are the questions and indicators relevant to various groups? Do we need to construct different instruments and separate norms for various groups? Does that risk separatism and stereotyping, in overemphasizing differences among groups? Are there simply too many variables for any norms to be meaningful? We will need to address these dilemmas if we are to strike a balance that allows us to identify key components of effective family functioning while taking differences into account.

In future research and theory construction, the challenges in defining family normality are twofold. First, we need to identify the family processes that are typical, or expectable, for families of varying forms and sociocultural contexts and in relation to particular life challenges. Second, we need to identify key family process components and mediating variables for effective family functioning, the well-being of members, and successful adaptation. To address both questions, we must continue to develop our constructs and methods to fit the diversity of family structural arrangements, values, and life challenges that comprise the wide spectrum of family normality.

Components of Healthy Family Functioning

Our growing knowledge of normal family processes can enable clinicians to identify key components of family functioning and guide interventions to draw on, expand, and reinforce family strengths and resources (Walsh, in press[a]). Diverse family challenges are not well served when therapy is driven by an invariant approach or set of techniques for every family and problem—akin to "one size fits all"—despite the lack of evidence to support all-purpose claims of efficacy (Gurman, Kniskern, & Pinsof, 1986). The recommendation of Gurman and Kniskern (1978) nearly two decades ago stands as a critical unmet challenge: A major task for family therapy and research is to determine which elements of intervention are most appropriate and effective with which presenting problems and with which elements of family functioning. It is crucial to assess each family's strengths and vulnerabilities, in relation to their particular social and developmental contexts, in order to set appropriate intervention objectives. A family functioning assessment framework can guide more informed selection of relevant family variables for problem resolution and strengthening family functioning. Attention to components of effective family functioning offers a positive and pragmatic frame for intervention, generating optimism in the therapeutic process while grounding changes in specific reachable objectives.

In addition to the empirically based Beavers Systems Model (Beavers & Hampson, 1990), Olson Circumplex Model (Olson, Russell, & Sprenkle, 1989), and McMaster Model (Epstein, Bishop, & Lewin, 1978; see Part II, this volume), a number of other family systems theorists and researchers have proposed a variety of conceptual schemas based on systems principles for mapping components of healthy family functioning (Barnhill, 1979; Fleck, 1980; Kantor & Lehr, 1975; Moos & Moos, 1986; Schumm, 1985; Skinner, Santa Barbara, & Steinhauer, 1983; Stinnett & DeFrain, 1985). In delineating and organizing variables, all researchers and clinicians bring their own selective focus and interpretations, such that these models can not be easily synthesized into a blueprint for a single unified model.

A quest for consensus is perhaps misguided, for we have come to question the generalizability and appropriateness of any single model for health, realizing the variety and complexity of contemporary family relationship patterns. Nevertheless, in surveying the major clinical and research-based models, despite selective emphasis of various aspects of family functioning and somewhat different definition of constructs, there is considerable overlap and agreement about key variables. With awareness of my own subjectivity in mapping a territory we all inhabit, and at the risk of oversimplification in selecting a set of basic elements, I do believe we can usefully identify a number of important processes for healthy family functioning:

1. Connectedness and commitment of members as a caring, mutually supportive relationship unit ("We are family").
2. Respect for individual differences, autonomy, and separate needs, fostering the development and well-being of members of each generation, from the youngest to the eldest.
3. For couples, a relationship characterized by mutual respect, support, and equitable sharing of power and responsibilities.
4. For nurturance, protection, and socialization of children and caretaking of other vulnerable family members, effective parental/executive leadership and authority.
5. Organizational stability, characterized by clarity, consistency, and predictability in patterns of interaction.
6. Adaptability: Flexibility to meet internal or external demands for change, to cope effectively with stress and problems that arise, and to master normative and nonnormative challenges and transitions across the life cycle.
7. Open communication characterized by clarity of rules and expecta-

tions, pleasurable interaction, and a range of emotional expression and empathic responsiveness.

8. Effective problem-solving and conflict-resolution processes.
9. A shared belief system that enables mutual trust, problem mastery, connectedness with past and future generations, ethical values, and concern for the larger human community.
10. Adequate resources for basic economic security and psychosocial support in extended kin and friendship networks and from community and larger social systems.

Each of these process elements reinforces other components. For instance, a core belief that problems can be mastered both furthers—and is reinforced by—effective problem-solving strategies. A counterbalance of processes is also important. For example, a balance between stability and flexibility is needed for continuity and change (see Olson, Chapter 3, this volume). Likewise, needs for connectedness and togetherness must be balanced by tolerence for individual autonomy and separateness.

It is important to keep in mind that these basic components of family functioning may be organized and expressed in quite diverse ways and to different degrees as they fit different family configurations, resources and constraints, family and cultural values, and the life challenges unique to each family. For example, specific roles and rules and an optimal balance of connectedness/separateness will vary for a dual-earner family, a single-parent household with extended family involvement, a stepfamily spanning two or more households, heterosexual and gay or lesbian domestic partners, or a single adult caring for aging parents.

In assessing normal family processes, it is important to distinguish clearly between typical and optimal patterns, and to emphasize that whereas certain interactional dilemmas are expectable and certain strategies are likely to be more effective than others, each family is unique and should be encouraged to invent its own optimal solutions. Just as there is no single type that should be held up for families to emulate, there are many pathways to healthy family functioning.

SUMMARY

In asking "What is a normal family?" we have been framing the wrong question. We need to focus on family processes, not on a singular or invariant family form or set of traits. Further, we must distinguish between "typical" and "optimal" meanings of the term "normal" and, from a systemic perspective, address each in relation to social and developmental contexts. While some might argue that the subjectivity of any constructions of normality make it impossible and unwise to address the topic at all, I would contend that this very subjectivity makes it all the more imperative to examine the notions of normality that powerfully influence all clinical theory and practice, family process research, and social policy.

The societal upheavals of recent decades and the growing diversity of families have complicated matters further, leaving many wary about defining *any* family pattern as normal—either typical or optimal. We need to be mindful that families in our society were always diverse. A sociohistorical perspective reveals that it was our illusion of a singular model of the normal family—as both average and ideal—that blinded us to this diversity and the potential for healthy functioning in a variety of family arrangements. It is the stigmatizing of differences as inherently pathological that must be addressed.

Just as therapeutic neutrality is impossible, since we can never be value-free, it is naive—and ethically questionable—to adopt a neutral position toward normality, dismissing it from consideration or maintaining a stance of "anything goes" or a "one-size-fits-all" model of intervention. We need to be aware of the implicit assumptions about normality we bring to our work with families from our own world view, including cultural standards, clinical theories, and personal experience. A well-intentioned silence on questions of normality may reinforce client expectations that, instead, we are judging them as abnormal because they have problems or fail to fit a cultural ideal of the normal family. We must be especially mindful that, in today's changing world, families are confused and concerned about their own normality and well-being as they question old myths and assumptions and experiment with new and complex family arrangements. We need to become more knowledgeable about family functioning *in its diversity* if we are to be attuned and responsive to the broad spectrum of families we serve.

Efforts to investigate and conceptualize normal (typical) and healthy (optimal) family processes are clarifying better questions as we seek to understand family functioning. How do ordinary families cope with life challenges? What are the mediating variables in well-functioning families that facilitate successful mastery and adaptation? Our most difficult challenge is to be aware of our assumptions and biases and to attempt to be true to the complexity and diversity of contemporary family forms and processes. Just as we need to see today's family diversity as part of the fabric of society, we need also to appreciate the commonalities that unite us all. It would be a grave error to swing from one extreme, of holding a single model of family normality and health, to the other extreme, of concluding that family diversity prevents us from identifying any commonalities or unifying principles for family well-being. The chapters that follow speak, from many perspectives, to the value in understanding normative family challenges and identifying key processes that enable family competence. A both/and position is needed in our clinical theory, practice, and research. We would err by replacing a denial of diversity with a blindness to our commonalities. As Maya Angelou, a poet for our times, reminds us, "Human beings are more alike than they are unalike."

REFERENCES

Ackerman, N. W. (1958). *The psychodynamics of family life.* New York: Basic Books.

Ahrons, C., & Rogers, R. H. (1989). *Divorced families: Meeting the challenges of divorce and remarriage.* New York: John Wiley & Sons.

Anderson, C. M. (1982). The community connection: The impact of social networks on family and individual functioning. In F. Walsh (Ed.), *Normal family processes* (1st ed., pp. 425–445). New York: Guilford Press.

Anderson, C. (1986). The all-too-short trip from positive to negative connotation. *Journal of Marital and Family Therapy, 12,* 351–354.

Anderson, C. M., Reiss, D., & Hogarty, G. (1986). *Schizophrenia and the family.* New York: Guilford Press.

Anderson, H., & Goolishian, H. (1988). Human systems as linguistic systems: Preliminary and evolving ideas about the implications for clinical theory. *Family Process, 27,* 371–393.

Aponte, H. (1976). Underorganization in the poor family. In P. Guerin (Ed.), *Family therapy: Concepts and methods.* New York: Gardner.

Aponte, H., & VanDeusen, J. (1981). Structural family therapy. In A. Gurman & D. Kniskern (Eds.), *Handbook of family therapy.* New York: Brunner/Mazel.

Aries, P. (1962). *Centuries of childhood: A social history of family life.* New York: Knopf.

Bane, M. J. (1976). *Here to stay: American families in the twentieth century.* New York: Basic Books.

Bank, S., & Kahn, M. (1982). *The sibling bond.* New York: Basic Books.

Barnhill, L. (1979). Healthy family systems. *Family Coordinator, 28,* 94–100.

Barton, C., & Alexander, J. (1981). Functional family therapy. In A. Gurman & D. Kniskern (Eds.), *Handbook of family therapy.* New York: Brunner/Mazel.

Bateson, G. (1979). *Mind and nature: A necessary unity.* New York: Dutton.

Bateson, M. C. (1989). *Composing a life.* New York: The Atlantic Monthly Press.

Beavers, W. R., & Hampson, R. B. (1990). *Successful families: Assessment and intervention.* New York: Norton.

Bellah, R., Madsen, R., Sullivan, W., Swidler, A., & Tipton, S. (1985). *Habits of the heart: Individualism and commitment in American life.* Berkeley: University of California Press.

Berardo, F. (1991). Family research in the 1980s: Recent trends and future directions. In A. Booth (Ed.), *Contemporary families: Looking forward, looking back.* Minneapolis, MN: National Council on Family Relations.

Bergman, J. (1985). *Fishing for Barracuda: The pragmatics of brief systemic therapy.* New York: Norton.

Bernard, J. (1982). *The future of marriage.* New Haven, CT: Yale University Press.

Bertalanffy, L. von. (1968). *General system theory: Foundation, developments, applications.* New York: Braziller.

Billingsley, A. (1992). *Climbing Jacob's ladder: The enduring legacy of African–American families.* New York: Simon & Schuster.

Bohannan, P. (1985). *All the happy families: Exploring the varieties of family life.* New York: McGraw-Hill.

Booth, A. (Ed.). (1991). *Contemporary families: Looking forward, looking back.* Minneapolis, MN: National Council on Family Relations.

Boscolo, L., Cecchin, G., Hoffman, L., & Penn, P. (1987). *Milan systemic family therapy: Conversations in theory and practice.* New York: Basic Books.

Boss, P. (1980). Family boundary changes across the life-span. *Family Relations.* 29, 445–450.

Boss, P. (1987). Family stress. In M. B. Sussman & S. K. Steinmetz (Eds.), *Handbook of marriage and the family.* New York: Plenum.

Boss, P. (1989). Family sociology and family therapy: A feminist linkage. In M. McGoldrick, C. Anderson, & F. Walsh (Eds.), *Women in families: Framework for family therapy.* New York: Norton.

Boszormenyi-Nagy, I. (1987). *Foundations of contextual family therapy.* New York: Brunner/Mazel.

Boszormenyi-Nagy, I., & Spark, G. (1973). *Invisible loyalties.* New York: Harper & Row.

Bott, E. (1957). *Family and social networks: Roles, norms, and external relationships in ordinary urban families.* London: Tavistock.

Bowen, M. (1978). *Family therapy in clinical practice.* New York: Jason Aronson.

Boyd-Franklin, N. (1989). *Black families in therapy: A multisystems approach.* New York: Guilford Press.

Breunlin, D., Schwartz, R., & MacKune-Karrer, B. (1992). *Metaframeworks: Transcending the models of family therapy.* San Francisco: Jossey-Bass.

Bronfenbrenner, U. (1979). *The ecology of human development.* Cambridge, MA: Harvard University Press.

Brooks-Gunn, J., & Chase-Lansdale, L. (1993). Correlates of adolescent pregnancy and parenthood. In C. G. Fisher & R. M. Lerner (Eds.), *Applied developmental psychology.* Cambridge, MA: McGraw-Hill.

Burton, L. (1990). Teenage childbearing as an alternative life-course strategy in multigeneration black families. *Human Nature, 1,* 123–143.

Carter, E., & McGoldrick Orfanidis, M. (1976). Family therapy with one person and the family therapist's own family. In P. Guerin (Ed.), *Family therapy: Theory and practice.* New York: Gardner.

Carter, E., & McGoldrick, M. (Eds.). (1980). *The family life cycle: Framework for family therapy.* New York: Gardner.

Carter, B., & McGoldrick, M. (Eds.). (1989). *The changing family life cycle: Framework for family therapy.* Boston: Allyn & Bacon.

Cecchin, G. F. (1987). Hypothesizing, circularity, and neutrality revisited: An invitation to curiosity. *Family Process, 26,* 405–414.

Chase-Lansdale, L., & Brooks-Gunn, J. (1991). Children having children: Effects on the family system. *Pediatric Annals, 20,* 467–481.

Cherlin, A., & Furstenberg, F. (1988). The American family in the year 2000. In J. Gipson Wells (Ed.), *Current issues in marriage and the family.* New York: Macmillan.

Chilman C, Nunnally, E. & Cox, F. (1988). *Variant family forms.* Beverly Hills, CA: Sage.

Cohler, B. (1987). Adversity, resilience, and the study of lives. In E. J. Anthony & B. Cohler (Eds.) *The invulnerable child.* New York: Guilford.

Cohler, B. & Geyer, S. (1982). Psychological autonomy and interdependence. In F. Walsh (Ed.), *Normal family processes* (1st ed.) New York: Guilford Press.

Combrinck-Graham, L. (1985). A developmental model for family systems. *Family Process, 24,* 139–150.

Combrinck-Graham, L. (1990). *Giant steps: Therapeutic innovations in child mental health.* New York: Basic Books.

Constantine, L. (1986). *Family paradigms.* New York: Guilford Press.

Cowen, P., & Hetherington, M. (1991). *Family transitions.* Hillsdale, NJ: Erlbaum.

de Shazer, S. (1988). *Clues: Investigating solutions in brief therapy.* New York: Norton.

Doherty, W. (1991). Postmodern family therapy. *Family Therapy Networker 15,* 36–42.

Doherty, W., Boss, P., LaRossa, R., Schumm, W., & Steinmetz, S. (1993). Family theories and methods: A contextual approach. In P. Boss, W. Doherty, W. LaRossa, W. Schumm, & S. Steinmetz (Eds.), *Sourcebook of family theories and methods: A contextual approach.* New York: Plenum.

Duvall, E. (1977). *Marriage and family development* (15th ed.). Philadelphia: Lippincott.

Edelman, M. W. (1992). *The measure of our success.* Boston: Beacon.

Ehrenreich, B. (1989). *Fear of falling: The inner life of the middle class.* New York: Pantheon.

Epstein, N., Bishop, D., & Levin, S. (1978). The McMaster model of family functioning. *Journal of Marriage and Family Counseling, 4,* 19–31.

Falicov, C. (Ed.). (1983). *Cultural perspectives in family therapy.* Rockville, MD: Aspen.

Falicov, C. (Ed.). (1988a). *Family transitions: Continuity and change over the life cycle.* New York: Guilford Press.

Falicov, C. (1988b). Learning to think culturally. In H. Liddle, D. Breunlin, & R. Schwartz (Eds.), *Handbook of family therapy training and supervision.* New York: Guilford Press.

Falicov, C. (in press). *Latino families in therapy.* New York: Guilford Press.

Falloon, I. (1991). Behavioral family therapy. In A. Gurman & D. Kniskern (Eds.), *Handbook of family therapy* (2nd ed.). New York: Jossey-Bass.

Falloon, I., Boyd, J., & McGill, C. (1984). *Family care of schizophrenia: A problem-solving approach to the treatment of mental illness.* New York: Guilford Press.

Faludi, S. (1991). *Backlash.* New York: Crown.

Figley, C. (1989). *Helping traumatized families.* San Francisco: Jossey-Bass.

Fisher, B., & Sprenkle, D. (1978). Therapists' perceptions of healthy family functioning. *International Journal of Family Counseling, 6,* 9–18.

Fleck, S. (1980). Family functioning and family pathology. *Psychiatric Annals, 10,* 46–57.

Framo, J. (1970). Symptoms from a family transactional viewpoint. In N. Ackerman (Ed.), *Family therapy in transition.* Boston: Little, Brown.

Framo, J. (1992). *Family-of-origin therapy: An intergenerational approach.* New York: Brunner/Mazel.

Furstenberg, F., & Cherlin, A. (1991). *Divided families: What happens to children when parents part?* Cambridge: Harvard University Press.

Furstenberg, F., & Spanier, G. (1987). *Recycling the family: Remarriage after divorce.* Beverly Hills: Sage.

Garbarino, J. (1992). *Children in danger: Coping with the consequences of community violence.* San Francisco: Jossey-Bass.

Gergen, K. (1991). *The saturated self.* New York: Basic Books.

Gilgun, J., Daly, K., & Handel, G. (Eds.) (1993). *Qualitative methods in family research.* Newbury Park, CA: Sage.

Glick, P. C. (1992). American families: The way they are and were. In A. Skolnick & J. Skolnick (Eds.), *Family in transition* (7th ed.). New York: Harper Collins.

Goldner, V. (1985). Feminism and family therapy. *Family Process, 24,* 31–48.

Goldner, V. (1988). Gender and generation: Normative and covert hierarchies. *Family Process, 27,* 17–33.

Goldstein, M., & Kopeikin, H. (1981). Short- and long-term effects of combining drug and family therapy. In M. Goldstein (Ed.), *New developments in interventions with families of schizophrenics*. San Francisco: Jossey-Bass.

Goodrich, T. J., Rampage, C., Ellman, B., & Halstead, C. K. (1988). *Feminist family therapy: A casebook*. New York: Norton.

Gordon, L. (1988). *Heroes of their own lives*. New York: Viking.

Gottman, J., & Levenson, R. (1992). Marital processes predictive of later dissolution: Behavior, physiology, and health. *Journal of Personality and Social Psychology, 63,* 221–233.

Gralnick, A. (1943). The Carrington family: A psychiatric and social study. *The Psychiatric Quarterly, 17,* 294–326.

Grinker, R. R. (1967). Normality viewed as a system. *Archives of General Psychiatry, 17,* 320–324.

Guerney, B. (1991). Marital and family enrichment research: A decade review and look ahead. In A. Booth (Ed.) *Contemporary families: Looking forward, looking back.* Minneapolis: National Council on Family Relations.

Gurman, A., & Kniskern, D. (1978). Research on marital and family therapy: Progress, perspective, and prospect. In S. Garfield & A. Bergin (Eds.), *Handbook of psychotherapy and behavior change* (2nd ed.). New York: John Wiley & Sons.

Gurman, A., Kniskern, D., & Pinsof, W. (1986). Research on marital and family therapy. In A. Bergin & S. Garfield (Eds.), *Handbook of psychotherapy and behavior change* (3rd ed.). New York: John Wiley & Sons.

Haley, J. (1973). *Uncommon therapy.* New York: Norton.

Haley, J. (1976). *Problem-solving therapy.* San Francisco: Jossey-Bass.

Haley, J. (1980). *Leaving home.* New York: McGraw-Hill.

Hare-Mustin, R. (1986). The problem of gender in family therapy theory. *Family Process, 26,* 15–27.

Hareven, T. (1982). American families in transition: Historical perspectives on change. In F. Walsh (Ed.), *Normal family processes* (1st ed.). New York: Guilford Press.

Hatfield, A., & Lefley, H. (Eds.). (1987). *Families of the mentally ill.* New York: Guilford Press.

Herz, F. (1991). *The family tapestry.* New York: Norton.

Hill, R. (1949). *Families under stress.* Connecticut: Greenwood Press.

Hill, R., & Rogers, R. (1964). The developmental approach. In H. T. Cristensen (Ed.), *Handbook of marriage and the family.* Chicago: Rand McNally, 1964.

Hochschild, A. (1989). *The second shift: Working parents and the revolution at home.* New York: Viking Penguin.

Hoffman, L. (1981). *Foundations of family therapy.* New York: Basic Books.

Hoffman, L. (1990). Constructing realities: An art of lenses. *Family Process, 29,* 1–12.

Holtzworth-Monroe, A., & Jacobson, N. (1991). Behavioral marital therapy. In A. Gurman & D. Kniskern (Eds.), *Handbook of family therapy* (Vol. 2). New York: Brunner/Mazel.

Imber-Black, E. (1988). *Families and larger systems.* New York: Guilford Press.

Imber-Black, E., Roberts, J., & Whiting, R. (Eds.) (1988). *Rituals in families and family therapy.* New York: Norton.

Jackson, D. D. (1965). The study of the family. *Family Process, 4,* 1–20.

Jackson, D. D. (1977). The myth of normality. In P. Watzlawick & J. Weakland (Eds.) *The interactional view.* New York: Norton.

Jacobson, N., & Margolin, G. (1979). *Marital therapy: Strategies based on social learning and behavior exchange principles.* New York: Brunner/Mazel.

Jordan, J. (1992, April). *Relational resilience.* Paper presented at Stone Center Colloquium series, Boston, MA.

Kaminer, W. (1992). *I'm dysfunctional, you're dysfunctional.* Reading, MA: Addison-Wesley.

Kantor, D., & Lehr, W. (1975). *Inside the family: Toward a theory of family process.* San Francisco: Jossey-Bass.

Karpel, M. (1986). *Family resources: The hidden partner in family therapy.* New York: Guilford Press.

Kazak, A. (1989). Perception of normality in families. *Journal of Family Psychology, 2,* 277–291.

Keeney, B., & Sprenkle, D. (1982). Ecosystemic epistemology: Critical implications for the aesthetics and pragmatics of family therapy. *Family Process, 21,* 1–19.

Kerr, M., & Bowen, M. (1988). *Family evaluation.* New York: Norton.

Kleinman, A. (1988). *The illness narratives: Suffering, healing, and the human condition.* New York: Basic Books.

Landau-Stanton, J. (1990). Issues and methods of treatment for families in cultural transition. In M. Mirkin (Ed.), *Social and political context of family therapy.* Boston: Allyn & Bacon.

Landau-Stanton, J. (1993). *AIDS, health and mental health: A primary sourcebook.* New York: Brunner/Mazel.

Lasch, C. (1977). *Haven in a heartless world: The family besieged.* New York: Basic Books.

Lazarus, R., & Folkman, S. (1984). *Stress, appraisal and coping.* New York: Springer.

Lebow, J. (1984). On the value of integrating approaches to family therapy. *Journal of Marital and Family Therapy, 10,* 127–138.

Lewis, J., Beavers, W. R., Gossett, J., & Phillips, V. (1976). *No single thread: Psychological health in family systems.* New York: Brunner/Mazel.

Lidz, T. (1963). *The family and human adaptation.* New York: International Universities Press.

Lidz, T., Fleck, S., & Cornelison, A. (1965). *Schizophrenia and the family.* New York: International Universities Press.

Luepnitz, D. (1988). *The family interpreted: Feminist theory and clinical practice.* New York: Basic Books.

Macklin, E. (1980). Nontraditional family forms: A decade of research. *Journal of Marriage and the Family, 42,* 905–922.

Madanes, C. (1991). Strategic family therapy. In A. Gurman & D. Kniskern (Eds.), *Handbook of family therapy* (Vol. II). New York: Brunner/Mazel.

Markman, H. (1981). Predictions of marital distress: A 5-year follow-up. *Journal of Consulting and Clinical Psychology, 49,* 760–762.

Masten, A. S., & Garmezy, N. (1989). Resilience in development: Implications of the study of successful adaptations for developmental psychopathology. In D. Cicchetti (Ed.), *The emergence of a discipline* (Vol. 1). Hillsdale, NJ: Erlbaum.

McAdoo, H. (Ed.) (1985). *Black families* (2nd ed.). Newbury Park, CA: Sage.

McCubbin, H., Joy, C., Cauble, A., Comeau, J., Patterson, J., & Needle, R. (1980). Family stress and coping: A decade review. *Journal of Marriage and the Family, 42,* 855–871.

McCubbin, H., & Patterson, J. M. (1983). The family stress process: the Double ABCX model of adjustment and adaptation. In H. McCubbin, M. Sussman, & J. M. Patterson, (Eds.), *Social stress and the family: Advances in family stress theory and research.* New York: Haworth.

McFarlane, W. (1991). Family psychoeducational treatment. In A. Gurman & D. Kniskern (Eds.), *Handbook of family therapy* (Vol. II). New York: Brunner/Mazel.

McGoldrick, M., Anderson, C., & Walsh, F. (1989). *Women in families: A framework for family therapy.* New York: Norton.

McGoldrick, M., & Gerson, R. (1985). *Genograms in family assessment.* New York: Norton.

McGoldrick, M., Pearce, J., & Giordano, J. (Eds.). (1982). *Ethnicity and family therapy.* New York: Guilford Press.

McGoldrick, M., & Walsh, F. (1991). A time to mourn: Death and the family life cycle. In F. Walsh & M. McGoldrick (Eds.), *Living beyond loss: Death in the family.* New York: Norton.

Meissner, W. W. (1978). The conceptualization of marital and family dynamics from a psychoanalytic perspective. In T. Paolino & B. McCrady (Eds.), *Marriage and marital therapy.* New York: Brunner/Mazel.

Metcoff, J., & Whitaker, C. (1982). Family micro-events: Communication patterns for problem solving. In F. Walsh (Ed.), *Normal family processes* (1st ed., pp. 251–274). New York: Guilford Press.

Meth, R., & Passick, R. (1991). *Men in therapy: The challenges of change.* New York: Guilford Press.

Mintz, S., & Kellogg, S. (1988). *Domestic revolutions: A social history of American family life.* New York: Free Press.

Minuchin, S. (1974). *Families and family therapy.* Cambridge, MA: Harvard University Press.

Minuchin, S. (1992). *Family healing.* New York: Macmillan.

Minuchin, S., Montalvo, B., Guerney, B., Rosman, B., & Schumer, F. (1967). *Families of the slums.* New York: Basic Books.

Mirkin, M. (Ed.) (1990). *The social and political contexts of family therapy.* Boston: Allyn & Bacon.

Montalvo, B. (1982). Interpersonal arrangements in disrupted families. In F. Walsh (Ed.), *Normal family processes* (1st ed., pp. 277–296). New York: Guilford Press.

Moon, S., Dillon, B., & Sprenkle, D. (1990). Family therapy and qualitative research. *Journal of Marital and Family Therapy, 16,* 357–373.

Moos, R., & Moos, B. (1976). A typology of family social environments. *Family Process, 15,* 357–371.

Moos, R. H., & Moos, B. S. (1986). *Family environment scale manual* (2nd ed.). Palo Alto, CA: Consulting Psychologists Press.

Napier, A., & Whitaker, C. (1978). *The family crucible.* New York: Harper & Row.

Neugarten, B. (1968). *Middle age and aging.* Chicago: University of Chicago Press.

Nichols, M., & Schwartz, R. (1991). *Family therapy: Concepts and methods* (2nd ed.). Boston: Allyn & Bacon.

Offer, D., & Sabshin, M. (1966, 1974). *Normality: Theoretical and clinical concepts of mental health* (1st & 2nd eds.). New York: Basic Books.

O'Hanlon, W., & Weiner-Davis, M. (1989). *In search of solutions: A new direction in psychotherapy.* New York: Norton.

Olson, D. H. (1977). Insider's and outsider's perspectives of relationships: Research strategies. In G. Levinger & H. Rausch (Eds.), *Close relationships.* Amherst, MA: University of Massachusetts Press.

Olson, D. H., Russell, C. S., & Sprenkle, D. H. (1989). *Circumplex model: Systemic assessment and treatment of families.* New York: Haworth.

Parsons, T., & Bales, R. F. (1955). *Family, socialization, and interaction processes.* Glencoe, IL: Free Press.

Patterson, G., Reid, J., Jones, R., & Conger, R. (1975). *A social learning approach to family interaction.* Eugene, OR: Castalia.

Paul, N., & Grosser, G. (1991). Operant mourning and its role in conjoint family therapy. In F. Walsh & M. McGoldrick (Eds.), *Living beyond loss.* New York: Norton.

Paul, N., & Paul, B. (1975). *A marital puzzle: Transgenerational analysis in marriage.* New York: Norton.

Penn, P. (1985). Feed forward: Future questions, future maps. *Family Process, 24,* 299–310.

Pittman, F. (1993). *Man enough.* New York: Putnam.

Rapaport, R. (1962). Normal crises, family structure, and mental health. *Family Process, 2,* 68–71.

Reiss, D. (1981). *The family's construction of reality.* Cambridge, MA: Harvard University Press.

Riskin, J. (1982). Research on non-labeled families: A longitudinal study. In F. Walsh (Ed.), *Normal family processes* (1st ed., pp. 67–93). New York: Guilford Press.

Riskin, J., & Faunce, E. (1972). An evaluative review of family interaction research. *Family Process, 11,* 365–455.

Roberto, L. G. (1992). *Transgenerational family therapies.* New York: Guilford Press.

Rolland, J. (In press). *Helping families with chronic and life-threatening disorders.* New York: Basic Books.

Rolland, J., & Walsh, F. (1993). Family systems approaches to assessment and treatment. In R. Hales, S. Yudofsky, & J. Talbott (Eds.), *Textbook of psychiatry* (2nd ed.). Philadelphia: American Psychiatric Press.

Rosenblatt, P., & Fischer, L. (1993). Qualitative family research. In P. Boss, W. Doherty, W. LaRossa, W. Schumm, & S. Steinmetz (Eds.), *Sourcebook on family theories and methods.* New York: Plenum.

Rutter, M. (1987). Psychosocial resilience and protective mechanisms. *American Journal of Orthopsychiatry, 57,* 316–331.

Saba, G., Karrer, B. M., & Hardy, K. (1989). *Minorities and family therapy.* New York: Haworth.

Satir, V. (1964). *Conjoint family therapy.* Palo Alto: Science & Behavior Books.

Satir, V. (1988). *The new peoplemaking.* Palo Alto, CA: Science & Behavior Books.

Scharff, D., & Scharff, J. S. (1987). *Object relations family therapy.* New York: Jason Aronson.

Schumm, W. (1985). Beyond relationship characteristics of strong families: Constructing a model of family strengths. *Family Perspective, 19,* 1–9.

Schwartzman, J. (1982). Normality from a cross-cultural perspective. In F. Walsh (Ed.), *Normal family processes* (1st ed., 383–398). New York: Guilford Press.

Selvini Palazzoli, M. (1986). Toward a general model of psychotic games. *Journal of Marital and Family Therapy, 12,* 339–349.

Selvini Palazzoli, M., Boscolo, L., Cecchin, G., & Prata, G. (1978). *Paradox and counterparadox.* Northvale, NJ: Jason Aronson.

Skinner, H., Santa Barbara, J., & Steinhauer, P. (1983). The family assessment measure. *Canadian Journal of Community Mental Health, 2,* 91–105.

Skolnick, A. (1991). *Embattled paradise: The American family in an age of uncertainty.* New York: Basic Books.

Skolnick, A., & Skolnick, J. (1992). *Family in transition* (7th ed.). New York: Harper/Collins.

Skynner, A. C. R. (1976). *Systems of family and marital psychotherapy.* New York: Brunner/Mazel.

Sluzki, C. (1979). Migration and family conflict. *Family Process, 18,* 379–390.

Sluzki, C. (1983). Process, structure, and world views in family therapy: Toward an integration of systemic models. *Family Process, 22,* 469–476.

Solomon, M. (1973). A developmental conceptual premise for family therapy. *Family Process, 12,* 179–188.

Spiegel, J. (1971). *Transactions: The interplay between individual, family, and society.* New York: Science House.

Sprey, J. (1991). Current theorizing on the family. In A. Booth (Ed.), *Contemporary families.* Minneapolis, MN: National Council on Family Relations.

Stacey, J. (1990). *Brave new families: Stories of domestic upheaval in late twentieth century America.* New York: Basic Books.

Stanton, M. D. (1981). An integrated structural/strategic approach to family therapy. *Journal of Marital and Family Therapy, 7,* 427–440.

Stierlin, H. (1974). *Separating parents and adolescents.* New York: Jason Aronson.

Stinnett, N., & DeFrain, J. (1985). *Secrets of strong families.* Boston: Little, Brown.

Taggart, M. (1985). The feminist critique in epistemological perspective: Questions of context in family therapy. *Journal of Marital and Family Therapy, 11,* 113–126.

Tomm, K. (1987). Interventive interviewing: Part II: Reflexive questioning as a means to enable self-healing. *Family Process, 26,* 167–183.

Vega, W. A. (1990). Hispanic families in the 1980s: A decade of research. *Journal of Marriage and the Family, 52,* 1015–1024.

Visher, E., & Visher, J. (1979). *Stepfamilies.* New York: Brunner/Mazel.

Visher, E., & Visher, J. (1988). *Old loyalties, new ties: Therapeutic strategies with stepfamilies.* New York: Brunner/Mazel.

Wallerstein, J., & Blakeslee, S. (1989). *Second chances: Men, women, and children a decade after divorce.* New York: Ticknor & Fields.

Walker, G. (1991). *In the midst of winter.* New York: Norton.

Walsh, F. (1982). Conceptualizations of normal family functioning. In F. Walsh (Ed.), *Normal family processes* (1st ed., pp. 3–42). New York: Guilford Press.

Walsh, F. (1983). Normal family ideologies: Myths and realities. In C. Falicov (Ed.), *Cultural dimensions in family therapy.* Rockville, MD: Aspen.

Walsh, F. (1987). The clinical utility of normal family research. *Psychotherapy, 24,* 496–503.

Walsh, F. (1988). The family in later life. In B. Carter & M. McGoldrick (Eds.), *The changing family life cycle.* Boston: Allyn & Bacon.

Walsh, F. (1989a). Perceptions of family normality: Refining our lenses. *Journal of Family Psychology, 2,* 303–306.

Walsh, F. (1989b). Reconsidering gender in the marital "quid pro quo." In M. McGoldrick, C. Anderson, & F. Walsh (Eds.), *Women in families.* New York: Norton.

Walsh, F. (1991). Promoting healthy functioning in divorced and remarried families. In A. Gurman & D. Kniskern (Eds.), *Handbook of family therapy.* New York: Brunner/Mazel.

Walsh, F. (1992, October). *Beyond the myths of the normal family.* Plenary paper presented at the 50th Annual Meeting of the American Association of Marriage and Family Therapy, Miami, FL.

Walsh, F. (in press[a]). *Promoting healthy family functioning.* New York: Guilford Press.

Walsh, F. (In press[b]). Research on normal family processes. In R. Mikesell, D. D. Lusterman, & S. McDaniel (Eds.), *Family psychology and systems therapy: A handbook*. Washington, DC: American Psychological Association.

Walsh, F., & Anderson, C. M. (1988). Chronic disorders and families: An overview. In F. Walsh & C. Anderson (Eds.), *Chronic disorders and the family*. New York: Haworth.

Walsh, F., & McGoldrick, M. (1991). Loss and the family: A systemic perspective. In F. Walsh & M. McGoldrick (Eds.), *Living beyond loss: Death in the family*. New York: Norton.

Walsh, F., & Olson, D. H. (1989). Utility of the circumplex model with severely dysfunctional families. In D. Olson, D. Sprenkle, & C. Russell (Eds.), *The circumplex model: Systemic assessment and treatment of families*. New York: Haworth.

Walsh, F., & Scheinkman, M. (1989). (Fe)male: The hidden gender dimension in models of family therapy. In M. McGoldrick, C. Anderson, & F. Walsh (Eds.), *Women in families*. New York: Norton.

Walters, M., Carter, B., Papp, P., & Silverstein, O. (1988). *The invisible web: Gender patterns in family relationships*. New York: Guilford Press.

Watzlawick, P. (1984). *The invented reality*. New York: Norton.

Watzlawick, P., Beavin, J., & Jackson, D. (1967). *Pragmatics of human communication*. New York: Norton.

Watzlawick, P., Weakland, J., & Fisch, R. (1974). *Change: Principles of problem formation and problem resolution*. New York: Norton.

Weakland, J., Fisch, R., Watzlawick, P., & Bodin, A. (1974). Brief therapy: Focused problem-resolution. *Family Process, 13*, 141–168.

Weiss, R. L. (1978). The conceptualization of marriage from a behavioral perspective. In T. Paolino & B. McCrady (Eds.), *Marriage and marital therapy*. New York: Brunner/Mazel.

Weston, K. (1991). *Families we choose: Lesbians, gays, kinship*. New York: Columbia University Press.

Wheeler, D., Avis, J., Miller, L., & Charney, S. (1989). Rethinking family therapy training and supervision: A feminist model. In M. McGoldrick, C. Anderson, & F. Walsh (Eds.) *Women in families*. New York: Norton.

Whitaker, C., & Keith, D. (1981). Functional family therapy. In A. Gurman & D. Kniskern (Eds.), *Handbook of family therapy*. New York: Brunner/Mazel.

White, M., & Epston, D. (1990). *Narrative means to therapeutic ends*. New York: Norton.

Wilson, W. J. (1987). *The truly disadvantaged*. Chicago: University of Chicago Press.

Wolin, S., & Wolin, S. (1993). *The resilient self: How survivors of troubled families rise above adversity*. New York: Villard.

Wood, B. (1985). Proximity and hierarchy: Orthogonal dimensions of family interconnectedness. *Family Process, 24*, 487–507.

Wynne, L. (1988). An epigenetic model of family process. In C. Falicov (Ed.), *Family transitions: Continuity and change over the life cycle*. New York: Guilford Press.

Wynne, L. C., McDaniel, S., & Weber, T. (Eds.). (1986). *Family consultation*. New York: Guilford Press.

Zacks, E., Green, R. J., & Marrow, J. (1988). Comparing lesbian and heterosexual couples on the Circumplex Model: An initial investigation. *Family Process, 27*, 471–484.

Research on Normal Family Processes

CHAPTER 2

MEASURING FAMILY COMPETENCE
The Beavers Systems Model

W. Robert Beavers and
Robert B. Hampson

$\mathbf{O}$UR STUDIES OF HEALTHY FAMILY processes have evolved over more than 30 years of clinical work and research with a wide range of individual and family functioning. Through observing, interviewing, and assessing families across a broad spectrum in a wide range of settings, we have developed a variety of measures and core constructs of interactional family functioning that clearly differentiate healthy from less healthy families. The first published study (Beavers, Blumberg, Timken, & Weiner, 1965) investigated communication patterns in family members of hospitalized adolescents. The Timberlawn study of healthy families (Lewis, Beavers, Gossett, & Phillips, 1976) was the first published report of a detailed examination of well-functioning families using an interactional, systemic viewpoint. From these and our continuing studies of nonlabeled and clinical families (Beavers, 1982; Beavers & Voeller, 1983; Beavers, 1985; Beavers, Hampson, & Hulgus, 1985; Hampson & Beavers, 1988; Hampson, Beavers, & Hulgus, 1988; Hampson, Beavers, & Hulgus, 1989; Beavers & Hampson, 1990), some cornerstone criteria for the study of family competence emerge. These concepts, central to the Beavers Systems Model, are:

1. Family *functioning*—observable, live, interactive functioning—takes precedence over symptoms or typology. Attempting to label clinical typologies, such as "schizophrenic," "addictive," or "codependent," yields little useful information about functional strengths and weaknesses or about qualities useful to the therapist.

2. Family competence, ranging from effective, healthy family function-ing to severely dysfunctional patterns, is viewed along a progressive con-tinuum, rather than in segmented categories. This concept promotes the view that observable and measurable growth and adaptation in families is possible.

3. Several families at similar competence levels may show different functional and behavioral *styles* of relating and interacting. The most compe-tent families are able to shift their functional style as developmental changes occur, whereas the most dysfunctional families show a marked rigidity in functional style.

4. Family assessment involves perceptions of family events from at least two sources: the observer/therapist ("outsider"), and each family member ("insider") (cf. Hampton et al., 1989).

5. Competence in small tasks (such as discussing an issue or resolving a conflict) is related to competence in the larger domains of living, raising children, and managing a family (Beavers, 1977; Lewis et al., 1976).

The major constructs and instruments of the Beavers Systems Model have emerged from this framework. In this chapter we present the constructs of Competence and Style, which define levels of family functioning, and the scales used to measure them. Next, we present clinically useful groupings of families based on the family assessment model. Finally, a brief presenta-tion of related studies is included to emphasize the model's validity and clini-cal utility.

FAMILY COMPETENCE AND STYLE

The Beavers Model emphasizes family competence, which defines how well the family, as an interactional unit, performs the necessary and nurturing tasks of organizing and managing itself. A major theme of this dimension is the structure of the family unit in which egalitarian leadership, strong parental or other adult coalition, and established generational boundaries are indica-tors of competence. Conversely, weak parental coalitions, or parent–child coalitions, ineffective leadership, and chaotic attempts at leadership are indi-cators of lower levels of system competence.

Also highly related to competence is the development of autonomy in individual family members, which carries with it increasing trust, clear boundaries, clear and direct communication, and the ability to resolve or accept differences. Competent families are more readily able to resolve con-flict and communicate openly and directly. The competent family is also quite spontaneous, shows a wide range of feelings, and is generally opti-mistic, whereas more dysfunctional families show more truncated ranges of feelings and a more pessimistic view of life. A more detailed presentation of the values and dimensions of family competence is presented in the next section.

However, it is important to recognize in assessing family competence that some families may perform certain tasks better than they do others, but it is highly unlikely that one family will show extremely competent interaction in one domain and dysfunctional levels in others (Beavers & Hampson, 1990). Hence, a global rating of family competence is a useful common denominator of the various components of family competence.

When assessed observationally, family competence is measured using the Beavers Interactional Competence Scale (Appendix A, pp. 96–98), a revision and update of the previously titled Beavers–Timberlawn Family Evaluation Scales (Beavers, 1982). Some of the scales have been reworded for clarity, and one ("Invasiveness") has been deleted as a Likert rating and included as a present/absent checklist. Currently, our interrater reliabilities for trained raters are consistently high for the subscales as well as the Global score. In terms of validity, scores on the Competence scale successfully discriminate clinic from nonclinic families (Beavers, Hampson, & Hulgus, 1990) and even between diagnostic subsamples of clinic families (Beavers & Hampson, 1990). We have found no significant differences among nonlabeled Anglo, African–American, and Mexican–American families on global competence (Hampson, Beavers, & Hulgus, 1990), which emphasizes the culture-fairness of the themes of competence.

Since the last edition of this volume was published, we have emphasized and refined the assessment of family style. Style refers to the degree of centripetal or centrifugal qualities in the family. Centripetal family members seek satisfaction more often from within the family, and children are slower in leaving home. Centrifugal family members look for satisfaction in the outside world, and the children often leave home earlier than the developmental norm. Erikson (1963) used this stylistic dimension in his description of American Indian tribes, as did Stierlin (1972) in describing binding versus expelling patterns of adolescents separating from their families.

Centripetal (CP) family members, looking for satisfaction within the family, are less trustful of the world beyond the family boundaries. Centrifugal (CF) family members, on the other hand, seeking gratification from beyond the confines of the family, often trust activities and relationships outside the family unit more than those within it. Ambivalent feelings in family members are handled quite differently, in that CP families try to repress, suppress, or deny negative or hostile feelings, and play up the positive, caring ones (hence, the "glue" in the CP style). In contrast, CF family members are wary of affectionate messages and are more comfortable with negative or angry feelings (hence the force for outward movement). Extremely CP families tend to bind children and make emancipation difficult, whereas extremely CF families tend to expel children before individuation is complete. It is not surprising, then, that our studies find more internalizing (anxiety, depressive) disorders in CP families and more externalizing (conduct, aggressive) disorders in CF families (Beavers & Hampson, 1990; Hampson & Pierce, 1992).

System health is system flexibility, and competent families alter their style according to developmental needs throughout the family life cycle. For those more competent families who are able to adapt their responses to temporal and developmental needs, style represents a functional adaptation. A young family is optimally centripetal. Small children's needs are met best by such a family style. As the family matures, it optimally becomes more centrifugal, with children and parents looking more to the outside world for satisfaction: the children in order to leave home successfully; the parents in order to sustain themselves after the children leave. Less competent families are rigid and find modification of style much more difficult.

Family Style is measured observationally by the Beavers Interactional Style Scale (Appendix B, pp. 99–100; Beavers & Hampson, 1990), a revision and update of the previously published Centripetal/Centrifugal Family Style Scale (Kelsey-Smith & Beavers, 1981). Seven observational ratings and a Global Style rating (ranged 1 to 5, with 1 being highly CP and 5 being highly CF) are completed, following the raters' completion of the Competence scale. The rating points represent behavioral correlates of CP or CF style (Beavers, 1977), and they are based on the present observation of the family's response to dependency needs of offspring, overt adult conflict, physical spacing and proximity (CP families tend to sit closer together), concern about social presentation to outsiders, professed family closeness, degree of expression of angry/hostile feelings, and the balance/skew of positive and negative feelings.

Our studies indicate acceptable to high interrater reliabilities for trained raters. Studies of clinic families also show significant differences between CP and CF families in the distribution of DSM-III-R diagnoses, with significantly more anxiety and unipolar depression in individual patients within CP families and more conduct and externalizing disorders in individuals within CF families (Hampson & Pierce, 1992). Family style differs slightly among ethnic groupings, with Mexican-American families rated as slightly more CP than Anglo or African-American families (Hampson et al., 1990). However, style is more clearly related to socioeconomic status of the family than to ethnicity; lower socioeconomic levels are associated with more CF style ratings (Hampson et al., 1990).

In addition to the observational instruments, we have developed a self-report instrument, the Self-Report Family Inventory (SFI) (Beavers & Hampson, 1990), which is able to access individual family members' perceptions of family competence, style, and several related domains. The 36-item questionnaire (Appendix C, pp. 101–103) is fairly simple to complete, such that children aged 10 or 11 have little difficulty completing the items independently. The SFI provides a Competence score for each member, and a

Cohesion score which is used as an estimate of Family Style. This factor addresses closeness, togetherness, and tendencies to enjoy time and activities together; as such, it is an approximation of some of the major family themes related to style. In addition, clinically useful scales of Conflict, Leadership, and Emotional Expressiveness are available.

The SFI allows a comparison of the "insider" and "outsider" perspective on the family. It serves as a brief and useful screening device to identify potential family dysfunction. The correlations between observational and self-report Competence scores are very high at the more dysfunctional end of the continuum. The determination of healthy family functioning by self-report has been more elusive, and we continue to study within-family agreement levels and patterns of self-report scores in healthy versus dysfunctional families.

BEAVERS SYSTEMS MODEL

Regardless of whether the assessment procedure utilizes observational instruments, self-report scales, or both, the dimensions of Competence and Style provide a useful map for identifying levels of family health/dysfunction. Figure 2.1 illustrates this systems model.

The horizontal axis represents the continuum of Family Competence, ranging from optimal functioning (ratings of 1 or 2, on the right) to severely dysfunctional (ratings 9–10, on the left). The continuum of Family Competence shows progression from extreme rigidity (chaotic, noninteractive), through marked dominance–submission patterns, to greater and greater capacity for equal-powered and successful transactions. The vertical axis represents Family Style, ranging from highly centripetal (rating of 1, lower end) to highly centrifugal (rating of 5, upper end). This representation is not intended to be a progressive continuum at all levels, as is competence but, rather, to suggest more extreme styles in the more dysfunctional families and a more blended and flexible style in healthier families.

Therefore, the figure is in the shape of an arrow, representing the clinical and empirical findings that healthy families show a flexible and blended family style, such that they can adapt stylistic behavior as developmental, individual, and family needs change over time. At the most dysfunctional end of the competence dimension are seen the most extreme and inflexible family styles. Here the extreme rigidity and limited coping skills preclude variation in style. The V-shaped "notch" on the left represents the finding that severely disturbed families show more extreme and inflexible styles, with no moderation or blending of stylistic behavior. All our empirical studies support this observation: system rigidity is system sickness (Von Bertalanffy, 1969).

Whereas this model and its assessment tools offer a here-and-now, snapshot view of current family functioning, the assessment system offers useful

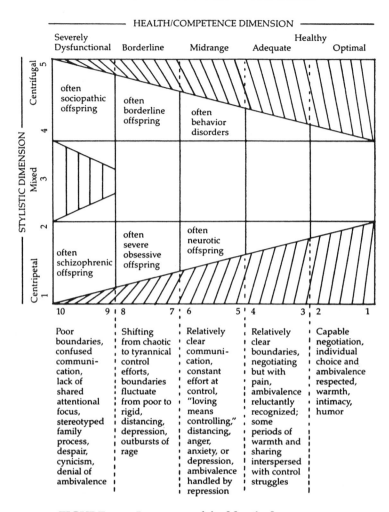

FIGURE 2.1. Beavers model of family functioning.

guidance to a therapist, especially in terms of useful information on strengths and weaknesses, and guidelines on most effective joining and structuring strategies. There is no doubt that current stressors and changes affect family functioning across time, and in some cases significant changes in competence levels have followed major life events. Still, we can speak in terms of common denominators of the different levels of competence and style. The model identifies nine clinically useful groupings of families, which are discussed below.

CLINICALLY USEFUL GROUPINGS OF FAMILIES

Optimal Families

Systems Orientation

These families score highest on our observational and self-report measures. The family members have what can be described as a *systems orientation*. This concept includes at least four basic assumptions:

1. An individual needs a group, a human system, for identity and satisfaction.
2. Causes and effects are interchangeable.
3. Any human behavior is the result of many variables rather than one "cause"; therefore, simplistic solutions are questioned.
4. Human beings are limited and finite. No one is absolutely helpless or absolutely powerful in a relationship.

Optimal family members know that people do not prosper in an interpersonal vacuum; human needs are satisfied in relationships. As children develop and mature, they leave their families, not for isolated independence but for other human systems. Whether they enter college or marriage, the military or a fast track career, the need for community continues, and interpersonal skills are required to adapt to these various networks.

The second hallmark of a systems view, the recognition that causes and effects are interchangeable, is equally significant. Optimal family members know, for example, that hostility in one person promotes deception in the other and that deception promotes hostility. Efforts at tyrannical control increase the possibility of angry defiance, just as uncooperative defiance invites tyrannical control. Thus, stimuli become responses and responses stimuli, in a process with shape and form but with no clearly defined villains or victims.

The third concept, that human behavior results from many variables, is evident in optimal families and painfully absent in dysfunctional families. For instance, when a child of 3 spills milk at the table, possible explanations include the following:

1. The incident happens accidentally, and no motive should be attached to the behavior.
2. The incident has interpersonal meaning; for example, the child has "a score" to settle with the mother or wishes to provoke her.
3. The child is attempting to express hostile, destructive drives unrelated to the mother.
4. The child is tired or anxious and therefore apt to make mistakes.

5. The problem is mechanical; the glass is too large for the child's small hands.

A characteristic of dysfunctional families is that they believe one or another of these explanations almost fanatically. In contrast, optimal families consider all these possibilities and more; they are not locked into an idea of single causation, and their responses vary with the situation in a pragmatic fashion.

Finally, a systems orientation includes an awareness that humans are finite, that they have limited power, and that self-esteem comes from achieving relative competence rather than from absolute control. Optimal family members know that success in human endeavors depends on variables beyond anyone's control; yet, they believe that if they possess goals and purpose, they can make a difference in their own lives and in others' lives. People are terribly vulnerable if they try to control others absolutely. Negotiation is essential for success in human enterprise, and individual choice must be taken into account. These family members accept that people have the capacity to envision perfection yet are destined to flounder, make mistakes, get scared, and need reassurance. This encourages a sense of humor, and an appreciation of paradox. We seek a measure of control over our children in order that they can become adult decision makers; we reach for closeness and support so that we can be free. We are never free from having mixed feelings about important people and things. We want to grow up, but the process is also frightening. We want our children to leave home, but we fear the loneliness their leaving engenders. We resolve mixed feelings by determining action *on balance*—the greater good or lesser evil. No compulsively linear thinkers need apply to entrance into optimal families!

Clear Boundaries

A useful parallel to the external boundary of an optimal family system is that of a living cell, possessing enough strength and integrity to allow a highly involved interaction within its borders, yet permeable to the outside world, allowing a satisfying interchange. Optimal family members are actively involved in the world beyond the family, relate to it with optimism and hope, and from their encounters outside bring varied interests and excitement back into the family. Openness to other viewpoints, lifestyles, and perceptions contribute to the congruent mythology seen in the optimal families studied. Their perception of their own family strengths and weaknesses coincides with observations of outside raters. In addition, these optimal families have clear boundaries between and among members. It is easy to distinguish a mother's feelings from a father's and one child's view of a specific situation from another child's view. Negotiation consists of accepting differences and working toward shared goals. In such a differentiated family unit, individual choice is expected, family members speak up, and even the youngest children are respected as significant sovereign individuals with valuable contributions.

There are clear generational boundaries. Though overt power is shared freely, there is no question as to who is parent and who is child. No parents feel obligated to disclaim their adult power, and no children feel called upon to assume a premature responsibility. Parents forego any possibility of exploiting their children by defining them as pseudo-adults.

Contextual Clarity

In any social context—family, friendship, patient–therapist—there is a useful rule of thumb in defining the degree of craziness or sanity: How clear is the context? When an optimal family interacts, it is generally clear to whom comments are addressed and what the relationship is between the speaker and the audience. There is a shared theme, and members can continue discussions over a period of time with effective results. Social roles, though flexible, are clear.

A central issue in normative development is the resolution of Oedipal issues. It is essential for relationship contexts to become clear, not blurred and muddied. One can be a parent, a spouse, or child, but not to the same person at the same time. A 4-year-old child is apt to say "I am going to grow up and marry Daddy (or Mommy). In dysfunctional families, a parent may smile, unperturbed, and even share the fantasy. In optimal families, children are assisted in accepting role limitations and context clarity by parents who present clear role definitions and generation boundaries.

Relatively Equal Power and the Process of Intimacy

A human being, when frightened, seeks some kind of power. Two choices are available:

1. The power of a loving relationship with others—the experiencing of closeness without coercion.
2. The power of control—control over one's inner self and/or control over others.

In an optimal family, there is a clear hierarchy of power, with leadership in the hands of the parents who form an egalitarian coalition. Children are less overtly powerful than their parents, but their contributions influence decisions, and their power becomes more nearly equal as the children grow toward adulthood. Frustrating, self-defeating power struggles seldom occur, and family tasks are undertaken with good-humored effectiveness. These fortunate individuals have learned to deal with fear by relating rather than by controlling.

Because the parents have relatively equal overt power, they must have complementary interaction in order to avoid competitive conflict. This can be through mutually agreed-upon complementary roles (you earn the living, I'll structure the home environment), complementary domains (you are responsible for maintaining the lawn, I'll clean the house), or complementary tasks (I'll make the main dish, you make the salad). Symmetrical roles, as in many dual-career families, require serious attention to domains and tasks in order that the necessary complementarity is developed and maintained.

It is important to emphasize that complementarity encompasses difference, not an inferior/superior dynamic. Perhaps a basketball analogy may best convey this point. On unskilled teams, everybody scrambles to get the ball and shoot baskets, whereas on very skilled teams, players cooperate and have complementary roles.

Optimal family members recognize and utilize both relationship and coercive controls. Authoritarian control is occasionally used to enforce family rules. It is neither compulsively denied nor virtuously touted. When under pressure the family can thus revert to a more control-oriented style, but it can enjoy relating intimately when circumstances are relatively stress-free by relaxing the overt power differences and sharing responsibilities as fellow humans.

These optimal families show the least amount of sexual stereotyping. Mothers are usually somewhat more involved in child care than are fathers, and in intact families, the fathers often take more responsibility in family support. In children, instead of gender dictating character, birth order is more significant. Oldest children are generally more controlled in emotional expression, better disciplined, and more achievement oriented. Second children show more affective openness, spontaneity, and less concern with achievement or with personal discipline. The younger children are often slower in social development.

The skill in operating with equal overt power, possessed by all family members, allows for intimacy. It is only when power differences are thrown aside that people can experience true intimacy—the sharing of their innermost selves achieved by the dropping of pretense in the presence of trust and the absence of fear. This experience is at once liberating and empowering. It provides a true "launching pad" for family members—enabling parents to go into the community with energy and confidence and children to approach their developmental tasks of leaving home with exceptional drive and performance.

Autonomy

Optimal family members take responsibility for their thoughts, feelings, and behavior. They are open to communication from others and respect the unique and different subjective views of reality found in any group of people. They express feelings and thoughts clearly. They show a striking absence of blame and personal attack, and there is no practice of scapegoating within the family unit. Because this family system accepts uncertainty, ambivalence, and disagreement, members risk little in being known and open. These families recognize people as mistake makers. The parents can issue pronouncements that later prove to be erroneous with little loss of face. Children can fail without being attacked or defined as inadequate. Because of this tolerance of uncertainty, ambivalence, and imperfection, family members can be honest. Honesty as a dynamic creates a climate in which mutual trust flourishes, since if people are not punished for telling the truth as they have experienced it, lying is unnecessary.

Joy and Comfort in Relating

Transactions among optimal family members are notable for their warm, optimistic tone of feeling and also for their intensity. Empathy for each other's feelings, interest in what each other has to say, and expectation of being understood encourage members to respond to each other with concern and action. Their orientation is affiliative, with each person expecting satisfaction and reward from relationships, and this reinforces the involvement with and investment in each other. Assessment of this affiliative attitude in a family is based on a complex synthesis of behavior, voice tone, verbal context, and communicative patterns.

As a corollary to an affiliative expectation, optimal family members see human nature as essentially benign. Human needs for sexual expression, intimacy, and assertiveness are recognized with a minimum of apprehension. People are understood to be struggling to do as well as possible under their particular circumstance, rather than to be fundamentally hostile or destructive. There is variability in the extent to which people outside the family are seen as benign, but all optimal families include at least their own members in this assumption. The belief that the other is basically benign and of good will is essential to the success of any effort at achieving closeness.

Skilled Negotiation

In shared tasks, optimal families excel in their capacity to accept directions, organize themselves, develop input from each other, negotiate differences, and reach closure coherently and effectively. Parents act as coordinators, bringing out others' ideas and voicing their own. They usually alternate this role several times in a short planning session. All the variables important in family systems come into play, including clarity of context, relatively equal power, affiliative expectations, and encouragement of choice. Family performance in specified small-scale tasks correlates with overall competence in parenting.

This negotiating skill is present in all groups of optimal families that we have studied—middle-class white, disadvantaged white, African-American, or Hispanic, single-parent, or unconventional family groups.

Significant Transcendent Values

Capable families accept change. Children grow up, themselves becoming parents. Parents grow old and die. To accept the inevitable risks and losses of loving and being close, families and individuals appear to require a system of values and beliefs that transcends the limits of their experience and knowledge. With such transcendent beliefs and values, families and their members can view their particular reality, which may be painful, uncertain, and frightening, from a perspective that makes some sense of events and allows for hope. Without such beliefs and perspectives, families and individuals are vulnerable to hopelessness and despair.

The ability to accept change and loss is closely tied to the acceptance of the idea of one's own death. Only by using the human capacity for symbolism, defining ourselves as part of a meaningful whole, can one's own death and that of loved ones be faced openly and courageously. Just as no individual person can survive and prosper without relating to a larger organizational unit—usually a family—no family can survive and prosper without a yet larger system. A transcendent value system, whether conventional or unique, allows persons and families to define themselves and their activities as meaningful and significant.

Implicit in the behavior and relationships of all families are certain attitudes about human nature and the nature of truth. For optimal families, these attitudes encompass a positive view of humanity as essentially good, or at least as neutral, and of human behavior as a response to experiences and an effort to deal with problems. The behavior and relationships of these family members also imply an understanding of truth as relative rather than as absolute; or, expressed another way, they permit family members to approach reality as subjective and different for each person. With these two underlying assumptions about people and reality, healthy families are able to relate with trust, without erecting ponderous interpersonal defenses.

It is important to put the foregoing description of optimal families in perspective. Yes, these skills are present, and these attitudes are found; but the overall description suggests a near perfection that is wondrously absent! Healthy families, like other healthy organisms, have defects and weaknesses resulting from the very processes that produce this health. Along with the capabilities, there are also relative fears of the unusual, or a need to control through affluence, or concerted efforts to blot out the non-normative or disturbing. Such defects are a part of health and part of the vibrancy of any competent family. These real defects represent vulnerability; no family can be confident that its skills can encompass all possible environmental stresses.

Adequate Families

Adequate families are also relatively effective, competent systems. Their boundaries are clear, and a gratifying presence of both intimacy and individual responsibility is encouraged. They contrast from optimal families, however, in that there is a greater emphasis on control efforts; conflicts are more often resolved through intimidation rather than negotiation.

The parental coalition in intact families is less effective; the emotional needs of each adult are short-changed, although the parents characteristically cooperate in parenting efforts. These families also exhibit more evidence of stress and emotional pain than do optimal ones. Family interaction produces less joy, less intimacy and trust, and is less spontaneous than in optimal families. Role stereotyping, particularly sex role stereotyping, however, is more evident and approaches that seen in midrange families. These families do, however, develop children that seem as competent as those from optimal families apparently because of family members' strong belief in the importance of family and of family life. Thus, tenacity and genuine caring prove effective in spite of modest parenting and negotiating skills.

Midrange Families

Midrange families constitute the most frequent of family groups. These families usually rear sane but limited offspring, although both parents and children are susceptible to psychiatric illness. They evidence obvious pain and difficulty in functioning over the life cycle. Characteristically, there is an emphasis on control efforts that reduces the possibility for intimacy.

Boundary problems are most evident in the abiding efforts of family members to control the thoughts and feelings of one another. "You shouldn't think that way." "You will disgrace the family by talking that way." "Loving means controlling" all represent midrange family mottos, whether expressed or not, derived from a pervasive belief that people are basically evil, and one shows caring by controlling oneself. It follows then that there will be a "war" in the nursery, with loving parenting understood as controlling the inborn antisocial impulses of the young.

There are frequently seen subtle or broad evidences of unresolved Oedipal conflicts. "Daddy's girl" and "Momma's boy" are phenomena often accepted as natural in family life. These both produce and result from parental conflict and make it more difficult for children to fulfill the immensely important task of leaving home.

It is in this group of families that one sees the most slavish repetition of cultural stereotyping. Stoic, insensitive males and emotive, overtly incompetent females abound. Healthier families are freer to make up their own minds about their roles in this society; very disturbed families are alienated from the culture and hence less influenced by it. It is the broad group of midrange families that continues to validate and pass on cultural stereotypes.

Midrange family members acknowledge mixed feelings in themselves and others, but these feelings are characteristically condemned. Fears of the outside world are defined as cowardice. Needs for independence are often characterized as willfulness and disrespect for elders.

With the greater problems with boundaries and with accepting ambivalence and the need for autonomy, negotiating becomes far more difficult. More decisions are unilateral, and more solutions are based on power plays and intimidation.

Children in these families grow up with many developmental tasks only partially completed. Effectively, leaving home is difficult in any style of midrange families, and the children may fall prey to the development of neurosis or behavior disturbances.

Midrange family members have a self-definition that is coherent but quite vulnerable because of its limited nature. Repression is a common way of handling the condemned half of mixed feelings, and the return of that which is repressed remains a continuing threat to emotional health.

Midrange Centripetal Families

These families manifest great concern for rules and authority; they expect overt, authoritarian control to be successful in controlling the base impulses of family members. Since the expressions of hostility and overt anger are disapproved and expressions of "love" and "caring" approved, raised and vented feelings of frustration and conflict are infrequent. Therefore, conflict resolution, clarity of expression, and competent negotiation are compromised. One sees only modest spontaneity shining through the web of concern for rules, order, and authority. Sex stereotyping is very strong in these families: Dependent, emotional women and strong, silent, authority-based men are predominant. Hence, the marital relationship takes on a flavor of a male-led unit, often with depressed females carrying out the vast majority of household and child-rearing duties.

These families promote internalizing and repression as means of dealing with distress and upset. When psychiatric illness occurs, it will usually manifest itself in anxiety disorders, mild depression, and somatizing disorders. The patients' concern for properness and authority make them "good" psychiatric patients who pay their bills, work hard, and keep their problems well hidden until their next week's session.

Midrange Centrifugal Families

Like midrange centripetal families, midrange centrifugal families attempt to control by authority and intimidation; however, they find over time that such control is ineffective and so come to expect that their control efforts will not be successful. Hence, the belief evolves that outsiders will find out about their inadequacies. These family members deal with this inevitable lack of control through frontal assaults and blame, usually spread across members from time to time, and through manipulation. Anger and derogatory blame are far more frequent manifestations of emotion than the anxiety-provoking expressions of warmth and tenderness. The parental dyad is openly conflictual and competitively hostile; the mother and father spend little time in the home; the coalition is tenuous, and unresolved power and control struggles are commonplace. Children observe that one survives through maneuvering and blaming others; they move out into the streets earlier than the norm and often have difficulty with authority figures. When they manifest psychiatric difficulties, these usually take the form of acting-out behavior disorders such as vandalism, sexual precocity, substance abuse, and conduct disorders.

Midrange Mixed Families

This group of families displays competing and alternating centripetal and centrifugal behavior, which reduces the rigidity of more extreme style but concomitantly increases inconsistency and uncertainty of position in the family. The attempts at control are consistent, but the effects vary at different times or with different children, depending on internal scapegoating patterns. Couples in this group experience role tension and struggles; they can present well socially but engage in blaming and hostile attacks on other occasions or in private. They distance through work or independent social activities. It is common for one child to manifest internalizing symptoms while another child is openly defiant and hostile.

Borderline Families

These families are more concerned about control issues than are midrange families; the centripetal borderline families pursue control more effectively than do the centrifugal group, but both family groupings are preoccupied with control to near exclusion of concerns for joy, satisfaction, or intimacy. Individual family members find little emotional support from the family. Developmental tasks are difficult to accomplish in these surroundings; resolution of ambivalence about important issues is accomplished infrequently, and both separation and individuation are compromised.

These families alternate between earnest efforts at control and a peculiar "zaniness," where the focus of conversation or interaction is lost and incoherence results.

Boundary problems are quite apparent, both of the "you should" variety (efforts at control of another's thinking and feeling) and the "you really think (or feel)" (invasions of another's experience of self). These invasions are, however, much less frequent than those seen in severely dysfunctional families. The mood of the family varies from overt depression to overt rage, with little evidence of satisfaction or joy.

Borderline Centripetal Families

These families represent the most difficult challenges for most family therapists. They are well enough organized to attempt control of the outside world, including therapists, as well as to pursue controlling efforts within the family.

Ambivalence is only reluctantly recognized or admitted, which leads to the frequent demonstration of incoherence in interactions (what we have termed "zaniness"). In watching this group of families, it is usual to see effective domination and control disintegrate into confusion and disorganization characteristic of severely dysfunctional families, and this disarray in turn chaotically reverts to controlled interaction.

Offspring are typically compulsive, whether defined as symptomatic or not. Symptom complexes include severe obsessive compulsive states, depression, and anorexia. The modal anorexic patient has dynamics quite isomorphic with the family dynamics—with both seeming to have given up hope or expectation of enjoyment for the dubious satisfaction of successful control. This goal of total control, however, is always out of reach unless it is clearly self destructive.

Borderline Centrifugal Families

These families are much more open than borderline centripetal families in the expression of anger, with ample leave-taking and frequent direct assaults. The parental coalition is loosely connected, and stormy battles occur with high regularity. These systems produce a sense of "no-man's land," with children left with little or no nurturance and support. Each individual is on his or her own to try to derive whatever goodies can be gained by manipulation or reckless attention seeking. Ambivalence is dramatically evident, but unacknowledged. Desired nurturance is never obtained, and the resulting impetus to depression is masked by anger and rebelliousness. Children learn to manipulate within this unstable oscillating system; many receive a label of "borderline personality disorder" as they carry these behaviors into the outside world.

Severely Dysfunctional Families

These families are the most limited in negotiating conflicts, in adapting to developmental demands and situational crises. The family members have the most trouble in resolving ambivalence and defining goals. The main lack that is evidenced, and the greatest need, is for coherence in interaction. Such families have poorly defined power structure; unclear, ineffective, and unsatisfying communication; extreme problems in interpersonal boundaries; few negotiation skills; and a pervasively depressed or cynical tone. The family power structure is difficult to define, and communication is chronically ineffective. Family members characteristically lack a shared focus of attention as the parental coalition is in shambles.

Family members in severely dysfunctional families deny the passage of time and its implications as to growth and development, aging and death. Behavior and feelings are quite often unresponsive to the changing abilities of family members, and the family members have great difficulty in looking forward to the future and making effective plans. Ambivalence is characteristically expressed in a sequential fashion. That is, family members tend to express first one side and then another of the strong mixed feelings that they feel toward one another. There is little "glue" in these ambivalent communications, and the listener is left to interpret and to make some sense out of quite opposite communications (Beavers et al., 1965).

The lack of individuality or differentiation of self in these families leads to profound difficulties in members' ability to decide on and move toward goals, as well as in the family's capacity to resolve conflicts and deal with pressing problems. The system wallows like a rudderless ship. The mood and tone of feeling are the most painful found in any of the family classifications. Expressions of warmth and affirmation are rare. Severely disturbed families feel chronically disappointed, frustrated, angry, resentful, and guilty. In these families and individuals, a basic developmental task, that of evolving trust, has been aborted and remains unfinished.

The child growing up in such a family develops a quite incomplete sense of self. Since choice is so important in the development of the self, children growing up in such a familial environment are deprived of a clear identity. Sharing powerful feelings with family members and reaching beyond the family to friends and loved ones are necessary to develop a sense of goals and purpose. It is also necessary to mourn the inevitable losses that are attendant to growth and development, aging and death. Because of the lack of a shared focus of attention, the boundary defects, and the communicational obscurity and isolation, no one in such families deals well with loss. Finally, the dysfunctional pattern becomes cyclical as such unmourned loss becomes crippling to the next generation in its efforts to develop competent families.

Severely Dysfunctional Centripetal Families

This group of severely disturbed families has a tough, nearly impermeable, outer boundary or perimeter. The family is usually seen as strange or odd by neighbors, and family loyalty requires remaining in the family and either physically or emotionally never leaving home. Family members are expected to think and feel alike with no comprehension of uniquely subjective human responses to the world. There are severe boundary problems. Children receive few clear messages and many confusing ones. Parents speak for children ("You don't really mean that; you really love your sister, you don't hate her"). Members of these families are unable to experience or express a sense of individual identity.

Because of the lack of a shared focus of attention and the pervasive communicational obscurity, dealing with loss by sharing is quite impossible.

The parental coalition is always poorly functioning. Its appearance is maintained through polite role playing, although the spouses' inability to relate to each other closely is obvious on direct observation. The parental coalition is often supplanted by a powerful parent–child coalition. This undermines the generational boundary and produces much of the confusing context and the resulting communicational obscurity.

The children in these families are characteristically quite inhibited and overcontrolled; for them, one solution to the conflict between developmental pressures toward separation and family rules of remaining loyal and static is a schizophrenic level of functioning. However, this reactive pattern seems to be possible only in those families that have a genetic predisposition to such illness.

Severely Dysfunctional Centrifugal Families

This group of families is characterized by an extremely diffuse boundary with the outside world. Family organization is unstable. Parents move in and out, children run away, and the very definition of who constitutes the family is often ambiguous. Family interaction is marked by competition, teasing, manipulation, and open conflict that is never resolved. Interpersonal skills are so limited that, although parents and children may leave home, they are usually unsuccessful in both personal and occupational endeavors and return to the family as needful and hostile as before.

Distinct patterns characterize this severely dysfunctional type of family. Discipline is attempted through intimidation, which usually fails because of the shifting, ineffective power structure and the lack of positive relationships. Family members are unreceptive to each other's efforts to communicate, and there is a marked lack of empathy. The quarrelsome, angry family interaction and the hostile, antisocial behavior of individual members can be seen as a defense against the pain and sadness of emotional deprivation. These family members find hostility easy to express, but tenderness, loneliness, and emotional pain are difficult or impossible for them to admit openly. Physical abuse is common in these families. Inept parenting and relating leads to great frustration, and family members' control of impulses is frequently inadequate.

Centrifugal severely disturbed families are likely to produce sociopathic offspring (antisocial personalities). Children in these families can find no way to be loved by obeying the rules, since the rules shift, and no behavior patterns are rewarded consistently by closeness or caring. They learn to present an "I don't care" facade and to share the family viewpoint that all those within its boundaries are bad, even evil. The resulting unacceptable behavior of these children provokes social rejection and punishment, which further encourages self-loathing. Self-defeating behavior expresses rage to an uncaring world.

Many of these families are embedded in a hostile community environment, and their functioning is affected by extreme poverty, by racism, and by a generalized sense of hopelessness regarding any improvement of circumstances. More often than not there is a negative interactive relationship between family and community, mirroring the negative relationship between individual and family.

PRACTICAL USE AND RESEARCH

The emphasis on coping and competence has been the driving force in the research and clinical work surrounding this model. Even in our studies of families with identified stressors or difficulties, common themes to look for those of coping and adaptation.

One set of studies examined adaptation and competence in families with a retarded child (Beavers, Hampson, Hulgus, & Beavers, 1986; Hampson, Hulgus, & Beavers, 1988). In this group, as in every large group of families, there was a wide range of family competence. This sample included a significant group of well-functioning families, as well as some dysfunctional families. Contrary to some previous research and clinical lore that such families are permeated by a sense of chronic sorrow leading universally to family dysfunction, we found that families who were able to deal openly with their feelings, including sorrow, were among the more competent families. Indeed, they were able to express a wide range of feelings including frustration, joy, and the fact that the presence of the handicapped child may have even contributed to their support of one another. What characterized the most dysfunctional group was an almost universal taboo on dealing with such feelings even though the interaction in these families would be characterized as despairing.

The above studies provide a perfect example of the need to "break set" and emphasize current interactional assets and liabilities when working with families. Unfortunately, there is great tradition, but very little utility, in describing families diagnostically or symptomatically. Labels such as "codependent," "alcoholic," or "schizophrenic" families tend to describe products rather than processes, and this factor is kept in mind as we develop any new study. We are currently beginning a study of single-parent families and expect to find as wide a variety of competence and style levels as have appeared with other studied groups. As with the families with retarded children, we will be asking family members how they deal with stress and change so advice may be gleaned for those with marginal coping skills who are exhibiting lower levels of success.

Other studies have examined family competence and style in relation to treatment outcome and compliance with medical regimens in a variety of medical (Foote, 1984; Steidl et al., 1980), and psychiatric settings (Beavers & Hampson, 1990; Kolevzon, Green, Fortune, & Vosler, 1988). In general, the more competent the family and the better the support system surrounding the patient in the immediate family, the better the response to treatment.

The ongoing study of the relationship between self-report and observational assessment is another major thrust of our research. Several studies with clinic and nonclinic samples are in process, and our research team is addressing such issues as whether a mean family score, variance patterns, or using certain individuals' scores is the most accurate means of assessing a family by self-report. In both clinic and nonclinic families, parents' SFI scores are in the more competent direction than that of the observer–rater, whereas in many cases an adolescent is more critical of the family, with lower SFI Competence ratings.

Most importantly, the assessment of competence and style is useful in guiding a therapist toward intervention strategies with a given family (Beavers & Hampson, 1990). We have found, for example, that more competent families gain more from therapy and that highly CF families come to fewer scheduled sessions and drop out of therapy more readily than CP families. Better treatment results are also attained when a therapist adapts his or her interactional style to the style of the family. Better treatment results for CP families are attained when the therapist actively joins the family, attends to disclosing therapeutic strategy with the family, and minimizes any perception of power differential and control (Beavers & Hampson, 1991). CF families, at least initially, respond better to the converse therapy conditions: lower levels of joining and disclosure and greater power differential.

The assessment methods and model, and the resultant family groupings, appear to be clinically useful and empirically reliable and valid. But throughout the discussion of healthy families and their assessment lies a nagging question, appropriately raised in the first edition of *Normal Family Processes*: Exactly what do we mean by "normal"? Across many studies, we have compiled assessment information, using observational and/or self-report data on over 1,800 families in clinical and nonclinical settings. This represents the sets of families we have studied since the original Timberlawn study (Lewis et al., 1976). In that initial study, middle-class non-clinical families were compared with middle-class families with hospitalized adolescents. Since then our research has evaluated groupings of nonclinical families across the socioeconomic and ethnic spectrum (Hampson et al., 1990), clinic families in an outpatient setting, volunteer families from school and university samples, and inner-city families with developmentally disabled children. Hence, these data and the model are based on a wide variety of family groups and situations, and the revisions and updates on the model and its scales presented in this chapter are reflective of the broad base of families we have studied.

Figure 2.2 presents a frequency histogram of the different levels of competence across this broad sample. Several important points can be derived from these data.

First, although the optimal family may serve as an ideal for effective family functioning, it cannot be considered the "normal" family on a statistical basis (Offer & Sabshin, 1976). Across the board, about 5% of families overall and up to 11% of a nonclinical sample were classified in this range.

Second, statistical "normality" appears to lie in the Adequate to Midrange levels of family Competence across groups.

Finally, and perhaps most importantly, severely dysfunctional families are a relatively small minority (3%, 11% of the clinical sample). This finding controverts the speculations of many "dysfunctional family" advocates, who attempt to convince us that the dysfunctional family represents the norm in modern America. Rather, the data suggest a reassuring bell-shaped curve, with extremes of health or incompetence small parts of the whole, and the bulk of American families doing reasonably well yet with considerable room for improvement.

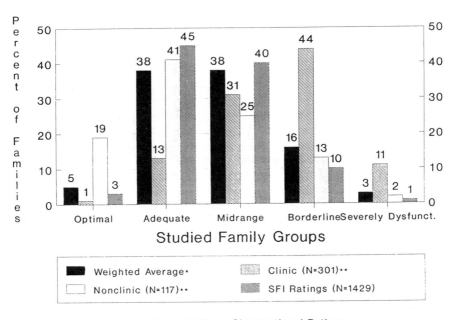

FIGURE 2.2. Distribution of levels of family competence in clinic and nonclinic families.

REFERENCES

Beavers, J. S., Hampson, R. B., Hulgus, Y. F., & Beavers, W. R. (1986). Coping in families with a retarded child. *Family Process, 25,* 365–378.

Beavers, W. R. (1977). *Psychotherapy and growth.* New York: Brunner/Mazel.

Beavers, W. R. (1982). Healthy, midrange, and severely dysfunctional families. In F. Walsh (Ed.), *Normal family processes* (1st ed., pp. 45–66). New York: Guilford Press.

Beavers, W. R. (1985). *Successful marriage: A family systems approach to marital therapy.* New York: W. W. Norton.

Beavers, W. R. (1988). A clinically useful model of family assessment. In C. Ramsay (Ed.), *Family systems in medicine* (pp. 120–138). New York: Guilford Press.

Beavers, W. R., Blumberg, S., Timken, K. R., & Weiner, M. D. (1965). Communication patterns of mothers of schizophrenics. *Family Process, 4,* 95–104.

Beavers, W. R., & Hampson, R. B. (1990). *Successful families: Assessment and intervention.* New York: W. W. Norton.

Beavers, W. R., & Hampson, R. B. (1991, October). *Successful families: Assessment guides intervention.* Workshop presented at annual convention of American Association of Marital and Family Therapy, Dallas.

Beavers, W. R., Hampson, R. B., & Hulgus, Y. F. (1985). The Beavers systems approach to family assessment. *Family Process, 24,* 398–405.

Beavers, W. R., Hampson, R. B., & Hulgus, Y. F. (1990). *Manual: Beavers Systems Model of Family Assessment.* Dallas: Southwest Family Institute.

Beavers, W. R., & Voeller, M. N. (1983). Family models: Comparing the Olson circumplex model with the Beavers systems model. *Family Process, 22,* 85–98.

Erikson, E. H. (1963). *Childhood and society.* New York: W. W. Norton.

Foote, M. S. (1984). *Psychological health and chronic illness in the family system.* Unpublished doctoral dissertation, Texas Women's University, Denton, Texas.

Hampson, R. B., & Beavers, W. R. (1988). Comparing males' and females' perspectives through family self report. *Psychiatry, 50,* 24–30.

Hampson, R. B., Beavers, W. R., & Hulgus, Y. F. (1988). Comparing the Beavers and Circumplex models of family functioning. *Family Process, 27,* 85–92.

Hampson, R. B., Beavers, W. R., & Hulgus, Y. F. (1989). Insiders' and outsiders' views of family: The assessment of family competence and style. *Journal of Family Psychology, 3,* 118–136.

Hampson, R. B., Beavers, W. R., & Hulgus, Y. F. (1990). Cross-ethnic family differences: Interactional assessment of white, black, and Mexican-American families. *Journal of Marital and Family Therapy, 16,* 307–319.

Hampson, R. B., Hulgus, Y. F., & Beavers, W. R. (1988). The assessment of competence in families with a retarded child. *Journal of Family Psychology, 2,* 32–53.

Hampson, R. B., & Pierce, J. A. (1993). Within-family patterns of self-report ratings. Unpublished manuscript, Southern Methodist University Press, Dallas.

Kelsey-Smith, M., & Beavers, W. R. (1981). Family assessment: Centripetal and centrifugal family systems. *American Journal of Family Therapy, 9,* 3–21.

Kolevzon, M. S., Green, R. G., Fortune, A. E., & Vosler, N. R. (1988). Evaluating family therapy: Divergent methods, divergent findings. *Journal of Marital and Family Therapy, 14,* 277–286.

Lewis, J. M., Beavers, W. R., Gossett, J. T., & Phillips, V. A. (1976). *No single thread: Psychological health in family systems.* New York: Brunner/Mazel.

Offer, D., & Sabshin, M. (1976). *Normality*. New York: Basic Books.

Steidl, J. H., Finkelstein, F. O., Wexler, J. P., Feigenbaum, H., Kitsen, D., Kliger, A. S., & Quinlan, D. M. (1980). Medical condition, adherence to treatment regimens, and family functioning. *Archives of General Psychiatry, 37*, 1025–1027.

Stierlin, H. (1972). *Separating parents and adolescents*. New York: Quadrangle Press.

Von Bertalanffy, L. (1969). General systems theory—An overview. In W. Gray, F. J. Duhl, & N. D. Rizzo (Eds.), *General systems theory and psychiatry* (pp. 33–46). Boston: Little, Brown.

APPENDIX A: Beavers Interactional Competence Scale

BEAVERS INTERACTIONAL SCALES: I. FAMILY COMPETENCE

Family Name_____ Rater_____

Segment_____ Date_____

Instructions: The following scales were designed to assess the family functioning on continua representing interactional aspects of being a family. Therefore, it is important that you consider the entire range of each scale when you make your ratings. Please try to *respond on the basis of the videotape data alone*, scoring according to what you see and hear, rather than what you imagine might occur elsewhere.

I. Structure of the Family

A. Overt Power: Based on the entire tape, check the term that best describes your general impression of the overt power relationships of this family.

1	1.5	2	2.5	3	3.5	4	4.5	5
Chaos		Marked dominance		Moderate dominance		Led		Egalitarian
Leaderless; no one has enough power to structure the inter- action.		Control is close to absolute. No nego- tiation; dominance and submission are the rule.		Control is close to absolute. Some nego- tiation, but dominance and submission are the rule.		Tendency toward dominance and sub- mission, but most of the interaction is through respectful negotiation.		Leadership is shared between parents, changing with the nature of the interaction.

B. Parental Coalitions: Check the terms that best describe the relationship structure in this family.

1	1.5	2	2.5	3	3.5	4	4.5	5
Parent-child coalition				Weak parental coalition				Strong parental coalition

C. Closeness

1	1.5	2	2.5	3	3.5	4	4.5	5
Amorphous, vague and indis- tinct boundaries among members				Isolation, distancing				Closeness, with distinct boundaries among members

Note any invasions (when a family member clearly "speaks for" the thoughts or feelings of another, without invitation):
--invasion(s) observed
--invasion(s) not observed

II. Mythology: Every member has a mythology; that is, a concept of how it functions as a group. Rate the degree to which this family's mythology seems congruent with reality.

1	1.5	2	2.5	3	3.5	4	4.5	5
Very congruent		Mostly congruent				Somewhat incongruent		Very incongruent

III. Goal-Directed Negotiation: Rate this family's overall efficiency in negotiating problem solutions.

1	1.5	2	2.5	3	3.5	4	4.5	5
Extremely efficient		Good				Poor		Extremely inefficient

IV. Autonomy

    A. Clarity of Expression: Rate this family as to the clarity of disclosure of feelings and thoughts. This is not a rating of the intensity or variety of feelings, but rather of clarity of individual thoughts and feelings.

1	1.5	2	2.5	3	3.5	4	4.5	5
Very clear				Somewhat vague and hidden				Hardly anyone is ever clear

    B. Responsibility: Rate the degree to which the family members take responsibility for their own past, present, and future actions.

1	1.5	2	2.5	3	3.5	4	4.5	5
Members regularly are able to voice responsibility for individual actions				Members sometimes voice responsibility for individual actions, but tactics also include sometimes blaming others, speaking in 3rd person or plural				Members rarely if ever, voice responsibility for individual actions

    C. Permeability: Rate the degree to which members are open, receptive and permeable to the statements of other family members.

1	1.5	2	2.5	3	3.5	4	4.5	5
Very open		Moderately open				Members frequently unreceptive		Members unreceptive

V. Family Affect

    A. Range of Feelings: Rate the degree to which this family system is characterized by a wide range expression of feelings.

1	1.5	2	2.5	3	3.5	4	4.5	5
Direct expression of a wide range of feelings		Direct expression of many feelings despite some difficulty		Obvious restriction in the expressions of some feelings		Although some feelings are expressed, there is masking of most feelings		Little or no expression of feelings

B. Mood and Tone: Rate the feeling tone of this family's interaction.

1	1.5	2	2.5	3	3.5	4	4.5	5
Usually warm, affectionate, humorous and optimistic		Polite, without impressive warmth or affection; or frequently hostile with times of pleasure		Overly hostile		Depressed		Cynical, hopeless and pessimistic

C. Unresolvable Conflict: Rate the degree of seemingly unresolvable conflict.

1	1.5	2	2.5	3	3.5	4	4.5	5
Severe conflict, with severe impairment of group functioning		Definite conflict, with moderate impairment of group functioning		Definite conflict, with slight impairment of group functioning		Some evidence of unresolvable conflict, without impairment of group functioning		Little, or no unresolvable conflict

D. Empathy: Rate the degree of sensitivity to, and understanding of, each other's feelings within this family.

1	1.5	2	2.5	3	3.5	4	4.5	5
Consistent empathic responsiveness		For the most part, an empathic responsiveness with one another, despite obvious resistance		Attempted empathic involvement, but failed to maintain it		Absence of any empathic responsiveness		Grossly inappropriate responses to feelings

VI. Global Health-Pathology Scale: Circle the number of the point on the following scale that best describes this family's health or pathology.

10	9	8	7	6	5	4	3	2	1
Most Pathological									Healthiest

APPENDIX B: Beavers Interactional Style Scale

BEAVERS INTERACTIONAL SCALES: II. FAMILY STYLE

Family Name_____ Date_____

Rater_____

1. All families must deal with the dependency needs of members. In this family, the dependency needs of members are:

1	2	3	4	5
discouraged, ignored		sometimes discouraged, sometimes attended		encouraged, alertly attended

2. Adults in all families have conflicts. In this family, adult conflicts are:

1	2	3	4	5
quite open	usually open		sometimes hidden covert	indirect, covert, hidden

3. All families, when together, space themselves physically in some way. In this family:

1	2	3	4	5
all members give and expect lots of room between members		some members touch, others stay apart		all members stay physically close, and there is much touching

4. All families have some attitude about how they look to outsiders. In this family, members:

1	2	3	4	5
try hard to appear well behaved and to make a good impression on others		sometimes appear concerned with making a good impression		seem unconcerned with appearances and social approval

Note whether internal scapegoating (one member bearing the burden of blame for family problems) is observed:

-----internal scapegoating observed
-----internal scapegoating not observed

5. This scale does not address family closeness, but rather how much family members profess that they are close. In this family, members:

1	2	3	4	5
consistently emphasize that they are close		don't make an issue of closeness		deny being close

6. All families must deal with the assertive and aggressive qualities of members. In this family, members:

1	2	3	4	5
discourage aggressive or disruptive behavior and expression				solicit or encourage assertive, even aggressive behavior and expression

7. All people have both positive and negative feelings. Rate this family in terms of the relative ease with which one or the other is expressed.

1	2	3	4	5
positive feelings are easier to express than negative		about the same		negative feelings are easier to express than positive

Global Centripetal/Centrifugal Family Style Scale.

1	1.5	2	2.5	3	3.5	4	4.5	5
Family has a strong, inner orientation, an inward pull. The outside world is seen as relatively threatening. The family is seen as the main hope for gratification of crucial needs.						Family has a strong outer orientation, an outward push. The outside world is less threatening than close family relationships. Main hope for gratification of crucial needs is seen as existing outside the family.		

APPENDIX C: Self-Report Family Inventory

SELF-REPORT FAMILY INVENTORY: VERSION II

For each question, mark the answer that best fits how you see your family now. If you feel that your answer is between two of the labeled numbers (the odd numbers), then choose the even number that is between them.

	YES: Fits our family very well		SOME: Fits our family some		NO: Does not fit our family
1. Family members pay attention to each other's feelings.	1	2	3	4	5
2. Our family would rather do things together than with other people.	1	2	3	4	5
3. We all have a say in family plans.	1	2	3	4	5
4. The grownups in this family understand and agree on family decisions.	1	2	3	4	5
5. Grownups in the family compete and fight with each other.	1	2	3	4	5
6. There is closeness in my family but each person is allowed to be special and different.	1	2	3	4	5
7. We accept each other's friends.	1	2	3	4	5
8. There is confusion in our family because there is no leader.	1	2	3	4	5
9. Our family members touch and hug each other.	1	2	3	4	5
10. Family members put each other down.	1	2	3	4	5
11. We speak our minds, no matter what.	1	2	3	4	5
12. In our home, we feel loved.	1	2	3	4	5
13. Even when we feel close, our family is embarrassed to admit it.	1	2	3	4	5

Southwest Family Institute

	YES: Fits our family very well		SOME: Fits our family some		NO: Does not fit our family
14. We argue a lot and never solve problems.	1	2	3	4	5
15. Our happiest times are at home.	1	2	3	4	5
16. The grownups in this family are strong leaders.	1	2	3	4	5
17. The future looks good to our family.	1	2	3	4	5
18. We usually blame one person in our family when things aren't going right.	1	2	3	4	5
19. Family members go their own way most of the time.	1	2	3	4	5
20. Our family is proud of being close.	1	2	3	4	5
21. Our family is good at solving problems together.	1	2	3	4	5
22. Family members easily express warmth and caring towards each other.	1	2	3	4	5
23. It's okay to fight and yell in our family.	1	2	3	4	5
24. One of the adults in this family has a favorite child.	1	2	3	4	5
25. When things go wrong we blame each other.	1	2	3	4	5
26. We say what we think and feel.	1	2	3	4	5
27. Our family members would rather do things with other people than together.	1	2	3	4	5
28. Family members pay attention to each other and listen to what is said.	1	2	3	4	5

	YES: Fits our family very well		SOME: Fits our family some		NO: Does not fit our family
29. We worry about hurting each other's feelings.	1	2	3	4	5
30. The mood in my family is usually sad and blue.	1	2	3	4	5
31. We argue a lot.	1	2	3	4	5
32. One person controls and leads our family.	1	2	3	4	5
33. My family is happy most of the time.	1	2	3	4	5
34. Each person takes responsibility for his/her behavior.	1	2	3	4	5

35. On a scale of 1 to 5, I would rate my family as:

1	2	3	4	5
My family functions very well together			My family does not function well together at all. We really need help.	

36. On a scale of 1 to 5, I would rate the independence in my family as:

1	2	3	4	5
(No one is independent. There are no open arguments. Family members rely on each other for satisfaction rather than on outsiders.)		(Sometimes independent. There are some disagreements. Family members find satisfaction both within and outside of the family.)	(Family members usually go their own way. Disagreements are open. Family members look outside of the family for satisfaction.)	

CIRCUMPLEX MODEL OF MARITAL AND FAMILY SYSTEMS
Assessing Family Functioning

David H. Olson

INTRODUCTION

The Circumplex Model of Marital and Family Systems was developed in an attempt to bridge the gaps that typically exist between research, theory, and practice. A variety of hypotheses have been developed and tested using the Circumplex Model. Some of the research has focused on types of family systems across the life cycle and how families cope effectively with normative stress (Olson, McCubbin, et al., 1989).

Family cohesion, flexibility and *communication* are the three dimensions in the Circumplex Model. These three dimensions emerged from a conceptual clustering of over 50 concepts developed to describe marital and family dynamics. Although some of these concepts have been used for decades (power and roles, for instance), many of the concepts have been developed more recently by individuals observing problem families from a general systems perspective (pseudomutuality, double-binds).

A variety of other theoretical models have focused independently on variables related to the *cohesion, flexibility* and *communication* dimensions. Most of these models have been developed in the last 10 years by individuals having a systems perspective on the family. Evidence regarding the value and importance of these three dimensions is the fact that these theorists have quite independently concluded that these dimensions were critical for understanding and treating marital and family systems.

Table 3.1 summarizes the work of 10 theorists who have worked on describing marital and family systems. Most of the recent theorizing about family dynamics and intervention has been strongly influenced by general systems theory. Current work has focused on describing both clinical and nonclinical families or has been concerned with clinical intervention with families.

Marital and Family Cohesion (Togetherness)

Family cohesion is defined as *the emotional bonding that family members have toward one another.* Within the Circumplex Model, some of the specific concepts or variables that can be used to diagnose and measure the family cohesion dimensions are: *emotional bonding, boundaries, coalitions, time, space, friends, decision-making* and *interests* and *recreation.* (See Clinical Rating Scales in Appendix A for how each concept is assessed.)

There are four levels of cohesion ranging from *disengaged* (very low) to *separated* (low to moderate) to *connected* (moderate to high) to *enmeshed* (very high) (see Figure 3.1). It is hypothesized that the central levels of cohesion (separated and connected) make for optimal family functioning. The extremes (disengaged or enmeshed) are generally seen as problematic.

In the model's Balanced area (separated and connected), individuals are able to *experience and balance* these two extremes and are also able to be both independent from and connected to their families. Many couples and families that go to marital or family therapy often fall into one of the extremes types. When cohesion levels are very high (enmeshed systems), there is too much consensus within the family and too little independence. At the other

TABLE 3.1. Theoretical Models Using Cohesion, Adaptability, and Communication

	Cohesion	Flexibility	Communication
Beavers & Hampson (1990)	Stylistic dimension	Adaptability	Affect
Benjamin (1977)	Affiliation	Interdependence	—
Epstein & Bishop (1983)	Affective involvement	Behavior control, problem solving	Communication, affective responsiveness
French & Guidera (1974)	—	Capacity to change, power	—
Gottman (1979)	Validation	Contrasting	—
Kantor & Lehr (1975)	Affect	Power	—
Leary (1975)	Affection, hostility	Dominance, submission	—
Leff & Vaughn (1985)	Distance	Problem solving	
Parsons & Bales (1955)	Expressive role	Instrumental role	—
Reiss (1981)	Coordination	Closure	—

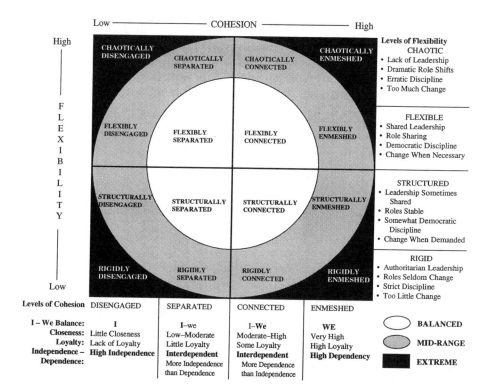

FIGURE 3.1. Circumplex Model: Couple and Family Map.

extreme (disengaged systems), family members "do their own thing," with limited attachment or commitment to their family.

Balanced couple and family systems (separated and connected types) tend to be more functional. More specifically, a *separated relationship* has some emotional separateness, but it is not as extreme as the disengaged system. Whereas time apart is more important, there are some times together, some joint decisions and marital support. Activities and interests are generally separate, but a few are shared. A *connected relationship* has emotional closeness and loyalty to the relationship. Time together is more important than time apart to be by oneself. There is an emphasis on togetherness. There are separate friends but also friends shared by the couple. Shared interests are common with some separate activities.

Conversely, unbalanced levels of cohesion are at extremes (very low or very high). A *disengaged relationship* often has extreme emotional separateness. There is little involvement among family members, and there is a lot of personal separateness and independence. Individuals often do their own thing, separate time, space, and interests predominate, and members are unable to turn to one another for support and problem solving. In the *enmeshed relationship* there is an extreme amount of emotional closeness, and loyalty is demanded. Individuals are very dependent on each other and reactive to one another. There is a general lack of personal separateness, and little private space is permitted. The energy of the individuals is mainly focused inside the marriage or family, and there are few outside individual friends or interests.

Based on the Circumplex Model, very high levels of cohesion (enmeshed) and very low levels of cohesion (disengaged) might be problematic for individuals and relationship development in the long run. On the other hand, relationships having moderate scores (separated and connected) are able to balance being alone versus together in a more functional way. Although there is no absolute best level for any relationship, some may have problems if they always function at either extreme of the Model (disengaged and enmeshed) for too long.

Marital and Family Flexibility

Family flexibility is the amount of *change in its leadership, role relationships, and relationship rules*. In order to describe, measure, and diagnose couples and families on this dimension, a variety of concepts have been taken from several social science disciplines, with heavy reliance on family sociology. These concepts include: *leadership* (control, discipline), *negotiation styles, role relationships*, and *relationship rules* (see Clinical Rating Scale in Appendix B for how each concept is assessed).

The four levels of flexibility range from *rigid* (very low) to *structured* (low to moderate) to *flexible* (moderate to high) to *chaotic* (very high) (see Figure 3.1). As with cohesion, it is hypothesized that central levels of flexibility (structured and flexible) are more conducive to marital and family functioning, with the extremes (rigid and chaotic) being the most problematic for families as they move through the family life cycle.

Basically, flexibility focuses on the *change* in a family's leadership, roles, and rules. Much of the early application of systems theory to families emphasized the rigidity of the family and its tendency to maintain the status quo. Until the work of recent theorists, the importance of potential for change was minimized. Couples and families need both stability and change, and the ability to change when appropriate distinguishes functional couples and families from others.

Balanced couple and family systems (structured and flexible types) tend to be more functional over time. A *structured relationship* tends to have a somewhat democratic leadership with some negotiations including the children. Roles are stable with some sharing of roles. There are few rule changes with rules firmly enforced. A *flexible relationship* has an equalitarian leadership with a democratic approach to decision making. Negotiations are open and actively include the children. Roles are shared and there is fluid change when necessary. Rules can be changed and are age-appropriate.

Unbalanced marriages and families tend to be either rigid or chaotic. A *rigid relationship* exists when one individual is in charge and is highly controlling. There tend to be limited negotiations with most decisions imposed by the leader. The roles are strictly defined, and the rules do not change. A *chaotic relationship* has erratic or limited leadership. Decisions are impulsive and not well thought out. Roles are unclear and often shift from individual to individual.

Based on the Circumplex Model, very high levels of flexibility (chaotic) and very low levels of flexibility (rigid) might be problematic for individuals and relationship development in the long run. On the other hand, relationships having moderate scores (structured and flexible) are able to balance some change and some stability in a more functional way. Although there is no absolute best level for any relationship, many relationships may have problems if they always function at either extreme of the Model (rigid and chaotic) for an extended period of time.

Marital and Family Communication

Family communication is the third dimension in the Circumplex Model and is considered a *facilitating dimension*. Communication is considered critical for facilitating couples and families to move on the other two dimensions. Because it is a facilitating dimension, communication is not graphically included in the model along with cohesion and flexibility (See Clinical Rating Scale in Appendix C for how communication is measured).

Family communication is measured by focusing on the family as a group with regard to their listening skills, speaking skills, self-disclosure, clarity, continuity–tracking, and respect and regard. In terms of listening skills, the focus is on empathy and attentive listening. Speaking skills include speaking for oneself and not speaking for others. Self-disclosure relates to sharing feelings about self and the relationship. Tracking is staying on topic, and respect and regard relate to the affective aspects of the communication. Several studies have investigated communication and problem-solving skills in couples and families and have found that Balanced systems tend to have very good communication, whereas Extreme systems tend to have poor communication.

Circumplex Model: A Couple and Family Map

Another way to consider the Model is as a descriptive map of 16 types of couple and family relationships, in other words, a Couple Map and a Family Map. The Couple Map is used to describe 16 types of marriages; the Family Map is used to describe 16 types of families (Figure 3.1).

The Family Map (Figure 3-1) is important because people often use their own family of origin as a reference for the type of marriage and family they either want or do not want. People often either recreate the type of family system they had as a child, or they sometimes react by doing the opposite. If a couple came from two quite different family systems or they prefer different types of family dynamics, it would be difficult for them to create a compatible relationship style that works for them. Thus, the *fit* between individuals is a critical variable in determining how functional and satisfying a relationship system is likely to be.

The Type of Marriage, as illustrated in the Couple Map (Figure 3.1), is important for individual and relationship development. Couples need to balance their levels of separateness–togetherness on cohesion and their levels of stability–change on flexibility. These levels can be adjusted by a couple to achieve a level that is acceptable to each individual.

An important distinction in the Circumplex Model (Figure 3.2) is between Balanced and Extreme types of couple and family relationships. There are four Balanced types that are "separated" or "connected" levels on cohesion and "structured" or "connected" on flexibility. Figure 3.1 illustrates the four balanced relationships and the four extreme or unbalanced relationships: *chaotically disengaged, chaotically enmeshed, rigidly disengaged* and *rigidly enmeshed.*

Three-Dimensional Circumplex Model: First- and Second-Order Change

Recently, a three-dimensional version of the Circumplex Model has been developed in order to make a variety of improvements in the measurement and utility of the model. Another advantage of the three-dimensional design is that it enables one to incorporate first order and second order change more effectively into the model, an idea that was suggested by Lee (1988).

First-order change is that which occurs within a given family system. It represents a "change in degree," whereas the basic family system does not change. First-order change is represented by the flexibility dimension.

First-order change is curvilinear in that too much or too little change is problematic. More specifically, either too much change (i.e., chaotic system) or too little change (i.e., rigid system) is related to a less functional pattern in families. In contrast, the two balanced types of flexibility are called "structured" and "flexible" because they represent more balanced levels of change.

Second-order change is change from one system type to another type of system. It is "change of the system itself" and can only be assessed over time. Also, under stress these patterns become more apparent. Second-order change can occur in times of normative stress, such as the birth of a child, or nonnormative change, such as when a parent is injured in a car accident or has a chronic illness.

Second-order change is linear with higher change in the balanced systems and the lowest level of change in unbalanced (extreme) systems. In times of stress, balanced systems will tend to change to another system type

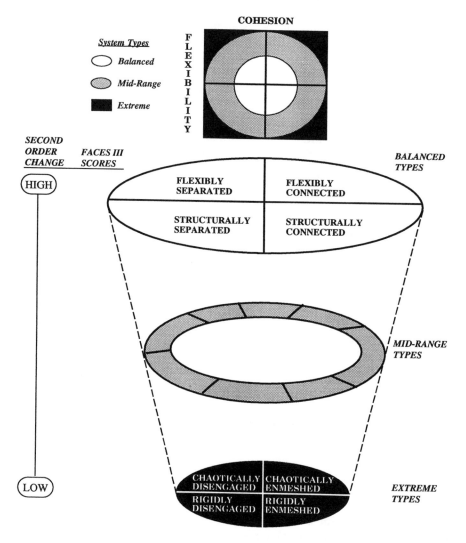

FIGURE 3.2. Three-dimensional family Circumplex Model.

to adapt, whereas unbalanced systems tend to stay stuck in their extreme pattern, which can often create more stress. Second-order change in this model is, thereby, similar to Beavers' concept of "competence" (Beavers & Hampson, 1990) and Constantine's family paradigm model (Constantine, 1986).

The three-dimensional model has the advantage of demonstrating more clearly the dynamic similarity of the types within the Balanced, Midrange and Extreme types. The three-dimensional model more clearly illustrates that the four Balanced types are more similar to each other dynamically in terms of second-order change than they are to any of the Extreme types. Conversely, the four Extreme types are similar to each other dynamically in that they are all low in second-order change. This clarifies the dynamic similarities within Balanced or Extreme types that are often lost when looking at the Circumplex Model when it is laid out in the two-dimensional (4 levels × 4 levels) design.

Methodologically, the assessment scale called FACES III measures the three-dimensional model in a more effective way than it does the traditional flat four-by-four design. It is clear from the various methodological studies and from a review of the specific questions in FACES III that high scores really measure Balanced family types and low scores measure Extreme family types. More specifically, high scores on cohesion are measuring "very connected" families (Balanced) and high scores on flexibility are measuring "very flexible" families (Balanced).

Studies with FACES III should assume it is a linear measure with high scores representing Balanced types and low scores representing Extreme types. This revised conceptual approach to FACES III also makes the three-dimensional model more similar to The Beavers System Model (see Beavers & Hampson, Chapter 2, this volume) and The McMaster Family Model (see Epstein et al., Chapter 4, this volume). It also helps clarify why FACES III statistically is correlated in a linear way to the Self-Report Family Inventory (SFI) by Beavers and Hampson (1990), the Family Assessment Measure (FAM III) by Skinner, Santa-Barbara, and Steinhauer (1983), and the McMaster Family Assessment Device (FAD) by Epstein and Bishop (1983).

DYNAMIC BALANCE AND SKIING: AN ANALOGY

An analogy can be made of a balanced or unbalanced family system with a balanced or unbalanced skier as was first presented by Walsh and Olson (1989). Whereas a professional skier is like a balanced system, a novice skier is more like an Unbalanced system.

In terms of cohesion, families need to balance separateness and togetherness. Likewise, in skiing these two aspects can be related to the two legs of the skier. A professional skier smoothly shifts his or her weight from one leg to another, whereas a novice skier tends to emphasize one leg or another. In balanced families, people are able to move in a more fluid manner between their separateness and togetherness, whereas unbalanced systems tend to be stuck at one extreme or the other and have a difficult time shifting between these two aspects of life.

In terms of flexibility, families need to balance both stability and change. This is parallel, in ways, to the ability of a skier to flexibly move his or her legs up and down. A professional skier is able to move his/her legs up and down in a fluid manner to absorb the moguls while keeping the upper part of the body upright, thereby providing general stability. In balanced families, people also require some basic stability while also being able to change. However, in unbalanced systems there is often too much rigidity or too much change, both of which lead to unstable systems.

Regarding communication, there is a clear correlation between family systems and skiing. Balanced families need good communication to maintain balance, whereas poor communication often keeps families out of balance. In skiing, a professional skier is very much "in touch" with all aspects of the hill, the type of snow conditions, and the structure of the moguls. Conversely, a novice skier often misreads the skiing conditions and misses the cues about the moguls. In order to stay balanced in skiing and in families, one needs to make small, subtle changes or adjustments over time. If one fails to make these small adjustments, one will become out of balance, and it will take more major adjustment to regain balance again. Another important characteristic of balanced families and professional skiers is that they tend to become more cohesive and flexible under stress. Conversely, unbalanced families often tend to become either too enmeshed or too separated, and often too rigid, which can lead to chaos. So like skiing, families need to become more flexible and cohesive to cope with life's moguls.

HYPOTHESES DERIVED FROM
THE CIRCUMPLEX MODEL

One of the assets of a theoretical model is that hypotheses can be deduced and tested in order to evaluate and further develop the model. The following are hypotheses derived from the Circumplex Model:

1. *Couples and families with Balanced types (two central levels) cohesion and flexibility will generally function more adequately across the family life cycle than those at the Unbalanced (Extreme) types.* An important issue in the Circumplex Model relates to the concept of balance. Individuals and family systems need to balance their separateness versus togetherness on cohesion and their level of stability versus change on flexibility. Even though a balanced family system is placed at the two central levels of the model, it should not be assumed that these families always operate in a "moderate" manner. Being Balanced means that a family system can experience the extremes on the dimension when appropriate, but it does not typically function at these extremes for long periods of time.

Families in the balanced area of the cohesion dimension allow family members to experience being both independent from and connected to their family. On flexibility, balance means maintaining some level of stability in a system with openness to some change when it is necessary. Extreme behaviors on these two dimensions might be appropriate for certain stages of the life cycle or when a family is under stress, but it can be problematic when families are stuck at the extremes.

Extreme types of family systems are not necessarily dysfunctional, especially if a family is under stress or if its members belong to a particular ethnic group (i.e., Hispanic, Southeast Asian) or religious groups (i.e., Amish, Mormon). If a family's expectations support more extreme patterns, families will then operate as a functional manner as long as all the family members desire the family to be that way. Ethnicity is a very central trait of families and needs to be seriously considered in assessing family dynamics. What might appear to be an "enmeshed" family of color to a white outsider may, in fact, be functional for various ethnic groups.

2. *Positive communication skills will enable Balanced types of couples/families to change their levels of cohesion and flexibility more easily than those Unbalanced (Extreme) types.* In general, positive communication skills are seen as helping marital and family systems facilitate and maintain a balance on the two dimensions. Conversely, negative communication skills impede movement into the Balanced types (central areas) and thereby, increase the probability that Unbalanced (Extreme) systems will remain extreme.

3. *To deal with situational stress and developmental changes across the family life cycle, families will modify their cohesion and adaptability to adapt to the stress.* This hypothesis deals with change in the family system (second-order change) to deal with stress or to accommodate changes in family members, particularly as family members change their expectations. The Circumplex Model is dynamic in that it assumes that couples and families will change types, and it hypothesizes that change can be beneficial to the maintenance and improvement of family functioning.

When one family member desires change, the family system must somehow deal with that request. For example, increasing numbers of wives want to develop more autonomy from their husbands (Cohesion dimension) and also want more power and equality in their relationships (Flexibility dimension). If their husbands are unwilling to understand and change in accordance with these expectations, the marriages will probably experience increasing levels of stress and dissatisfaction. Another common example of changing expectations occurs when a child reaches adolescence. Like the wives in the previous example, adolescents often want more freedom, independence, and power in the family system. These pressures to change the family system by one member can facilitate change in the family, which will often tend to resist any change.

FAMILY SYSTEMS AND STRESS ACROSS THE FAMILY LIFE CYCLE

Empirically, this chapter builds on and extends the findings from a national survey of nonclinical families described in the book, *Families: What Makes Them Work* (Olson, McCubbin, et al., 1989). The operationalization of family developmental stages, family stress, and adaptation, family system types and the analyses in the present chapter are updated from the results in that book.

The overall sample comprised 1,251 families, with more than 100 families in seven family life stages and more than 200 families with adolescents. Data were collected from both spouses in each family and from adolescents in families that included adolescent(s) at home. The present analysis is based on responses of adults (husband, wives).

The sample consisted of predominantly Caucasian, middle-class, Protestant, intact families from both rural and urban areas. Husbands' ages ranged from 20 to 85 (mean = 46) and wives' ages ranged from 19 to 84 (mean = 43). Children's ages ranged from less than 1 year in the preschool stage to more than 40 in retirement-stage families. A large variety of occupations were represented in the sample. Average family income fell in the $20,000 to $30,000 range. Data on education showed that 30% of the husbands and 20% of the wives had at least a college education.

Levels of Cohesion and Flexibility

Figures 3.3 and 3.4 represent the frequency of families at each of the four developmental stages classified by the Circumplex's main dimensions of Cohesion (connected vs. separated) and Flexibility (flexible vs. structured) families.

In terms of family cohesion, younger couples had the highest percentage that felt "connected" (71%) versus felt "separated" (29%). The percentage feeling "connected" dropped to 63% in families with younger children and more dramatically to 40% in families with adolescents (see Figure 3.3).

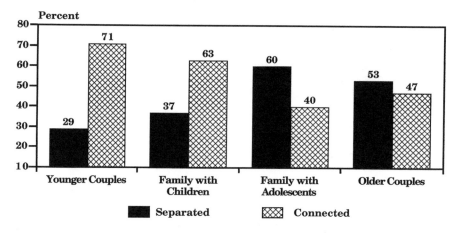

FIGURE 3.3. Family cohesion across the family life cycle.

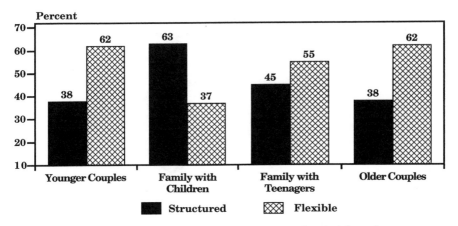

FIGURE 3.4. Family flexibility across the family life cycle.

After the adolescent left home, about an equal number of older couples felt "connected" or "separated."

As might be expected, younger couples felt their relationship was more "flexible" (62%), and this dropped to 37% with families with younger children. As expected, the flexibility increased to 55% with families with adolescents. What is somewhat surprising is that 62% of older couples who had already launched their children still felt "flexible," and only 38% felt "structured," which is identical with the pattern in younger couples (see Figure 3.4).

Family Stressors, Strains, and Well-Being across the Family Life Cycle

This analysis examined the accumulation of stressors and strains and the level of family well-being across the family life cycle. The results of this analysis are graphically presented in Figure 3.5. There was very little difference in the number of stressor events across the four family life stages. An analysis of variance, indeed, indicated no significant differences in the number of stressor events [$F(3) = 2.38$, $p > .10$], with all stages having about three major stressor events.

On the other hand, there was a significant difference among families' levels of strain at the four stages [$F(3) = 32.63$, $p > .01$]. The results in Figure 3.5 indicate that families with children, either preschool and school-age or adolescents, experience higher levels of interfamily strain than do childless couples or families at the empty-nest stage and retirement stage. The results indicate that both younger and older couples have the lowest level of strain.

Couples at the first stage of family development (i.e., before children are born) and at the last stage of the family development (i.e., after all chil-

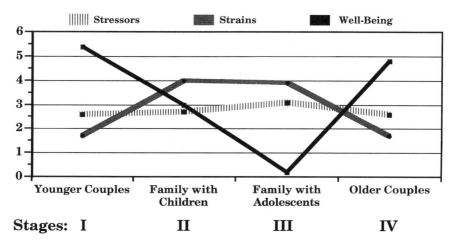

FIGURE 3.5. Stressors, strains, and well-being across the family life cycle.

dren have left home) are also more satisfied with their marriage, their families, and their quality of life than are those with children at home. Families with adolescents have lower levels of well-being than those families with younger children, despite having similar levels of stressors and strains.

CHANGES IN A COUPLE SYSTEM
IN EARLY MARRIAGE

The Circumplex Model allows one to integrate systems theory within family development, a proposal made more than two decades ago by Reuben Hill (1970). Building on the family developmental approach, it is hypothesized that the stage of the family life cycle and composition of the family will have considerable impact on the type of family system (Carter & McGoldrick, 1988).

It is hypothesized that at any stage of the family life cycle, there will be a diversity in the types of family systems as described in the Circumplex Model. In spite of this diversity, it is predicted that at different stages of the family life cycle many of the families will cluster together, in some types more frequently than others. For example, it would be predicted that premarital couples would tend toward the high range on Cohesion (enmeshed and connected) and toward the higher range on Flexibility (flexible and chaotic). In other words, they would fall into the upper-left quadrant of the Circumplex Model.

The model is dynamic in that it assumes that changes can occur in family types over time (Olson, McCubbin, et al., 1989). Families can move in any direction that the situation, stage of the family life cycle, or socialization of family members may require. A look at a couple illustrates the dynamic nature of the Circumplex Model. The Circumplex Model can be used to illustrate developmental change of a couple as the pair progress from dating to marriage, to pregnancy, childbirth, and childrearing. Even in the early years of marriage, Cohesion and Flexibility can change relatively dramatically. Figure 3.6 illustrates the changes one young couple faced in a period of only 5 years.

During the dating period (1), the couple indicates a *flexibly connected* relationship. They feel close (connected) and have a flexible style in terms of leadership and decision making. After marriage (2), the newlywed couple

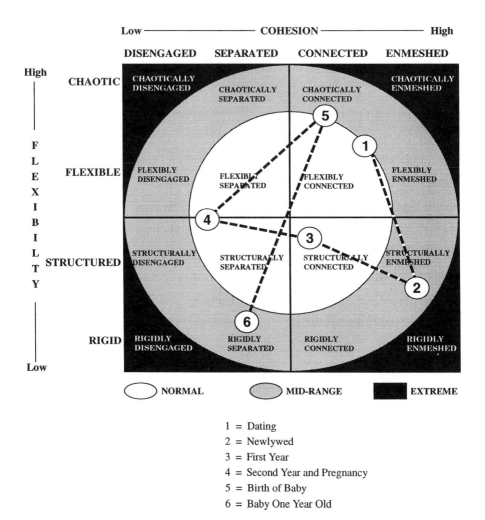

1 = Dating
2 = Newlywed
3 = First Year
4 = Second Year and Pregnancy
5 = Birth of Baby
6 = Baby One Year Old

FIGURE 3.6. Changes in early marriage.

could best be described as *structurally enmeshed*. They are structured because they are still getting organized in terms of their roles and leadership. Being in love and enjoying spending maximum time together, they are still enmeshed.

By the end of their first year of marriage (3), the so-called "honeymoon" effect has worn off, and the couple has become *structurally connected*. The excitement with each other isn't as great as it had been, and their togetherness has become more balanced on both Cohesion and Flexibility. During the second year of the marriage the woman becomes pregnant (4). The couple now becomes *flexibly separated* and move somewhat apart as she focuses on the pregnancy experience, and her husband invests more time in his job. Their roles become a little more flexible.

Another year passes (5), and the family can be described as *chaotically connected*. The birth of a baby is a momentous time in any couple's relationship. Change is high at this time, and the couple is forced to adapt to the advent of this new member. Their life is in relative turmoil because they are up each night to feed and attend to the baby, the wife may have had to leave her job, they lack couples' time and can't go out with friends the way they used to, they are short on money, there are 10 or 15 diapers to change each day, and so forth. They are so busy they don't have time to think about how chaotic life is now. The baby's presence has also increased the sense of bonding between the husband and wife; they feel united in their goal of rearing their child.

The baby is 1 year old, and life has stabilized for this family (6). They are now functioning as a *rigidly separated* family and are experiencing very few changes. She is home with a 1-year-old and enjoying the baby. He spends little time with the infant. Their cohesion scores have dropped off dramatically. She is more involved with the baby than her husband, and he is focused on the demands of his work. The couple has invested little time into their marriage and their closeness has declined.

In summary, this example illustrates how a couple's relationship can change across the early stages of marriage. The changes can occur gradually over months or more rapidly after the birth of a child. These changes often occur without specific planning; however, couples can negotiate the type of relationship they want and be more proactive in creating the type of relationship they both want.

CHANGES IN A FAMILY SYSTEM
RELATED TO PHYSICAL ILLNESS

Although some hypotheses have been developed relating family systems described by the Circumplex Model and family stress (Olson, Russell, & Sprenkle, 1989), little research has been done that would help us understand the changes that take place in family processes related to physical and emotional illness. Short-term longitudinal studies are needed if we are to understand better the changes that occur in the family system, with comparisons between those individuals who recover more quickly and those who have difficulty recovering.

An example of *second order change* occurs when the family changes its type of system to adapt to the major stressor. One hypothesis from the Circumplex Model is that Balanced types of families, compared to Extreme types of families, will do better because they are able to change their family system in order to cope more effectively with the illness in a family member.

An example of how the Circumplex Model can be used in both understanding and graphing the changes in family system over time is a family where the husband had a heart attack. In this family crisis, the husband, Peter, (age 53) had a massive heart attack. His wife, Martha, was a homemaker, and they had three teenagers living at home, one of whom was attending college.

The changes in this family system before and after Peter's heart attack are illustrated in Figure 3.7. Before the heart attack (point A), the family was *structurally separated*, which was generally appropriate for that stage of the family life cycle. Once the heart attack occurred, however, the family quickly shifted to becoming more *chaotically enmeshed* (point B). Very high levels of closeness, characterized by enmeshment, occurred because the illness brought the family closer together emotionally. It also created chaos in the family because they needed to dramatically shift many of their daily routines.

From about the third to sixth week, the family continued to be enmeshed but became more rigid in their structure. This rigidly was an attempt to stabilize the chaos by reorganizing some of the routines in their family system (point C). Six months later, the family was functioning as a *structurally connected* family (point D). Some of the previous rigidity and extreme cohesion decreased, but they remained a rather close family with a more structured system because of Peter's disability.

In summary, because of Peter's heart attack, this family's system changed several times over the course of the next 6 months as they adapted to this family crisis. They started as a Balanced system (flexibly separated), moved to two Extreme types (chaotically enmeshed and structurally enmeshed), before ending up once again as a Balanced system (structurally connected).

It is expected that family systems will change in response to a crisis. As hypothesized with the Circumplex Model, it is the Balanced families that would have the resources and skills to shift their system in an appropriate way to cope more effectively with a crisis. In contrast, it is hypothesized that Extreme families would not have the resources that are needed to

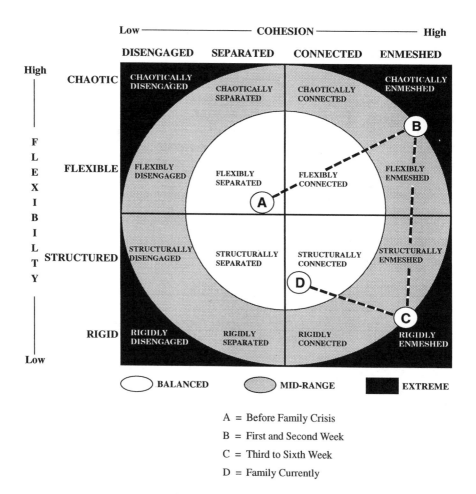

FIGURE 3.7. Family change before and after husband's heart attack.

change their family and, therefore, would have more difficulty adapting to a crisis. In other words, Balanced families are higher in *second-order change* because they are able to alter their family system to adapt to family crises.

Change in Family Systems

There are a few generalizations that can be made about how relationships successfully change as time passes:

1. An intimate relationship is able to *balance* between too much change (chaos) and too little change (rigidity).

2. Too much change leads to a lack of predictability and chaos, whereas too little change leads to too much predictability and rigidity.
3. An intimate relationship is able to change its system type when appropriate (second-order change).
4. Staying unbalanced (Extreme system type) too long can create problems in an intimate relationship.

STUDIES VALIDATING THE CIRCUMPLEX MODEL

Balance versus Extreme Families

A central hypothesis derived from the model is that Balanced couples/families will function more adequately than Extreme couples/families. This hypothesis is built on the assumption that families Extreme on both dimensions will tend to have more difficulties functioning across the life cycle. This assumes a curvilinear relationship between family functioning and the dimensions of Cohesion and Flexibility. This means that too little or too much cohesion or flexibility is seen as dysfunctional to the family system. However, families that are able to balance between these two extremes seem to function more adequately.

To test the major hypothesis that Balanced family types are more functional then Extreme types, a variety of studies have been done focusing on a range of emotional problems and symptoms in couples and families. A study by Clarke (1984) focused on families with schizophrenics, neurotics, families who had completed therapy sometime in their past, and a no-therapy control group (see Figure 3.8). He used FACES II, a self-report scale that assesses family Cohesion and Flexibility. In general, he found a very

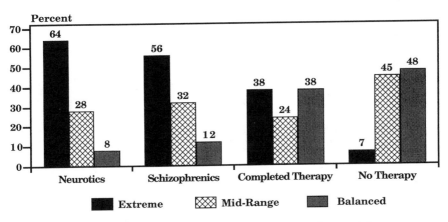

FIGURE 3.8. Problem families and Circumplex Model.

high level of Extreme families in the neurotic and schizophrenic groups compared to the no-therapy group. Conversely, he found a significantly higher level of balanced families in the no-therapy group compared to the other groups.

Figure 3.8 illustrates the differences in the levels of Cohesion and Flexibility between these groups. Whereas the percentage of Extreme family types decreased dramatically from the symptomatic to no-therapy groups (neurotic, 64%; schizophrenic, 56%; completed therapy, 38%; no therapy, 7%), the percentage of Balanced families increased (neurotic, 8%; schizophrenic, 12%; completed therapy, 38%; no therapy, 48%) as hypothesized.

A study by Carnes (1989) that used FACES II investigated the family systems in sex offenders and found high levels of Extreme family types in both their family-of-origin and their current families (see Figure 3.9). Whereas 49% had Extreme family types in their family-of-origin and 66% of their current families were Extreme types, only 19% of the nonoffender families were Extreme. Conversely, whereas only 11% of their family-of-origin and 19% of their current families were Balanced types, and 47% of the nonoffender families were Balanced.

In summary, these studies of clinical samples clearly demonstrate the discriminate power of the Circumplex Model in distinguishing between problem families and nonsymptomatic families. There is a strong empirical support for the hypothesis that Balanced types of families are more functional than Extreme family types. There is, however, a lack of evidence that any of these symptoms are specifically linked with a specific type of family system, for example, the chaotically enmeshed. This was a misplaced hope of early family research linking family symptoms (a schizophrenic offspring) and family systems (Walsh & Olson, 1989).

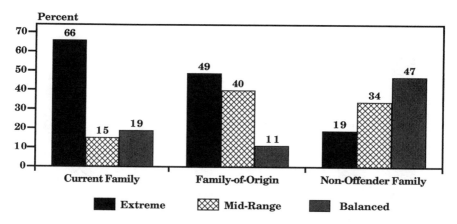

FIGURE 3.9. Sex offenders and Circumplex Model.

Balanced Families and Communication

Another hypothesis is that Balanced families will have more positive communication skills than Extreme families. Communication can be measured at both the marital and family levels. Using data from the national survey of 1,000 families, Barnes and Olson (1983, 1986) investigated parent–adolescent communication and family functioning. Using "nonproblem" families, the hypothesis that Balanced families would have better communication skills was supported when relying on data from the parents' reports. However, this hypothesis was not supported for adolescents, whose perceptions of their families differed from their parents.

In addition to testing the hypothesis regarding Balanced versus Extreme families reviewed earlier, Rodick, Henggler, and Hanson (1986) found strong support for the hypothesis that Balanced families have more positive communication skills. Using observational measures of mother–adolescent interaction, they found that mothers in the Balanced group had significantly higher rates of supportive communication, explicit information and positive affect than did mothers in the Extreme type with the majority of problem dyads (chaotically enmeshed).

UPDATE ON INVENTORIES
FOR FAMILY ASSESSMENT

In order to assess adequately the three major dimensions of the Circumplex Model and other related concepts, Olson, McCubbin, and colleagues (1986) developed a variety of self-report instruments. These assessment tools were designed to provide not only an "insider's perspective" on their own family system, but also an "outsider's perspective" (Olson, 1977). The self-report instrument called the Circumplex Assessment Package (CAP) provides the insider's perspective, whereas the Clinical Rating Scale (CRS) provides the outsider's perspective. Both perspectives are useful, but they often yield apparently conflicting data. Used together, however, they help capture the complexity of marital and family systems.

Assessment Criteria: Multimethod, Multitrait, and Multisystem Levels

Multimethod assessment utilizes both self-report scales that provide an "insider's perspective" on their own relationship and the therapists' or observers' ratings that provide an "outsider's perspective" on that same system. Both clinical work and research with families have indicated that there is often a discrepancy between these two perspectives and related methodologies (Olson, 1986). Because these two methodologies often provide different perspectives, this provides an important rationale why both approaches should be used in work with families.

If an investigator only relies on his or her own perception of the system (an outsider's perspective), our data indicate that it will often differ in significant ways from one or more of the family members' perceptions. It is also problematic to rely on only one family member because family members often do not agree with each other in describing their family system (Olson, McCubbin, et al., 1989). Assessment using multiple family members, therefore, provides a more complete picture of how each family member views the system and the level of agreement or disagreement between them.

Multitrait assessment is based on the three central dimensions of the Circumplex Model: Cohesion, Flexibility, and Communication. Although other traits can be incorporated into couple and family assessment, these three dimensions provide the foundation and central core of the relationship systems.

Multisystem assessment ideally focuses on the individual, the marital system, parent–child system, and total family—including extended family relationships. One important question to ask family members is who they each consider to be members of their family. It is surprising to us how often family members disagree regarding who is currently in their family system. This raises important questions about boundary issues and who is psychologically and/or physically present in a given family system (Boss & Greenberg, 1984). This is especially important given the increasing diversity of family forms, particularly the changes accompanying divorce and remarriage.

Circumplex Assessment Package and Clinical Rating Scale

The *Circumplex Assessment Package* (CAP) is the latest in a series of a self-report assessments developed that are based on the Circumplex Model. This assessment procedure is multidimensional in that it assesses the three Circumplex dimensions of cohesion, adaptability, and communication. It also includes the satisfaction dimension, which focuses on each person's satisfaction with various aspects of the family system. It is a multisystem level as well in that assessment procedures focus on both the marital system and the family system. More specifically, each of the four dimensions is assessed at the couple and family levels. Two-parent families (nuclear or blended) would complete both the marital and family scales. Single-parent families would complete the family scales and would complete the marital scales if the single parent has a significant other. Couples (married or cohabiting) would complete the couple scales.

FACES III is an acronym for Family Adaptability and Cohesion Evaluation Scales, and *MACES III* is an acronym for Marital Adaptability and Cohesion Evaluation Scales. The communication dimension is assessed at the couple level using a subscale from the *ENRICH* instrument (Olson, Fournier,

& Druckman, 1986), and family communication is based on the Parent–Adolescent Communication Scale (Barnes & Olson, 1983, 1986). The satisfaction dimension is assessed at the couple level using a subscale from the ENRICH instrument (Olson, Fournier, et al., 1986), and the Family Satisfaction Scale (Olson & Wilson, 1986) is based on the Circumplex dimensions.

For clinical work with premarital and married couples, there are two comprehensive inventories that can be used called *PREPARE* and *ENRICH* (Olson, Fournier, et al., 1986). PREPARE, for premarital couples, has been found to predict which couples will divorce with 80–85% accuracy. ENRICH is designed for married couples and is able to discriminate happy from clinical couples with 90% accuracy. Both PREPARE and ENRICH Inventories contain 14 content categories, are computer scored, and have norms based on over 100,000 couples.

The reliability of these scales has been assessed in a variety of studies. The most comprehensive summary is provided in the volume entitled *Family Inventories* (Olson, McCubbin, et al., 1986). As indicated in Table 3.2, both the internal consistency and test-retest reliability of these scales are consistently high ($r = .80$). In terms of validity, therapists and researchers have evaluated the items in terms of face validity and find them to meet acceptable criteria. The scales also demonstrated having discriminate validity in that they distinguish between clinical and nonclinical families (Olson, 1986).

The *Clinical Rating Scale* (*CRS*) was developed by Olson (1990) in order to do clinical assessment on cohesion, adaptability, and communication. It describes specific indicators for each level of the three dimensions. This scale is a useful training device for helping individuals learn more about the

TABLE 3.2. Circumplex Assessment Package (CAP): Reliability*

	Internal consistency	Test–retest
FACES III (Family)		
Cohesion	.84	.83
Adaptability	.79	.80
MACES III (Marital)		
Cohesion	.82	.83
Adaptability	.78	.80
Communication		
Couple (ENRICH)	.82	.90
Parent-Adolescent	.88	.88
Satisfaction		
Couple (ENRICH)	.86	.86
Family	.92	.81
Average	.84	.83

*Scales are contained in the *Family Inventories* by Olson, Portner, and Lavee (1985).

Circumplex Model and its value for family assessment and planning treatment intervention. A copy of the CRS is included in Appendices A–C.

GOALS OF FAMILY THERAPY
USING THE CIRCUMPLEX MODEL

Whereas family therapists have as a central goal reduction of the presenting problems and symptoms of family members, this is achieved by intervention focused on changing a dysfunctional type of couple and/or family system. The basic assumption is that the current family system dynamics are helping to maintain symptomatic behaviors. In other words, the current pattern of interaction in the family needs to be changed before the symptoms or presenting problems will be alleviated.

Table 3.3 summarizes the specific goals of family therapy based on the Circumplex Model. The first goal is ultimately to reduce any problems and symptoms. Since most dysfunctional families coming for therapy represent Midrange or Extreme types on the Model, change often involves trying to shift the system one level on Cohesion and one level on Flexibility toward the Balanced levels. It is, therefore, typically assumed that the family will function more adequately if the marital and/or family system is moved toward the Balanced types.

Because the Model is dynamic, intervention on Cohesion or Flexibility often has a ripple effect in that it influences the system on the other dimension. In terms of Cohesion, problems in couples and families often occur because of their inability to balance separateness (autonomy) and togetherness (intimacy). In couples coming for therapy, often there is a difference in the amount of separateness and togetherness a couple experiences or desires. For example, in disengaged couples, one or both individuals have emphasized looking out for themselves, and thus, they have not maintained their emotional bond of intimacy.

TABLE 3.3. Goals of Marital and Family Therapy Based on Circumplex Model

---

Goal regarding symptoms
 • Reduce presenting problems and symptoms
Goals regarding system (marital and/or family)
 • Change system one level on cohesion and adaptability toward balanced types
 • On cohesion, balancing separateness and togetherness
 • On adaptability, balancing stability and change
 • Improve communication skills
Metagoal regarding system (preventive)
 • Increase ability to negotiate system change over time

In families, the dynamics on cohesion are often more complicated. One type of problem family might have an enmeshed mother–adolescent coalition with a disengaged father. In this case, the marital dyad would not be emotionally close. Increasing their marital–parental collaboration is an effective strategy for breaking up the strong parent–child coalition.

In terms of flexibility, couples and families with problems often have difficulty balancing stability and change. Often these relationships are either too rigid or too chaotic. With rigid systems, often the behavioral repertoire is very narrow. When people in the relationships are confronted with increasing stress, they tend to become more rigid and inflexible. These families can often benefit from learning and using more democratic decision-making and better problem-solving skills. On the other hand, chaotic relationships often need increasing structure, and they can also benefit from improved problem-solving skills.

Increasing the positive communication skills of couples and families can also facilitate system change. Individuals in problem families often need to learn how to be more assertive in expressing their wants and desires. They usually can benefit as well from learning how to express their feelings in a constructive manner and how to listen and give empathic feedback to each other.

However, improving the communication skills in a family is a necessary but not sufficient condition for change on the dimensions of Cohesion and Flexibility. Communication skills can help increase awareness of current needs and preferences. However, system change on cohesion and adaptability is more difficult and complex. Having good communication skills enables families to express more clearly the type of relationship they would like to have on cohesion and Flexibility.

One desirable goal of couple and family therapy is ultimately to teach the couple not only to deal with their current issues but to provide them with the necessary skills to negotiate system change over time. It is an assumption of the Model that couples and families need to change their system as their individual needs and preferences change. Being able to articulate and negotiate these changes on cohesion and adaptability will also enable the couple or family to cope more adequately with stress and the other problematic issues that they will encounter over time. This is an important preventive goal that moves beyond dealing with the current and presenting symptoms. Unfortunately, this metagoal is rarely achieved in therapy because most families, and even some therapists, are too focused on only reducing the current presenting problems.

Treatment Planning Using the Circumplex Model

The Circumplex Model is a valuable resource in assessment-based treatment planning with severely dysfunctional families, illustrated in some detail by Walsh and Olson (1989). A major task for family therapy and outcome is to determine which elements of intervention are most appropriate and effective with which presenting problems and with which elements of family functioning. The Circumplex Model and accompanying self-report scale (FACES III) and Clinical Rating Scale (CRS) offer an empirically based family assessment tool that can be used for treatment planning and outcome evaluation (Walsh & Olson, 1989).

The model provides a conceptual framework for assessing family system functioning on two fundamental dimensions of family organization, cohension and flexibility. This descriptive typology of transactional patterns can be used to determine a family's current level and style of functioning on each dimension and to guide treatment planning to strengthen particular components of functioning toward clearly specified and realistic objectives. Thus, family therapy is not limited to reduction or interruption of extreme dysfunctional patterns but is directed systematically toward promotion of more functional patterns.

For families assessed at either Extreme on the dimensions, intervention strategies can be targeted to fit their particular pattern of organization and to guide change, in a stepwise progression, toward a more Balanced system. In most cases of severe and chronic dysfunction, a reachable therapeutic goal would be the achievement of higher functioning at the next, adjacent pattern, such as a shift from disengaged to separated or from enmeshed to connected. It would be unrealistic to attempt to change family patterns to a quite different type of organization, such as pushing a disengaged family to be strongly connected, or an enmeshed family to become separated. Such goals might even be inappropriate to a family's values relative to their socioeconomic context or to demands in their life-cycle stage. A common therapeutic error with severely dysfunctional families is to assume either that patterns are unchangeable or that change toward the opposite pattern is necessary and desirable.

In our experience, severely dysfunctional families often assume such extreme all-or-none positions regarding change. They are likely to alternate between feelings of hopelessness that any change can occur and unrealistic expectations for goals that are unlikely to be met. They commonly fluctuate between Extremes of enmeshed/disengaged and extremes of rigidity/chaos. An enmeshed family may resist a clinician's efforts to promote physical separation, such as leaving home at launching, when its members hold catastrophic expectations that any separation will result in a total cut-off.

Opposite extremes may also be found in different subsystems within a family. In many enmeshed families, some siblings may disengage completely from the family in order to avoid fusion, assuming positions of pseudo-autonomy that dissolve in contact with the family. Clinicians must be cautious not to collude with presuppositions of either all-or-none position. Fears of runaway change or loss of patterns considered to be essential to individual or family survival are common sources of "resistance" to change and therapy drop-out. Clinicians need to be alert to prevent extreme family oscillation that can occur much like a "short-circuiting" process.

A therapist must be active in structuring and monitoring family interaction to block or interrupt the all-or-none tendency in these families to flip to the other extreme from their current organizational pattern. In work with families with extreme patterns, it is essential to set modest, concrete objectives to be reached through small increments of change in order to reduce anxiety to a manageable level, to prevent extreme fluctuations, and to help the family to modulate and moderate changes that can be maintained over time.

In the section that follows, characteristics of families at each extreme on the Circumplex Model will be described, with interaction objectives and guidelines suggested to fit the challenges of each system pattern and to shift interaction to a more functional level. In each of these four illustrations, the system level is shifted from an extreme, to the next level, moving the system to a more balanced position. In each case, refer to the Clinical Rating Scale in Appendix A–C for the specific clinical variables involved in each Cohesion or Adaptability. For more details on the specific therapeutic interventions, see Walsh and Olson (1989).

Moving Families from Rigid to Structured Systems (Flexibility Dimension)

In families with extremely rigid interactional patterns, leadership tends to be authoritarian, with one or both parents highly controlling. Discipline is typically autocratic, based on a simplistic principle of "law and order," and consequences are strict, even harsh, without leniency. Negotiations tend to be limited, with decisions imposed by parents, often arbitrarily, or by applying a single solution to all problems regardless of its applicability. Rigid families have a very limited repertoire of roles, which are strictly defined and inflexible. Rules are unbending and strictly enforced. These tendencies prevent the family from making adaptive changes when confronted by new circumstances and demands.

Applying the Circumplex Model, we would propose that therapy with rigid families target interventions to shift their organization to the structured range on the family Flexibility dimension. Leadership, while still primarily authoritarian, would become less controlling and more egalitarian. Discipline would become somewhat more democratic, with consequences predictable, although still seldom lenient. Roles would be stable, with somewhat greater flexibility and sharing. Rules would allow for few changes and be firmly, yet less strictly, enforced.

The chief therapeutic task with rigid families is to promote the interaction flexibility that is lacking. Tasks that facilitate more open communication, negotiated decision making, and experimental problem solving can be useful. At the same time, it is crucial to maintain stability in the family. A common clinical error with extremely rigid families is to push for too much change too fast, which typically only heightens these families' resistance to change.

Moving Families from Chaotic to Flexible Systems (Flexibility Dimension)

Families at the chaotic extreme on the adaptability dimensions are characterized by a lack of structure, order, and predictability in their interactions. Leadership tends to be limited and erratic. Decisions are impulsive, with a lack of consistent follow-through in action. Roles and rules are unclear and shifting. Loss of control is frequently experienced in escalating conflict and run-away change. Chaotic families tend to be crisis-prone, as unanticipated and unresolved problems pile up to overwhelming proportions, and members rebound from one crisis into the next.

We propose that therapy with chaotic families be aimed to shift their organizational pattern toward the flexible range on the family adaptability dimension. Objectives would include stronger and more consistent parental leadership and control of the family process, with authority shared by parents and changes fluid but not erratic. Discipline, while remaining somewhat lenient, would become more democratic and effective, with consequences more often negotiated and consistent. Negotiation would be flexible, yet with more careful consideration, agreement, and closure. Greater clarity and consistency of roles and rules would be important objectives.

The chief therapeutic task with chaotic families is building structure. The extreme disorganization makes it imperative for therapists to assume an active and at times even authoritarian position of leadership in the initial phase of therapy, gradually strengthening the leadership capacities of parents and family. The therapist needs to take charge of the therapy rather than follow the family process, which is likely to become diffuse or to spiral out of control. This involves establishing clear and consistent ground rules and limits for the structure of the therapy, setting concrete problem-solving objectives with the family, and defining therapist and family roles and mutual expectations.

Moving Families from Disengaged to Separated Systems (Cohesion Dimension)

A disengaged relationship is characterized by extreme emotional and physical separateness. The paradigmatic rule in disengaged families tends to be: everyone for him- or herself. There is little interest, involvement, or sense of mutual caring between or among family members. Each member goes his or her own way, with limited attachment or commitment to the family.

There is little expectation that others can be counted on to support a member in distress.

Although extreme separateness may be confused with autonomy, in fact, genuine autonomy involves the maintenance of self in the context of relationships with others, as is found in the balanced levels of Cohesion. Disengagement, instead, is a distancing or total cut-off from family relationships, resulting in an isolated pseudoautonomous position.

We would propose that therapy with disengaged family systems aim toward the separated level of family Cohesion. A separated relationship (low to moderate Cohesion) has a good deal of emotional and physical separateness, yet it is more balanced with some connectedness among family members. Family loyalty and affective responsiveness are occasionally demonstrated. Although time and space apart may be preferred, there is some time together and some joint decisions. Activities, interests, and friendships tend to be separate, but a few are shared.

A chief therapeutic goal with disengaged families is to promote connectedness through shared problem solving. Intervention is often problematic from the start because it is difficult even to convene members at the same time and place. A major therapeutic challenge is to engage family members to work together on behalf of a symptomatic member. The therapist needs to frame treatment as a collaborative effort—valuing the input of each member and offering potential benefit to all who participate.

Moving Families from Enmeshed to Connected Systems (Cohesion Dimension)

Enmeshed relationships are characterized by an extreme amount of emotional closeness and demands for loyalty and consensus. The paradigmatic rule operating in enmeshed family systems is, "All for one and one for all." Individual needs are sacrificed for the group. Members are highly dependent and emotionally reactive to one another. There is a general lack of personal separateness, and little private space or time is permitted. Individual boundaries are blurred to the extreme of fusion, with members poorly differentiated, lacking a coherent sense of self as distinct from family role expectations. Generational boundaries are breached, with children treated as parents or mates (at times sexualized) as parents. Attention is focused inside the family, with a paucity of outside friendships or interests. Members are unable to tolerate separation from the family, with developmental transitions involving launching or loss especially problematic.

We would propose that therapy with enmeshed family systems aim at shifting the family organization toward the connected level of the Cohesion dimension of family functioning. Emotional closeness, while high, is better balanced with tolerance and respect for separateness. Loyalty and involvement are expected, yet some personal choice and separate time, space, friendships, and interests are allowed. Social markers of independence, such as leaving home, may not be emphasized, as family members are likely to remain in close emotional and physical contact over the course of the life cycle. The major goal of therapy with enmeshed family systems is to encourage a tolerance for some separateness and boundaries in relationships, while respecting needs for maintaining high connectedness.

Unlike disengaged families, enmeshed families are likely to come together for therapy, even when individual sessions are scheduled. Because of difficulties with separation, they are more likely to have difficulty leaving therapy, both at the end of a session and at termination. They are likely to become overinvolved and helplessly dependent on the therapist, expecting unrealistic amounts of all-giving attention and responsibility for rescuing them. They often call in the middle of the night, invite the therapist home to dinner, and even express the wish that the therapist could move in with them. Clinicians need to guard against becoming overcommitted and overresponsible in ways that do not strengthen the family but, instead, contribute to therapist burnout. Therapists need to communicate clear expectations for their own roles and boundaries and to model a balanced position of caring involvement with limits.

In summary, clinical intervention using the Circumplex Model helps the therapist move beyond limited focus on the present problems to the clinically relevant dynamics of family cohesion, family adaptability, and family communication. Treatment goals based on the Model focus on moving family extremes on one or both dimensions to more balanced levels of functioning. A range of therapeutic techniques can be used for helping move families from extreme levels of Cohesion and Flexibility to more balanced levels.

A metagoal of therapy is to help couples and families better learn how to negotiate system change over time. Families need to learn how to balance their separateness versus togetherness on Cohesion, and their stability versus change on Flexibility, without getting stuck at the extreme levels. Balance is a dynamic process that continually needs adjustment and change to remain functional as a system.

REFERENCES

Barnes, H., & Olson, D. H. (1983). Parent–adolescent communication and the Circumplex Model. *Child Development, 56,* 438–447.

Barnes, H., & Olson, D. H. (1986). Parent–adolescent communication scale. In D. H. Olson, H. I. McCubbin, H. Barnes, A. Larsen, M. Muxen, & M. Wilson (Eds.), *Family inventories* (pp. 35–44). St. Paul, MN: Family Social Science, University of Minnesota.

Beavers, W. B., & Hampson, R. B. (1990). *Successful families: Assessment and intervention.* New York: W. W. Norton.

Benjamin, L. S. (1977). Structural analysis of a family in therapy. *Journal of Counseling Clinical Psychology, 45*, 391–406.

Boss, P. G., & Greenberg, J. (1984). Family boundary ambiguity: A new variable in family stress theory. *Family Process, 23*, 535–546.

Carnes, P. (1989). *Contrary to love: Helping the sexual addict*. Minneapolis, MN: Comp-Care Publications.

Carter, B., & McGoldrick, M. (Eds.). (1988). *The changing family life cycle*. New York: Gardner Press.

Clarke, J. (1984). *The family types of neurotics, schizophrenics and normals*. Unpublished doctoral dissertation. St. Paul, MN: Family Social Science, University of Minnesota.

Constantine, L. (1986). *Family paradigms*. New York: Guilford Press.

Epstein, N. B., & Bishop, D. S. (1983). The McMaster Assessment Device (FAD). *Journal of Marriage and Family Counseling, 9*, 171–180.

French, A. P., & Guidera, B. J. (1974). *The family as a system in four dimensions: A theoretical model*. Paper presented at the American Academy of Child Psychology, San Francisco.

Gottman, J. M. (1979). *Marital interaction*. New York: Basic Books.

Hill, R. (1970). *Family development in three generations*. Cambridge, MA: Schenkman.

Kantor, D., & Lehr, W. (1975). *Inside the family*. San Francisco: Jossey-Bass.

Leary, T. (1975). *Interpersonal diagnosis of personality*. New York: Ronald Press.

Lee, C. (1988). Theories of family adaptability: Toward a synthesis of Olson's Circumplex Model and Beavers' Systems Model. *Family Process, 27*(2), 73–85.

Leff, J., & Vaughn, C. (1985). *Expressed emotion in families*. New York: Guilford Press.

Olson, D. H. (1977). Insider's and outsider's perspectives of relationships: Research strategies. In G. Levinger & H. Rausch (Eds.), *Close relationships*. Amherst, MA: University of Massachusetts Press.

Olson, D. H. (1986). Circumplex Model VII: Validation studies and FACES III. *Family Process, 25*, 337–351.

Olson, D. H. (1990). *Clinical rating scale for Circumplex Model*. St. Paul, MN: Family Social Science, University of Minnesota.

Olson, D. H., Fournier, D. G., & Druckman, J. M. (1986). *PREPARE, PREPARE-MC and ENRICH inventories* (2nd ed.). Minneapolis, MN: PREPARE/ENRICH, Inc.

Olson, D. H., McCubbin, H. I., Barnes, H., Larsen, A., Muxen, M., & Wilson, M. (Eds.). (1986). *Family inventories*. St. Paul, MN: Family Social Science, University of Minnesota.

Olson, D. H., McCubbin, H. I., Barnes, H., Larsen, A., Muxen, M., & Wilson, M. (1989). *Families: What makes them work* (2nd ed.). Los Angeles: Sage Publishing.

Olson, D. H., Portner, J., & Lavee, Y. (1985). *FACES III*. St. Paul, MN: Family Social Science, University of Minnesota.

Olson, D. H., Russell, C. S., & Sprenkle, D. H. (Eds.). (1989). *Circumplex Model: Systemic assessment and treatment of families*. New York: Haworth Press.

Olson, D. H., & Wilson, M. (1986). Family satisfaction. In D. H. Olson, H. I. McCubbin, H. Barnes, A. Larsen, M. Muxen, & M. Wilson (Eds.), *Family inventories*. St. Paul, MN: Family Social Science, University of Minnesota.

Parsons, T., & Bales, R. F. (1955). *Family socialization and interaction process*. Glencoe, IL: Free Press.

Reiss, D. (1981). *The family's construction of reality*. Cambridge, MA: Harvard University Press.

Rodick, J. D., Henggler, S. W., & Hanson. C. L. (1986). An evaluation of family adaptability, cohesion evaluation scales (FACES) and the Circumplex Model. *Journal of Abnormal Child Psychology, 14,* 77–87.

Skinner, H. A., Santa-Barbara, J., & Steinhauer, P. D. (1983). The family assessment measure. *Canadian Journal of Community Mental Health, 2,* 91–105.

Walsh, F., & Olson, D. H. (1989). Utility of the Circumplex Model with severely dysfunctional family systems. In D. H. Olson, C. S. Russell, and D. H. Sprenkle (Eds.), *Circumplex Model: Systemic assessment and treatment of families* (2nd ed.). New York: Haworth.

APPENDIX A: Family Cohesion

Couple/Family Score	Disengaged (1–2)	Separated (3–4)	Connected (5–6)	Enmeshed (7–8)
EMOTIONAL BONDING	Extreme emotional separateness. Lack of family loyalty.	Emotional separateness. Limited closeness. Occasional family loyalty.	Emotional closeness. Some separateness. Loyalty to family expected.	Extreme emotional closeness. Little separateness. Loyalty to family demanded.
FAMILY INVOLVEMENT	Very low involvement or interaction. Infrequent affective responsiveness.	Involvement acceptable. Personal distance preferred. Some affective responsiveness.	Involvement emphasized. Personal distance allowed. Affective interactions encouraged and preferred.	Very high involvement. Fusion, over-dependency. High affective responsiveness and control.
MARITAL RELATIONSHIP	High emotional separateness. Limited closeness.	Emotional separateness. Some closeness.	Emotional closeness. Some separateness.	Extreme closeness, fusion. Limited separateness.
PARENT-CHILD RELATIONSHIP	Rigid generational boundaries. Low p/c closeness.	Clear generational boundaries. Some p/c closeness.	Clear generational boundaries. High p/c closeness.	Lack of generational boundaries. Excessive p/c closeness.
INTERNAL BOUNDARIES	**Separateness dominates.**	**More separateness than togetherness.**	**More togetherness than separateness.**	**Togetherness dominates.**
TIME (Physical & Emotional)	Time apart maximized. Rarely time together.	Time alone important. Some time together.	Time together important. Time alone permitted.	Time together maximized. Little time alone permitted.
SPACE (Physical & Emotional)	Separate space needed and preferred.	Separate space preferred. Sharing of family space.	Sharing family space. Private space respected.	Little private space permitted.
DECISION-MAKING	Individual decision-making. (Oppositional)	Individual decision-making, but joint possible.	Joint decisions preferred.	Decisions subject to wishes of entire group.
EXTERNAL BOUNDARIES	**Mainly focused outside the family.**	**More focused outside than inside family.**	**More focused inside than outside family.**	**Mainly focused inside the family.**
FRIENDS	Individual friends seen alone.	Individual friendships seldom shared with family.	Individual friendships shared with family.	Family friends preferred. Limited individual friends.
INTERESTS	Disparate interests.	Separate interests.	Some joint interests.	Joint interests mandated.
ACTIVITIES	Mainly separate activities.	More separate than shared activities.	More shared than individual activities.	Separate activities seen as disloyal.
Global Cohesion Rating (1–8)	Very Low	Low to Moderate	Moderate to High	Very High

135

APPENDIX B: Family Flexibility

Couple/Family Score	Rigid		Structured		Flexible		Chaotic	
	1	2	3	4	5	6	7	8
LEADERSHIP (Control)	Authoritarian leadership. Parent(s) highly controlling.		Primarily authoritarian but some equalitarian leadership.		Equalitarian leadership with fluid changes.		Limited and/or erratic leadership. Parental control unsuccessful. Rebuffed.	
DISCIPLINE (For families only)	Autocratic "law & order." Strict, rigid consequences. Not lenient.		Somewhat democratic. Predictable consequences. Seldom lenient.		Usually democratic. Negotiated consequences. Somewhat lenient.		Laissez-faire and ineffective. Inconsistent consequences. Very lenient.	
NEGOTIATION	Limited negotiations. Decisions imposed by parents.		Structured negotiations. Decisions made by parents.		Flexible negotiations. Agreed upon decisions.		Endless negotiations. Impulsive decisions.	
ROLES	Limited repertoire. Strictly defined roles. Unchanging routines.		Roles stable, but may be shared.		Role sharing and making. Fluid changes of roles.		Lack of role clarity. Role shifts and role reversals. Few routines.	
RULES	Unchanging rules. Rules strictly enforced.		Few rule changes. Rules firmly enforced.		Some rule changes. Rules flexibly enforced.		Frequent rule changes. Rules inconsistently enforced.	
Global Cohesion Rating (1-8)	Very Low		Low to Moderate		Moderate to High		Very High	

Note: The global rating is based on your overall evaluation, not a sum score of the sub-scale.

APPENDIX C: Family Communication

Low ← Facilitating → High

Couple/Family Score	1	2	3	4	5	6
LISTENER'S SKILLS Empathy Attentive listening	Seldom evident Seldom evident		Sometimes evident Sometimes evident		Often evident Often evident	
SPEAKER'S SKILLS Speaking for self Speaking for others* *Note reverse scoring	Seldom evident **Often evident**		Sometimes evident **Sometimes evident**		Often evident **Seldom evident**	
SELF-DISCLOSURE	Infrequent discussion of self, feelings and relationships.		Some discussion of self, feelings and relationships.		Open discussion of self, feelings and relationships.	
CLARITY	Inconsistent and/or unclear verbal messages. Frequent incongruences between verbal and non-verbal messages.		Some degree of clarity, but not consistent across time or across all members. Some incongruent messages.		Verbal messages very clear. Generally congruent messages.	
CONTINUITY/ TRACKING	Little continuity of content. Irrelevant/distracting non-verbals and asides frequently occur. Frequent/inappropriate topic changes.		Some continuity, but not consistent across time or across all members. Some irrelevant/distracting non-verbals and asides. Topic changes not consistently appropriate.		Members consistently tracking. Few irrelevant/distracting non-verbals and asides. Facilitative non-verbals. Appropriate topic changes.	
RESPECT AND REGARD	Lack of respect for feelings or message of other(s). Possibly overtly disrespectful or belittling attitude.		Somewhat respectful of others, but not consistent across time or across all members. Some incongruent messages.		Consistently appears respectful of other's feelings and messages.	

Global Family Communication Rating (1-6)

Note. The global rating is based on your overall evaluation, not a sum score of the subscale.

137

CHAPTER 4

THE McMASTER MODEL
View of Healthy Family Functioning

Nathan B. Epstein, Duane Bishop,
Christine Ryan, Ivan Miller, and
Gabor Keitner

I N THIS CHAPTER WE DISCUSS our view of healthy family functioning and the findings from our research and the research of other investigators that relate to normal families. We describe the McMaster Model of Family Functioning (MMFF) from many points of view including the significant historical issues in its development and elaboration, the definition of the model, and its concepts. As an example, we describe one family according to the MMFF and discuss the variations that could occur within a normal range.

HEALTH AND NORMALITY

To attempt to arrive at a definition of a healthy or normal family may seem like, or indeed actually be—a fool's errand. It is exceedingly difficult to describe a healthy or normal individual. When we attempt to describe a normal family, the variables to consider multiply by quantum leaps. Those of us who conceptualize the family as a system of interacting individuals, being acted upon and in turn acting on a number of other systems at obvious levels such as surrounding subculture, culture, economic domain, and biological substrates of the individuals concerned, are often tempted to avoid this particular exercise. Nevertheless, the demands of systematic empirical research of the family are such that a series of benchmarks of family function must be developed. Thus, the markers of something approaching what is meant by normal and/or healthy are of greatest importance.

Normality is an ill-defined concept. It often seems to mean "not displaying any particular problems." For instance, when we conducted a computer search of papers on the normal family, "normal" was not a category; we had to specify "not reconstituted," "not alcoholic," and so forth. When defined in this exclusionary way, "normal" is not a very useful concept. A normal family is described as not having a number of features, but there is no positive statement about what a normal family actually is.

Another common approach has been to equate "normal" with the statistical average. Using this approach, measurements are taken on some sample, and the average score is taken to be the normal score for the population. If the sample is representative of the total population, then something is known of the distribution of the characteristic being measured in the whole population. But, for example, if the characteristic is the frequency with which husbands and wives discuss financial problems, and the average is once a week, it does not tell us much of use about families. For one thing, the current life situation of the family may influence the amount of discussion that is required. For another thing, if it could be assumed that other families were in similar life situations, could we think that families discussing finances once a week are functioning better than those discussing finances more or less often?

We argue that a clinically useful concept is "health." A healthy family is neither necessarily average nor merely lacking in negative characteristics. Rather, it has described positive features. The MMFF contains a description of such a set of features.

McMASTER MODEL OF FAMILY FUNCTIONING

The MMFF does not cover all aspects of family functioning. It focuses on the dimensions of functioning that are seen as having the most impact on the emotional and physical health or problems of family members. We have defined each dimension as ranging from "most ineffective" to "most effective." We hypothesize that "most ineffective" functioning in any of these dimensions can contribute to a clinical presentation, whereas, "most effective" functioning in all dimensions supports optimal physical and emotional health.

The MMFF has evolved over a period of more than 25 years. The initial study in the evolution of the model was conducted in the late 1950s at McGill University and was reported in *The Silent Majority* (Westley & Epstein, 1969). (This research is discussed in more detail later in this chapter "Research on Normal Families.") The next stage in the development, described in the *Family Categories Schema* (Epstein, Sigal, & Rakoff, 1962), occurred in the early 1960s, also at McGill. In the late 1960s and through the 1970s, work on the model took place at McMaster University. The model in its current form was described by Epstein, Bishop, and Levin (1978). Currently, work on the model is taking place at Brown University.

Useful ideas from the family literature, as well as from clinical, teaching, and research experience, have been incorporated into the model. The model has been continually refined and reformulated. Aspects of family functioning were conceptualized and then tested in clinical work, research, and teaching. Problems arising in applying the model became the basis for reformulations. The result is a pragmatic model containing ideas that have worked. Those not meeting the test in treatment, teaching, or research have been discarded or modified.

The model has been used extensively in a variety of psychiatric and family practice clinics (Comley, 1973; Epstein & Westley, 1959; Guttman, Spector, Sigal, Rakoff, & Epstein, 1971; Guttman, Spector, Sigal, Epstein, & Rakoff, 1972; Postner, Guttman, Sigal, Epstein, & Rakoff, 1971; Rakoff, Sigal, Spector, & Guttman, 1967; Sigal, Rakoff, & Epstein, 1967; Westley & Epstein, 1960) and by therapists who treated families as a part of a large family therapy outcome study (Guttman et al., 1971; Santa-Barbara et al., 1975; Woodward et al., 1975; Woodward, Santa-Barbara, Levin, Epstein, & Streiner, 1977; Woodward et al., 1974). The framework has also been used in a number of family therapy training programs and found to be readily teachable (Bishop & Epstein, 1979).

The model is based on a systems approach:

> In this approach the family is seen as an open system consisting of systems within systems (individual, marital dyad) and relating to other systems (extended family, schools, industry, religions). The unique aspect of the dynamic family group cannot be simply reduced to the characteristics of the individuals or interactions between pairs of members. Rather, there are explicit and implicit rules, plus action by members, which govern and monitor each other's behavior. (Epstein & Bishop, 1973, p. 176)

The crucial assumptions of systems theory that underlie our model can be summarized as follows:

1. The parts of the family are interrelated.
2. One part of the family cannot be understood in isolation from the rest of the system.
3. Family functioning cannot be fully understood by simply understanding each of the parts.
4. A family's structure and organization are important factors determining the behavior of family members.
5. Transactional patterns of the family system are among the most important variables that shape the behavior of family members.

In addition to the systems approach, another feature we should note is that of values. We describe how a healthy, or, in our view, a normal family should look on each of the dimensions. Often such a description involves a value judgment. For instance, we would say that family members ought to be able to show sadness at the appropriate times and to the degree called for by the situation. The judgment of appropriateness with respect to sadness is not clear-cut and varies among cultures. We take the position that knowledge of the culture to which a family belongs is necessary for understanding a family, and the judgments of health or normality are relative to the culture of the family. We comment more on values later.

We assume that a primary function of today's family unit is to provide a setting for the development and maintenance of family members on the social, psychological, and biological levels (Epstein, Levin, & Bishop, 1976, p. 1411). In the course of fulfilling this function, families will have to deal with a variety of issues and problems or tasks, which we group into three areas. These are the Basic Task Area, the Developmental Task Area, and the Hazardous Task Area.

The Basic Task Area is the most fundamental of the three; it involves instrumental issues. For example, families must deal with the problems of providing food, money, transportation, and shelter.

The Developmental Task Area encompasses those family issues that arise as a result of development over time. These developments are often conceptualized as a sequence of stages. On the individual level, these include crises of infancy, childhood, adolescence, and middle and old age. On the family level, these might be the beginning of the marriage, the first pregnancy, or the last child leaving home. Developmental concepts and family functioning have been referred to by a number of authors (Berman & Lief, 1975; Brody, 1974; Carter & McGoldrick, 1980; Group for the Advancement of Psychiatry, 1970; Hadley, Jacob, Milliones, Caplan, & Spitz, 1974; Scherz, 1971; Solomon, 1973).

The Hazardous Task Area involves the handling of crises that arise as a result of illness, accident, loss of income, job change, and so forth. There is also substantial literature dealing with these topics (Comley, 1973; Hill, 1965; Langsley & Kaplan, 1968; Minuchin & Barcai, 1969; Parad & Caplan, 1965; Rappaport, 1965).

We have found that families who are unable to deal effectively with these three task areas are most likely to develop clinically significant problems and/or chronic maladaptive problems.

Dimensions of Family Functioning

To understand the structure, organization, and transactional patterns of the family, we focus on the following six dimensions: "problem solving," "communication," "roles," "affective responsiveness," "affective involvement," and "behavior control." These are outlined briefly in Table 4.1. As stated by Epstein and Bishop (1981):

TABLE 4.1. Summary of Dimension Concepts in the McMaster Model of Family Functioning

Problem solving
Two types of problems:
    Instrumental and affective
Seven stages to the process:
    1. Identification of the problem
    2. Communication of the problem to the appropriate person(s)
    3. Development of action alternatives
    4. Decision on one alternative
    5. Action
    6. Monitoring the action
    7. Evaluation of success
Postulated:
    • Most effective when all seven stages are carried out.
    • Least effective when families cannot identify problem (stop before step 1).

Communication
Instrumental and affective areas
Two independent dimensions:
    1. Clear and direct
    2. Clear and indirect
    3. Masked and direct
    4. Masked and indirect
Postulated:
    • Most effective: Clear and direct.
    • Least effective: Masked and indirect.

Roles
Two family function types:
    Necessary and other
Two areas of family functions:
    Instrumental and affective
Necessary family function groupings:
    1. Instrumental
      a. Provision of resources
    2. Affective
      a. Nurturance and support
      b. Adult sexual grafitication
    3. Mixed
      a. Life skills dvelopment
      b. Systems maintenance and management
Other family functions:
    Adaptive and maladaptive
Role functioning is assessed by considering how the family allocates responsibilities and handles accountability for them.
Postulated:
    • Most effective when all necessary family functions have clear allocation to reasonable individual(s) and accountability is built in.
    • Least effective when necessary family functions are not addressed and/or allocation and accountability are not maintained.

Affective responsiveness
Two groupings:
    Welfare emotions and emergency emotions

Postulated:
- Most effective when a full range of responses is appropriate in amount and quality to stimulus.
- Least effective when range is very narrow (one or two affects only) and/or amount and quality is distorted, given the context.

Affective involvement
A range of involvement with six styles identified:
1. Absence of involvement
2. Involvement devoid of feelings
3. Narcissistic involvement
4. Empathic involvement
5. Overinvolvement
6. Symbiotic involvement

Postulated:
- Most effective: Empathic involvement
- Least effective: Symbiotic involvement and absence of involvement

Behavior control
Applies to three situations:
1. Dangerous situations
2. Meeting and expressing psychobiological needs and drives (eating, drinking, sleeping, eliminating, sex, and aggression)
3. Interpersonal socializing behavior inside and outside the family

Standard and latitude of acceptable behavior determined by four styles:
1. Rigid
2. Flexible
3. Laissez-faire
4. Chaotic

To maintain the style, various techniques are used and implemented under "role" functions (systems maintenance and management)
Postulated:
- Most effective: Flexible behavior control
- Least effective: Chaotic behavior control

The McMaster model does not focus on any one dimension as the foundation for conceptualizing family behavior. We argue that many dimensions need to be assessed for a fuller understanding of such a complex entity as the family. Although we attempt to clearly define and delineate the dimensions, we recognize the potential overlap and/or possible interaction that may occur between them. Further clarification will undoubtedly result from our continuing research. (p. 448)

We discuss the dimensions separately and present brief definitions of each. We then describe how one very effectively functioning family appeared on that dimension. (This particular family, whom we call the Sampsons, consisted of father, mother, and two sons, ages 3 and 4. The description we present is excerpted from material obtained during an in-depth interview.) Finally, we consider the range of functioning that we consider healthy or normal. The case material and the description of the range of effective functioning provide other ways to understand the workings of the Model.

A more detailed discussion of the Model is presented elsewhere (Epstein & Bishop, 1981b; Epstein et al., 1978). The 1978 presentation discussed the relationship of family functioning to preventive medicine, which might also be of interest to some readers.

Problem Solving

Definition

The term "family problem solving" refers to a family's ability to resolve problems to a level that maintains effective family functioning. Prior to Epstein's earlier research studies (Westley & Epstein, 1969), it had been postulated that ineffective families would have more problems than would more effectively functioning families. Surprisingly, studies showed that this was not the case; in fact, all families encountered more or less the same range of difficulties. However, differences did occur. Effective families solved their problems, whereas ineffectively functioning families did not deal with at least some of their problems.

Family problems can be divided into two types: "instrumental" and "affective." Instrumental problems relate to issues that are mechanical in nature, such as provision of money, food, clothing, housing, transportation, and so forth. Affective problems relate to issues of emotion or feeling, such as anger or depression. Families whose functioning is disrupted by instrumental problems rarely, if ever, deal effectively with affective problems. However, families whose functioning is disrupted by affective problems may deal adequately with instrumental problems.

Effective problem solving can be described as a sequence of seven steps:

1. Identifying the problem.
2. Communicating with appropriate people about the problem.
3. Developing a set of possible alternative solutions.
4. Deciding on one of the alternatives.
5. Carrying out the action required by the alternative.
6. Monitoring to ensure that the action is carried out.
7. Evaluating the effectiveness of the problem-solving process.

Effective families solve most problems efficiently and easily. Therefore, at times, it can be difficult to elicit information about the problem-solving steps that they have gone through. In families that have difficulty solving problems, it is easier to analyze their stepwise attempts at solving problems.

Families range along a dimension of problem-solving ability. Most effective families will have few, if any, unresolved problems. Problems that exist are relatively new, and they are dealt with effectively. When a new problem situation occurs, the family approaches the problem systematically. As family functioning becomes less effective, family problem-solving behavior becomes less systematic, and fewer problem-solving steps are accomplished.

Clinical Description

The Sampsons cannot identify any major unresolved problems. A visit by the maternal grandmother led to some difficulties with the children. They describe one son as cuddly, whereas the other is more active and independent. The independent grandson, who did not receive as much attention from his grandmother, became jealous and acted up a bit when she visited. When his grandmother scolded him, his behavior then became mildly problematic. Mrs. Sampson first identified this problem and then discussed it with her husband. At the earliest reasonable opportunity, they discussed it with the grandmother. This was done in such a way that she was able to support them in maintaining discipline; at the same time, they helped her relate more appropriately with each boy. The couple was flexible and made reasonable allowances for the grandmother, as she had come from a great distance and was only with them for a brief time; they respected her individuality.

They described another problem with the older son. He would not follow the rules they had laid down regarding where he could and couldn't play. Initially, they tried a number of disciplinary measures. Then the mother realized that this was not working, and they reverted to a previously effective pattern of using rewards. Returning to a previously adaptive approach quickly led to positive results.

This family can discuss all problems in an open and clear way and can also identify both the instrumental and the affective components of each. They communicate about problems at the earliest possible time, process alternatives quickly, make a decision, and begin to act. They make sure their actions are carried out, and they can describe reviewing previously effective and ineffective methods.

Variations within Normal

Not all normal families demonstrate problem solving as effective as that just described. The Sampsons represent the positive extreme of healthy functioning. We conceptualize that a normal family can have some minor unresolved problems. However, such problems will not be of a degree or duration that creates major disruption in the family. A normal family can also be a little slower than the Sampsons to identify problems, to communicate with each other about them, and to act. Despite this reduction in efficiency, however, they will still manage to resolve the majority of problems. They will resolve all instrumental problems; affective problems may present a little more difficulty. We also expect that only the most effective families will actually evaluate the problem-solving process.

Communication

Definition

We define "communication" as the exchange of information within a family. "Communication" is also subdivided into instrumental and affective areas, with the same ramifications for each as are discussed for the dimension of "problem solving."

In addition, two other aspects of communication are also assessed. Is the communication clear or masked, and is it direct or indirect? The clear versus masked continuum focuses on whether the content of the message is clearly stated or is camouflaged, muddied, or vague. The direct versus indirect continuum focuses on whether messages go to their appropriate targets or tend to be deflected to other people. These two aspects are independent, and we can therefore identify four styles of communication as follows: clear and direct; clear and indirect; masked and direct; masked and indirect.

Although we focus primarily on verbal communication, we pay attention to nonverbal behavior especially when it contradicts the verbal information exchange. Contradictory nonverbal behavior contributes to masking and may reflect indirectness of communication as well.

At the healthy end of the dimension, the family communicates in a clear and direct manner in both the instrumental and the affective areas. As we move towards the less effective end of the dimension, communication becomes less clear and less direct.

Clinical Description

The Sampson family is clear and direct in all their patterns of communication. There was no sense of hesitation or holding back, no talking around the issues; in addition, family members always direct their comments to the person for whom they are intended. Their talking is efficient and effective. This is equally true of the children, who were open and straightforward with the parents and the interviewer.

Variations within Normal

Toward the lower end of the normal functioning range, communication about conflictual issues may not be clear and direct. There can be some brief occasions of hesitations or beating around the bush (masking); having trouble clearly hearing each other (masking and/or indirectness); or not clearly stating a personal point of view (indirectness).

Role Functioning

Definition

"Family roles" are defined as the repetitive patterns of behavior by which family members fulfill family functions. There are some functions that all families have to deal with repeatedly in order to maintain an effective and healthy system. We identify five such necessary family functions, and they are the basis for necessary family roles. Each of these areas subsumes a number of tasks and functions.

1. Provision of resources. This area includes those tasks and functions associated with providing money, food, clothing, and shelter.
2. Nurturance and support. This involves the provision of comfort, warmth, reassurance, and support for family members.
3. Adult sexual gratification. Both husbands and wives must personally find satisfaction within the sexual relationship and also feel that they can satisfy their partners sexually. Affective issues are therefore prominent. A reasonable level of sexual activity is generally required. It has been our experience that in some instances, however, both partners may express satisfaction with little or no activity.
4. Personal development. This includes those tasks and functions necessary to support family members in developing skills for personal achievement. Included are tasks relating to the physical, emotional, educational, and social development of the children, and those relating to the career, avocational, and social development of the adults.
5. Maintenance and management of the family system. This area includes a variety of functions.
   a. Decision-making functions include leadership, major decision making, and the question of final decisions when there is no agreement. In general, these functions should reside at the parental level and within the nuclear family.
   b. Boundary and membership functions include functions and tasks concerned with extended families, friends, neighbors, the taking in of boarders, family size, and dealings with external institutions and agencies.
   c. Behavior control functions include disciplining of children and the maintenance of standards and rules for the adult family members.
   d. Household finance functions include the tasks of dealing with monthly bills, banking, income tax, and household money handling.
   e. Health-related functions include caregiving, making appointments, identifying appropriate health problems, and maintaining compliance with health prescriptions.

We consider two additional aspects of role functioning: "role allocation" and "role accountability."

1. Role allocation is concerned with the family's pattern in assigning roles, and it includes a number of issues. Does the person assigned a task or function have the power and skill necessary to carry it out? Is the assignment done clearly and explicitly? Can reassignment take place easily? Are tasks distributed and allocated to the satisfaction of family members?
2. Role accountability looks at the procedures in the family for making sure that functions are fulfilled. This includes the presence of a sense of responsibility in family members and the existence of monitoring and corrective mechanisms.

At the healthy end of this dimension, all necessary family functions are fulfilled. Allocation is reasonable and does not overburden one or more members. Accountability is clear.

Clinical Description

The Sampsons are very clear regarding who carries out each of a variety of family tasks. They discuss the jobs each has, are comfortable with them, and do not feel overburdened. They share tasks in many areas but are also clear about their separate areas of responsibility. For example, the wife does the flower garden, while the husband does the vegetable garden, lawns, and shrubbery.

The task of getting up with the children on weekend mornings is split, one taking Saturday, the other Sunday. Their mutual involvement in dealing with the children was repeatedly demonstrated during the course of the interview, and the children showed no preference for one parent or the other.

The couple are satisfied with their financial resources but would not mind a larger income. They are quite clear about their roles in handling budgeting and financial organization. They set priorities and handle their finances so that they can maximize their resources. The children clearly go to both parents for nurturance and support as appropriate, and the parents obtain their main support from each other.

Both partners are satisfied with their sexual functioning. They can discuss this in an open and straightforward manner and can indicate their enjoyment in being personally satisfied as well as in satisfying each other. In the course of their marriage, the wife has increasingly become more active in initiating sexual activity. They can handle issues such as one partner's saying "no" to sex with tact and sensitivity and without either of them having a sense of being rebuffed.

The wife is actively involved in decisions regarding the husband's career and his pursuit of avocational interests. He is aware of her need to be active outside the home, and he organizes his schedule to support this. She is a Girl Guide commissioner and had an active job early in the marriage. They fully discussed her leaving the job to have children and their long-range plans. The wife enjoys her active role with the children, which led after discussions to their involvement in a parent–therapist program (which we discuss later). They are always able to agree on major decisions.

In all of the above role functioning, this family is amazingly clear in its member's ability to discuss the allocation of roles; in doing so, they play to individual strengths and interests. They keep track of whether the jobs allocated to each are carried out. When one does not carry out a task, the other will either fill in or point out the problem.

Variations within Normal

Functioning somewhat less effectively than the Sampsons' would still fall appropriately within the normal range. In our society, normally functioning families will generally not have difficulties with provision of resources except when circumstances are out of their control (e.g., times of economic depression, labor action, etc.). Nurturance and support will be provided, although it may not always be immediately available. The couple may have minor dissatisfaction with the sexual relationship. Similarly, slight deficiencies in personal development and systems management and maintenance may also occur.

In general, these deviations from effective role functioning should not lead to conflict. In some normal families, roles can be effectively handled even though most functions are carried out by one individual. In the most effective families, there is role sharing. This allows the family to deal with changes from the usual pattern (e.g., those that might be caused by illness.) Within the normal range of families, individuals carry out role functions willingly and possess the required skills and abilities. Individuals are not overburdened. Normally functioning families do not always maintain complete accountability, and there can be occasions when some tasks are not carried out or there is a delay. But, again, this should not lead to conflict.

Affective Responsiveness

Definition

In this dimension, we examine the family's potential range of affective responses, both qualitatively and quantitatively. We define "affective responsiveness" as the ability to respond to a given stimulus with the appropriate quality and quantity of feelings.

We are concerned with two aspects of the quality of affective responses. First, do family members demonstrate an ability to respond with the full spectrum of feelings experienced in human emotional life? Second, is the emotion experienced at times consistent with the stimulus and/or situational context?

The quantitative aspect focuses on the degree of affective response and can be described along a continuum from absence of response through reasonable or expected responsiveness to overresponsiveness. Whereas the dimension considers the overall pattern of the family's responses to affective stimuli, it focuses more than any other dimension on the behaviors of individual members.

It is important to remember that this dimension does not assess the ways in which family members will convey their feelings. How affect is conveyed is an aspect of affective communication.

We distinguish between two categories of affect: *welfare emotions* and *emergency emotions*. Welfare emotions consist of affection, warmth, tenderness, support, love, consolation, happiness, and joy. Emergency emotions consist of responses such as anger, fear, sadness, disappointment, and depression.

At the healthy end of the dimension, we conceive of a family that possesses the capability of expressing a full range of emotions. In most situations, members experience the appropriate emotion, and when an emotion is experienced, it is of reasonable intensity and of reasonable duration. Obviously, cultural variability must be considered in evaluating the affective responsiveness of families.

Clinical Description

All members of the Sampson family display a wide range of affect that is appropriate and in keeping with the situation. They have suffered no major losses in their extended family but can describe periods of sadness and loss in other circumstances. They respond with appropriate anger and disappointment to situations. They have a good sense of humor and are able to be affectionate and caring. They describe how earlier the husband was more responsive across the range of emotions than the wife but also how he has helped her to become more responsive. They communicate all feelings in a clear and direct manner.

Variations within Normal

Even at a fairly healthy level on this dimension, families may contain a member who is not capable of experiencing a particular affect. There may also be instances where members occasionally respond with inappropriate affect and/or experience occasional episodes of underresponding or overresponding. However, the inappropriateness is not disruptive.

Affective Involvement

Definition

Affective involvement is the extent to which the family shows interest in and values the particular activities and interests of individual family members. The focus is on the amount of interest the family demonstrates, as well as the manner in which the family members show interest in and invest themselves in one another. There is a range of styles from a total lack of involvement at one end of the continuum to extreme involvement at the other. We identify six types of involvement as follows:

1. Lack of involvement: no interest or investment in one another.
2. Involvement devoid of feelings: some interest and/or investment in one another. This interest is primarily intellectual in nature.
3. Narcissistic involvement: interest in others only to the degree that their behavior reflects on the self.
4. Empathic involvement: interest and/or investment in one another for the sake of the others.
5. Overinvolvement: excessive interest and/or investment in one another.
6. Symbiotic involvement: an extreme and pathological interest and/or investment in others. Symbiotic involvement is seen only in very disturbed relationships. In such families, there is marked difficulty in differentiating one person from another.

We consider empathic involvement optimal for health. As families move in either direction away from empathic involvement, family functioning becomes less effective in this area.

Clinical Description

In the Sampson family, all members show an active interest in each other. The children respond appropriately for their age. The parents take an active interest in what is important to each other, even though their interests vary in several areas. They can respond to what is going on with each other without overidentifying or personalizing.

Variations within Normal

The Sampsons function very effectively on this dimension. However, some variation can occur within the healthy range. There may be some instances of narcissistic interest of some members in others. There may also be occasional episodes of overinvolvement. However, these patterns are focused on a single individual and are not consistent.

Behavior Control

Definition

This dimension is defined as the pattern a family adopts for handling behavior in three areas: physically dangerous situations; situations that involve the meeting and expressing of psychobiological needs and drives; and situations involving interpersonal socializing behavior both between family members and with people outside the family.

We are interested in the standards or rules the family sets in these areas and in the latitude they allow around the standard. We describe four styles of behavior control based on variations of the standard and latitude:

1. Rigid behavior control. Standards are narrow and specific for the culture, and there is minimal negotiation or variation across situations.
2. Flexible behavior control. Standards are reasonable, and there is opportunity for negotiation and change, depending on the context.
3. Laissez-faire behavior control. At the extreme, no standards are held, and total latitude is allowed, regardless of the context.
4. Chaotic behavior control. There is unpredictable and random shifting between other styles, so that family members do not know what standards apply at any one time or how much negotiation is possible.

We view flexible behavior control as the most effective style and chaotic behavior control as the least effective.

Clinical Description

Mr. and Mrs. Sampson are very clear about rules of behavior. They take a basic stance of allowing considerable exploration and activity by the children, and they tolerate a higher level of activity and noise than many couples would. However, they are very clear about what behavior is unacceptable, and they intervene consistently when such behavior occurs.

They support each other in this regard. They handle the children in a mutually supportive and consistent fashion. They make allowances when the situation calls for it (for example, a visit by grandmother), but they still maintain consistent patterns within that framework. They demonstrate superior techniques for handling the children's behavior. For example, during the interview when one child went to leave the room, he was politely told to stay and close the door. When he persisted, he was told again, in a clear and slightly more forceful way. He responded and was immediately told, "Thank you, that's very good." On another occasion, when one boy was making quite a bit of noise, the father said, "Please yell more quietly." The child immediately spoke in a quieter voice.

This family was considering becoming foster parents for a disturbed child. They could indicate with considerable insight the problems they felt they would face in this role. They knew that taking a disturbed child into the family setting would require a shift in their standards of behavior and control. While they had standards for their own children, they realized that tighter standards might initially be required when the disturbed child came to stay with them.

Variations within Normal

Within the range of normal functioning, there can be a number of variations on the above example of very effective functioning. The family may be clear about the rules of behavior in general, while being indecisive, unclear, or lacking in agreement in one or two relatively minor areas (e.g., the parents may disagree about minor aspects of table manners, but the family members are aware of the general range). Such inconsistency should not, however, be a source of major conflict. Normally functioning families also may not use the most effective of techniques and therefore may require more time to establish control.

It should be noted that this dimension also applies to the parents in the family. In normally functioning families, parents are able to describe what they expect from their partners and what their partners expect of them. When one partner does not meet the other's expectations, they address the problem.

RESEARCH ON NORMAL FAMILIES

The Silent Majority (Westley & Epstein, 1969) was a report on a large study that proved to be the forerunner of much of the work reported in this chapter. The study was of college students and their families carried out from 1955 to 1964 at McGill University. The aim of the study—as of most of our work since then—was to determine how the emotional health of individuals related to the overall structure and function of their families. We will not review the details of this study at this time, as they can be obtained elsewhere in other published articles by our group.

On reviewing the study, it is striking to note the rapidity and extent of the changes in our society in values and morals in the three decades since the completion of the study. These changes have not only affected family life, but they have radically changed the methods of examining and evaluating families in many areas. The largest value shifts are those arising from changes relating to the position of women in society and especially their role in today's family and the economy. These changes have had enormous effects on both spousal and parent–child relationships. The multiple varieties of family structure and organization that are common at this time could not have even been imagined when the study was done.

Despite all these changes that have taken place in families, we feel that two of the basic findings in the original study are still applicable. This statement is based on clinical impressions only, as we have no experimental or empirical information to support it.

First, we feel that the organizational, structural, and transactional pattern variables are more powerful in determining the behavior of family members than are the intrapsychic variables. This statement refers to the relative power of the variables only and does not invalidate the contribution of intrapsychic factors to behavior.

Second, the most important finding of the *Silent Majority* study was that the emotional health of the children is closely related to the emotional relationships between their parents. When these relationships were warm and supportive, so that the husband and wife felt loved, admired, and encouraged to act in ways that they themselves admired, the children were happy and healthy. Couples who were emotionally close, met each other's needs, and encouraged positive self-images in each other were good parents. This positive relationship between husband and wife did not depend on their being emotionally healthy themselves as individuals, though obviously this was most beneficial. In some cases, one or both parents were emotionally disturbed, but they still managed to develop a good marital relationship. When this occurred, the children were emotionally healthy. It was as if the positive marital relationship had insulated the children and prevented contagion from the individual psychopathology of the parents.

In our ongoing clinical and research work, we continue to be impressed by the importance of a loving and supportive relationship between the parents. The presence of such strong support, genuine concern and loving care, and the absence of chronically persistent and nagging destructive hostility in the relationships of the parental couple, apparently serve as a foundation that can bear the weight of much strain inside and outside the family group in a manner that protects the ongoing interrelationships and development of the family members. We go so far as to predict that in the absence of such a relationship between parents, no family system could be expected to function at a satisfactory level.

Over the years there have been a number of studies utilizing the MMFF and the psychometric instruments derived from it that have investigated different aspects of normal families. We are not acquainted with all of them, but we will herein mention just a few that hold interest.

The Parent–Therapist Study

Colleagues in our research group tested the hypothesis that placing disturbed children in very effectively functioning families could have a remedial influence (Levin, Rubenstein, & Streiner, 1976; Rubenstein, Armentrout, Levin, & Herald, 1978). Their project, "The Parent–Therapist Program: An Innovative Approach to Treating Emotionally Disturbed Children," compared the relative effectiveness of placing emotionally disturbed children in superior—functioning families (i.e., with parent–therapists) with placing them in residential child-treatment centers. The families involved were interviewed and assessed using the MMFF. Superior-functioning families were quite identifiable. This supported our view that the model could be applied to and discriminate among families of widely varying levels of functioning.

It was found that the families were as effective as the institutions in improving the functioning of the children. This finding supports the assumption that the behavior of individuals is strongly influenced by the structure and organization of the family of which they are a part.

The original design of the study called for the children to be placed in three different settings: in institutions, in families that were part of a collaborative network of parent–therapist families, and with individual parent–therapist families not tied into a network. It was quickly discovered that the last group could not deal with the assigned children. Even such highly effective families had limits to the stress they could handle. Less effective, but still healthy, families are probably even less able to handle such stresses. Presumably, they too can cope more effectively if they are part of a social network for support. These findings shed light on the popularity and apparent effectiveness of self-help groups—a phenomenon that has arisen in an explosive fashion in the past decade to help people cope with a very wide range of human problems.

As a final comment on the parent–therapist project, it is interesting to note that none of the children treated were incorporated to the level of complete family membership. This supports the notions that aberrant behavior in an individual is not tolerated by a healthy family and that healthy, well-functioning families deal clearly and effectively with boundary and membership issues.

The London Study

In 1979, Byles conducted a study of families being seen at a family medicine clinic for nonpsychiatric problems in London, Ontario, Canada. He collected data on 30 couples who had at least one child using an early version of our Family Assessment Device (FAD) for the problem-solving dimension only. Although these families were not seeking help for psychiatric problems, there is no evidence they were functioning extremely well according to our model; however they can probably be considered as "normal" in the statistical sense discussed at the beginning of this chapter.

Without going into the methodological details of this study (Epstein, Bishop, & Baldwin, 1982) it was found that some of these nonclinical families had ineffective problem-solving techniques and a fairly high incidence of problems. The families that had the most trouble with the process of problem solving had the most areas of difficulty ($r = +.80$). These data are consistent with the findings in *The Silent Majority*.

Another interesting finding in this study was that families in which the oldest child was an adolescent had the most difficulties with problem solving. This finding has since been repeated in a number of studies from many different vantage points—that families with adolescent children experience more stress than those families with children of other ages. These findings clearly highlight statements made by most family researchers to the effect that families vary according to developmental stage and therefore all stages of family development must be studied.

The Ontario Child Health Study

Byles and his colleagues in the Ontario Child Health Study reported on the reliability and validity of the General Functioning (GF) Subscale of the McMaster FAD (Byles, Byrne, Boyle, & Offord, 1988). The scale was used to measure family functioning in a large, random sample (*n* = 1,869) of Ontario families participating in the Ontario Child Health Study. In finding that "the results support confidence in the construct validity of the GF scale as a measure of family functioning" (Byles et al., 1988), Byles et al. confirm the approaches developed in the MMFF to assessing family function with reference to healthy function as well as pathological function.

The Retirement Study

In this project our group studied the effect of family functioning, couple health, and retirement on the morale of 178 couples in their 60s (Bishop, Epstein, Baldwin, & Miller, 1988). The sample studied was a subset of Providence, Rhode Island, households selected originally by the Population Research Laboratory at Brown University in 1969 for a study of health and mobility (Speare & Kobrin, 1980). The proportion who reported optimal and less than optimal family function in the FAD were 63.5% and 36.5% for husbands and 67.0% and 33.0% for wives. This study was particularly interesting in highlighting differences among individual family members. As reported in the study

> the difference between predictors of family functioning for husbands and wives is striking. For husbands, health is more predictive of psychological well-being than family functioning and retirement status, whereas for wives, family functioning is more predictive than health, and husband's retirement status does not significantly relate. The psychological well-being of a married man in his sixties [sic] appears to be strongly indicated by issues of health, and only to a lesser degree by family functioning and retirement status. For a married woman in her sixties [sic], psychological well-being is most strongly predicted by family issues and only to a lesser degree by health. It is most important to note that this difference between predictors of morale for men and women occurs despite the fact that husbands and wives agree in their perceptions about the effectiveness of their family functioning across several dimensions. (p. 245)

Such findings of differences in individual family members and differences in findings at various stages in the family developmental cycle continually recur in research on family function.

The Psychometric Study

In a recently published study (Kabacoff, Miller, Bishop, Epstein, & Keitner, 1990), our group investigated the psychometric properties of the McMaster

FAD. Data for this investigation were obtained from large clinical, nonclinical, and medical samples. In general, scale reliabilities were favorable, and the hypothesized factor structure of the FAD was supported. As an answer to previously repeated criticisms that the FAD was not developed through factor analytic methods (Epstein, Baldwin, & Bishop, 1983), this study reported: "over 90% of FAD items loaded on factors hypothe-sized by the McMaster Model" (p. 438). The authors summarized thus, "combined with previous reports (Epstein et al., 1983; Miller, Epstein, Bishop, & Keitner, 1985), the results from this study suggest that the FAD can provide reliable and valid assessment of a wide range of families" (p. 438).

The Quebec Group

An extremely productive research group led by Maziade and Thivierge in Quebec City have been utilizing the MMFF and the FAD in their ongoing investigations in child psychiatric epidemiology.

Some of the findings they have reported include: (1) the dimension of behavior control has been found to interact with the child's temperament in predicting clinical disorders in middle childhood (Maziade et al., 1985) but not to predict academic achievement (Maziade et al., 1986); (2) the communication dimension was shown to interact with extreme infant temperament to predict IQ in preschool years (Maziade, Cote, Boutin, Bernier, & Thivierge, 1987).

In another study (Maziade, Bernier, Thivierge, & Cote, 1987), the authors report that

> In an epidemiological framework, that is, when used in samples of the general population, the two MMFF dimensions under study [i.e., behavioral control and communication (our addition)] displayed a satisfactory level of interactor reliability. This suggests that trained investigators can deliver a satisfactory agreement when basing their rating on the process as well as on the content of the family interview. In addition, our data from this normal nonclinical sample to some degree confirm that what the scale defines as a normative level of functioning (ratings of 4–5), corresponds to the functioning of a majority of nonclinical families in the population. The present data also bring into focus an important empirical quality that such an assessment device of family functioning must present: independence of SES. (pp. 529–530)

RECENT DEVELOPMENTS

Our group recently convened a research conference of investigators utilizing the, MMFF, FAD, CRS, and McSiff. These are psychometric instruments developed by our research group over the years and are all developed from, and based on, the McMaster Model of Family Functioning. Groups from the United States, England, Holland, Hungary, Australia, and Brazil were represented. They reported on works completed, and in progress—some of which will be published in relevant journals in the near future. This conference, as well as the detailed sampling of research work presented above, are indicators of the vitality and intensity of family studies being generated by the theoretical issues developed by the MMFF and the ability to do more exact empirical investigation facilitated by the instruments developed from this model. They all serve to throw further light on the functioning of healthy as well as pathological families.

REFERENCES

Berman, E. M., & Lief, H. I. (1975). Marital therapy from a psychiatric perspective: An overview. *American Journal of Psychiatry, 132,* 583–592.

Bishop, D. S., & Epstein, N. B. (1979). *Research on teaching methods.* Paper presented at the International Forum for Trainers and Family Therapists, Tavistock Clinic, London, England.

Bishop, D. S., Epstein, N. B., Baldwin, L. M., & Miller, I. W. (1988). Older couples: The effect of health, retirement, and family functioning on morale. *Family Systems Medicine, 6*(2), 238–247.

Brody, E. M. (1974). Aging and family personality: A developmental view. *Family Process, 13,* 23–37.

Byles, J. (1939). [Study of families being seen at a family medicine clinic for nonpsychiatric problems.] Unpublished manuscript.

Byles, J., Byrne, C., Boyle, M., & Offord, D. (1988). Ontario child health study: Reliability and validity of the general functioning subscale of the McMaster Family Assessment Device. *Family Process, 27,* 97–104.

Carter, E., & McGoldrick, M. (Eds.). (1980). *The family life cycle: A framework for family therapy.* New York: Gardner Press.

Comley, A. (1973). Family therapy and the family physician. *Canadian Family Physician, 19,* 78–81.

Epstein, N. B., Baldwin, L. M., & Bishop, D. S. (1983). The McMaster Family Assessment Device. *Journal of Marital and Family Therapy, 9*(2), 171–180.

Epstein, N.B., & Bishop, D.S. (1973). State of the art—1973. *Canadian Psychiatric Association Journal, 18,* 175–183.

Epstein, N. B., & Bishop, D. S. (1981b). Problem centered systems therapy of the family. In A. S. Gurman & D. P. Kniskern (Eds.), *Handbook of family therapy.* New York: Brunner/Mazel.

Epstein, N. B., Bishop, D. S., & Baldwin, L. M. (1982). McMaster model of family functioning: A view of the normal family. In F. Walsh (Ed.), *Normal Family processes* (1st ed., pp. 115–141). New York: Guilford Press.

Epstein, N. B., Bishop, D. S., & Levin, S. (1978). The McMaster model of family functioning. *Journal of Marriage and Family Counseling, 4,* 19–31.

Epstein, N. B., Levin, S., & Bishop, D. S. (1976). The family as a social unit. *Canadian Family Physician, 22,* 1411–1413.

Epstein, N. B., Sigal, J. J., & Rakoff, V. (1962). *Family categories schema.* Unpublished manuscript, Jewish General Hospital, Department of Psychiatry, Montreal.

Epstein, N. B., & Westley, W. A. (1959). Patterns of intra-familial communication. In *Psychiatric Research Reports 11* (pp. 1–9). Washington, DC: American Psychiatric Association.

Group for the Advancement of Psychiatry. (1970). *The field of family therapy, Report 78, Vol. 7.*

Guttman, H. A., Spector, R. M., Sigal, J. J., Epstein, N. B., & Rakoff, V. (1972). Coding of affective expression in conjoint family therapy. *American Journal of Psychotherapy, 26,* 185–194.

Guttman, H. A., Spector, R. M., Sigal, J. J., Rakoff, V., & Epstein, N. B. (1971). Reliability of coding affective communication in family therapy sessions: Problems of measurement and interpretation. *Journal of Consulting and Clinical Psychology, 37,* 397–402.

Hadley, T. R., Jacob, T., Milliones, J., Caplan, J., & Spitz, D. (1974). The relationship between family developmental crisis and the appearance of symptoms in a family member. *Family Process, 13,* 207–214.

Hill, R. (1965). Generic features of families under stress. In H. N. Parad (Ed.), *Crisis intervention: Selected readings* (pp. 32–52). New York: Family Services Association of America.

Kabacoff, R. I., Miller, I. W., Bishop, D. S., Epstein, N. B., & Keitner, G. I. (1990). A psychometric study of the McMaster Family Assessment Device in psychia-tric, medical, and nonclinical examples. *Journal of Family Psychology, 3*(4), 431–439.

Langsley, D. G., & Kaplan, D. M. (1968). *The treatment of families in crisis.* New York: Grune & Stratton.

Levin, S., Rubenstein, J., & Streiner, D. L. (1976). The parent–therapist program: An innovative approach to treating emotionally disturbed children. *Hospital and Community Psychiatry, 27,* 407–410.

Maziade, M., Bernier, H., Thivierge, J., & Cote, R. (1987). The relationship between family functioning and demographic characteristics in an epidemiological study. *Canadian Journal of Psychiatry, 32*(7), 526–533.

Maziade, M., Caperaa P., Boudreault, M., Thivierge J., Cote, R., & Boutin, P. (1986). The effect of temperment on longitudinal academic achievement in primary school. *Journal of the American Academy of Child Psychiatry, 25,* 692–696.

Maziade, M., Caperaa, P., Laplante, B., Boudreault, M., Thivierge, J., Cote, R., & Boutin, P. (1985). Value of difficult temperament among 7–year-olds in the general population for predicting psychiatric diagnosis at age 12. *American Journal of Psychiatry, 142,* 943–946.

Maziade, M., Cote, R., Boutin, P., Bernier, H., & Thivierge, J. (1987). Temperament and intellectual development: A longitudinal study from infancy to four years. *American Journal of Psychiatry, 144,* 144–150.

Miller, I. W., Epstein, N. B., Bishop, D. S., & Keitner, G. I. (1985). The McMaster Family Assessment Device: Reliability and validity. *Journal of Marital and Family Therapy, 11*(4), 345–356.

Minuchin, S., & Barcai, A. (1969). Therapeutically induced family crisis. In J. H. Masserman (Ed.), *Science and psychoanalysis: Vol. XIV. Childhood and adolescence* (pp. 199–205). New York: Grune & Stratton.

Parad, H. J., & Caplan, G. (1965). A framework for studying families in crisis. In H. J. Parad (Ed.), *Crisis intervention: Selected readings* (pp. 53–72). New York: Family Service Association of America.

Postner, R. S., Guttman, H. A., Sigal, J. J., Epstein, N. B., & Rakoff, V. (1971). Process and outcome in conjoint family therapy. *Family Process, 10,* 451–473.

Rakoff, V., Sigal, J. J., Spector, R., & Guttman, H. A. (1967). *Communications in families.* Report on investigation aided by grants from Foundations Fund for Research in Psychiatry, Laidlaw Foundation.

Rapoport, L. (1965). The state of crisis: Some theoretical considerations. In H. J. Parad (Ed.), *Crisis intervention: Selected readings* (pp. 22–31). New York: Family Service Association of America.

Rubenstein, J., Armentrout, J., Levin, S., & Herald, D. (1978). The parent–therapist program: Alternative care for emotionally disturbed children. *American Journal of Orthopsychiatry, 48,* 654–662.

Santa-Barbara, J., Woodward, C. A., Levin, S., Steiner, D., Goodman, J., & Epstein, N. B. (1975). *The relationship between therapists' characteristics and outcome variables in family therapy.* Paper presented at the Canadian Psychiatric Association, Banff, Alberta.

Scherz, F. H. (1971). Maturational crisis and parent–child interaction. *Social Casework, 52,* 362–369.

Sigal, J. J., Rakoff, V., & Epstein, N. B. (1967). Indicators of therapeutic outcome in conjoint family therapy. *Family Process, 6*(2), 215–226.

Solomon, M. A. (1973). A developmental, conceptual premise for family therapy. *Family Process, 12,* 179–188.

Speare, A., & Kobrin, F. (1980). *Biases in panel studies of migration.* Paper presented at the American Statistical Association.

Westley, W. A., & Epstein, N. B. (1960). Report on the psychosocial organization of the family and mental health. In D. Willner (Ed.), *Decisions, values, and groups* (Vol. 1, pp. 278–303). New York: Pergamon Press.

Westley, W. A., & Epstein, N. B. (1969). *The silent majority.* San Francisco: Jossey-Bass.

Woodward, C. A., Santa-Barbara, J., Levin, S., Epstein, N. B., & Streiner, D. (1977). *The McMaster family therapy outcome study III: Client and treatment characteristics significantly contributing to clinical outcomes.* Paper presented at the American Orthopsychiatric Association, New York.

Woodward, C. A., Santa-Barbara, J., Levin, S., Goodman, J., Streiner, D., & Epstein, N. B. (1975). *Client and therapist characteristics related to family therapy outcome: Closure and follow-up evaluation.* Paper presented at the Society for Psychotherapy Research, Boston.

Woodward, C. A., Santa-Barbara, J., Levin, S., Goodman, J., Streiner, D., Muzzin, L., & Epstein, N. B. (1974). *Outcome research in family therapy: On the growing edginess of family therapists.* Paper presented at the Nathan W. Ackerman Memorial Conference, Margarita Island.

GENETIC INFLUENCES ON FAMILY PROCESS
The Emergence of a New Framework for Family Research

Danielle A. Bussell and David Reiss

INTRODUCTION

For years, family researchers and practitioners have accepted the premise that being reared in one family versus another has important developmental consequences for children's personality and psychological well-being. Factors such as social class, an intellectually impoverished home environment, and parental psychiatric disorder or marital conflict have been studied as potential risk factors for children (e.g., Shaffer, Phillips, Enzer, Silverman, & Anthony, 1989). Typically, the research designs used to study the influence of family environment on child development have assessed one child per family, often implicitly assuming that the effects of environmental variables such as parenting and stressful life events on one child would generalize to other children in the family. However, this assumption that shared or common family experiences are critical to child development has been called into question by recent findings in the field of behavioral genetics that suggest the general family environment is not a very important determinant of variations in children's outcomes (Loehlin & Nichols, 1976). Instead, it appears that children in the *same* family have markedly different experiences, and it is these differences that seem to shape development.

The idea that common childrearing conditions make little difference in children's development challenges the interpretation of a large literature base examining the relationship of familial characteristics to child well-being. These findings somehow violate our expectations of family life. Yet, at the same time, these seemingly "anomalous" findings are strangely familiar when viewed from within a family systems framework, which historically has argued that the family environment consists of changing patterns of relationships rather than any single, continuous condition experienced equally by all family members (e.g., Gilbert, Christensen, & Margolin, 1984; McGoldrick & Carter, 1982; Minuchin, 1974).

To the family therapist, it is not surprising that children's socialization cannot be explained in isolation from the entire family context, including transactions within and between marital and offspring subsystems. In a sense, recent research may be confirming aspects of family systems that therapists, in clinical reports, have described for many years. Perhaps, as behavioral genetics research begins to underscore the developmental importance of nonshared environments, comparable family systems ideas such as alliances, boundaries, and roles may become the subject of widespread interest across disciplines. Further, behavioral genetics research may permanently alter family scientists' measurement and models of family environment. The primary objective of this chapter is to encourage such interdisciplinary dialogue by briefly describing important behavioral genetic findings and by demonstrating the broad implications of genetic research designs for our understanding of family process and child development.

GENETIC DATA AND THE REDEFINITION
OF FAMILY ENVIRONMENT

Behavioral differences among individuals can arise from both genetic differences and environmental variations. This section summarizes important findings from behavioral genetics research, an application of quantitative genetic methods to behavioral phenomena. Importantly, the quantitative genetic applications discussed in this chapter focus on the study of traits that are probably influenced by many genes as well as environment, in contrast to molecular genetics, which emphasizes DNA structure and function. Behavioral genetics research uses twin and adoption designs to decompose observed variation in behavior in a population into genetic and environmental components. That is, these studies are simple natural experiments that control for genetic relatedness while studying environmental effects (e.g., identical twins adopted into separate homes) or control for environmental effects while studying genetic relatedness (e.g., comparing adoptive to non-adoptive siblings in the same home) (Plomin, Chipuer, & Neiderhiser, 1994).

Behavioral genetics research typically examines the correlation between siblings on some trait or personality attribute as an index of familial resemblance. As noted above, two major designs predominate: twin and adoption studies. In the former, the degree of similarity between identical (monozygotic or MZ) and fraternal (dizygotic or DZ) twins is estimated. A genetic effect is indicated when MZ twins, who carry identical genes, are more similar than DZ twins, who only share 50% of their genes (Plomin, Chipuer, & Neiderhiser, 1994). Heritability, an estimate of variance in an observed behavior or trait resulting from genetic factors, is computed from the difference between these correlations.[1] Similarity between the twins that is not explained by common genes is attributed to the effects of a common rearing environment that has acted to produce a familial resemblance.[2] To the behavioral geneticist, any dissimilarity between the identical twins $(1 - r_{mz})$ must result from environmental effects not shared by the siblings or measurement error.

The model applied to adoption designs is similar in approach to the twin method. For example, if sibling similarity results from shared family environment, adoptive siblings must resemble each other. Heritability can be estimated by comparing the correlation between biologically related siblings reared together (50% genetically alike) to the resemblance of the adoptive siblings reared together (0% genetic similarity). Additional details about the logic of twin and adoption designs can be found in any of several behavioral genetics textbooks (e.g., Plomin, 1990).

Regardless of the design used, behavioral genetics research has consistently pointed to two conclusions: (1) The heritability of behavioral phenomena rarely exceeds .50. That is, although evidence supports significant genetic influence on behavior, environmental effects are also critical in explaining individual variation (Plomin, Chipuer, & Neiderhiser, 1994; Plomin & Daniels, 1987). (2) Familial resemblance is largely explained by heritability. Typically estimates of the effects of shared environment are quite negligible (Plomin, Chipuer, & Neiderhiser, 1994; Scarr & Weinberg, 1991). The surprising corollary to this finding is that nonshared environmental influences explain substantially more of the variation in children's personalities, interests, and adjustment levels than the common family environment. As Plomin has described:

> The data imply that environmental influences important to behavioral development operate in such a way as to make children in the same family different from one another. That is, environmental influences do not operate on a family-by-family basis but rather on an individual-by-individual basis. They are specific to each child rather than general for an entire family. (1989, p. 109)

Although it is beyond the scope of this chapter to review extensively the behavioral genetics literature, for purposes of clarifying the implications of genetic data, it is useful to examine an exemplary study conducted by Scarr and Weinberg (1991). These investigators set out to assess the effects of shared rearing environment by measuring familial resemblance in intellectual and personality development between genetically unrelated adoles-

[1]Heritability = $2 (r_{mz} - r_{dz})$.
[2]Shared environment = $(r_{mz} -$ heritability$)$.

cents adopted into the same family shortly after birth. The adolescents in the study had spent an average of 18 years in the adoptive families. Strengthening the design, Scarr and Weinberg recruited a comparable sample of biologically related siblings reared by their biological parents.

The findings related to children's intellectual development were particularly striking. The parent–child IQ correlation in the biologically related families was approximately .40, as compared to the adoptive parent–child correlation of .13. In contrast, the adopted children's IQ scores were closely correlated with the educational level of their birth mothers (.28) and birth fathers (.43) as obtained from the adoption agency's records. Adopted children's IQs did not correlate strongly with their adoptive mothers' (.09) and adoptive fathers' (.11) educational levels. Finally, the IQ correlation of the biologically related siblings was .35, whereas the IQ correlation of adopted children who had lived together in the same family almost all of their lives was .00!

Scarr and Weinberg's finding that older adoptive siblings showed no resemblance in intellectual ability is remarkable given their objective of demonstrating the influence of shared family environment. Instead, the lack of resemblance between the adoptees and to their adoptive parents at the end of the childrearing period argued that the influence of shared family environment was negligible in the long run. Further, the adoptees' continued resemblance to their birth parents even after living with their adoptive parents for so many years indicated the importance of genetic effects on intelligence.

Scarr and Weinberg's discovery and similar evidence from research examining other behavioral constructs have pointed to a limitation in our existing developmental and family research paradigm, which has emphasized variation in environmental factors across families, such as educational level of parents. These findings argue for further exploration of which kinds of environmental factors predict variations in children's developmental trajectories. Extant literature demonstrating a link between childrearing and child outcomes clearly indicates family experiences are important in shaping children's personality and behavior. Now, the challenge becomes discovering how the relevant environmental influences come to operate in specific and unique ways for each child rather than operating generally for all children within the family (Dunn & Plomin, 1990; Hoffman, 1991).

FAMILY ENVIRONMENT REDEFINED: A NEW RESEARCH PARADIGM

Although most mental health professionals and scientists concede that both family environment and genes influence intellectual and emotional development, how developmentalists, clinicians, behavioral geneticists, and related disciplines come to see the world and practice science in it are not always compatible. The discovery that common familial background does not explain much of the variance in child personality and well-being challenges various fields of inquiry to reconstruct elementary generalizations as well as research methods. For example, much of the extant child socialization literature has not explored sibling differences because only one child is included in the research design (e.g., Baumrind, 1991; Forehand, Thomas, Wierson, Brody, & Fauber, 1990). Similarly, behavioral geneticists' understanding of sibling differences has been hindered by the failure of the design of most genetic studies to actually operationalize and measure environmental processes.

Thus, at this critical juncture, scientists from various fields have become increasingly aware that family members are not very similar on personality traits, yet this recognition has precipitated a crisis as researchers from different backgrounds try to integrate genetics with family systems and developmental models (Hoffman, 1991). For example, given that behavioral geneticists practically discovered the significance of nonshared environment by accident in their search for genetic influences on behavioral phenomena, researchers from diverse backgrounds are now struggling to clarify the definition of nonshared environment, what methods to use to explore its effects, and how to apply what we learn. The remainder of this chapter explores the emergence of new methods and research designs that attempt to integrate genetic and environmental data in family research. Some of the approaches described are the product of our own longitudinal investigation of nonshared environment in 720 families nationwide (Reiss et al., 1994). This project, which integrates behavioral genetics methods with a comprehensive assessment of adolescents' social environments, is one of the first to attempt to participate in a new paradigm of child development research on a large-scale basis. The significance of this work and the details of its design will be elaborated below.

WHAT IS NONSHARED ENVIRONMENT?

Although behavioral geneticists make no attempt to measure the environment directly, their models are built on a broad conception of environment as all biological, social, and behavioral events experienced by the child since conception. In attempts to define facets of children's observable social environments that could lead to nonshared effects, behavioral geneticists have proposed at least four important classes of sibling differential experience: (1) differential parenting; (2) differential experiences with one another (differential sibling treatment); (3) differential experiences in peer groups; and (4) differential exposure to life events (e.g., Daniels, Dunn, Furstenberg, & Plomin, 1985; Plomin, 1989). Simpler sources of differential experience of the environment—such as birth order—have shown very few consistent effects across studies (Schooler, 1972). Differences in gender between siblings may elicit great differences in parenting and sibling relationships. However, finding of gender differences have typically been based on comparisons of children in different families rather than within families. In keeping with our objective of elucidating the importance of genetic and nonshared environmental data for family research, this chapter focuses on differential family experiences.

Generally, although aspects of family structure such as birth order and gender appear to contribute to siblings' nonshared experiences, their effects are typically quite small. For example, in our investigation of the relationship of nonshared environment to adolescent development, the set of variables including siblings' combined age, their age difference, gender, birth order, and total number of siblings in the family accounted for less than 5% of the total variance in how similarly or dissimilarly siblings were exposed to parental threatening behavior (Reiss et al., 1994). Other investigators have reported similar results, with differential family constellation variables explaining as little as 1% of the variance in children's achievement, ability, and sibling differences in self-reported delinquent behavior (Plomin & Foch, 1981; Rowe, Rodgers, & Meseck-Bushey, 1992; Scarr & Grajeck, 1982). Given that obvious differences between siblings, such as age and birth order, do not account for their degree of resemblance to one another, attention has turned to the microenvironments that children experience within their families.

The principal starting point for elucidating findings that sibling resemblance is largely the result of genetics has been exploration of how similar are the experiences of children within the same family. In a sense, researchers have begun to explore the phenomenology of nonshared family environments, which until recently existed only as a residual mathematical term resulting from heritability calculations. Indeed, parents do seem to direct different rates of affectionate and controlling behaviors toward different children (Brody & Stoneman, 1994; Brody, Stoneman, & Burke, 1987; Bryant & Crockenberg, 1980; Daniels et al., 1985; Dunn & McGuire, 1994; Stocker, Dunn, & Plomin, 1989). Children as young as 5 years old have reported that their parents treat them differently than their siblings (Koch, 1960). Further, observational research suggests children, in their earliest years, closely monitor their mothers' interactions with their siblings and react strongly to those interactions (e.g., interrupting a conversation to draw attention away from the sibling and back to themselves) (Dunn & McGuire, 1994).

In summarizing her work on the Colorado Adoption Project, a longitudinal study of 100 sibling pairs who were initially 4–7 years old, Dunn notes that in this sample, approximately 50% of the children said they were treated differently from their siblings. Interestingly, the number of siblings who reported receiving more favorable treatment than their sibling was about equal to the number who reported being treated worse. Only one-third of the mothers reported similar intensity and extent of affection for their two children, and only 12% reported equally easy or problematic experiences disciplining the two children (Dunn & McGuire, 1994).

Importantly, evidence is emerging that differential parental treatment plays a significant role in child development as the findings from behavioral genetics predicted. For example, in the Colorado Adoption Project, differential maternal affection and control were linked to children's worrying, anxiety, and depression (Dunn, Stocker, & Plomin, 1990). Children who experienced greater maternal control or less maternal affection than their siblings were more likely to be anxious or depressed. Likewise, in a longitudinal study of preschoolers assessed before and after their siblings were born, differential parental behavior was related to child self-esteem both longitudinally and concurrently, even when temperamental differences between the siblings were taken into account (Dunn & McGuire, 1994). Finally, in their study of 11- to 17-year-old sibling pairs, Daniels et al. (1985) found better adjusted adolescents experienced more maternal closeness, more say in family decision-making, and more parental chore expectations as compared to more poorly adjusted siblings. Further longitudinal research will be necessary to explore the etiology of differential treatment in families and how it may predict different developmental trajectories.

In addition to differential parental treatment, differing experiences with one's siblings appear to be an important component of nonshared environment. For example, in Daniels and Plomin's (1985) study of adoptive and biological adolescent and young adult sibling pairs, 47.7% of the participants reported a "bit of difference" and 18.7% reported "much difference" in the mutuality of their interactions with their siblings. Further, the inclusion of adoptees in the design allowed the investigators to determine that the origin of nonmutuality of sibling interactions was primarily environmental rather than genetic. Likewise, in an observational study of preschool and young school-aged children, only 23% of the siblings were rated as expressing similar degrees of sibling closeness as their sibling expressed (Dunn & McGuire, 1994). Importantly, in this same study, children who behaved more negatively to their siblings had higher self esteem than the children who received more hostility than they directed.

Relatedly, Brody et al. (1987) examined the influence of one sibling's temperament on the sibling relationship in same-sex, school-aged siblings. They found evidence of nonshared experiences such as that older siblings direct more prosocial behavior toward younger siblings than younger siblings directed toward them, and younger brothers behaved more negatively toward older brothers than vice versa. Further, sibling dyads which included an active, emotionally intense, or nonpersistent child tended to experience higher rates of conflictual, negative interactions. Other studies have focused on the developmental significance of nonshared sibling relationships. These studies include Baker and Daniels' (1990) retrospective examination of adult twins, Daniels et al.'s (1985) investigation of adolescent sibling pairs, and Zahn-Waxler, Robinson, & Emde's (1992) study of the development of empathy in preschool twins.

As researchers begin to explore the effects of differential treatment, it is becoming increasingly important to consider the role of perceptual processes in shaping nonshared environmental effects. That is, how do different family members *subjectively* define nonshared environment, and how does the family's view relate to researchers' definitions of nonshared experiences? Interestingly, across several studies, siblings report a greater degree of differential treatment than reflected in parental reports (Daniels et al., 1985; Dunn & McGuire, 1994; Reiss et al., 1994). In some of these investigations, a rater effect may be inflating the correlations in parental treatment between the two siblings, given that the same parental rater provided reports on both children, whereas different children reported on the same parent.

However, recent data suggest the consistency of this reporting bias may reflect an underlying finding that perception of differential treatment is a proxy for important family processes. For example, in the Colorado Adoption Project, which examined mothers' behavior toward their different children over a 3-year period, Dunn and colleagues found that mothers treated each of their successive children very similarly when the children were at the same age (e.g., a mother treated her second-born 2-year-old similarly to how she had treated her first born when that child was 2), although they did not treat the same child consistently as that child grew up (i.e., parenting for a particular child varied with the age of that child) (Dunn & McGuire, 1994). Thus, parents may subjectively perceive they treat their children similarly because they believe they use a consistent parenting approach to each child according to their developmental stage. In other words, a parent may believe an infant needs coddling but a 2-year-old needs strict limit setting. Consequently, the parent is similarly affectionate to all her children when they are infants and similarly strict when they are preschoolers. Yet, the children of this parent are likely to report they are treated differently from their siblings because they do not have the historical perspective to realize their parent had taken the same approach to them as to their sibling when they were the same age.

The interaction between parenting beliefs and behavior with variation in children's unique stimulus values, such as siblings at different developmental stages or with different activity levels, is only beginning to be explored in research sensitive to sibling differences. For example, McGillicuddy-DeLisi and colleagues (McGillicuddy-DeLisi, 1990) are pursuing a program of research exploring both how parents construct their beliefs about developmental processes and childrearing strategies and whether the parental belief–behavior relationship is affected by differences among children in the family. Gender differences and socialization in the family of origin, as well as experience with the first-born child, are some of the variables being examined to explain how parents adapt their posture toward different children (Deal, Halverson, & Wampler, 1994; McGillicuddy-DeLisi, 1990).

In addition to the role of adult belief systems in creating children's nonshared experiences, the importance of children's perceptual processes in mediating nonshared effects on development has been suggested by a few studies (e.g., Brody, Stoneman, & MacKinnon, 1986; McHale and Pawletko, 1992). In their study of differential maternal treatment of siblings in families with and without a disabled child, McHale and Pawletko (1992) found the poorest levels of child adjustment when children received more positive treatment than a disabled sibling. In contrast, children with able-bodied siblings who received preferential treatment reported the highest levels of adjustment. These researchers suggest that receiving more favorable treatment than a sibling may make a child feel good *except* when the sibling is disabled. That is, children with handicapped siblings may feel guilty and anxious about being treated more positively than a sibling who is struggling with the difficulties of being disabled.

Additionally, McHale and Pawletko's data suggest that the child's interpretations about what is legitimate behavior in a family (e.g., that a disabled child may need more attention than an able-bodied sibling) can impact the siblings' relationship with each other. They found the most positive sibling relationships between a disabled and able-bodied sibling when the latter received more favorable maternal treatment. Hypothetically, the able-bodied child's guilt about receiving preferential treatment may motivate that child to respond with high levels of kindness and concern toward his or her less advantaged sibling. In contrast, the poorest sibling relationships occurred between able-bodied siblings experiencing differential treatment. Presumably, when one child is slighted and one treated specially, the former child may develop feelings of resentment toward the favored child, who may treat the other in a derogatory way because he or she was not worthy of similar parental favor. In sum, McHale and Pawletko's research is an exemplar of how the same family processes may be mediated by children's interpretations and the family context. Clearly, the factors mediating the effects of nonshared environment merit further investigation.

GENETIC INFLUENCE
ON ENVIRONMENTAL MEASURES

At the same time as family researchers have been exploring the significance of genetic findings concerning the nonshared environment, behavioral genetics are reporting a new set of findings that are equally portentous. Several geneticists have asked why genetic analyses should be confined to measures that are usually the outcomes of family process such as depression, antisocial behavior, self esteem, and social responsibility. Whereas differences among individuals along all of these dimensions may be influenced, in part, by genes, other behaviors more typically regarded as part of family process may also be influenced by genes. All of these outcomes can be thought of as transactional processes as well as internal properties of individual persons. A depressed mother may be socially withdrawn, hypersensitive to criticism, and irritable, and this could affect her parenting and marital relationships as well as her interior mood states and self esteem. Thus, it is matter of perspective whether we choose to call a stream of behavior "depression" or "impaired relationships." Given this continuity between intrapersonal and interpersonal processes, it was reasonable to ask whether transactional variables such as parental warmth toward their children, or sibling conflict, or the quality of an adolescents' peer group might also show strong genetic influence.

Two sorts of genetic mechanisms may influence transactional processes. First, the parents' genes may shape, in part, the kinds of perceptions and reaction patterns they have while involved in relationships with others. Second, heritable characteristics of the child might elicit from the parent certain kinds of parenting, stimulate certain kinds of interaction from siblings, and influence the chances of being accepted and retained by certain kinds of peer groups. For example, a fussy infant—whose fussiness is influenced by genetic factors—may, very effectively, elicit irritability in his mother. Or an impulsive adolescent, where impulsivity may be partially shaped by genes, may be more acceptable to a delinquent peer group and be more likely to be retained by such a group.

Using our sample of 720 families (described in detail in the next section), we have recently completed a systematic exploration of genetic influence on a diverse collection of measures of the family environment (Plomin, Reiss, Hetherington, & Howe, 1994). Behavioral genetics model fitting analyses indicated on average approximately 26% of the variance of our environmental measures were explained by genetic differences between children. In some cases, as in a measure of maternal closeness, genetic effects accounted for as much as 51% of the variance. Interestingly, it appears that some dimensions of family experience may show more heritability than others. Our analyses provided moderate support for preliminary evidence in other research that measures of parental closeness (e.g., warmth, cohesion) are mediated more by genetic factors than measures of parental control (Plomin & Bergeman, 1991; Rowe, 1981, 1983).

Additionally, preliminary analyses of the heritability of observer ratings of family environment in our sample suggest family interaction coded by observers is also influenced by genetic factors. Given that the NEAD design hinges on the genetic relatedness of the children, this is particularly true for behavior of children directed at both parents but is less true for parents' behavior directed at their children (T. O'Connor, unpublished data).

The next stage in this research is to discover the specific mechanisms leading from genetic influences to family transactions. As mentioned, one mediating factor may be the temperament or personality of the child. Many other mediating factors are possible including intelligence, perceptual style, and physical appearance. However, the long-term importance of this research lies in sensitivity to confounds in relationships among variables, confounds that now go completely undetected in research on families. If, in any set of research observations, the environmental and outcome variables are influenced by genetic processes, the observed association between the two may be attributable in part or entirely to genetic mechanisms. By failing to identify this kind of confound, we could make serious errors in interpreting developmental models and in designing interventions. Only designs that allow for examination of genetic effects can control for genetic confounding of environment-outcome associations.

For example, the relationship between intellectually stimulating features of the home environment and mental development of toddlers is a well-established finding in family research. However, this relationship holds mainly when the parents and children are genetically related. The relationship is far less for adopting parents and their adoptees (Braungart, Plomin, Fulker, & DeFries, 1992). This suggests that the observed association is attributed, in part, to genes shared by parents and children; these genes influence parents in their structuring of the home environment (perhaps through their influence on the parents' intelligence), and the same genes influence variation in mental development in toddlers.

THE EMERGENCE OF NEW FAMILY RESEARCH DESIGNS AND METHODS TO INTEGRATE GENETIC AND ENVIRONMENTAL DATA

As we have argued above, a new paradigm is emerging that redefines family environments. This paradigm is marked by an increasing number of studies that combine genetic designs with direct measurement of environmental effects. Although more and more professionals are becoming familiar with this new way of looking at families, methods and measures to capture our changing view of child development are only beginning to be explored. The focus of this section is the description of some new tools or methods for family research that have arisen from research integrating environmental and genetic data.

Building on the findings discussed above, the research designs presented below reflect a new set of fundamental assumptions: (1) If environments are child-specific, it is necessary to include more than one child within a family in a research design; (2) "environment" is a multidimensional construct, which includes common exposure and differential experiences. Further, both objective and subjective indices of environment are necessary to fully understand how heritability and perceptual processes may be operating to produce observed effects; and (3) different mechanisms, including genetics, family dynamics and perceptual processes, can mediate environmental effects.

The primary tools emerging from the use of genetic designs to study family environment are methods to distinguish *specific* kinds of environmental effects. For example, for the past 5 years, we have been following a national sample of 720 two-parent families with pairs of same-sex adolescent siblings no more than 4 years apart in age (Reiss et al., 1994). This study (hereafter referred to as NEAD) is a unique combination of socialization and behavioral genetics research in that we have comprehensively assessed the adolescents' family and peer environments with observational and self-report methods in a sample sensitive to genetic effects. Specifically, our sample consists of six groups: families of MZ twins (100% genetically identical); families of DZ twins (50% genetically similar); step families and nondivorced families with full siblings (50% genetic similarity); stepfamilies with half siblings (25% genetic similarity); and step families with unrelated siblings (0% genetic relationship). Not only is this research design yielding an extensive data set on the role of genetics in shaping family and peer processes, it promises to provide more accurate estimates of environmental effects, including nonshared influences, on adolescent development. To date, these kinds of research questions are uncharted terrain because few studies have attempted to examine nonshared environments systematically. The tools we are developing to define and analyze genetic and nonshared environmental effects are discussed in various places in this section.

Whereas NEAD is an example of a research design to specify nonshared environmental effects, research tools to examine the effects of *specified* common environments within families are also emerging. For example, Kendler and his associates (Kendler, Neale, Kessler, Heath, & Eaves, 1992) have examined the relationship between childhood parental loss and adult psychopathology in pairs of female twins. As Kendler's group points out, given the consistency of findings that major psychiatric disorders tend to aggregate in families, examination of environmental sources of familial resemblance could provide important clues to the epidemiology of psychopathology. This approach is an innovative elaboration of prior methods. In earlier twin research, shared or common environment was not specified or even measured directly. Further, whereas epidemiologists have measured environmental risk factors, they have paid little attention to familial aggregation of disorders even when multiple family members are exposed to the same risk factor, such as parental death.

Thus, in setting out to examine familiar data in a new way, Kendler and colleagues (1992) have generated an important set of epidemiological findings, which in and of themselves challenge assumptions built on the behavioral genetics framework. Although a discussion of how and why Kendler and his associates' findings challenge prior behavioral genetics investigations is beyond the scope of this chapter, their work is presented as an exemplar of a design combining genetic and environmental data. Whereas, behavioral geneticists have typically reported the effects of shared environment are negligible, Kendler and colleagues found the best fitting genetic model resulted from inclusion of genetic effects, nonshared and *specified* shared environmental effects. Parental loss as a specified shared environmental variable accounted for between 7.0% and 20.5% of the tendency for disorders to aggregate in siblings, depending on the disorder, and for between 1.5% and 5.1% of the liability to disorder.

Importantly, Kendler's group found no effects of shared family environment on the etiology of depression when they used traditional methods (i.e., treating family environment as an unspecified latent variable rather than a specified, measured variable). Further, they report that the effects of parental loss differed qualitatively depending on whether the twins experienced parental separation or parental death. Specifically, parental death was associated with phobias or panic disorder; whereas parental separation was associated with major depression, generalized anxiety disorder, and panic disorder. Kendler and colleagues (1992, p. 114) suggest this type of "genetic epidemiological" design is an important advance in quantifying the relative impact of environmental risk factors (e.g., parental loss) on liability to illness compared to other risk factors, such as genetic predisposition. Additionally, the genetic epidemiological design can be an important tool in exploring how exposure to a common environmental risk factor can contribute to familial aggregation.

By nature of the two-sibling design prerequisite for genetic modeling, research in this emerging paradigm provides some unique opportunities to explore important mechanisms of family process in new ways. For example, the function and impact of differential treatment for child and family well-being are topics that have been widely discussed by structural family therapists (e.g., Minuchin, 1974). Yet, little empirical research has been done in this area. Building on behavioral genetics findings, several family investigators are currently exploring how to assess nonshared experiences within families, including differential treatment, with the objective of learning about features of the family system that might develop and maintain separate worlds for siblings in the same family.

As an example of the opportunities provided by two-sibling designs, in NEAD we have begun to study the hypothesis that nonshared environments may arise as a family-level strategy for managing conflict within the family system (Reiss et al., 1994). Briefly, based on clinical data that some children may be triangulated into a troubled marriage (e.g., Gilbert et al., 1984), nonshared environment may reflect different triadic experiences in the family. Whereas one child may be pulled into a troubled marriage, another may be distanced (e.g., in the case of scapegoating). Recent data suggest that conflict in the marriage may stimulate sibling conflict (MacKinnon, 1988, 1989). Siblings then create a nonshared microenvironment in the sibling subsystem by distancing from each other. One suggested process siblings may use to create space in the relationship is "deidentification" whereby the siblings try to make themselves as different as possible from one another (Schachter, 1982). In sum, we are hypothesizing that marital instability may drive a process of increased polarization of environments, leading to more nonshared or unique experiences in the family. In exploring hypotheses of this type, while accounting for genetic mediation of environmental and outcome variables, we aim to describe what relational configurations create unique microenvironments within the family for each child.

Relatedly, designs that integrate genetic and environmental data can be used to examine how social and genetic influences may interact to shape family process. In the NEAD project, we have begun to examine family processes that may create nonshared experiences for full siblings raised in a blended family that full siblings in nondivorced families may not experience. Importantly, because these two types of siblings are both 50% genetically similar, we can begin to tease apart differential treatment due to social processes from that due to genetic effects. Further, we are beginning to explore how much of the nonshared experiences of stepsiblings might be mediated by the parents' beliefs about their genetic likenesses to their children. To examine this question, we have constructed two new instruments to assess parents' beliefs about what kind of characteristics are heritable and their perceptions of their similarity to their children on each of these characteristics. Given that people have different ideas about the proportion of genes transmitted to children by mothers and fathers, we are predicting variation in beliefs about heritability within all the family types in the NEAD sample. Ideally, these instruments will allow us to explore the role of subjective genetic linkages in nonshared experiences.

Initial analyses of the NEAD sample provide tentative evidence for the noncomparability between step and nondivorced families. For example, the correlation between full siblings in stepfamilies on a measure of maternal closeness (when the mother was the biological parent of both children) was .04 as compared to the .28 correlation obtained for maternal closeness for full siblings in nondivorced families. Thus, siblings in stepfamilies do not seem to have as similar experiences of closeness with their mothers as siblings in nondivorced families. Analyses of measures of disciplinary strategies, threatening parent–child interaction, and parent monitoring and control of child's activities also indicated more shared experiences between siblings in nondivorced families than in stepfamilies (Plomin, Reiss, & Neiderhiser, 1994). Interestingly, we did not find any effect of parent–offspring genetic relatedness on similarity of sibling experiences. That is, although the full siblings in the stepfamilies were biologically related only to their mothers, our measures did not indicate greater similarity between siblings' experiences with mothers than with their stepfathers.

Part of the challenge in utilizing two-sibling designs to study family dynamics is how to measure differential sibling experiences. One general approach we have used to explore the linkage between unique family experiences and child outcomes is the sibling difference score (Reiss et al., 1994). Although we are not necessarily arguing that the difference score approach is the best way to capture unique family experiences, we briefly describe it here as an example of how this new paradigm is forcing researchers to adapt familiar tools to look at data in novel ways.

In brief, two kinds of difference scores can be computed: relative difference scores and absolute difference scores. Relative difference scores are calculated by selecting some invariant property of the children, such as birth order, and systematically subtracting the score of one sibling from another based on that property (e.g., subtract the youngest from the oldest). Absolute difference scores are simply the unsigned differences between the two siblings. Importantly, relative and absolute difference scores can be uncorrelated and may index different environmental processes. Additional detail about the use of difference scores in family designs can be found in Rovine (in press).

Our recent report on the relationship of the Symbolic Aggression subscale of the Conflict Tactics Scale (Straus, 1979) to adolescent outcomes in the NEAD sample using the difference score technique (Reiss et al., in press) is an example of how the two kinds of difference scores address different family phenomena. In general, the Conflict Tactics Scale assesses a family's approach to conflict resolution, with the Symbolic Aggression subscale tapping intermediate levels of aggression such as "threatened to hit." In the NEAD sample, the mean of relative difference scores ranged from .25 to 1.85 depending on reporter. In contrast, the mean of absolute difference scores ranged from 2.35 to 5.54, with children's scores indicating more differential parental treatment than parents reported. Because only relative difference scores are signed, they are widely accepted as a sensitive index of birth-order effects (i.e., negative scores indicate the younger child receives more of the given variable than the older sibling, and positive scores indicate the converse). Given that the relative differences were almost zero, it appears there is no systematic birth order effect across families on threatening parent–child interactions.

As part of a series of analyses to next determine the extent of genetic and nonshared environmental influences on children's outcomes, we noted that siblings reported little or no common experience in threatening parent–child interactions. These results suggest substantial nonshared effects in symbolic aggression in families. To answer the question of whether such differential parental treatment has important implications for development, we first calculated the relative difference in experienced symbolic aggression by subtracting the younger child's scores from the older child. These relative difference scores were then correlated with a standardized measure of internalizing and externalizing symptoms (Zill, 1985) based on the Achenbach Child Behavior Checklist (Achenbach & Edelbrock, 1983). Correlations using absolute difference scores were computed separately.

Hypothetically, these analyses can inform our understanding of how parental aggression increases the risk of child dysfunction. For example, if the relative difference score correlates positively with symptomatology for older children and negatively for younger children, these results suggest that any child who has more aggressive interactions with parents is at risk for psychological disturbance, regardless of whether the child is the older or younger sibling. Additionally, if there is no interaction between the level of aggression experienced and symptomatology (i.e., the effects are comparable across families regardless of the mean level of symbolic aggression), then it would appear that it is the *relative* difference between the siblings that matters most for child well-being. That is, even in a relatively nonaggressive household, the child who experiences more threatening behavior will be uniquely at risk for psychopathology, whereas his or her sibling will be protected from it. This type of family process would rely on children being very keenly sensitive to differential treatment in the family.

The logic of absolute difference scores implies different family mechanisms. Assuming a positive correlation between absolute difference scores and symptomatology and no interaction effect for mean level of aggression in the families, these findings would suggest that parental aggression does not uniquely affect the targeted child. Instead, if either child experiences aggressive behavior, both would be at risk. We have described two kinds of social comparison processes that could lead to this type of effect: (1) Even if one child is mostly singled out for the aggressive interaction, both children will show signs of disturbance in anticipation that either he or she could be next. (2) Obvious differential treatment may signal to the children that family norms allow them to experience very different rewards and punishments, isolating the children within their own worlds.

Our preliminary results from this strategy were fairly consistent regardless of reporter. First, absolute and relative difference scores both were generally positively related to symptomatology. That is, high levels of differential treatment are associated with high levels of disturbance, and high relative difference scores were related to more symptomatology for older children and less for younger siblings. More detailed analyses indicated that relative differences appear more important to child functioning at high levels of family aggression, whereas absolute differences contributed most to variance in child well-being at low levels of family aggression. Further, absolute differences had a greater impact for full and half siblings, in contrast to relative difference scores, which were more important between stepsiblings than in the other two groups. Finally, boys seemed more affected by large relative differences in contrast to girls who were more impacted by absolute differences. Given that children would need to be very sensitive to differential treatment to pick up absolute differences in families with typically low levels of aggression, we have tentatively proposed that parents and children must be very close or connected to one another for children to detect small shifts in parental affect which had been expressed toward themselves but which were now being directed more at a sibling. Girls may be more susceptible to this type of family process because, as some studies suggest (Hill, 1988) they tend to be more emotionally embedded in the family system than boys during adolescence. Similarly, families with full and half-siblings have lived together for an extended period of time, so they may be more attuned to family norms and behavior patterns. Finally, low aggression homes may allow more intimacy between parents and children, which could lead to enhanced sensitivity to one another's actions.

Other investigators have begun exploring alternative ways to capitalize on multiple sibling designs to further delineate what kinds of childrearing variations are most predictive of child health and psychopathology. In their longitudinal study of 178 1- to 10-year-old children and their 12- to 18-year-old siblings, Tejerina-Allen, Wagner, and Cohen (1994) attempted to contrast the effects of differential parenting on children in different families with differences in parenting of children in the same family. That is, does parenting universally affect children the same way regardless of what family they belong to (e.g., exposure to high amounts of conflict always increases risk of antisocial behavior), or is it really the experience of being treated in a particular way within a specified family environment that impacts development (e.g., although a child is exposed to a small amount of conflict, if that child experiences more conflict than his or her siblings, is he or she at risk for antisocial behavior)?

This direction of research is particularly important in light of recent developmental models suggesting that within normal ranges, childrearing variations between families are of little consequence for child well-being. That is, wide variations in environments within this normal range can present "functionally equivalent" opportunities for normal developmental patterns (Scarr, 1992). Although the work of Tejerina-Allen and colleagues cannot fully test such a hypothesis because their design does not allow them to estimate genetic contributions to outcomes and variance in environmental experiences, the method they propose is a first step toward defining "the normal range" of childrearing variation.

In brief, Tejerina-Allen et al. (1994) used the average parenting experienced by the siblings as an index of shared or common parenting environment. The average parenting across families was considered to reflect variation between different families in childrearing (as in a simple analysis of variance model). In contrast, the degree of nonshared or unique parenting experienced within the same family was estimated by calculating the difference score between siblings in the same family (parenting directed at older sibling minus parenting directed toward younger sibling). The effects of age and gender were removed from all analyses. Further, difference scores were partialed out of analyses focusing on between-family variations to get a clear picture of how influential variation in childrearing across families was to child wellbeing. Likewise, the average level of parenting in the families (the shared environment) was partialed out of the difference score analyses in order to cleanly examine the impact of within-family differential treatment on child outcome. A subset of the analyses examined how well shared and nonshared experiences predicted the differences in depression, suicidal ideation, and oppositional behavior of children in the same family (calculated by subtracting the younger child's score on the outcome measure from the older child's score).

The results of these analyses suggest certain relational experiences are risky for all children across families, whereas other patterns of interaction are uniquely risk-producing for children if they are treated differently than their siblings. For example, Tejerina-Allen and colleagues (1994) report that close maternal–child relationships seem universally to protect children from suicidal ideation regardless of whether a sibling in the same family receives more or less maternal affection. However, the sibling in the family who receives the most punishment is uniquely at risk for higher suicidal ideation. These results can be viewed as evidence that both childrearing variations across and within families are consequential for child well-being. However, a specific parenting behavior may be most likely to promote child psychopathology in the context of differential treatment of children within the same family. Interestingly, differential sibling exposure to maternal warmth and supportiveness was only marginally related to sibling differences in suicidal ideation, suggesting the sibling with higher suicidal ideation does not necessarily see his or her mother as less emotionally supportive than the sibling with lower suicidal ideation.

Analyses conducted with the NEAD sample (Reiss et al., 1994) show quite similar results. Specifically, differential exposure to parental punitiveness is more highly correlated with adolescent antisocial and depressive symptoms than differential receipt of parental warmth and support. In fact the more parental negativity is targeted to another sibling in the family, the less antisocial behavior is shown by a particular child. In other words, having a sibling who is treated more punitively by your parents than you are can reduce your risk for psychopathology. The effects of such a "sibling barricade" would be unobservable in traditional single-child designs.

CONCLUSION

The limited scope of this chapter did not permit us to fully discuss the theoretical and methodological debate involved in integrating genetic data into family research. Within the NEAD team alone, which unites developmental psychologists, behavioral geneticists, and family researchers, we have run through several models already, and we have not yet tackled the challenge of our longitudinal data. Each of the models we have explored has represented a minirevolution, brought on by the crisis of a prior model failing to fit the data. However, as we have argued in this chapter, each of these crises, brought on by the difficulties of integrating genetic and environmental data into family research, represents an opportunity. Thus, a new model emerges, and we hope we are getting closer to understanding how families work.

ACKNOWLEDGMENTS

This chapter is partly based on a project entitled Nonshared Environment in Adolescent Development. The project is supported by the National Institute of Mental Health (MH-43373 and MH-48825) and the William T. Grant Foundation.

REFERENCES

Achenbach, T. M., & Edelbrock, C. (1983). *Manual for the child behavior checklist and revised child behavior profile.* Burlington, VT: Queen City Printers.

Baker, L. A., & Daniels, D. (1990). Nonshared environmental influences and personality differences in adult twins. *Journal of Personality and Social Psychology, 58*(1), 103–110.

Baumrind, D. (1991). The influence of parenting style on adolescent competence and substance use. *Journal of Early Adolescence, 11*(1), 56–95.

Braungart, J. M., Plomin, R., Fulker, D. W., & DeFries, J. C. (1992). Genetic influence on the home environment during infancy: A sibling adoption study of the home. *Developmental Psychology, 28*(6), 1048–1055.

Brody, G., & Stoneman, Z. (1994). Sibling relationships and their association with parental differential treatment. In E. M. Hetherington, D. Reiss, & R. Plomin (Eds.), *Separate social worlds of siblings: The impact of nonshared environment on development.* Hillsdale, NJ: Lawrence Erlbaum Associates.

Brody, G. H., Stoneman, Z., & Burke, M. (1987). Child temperaments, maternal differential behavior and sibling relationships. *Developmental Psychology, 23*(3), 354–362.

Brody, G. H., Stoneman, Z., & MacKinnon, C. E. (1986). Contributions of maternal childrearing practices and play contexts to sibling interactions. *Journal of Applied Developmental Psychology, 7,* 225–236.

Bryant, B. K., & Crockenberg, S. B. (1980). Correlates and dimensions of prosocial behavior: A study of female siblings with their mothers. *Child Development, 51,* 529–544.

Daniels, D., Dunn, J., Furstenberg, F. F., Jr., & Plomin, R. (1985). Environmental differences within the family and adjustment differences within pairs of adolescent siblings. *Child Development, 56,* 764–774.

Daniels, D., & Plomin, R. (1985). Differential experience of siblings in the same family. *Developmental Psychology, 21*(5), 747–760.

Deal, J. E., Halverson, C. F., Jr., & Wampler, K. S. (in press). Sibling similarity as an individual difference variable: Within family measures of shared environment. In E. M. Hetherington, D. Reiss, & R. Plomin (Eds.), *Separate social worlds of siblings: The impact of nonshared environment on development.* Hillsdale, NJ: Lawrence Erlbaum Associates.

Dunn, J. & McGuire, S. (1994). Young children's nonshared experiences: A summary of studies in Cambridge and Colorado. In E. M. Hetherington, D. Reiss, & R. Plomin (Eds.), *Separate social worlds of siblings: The impact of nonshared environment on development.* Hillsdale, NJ: Lawrence Erlbaum Associates.

Dunn, J., & Plomin, R. (1990). *Separate lives: Why are siblings so different?* New York: Basic Books.

Dunn, J., Stocker, C., & Plomin, R. (1990). Assessing the sibling relationship. *Journal of Child Psychology and Psychiatry, 31,* 983–991.

Forehand, R., Thomas, A. M., Wierson, M., Brody, G., & Fauber, R. (1990). Role of maternal functioning and parenting skills in adolescent functioning following parental divorce. *Journal of Abnormal Psychology, 99*(3), 278–283.

Gilbert, R., Christensen, A., & Margolin, G. (1984). Patterns of alliances in nondistressed and multiproblem families. *Family Process, 23,* 75–87.

Hill, J. P. (1988). Adapting to menarche: Familial control and conflict. In M. R.

Gunnar & W. A. Collins (Ed.), *Development during the transition to adolescence* (pp. 43–77). Hillsdale, NJ: Lawrence Erlbaum Associates.

Hoffman, L. W. (1991). The influence of the family environment on personality: Accounting for sibling differences. *Psychological Bulletin, 110*(2), 187–203.

Kendler, K. S., Neale, M. C., Kessler, R. C., Heath, A. C., & Eaves, L. J. (1992). Childhood parental loss and adult psychopathology in women: A twin study perspective. *Archives of General Psychiatry, 49*, 109–116.

Koch, H. L. (1960). The relation of certain formal attributes of siblings to attitudes held toward each other and toward their parents. *Monographs of the Society for Research in Child Development, 25*(4, Serial No. 78).

Loehlin, J. C., & Nichols, R. C. (1976). *Heredity, environment and personality.* Austin, TX: University of Texas Press.

MacKinnon, C. E. (1988). Influences on sibling relations in families with married and divorced parents: Family form or family quality. *Journal of Family Issues, 9*(4), 469–477.

MacKinnon, C. E. (1989). An observational investigation of sibling interactions in married and divorced families. *Developmental Psychology, 25*(1), 36–44.

McGillicuddy-DeLisi, A. V. (1990). Parental beliefs within the family context: Development of a research program. In I. E. Sigel & G. H. Brody (Eds.), *Methods of family research: Biographies of research projects:* Vol. 1: *Normal families* (pp. 53–85). Hillsdale, NJ: Lawrence Erlbaum Associates.

McGoldrick, M., & Carter, E. A. (1982). The family life cycle. In F. Walsh (Ed.), *Normal family processes* (1st ed., pp. 167–195). New York: Guilford Press.

McHale, S. M., & Pawletko, T. M. (1992). Differential treatment of siblings in two family contexts. *Child Development, 63*, 68–81.

Minuchin, S. (1974). *Families and family therapy.* Cambridge: Harvard University Press.

Plomin, R. (1989). Environment and genes: Determinants of behavior. *American Psychologist, 44*(2), 105–111.

Plomin, R. (1990). *Nature and nurture: An introduction to human behavioral genetics.* Pacific Grove, CA: Brooks/Cole.

Plomin, R., & Bergeman, C. S. (1991). The nature of nurture: Genetic influence on "environmental" measures. *Behavior and Brain Sciences, 14*, 373–386.

Plomin, R., Chipuer, H. M., & Neiderhiser, J. (1994). Behavioral genetic evidence for the importance of nonshared environment. In E. M. Hetherington, D. Reiss, & R. Plomin (Eds.), *Separate social worlds of siblings: The impact of nonshared environment on development.* Hillsdale, NJ: Lawrence Erlbaum Associates.

Plomin, R., & Daniels, D. (1987). Why are children in the same family so different from one another? *Behavioral and Brain Sciences, 10*, 1–16.

Plomin, R., & Foch, T. (1981). Sex differences and individual differences. *Child Development, 52*, 383–385.

Plomin, R., Reiss, D., Hetherington, E. M., & Howe, G. H. (1994). Nature and nurture: Genetic contributions to measures of the family environment. *Developmental Psychology.*

Reiss, D., Plomin, R., Hetherington, E. M., Rovine, M., Tryon, A., & Stanley-Hagen, M. (1994). The separate world of teenage siblings: An introduction to the study of the nonshared environment and adolescent development. In E. M. Hetherington, D. Reiss & R. Plomin (Eds.), *Separate social worlds of siblings: The impact of nonshared environment on development.* Hillsdale, NJ: Lawrence Erlbaum Associates.

Rovine, M. J. (1994). Estimating nonshared environment using sibling discrepancy scores. In E. M. Hetherington, D. Reiss & R. Plomin (Eds.), *Separate social worlds of siblings: The impact of nonshared environment on development*. Hillsdale, NJ: Lawrence Erlbaum Associates.

Rowe, D. C. (1981). Environmental and genetic influences on dimensions of perceived parenting: A twin study. *Developmental Psychology, 17*, 203–208.

Rowe, D. C. (1983). A biometrical analysis of perceptions of family environment: A study of twin and singleton siblings. *Child Development, 54*, 416–423.

Rowe, D. C., Rodgers, J. L., & Meseck-Bushey, S. (1992). Sibling delinquency and the family environment: Shared and unshared influences. *Child Development, 63*, 59–67.

Scarr, S. (1992). Developmental theories for the 1990s: Development and individual differences. *Child Development, 63*, 1–19.

Scarr, S., & Grajeck, S. (1982). Similarities and differences among siblings. In M. E. Lamb & B. Sutton-Smith (Eds.), *Sibling relationships: Their nature and significance across the lifespan* (pp. 357–381). Hillsdale, NJ: Lawrence Erlbaum Associates.

Scarr, S., & Weinberg, R. A. (1991). The nature-nurture problem revisited: The Minnesota Adoption Studies. In I. E. Sigel & G. H. Brody (Eds.), *Methods of family research: Biographies of research projects: Vol. 1: Normal families* (pp. 121–152). Hillsdale, NJ: Lawrence Erlbaum Associates.

Schachter, F. F. (1982). Sibling deidentification and split-parent identification: A family tetrad. In M. E. Lamb & B. Sutton-Smith (Eds.), *Sibling relationships: Their nature and significance across the lifespan* (pp. 123–151). Hillsdale, NJ: Lawrence Erlbaum Associates.

Schooler, C. (1972). Birth order effects: note here, not now! *Psychological Bulletin, 78*, 161–175.

Shaffer, D., Phillips, I., Enzer, N. B., Silverman, M. M., & Anthony, V. (Eds.). (1989). *Prevention of mental disorders, alcohol and other drug use in children and adolescents*. Rockville, MD: Office of Substance Abuse Prevention.

Stocker, C., Dunn, J., & Plomin, R. (1989). Sibling relationships: Links with child temperament, maternal behavior, and family structure. *Child Development, 60*, 715–727.

Straus, M. A. (1979). Measuring intrafamily conflict and violence: The Conflict Tactics Scale. *Journal of Marriage and the Family, 41*, 75–85.

Tejerina-Allen, M., Wagner, B. W., & Cohen, P. (1994). A comparison of across-family and within-family parenting predictors of adolescent psychopathology and suicidal ideation. In E. M. Hetherington, D. Reiss, & R. Plomin (Eds.), *Separate social worlds of siblings: The impact of nonshared environment on development*. Hillsdale, NJ: Lawrence Erlbaum Associates.

Zahn-Waxler, C., Robinson, J., & Emde, R. N. (1992). The development of empathy in twins. *Developmental Psychology, 28*(6), 1038–1047.

Zill, N. (1985). *Behavior problems scales developed from the 1981 Child Health Supplement to the National Health Interview Survey*. Washington, DC: Child Trends, Inc.

PART III

Emerging Family Forms and Challenges

CHAPTER 6

DUAL-EARNER FAMILIES IN CONTEXT
Managing Family and Work Systems

*Chaya S. Piotrkowski and
Diane Hughes*

INTRODUCTION

Families fulfill a number of formidable functions that include the socialization of children, the care of dependents, and the maintenance of the household. They manage the psychodynamics of family life by regulating cohesion and conflict and by helping family members interpret, organize, and recuperate from daily experiences in the outside world. Families also develop and maintain relations with extended kin networks, their communities, and larger social institutions. Historically, the gender-based division of labor in so-called traditional male-breadwinner families structured how these normative family functions were performed: Men supported the household financially; women—even at considerable cost to their own development—were responsible for most other functions, including providing a "haven in a heartless world" (Lasch, 1977), a private sphere distinct from the public world of work.

Although these functions and their associated tasks have remained relatively constant since industrialization, the shift from the traditional male-breadwinner family to the contemporary dual-earner family structure has resulted in new challenges in performing them. As used here, the term "dual-earner" refers to two-parent families in which both partners participate in market work for pay. Our emphasis is on dual-earner families with children because they are most common. We do not use the term "dual-worker" because it obscures unpaid household work.

Almost two-thirds of all two-parent families are now dual-earners (Hayghe, 1990), a number that will increase as women of childbearing age continue to enter the workforce. Although the dual-earner family has many benefits, especially for women, it comes with a host of new challenges. Unlike male-breadwinner families, dual-earners must perform three jobs: two market jobs for pay and one unpaid job in the family. When both parents work outside the home, who cares for children, does the shopping, goes to parent–teacher conferences, finds time to play and talk? When can husbands and wives spend private time together when both have worked hard in their paid jobs and come home each evening to their children and to household chores? And, equally important, how do family members make decisions about these matters?

Contemporary dual-earner couples face a new dilemma: In a social context that is largely nonsupportive, they have to do more work than their parents did while reshaping family roles, with little to guide them. Thus, traditional and dual-earner families differ in the challenges they face in performing basic family tasks. The ways of being a family can no longer be assumed, as dual-earner families invent new paradigms for being a family (Walsh, 1989). But when resources are limited and social policies and practices constrain the solutions and adaptations families can find, family tasks turn into challenges that can become stressors.

In this chapter we provide a framework for conceptualizing the normative tasks that dual-earner families must accomplish that is informed both by research and by the experiences of dual-earner families in our society. We begin our discussion with an overview of historical factors that have given rise to the dual-earner family in its current form. Next, we describe contextual factors that shape both these central normative tasks and families' solutions to the difficulties they confront in effectively accomplishing them. Finally, we describe the tasks themselves, focusing on the new challenges in managing housework and childcare, two paid jobs, and family relationships.

HISTORICAL BACKGROUND

Two important social and economic changes have given rise to the contemporary dual-earner family. The first was the separation of work from family-based activities that occurred with industrialization and the centralization of work in the 19th century (e.g., Scott & Tilly, 1975; Smelser, 1959; Thompson, 1966). In preindustrial societies, subsistence activities and production for exchange centered around the family "homestead" (Turner, 1971). All family members, even young children, participated in the production of goods, food, and clothing. However, this situation changed dramatically with industrialization, when productive activity became centralized outside the home. Eventually, protective legislation restricted child labor and the hours women could be employed in certain industries (Baron, 1981), thereby restricting women's participation in market work for pay.

By the early 20th century, only about 10% of white women were employed outside the home (Chafe, 1976; Scott & Tilly, 1975).[1] They tended to be single and to leave the labor force upon marriage, becoming economically dependent on their husbands. The cult of domesticity and the domestic science movement reinforced the idea that women's natural place was in the home, caring for the physical and moral development of children and nurturing husbands after their daily travails in the world outside (Cowan, 1976; Ehrenreich & English, 1975). Wives were housewives, responsible for housework and childcare; men were breadwinners, responsible for market work. Long working hours away from family members most likely hindered men from taking an active part in domestic life (Kanter, 1977). A new family ideal emerged: that of the housewife who could—and should—remain at home because her husband was a good provider. This family ideal eventually extended from the middle to the working classes. By 1940 only 9% of all families were dual-earners (Hayghe, 1990).

The second change was the dramatic and consistent increase in the labor force participation rate of married women since World War II. Fueled by the necessity for additional labor, employment rates of married women rose dramatically during the War to nearly 22% (Hayghe, 1990). After a brief postwar decline, the labor force participation of wives continued to grow steadily, with sharp increases in the 1960s and thereafter, particularly among mothers. In 1988, 64% of white married women with children under 18 and almost 76% of their African-American counterparts were in the labor force. Fifty-six percent of white married women and 72% of African-American married women with children under 6 were employed in 1988 (US Bureau of the Census, 1990).

In the last 15 years or so, the fastest growing segment of the female labor force has been women with very young children. In 1970, approximately one-fourth of married women with children 1 year of age or younger were employed. By 1988, this figure had risen to more than one-half (Select Committee on Children, Youth, and Families, 1989). Forty-four percent of all women return to the labor force within the first 6 months after the birth

---

[1]To some extent, early United States Census data probably underestimated the financial contributions women made to families (Tentler, 1979; Aldous, 1981). Women frequently worked on farms. Married working-class women often took in boarders and did laundry at home, work-for-pay that was largely invisible. Moreover, nonwhite women historically maintained higher labor-force participation rates, making substantial economic contributions to the family.

of their child. More than two-thirds of these return on a full-time basis (O'Connell, 1989). In this decade, half of new workers entering the labor force will be women (Fullerton, 1987; Kutscher, 1987).

These increases in employment among married women and mothers have resulted in a dramatic decline in the traditional family. In 1975, 43% of all married-couple families with children were dual-earners. By 1988, such dual-earner families represented 63% of all families (Hayghe, 1990). The child born into a two-parent family is now more likely than not to have a mother who is employed outside the home. Dual-earner families have emerged as a dominant family form not only because women want to be employed but also because of economic necessity and declines in real family income. Most families in the United States today require two incomes to maintain their standard of living. Those without two-earners may have difficulty keeping poverty at bay and may see their real incomes decline (Hayghe, 1989).

CONTEXTS FOR UNDERSTANDING DUAL-EARNER FAMILIES

To appreciate the particular challenges dual-earner families face and the strategies they develop in meeting them, the contexts of family life must be acknowledged. Of particular relevance are the social-structural, cultural, and developmental contexts. The social-structural context includes the social class structure, workplace policies and practices, the balance of power between home and work, gender relations, and public policies regarding families. The cultural context includes the beliefs, attitudes, and values held by individuals and families, by ethnic groups, and by society as a whole. The content and structure of family tasks also change throughout the family life cycle, which is driven by the birth, development, and eventual departure of children.

Some contexts are invariant for almost all dual-earner families. One overarching context is the essential imbalance of power between workplace and home. Although individual families may shape the choice of their members to change jobs or forgo employment altogether, overall they have little individual power to change workplace policies and practices to better suit their needs. Therefore, families accommodate to the workplace more than the workplace accommodates to them. Another important and invariant power asymmetry is gender inequality, which infuses work and family life (Thompson & Walker, 1989). Gender inequality means that wives are paid less than husbands, influencing family decisions about who takes time off for the care of a sick child, whose job takes a "backseat," and so forth.

The public policy context also strongly affects dual-earner families. Especially important are policies regarding family leaves from work and the provision of affordable, high-quality childcare. Although there is some state-to-state variation, in general, the United States is notoriously behind other developed countries in its provision of policy supports for families, especially two-earners (Zigler & Lang, 1991). Other developed Western countries provide paid paternity and maternity leaves and affordable, high-quality, out-of-home childcare for all who need it (Allen, 1988; Kamerman, Kahn, & Kingston, 1983; Zigler & Frank, 1988). In the United States, the struggle to provide unpaid family leave has been a long one, and high-quality childcare is unaffordable and unavailable to most families, except the most affluent. As a result, each dual-earner family struggles to invent its own solutions to the problems caused by a paucity of coherent and supportive public policies.

Societal attitudes toward male and female roles in the family are yet another context common to dual-earner families. The family is still viewed as a woman's domain, so that women continue to take primary responsibility for children and the elderly. Thus, men's and women's family roles lag behind changes in women's employment roles. However, some attitudes have undergone change. For example, women's work outside the home has become relatively acceptable, childrearing increasingly is viewed as the responsibility of both parents (e.g., Harris & Associates, 1981; Szinovacz, 1984), and men are increasing somewhat the time they spend in household work, particularly childcare. But whereas the employment of mothers with school-aged children has become more socially acceptable, the employment of mothers with very young children has not (Thornton, 1989).

Whereas the prevailing sex-role ideology is a common context for families, notions about the proper division of work within the family and the meaning of employment vary with ethnic group membership.[2] For example, married African-American women historically have maintained higher labor-force participation rates than their white counterparts (Beckett, 1976), with African-American women and their husbands defining women's occupational roles as part of their obligation to the family (Leggon, 1983). This has been accompanied by supportive family and community ideologies.

Other contexts vary systematically as well. Social class is a powerful structural force that influences life in dual-earner families. Occupational position and socioeconomic status affect experiences at work, orientations toward jobs, remuneration, material and other resources, and even values (e.g., Kohn, 1959; Piotrkowski & Katz, 1982). Past research on dual-earner families has tended to focus on the special normative tasks of a visible minority of upper socioeconomic, "dual-career" families. Careers offer greater self-determination and autonomy than most jobs do and substantial financial rewards, all of which facilitate the integration of work and family roles.

---

[2]Within the constraints of the limited available research, in this chapter we use African-Americans to illustrate how cultural contexts can shape the experiences of dual-earner families.

However, most men and women in dual-earner families have jobs that offer limited opportunities for advancement and control and inadequate pay, necessitating two breadwinners for each family. Lacking financial and other resources to manage work and family responsibilities, normative family tasks become difficult and stressful. In this chapter, we concentrate primarily on the majority of these low- and middle-income dual-earner families.

Workplace policies regarding families also can vary. At best, such policies can include paid family leave to care for a new baby or adopted child and paid health benefits while one is on leave; provisions for sick children; flexible scheduling; employer-supported childcare such as on- or near-site childcare, resource and referral services, and various forms of financial assistance (e.g., dependent-care deductions and childcare vouchers). Although such family-friendly policies facilitate the functioning of dual-earner families, currently few workplaces provide adequate programs for their employees, even though awareness of the problems has increased. Large employers are more likely than small ones to provide some assistance (Hayghe, 1988).

Workplace policies and practices also structure how jobs are to be carried out. Job design can make jobs more or less stressful and demanding, with psychological and physical consequences for husbands and wives that families also must handle (Piotrkowski, 1979; Piotrkowski & Staines, 1991). When both parents are employed, job stressors may be doubled.

How the workplace structures time is especially important for dual-earner families, who must mesh the schedules of two employed adults. Although most people work a standard work week, many work evenings, night times, and/or weekends. Some jobs require employees to be away from home for extended periods of time. These variations in work schedules structure the rhythms of daily life by determining the pattern and length of daily absences from home (Staines & Pleck, 1983), with important implications for how dual-earner families care for and socialize their children, perform housework, and regulate intimacy and conflict.

A final significant source of variation is the developmental context. Dual-earners face qualitatively different tasks throughout their life cycles, and therefore they experience greater developmental discontinuities than traditional male-breadwinner families. For example, job and family demands are especially high and resources limited in young dual-earner families, who face the daunting task of finding high-quality, affordable childcare for infants and toddlers. When their children enter school, dual-earner families face the new tasks of locating before- and after-school care and coordinating their work schedules with the demands created by their children's increasing involvement in extracurricular activities. Because of the lack of institutional and policy supports, dual-earner families are required to be especially inventive as they juggle such competing demands. For many dual-earner families, this translates into increased stress. In contrast, in male-breadwinner families, mothers are available, if pressed, to manage these tasks.

CONFRONTING THE CHALLENGES

Dual-earner families face common tasks. But with few supports, these tasks become challenges as parents struggle to accomplish family work, including the care of their children, to manage their jobs, and to maintain their relationships within the family.

Family Work

Pleck (1977) coined the term "family work" to represent the household chores and childcare tasks that must be performed by families to maintain the household and its members. In traditional families, the unspoken assumption is that women are responsible for family work, whereas in contemporary dual-earner families, managing housework and childcare are major challenges.

Despite women's changing roles outside the family, traditional sex-role attitudes largely shape dual-earners' approach to family work. As noted above, in most families, women still do the lion's share of housework, regardless of ethnicity or wives' employment or socioeconomic status, so that women in dual-earner families carry two jobs (Hochschild & Machung, 1990). Many factors inhibit men's participation in family work: the idea that family work is "women's work" and the general devaluation of what women do; the lack of male role models for sharing family work; men's inexperience; and even women's difficulty in sharing control over the household domain. In fact, men do not appreciably increase the number of hours spent in housework when their wives are employed, and their family work is relatively insensitive to the number of hours their wives work outside the home (Hiller & Philliber, 1986; Barnett & Baruch, 1987; Spitze, 1988). Some studies have reported that women do two to five times more family work than their husbands (e.g., Berk, 1985; Rexroat & Shehan, 1987; Thompson & Walker, 1989). Although employed women manage their load by lowering their standards for housework, working fewer hours, finding jobs with some flexibility, and giving up personal time (Piotrkowski & Repetti, 1984), this workload imbalance may lead to marital conflict (Walsh, 1989).

The gender differential in the performance of family work is magnified at earlier stages of the family life cycle, when the family workload is greatest. The addition of young children increases household chores dramatically (Walker & Woods, 1976). Laundry, changing diapers, preparing meals, cleaning up children's toys—all of these increase the sheer amount of work to be accomplished. Most researchers find that women assume a greater share of the expanding family workload, even if they are employed (Belsky, Lang, & Rovine, 1985; Gray, Lovejoy, Piotrkowski, & Bond, 1990; MacDermid, Huston, & McHale, 1990; Rexroat & Shehan, 1987). One can imagine the scenario: Even if couples shared family work prior to the birth of the child, the new mother begins to take on a greater proportion of the family work because she is home. As the father, in turn, becomes the primary breadwinner, his work hours may increase (see Gray et al., 1990), and his job takes priority. Thus, the couple assumes more traditional gender roles, which can solidify further with the arrival of a second child (Walsh, 1989). Moreover, for dual-earner families, the combination of job and family demands can easily lead to role overload from too much to do, to interrole conflict and to strain in managing work–family relations.

The sheer amount of work to be done, the new feminist values that women and many men endorse, and the increased power women have gained as breadwinners have resulted in some renegotiation of family work. Husbands' increased participation in family work appears to be partly a function of their wives earnings' relative to their own and their wives' occupational prestige (Marat & Finlay, 1984; Model, 1981; Spitze, 1988; Scanzoni, 1978). Reviewing the available research, Pleck (1990) concludes that fathers have been increasing their share of family work. Much of this increase is in childcare, rather than more mundane and boring household tasks, creating another type of inequity. This inequity generally is not noted, as women may be grateful for any increased involvement on the part of their husbands.

The politics of family work can create an undercurrent of tension in dual-earner families, as everyday realities confront traditional sex-role ideology. For example, some husbands subscribe to an ideology of equality, without the practice. Among a sample of midwestern married couples, Hiller and Phillber (1986) found that 58% of husbands thought that housework should be shared but not more than 33% of them actually shared or did regular housework. Even though couples may believe in sharing family work equally, they may disagree on the "rules" to ensure equality, the standards for how clean the house should be, and so forth. And in those relatively infrequent cases when the workload is balanced, wives still may serve as managers and coordinators of family work.

How family work is accomplished also varies by ethnicity and by social class. Ethnic groups have different norms, values, and attitudes about the division of household labor. For example, data from the 1970s suggest that African-American men participate more in family work and childcare than do their white counterparts. Husbands and wives in African-American families socialize their children to maintain more interchangeable family roles (Young, 1970; Lewis, 1976). Because they define employment as part of their obligation to the family, African-American women believe it acceptable to delegate some routine childrearing and domestic functions to others (Leggon, 1983). Moreover, African-American families are embedded in a network of extended kin, who help with childcare and domestic tasks (Hays & Mindel, 1973; McAdoo, 1983; Malson, 1983).

Upper-income, dual-earner families can solve the problem of housework by hiring domestic help, that is, the labor of poor women who themselves may be members of dual-earner families (e.g., Angrist, Lave, & Mickelsen, 1976; Hunt & Hunt, 1982). But the majority of dual-earner families lack these financial resources. Young dual-earners, who face a particularly daunting workload, are usually least well-equipped financially to afford help.

Managing Childcare

The greatest challenge faced by dual-earner families is arranging for and coordinating the care of their children while they are at work (Galinsky, 1988; Galinsky & Hughes, 1987). The search for quality nonparental care for young children is daunting at best and can reach crisis proportions at worst, because our nation currently lacks a policy that ensures reliable, affordable, developmentally-appropriate care for all children who need it. In 1987, there were only 2.5 million slots in licensed centers and family day care programs to accommodate 10.5 million children under age 6 with mothers in the labor force (Hayghe, 1988; Hofferth & Phillips, 1987). Parents may be unable to obtain care because of long waiting lists, prohibitive costs, inconvenient locations, or unsatisfactory choices (Galinsky, 1988). Moreover, the hours of many childcare centers and family day care homes do not conform to parents' work schedules. Although there has been some expansion in the availability of childcare overall, it has mostly taken place in the facilities used by upper-income families (Wash & Brand, 1990). Thus, finding adequate childcare is particularly difficult for low-income families and can pose a serious obstacle to employment (Cattan, 1991).

In addition to difficulty finding childcare at all, families have trouble locating affordable, high-quality care. Indicators of quality include: an adequate staff:child ratio, small group size, developmentally-appropriate structures and activities, caring, nurturing, and adequately trained caregivers, and low caregiver turnover. Childcare regulations regarding these features of childcare vary from state to state, with many critical features of quality being basically unregulated, even in the best circumstances (Zigler & Lang, 1991). In addition, many family day care homes operate without registration, licensing, or state monitoring; unlicensed family day care varies enormously in quality—from terrible to outstanding.

The quality of care for children in formal childcare centers also varies widely. In a study of 120 childcare centers in three states, Phillips (1992) reported that the majority were of mediocre quality or worse. State regulations varied widely in how stringent childcare standards were, noncompliance was high, and a large percentage of centers studied did not meet standards that developmentalists deem necessary to ensure high-quality care for young children. Those responsible for licensing and monitoring childcare facilities carry an extensive caseload, so that centers that are out of compliance with state regulations can operate unnoticed for extended periods of time (Zigler & Lang, 1991).

Quality childcare is expensive, and many families are unable to afford it. Because financial supports for childcare are limited, families bear the primary burden of paying for these aspects of quality, and there is a direct relationship between childcare quality and cost. The ability to find reliable, high-quality childcare differs according to families' socioeconomic positions. Upper-income families can more easily afford private centers, whereas poorer families are more likely to use public centers (Veum & Gleason, 1991). Families who are not poor spend about 10% of their budget on child care; for poor families the proportion spent is considerably higher (Hofferth, 1989).

The challenges families face in arranging and coordinating childcare also vary with the developmental stage of the family. After childbirth, a family must make a difficult decision about when the primary caregiver (almost always the mother) will return to work and who will care for the baby. This decision about when a mother is to return to work should be a private one that takes into account the temperament of the child and the values and feelings of parents. But it is constrained by inadequate policies, such as the unwillingness of many employers to offer temporary part-time employment for their fulltime employees (Zigler & Lang, 1991). The Family and Medical Leave Act of 1993 is an historic step forward in public policy that supports dual-earner families, by providing 12 weeks of job-protected leave—albeit unpaid—for the birth or adoption of a child. Nonetheless, the new legislation does not cover all who need it; exempted are new hires, part-timers and those working for small organizations.

If families have managed the childcare crisis when their children are infants and preschoolers, they often have to begin anew when their children enter school and only need care before and after formal school hours. In 1987, 15.7 million children aged 6 through 13 needed before- and after-school care (Hayghe, 1988). The school-aged child has been seriously overlooked in employer and government considerations of the childcare issue.

As noted above, few workplaces provide any childcare assistance programs for their employees. But an often overlooked workplace practice that can facilitate or impede dual-earners' attempts to care for their children is the provision of *control*—over work schedules, over leave time, over the permeability of workplace boundaries to family members (Piotrkowski, 1979). Since families are not static systems, their needs change. Some control at work allows families to modify their solutions to the childcare dilemma according to their needs. For example, families might choose split-shift arrangements until children enter school, then change to regular day-time schedules, or have one spouse work part time.

An example of the importance of schedule control is seen in a study by Staines and Pleck (1983), who found that the negative effects of shift work on participation in childcare were reversed when people had some control over the hours they worked. Flexibility in starting and ending times also facilitates family functioning; however, it is available only to about 12% of full-time employees according to 1985 data, and to men more than women (Flaim, 1986; Mellor, 1986). Again, the amount of control dual-earner families have at work is partly a function of their position in the social structure:

Control increases as one rises in the occupational hierarchy. Thus, dual-career families are more able than blue-collar or service workers to take time off from work to manage childcare problems (Veum & Gleason, 1991).

The interpretation of formal policies by supervisors, as well as the implementation of informal policies, also can facilitate or hinder family adaptations (Piotrkowski, Hughes, Pleck, Kessler-Sklar & Staines, 1993). A sympathetic supervisor may allow a new father to miss a few days of work, even when no formal leave policy is in place (e.g., Pleck, 1990). Conversely, a supervisor may subtly discourage paternity leave, even when such policies exist.

In light of the limited availability of affordable, high-quality care for young and school-aged children, how do dual-earner parents manage? Most parents choose relatives, often grandmothers, or family day care homes to care for their very young children. About 44% of children under age 1 with full-time employed mothers are cared for in family day care homes (Hofferth & Phillips, 1987), which are often unregulated and unlicensed. Another solution for young families is care by parents themselves, through split-shift arrangements, where parents work different shifts (Presser, 1988). Interestingly, the shaping role of gender is also seen in split-shift couples, as mothers are still more likely to care for their young children than fathers (Presser, 1988). When children enter school, self-care is a solution some parents must resort to, and this issue is of particular concern to parents, researchers, and policy makers. (See Galambos & Garbarino, 1983; Rodman, Pratto, & Nelson, 1985, 1988; Steinberg, 1986; and Woods, 1972 for the debate surrounding this issue.)

Most parents put together what has been called "a patchwork system" to accommodate varied work schedules, work emergencies, sick children, school holidays and breaks, and coverage when a family day care provider is sick or when a childcare center is closed. Parents expend considerable effort in coordinating and maintaining the multiple arrangements for each child under 13 (1.7 on average). Nonetheless, despite parents' best efforts, these "patchwork" arrangements frequently fall apart (Galinsky & Hughes, 1987; Shinn, Ortiz-Torres, Morris, Simko, & Wong, 1987), reminding us how fragile are dual-earners' solutions to the childcare crisis.

Managing Family Relationships

To successfully maintain their stability, families need to balance cohesion and conflict, maintain attachments and bonds, and arrive at consensus about family values and roles. These difficult tasks require regular face-to-face contact among family members (Piotrkowski & Gornick, 1987). Among adults, face-to-face contact allows for displays of physical affection and support, subtle forms of communication, and the bonds that grow from sharing family tasks. For children, face-to-face contact is necessary for the development of secure attachments and for healthy development.

Workplace schedules determine the timing of separations and the length of absences, thereby patterning face-to-face interactions among family members. Most full-time employees work over 40 hours per week, during the day (8 AM to 5 PM) and from Monday to Friday (Flaim, 1986; Wiatrowski, 1988). But there are important exceptions. In 1985, for example, about one-fourth of employees worked on Saturday, and one in eight worked on Sunday (Flaim, 1986). In one national survey, researchers found that in over one-third of couples studied, one or both spouses regularly worked on the week-end (Staines & Pleck, 1983), with men being more likely to do so than women. In general, married men work longer hours than employed married women in their jobs (not counting housework). They also are more likely to hold second jobs, especially if they have children (Sekscenski, 1980; Staines & Pleck, 1983), although the incidence of second jobs is increasing among women (Stinson, 1986). At least one in six full-time workers regularly works a nonstandard shift, i.e., during the evenings (most common), nights, or both by rotating shifts (Flaim, 1986; Mellor, 1986). Shift work is governed by complex seniority rules and sometimes comes with pay differentials, with the youngest workers with young children tending to work the less desirable shifts and longer hours (Moen & Moorehouse, 1983).

Although the workplace structures time in all families with an employed member, dual-earner families face unique "relationship challenges." The first challenge occurs when mothers return to work following the birth of their child. Confronted by societal expectations that the mother be the child's primary caretaker, by psychological theory that stresses the centrality of the mother–infant tie as critical in the development of secure "attachment" (e.g., Bowlby, 1951, 1973)[3] and by the heated debate within psychology about the effects of "nonmaternal" care on infants, parents—especially, mothers—must manage feelings of anxiety and loss when placing an infant or even a pre-schooler in the care of another adult (e.g., Hock, Demeis, & McBride, 1987). The perceived centrality of the maternal role is evidenced by the fact that, even in countries such as Sweden—where paid leave is equally available to men and women—only a small proportion of men take time off to care for their infants (Lamb, Frodi, Hwang, & Frodi, 1983).

Experts agree that all children, especially infants, require the presence of a stable, accessible, sensitive adult for healthy development. What is disputed is whether this stable adult must be a parent—particularly a mother. Rather than engaging in this debate, like others we take the stance that it is society's responsibility to support families by providing choices and enabling policies for them. Moreover, by and large, employed mothers and fathers manage to have securely attached children, indicating that many dual-earner

---

[3]Interestingly, prior to mothers' participation in the labor force, psychological theory paid virtually no attention to attachment between infants and (employed) fathers, implicitly assuming that this attachment was not problematic. Even the term "nonmaternal care" reflects this emphasis on the centrality of the mother's role in childcare.

families have solved the problem of how to care appropriately for their children, even when time with them is constrained by work schedules. As Ainsworth (1979) has noted, we do not know how much time infants must be with parents to develop secure attachments.

A second unique relationship challenge for dual-earner families is the socialization of school-aged children. As children grow older, parents are called upon to balance age-appropriate autonomy with adequate supervision. Even teenage children need to feel safe and protected, while being allowed increasing independence. In the case of school-aged children, at-home mothers are able to provide necessary guidance and supervision, although some mothers may allow too little independence. But allowing age-appropriate autonomy for school-aged children is especially difficult for many dual-earner families because self-care may be the only available option while parents are at work. Thus, some children may have too much independence and become subject to excessive peer pressure (Steinberg, 1986). Dual-earner parents need to find "indirect supervising mechanisms" (Steinberg, 1986) that structure their children's activities while they are at work. They must provide their children with explicit rules and instructions for self-care, prepare children's meals ahead of time, and maintain daily telephone contact with them. They need to know their children's whereabouts, and they need to be able to stay in contact with them.

But for many parents, being able to have telephone contact with children while they are at work is not a simple matter. Employees differ in the amount of control they have over the permeability of workplace boundaries for family members (Piotrkowski, 1979). The higher up in the occupational hierarchy one is, the more likely it is that family members can call work, can visit work, and so forth. In contrast, many people have difficulty gaining access to telephones at the workplace so that parents cannot readily call home, and children cannot easily call their parents.

Because two work schedules must be accommodated in the context of a considerable workload, additional relationship challenges for dual-earner couples are the development and maintenance of marital consensus and the regulation of intimacy and tension. For example, although childcare may be facilitated when young husbands and wives work different shifts (Hood & Golden, 1979; Presser, 1988), dual-earner marriages can suffer. Husbands and wives may feel like "trains on separate tracks, pausing to unload at the station before racing on" (Walsh, 1989). This split-shift arrangement is common in families that are most vulnerable to disruption—young couples with children and families of low socioeconomic status. Unfortunately, this is a subject that has received relatively little empirical attention.[4]

Also unstudied are the rituals—so important in maintaining family cohesion and attachments—that dual-earner families develop to handle depar-

---

[4] See Mott, Mann, McLoughlin, and Warwick (1965) for a classic study of the effects of shift work on traditional breadwinner families.

tures and reunions (Piotrkowski & Gornick, 1987). Complex issues about power, privilege, and entitlement are worked out at departures and reunions. In one study, for example, the interaction between employed mothers and their infants at homecomings was so intense—perhaps to make up for the time they were away—that the young fathers were literally "crowded out." These fathers actually interacted less with their infants than fathers in traditional families (Zaslow, Pedersen, Suwalsky, & Rabinovich, 1983). Other studies suggest that little boys receive less positive attention than girls and less attention at homecoming than boys in traditional families (e.g., Bronfenbrenner, Alvarez, & Henderson, 1984; Stuckey, McGhee, & Bell, 1982).

One can imagine an all too familiar scenario: Mother comes home exhausted, wanting support from Father; Father comes home irritable and withdrawn and wants to be left alone; neither can give the other the support he or she needs, and their interactions are tense and brief. Meanwhile, the children are demanding attention—the little one needs diapering, while the older one is watching television instead of doing his homework. Both parents are emotionally drained. Dinner still needs to be prepared.

In addition to completing the family workload, dual-earners must develop rules about how to handle such homecomings. Are there agreed-upon rules about when people come home—are homecomings expectable? What rules govern exceptions? Who talks to whom first? Is the parent–child or marital subsystem given priority or does everyone compete for attention? Which child's needs will be met first? As dual-earner families struggle to develop flexible consensus around these issues and to actually get family work accomplished, they may not connect the strains they experience to the intricate balancing act in which they are engaged. Instead, partners may blame each other for not helping enough at home, for not listening to them or understanding their problems, for being too demanding.

Managing Two Jobs

Jobs vary enormously in their demands and the conditions under which tasks are performed, with differing psychological and physical consequences. Many factors make jobs stressful, including high pressure for output, lack of control over job tasks, poor interpersonal relationships, the threat of job loss, physically noxious environments, nonsupportive supervision, and so forth (e.g., Cottington & House, 1985; House & Wells, 1978; Karasek, Theorell, Schwartz, & Alfredson, 1982).

Excessive demands coupled with lack of control over those demands are especially stressful. Jobs with these characteristics tend to be disproportionately located at the bottom of the occupational hierarchy. Job and family demands can lead to overload, role conflict, and work–family strain, which may, in turn, be exacerbated by stressful job conditions (Katz & Piotrkowski, 1983; Hughes, Galinsky, & Morris, 1992). As we move up the social ladder, the nature of job stressors changes somewhat. The families of managers and executives must determine how permeable family boundaries will be to workplace demands, such as bringing work home, working long hours, and so forth (Frone, Russell, & Cooper, 1992). Many of these jobs are highly absorbing, and they may attract and reward job-involved people (Piotrkowski, Rapoport, & Rapoport, 1987).

Some job stressors are particular to women and to nonwhites. Women frequently experience sexual harassment and gender discrimination in the workplace, including limited opportunities for advancement. African-American workers encounter overt racism and discrimination (Alderfer, Alderfer, Tucker, & Tucker, 1980; Davis & Watson, 1982). Insidious manifestations of racism include assignments to undesirable work shifts and dirty jobs with low pay and few benefits.

Generally, occupational stress has been treated as an individual problem. However, it also is a family-system problem (Hughes et al., 1992; Piotrkowski, 1979; Piotrkowski & Staines, 1991). Traditionally, women have been expected to provide a home environment that facilitates the recuperation of the job holder under stress and to develop strategies to manage physical and psychological consequences of occupational stress as they express themselves in the worker at home—coming home exhausted, tense and irritable, anxious, even feeling deadened from boredom (Hughes, et al., 1992; Piotrkowski, 1979). Such strategies have included keeping children quiet while Father rests and taking on additional family responsibilities. But in the dual-earner family, both partners may be experiencing the adverse effects of stressful jobs, with no one available to provide the recuperative environment each needs. Moreover, job stressors such as job loss, business failure, and arguments may also have adverse effects on other family members similar to those on the job holder (Rook, Dooley, & Catalano, 1991).

Additionally, dual-earner families must contain the interpersonal tensions *created by* work-related stressors. For one, job stress may have an adverse impact on marriage. When workers experience their jobs as stressful, or react negatively to them, they report less satisfying marital relationships and more marital tension (Crouter, Perry-Jenkins, Huston, & Crawford, 1989; Jackson & Maslach, 1982; Jackson, Zedeck, & Summers, 1985). Workplace experiences, such as arguments at work, nonsupportive work relationships, high pressure for output, and fear of job loss are also associated with more marital disagreements (Bolger, DeLongis, Kessler, & Wethington, 1989; Hughes et al., 1992; Repetti, 1989).

Parents' job stress also may have an adverse effect on parent–child relations. For example, when parents experience job stress, work–family role strain, and role conflict, they are more restrictive, and they withdraw more and are less positive when interacting with their children (e.g., Hoffman, 1963; Kosciw & Hughes, 1991; Lerner & Galambos, 1988; Piotrkowski & Katz, 1983; Piotrkowski & Stark, 1984; Repetti, 1989). Researchers also have found inverse relationships between parental job satisfaction and children's behavioral problems (Barling & Van Bart, 1984; Barling, 1986) and between parental role conflict and childrens' academic achievement and school behavior (Gottfried & Gottfried, 1988), suggesting changes in parental behavior caused by occupationally-related strain. Job loss and unemployment also have been associated with increased rates of child abuse (Steinberg, Catalano, & Dooley, 1981).

Men and women may express occupational strain differently in the family. Men have been found to withdraw from marital interaction, whereas women seek support from their spouses (Kosciw & Hughes, 1991; Weiss, 1990). Also, wives are more likely to respond to their husbands' job-related strain by assuming some of their family responsibilities (Billings & Moos, 1982; Bolger, DeLongis, Kessler, & Wethington, 1990). In general, wives probably give more job-related support to their husbands than they receive (Lopata, Barnelwolt, & Norr, 1980). Moreover, there is some limited evidence that mothers and fathers interact differently with their male and female children when experiencing occupationally-related stress (e.g., Kosciw & Hughes, 1991; Piotrkowski & Stark, 1984; Stuckey et al., 1982). Thus, any understanding of the impact of job stressors on the dual-earner family must be filtered through the lens of gender.

The research on job stress and family relations suggests that the management of job-related stress can be especially difficult in dual-earner families. The negative effects on family interaction are likely compounded when both spouses' jobs are stressful. Moreover, spouses' abilities to buffer the effects of stressful jobs for each other can be undermined by their own job strain.

SUMMARY AND CONCLUSIONS

Dual-earner families are now the dominant family form for two-parent families with children. But the contemporary dual-earner family is under pressure. With inadequate public policies and few workplaces that are family-friendly, we have described some of the normative difficulties families face in managing basic tasks including housework and childcare, the stresses and work–family conflict associated with two jobs, and the relationship dilemmas created by complex work schedules. The dual-earner family is a team short of players: These are really three-job families (if we count housework and childcare), and with children there are simply not enough hands to do the work. Perhaps the greatest challenge currently confronting modern dual-earner families in our society is finding reliable, high-quality, affordable childcare.

We have also described some of the contexts that influence the functioning of dual-earner families. Young families are under particular pressure because of excessive demands, as are those lower in the socioeconomic structure, where jobs are especially stressful, schedules less flexible, and resources limited. Gender is a cross-cutting force that shapes how tasks are handled and challenges met, with women still having primary responsibility for family work. At considerable cost, women absorb many of the strains inherent in being a three-job family. Because our society has not yet fully accepted and faced the fact that wives and mothers are and will continue to be employed, few social, organizational or community supports exist to help dual-earners accomplish their fundamental tasks. Therefore, each family must struggle to derive its own solutions.

Although the picture we have painted is not positive, it is important to remember that it is possible for community and social institutions and values to support rather than to create obstacles for families. Many European countries provide examples of the possibilities for creating family-friendly policies. Although policy in the United States lags far behind, work and family issues are now on the public agenda. Increasingly, employers are coming to understand that facilitating childcare and other family functions can be good business; one challenge for them is to create policies that distribute new benefits across all occupational groups. The example of African-American families, who have long valued women's labor-force participation, also reminds us that attitudes toward married women's employment can be positive. And the increasing participation of men in family work, especially childcare, suggests that traditional sex-role attitudes are changing, albeit slowly.

This discussion of dual-earner families underscores that families are open systems influenced by their social context. With some notable exceptions, family systems theory lacks descriptions and conceptualizations of how significant social systems outside the family affect life inside it. One consequence of treating the family as a closed system is believing that a family's problems result primarily from its own deficiencies, that is, a deficit model of family functioning.

Practitioners serving dual-earner families with problems may find it difficult to see their embeddedness in an inhospitable social context. Dual-earner families themselves often do not understand the extent to which the stresses they experience are normative and result from lack of support. Men and women in contemporary dual-earner families grew up with traditional views about family and work roles that provided a blueprint for how to be a family. But the influx of women into the labor force, the new feminism, and the rise of the dual-earner family as a dominant family structure for two-parent families with children has introduced uncertainty into how to be a viable family. Not only are dual-earner families faced with additional task demands, for which old solutions do not work, but they also lack clear socially prescribed and supported roles for accomplishing basic family functions. Contemporary dual-earners are struggling to construct new relationship "bargains" for how to be a family. Thus, what the practitioner sees is a family groping for solutions to normative dilemmas where few models for solving them exist. The fact that most dual-earner families manage their day-to-day lives effectively and rear their children successfully is a testament to their resourcefulness and strength.

REFERENCES

Ainsworth, M. D. S. (1979). Infant–mother attachment. *American Psychologist, 34*, 932–937.

Alderfer, C., Alderfer, C., Tucker, L., & Tucker, S. (1980). Diagnosing race problems in management. *Journal of Applied Behavioral Science, 16*, April–June, 135–166.

Aldous, J. (1981). From dual-earner to dual-career families and back again. *Journal of Family Issues, 2*, 115–125.

Allen, J. P. (1988). European infant care leaves: Foreign perspectives on the integration of work and family roles. In E. Zigler & M. Frank (Eds.), *The parental leave crisis: Toward a national policy* (pp. 245–275). New Haven: Yale University Press.

Angrist, S. S., Lave, J. R., & Mickelsen, R. (1976). How working mothers manage: Socioeconomic differences in work, child care and household tasks. *Social Science Quarterly, 56*, 631–637.

Barling, J. (1986). Fathers' work experiences: The father–child relationship and children's behavior. *Journal of Occupational Behavior, 7*, 61–66.

Barling, J., & Van Bart, D. (1984). Mothers' subjective work experiences and the behavior of their preschool children. *Journal of Occupational Psychology, 54*, 49–56.

Barnett, R. C., & Baruch, G. K. (1987). Determinants of father's particpation in family work. *Journal of Marriage and the Family, 49*, 29–40.

Baron, A. (1981). Protective legislation and the cult of domesticity. *Journal of Family Issues, 2*, 25–38.

Beckett, J. O. (1976). Working wives: A racial comparison. *Social Work, 21*, 463–471.

Belsky, J., Lang, M., & Rovine, M. (1985). Stability and change in marriage across the transition to parenthood: A second study. *Journal of Marriage and the Family, 47*, 855–866.

Berk, S. F. (1985). *The gender factory: The apportionment of work in American households.* New York: Plenum Press.

Billings, A. G., & Moos, R. H. (1982). Work stress and the stress-buffering roles of work and family resources. *Journal of Occupational Behavior, 3*, 215–232.

Bolger, N., DeLongis, A., Kessler, R., & Wethington, E. (1989). The contagion of stress across multiple roles. *Journal of Marriage and the Family, 51*, 175–183.

Bolger, N., DeLongis, A., Kessler, R. C., & Wethington, E. (1990). The microstructure of daily role-related stress in married couples. In J. Eckenrode & S. Gore (Eds.), *Stress between work and family* (pp. 95–116). New York: Plenum Press.

Bowlby, J. (1951). *Maternal care and mental health: Monograph 2.* Geneva: World Health Organization.

Bowlby, J. (1973). *Attachment and loss: Vol. 2. Separation: Anxiety and anger.* New York: Basic Books.

Bronfenbrenner, U., Alvarez, W. F., & Henderson, C. R. (1984). Working and watching: Maternal employment status and parents' perceptions of their three year-old children. *Child Development, 55*, 1362–1378.

Cattan, P. (1991). Child-care problems: An obstacle to work. *Monthly Labor Review, 114*(10), 3–9.

Chafe, W. H. (1976). Looking backward in order to look forward: Women, work and social values in America. In J. M. Kreps (Ed.), *Women and the American economy.* Englewood Cliffs, NJ: Prentice-Hall.

Cottington, E. M., & House, J. S. (1985). Occupational stress and health: A multivariate relationship. In A. R. Baum & J. E. Singer (Eds.), *Handbook of psychology and health:* Vol. 5. Hillsdale, NJ: Lawrence Erlbaum Associates.

Cowan, R. (1976). The "Industrial Revolution" in the home: Household technology and social change in the 20th century. *Technology and Culture, 17,* 1–23.

Crouter, A. C., Perry-Jenkins, M., Huston, T. L., & Crawford, D. (1989). The influence of work-induced psychological states on behaviors at home. *Basic and Applied Social Psychology, 10*(3), 273–292.

Davis, G., & Watson, G. (1982). *Black life in corporate America.* New York: Doubleday.

Ehrenreich, B., & English, D. (1975). The manufacture of housework. *Socialist Revolution, 5*(4), 5–40.

Flaim, P. O. (1986). Work schedules of Americans: An overview of new findings. *Monthly Labor Review, 109*(11), 3–6.

Frone, M. R., Russell, M., & Cooper, M. L. (1992). Antecedents and outcomes of work–family conflict: Testing a model of the work–family interface. *Journal of Applied Psychology, 77*(1), 65–78.

Fullerton, H. N., Jr. (1987). Labor force projections: 1986 to 2000. *Monthly Labor Review, 110*(9), 19–29.

Galambos, N. L., & Garbarino, J. (1983). Identifying the missing links in the study of latchkey children. *Children Today,* July–August, 2–4, 40–41.

Galinsky, E. (1988). *Child care and productivity.* Paper presented at the Child Care Action Campaign Conference: Child care: The Bottom Line, New York, NY.

Galinsky, E., & Hughes, D. (1987). *The Fortune magazine child care study.* Unpublished manuscript, Bank Street College of Education, New York.

Gottfried, A., & Gottfried, A. W. (1988). Maternal employment, family environment, and children's development: Infancy through school years. In A. Gottfried & A. W. Gottfried (Eds.), *Maternal employment, family environment, and children's development.* New York: Plenum Press.

Gray, E., Lovejoy, M., Piotrkowski, C., & Bond, J. (1990). Husband supportiveness and the well-being of employed mothers of infants. *Families in Society, 71,* 332–341.

Harris, L., & Associates, Inc. (1981). *Families at work: Strengths and strains.* Minneapolis: General Mills.

Hayghe, H. V. (1988). Employers and child care: what roles do they play? *Monthly Labor Review, 111*(9), 38–44.

Hayghe, H. V. (1989). Children in 2-worker families and real family income. *Monthly Labor Review, 112*(12), 48–52.

Hayghe, H. V. (1990). Family members in the work force. *Monthly Labor Review, 113*(3), 14–19.

Hays, W. C., & Mindel, C. H. (1973). Extended kinship relations in black and white families. *Journal of Marriage and the Family, 35*(1), 51–56.

Hiller, D. V., & Philliber, W. W. (1986). The division of labor in contemporary marriage: Expectations, perceptions, and performance. *Social Problems, 33,* 191–201.

Hochschild, A., & Machung, A. (1990). *The second shift.* New York: Avon.

Hock, E., Demeis, D., & McBride, S. (1987). Maternal separation anxiety: Its role in the balance of employment and motherhood in mothers of infants. In A. Gottfried & A. Gottfried (Eds.), *Maternal employment and children's development: Longitudinal research* (pp. 191–232). New York: Plenum Press.

Hofferth, S. L. (1989). Testimony before the Subcommittee on Children, Families, Drugs and Alcoholism, U.S. Senate, Washington, DC.

Hofferth, S. L., & Phillips, D. A. (1987). Child care in the United States, 1970–1995. *Journal of Marriage and the Family, 49,* 559–571.

Hoffman, L. W. (1963). Effects on the child. In F. I. Nye & L. W. Hoffman (Eds.), *The employed mother in America* (pp. 126–166). Chicago: Rand McNally.

Hood, J., & Golden, S. (1979). Beating time/making time: The impact of work scheduling on men's family roles. *Family Coordinator, 28,* 575–582.

House, J. S., & Wells, J. (1978). Occupational stress, social support, and health. In A. McLean, G. Black, & M. Colligan (Eds.), *Reducing occupational stress: Proceedings of a conference* (pp. 8–29). Cincinnati: National Institute of Occupational Safety and Health.

Hughes, D., Galinsky, E., & Morris, A. (1992). Job characteristics and marital quality: Specifying linking mechanisms. *Journal of Marriage and the Family, 54*(1), 31–41.

Hunt, J. G., & Hunt, L. L. (1982). Dual-career families: Vanguard of the future or residue of the past. In J. Aldous (Ed.), *Two paychecks: Life in dual-earner families* (pp. 41–59). Beverly Hills: Sage.

Jackson, S., & Maslach, C. (1982). After-effects of job related stress: Families as victims. *Journal of Occupational Behavior, 3,* 63–77.

Jackson, S., Zedeck, S., & Summers, E. (1985). Family life disruptions: Effects of job-induced structural and emotional interference. *Academy of Management Journal, 28*(3), 574–586.

Kamerman, S., Kahn, A. J., & Kingston, P. (1983). *Maternity policies and working women.* New York: Columbia University Press.

Kanter, R. M. (1977). *Work and family in the United States: A critical review and agenda for research and policy.* New York: Russell Sage Foundation.

Karasek, R. A., Theorell, T., Schwartz, J., & Alfredson, L. (1982). Job, psychological factors, and coronary heart disease. *Advanced Cardiology, 29,* 62–67.

Katz, H. H., & Piotrkowski, C. S. (1983). Correlates of family role strain among employed black women. *Family Relations, 32,* 331–339.

Kohn, M. L. (1959). Social class and parental values. *American Journal of Sociology, 64,* 337–354.

Kosciw, J., & Hughes, D. (1991, June). *The impact of job stress on family functioning.* Paper presented at the Third Biennial Conference on Community Research and Action, Tempe, AZ.

Kutscher, R. E. (1987). Overview and implications of the projections to 2000. *Monthly Labor Review, 110*(9), 3–9.

Lamb, M., Frodi, A. M., Hwang, C., & Frodi, M. (1983). Varying degrees of paternal involvement in infant care: Attitudinal and behavioral correlates. In M. E. Lamb (Ed.), *Nontraditional families: Parenting and child development* (pp. 117–138). Hillsdale, NJ: Lawrence Erlbaum Associates.

Lasch, C. (1977). Haven in a heartless world. *The family beseiged.* New York: Basic Books.

Leggon, C. (1983). Career, marriage and motherhood: "Copping out" or coping. In C. E. Obudho (Ed.), *Black marriage and family therapy.* Westport, CT: Greenwood Press.

Lerner, J. V., & Galambos, N. L. (1988). The influences of maternal employment across life: The New York longitudinal study. In A. Gottfried & A. Gottfried

(Eds.), *Maternal employment, family environment, and children's development.* New York: Plenum Press.

Lewis, D. K. (1976). The black family: Socialization and sex roles. *Phylon, 36*(3), 221–237.

Lopata, H. Z., Barnewolt, D., & Norr, K. (1980). Spouses' contributions to each others' roles. In F. Pepitone-Rockwell (Ed.), *Dual-career couples* (pp. 111–142). Beverly Hills: Sage.

MacDermid, S. M., Huston, T. L., & McHale, S. M. (1990). Changes in marriage associated with the transition to parenthood: Individual differences as a function of sex-role attitudes and changes in the division of household labor. *Journal of Marriage and the Family, 52,* 475–486.

Malson, M. R. (1983). Black families and childrearing support networks. In H. Z. Lopata & J. H. Pleck (Eds.), *Research in the interweave of social roles: Jobs and families:* Vol. 3 (pp. 131–142). Greenwich, CT: JAI Press.

Marat, E., & Finlay, B. (1984). The distribution of household labor among women in dual-earner families. *Journal of Marriage and the Family, 46,* 357–364.

McAdoo, J. L. (1983). Involvement of fathers in the socialization of black children. In H. P. McAdoo (Ed.), *Black families* (pp. 225–238). Beverly Hills: Sage.

Mellor, E. F. (1986). Shift work and flexitime: How prevalent are they? *Monthly Labor Review, 109*(11), 14–21.

Model, S. (1981). Housework by husbands. *Journal of Family Issues, 2,* 225–237.

Moen, P., & Moorehouse, M. (1983). Overtime over the life cycle: A test of the life cycle squeeze hypothesis. In H. Z. Lopata & J. H. Pleck (Eds.), *Research in the interweave of social roles: Vol. 3. Families and jobs.* Greenwich, CT: JAI Press.

Mott, P. E., Mann, F. C., McLoughlin, Q., & Warwick, D. P. (1965). *Shift work.* Ann Arbor: University of Michigan Press.

O'Connell, M. (1989, August 7). *Maternity leave arrangements, 1961–85.* Paper presented at the Annual Meeting of the American Statistical Association, Washington, DC.

Phillips, D. (1992). Public policy, quality of child care, and children's development [Summary]. In F. L. Parker, R. Robinson, S. Sambrano, C. S. Piotrkowski, J. Hagen, S. Randolph, & A. Baker (Eds.), *New directions in child and family research: Shaping Head Start in the 90's* (pp. 221–223). Washington, DC: Administration on Children, Youth and Families.

Piotrkowski, C. S. (1979). *Work and the family system.* New York: Macmillan.

Piotrkowski, C. S., & Gornick, L. (1987). Effects of work-related separations on children and families. In J. Bloom-Feshback, S. Bloom-Feshback, & Associates (Eds.), *The psychology of separation and loss.* San Francisco: Jossey-Bass.

Piotrkowski, C. S., Hughes, D., Pleck, J. H., Kessler-Sklar, S., & Staines, G. L. (1993). *The experience of childbearing women in the workplace: The impact of family-friendly policies and practices.* (Contract No. J-9-M-1-0076). Report to the U.S. Department of Labor, Women's Bureau.

Piotrkowski, C. S., & Katz, M. H. (1982). Indirect socialization of children: The effects of mothers' jobs on academic behavior of children. *Child Development, 53,* 1520–1529.

Piotrkowski, C. S., & Katz, M. H. (1983). Work experience and family relations among working-class and lower middle class families. In H. Z. Lopata & J. H. Pleck (Eds.), *Research in the interweave of social roles: Vol. 3. Families and jobs.* Greenwich, CT: JAI Press.

Piotrkowski, C. S., Rapoport, R. N., & Rapoport, R. (1987). Families and work. In

M. B. Sussman & S. K. Steinmetz (Eds.), *Handbook of marriage and the family* (pp. 251–283). New York: Plenum Press.

Piotrkowski, C. S., & Repetti, R. L. (1984). Dual-earner families. *Marriage and Family Review, 7*(2/3), 99–124.

Piotrkowski, C. S., & Staines, G. L. (1991). Job Stress and the Family. *Business Insights, 7*(1) 22–36.

Piotrkowski, C. S., & Stark, E. (1984). *Job stress and children's mental health: An ecological study.* Report prepared for the W. T. Grant Foundation: New York.

Pleck, J. H. (1977). The work–family role system. *Social Problems, 24,* 417–427.

Pleck, J. H. (1990). Family-supportive employer policies: Are they relevant to men? In J. C. Hood (Ed.), *Men's work and family roles.* Newbury Park, CA: Sage.

Presser, H. B. (1988). Shift work and child care among young dual-earner American parents. *Journal of Marriage and the Family, 50,* 133–148.

Repetti, R. (1989). The effects of daily workload on subsequent behavior during marital interaction: The roles of social withdrawal and spouse support. *Journal of Personality and Social Psychology, 57*(4), 651–659.

Rexroat, C., & Shehan, C. (1987). The family life cycle and spouses' time in housework. *Journal of Marriage and the Family, 49,* 737–750.

Rodman, H., Pratto, D., & Nelson, R. (1985). Child care arrangements and children's functioning: A comparison of self-care and adult-care children. *Developmental Psychology, 21*(3), 413–418.

Rodman, H., Pratto, D., & Nelson, R. (1988). Toward a definition of self-care children: A commentary on Steinberg (1986). *Developmental Psychology, 24,* 292–294.

Rook, K., Dooley, D., & Catalano, R. (1991). Stress transmission: The effects of husbands' job stressors on the emotional health of their wives. *Journal of Marriage and the Family, 53,* 165–177.

Scanzoni, J. H. (1978). *Sex roles, women's work, and marital conflict.* Lexington, MA: D. C. Heath.

Scarr, S., Phillips, D., & McCartney, K. (1989). Working mothers and their families. *American Psychologist, 44*(11), 1402–1409.

Scott, J. W., & Tilly, L. A. (1975). Women's work and the family in nineteenth-century Europe. In C. E. Rosenberg (Ed.), *The family in history.* Philadelphia: University of Pennsylvania Press.

Sekscenski, E. S. (1980). Women's share of moonlighting nearly doubles during 1969–79. *Monthly Labor Review, 103*(5), 36–39.

Select Committee on Children, Youth & Families (1989, November 14). U.S. House of Representatives, *Report 101-356.* Washington, DC: U.S. Government Printing Office.

Shinn, M. B., Ortiz-Torres, B., Morris, A., Simko, P., & Wong, N. (1987, August). *Child care patterns, stress, and job behaviors among working parents.* Paper presented at the annual convention of the American Psychological Association, New York.

Smelser, N. (1959). *Social change in the industrial revolution: An application of theory in the Lancashire cotton industry 1770–1840.* London: Routledge.

Spitze, G. (1988). Women's employment and family relations: A review. *Journal of Marriage and the Family, 50,* 595–618.

Staines, G. L., & Pleck, J. H. (1983). *The impact of work schedules on the family.* Ann Arbor: Survey Research Center, University of Michigan.

Steinberg, L. (1986). Latchkey children and susceptibility to peer pressure: An eco-logical analysis. *Developmental Psychology, 22,* 433–439.

Steinberg, L., Catalano, R., & Dooley, D. (1981). Economic antecedents of child abuse. *Child Development, 52,* 975–985.

Stinson, J. F., Jr. (1986). Moonlighting by women jumped to record highs. *Monthly Labor Review, 109*(11), 22–25.

Stuckey, M. F., McGhee, P. E., & Bell, N. J. (1982). Parent–child interaction: The influence of maternal employment. *Developmental Psychology, 18,* 635–644.

Szinovacz, M. E. (1984). Changing family roles and interaction. *Marriage and Family Review, 3/4,* 163–201.

Tentler, L. (1979). *Wage-earning women, industrial work, and family life in the United States, 1900–1930.* New York: Oxford University Press.

Thompson, E. P. (1966). *The making of the English working class.* New York: Vintage.

Thompson, L., & Walker, A. J. (1989). Gender in families: Women and men in mar-riage, work and parenthood. *Journal of Marriage and the Family, 51,* 845–872.

Thornton, A. (1989). Changing attitudes toward family issues in the United States. *Journal of Marriage and the Family, 51,* 873–893.

Turner, C. (1971). Dual work households and marital dissolution. *Human Relations, 24,* 535–548.

U.S. Bureau of the Census. (1990). *Statistical Abstract of the United States.* Washing-ton, DC: U.S. Government Printing Office.

Veum, J. R., & Gleason, P. M. (1991). Child care: Arrangements and costs. *Monthly Labor Review, 114,* 10–17.

Walker, K. E., & Woods, M. E. (1976). *Time use: A measure of household production of family goods and services.* Washington, DC: American Home Economics Asso-ciation.

Walsh, F. (1989). Reconsidering gender in the marital quid pro quo. In M. McGold-rick, C. Anderson, & F. Walsh (Eds.), *Women in families* (pp. 267–285). New York: Norton.

Wash, D. P., & Brand, L. E. (1990). Child care services: An industry at the crossroads. *Monthly Labor Review, 113,* 17–24.

Weiss, R. S. (1990). Bringing work stress home. In J. Eckenrode & S. Gore (Eds.), *Stress between work and family* (pp. 17–38). New York: Plenum Press.

Wiatrowski, W. J. (1988). Comparing employee benefits in the public and private sectors. *Monthly Labor Review, 111*(12), 3–8.

Woods, M. B. (1972). The unsupervised child of the working mother. *Developmental Psychology, 6,* 14–25.

Young, V. H. (1970). Family and childhood in a southern Negro community. *Ameri-can Anthropologist, 72,* 269–288.

Zaslow, M., Pedersen, F. A., Suwalsky, J., & Rabinovich, B. (1983, April). *Maternal employment and parent–infant interaction.* Paper presented at the meeting of the Society for Research in Child Development, Detroit.

Zigler, E., & Frank, M. (Eds.). (1988). *The parental leave crisis: Toward a national policy.* New Haven: Yale University Press.

Zigler, E., & Lang, M. (1991). *Child care choices: Balancing the needs of children, fami-lies, and society.* New York: Free Press.

CHAPTER 7

DIVORCE
Challenges, Changes, and New Chances

*E. Mavis Hetherington,
Tracy C. Law, and
Thomas G. O'Connor*

$\mathbf{S}$TUDIES OF THE EFFECTS OF divorce on family members traditionally have centered around the development of problem behaviors subsequent to marital dissolution. Recent findings, however, have emphasized the wide variation in responses to stressful experiences and life transitions, including divorce and remarriage (e.g., Rutter, 1987; Werner, 1987; Hetherington, 1991a). Although debate still exists over the question of the magnitude and duration of the effects of parental divorce on children, work in the past 10 years has converged in suggesting that the interaction among individual differences in personal and familial characteristics and extrafamilial factors that support or undermine coping efforts by family members must be examined in order to understand the spectrum of responses to divorce. This spectrum can range from enhanced competence to clinical levels of problem behavior (Hetherington, 1989, 1991a; Stolberg, Camplair, Currier, & Wells, 1987).

In addition, it is becoming increasingly apparent that divorce should be viewed not as a discrete event but as part of a series of family transitions and changes in family relationships. The response to any family transition will depend both on what precedes and follows it. The response to divorce and life in a single-parent household will be influenced by individual adjustment and the quality of family relationships before the divorce as well as circumstances surrounding and following the divorce. In many families, divorce may trigger a series of adverse transactional factors such as economic decline, parenting stress, and physical and psychological dysfunction in family members. For others, it may present an escape from conflict and an unsatisfying marital relationship, a chance to form more gratifying and harmonious relationships, and an opportunity for personal growth and individuation (Gore & Eckenroade, 1992; Hetherington, 1989).

The recognition that divorce is part of a chain of marital transitions and shifting life experiences, and that individual responses to these experiences demonstrate marked variability, has been a powerful influence on recent theoretical models developed to explain children's adjustment to parental divorce. In understanding these findings, many researchers have adopted a developmental contextual framework (Gore & Eckenroade, 1992; Nock, 1982; Hetherington & Clingempeel, 1992; Hetherington & Martin, 1986). This approach examines adjustment across time, and on multiple levels, including interactions among the overarching social and historical context, changing dynamics within the family system, individual ontogenic characteristics of child and parent, and influences external to the family such as the extended family, peer relationships, and the educational, occupational, mental health, legal, religious, and welfare systems.

The purpose of this chapter is not to present a comprehensive review of research and clinical findings concerning the adjustment to divorce. Selected recent research examples and a developmental, contextual, interactive model will be used as an organizational framework in which to examine factors that contribute to individual differences in the way family members negotiate the changes and challenges associated with divorce. Many of the research findings will be drawn from the longitudinal studies of Hetherington and her colleagues. Before discussing the factors implicated in a developmental, contextual, interactive approach, it is important to place the findings in the larger context of demographic and social changes that have occurred in the last 20 years.

THE CHANGING WORLD OF THE FAMILY: DEMOGRAPHIC AND SOCIAL FORCES

Although the divorce rate doubled between 1960 and 1980, it has leveled off and even declined slightly in the past decade (Glick, 1988). Currently, it is estimated that half of all marriages will end in divorce and that approximately 60% of these dissolutions will involve children. Although the percentage of marriages ending in divorce has not changed appreciably since the early 1980's, the number of children affected by parental divorce, as well as the number of children from divorced families now of marriageable age themselves, has continued to increase (Bumpass, 1984). It has been estimated that 38% of white children and 75% of African-American children born to married parents in the United States will experience their parents' divorce before their 16th birthday (Bumpass, 1984). In addition, African-Americans not only have a higher rate of divorce than whites, they are also more likely to separate but not go through a legal divorce procedure, to experience a longer time-lag between time of separation and divorce, and are less likely to remarry (Glick, 1988; Teachman, Polonko, & Scanzoni, 1987). Although families who are poor, African-American. and suffering multiple life stresses are more likely to divorce, the rise in economic independence for well-educated women also has led to a greater likelihood that these women will divorce compared to their less-educated peers. Furthermore, since most divorced men and women remarry, and since the rate of divorce in second marriages is even higher than in first marriages (61% of men and 54% of women go through a second divorce), many children and parents encounter a series of marital transitions and reorganizations in family roles and relationships (Glick, 1988; Chase-Lansdale & Hetherington, 1990). These statistics indicate that divorce, once considered an atypical family event, is now a "normative," even if not a "normal," experience in the life cycle of many contemporary American families (Emery & Forehand, 1992).

Shifting social and historical factors affect patterns of both marriage and divorce (Cherlin, 1981; Teachman et al., 1987; Glick, 1988). Wars, whether the Civil War, World War II, the Korean War, or the Vietnam War, have been associated with hasty marriages followed by increased rates of divorce (Glick, 1988). Current high rates of divorce have also been attributed to greater labor force participation and economic independence of women, improved contraception, the emergence of the welfare system, an increase in the proportion of marriages involving premarital births, changing ideologies associated with the women's movement, and the liberalization of divorce laws. The family is being reshaped in response to transformations in social values and roles. Greater diversity in attitudes and accepted behaviors are found not only in family and gender roles but also in other social systems—in law, politics, religion, education, and the workplace. Divorce and the concommitment experiences of family members are only one reflection of the need for social institutions, such as the family, to adapt to historical and social change.

WHY MARRIAGES FAIL:
THE PRECURSORS OF DIVORCE

Neither marital satisfaction nor sheer frequency of disagreements is a good predictor of divorce. Instead, styles of conflict resolution involving disengagement, stonewalling, contempt, denial, and blaming are likely to be associated with divorce (Gottman, in press; Hetherington, 1989). One of the most common patterns of marital relations leading to divorce is a conflict-confronting, conflict-avoiding pattern where one spouse, usually the wife, confronts areas of concern and disagreements in the marriage and expresses her feelings about these problems, while the other spouse responds with defensiveness, avoidance, withdrawal, whining, and, if prodded, with resentment and anger. A second common marital pattern associated with later divorce is one in which couples have little overt conflict, but have different expectations and perceptions about family life, marriage and their children, and have few shared interests, activities, or friends (Hetherington & Tryon, 1989; Notarius & Vanzetti, 1983).

These patterns of relating in dysfunctional couples means that many children before the divorce are likely to have been exposed to unresolved disagreements, resentment, anger, and ineffective marital problem solving. Prospective studies indicate that troubled marital relations and interparental tension accompanied by unsupportive parenting and high rates of behavior problems in children occur years before the dissolution of the marriage (Block, Block, & Gjerde, 1986, 1988; Cherlin et al., 1991). The inept parenting and behavior disorders usually attributed to divorce and life in a one-parent household may, to some extent, be a continuation of predivorce functioning and be associated with disrupted processes in the nuclear family. Although the popular interpretation of these findings is that marital tension, alienation, and conflict cause inept parenting and behavior problems in children, it may be that the stress of dealing with a difficult, noncompliant, antisocial child helps to undermine an already fragile marriage and precipitates divorce.

Recently, another explanation, based on the findings of twin studies, has been proposed. It suggests that divorce and problem behaviors in children are genetically linked, and that this may help to explain the slightly higher rates of divorce found in offspring of divorced parents (McGue & Lykken, in press). Irritable, antisocial behavior in parents may provoke marital problems and be genetically associated with behavior problems in children, with the subsequent marital difficulties of adult offspring of divorced parents, and with the intergenerational transmission of divorce. Whatever the reasons may be for the dysfunctional precursors of divorce, it is against a background of disrupted family relationships and disordered behavior in parents and children that family members move into the changes and challenges associated with separation, divorce, and life in a one-parent household.

CHANGES IN THE LIVING SITUATION

An established family system can be viewed as a mechanism for identifying and framing the roles, activities, and daily life of each family member. When a divorce occurs, it means not only the loss of patterns of everyday family interaction and a family member, but loss of a way of life. Pervasive alterations in expectations, life experiences, and the sense of self in parents and children are associated with the uncertainty, found not only in divorce, but also in other transitions, such as loss of a family member through death (Silverman, 1988) or even with the addition of a family member through remarriage (Hetherington, in press).

Immediately following divorce, household routines and roles break down and parents experience task overload as a single parent attempts to perform the tasks usually assumed by two parents. In such situations, children, especially daughters, in divorced families are often asked to assume responsibility for household chores and care of younger siblings. Many of the interactions between custodial mothers and their children, are instrumental in nature and occur in the context of shared tasks. The problems of overwhelming responsibility for parent and child are often exacerbated when divorced mothers must begin working or increase their workload because of economic necessity (Duncan & Hoffman, 1985).

In the first year following divorce, the average family income of women decreases by almost 40%. Although income relative to needs gradually increases, even 5 years after divorce, the income of divorced mothers remains at 94% of their predivorced income, in contrast to 130% for divorced fathers and 125% for remarried women (Duncan & Hoffman, 1985). This is the result, in part, of partial or intermittent payment, or nonpayment, of child support by 70% of divorced noncustodial fathers. This loss of income following martial dissolution often determines where families live, where children go to school, the quality of neighborhoods and peer groups, and the accessibility of jobs, health care, and support networks. Although income level or loss explains only a small amount of the variance related to childrens' adjustment following divorce, poverty does increase the probability of encountering these other transactional factors associated with the ability of parents and children to manage stress successfully and with developmental outcomes for children. Negative life stresses are most marked for members of divorced families in the first 2 years following divorce and gradually decline with time; however, they always remain higher than those in nondivorced families (Forgatch, Patterson, & Ray, in press; Hetherington, Cox, & Cox, 1985). An unexpected bill, illness, or a school closing may present a greater emergency for a divorced mother than for parents in a two-parent household with mutual support and greater resources.

In spite of the difficulties encountered by divorced women, by 2 years after divorce, whether or not they initiate the divorce, the vast majority of women report being more satisfied with their family situation than they had been in the last year of their marriage. Furthermore, although divorced mothers report more childrearing stress than do nondivorced mothers, they also say that parenting is easier without a nonsupportive spouse who undermines or disagrees with their parenting practices. The balance between increased risk and stressors and positive life changes must be considered in examining the response to divorce (Hetherington, in press).

CUSTODY, CONTACT, AND CO-PARENTAL RELATIONS

In the vast majority of divorces, the mother is awarded custody of children; only 13% of fathers are awarded sole custody of their children at the time of divorce (Emery, 1988). In these cases, it is often because mothers are deemed incompetent, do not want custody of their children, or because male or adolescent children are involved. In spite of the overt or covert legal preference for mothers as custodians under the guise of best interests of the child or primary caregivers guidelines, there is no consistent evidence that fathers who seek custody are less competent parents than mothers (Warshak, 1992). In fact, by 2 years after divorce, custodial fathers report better family relations and fewer problems with their children than do custodial mothers (Furstenberg, 1988). This may be because custodial fathers, in contrast to custodial mothers, have higher incomes, more available supports, and are more likely to be caring for older children. In addition, fathers may be less sensitive and responsive than mothers to family dysfunction and behavior problems in children. However, reluctant fathers who assent to assume custody because of their wives' inability or disinclination to care for their children are less involved and able parents. A finding relevant to decisions involving custody is that, although there is some continuity in the pre- and postdivorce quality of parenting for mothers, there is little for fathers (Hetherington, Cox, & Cox, 1982). Some custodial fathers seem to exhibit a "Kramer versus Kramer" response and develop an involvement and parenting skills they had not had before the divorce, but some intensely attached noncustodial fathers find intermittent parenting painful and withdraw from their children. On the other hand, a substantial number of noncustodial fathers report that their relationship with their children improves after divorce.

On the average, noncustodial fathers become increasingly less available to their children. In the most recent national study using a probability sample, mothers reported that, following divorce, only one-quarter of children see their fathers once a week or more, and over a third do not see their father at all or see them only a few times a year (Seltzer, 1991). Physical distance in residence, low socioeconomic status, remarriage, and having only female rather than male children are associated with less visitation by noncustodial fathers. Noncustodial mothers are more likely to maintain contact with their children than are noncustodial fathers (Furstenberg, 1988; Zill, 1988). This leads to the rather intriguing issue as to whether differences found in children in a mother's custody, and a father's custody are attributable to the relationship with the custodial parent or to differences in the child's contact with the noncustodial parent and additional support in childrearing for custodial fathers provided by noncustodial mothers.

The move toward facilitating visitation and joint custody has been based on the premises that continued contact with both parents is desirable and that noncustodial parents with joint custody will be more likely to maintain contact and financial support. The response to the first premise must be that it depends on who is doing the visiting and on the relationship between the parents. If the noncustodial parent is reasonably well-adjusted, competent in parenting, and has a close relationship with the child, and if the child is not exposed to conflict between the two parents, continued contact can have a salutary effect on the child's adjustment. However, it takes an exceptionally close relationship with a noncustodial parent to buffer a child from the deleterious effects of a conflictual, nonsupportive relationship with a custodial parent (Hetherington et al., 1982). If there is high conflict between the parents, joint custody and continued contact can have adverse effects on the child (Maccoby, Depner, & Mnookin, 1988; Wallerstein & Blakeslee, 1989). Furthermore, there is some evidence that, after remarriage, although continued involvement of the noncustodial father with the child does not interfere with family functioning in the stepfamily, frequent visits by the noncustodial mother may be associated with negative relations between children, especially daughters, and their stepmothers (Brand, Clingempeel, & Bowen-Woodward, 1988).

Although cooperative, consensual coparenting following divorce is the ideal relationship (Camara & Resnick, 1988), in most cases the best that can be attained is one of independent but noninterfering parental relations. In a substantial group of families, conflict is sustained or accelerates following divorce (Hetherington et al., 1982; Kline, Johnston, & Tschan, 1991; Maccoby, Depner, & Mnookin, 1990). Interparental conflict in the long run is related to diminished contact and fewer child support payments by noncustodial fathers (Seltzer, 1991). In addition, in such conflicted relationships, children may feel caught in the middle as they are sometimes asked to carry messages between parents, to inform each parent of the other's activities, to defend one parent against the other's disparaging remarks, or to justify wanting to spend time with the other parent (Buchanon, Maccoby, & Dornbusch, 1991; Hetherington, in press). Being "caught in the middle," rather than divorce per se, or loss of contact with a noncustodial parent, has the most adverse effect on children's behavior and psychological well-being. Parental conflict provides children with an opportunity to exploit parents and play one off against the other, and when they are older, to escape careful monitoring of their activities. However children, especially older children, are able to function well over time in independent, noninterfering households. As long as they are not involved in parental conflict, children are able to cope well even if these households have different rules and expectations. Children are able to learn the differing role demands and constraints required in relating to diverse people in a variety of social situations such as in the peer group, church, the classroom, on the playing field, or at grandmother's house. In view of children's adaptability and differentiated responses to a broad range of social situations, the resistance to recognizing that children can cope with two different home situations is remarkable. Problems in joint custody come when parents interfere in each other's child rearing, and when children don't want to leave their friends, neighborhoods, or regular routines. In the rare cases where joint custody requires shifts between schools, this too may become a burden. Difficulty in visitation under any custody arrangement may emerge as children grow older and want to spend more time with their peers and less with parents.

Joint custody does tend to promote greater contact and financial support by noncustodial parents (Maccoby et al., 1988). Noncustodial fathers or fathers with joint custody are more likely to support children when they feel they have power in decisions relating to their children's life circumstances and activities. However, under conditions of high conflict, the increased contact associated with joint custody can be detrimental to the well-being of the child. Under conditions of low or encapsulated conflict, or emotional distancing between the parents, the effects of contact will be positive or at least neutral. Most children want to maintain contact with both parents and are more satisfied with continued contact. However, if the custodial parent has formed a hostile alliance with the child against the noncustodial parent, if the child feels caught in the middle of the parental conflict, or if the noncustodial parent has been extremely dysfunctional (e.g., abusive), children may seek to limit their contact with the nonresidential parent.

ADJUSTMENT OF DIVORCED PARENTS

Separation and divorce place both men and women at risk for psychological and physical dysfunction (Chase-Lansdale & Hetherington, 1990). In the immediate aftermath of marital dissolution, both men and women often exhibit extreme emotional lability, anger, depression, anxiety, and impulsive, and antisocial behavior, but for most this is gone by 2 years following divorce. However, even in the long run, alcoholism, drug abuse, psychosomatic problems, accidents, depression, and antisocial behavior are more common in divorced than nondivorced adults (Bloom, Asher, & White, 1978). Furthermore, recent research suggests that marital disruption alters the immune system, making divorced persons more vulnerable to disease, infection, chronic and acute medical problems, and even death (Kiecolt-Glaser et al., 1987). Some of these postdivorce symptoms in adults, such as depression and antisocial behavior, seem likely to have been present before divorce and even to have contributed to a distressed marriage and to marital dissolution. Depression and antisocial behavior are related to irritable, conflictual marital interactions. Adults exhibiting antisocial behavior are more likely to have disordered social relationships, to encounter negative life events, and to undergo multiple marital transitions (Forgatch et al., in press). Our own work, examining couples who later divorced, suggests that, especially for women in distant or hostile, conflicted marriages, depression is likely to decline following divorce, whereas antisocial behavior is likely to remain constant or to increase. Continued attachment to the ex-spouse is associated both with health problems and depression (Kiecolt-Glaser et al., 1987). This connection, however, declines with repartnering and the formation of a close meaningful relationship (Hetherington et al., 1982; Forgatch et al., in press).

We spoke earlier of divorce, like death of a spouse, involving loss of a way of life. It also involves loss of aspects of the self sustained by that way of life (Silverman, 1988). Because of this, the early years of separation and divorce offer great opportunity for positive and negative change. In this early phase, separated and divorced men and women often complain of being disoriented, of not knowing who they are or who they want to be, and of behaving in ego alien ways. They speak of having "not me experiences" where previously rational, self-controlled individuals report such things as smearing dog feces on their exspouse's face, following them and peering into their bedroom windows, defacing their property, fantasizing and sometimes acting out violent impulses, or whining and begging for reconciliation. "I can't believe I did that" or "That wasn't really me" is repeatedly heard in interviews with divorcing adults. Many noncustodial fathers feel rootless, disoriented, shut out of regular contact with their children and nurture unrealistic fantasies of reconciliation. Others throw themselves into a frenzy of social activity and try to develop a more open, free-living persona.

Conventional women have more problems in adapting to their new life situation than do less conventional, more internally controlled, androgynous, or working women. Nonemployed women in traditional marriages have often organized their identities around the achievements of their husbands and children. One said, "I used to be Mrs. John Jones, the bank manager's wife. Now I'm Mary Jones! Who is Mary Jones?" In spite of the problems with income, housing, inadequate childcare, loneliness, and limited resources and support encountered by many divorced women, our work shows that about 70% in the long run, prefer their new life to an unsatisfying marriage. Most think that divorce and raising children alone have provided an experience of personal growth, albeit sometimes painful growth. Some of these women were competent, autonomous women before the divorce. Others, in coping with the demands of their new situation, discovered strengths, developed skills, and attained levels of individuation that might never have emerged if they had remained in the constraints of a dysfunctional marriage. It should be noted however, that in comparison to married women, divorced women are overrepresented at both extremes of competence and adjustment. Some are found in a group with high self-esteem and few psychological problems who function ably in social situations, in the workplace, and in the family. Others seem permanently overwhelmed by the losses and changes in their lives, show little adequate coping behavior, and exhibit low self-esteem and multiple problems such as depression, antisocial behavior, substance abuse, and repeated, unsuccessful intimate relationships. Job training, continued education, and professional enhancement play important roles not only in the economic, but also the psychological, well-being of women. Adequate childcare is critical in facilitating these activities (Burns, 1992). Although work satisfaction plays an important role in the self-esteem of divorced adults, most custodial mothers and fathers restrict their social, and to some extent, work activities, and organize their lives around providing and caring for their children. Adequacy in these roles is central to their self-esteem.

Repartnering is the single factor that contributes most to the life satisfaction of divorced men and women; however, it seems more critical to men. Divorced fathers are less likely than divorced mothers to show marked personal growth and individuation while they are single. Men show more positive development in the security of a marriage.

The significance for children of these psychological, emotional, and physical changes in parents is that, in the early years following divorce, children are encountering an altered parent at a time when they need stability in a rapidly changing life situation. A physically ill, emotionally disturbed, or preoccupied parent and a distressed, demanding, angry child may have difficulty giving each other support or solace. Over time, the well-being of the child is associated with the adjustment of the custodial parent, and this is largely an indirect path mediated by parenting behaviors. If parent distress, low self-esteem, depression, or antisocial behavior results in disrupted parenting, behavior problems in children increase (Hetherington & Clingempeel, 1992; Patterson & Bank, 1989; Forgatch et al., in press). If a disturbed parent is able to maintain authoritative qualities, such as responsiveness, warmth, firm control, monitoring, and communication, adverse effects on children are less likely to occur.

There is an exception to the finding that the well-being of the parent is related to the well-being of the child. We identified one small cluster of egocentric, self-fulfilling women who, on standardized personality tests and measures of self-esteem, were functioning well. They reported high levels of life satisfaction and success in the workplace and in social relations, and were adapting remarkably well to their new life situation. Following divorce, they threw themselves into continued education, job enhancement, and self-improvement programs, were socially active, systematically built a new social network, and sought out new stable intimate relationships. However, their success came at the expense of their children's well-being. They spent little time with their children, were emotionally disengaged, and preoccupied with their own needs and activities. These children were among the most dysfunctional in our study, showing high levels of depression and acting-out behavior and low levels of self-esteem, social competence, and academic competence. For most families, however, maternal self-esteem and individuation were associated with more competent parenting and fewer behavior problems in children in divorced families.

PARENT–CHILD RELATIONS

The first 2 years following divorce are associated with a period of diminished parenting in divorced custodial mothers characterized by preoccupation, irritability, and nonsupportive, erratically punitive discipline. The decline in monitoring and control of children's behavior is marked, with parents not consistently enforcing their demands. Divorced custodial parents in comparison to nondivorced parents are less likely to know where their children are, what they are doing, or who they are with (Forgatch et al., in press; Hetherington et al., 1982). Children in the early years following divorce are likely to exhibit increased noncompliant, angry, demanding, dependent behavior with their custodial mothers. Divorced mothers and their sons are particularly likely to engage in escalating, mutually coercive interchanges. By 2 years after divorce, as the family adapts to its new situation and begins to establish a new equilibrium, the problems in mother–son relations diminish but always remain more disturbed than those in nondivorced families. In contrast, mothers and daughters usually have constructed a close, harmonious, often companionate, relationship by this time. In established mother-custody families, there is both intense positive and negative affect, considerable time spent in shared activities, and relative autonomy of family members.

One of the most notable results of divorce is a shift in the distribution of power within the family system. As Robert Weiss (1979) has said, children in these families do "grow up faster." Sons and daughters in post-divorce homes often are given additional responsibilities, independence, and increased power in decision-making (Weiss, 1979; Hetherington, 1991b). It is on daughters that the greatest responsibility for household tasks, care of younger siblings, and the role of confidant for the mothers personal concerns are likely to fall. Whether these demands lead to positive or negative child outcomes seems to be a function of the age appropriateness of the demands and the capacities and resources of the child. Age-inappropriate parental expectations, or demands that interfere with normative activities, are related to resentment and sometimes to anxiety and depression or rebellious, antisocial child behavior, including elevated rates of drug use, delinquency, and psychopathology (Peterson & Zill, 1986). However, if mothers are supportive, and foster an egalitarian atmosphere, children may actually benefit from increased participation and responsibility in family life.

Adolescence is a time when problems may reemerge in renewed conflict and coercive discipline between divorced mothers and daughters. These parenting behaviors are often in response to daughters', especially early-maturing daughters', precocious sexual or acting-out behavior. Divorced mothers may increase their monitoring and control of adolescent daughters, but this seems to be a reactive rather than proactive attempt at influence and is usually unsuccessful (Hetherington, 1989; in press; Hetherington & Clingempeel, 1992).

Custodial fathers, like custodial mothers, complain of task overload. However, they are more willing to assign responsibilities to their children, have fewer problems in discipline, and have more economic and social supports available to help them in childrearing (Hetherington & Stanley-Hagan,

1986; Furstenberg, 1988). In adolescence, however, they do have more difficulty with their daughters' sexual education and activities, and they monitor their children less well than do mothers. This lack of adequate paternal monitoring is related to the higher levels of problem behavior reported in adolescents from father- than mother-custody homes (Maccoby, Buchanan, Mnookin, & Dornbusch, in press).

Authoritative parenting, in contrast to disengaged, authoritarian, or permissive parenting, is associated with higher levels of social and academic competence and lower levels of psychopathology in children from both nondivorced and divorced families (Baumrind, 1991; Hetherington & Clingempeel, 1992; Steinberg, Mounts, Lamborn, & Dornbusch, 1991). The effects on children of a wide range of ecological stressors and parent distress and psychopathology are, to a large extent, moderated or mediated by positive parenting (Lempers, Clark-Lempers, & Simons, 1989; Forgatch et al., in press; Hetherington & Clingempeel, 1992). Authoritative parenting by the custodial parent is more influential than that of the noncustodial parent, particularly as the salience of the noncustodial parent decreases with time. With younger children, authoritative parenting by the custodial parent eventually obliterates the effects of divorce. However, adolescents in restabilized divorced families with an authoritative custodial mother exhibit more behavior problems than do children in nondivorced families with authoritative parents (Hetherington & Clingempeel, 1992). This suggests that factors other than parent–child relations, such as relationships with siblings and peers and experiences in extrafamilial settings, play an increasingly salient role as children grow older.

It must be recognized that the parent–child relationship involves bidirectional processes. It is much easier to be an authoritative parent when dealing with a competent, well-adjusted, responsive child. There is considerable evidence that, as children grow older, they are more influential in shaping their parents' behavior (Hetherington, in press). Under stressful life conditions or when the family is in a state of transition or disequilibrium, antisocial, externalizing behavior in adolescents is especially likely to lead to coercive, erratic, nonauthoritative responses in parents. Under such conditions, the adolescent often has more influence in steering parent–child interactions, and in modifying the subsequent behavior of the parent, than vice versa (Hetherington & Clingempeel, 1992; Forgatch et al., in press).

In older children and adolescents, about one–third of children, especially sons, in divorced or remarried families become disengaged from their families. If this disengagement also involves association with an antisocial peer group, it is related to delinquent behavior in children. However, if a close supportive relationship with a competent adult outside of the family is available, (e.g., the parent of a friend, a grandparent, a teacher or neighbor) disengagement may be a positive solution to an adverse family situation (Hetherington, 1989).

SIBLING RELATIONSHIPS IN DIVORCED FAMILIES

Changes in family relationships following divorce are found not only in parent–child relationships, but also in sibling relationships. Divorce is associated with conflict, aggression, rivalry, and disengagement in sibling relationships, which, in turn, are correlated with externalizing behavior in children (Hetherington, 1989; Hetherington & Clingempeel, 1992). Conflict between divorced spouses as well as marital conflict in nondivorced families are related to the quality of sibling relationships (MacKinnon, 1989). However, the effects on child adjustment of conflict in the marital relationship are usually found to be mediated by inept, nonauthoritative parenting (Hetherington & Clingempeel, 1992). In divorced families, sibling dyads in which there is a male exhibit more disengagement and negativity than pairs of female siblings or siblings in nondivorced families. Boys in divorced families tend to receive less support from either mothers or female siblings than do girls. In contrast, a subgroup of female siblings in divorced families form mutually supportive relationships. When a buffering effect for positive sibling relations occurs, it is most likely to emerge with female siblings and in adolescents, rather than younger children (Hetherington, 1988; in press; Hetherington & Clingempeel, 1992; Kempton et al., 1991).

EXTRAFAMILIAL SUPPORT SYSTEMS

Extrafamilial support systems can serve as sources of practical and emotional support for both parents and children experiencing family transitions. Just as authoritative parents can offer support to children going through their parents' marital transitions, authoritative schools can offer support to children undergoing stressful experiences (Hetherington, in press). Day care centers and schools that provide warm, structured, and predictable environments can offer stability to children experiencing a rapidly changing family environment, chaotic household routines, an altered parent, and inconsistent parenting. However, it has been found that although an authoritative school environment can, to some extent, buffer children from the adverse effects of having no authoritative parent in the home, it adds less with one authoritative parent (Hetherington, in press; C. E. MacKinnon, personal communication). In addition, responsive peers and school personnel can validate the self-worth, competence, and personal control of the adolescent who has access to these extrafamilial supports, whereas academic difficulties and dysfunctional peer relations exacerbate children's behavior problems (Patterson & Bank, 1989; Hetherington, 1989; Rutter, 1987).

Supports offered by friends and family also can increase divorced parents' positive attitudes toward themselves and their life situation and can facilitate the parenting role (Hetherington, 1989). Following divorce, often for economic reasons, between 25% and 33% of newly divorced custodial mothers reside with a relative, usually their own mothers (Hernandez, 1988). The grandmother often provides economic resources and shares in child care and household responsibilities. Thus, the grandmother may partially relieve the mother's financial concerns and sense of task overload, as well as provide the child with another source of needed emotional support. Researchers have found that, in African-American families, children who live with both mother and grandmother adjust better than do children who reside with a divorced mother alone (Kellam, Ensminger, & Turner, 1977). Furthermore, sons in the custody of mothers show fewer behavior problems when they have an involved, supportive grandfather than when none is available (Hetherington, 1989). When they have the economic resources to do so, most custodial mothers prefer to establish their own households, thus avoiding feelings of dependency and conflict over childrearing issues that may arise when they share a residence with their own parents. Such conflicts between custodial mothers and their parents occur less often with grandfathers than with grandmothers (Hetherington, 1989).

In the past decade, formal intervention programs for divorced families have been introduced. These interventions usually focus on one of three levels: coping skills training for children (child level) (Alpert-Gelles, Pedro-Carrol, & Cowen, 1989; Stolberg & Garrison, 1985); divorce mediation or coping skills training for parents (parent level) (Emery, Matthews, & Wyer, 1991; Forgatch et al., in press); or changes in divorce and child custody laws (legal level) (Albiston, Maccoby, & Mnookin, 1990; Furstenberg, 1990; Maccoby et al., 1988). Although all of these forms of intervention have been demonstrated to be helpful in promoting child adjustment, which intervention, or combination of interventions, is most advantageous is still open to question (Grych & Fincham, in press; Forgatch et al., in press).

THE ADJUSTMENT OF CHILDREN FOLLOWING DIVORCE

We have emphasized that divorce should be regarded not as an isolated event but as part of an extended series of transitions involving multiple changes in the experiences of parents and children. The point at which we tap into the course of these transitions will, to a large extent, determine our evaluation of the impact of divorce on family members. Since a chapter by the Vishers' on remarriage (see Chapter 8, this volume) is included in this volume, we have avoided discussing the effects of remarriage on parents and children. This misrepresents the role of marital transitions in childrens' development since, for most children, life in a single-parent household following divorce is a way station not a destination; about half of divorced adults remarry within 3–5 years of divorce, and children spend an average of 5 years in a single-parent household (Glick & Lin, 1986). Remarriage has a marked influence on the experiences and adjustment of both parents and children; however in this chapter we focus only on divorce and childrens' adjustment in families in which the custodial parent has not remarried (Hetherington, Stanley-Hagan, & Anderson, 1989; Hetherington, 1991a; Hetherington & Clingempeel, 1992).

Divorce and Children's Distress

The decision to divorce is usually made on the basis of the possibility of improving the life situation of parents, in many instances with little or no consideration for the concerns of the child. Few children wish for their parents divorce, and they initially respond with considerable anger, resentment, anxiety, and unhappiness. Even as adults, offspring of divorced parents often have painful memories and feelings about their parents' divorce (Wallerstein & Blakeslee, 1989) in spite of the fact that most eventually have coped well with their new life situation. Although resiliency, not enduring adverse consequences, is most characteristic of childrens' responses to divorce, divorce is not an easy experience (Emery & Forehand, 1992). Children often fantasize about their parents' reconciliation, fear abandonment by both parents, and are discomforted by their peers knowing about their family situation (Kurdek & Berg, 1987; Wallerstein & Kelly, 1980). Adults whose parents divorced when they were children, unlike those from intact families, report that childhood was the most unhappy time in their lives (Kulka & Weingarten, 1979; Wallerstein & Blakeslee, 1989). The discussion that follows, although it focuses on diversity and resiliency in response to divorce, in no way negates the importance of the experience of divorce. Painful experiences, even if positively coped with, are important.

Social, Emotional, and Academic Adjustment of Children and Adolescents

Most children show some problems in the first 2 years following their parents' divorce. After this initial crisis period, some children exhibit remarkable resiliency and emerge as well-functioning, competent, or even enhanced individuals. Other children suffer sustained developmental delays or disruptions, and still others appear to adapt well in the early stage of the transition but show delayed effects, especially in adolescence and early adulthood (Hetherington, 1989; Chase-Lansdale & Hetherington, 1990).

A recent meta-analysis of 92 studies on the effects of divorce on children's adjustment concluded that, in comparison to children in nondivorced families, children in divorced families show more problems in social and psychological adjustment (Amato & Keith, 1991a). It should be noted, however, that the effect sizes are small. Furthermore, the effect sizes have decreased over time as divorce has become more common and accepted. Effect sizes are also larger in clinical studies than in research involving representative samples of the population. It may be that the use of mean levels on various measures of adjustment and psychopathology obscures differences between children from divorced and nondivorced families, since there is considerable variability in the adjustment of children from divorced families. Children from divorced families tend not only to be overrepresented in clusters of children with multiple problems and high levels of dysfunctional behavior, but also girls from divorced families are overrepresented in groups of exceptionally competent, resilient children. Studies that use clinical cutoffs on standardized measures, rather than mean levels, indicate that almost twice as many children from divorced families (20%) as from nondivorced families (10%) score above the clinical cutoff on such scales as total behavior problems or externalizing on the Child Behavior Checklist (Achenbach & Edelbrock, 1983; Forgatch et al., in press; Hetherington & Clingempeel, 1992; Hetherington, 1991a; in press; Zill, Morrison, & Cairo, in press). This overrepresentation at extreme levels of deviant behavior may be one reason that effects of divorce are more often found in clinical studies. It should be kept in mind however, that although 20% of children are showing extreme levels of behavior problems even beyond the crisis period of the divorce transition, 80% are functioning within the normal range.

In the first 2 years following divorce, children tend to show increases in externalizing and internalizing behavior and decreases in social and academic competence (Allison & Furstenberg, 1989; Camara & Resnick, 1988; Forehand et al., 1991; Guidubaldi, Clemshaw, Perry, & McLoughlin, 1983; Hetherington et al., 1985; Peterson & Zill, 1986). Furthermore, although pre-adolescent girls usually rapidly adjust to their new life situation in a mother custody home, boys continue to exhibit noncompliant, impulsive, aggressive, antisocial behavior as long as 4–8 years after divorce (Guidubaldi & Perry, 1985; Hetherington, 1991a; Hetherington & Clingempeel, 1992).

Although most research on the effects of divorce has been done with preadolescent children, recent work suggests that adolescents from divorced families are at risk for problems in social adjustment and school dropout (Forgatch et al., in press; Hetherington, 1991a; Hetherington & Clingempeel, 1992; Krein & Beller, 1988). It may be that adolescence actually triggers behavior problems in children who previously have been adapting well in divorced and remarried families (Hetherington, 1991a; Bray, 1988). Gender differences often obtained with younger children are rarely found with adolescents. In adolescence, the behavior of girls in divorced families becomes increasingly less similar to that of girls in nondivorced families and more similar to boys in divorced families (Baumrind, 1991; Hetherington, 1991a; Hetherington & Clingempeel, 1992). Adolescents in divorced families are less socially competent, more aggressive, noncompliant and sexually active, and more likely to use drugs and alcohol and to become substance abusers (Baumrind, 1989; Doherty & Needle, 1991; Dornbusch et al., 1985; Hetherington, 1991a; Hetherington & Clingempeel, 1992; Kalter, 1977; Newcomer

& Udry, 1987; Needle, Su, & Doherty, 1990; Steinberg, 1987). Early physical maturation, an overtly sexually active mother, older friends, and the belief that friends are sexually active, play an important role in the precocious sexual behavior of girls in divorced families (Hetherington, in press).

Differences between adolescents in divorced and nondivorced families are also found in academic performance and rates of school dropouts, even after controlling for differences in socioeconomic status (Giudubaldi et al., 1983; Hetherington, 1991a; Krein & Beller, 1988; McLanahan, 1985; McLanahan & Bumpass, 1988). A recent study (Zimiles & Lee, 1991) found that low achievement was the primary factor associated with dropout in nondivorced families whereas social and behavior problems were more likely to lead to dropout in children from divorced families. Moreover, the finding that girls were at greater risk if they lived in a remarried family with a stepmother, and boys were more vulnerable if they lived with a divorced custodial mother, suggests that having a same-sex biological parent in the household can act as a buffer against dropout.

There is other evidence that school-aged children adapt better in the custody of a parent of the same sex (Camara & Resnick, 1988; Zill, 1988). Boys in the custody of their fathers are more mature, social, and independent, are less demanding, and have higher self-esteem than boys in the custody of their mothers. Sons in father-custody homes, however, are also less communicative and less overtly affectionate, perhaps as a result of less exposure to a mother's expressiveness. Girls, in the custody of their fathers, show higher levels of aggression and behavior problems and less prosocial behavior than do girls in the custody of their mothers (Furstenberg, 1988; Maccoby et al., in press). There are so few studies of father-custody families using representative samples and sophisticated measures of family process and children's adjustment that these provocative findings need further replication.

Individual Differences in Children's Response to Divorce

Many investigators have examined individual characteristics of the child, such as age at time of divorce, gender, intelligence, temperament, and personality in attempting to explain diversity in children's response to divorce. Research findings on the effects of age at the time of divorce on children's adjustment are inconsistent. Some studies have reported that young children are most adversely affected (Allison & Furstenberg, 1989; Kalter & Rembar, 1981; Zill et al., in press); other studies have found that the deleterious impact of divorce in adolescence is equal or sometimes greater than that found when divorce occurs earlier (Frost & Pakiz, 1990; Needle et al., 1990). It is clear, however, that adolescents are better able to understand the reasons for their parents' divorce and to utilize extrafamilial sources of support in dealing with the divorce (Hetherington, 1991b). One of the problems in interpreting age effects in longitudinal studies is that age at the time of divorce and length of time since divorce are often confounded. In studies that report more current adjustment problems when the divorce occurred during children's early years, it is usually impossible to discern whether this is attributable to the timing of divorce or to the longer period of time children have been exposed to the concommitant stressors found in one-parent families or stepfamilies.

Although in older studies gender differences were frequently reported, with the effects of divorce being more severe and enduring for boys, consistent gender effects are less likely to be found in more recent studies (Amato & Keith, 1991a). When gender differences are found, they are most likely to be obtained in preschool and elementary school children but not in adolescents (Zaslow, 1988). It has been argued that, when boys are found to be more disturbed than girls, it is because most studies involve mother-custody families, and young boys are more likely than girls to get involved in coercive cycles with their divorced custodial mothers. They also are more likely to be exposed to parental conflict. Parents fight more and their fights are longer in the presence of sons than daughters (Hetherington et al., 1982). Furthermore, families with sons are less likely to divorce than are those with daughters (Glick & Lin, 1986). This may be attributable to the greater involvement and attachment of fathers to sons or to the reluctance of mothers to attempt raising male children alone. Whatever the reason, it seems likely that parents of sons may remain together longer, even in an acrimonious marriage, and that sons may be exposed to more conflict, both before and after divorce. In addition, in times of family stress, boys, like their fathers, are less able than girls to disclose their feelings and solicit support from parents, other adults, and peers (Hetherington, 1989).

Characteristics other than age and gender, such as intelligence, temperament, personality, and psychopathology, also protect or put children at risk as they confront stressful life events. Children who already have vulnerabilities, such as poor cognitive competence, behavior problems, or a difficult temperament, may have these difficulties exacerbated or amplified by stress (Rutter, 1987; Hetherington, 1991a). In contrast cognitively or socially competent children, or children with easy temperaments, are more able to cope with adverse life experiences, such as divorce. It has even been found that temperamentally easy girls, with some supports available, may experience enhanced social competence after encountering moderate levels of stress (Hetherington, 1991a). This has been called an inoculation or steeling effect where some experience in coping with stress under supportive conditions facilitates the ability to adjust to new stressors (Rutter, 1987). Thus, under conditions of stress, the psychologically poor get poorer and the psychologically rich may get richer. To some extent this is because children who already have personal problems, in contrast to less vulnerable children, are more likely to encounter multiple, aversive experiences in interpersonal relations and have fewer resources to serve as buffers against them during or following stressful events or transitions (Caspi & Elder, 1988).

The role of intelligence and temperament may be of special interest, since behavior genetics studies of identical and fraternal twins and adopted children find a substantial contribution of heritability to these characteristics and considerable stability in these attributes beyond age 3. Garmezy (1991) reports that 30% of the individual differences in children's adaptation to stressful life events are attributable to intelligence. Even with the relatively restricted range of intelligence in the white middle-class families with which we work, we find that 15% of the variance in coping with parental divorce and remarriage is attributable to intelligence. This is not just because bright children are better problem solvers but because bright children are more skilled in peer relations, more popular, and have greater scholastic success. Positive relations in the peer group, academic success, and, to a lesser extent, attainments in extracurricular activities and athletics (particularly for boys), can serve as buffers against the effects of adverse family relations. These factors become increasingly important in adolescence.

Temperamentally difficult children have been described as being irritable and fearful, active and inattentive, low in sociability, distressed by new situations, and difficult to soothe. They are less adaptable to change and more vulnerable to adversity than are temperamentally easy children. Rutter (1987) proposes that the difficult child is more likely to be both the elicitor and target of aversive responses by the parents, especially when the parents are experiencing stress. The temperamentally easy child not only is less likely to be the recipient of criticism, displaced anger, and anxiety but also is more able to cope with these responses. Mothers are more responsive than fathers to temperamental differences in children and are more likely to target temperamentally difficult boys than girls when they are under stress. These effects are particularly marked under the conditions of the multiple changes and stresses found in divorced and remarried families (Hetherington, 1989, 1991a). Thus, boys who have been identified as temperamentally difficult before their parents' divorce or remarriage are more likely than "easy" boys to exhibit high levels of behavior disorders in response to their parents' martial transitions, especially under conditions of high stress and low support.

Although intelligence, an easy temperament, internal locus of control, and high self-esteem are associated with lower rates of psychopathology and higher competence in both divorced-and-nondivorced families, the differences in adjustment between children who are high and low on these attributes are most marked in conflicted, dysfunctional, intact families and in stressed, divorced families. This is especially the case in families with non-authoritative custodial mothers who have few available supports. However, in general, if children move from highly conflicted, intact families into a more harmonious, supportive situation in a single-parent family, behavior problems eventually decline. In contrast, children exhibit an increase in behavior problems over time when they move from a predivorce situation that involved little overt conflict or stress and a close attachment to a parent who becomes less available following divorce, to a home situation with an inept custodial parent, overt conflict between the divorced spouses, and multiple life stressors. These effects are most marked for the less competent, more difficult children. Although there is some continuity in children's behavior problems across time, in the long run, current family relationships, adversity, and supports, rather than past conflict and divorce, are most strongly associated with emotional and behavioral problems and the adjustment of children.

CONSEQUENCES OF DIVORCE IN ADULTHOOD

Although there is less research on the impact of marital dissolution when children of divorce reach adulthood than in childhood or adolescence, the results of a recent meta-analysis indicate not only that effect sizes have declined in recent cohorts as divorce has become more common but also that effects may be larger for adults than children (Amato & Keith, 1991a, 1991b). Adults whose parents divorced when they were children are more likely than those with nondivorced parents to have problems in intimate relations and in work. They are more likely to marry early and have marital problems, to choose unstable partners, to have children before marriage, and to divorce earlier and with greater frequency (Amato & Keith, 1991a; Glenn & Kramer, 1985; Hetherington, 1972; Hetherington & Parke, 1986; Kurdek, 1991; McLanahan & Bumpass, 1988; Wallerstein & Blakesley, 1989). In view of higher rates of school dropouts in children from divorced families, it is perhaps not surprising that they also have lower educational attainments, income, and occupational prestige. These unsuccessful relationships and experiences are associated with less general life satisfaction, especially with friends and family relations, less happiness, and more depression and health problems. The effects of earlier parental divorce on later functioning in adulthood, as in childhood and adolescence, are less marked for African–Americans than for whites. Perhaps, this is because mother-headed households are more common among African-Americans and because African-Americans, whether in divorced or nondivorced families, suffer more adversity in general (Amato & Keith, 1991a).

Why should sleeper effects of divorce in work and intimate relations emerge in adolescence and adulthood? It seems likely that delayed effects may emerge when a new set of developmental tasks related to intimacy and sexuality, autonomy and individuation, and educational and occupational attainment, emerge in adolescence and continue into adulthood.

There has been some suggestion that the presence of two parents permits children to learn how to be skillful and secure both in loving and being loved by a member of the opposite sex. Children also acquire problem-

solving skills by viewing two adults of similar status attempting to negotiate and resolve their differences (Hetherington & Parke, 1986). These are
skills essential to developing and maintaining successful intimate relationships. Adult offspring of divorced parents have more unrealistic views of their
spouses and their relationships and are less adept at marital problem solving. Even before marriage, they are more likely than those from nondivorced
families, to expect to distrust a future spouse and to have expectations of an
unsuccessful marriage. Furthermore, they are more likely to believe that the
success of a marriage is externally controlled and depends not on their own
but on the other person's attributes and behavior. These expectations are
strongest for those adults who report the greatest degree of continued conflict between their divorced parents (Franklin, Janoff-Budman, & Roberts,
1990). These findings suggest that experiencing parental divorce as a child
has an impact in adulthood on beliefs and behaviors that are linked specifically to attitudes, expectations, and behavior in their own intimate relationships and marriages.

SUMMARY AND CONCLUSIONS

Most parents and children initially experience divorce as stressful, however
most are able to adapt to their new life situation in a few years if it is not
accompanied by sustained or new adversity. In the long run, children are
better adjusted in a well-functioning, single-parent family with low conflict
and an authoritative custodial parent than in a conflict-ridden, two-parent
household. Although divorce places children and parents at risk for encountering new challenges and multiple life stressors, it also can offer opportunities for personal growth, more gratifying relationships, and a more harmonious family situation. In general, the sustained adverse effects of divorce
on children's adjustment are small, and to some extent may be a legacy of
dysfunctional relations in the predivorce family. However, the customary
reliance on differences in the average levels of family member's adjustment
in divorced and nondivorced families may obscure the diversity found in
responses to divorce. Most parents and children eventually emerge as competent, even enhanced, individuals following divorce. However, a substantial minority exhibit problems in health and in emotional, psychological, and
social adjustment. Some of these problems are delayed and emerge only
when confronting the normative developmental tasks associated with intimacy, individuation, and achievement in adolescence and early adulthood.
Only by taking a developmental contextual approach will we begin to understand individual differences in risk and resiliency in response to divorce, the
multiple pathways leading to diverse outcomes, and variations in the timing
of the emergence of the sequelae of divorce. It is the diversity rather than
the inevitability of outcomes that is notable in response to divorce and
remarriage.

REFERENCES

Achenbach, T., & Edelbrock, C. S. (1983). *Manual for the Child Behavior Checklist and revised Child Behavior Profile.* New York: Queen City Printers.

Albiston, C. R., Maccoby, E. E., & Mnookin, R. H. (1990). Does joint legal custody matter? *Stanford Law and Policy Review, 42,* 167–179.

Allison, P. D., & Furstenberg, F. F. (1989). How marital dissolution affects children: Variations by age and sex. *Developmental Psychology, 25,* 540–549.

Alpert-Gillis, L. H., Pedro-Carroll, J. L., & Cowan, E. L. (1989). The Children of Divorce Intervention Program: Development, implementation and evaluation of a program for young urban children. *Journal of Consulting and Clinical Psychology, 57,* 583–589.

Amato, P. R., & Keith, B. (1991a). Parental divorce and the well-being of children: A meta-analysis. *Psychological Bulletin, 110,* 26–46.

Amato, P. R., & Keith, B. (1991b). Parental divorce and adult well-being: A meta-analysis. *Journal of Marriage and the Family, 53,* 43–58.

Baumrind, D. (1989, April). *Sex-differentiated socialization effects in childhood and adolescence in divorced and intact families.* Paper presented at the biennial meetings of the Society for Research on Child Development, Kansas City, MO.

Baumrind, D. (1991). Effective parenting during the early adolescent transition. In P. A. Cowan & E. M. Hetherington (Eds.), *Family transitions* (pp. 111–163). Hillsdale, NJ: Lawrence Erlbaum Associates.

Block, J. H., Block, J., & Gjerde, P. (1986). The personality of children prior to divorce. *Child Development, 57,* 827–840.

Block, J., Block, J. H., & Gjerde, P. F. (1988). Parental functioning and the home environment in families of divorce: Prospective and concurrent analyses. *Journal of the American Academy of Child and Adolescent Psychiatry, 27,* 207–213.

Bloom, B. L., Asher, S. J., & White, S. W. (1978). Marital disruption as a stressor: A review and analysis. *Psychological Bulletin, 85,* 867–894.

Brand, E., Clingempeel, W. G., & Bowen-Woodward, K. (1988). Family relationships and children's psychological adjustment in stepmother and stepfather families. In E. M. Hetherington & J. D. Arasteh (Eds.), *Impact of divorce, single parenting, and stepparenting on children* (pp. 299–324). Hillsdale, NJ: Lawrence Erlbaum Associates.

Bray, J. H. (1988). Children's development during early remarriage. In E. M. Hetherington & J. D. Arasteh (Eds.), *Impact of divorce, single parenting, and stepparenting on children* (pp. 279–298). Hillsdale, NJ: Lawrence Erlbaum Associates.

Buchanon, C. M., Maccoby, E. E., & Dornbusch, S. M. (1991). Caught between parents: Adolescents experience in divorced homes. *Child Development, 62,* 1008–1029.

Bumpass, L. L. (1984). Children and marital disruption: A replication and update. *Demography, 21,* 71–82.

Burns, A. (1992). Mother-headed families: An international perspective and the case of Australia. *Social Policy Report: Society for Research in Child Development, VI,* 1–22.

Camara, K. A., & Resnick, G. (1988). Interparental conflict and cooperation: Factors moderating children's post-divorce adjustment. In E. M. Hetherington & J. D. Arasteh (Eds.), *Impact of divorce, single-parenting and stepparenting on children* (pp. 169–195). Hillsdale, NJ: Lawrence Erlbaum Associates.

Caspi, A., & Elder, G. H. (1988). Emergent family patterns: The intergenerational construction of problem behavior and relationships. In R. A. Hinde & J. Stevenson-Hinde (Eds.), *Relationships within families* (pp. 218–240). Oxford: Clarendon Press.

Chase-Lansdale, P. L., & Hetherington, E. M. (1990). The impact of divorce on life-span development: Short and long term effects. In P. B. Baltes, D. L. Featherman, & R. M. Lerner (Eds.), *Life development and behavior* (Vol. 10, pp. 105–150). Hillsdale, NJ: Lawrence Erlbaum Associates.

Cherlin, A. (1981). *Marriage, divorce and remarriage: Changing patterns in the postwar United States.* Cambridge, MA: Harvard University Press.

Cherlin, A. J., Furstenberg, F. F., Chase-Lansdale, P. L., Kiernan, K. E., Robins, P. K., Morrison, D. R., & Teitler, J. O. (1991). Longitudinal effects of divorce in Great Britain and the United States. *Science, 252,* 1386–1389.

Doherty, W. J., & Needle, R. H. (1991). Psychological adjustment and substance abuse among adolescents before and after a parental divorce. *Child Development, 62,* 328–337.

Dornbusch, S., Carlsmith, J., Bushwall, S., Ritter, P., Leiderman, H., Hastorf., A., & Gross, R. (1985). Single parents extended households and the control of adolescents. *Child Development, 56,* 326–341.

Duncan, G. J., & Hoffman, S. D. (1985). Economic consequences of marital unstability. In M. David & T. Smeeding (Eds.), *Horizontal equity, uncertainty and well being* (pp. 427–469). Chicago: University of Chicago Press.

Emery, R. E. (1988). *Marriage, divorce, and children's adjustment.* Newbury Park, CA: Sage.

Emery, R. E., & Forehand, R. (1992, June). *Parental divorce and children's well being: A focus on resilience.* Paper presented at the William T. Grant Foundation's conference on "Risk, resiliency, and development: Research and intervention," Kiawah Island, South Carolina.

Emery, R. E., Matthews, S. G., & Wyer, M. M. (1991). Child custody mediation and litigation: Further evidence on the differing views of mothers and fathers. *Journal of Consulting and Clinical Psychology, 59,* 410–418.

Forehand, R., Wierson, M., Thomas, A. M., Fauber, R., Armistead, L., Kempton, J., & Long, N. (1991). A short-term longitudinal examination of young adolescent functioning following divorce: The role of family factors. *Journal of Abnormal Child Psychology, 19,* 97–111.

Forgatch, M. S., Patterson, G. R., & Ray, J. A. (in press). Divorce and boys' adjustment problems: Two paths with a single model. In E. M. Hetherington (Ed.), *Stress, coping, and resiliency in children and the family.* Hillsdale, NJ: Lawrence Erlbaum Associates.

Franklin, K. M., Janoff-Bulman, R., & Roberts, J. E. (1990). Long-term impact of parental divorce on optimism and trust: Changes in general assumptions or narrow beliefs? *Journal of Personality and Social Psychology, 59,* 743–755.

Frost, A. K., & Pakiz, B. (1990). The effects of marital disruption on adolescents: Time as a dynamic. *American Journal of Orthopsychiatry, 60,* 544–555.

Furstenberg, F. F. (1988). Child care after divorce and remarriage. In E. M. Hetherington & J. D. Arasteh (Eds.), *Impact of divorce, single parenting and stepparenting on children* (pp. 245–261). Hillsdale, NJ: Lawrence Erlbaum Associates.

Furstenberg, F. F. (1990). Divorce and the American family. *Annual Review of Sociology, 16,* 379–403.

Garmezy, N. (1991). Resilience in children's adaptation to negative life events and stressed environments. *Pediatric Annals, 20*(9), 459–466.

Glenn, N. D., & Kramer, K. B. (1985). The psychological well-being of adult children of divorce. *Journal of Marriage and the Family, 47,* 905–913.

Glick, P. C. (1988). The role of divorce in the changing family structure: Trends and variations. In S. A. Wolchik & P. Karoly (Eds.), *Children of divorce* (pp. 3–34). New York: NY: Gardner Press.

Glick, P. C., & Lin, S. (1986). Recent changes in divorce and remarriage. *Journal of Marriage and the Family, 48,* 737–747.

Gore, S., & Eckenroade, J. (1992, May). *Context and process in research on risk and resilience.* Paper presented at the William T. Grant Foundation Conference on Risk, Resiliency and Development: Research and Interventions, Kiawah Island, South Carolina.

Gottman, J. M. (in press). *Why marriages fail.* Hillsdale, NJ: Lawrence Erlbaum Associates.

Grych, J. H., & Fincham, F. D. (1992). Interventions for children of divorce: Toward greater integration of research and action. *Psychological Bulletin, 111*(3), 434–454.

Guidubaldi, J., Cleminshaw, H. K., Perry, J. D., & McLoughlin, C. S. (1983). The impact of parental divorce on children: Report of the nationwide NASP study. *School Psychology Review, 12,* 300–323.

Guidubaldi, J., & Perry, J. D. (1985). Divorce and mental health sequelae for children: A 2-year follow-up study of a nationwide sample. *American Journal of Child Psychiatry, 24,* 531–537.

Hernandez, D. J. (1988). Demographic trends and the living arrangements of children. In E. M. Hetherington & J. D. Arasteh (Eds.), *Impact of divorce, single-parenting, and stepparenting on children* (pp. 3–22). Hillsdale, NJ: Lawrence Erlbaum Associates.

Hetherington, E. M. (1972). Effects of father absence on personality development in adolescent daughters. *Developmental Psychology, 7,* 313–326.

Hetherington, E. M. (1988). Parents, children and siblings six years after divorce. In R. Hinde & J. Stevenson-Hinde (Eds.), *Relationships within families* (pp. 311–331). Oxford: Clarendon Press.

Hetherington, E. M. (1989). Coping with family transitions: Winners, losers, and survivors. *Child Development, 60,* 1–14.

Hetherington, E. M. (1991a). The role of individual differences and family relationships in children's coping with divorce and remarriage. In P. A. Cowan & E. M. Hetherington (Eds.), *Family transitions.* Hillsdale, NJ: Lawrence Erlbaum Associates.

Hetherington, E. M. (1991b). Families, lies and videotapes. *Journal of Research on Adolescence, 1,* 323–348.

Hetherington, E. M. (in press). A review of the Virginia Longitudinal Study of Divorce and Remarriage with a Focus on Early Adolescence. *Journal of Family Psychology.*

Hetherington, E. M., & Clingempeel, W. G. (1992). Coping with marital transitions: A family systems perspective. *Monographs of the Society for Research in Child Development, 57*(2–3, Serial No. 227).

Hetherington, E. M., Cox, M., & Cox, R. (1982). Effects of divorce on parents and children. In M. Lamb (Ed.), *Nontraditional families: Parenting and child development.* Hillsdale, NJ: Lawrence Erlbaum Associates.

Hetherington, E. M., Cox, M., & Cox, R. (1985). Long-term effects of divorce and remarriage on the adjustment of children. *Journal of the American Academy of Child Psychiatry, 24*, 518–530.

Hetherington, E. M., & Martin, B. (1986). Family factors and psychopathology in children. In H. C. Quay & J. S. Werry (Eds.), *Psychopathological disorders of childhood* (3rd ed., pp. 332–390). New York: John Wiley & Sons.

Hetherington, E. M., & Parke, R. D. (1986). *Child psychology: A contemporary viewpoint* (3rd ed.). New York: McGraw-Hill.

Hetherington, E. M., & Stanley-Hagan, M. (1986). Divorced fathers: Stress, coping, and adjustment. In M. E. Lamb (Eds.), *The father's role: Applied perspectives* (pp. 103–134). New York: John Wiley & Sons.

Hetherington, E. M., Stanley-Hagan, M., & Anderson, E. A. (1989). Marital transitions: A child's perspective. *American Psychologist, 44*, 303–312.

Hetherington, E. M., & Tryon, A. S. (1989). His and her divorces. *The Family Therapy Networker, 13*(6), 58–61.

Kalter, N. (1977). Children of divorce in an outpatient psychiatric population. *American Journal of Orthopsychiatry, 47*, 40–51.

Kalter, N., & Rembar, J. (1981). The significance of a child's age at the time of parental divorce. *American Journal of Orthopsychiatry, 51*, 85–100.

Kellam, S. G., Ensminger, M., & Turner, R. J. (1977). Family structure and the mental health of children: Concurrent and community-wide studies. *Archives of General Psychiatry, 54*, 1017–1022.

Kline, M., Johston, J. R., & Tschann, J. (1991). The long shadow of marital conflict: A model of post-divorce adjustment. *Journal of Marriage and the Family, 53*, 297–309.

Krein, S. F., & Beller, A. H. (1988). Educational attainment of children from single-parent families: Differences by exposure, gender, and race. *Demography, 25*, 221–234.

Kiecolt-Glaser, J. K., Fisher, L. D., Ogrocki, P., Stout, J. C., Spucler, B. S., & Glaser, R. (1987). Marital quality, marital disruption and immune function. *Psychosomatic Medicine, 40*, 13–34.

Kulka, R. A., & Weingarten, H. (1979). The long-term effects of parental divorce in childhood on adult adjustment. *Journal of Social Issues, 35*, 50–78.

Kurdek, L. A., & Berg, B. (1987). Childrens' beliefs about parental divorce scale: Psychometric characteristics and concurrent validity. *Journal of Consulting and Clinical Psychology, 55*, 712–718.

Kurdek, L. R. (1991). Divorce history, marital status, gender, and well-being. *Journal of Marriage and the Family, 53*, 71–78.

Lempers, J. D., Clark-Lempers, D., & Simons, R. (1989). Economic hardship, parenting and distress in adolescence. *Child Development, 60*, 25–39.

Maccoby, E. E., Buchanan, C. M., Mnookin, R. H., & Dornbusch, S. M. (in press). Post-divorce roles of mothers and fathers in the lives of their children. *Journal of Family Psychology.*

Maccoby, E. E., Depner, C. E., & Mnookin, R. H. (1988). Custody of children following divorce. In E. M. Hetherington & J. D. Arasteh (Eds.), *Impact of divorce, single parenting and stepparenting on children* (pp. 91–114). Hillsdale, NJ: Lawrence Erlbaum Associates.

Maccoby, E. E., Depner, C. E., & Mnookin, R. H. (1990). Co-parenting in the second year after divorce. *Journal of Marriage and the Family, 52*, 141–155.

MacKinnon, C. E. (1989). An observational investigation of siblings in divorced families. *Developmental Psychology, 25,* 36–44.

McGue, M., & Lykken, D. T. (1992). Genetic influences on risk for divorce. *Psychology Science, 3,* 368–373.

McLanahan, S. (1985). Family structure and the reproduction of poverty. *American Journal of Sociology, 90,* 873–901.

McLanahan, S., & Bumpass, L. (1988). Intergenerational consequences of family disruption. *American Journal of Sociology, 94,* 130–152.

Needle, R. H., Su, S. S., & Doherty, W. J. (1990). Divorce, remarriage and adolescent substance use: A prospective longitudinal study. *Journal of Marriage and the Family, 52,* 157–169.

Newcomer, S. F., & Udry, J. R. (1987). Parental marital status effects on adolescent sexual behavior. *Journal of Marriage and the Family, 49,* 235–240.

Nock, S. L. (1982). The life-cycle approach to family analysis. In B. B. Wolman (Ed.), *Handbook of marriage and the family.* New York: Plenum Press.

Notarius, C. J., & Vanzetti, N. A. (1983). The marital agenda protocol. In E. E. Filsinger (Ed.), *Marital and family assessment.* Beverly Hills, CA: Sage.

Patterson, G. R., & Bank, L. (1989). Some amplifying mechanisms for pathologic processes in families. In M. R. Gunnar & E. Thelan (Eds.), *Minnesota symposia on child psychology:* Vol. 22. *Systems and development.* Hillsdale, NJ: Lawrence Erlbaum Associates.

Peterson, J. L., & Zill, N. (1986). Marital disruption, parent–child relationships, and behavior problems in children. *Journal of Marriage and the Family, 48,* 295–307.

Rutter, M. (1987). Psychosocial resilience and protective mechanisms. *American Journal of Orthopsychiatry, 57,* 316–331.

Seltzer, J. A. (1991). Relationships between fathers and children who live apart: The father's role after separation. *Journal of Marriage and the Family, 53,* 79–101.

Silverman, P. R. (1988). In search of new selves: Accommodating to widowhood. In L. A. Bond (Ed.), *Families in transition: Primary prevention programs that work* (pp. 200–220). Beverly Hills, CA: Sage.

Steinberg, L. (1987). Single parents, stepparents, and the susceptibility of adolescents to antisocial peer pressure. *Child Development, 58,* 269–275.

Steinberg, L., Mounts, N. S., Lamborn, S. D., & Dornbusch, S. M. (1991). Authoritative parenting and adolescent adjustment across varied ecological niches. *Journal of Research on Adolescence, 1,* 19–36.

Stolberg, A. L., Camplair, C., Currier, K., & Wells, M. J. (1987). Individual, familial and environmental determinants of children's post-divorce adjustment and maladjustment. *Journal of Divorce, 11,* 51–70.

Stolberg, A. L., & Garrison, K. M. (1985). Evaluating a primary prevention program for children of divorce. *American Journal of Community Psychology, 13,* 111–124.

Teachman, J. D., Polonko, K. A., & Scanzoni, J. (1987). Demography of the family. In M. B. Sussman & S. K. Steinmetz (Eds.), *Handbook of marriage and the family* (pp. 3–36). New York: Plenum Press.

Wallerstein, J. S., & Blakeslee, S. (1989). *Second chances: Men, women and children a decade after divorce.* New York: Ticknor & Fields.

Wallerstein, J. S., & Kelly, J. (1980). *Surviving the breakup: How children and parents cope with divorce.* New York: Basic Books.

Warshak, R. A. (1992). *The custody revolution.* New York: Poseiden Press.

Weiss, R. S. (1979). Growing up a little faster: The experience of growing up in a single-parent household. *Journal of Social Issues, 35*, 97–111.

Werner, E. E. (1987). Vulnerability and resiliency in children at risk for delinquency: A longitudinal study from birth to young adulthood. In J. D. Burchard & S. M. Burchard (Eds.), *Prevention of delinquent behavior*. Beverly Hills, CA: Sage.

Zaslow, M. J. (1988). Sex differences in children's response to parental divorce: 1. Research methodology and postdivorce family forms. *American Journal of Orthopsychiatry, 58*, 355–378.

Zill, N. (1988). Behavior, achievement, and health problems among children in stepfamilies: Findings from a national survey of child health. In E. M. Hetherington & J. D. Arasteh (Eds.), *Impact of divorce, single-parenting and stepparenting on children* (pp. 325–368). Hillsdale, NJ: Lawrence Erlbaum Associates.

Zill, N., Morrison, D. R., & Coiro, M. J. (in press). Long-term effects of parental divorce on parent–child relationships, adjustment and achievement in young adulthood. *Journal of Family Psychology*.

Zimilees, H., & Lee, V. E. (1991). Adolescent family structure and educational progress. *Developmental Psychology, 27*, 314–320.

CHAPTER 8

REMARRIAGE FAMILIES AND STEPPARENTING

*Emily B. Visher
and John S. Visher*

INTRODUCTION

Stepfamilies are no longer an alternative form of the American family. During the past decade the number of households that include stepparents and stepchildren has increased dramatically. In fact, using a broad definition of a stepfamily (a household containing a child who is biologically related to only one of the adults), the well-known demographer, Paul C. Glick, using data from the 1987 National Survey of Families and Households (NSFH) estimated that 35% of *all* adults in the United States were in step situations either as stepparents, parents who had remarried, or adult stepchildren, and 20% of children under 19 were stepchildren or half-siblings. Thus, in 1987, 33% of the entire population was in a step situation (Glick, 1991).

Since many individuals have lived at one or more times in stepfamily situations that ended in death or divorce, and others will experience stepfamily life in their futures, Glick concluded his analysis by saying, "In this perspective, it would not be unreasonable to expect that more than half of all Americans alive today have been, are now, or will eventually be in one or more step situations before they die" (Glick, 1991).

American institutions such as the law, the schools, and the church, as well as American society in general, have not kept pace with these important family changes. Even though it is predicted that 35% of children born during the 1980s will live with a stepparent before they are 18 years old (Glick & Lin, 1986), and that by the year 2000 there will be more stepfamilies than any other type of American family (Glick & Lin, 1986), the general perception of "family" continues to be Mom, Dad, two children, and a dog.

Although there certainly is more recognition today of stepfamilies, they continue to exist under a dark cloud of negative stereotyping (Coleman & Ganong, 1987), and the term "stepchild" still is used extensively to connote less than adequate attention. This uncomfortable status no doubt contributes to the search for bland and neutral synonyms such as "reconstituted," "blended," or "remarriage" family in place of the more descriptive term: stepfamily. Our impression is that it will take many more years for society to overcome the influence of the old fairy tales, the negative bias toward divorce and remarriage, and the idealization of the nuclear family, so that marriages other than first marriages will be accepted as positive, albeit challenging, life cycle stages.

It is in this current problematic milieu that stepfamilies are created and attempt to move toward successful integration. We estimate that approximately 1,300 new stepfamilies are formed every day in the United States (Visher & Visher, 1979), and unfortunately, the divorce rate for second marriages is slightly higher than the generally accepted 50% figure for first marriages (Bumpass, Sweet, & Martin, 1990). In addition, about 20% of American children will experience more than one divorce before they become adults. Research is helpful in suggesting that it is not the structure per se of remarried families that is responsible for these divorces; as with other types of families, it is basically the quality of the relationships between the individuals in the family that determines its success (Pasley, 1987). However, within the more complex stepfamily structure, forming satisfactory relationships is often difficult and the uneasy interface between stepfamilies and the culture does not help with this process. A stepmother's words may mirror those of other stepparents when she says, "I feel as though everyone I know is looking over my shoulder waiting for me to screw up."

Unfortunately family pathologizing is prevalent in American society today. A recent cartoon shows a large auditorium with a banner overhead that identifies the gathering as the "Annual Convention of Adult Children of Normal Parents." Only two seats are occupied; the remaining auditorium is empty. For stepfamilies, as for other families, societal validation and support is an important ingredient for the maximization of individual and family potential. If this affirmation does develop it could lead stepfamilies to value their type of family more fully and view themselves as making a positive contribution to the diversity of family life in America.

STEPFAMILY RESEARCH

Over the past 10 years, empirical research concerned with stepfamily life has flourished in both quantity and quality. To date most normative stepfamily research concerns three types of remarriage families; the first are families in which the wife has children in the household; the second, those in which the husband has children in the household; and third, families in which both adults have children in the household. More recently, stepfamilies with a mutual child have also received attention. In the following, we discuss findings that have been corroborated by several studies.

Stepfather Families

Stepfather families are stepfamilies in which the man is the stepparent. Studies indicate that this type of stepfamily tends to have less stress than other types of stepfamilies (Clingempeel, Ievoli, & Brand, 1984; Crosbie-Burnett, 1984; Visher & Visher, 1979). Boys respond more favorably than girls to having a stepfather in the household (Santrock, Sitterle, & Warshak, 1988), and many children develop satisfying relationships with their stepfathers over time (Bohannan & Yahraes, 1979). For boys, having contact with their biological father tends to enhance the relationship with their stepfathers. Also, having no children other than stepchildren enhances the stepfather's ability to bond with his stepchildren (Furstenburg, 1987).

Stepmother Families

Families in which the woman is the stepparent are called stepmother families. This type of family tends to have more stress than do stepfather families (Clingempeel et al., 1984; Hetherington, 1989; Santrock & Sitterle, 1987; White & Booth, 1985). Children, particularly girls, also experience higher stress when they are living with their father and stepmother than when they are living with their mother and stepfather (Jacobson, 1987).

These findings are consistent and important because they indicate that there are strong situational dynamics at work that create special relationship problems for stepmother families. Since stepmother families are usually defined as stepfamilies in which the father has physical custody of at least one of his children, it may be that disturbances in mother–child bonding patterns, particularly mother–daughter bonding, are more upsetting to children than disturbances in the father–child relationship during and after divorce. Difficulty between the children's mother and stepmother also has been mentioned as a possible contribution to the greater stress in stepmother families (Visher & Visher, 1988).

The fact that women are still expected to set the emotional tone for the family probably contributes strongly to the differences in functioning between stepfather and stepmother families. As Walsh (1991) has commented,

> With traditional cultural expectations for women in families to assume responsibility for the well-being of all members, stepmothers tend to get into an over-responsible position for stepfamily integration and harmony and to assume it

is their fault if expectations aren't met. Because a woman's identity and self-esteem are so bound up with success in her role as mother and wife and with gaining love and approval, she is likely to feel the rebuffs of stepchildren as her inadequacy. (p. 541)

Another factor that may contribute to these differences is that in America, fathers, as a rule, move out after a divorce, and boys lose the person with whom they can most readily identify; after a remarriage, since 90% of the time children live with their mother, boys have gained an important male figure, whereas girls have retained their relationship with their biological mother and now need to share her with a new partner. Girls also may become competitive with their mothers for the attention of their stepfather (Hetherington, Cox, & Cox, 1985).

Complex Stepfamilies

Complex stepfamilies account for approximately 7% of stepfamilies and are those in which both adults have children from a previous marriage living in the household (White & Booth, 1985). These researchers have also found that the greatest likelihood of a redivorce is in complex stepfamilies. This finding has been confirmed by Becker, Landes, and Michael (1977), Cherlin (1978), and McCarthy (1978). Indeed, the greater the number of children, the more likely it will be that the couple will divorce (Hetherington, 1989). Working out these complex relationships is not easy.

Stepfamilies with a Mutual Child

About half of all remarried families have an "ours" child. Bernstein (1989) interviewed 150 people from 55 stepfamilies with a mutual child born during the remarriage. In general, if the child was born prior to successful stepfamily integration, there was likely to be increased stress and difficulty. For example, a stepmother who had no children of her own following the birth of a mutual child tended to devote more loving attention to her biological child than to her stepchildren. The husband, who was the parent of all the children, was upset with these differences in overt expression of feelings and emotional attachments. This created severe tension between the couple.

A child conceived early in the stepfamily integration process in an attempt to make a failing relationship work may in fact have an effect in the opposite direction. In most instances, however, if the child was born after the couple had formed a solid relationship, the parents considered that the birth of the child contributed positively to the integration of the family (Bernstein, 1989).

Knowing what is common in different types of stepfamilies can provide involved individuals with some understanding of the typical causes of stress in their particular stepfamily. This knowledge can enable them to deal more effectively with situations that arise. It also can enhance their self-esteem and coping skills by giving them a helpful perspective of common behaviors and situations. They can then experience the difficulties as typical challenges rather than as signals that the family is not successful.

THE INTEGRATION PROCESS

Remarriage families are families in transition from former households to an integrated stepfamily household (Whiteside, 1982; Walsh, 1991). It is a process that takes time, one that may be likened to the acculturation process of immigrating families as they move to a new country. In fact, the work of Judith Landau-Stanton (1985) with such families defines important similarities: There are many necessary adjustments to be made, and individuals and subgroups in the extended family often move toward acculturation at differing rates. This discrepancy of movement can lead to stressful interpersonal relations. What is important is that these symptoms are related to transitional difficulties rather than being manifestations of serious intrapsychic problems (Visher & Visher, 1988).

Although everyone in stepfamilies must make many adjustments to new situations, children frequently have additional complexities because they retain "dual citizenship" (M. Weston, personal communication) in two households and cultures, with different languages, different foods, and many different customs and ways of doing things. Not surprisingly, there is often tension as they pack to leave, unpack when they arrive, or overstep the unwritten proprieties of a particular family culture. There is richness in the diversity too, but it takes acceptance, tolerance, understanding, and familiarity for children to experience the special rewards of each family. Parents and stepparents who allow their children to enjoy these varied experiences reduce the children's loyalty conflicts and contribute much toward creating their own successful families. Slowly, former alliances and ways of doing things become transformed, as stepfamily members move from having little or no emotional connections between them to the establishment of bonds that give them a sense of belonging together as a family unit.

Papernow (1993) describes seven emotional and developmental stages in the integration process, beginning with Fantasy, followed by Immersion and then Awareness, in which the household tends to split apart along biological lines when tensions appear; only gradually do the adults become aware that relationship changes need to occur. In the middle stages of Mobilization and Action, the tensions have become acute, and it is at this point that many stepfamily couples divorce because the two adults are not able to resolve their many differences and to work together as a team. For many families it may take 5–6 years before the adults have formed a solid couple bond and are working as a team to meet the challenges of the family. The final stages, Contact and Resolution, mark a time of deepening stepparent–stepchild relationships and a growing recognition that the family has achieved stability as a unit. Even the frequent household changes resulting from the dual citizenship of the children, who spend time in different households, can become a natural and normal process. Remarriage families have now achieved satisfactory bonding between the couple and between steprelatives so that the family members feel connected and find satisfaction in their relationships.

Related to these findings is research carried out by Margaret Crosbie-Burnett (1984) in which she found that the best predictor of stepfamily happiness was the quality of the relationship between the stepparent and the stepchildren. As outlined, Papernow (1993) also found that satisfactory step-relationships formed following the establishment of a good couple relationship. Satisfactory *family* integration requires the development of good step-relationships as well as the creation of a solid couple bond.

Looking at these studies, it becomes clear that, unlike many first-marriage families, couples in stepfamilies may form good couple bonding but good stepparent–stepchild relationships do not necessarily follow. Indeed, couples may often divorce even when the two adults are happy together, because they have not been able to form satisfactory stepparent–stepchild relationships. Research is indicating that these new relationships are relatively independent of one another and need to be individually developed. As Papernow's work indicates, the usual pattern is for the couple to first learn to work together, which can then provide a foundation with enough stability for satisfactory relationships to be developed between stepparent and stepchildren (Papernow, 1993).

DYNAMIC ISSUES IN STEPFAMILY SYSTEMS

As a family system, stepfamilies are more complex in their structure, with a greater number of built-in subsystems and greater ambiguity than is found in nuclear families. Boundaries are less clear, and homeostatic stability is lacking because of the constant fluctuations within the household. "We have an accordion family," said one parent/stepparent, "One day there are the two of us, the next there are nine." There are continual transitions, greater stress, and less cohesiveness. The household must deal with the following major dynamic issues:

1. Outsiders versus insiders.
2. Boundary disputes.
3. Power issues.
4. Conflicting loyalties.

5. Rigid, unproductive triangles.
6. Unity versus fragmentation of the new couple relationship.

Outsiders versus Insiders

Although individuals in nuclear families may experience being "left out," in stepfamilies with the many types of "mergers" that take place, there is a constant problem of helping outsiders to become insiders if there is to be household unity. Very often the outsider is a stepfather joining an ongoing group of a mother and her children; or it may be a woman marrying a man with custody of his children; or children coming to stay in the household every other weekend or for the summer; or a teenager changing residence from the mother and stepfather's household to the father and stepmother's household. Being a newcomer in any type of group can cause discomfort, both for the person or persons trying to be "one of the gang" and for the original group, who may feel intruded on and protective of the status quo. In the less "neutral" emotional climate of the stepfamily group, the feeling of exclusion, intrusion, rejection, and resultant anger and depression can be extremely strong. Working out ways of dealing with the shifts and transitions takes time and understanding, patience, and tolerance for ambiguity.

Boundary Disputes

Because children are often members of two separate households, the step-family boundaries may get blurred as the adults in the two households need to cooperate in arrangements involving the children. It is, however, necessary in most instances for each household to recognize that there are boundaries to that particular unit. The individuals in each household do have control over how they decide to deal with the individuals and events that take place within that sphere. In fact, if some separation is not made between the two households, there is little chance for a stepfamily to develop any sense of cohesiveness and unity.

Within the household there are also many "turf" problems to be worked out as well: who sleeps where; what personal privacy is possible; what space can be reserved for whom? As an example of what can happen, consider the stepfamily in which the husband's three children rejoined the household every 3–4 days for a few days' time. The house was small, and the mother's three children who lived in the household had to shift where they slept, where they put their clothes, and where they could go to relax or to be alone in order to make the available space accommodate the extra family members. Bedrooms became dormitories, and the continual chaos created tension and instability for everyone. This family needed to work out ways in which to ameliorate the impact of such major changes so that "property rights" became clear and consistent and there was a stable place for each person.

Power Issues

Power issues in stepfamilies can be exaggerated for many reasons. Women who have been on their own for the first time in their lives because of a divorce or the death of a husband, and who take pride in having "proved" their capabilities, frequently have no desire to return to a relationship that is not an egalitarian one. They have discovered that they can indeed take care of themselves and of their children too if they have children. For many, there is a fear of sharing this new-found control or power with another adult for fear of falling back into previously dissatisfying patterns.

Money is often equated with power, and men who are divorced and remarried often feel that they have been robbed of their power and control and have become "walking wallets." Secrecy in regard to financial matters may be practiced by both adults, and this often exacerbates power issues that affect many relationship areas.

In stepfamilies, children can often gain power in the age-old game of "divide and conquer," because their two biological parents now live in two separate households. If, in addition, they maintain only minimal and hostile contact with each other, there is a built-in system that makes it extremely easy for children to gain tremendous power. "If you don't treat me right, I'll go live with my Dad." "You are really mean! My mother lets me watch TV until midnight." And while the children want and need to feel a sense of mastery and power, they also need and want to know that there are adults who are stronger than they are and on whom they can depend.

Conflicting Loyalties

Loyalty conflicts for children and for remarried parents can hardly be avoided. In a biological family, children may feel more comfortable with one parent than with the other, but they are not placed in the position of choosing whom to ask to a special event or with whom they are to spend the weekend. They are part of each parent and feel torn apart when their parents are no longer together, with divided loyalties perhaps increasing when another adult enters the picture because of a parental remarriage. Naturally, the more amicable the relationships between all the parental adults, the fewer loyalty conflicts the children will have.

When one parent has died and the surviving biological parent remarries, the remarriage is often seen by the children as a betrayal of the former spouse (Walsh & McGoldrick, 1991). It may appear to the children that the new couple relationship negates the former couple relationship. Therefore, the stepparent stirs many strong emotions, particularly in older children who have lived with their other biological parent longer, and it is difficult for the children to accept their new stepparent.

As for remarried parents, since the parent–child relationships have preceded the new couple relationship, the adults often feel caught between their children and their new partners. It may, indeed, seem to remarried parents that it is a betrayal of the older parent–child bonds to form the new primary adult relationships. However, a satisfactory couple bond is usually necessary for a remarriage to continue. Therefore, if a new primary couple bond is not established, it is likely that the children in the stepfamily will experience still more loss and disruption in their lives as their second family unit breaks apart.

Rigid, Unproductive Triangles

There are triangles in all families. However, the subgroupings present in stepfamilies can produce particularly rigid, unproductive triangles. Unproductive triangles involve three individuals in a struggle so that clear dyadic relationships are not possible. Important triangles in stepfamilies include the following:

1. Remarried parent in the middle, not allowing a direct relationship between a stepparent and a stepchild.
2. Remarried parent and stepparent standing united against an ex-spouse.
3. Child caught in the middle between hostile ex-spouses.
4. Child caught in the middle between parent and stepparent of the same sex.

Because of the complexity of the subgroups in a stepfamily, and because of the heightened emotions involved and the long duration of some of the relationships, it can become difficult to break down these groupings so that simple and direct dyadic relationships are possible.

Unity versus Fragmentation of the New Couple Relationship

There are many internal and external pulls on the new couple relationship. A number have already been mentioned, such as the feelings of betrayal at the formation of a primary couple relationship, and the pull of grandparents who are having difficulties adjusting to new branches being grafted onto their family tree. There is also the divisiveness of children who still hope that disruption can lead to the reuniting of their biological parents; the insecurity of being a "second" spouse and perhaps not being seen by others as the "real" mate; and, initially, the absence of a shared family history or way of doing things.

The interface between the stepfamily and the community can also produce tensions that strain the couple. Schools, churches, the legal system, and social institutions of all types continue to consider the biological parents together and to leave out stepparents, even though these persons may in fact have been primary parental figures in children's lives for many months or even years. Often stepparents do not receive graduation tickets, are not included in PTA activities, are not asked to help with the Little League, or are not included in legal discussions when a stepchild may in fact be joining the household in which they live. Human flexibility exceeds institutional flexibility, and the social system is only now becoming responsive to the need for many changes in these areas.

CHARACTERISTICS OF SUCCESSFUL REMARRIED FAMILIES

Only recently has research begun to move away from a "deficit model" for stepfamilies (Clingempeel, Brand, & Segal, 1987) to look at what makes a remarriage family successful. Although this work is just beginning, important characteristics of successful stepfamilies are emerging. This knowledge provides supportive goals that give the adults a direction in which to move the family. As with any type of family there is a range within which family members will find satisfaction and a sense of well-being; it is not as though the family must achieve the "ideal" to be successful. As Kelley (1993) states, "The concept of healthy or good family functioning is a relative concept . . . families act in more or less functional ways at different times under different circumstances." The following characteristics can be observed and are repeated by remarriage families in which children and adults experience warm interpersonal relationships and satisfaction with their lives.

Expectations Are Realistic

With few exceptions, individuals in successful stepfamilies are realistic about what they can expect for their families, and they do not accept the common myths about stepfamily life—the myth of instant love and adjustment or the myth that stepfamilies are the same as first-marriage families. They are aware that love and caring take time to achieve, and they are aware of the differences between remarriage families and first-marriage families and do not attempt to force their family into a nuclear family mold.

They recognize that instant love or adjustment is a myth because relationships take time to grow and cannot be forced. In all families, parent–child relationships run from hot to cold, and to expect reciprocal caring from individuals who suddenly find themselves living together after remarriage can lead to disappointment, insecurity, and anger.

Successful stepfamilies realize that satisfactory ways of doing things can be worked out much faster than can emotional bonding between people, and they relax and let the children set the pace for the new relationships. They accept the fact that younger children can more easily develop relationships with stepparents than teenagers who are struggling with their own sense of identity and are already growing away emotionally from their family or families. As one teenager in a stepfamily put it, "Two parents are more than enough. I don't need another telling me what to do."

Often remarried parents and stepparents cling to the myth of "instant love" because of their strong desire to erase past hurts for themselves and their children. They frequently feel guilty about their children's reactions to the divorce or death of a parent, and they wish to make up for the children's pain. However, the pressure to *feel* a certain way, and then be unable to feel that way, creates anger and guilt for stepparents and stepchildren. Attempts to force friendship and caring create a pressure that usually leads to just the opposite. When everyone tries too hard or "pussyfoots" around issues and finds it impossible to relax, then anger rather than love reigns. In successful remarriage families, this myth of instant love is understood and rejected; the stepfamily members relax their expectations about their feelings, and often relationships slowly blossom into caring and loving bonds that last a lifetime.

Closely related to this myth is the one that states that stepfamilies are the same as first-marriage families. Children in remarriage families usually are acutely aware of differences, and almost universally the adults in well-functioning stepfamilies at some psychological level recognize and accept that the following stepfamily characteristics are not shared by those in first marriage families (Visher and Visher, 1979):

1. Stepfamilies are formed following many losses and changes. Parent–child relationships have been altered, marriage dreams shattered, and many changes have occurred in living arrangements.

2. The members of a stepfamily come together at different phases in their individual, marital, and family life cycles. For example, a woman who has not been previously married may marry a man with three children, or a couple may be forming a new family unit containing a teenager who is in the developmental stage of moving emotionally toward peers and away from a close family group.

3. Children as well as adults have experienced differing traditions and ways of doing things in previous families in which they have lived. As a result, they may have many different values and convictions about how families "should" operate.

4. Parent–child relationships have preceded rather than followed the relationship between the couple. Therefore, there are numerous alliances already in existence when the stepfamily is formed.

5. The children have a parent elsewhere, in reality or in memory (if their parent has died or disappeared.) Thus there is an important person to the children in another household.

6. Fifty percent of children of divorce have some contact with their other parent (Furstenburg, 1987). This means that there are shifts in household membership when children move between the households of their two parents.

7. There is little or no legal relationship between stepparents and stepchildren. This can lead to uncomfortable situations in which stepparents cannot sign consent forms for their stepchildren, include them in insurance policies, or ask a court for visitation after a divorce or death of their spouse.

The acceptance of these characteristics and mastery of the challenges they represent can result in families finding special rewards that are available in this more complex remarriage family structure. For example, there are more parenting adults who can share child-rearing responsibilities; and couples can have times to themselves when the children are staying in their other household.

Losses Can Be Mourned

We often say that stepfamilies are families "born of loss," since they are formed following a death or a divorce. Even adults who wanted to divorce have lost a relationship that they had expected to continue. For the partner who has not been married before, losses come from a discrepancy between fantasies of what their marriage would be like and the realities of stepfamily life, with a former spouse and instant stepchildren in the picture. When these losses as well as other losses are acknowledged and grieved, unrecognized sadness does not prevent and block embracing the process of moving toward satisfying step-relationships.

In well-functioning remarriage families, the adults are sensitive to the sadness of the children when they are upset and depressed, partly because they have not had control over these major changes in their lives. The adults support the children in the verbal expression of their feelings—their fears, their anticipations, and their anger, and they allow the children time to adjust to the many changes.

There Is a Strong Couple Relationship

The presence of a strong couple working together as a team is an important characteristic of successful stepfamilies, just as it is in first-marriage families. Using the Olson Circumplex measures with nuclear families and stepfamilies, successful stepfamilies have been found to be less cohesive than first-marriage families (Chollak, 1989), and successful stepfamilies have been found to retain stronger parent–child alliances than exist in successful first-marriage families (Anderson & White, 1986). Such findings are not surprising when one considers the structural characteristics of this type of family.

The adults in well-functioning stepfamilies understand the importance of providing an atmosphere of stability. Although they continue to pay attention to the needs of their children, they do not consider it a betrayal of their earlier relationship with them to form a primary relationship with their new partner. Not only does their new couple relationship bring happiness to the adults, it reduces the children's anxiety about another parental break-up, creates an atmosphere in which the maintaining of the parent/child relationship can be respected by the stepparent, and encourages warm step-relationships. It also provides the children with a model of a couple who are happy together and can work as a team to meet family challenges; this is important for children as they grow to adulthood and form their own couple relationships.

Satisfactory Steprelationships Have Formed

In most nuclear families, relationships within the family tend to be satisfy-ing if the couple relationship is good. Since this does not necessarily follow in remarriage families, separate attention needs to be paid to the develop-ment of interpersonal relationships between stepparent and stepchildren and between/among stepsiblings. For the family to be successful as a family, step-relationships are of great importance, and as a rule, well-functioning step-families illustrate the validity of the following guidelines for successful inte-gration:

The stepparent has entered into a parenting role slowly and gradually. This is important because a new stepparent has little or no authority so far as the children are concerned, unless the children are of preschool age. For a stepparent, status with the children in a stepfamily is an "earned" one, not an "acquired" one like the status of the biological parent of the child or children.

Successful stepparents do not "come in like the cheerleader of the West-ern World," as one initially unsuccessful stepmother said. Instead they gradu-ally build relationships with their stepchildren and slowly take on disciplinary functions (Stern, 1978; Hetherington, 1989). If the stepchildren are teenagers when the integration process is just beginning, the adolescents may be on their own before the stepparent has taken a parenting role. The successful couple will be working together as a team, with the parent initially taking the active parent role with his or her children and the stepparent support-ing this behavior. Roles are not based on society's stereotypes of the nurtur-ing mother and financially responsible, disciplinary father. The relationship is basically egalitarian, and role function is determined by parenthood rather than by gender. As the stepparent is able to form a satisfactory relationship with the children, a parenting role may become appropriate.

Some remarried parents are able to form good couple relationships but find it difficult to encourage and support stepparent–stepchild bonding, as this usually requires a shift in the parent–child relationship to make room for this to occur. In successful stepfamilies, the parent of the children is sup-portive of the stepparent's relationship with them. The important sequence appears to be the following:

1. The couple becomes solidified, and the remarried parent is support-ive of the stepparent's relationship with his or her stepchildren.

2. Satisfactory relationships are developed between the stepparent and stepchildren.
3. Now there are connections between adults and children, and the household can function satisfactorily.

In well-functioning remarriage families, the relationship between a stepparent and a stepchild can be quite varied, and need not become a parent role (Crosbie-Burnett, 1984; Mills, 1984). Having the freedom to form whatever type of interpersonal relationship is satisfying both to the adult and to the young person allows for many different types of relationships. One young person thanked her stepfather by saying, "I really love my stepfather, and I appreciate the fact that he is a good companion to me, a confidante and friend to my brother, and a parent to my little sister" (Visher & Visher, 1990, p. 10).

At times steprelationships between stepsiblings may not be particularly warm. It takes effort from each person to develop a bond between them, and children sometimes are reluctant to make this type of commitment. Even when the adults are fair to all the children and adequately meet their individual needs so that strong jealousies are absent, stepsiblings may differ greatly in their life styles and values and may never form close relationships. Similarly, stepparents and stepchildren, for a variety of reasons, may not develop warm interpersonal ties. In these families tolerance and respect for differences enable many such individuals to live together until the children have matured and are living on their own. Well-functioning remarriage families often remain open to the possibility of building positive relationships in later years when the stresses of earlier relationships may have shifted to warmth and caring.

Satisfying Rituals Are Established

Stepfamily members come together from a number of different family backgrounds. Indeed, if both adults have been married once previously, this marriage will represent a seventh household forged from the six previous family systems experienced by the two adults:

Wife	*Husband*
Family of origin	Family of origin
First marriage family	First marriage family
Single-parent household	Single-parent household
Present stepfamily household	

This household will also be the third family unit experienced by each child.

The difficult side of all these family experiences is the need to recognize that there is more than one way to do the laundry, cook a turkey, or celebrate a birthday. It is not a matter of one right or wrong way. The positive side of the past family experiences is the opportunity to share and decide from diverse and varied backgrounds what rituals and ways of doing things this unit would like to adopt (Whiteside, 1988). It may be following a former way of celebrating Thanksgiving, the combination of previous ways of sharing household tasks, developing an entirely new method of deciding what to do together on the weekends, or trying various ways to ease the children's transition from one household to the other.

The flexibility and creativity that flow from the necessity of actually working out such arrangements can bring rewards to all those involved. One stepfather put it this way, "I used to be a pretty rigid guy, but I've had to be more flexible, and this has helped me at work as well as at home." Successful stepfamilies have worked out positive rituals and appreciate the creativity and cooperation that accompanies these decisions.

The Separate Households Cooperate

Well-functioning stepfamilies have worked out satisfactory arrangements between the children's households. This is an important characteristic because when the children's two households cooperate rather than compete with one another in raising the children, the young people experience less intense loyalty conflicts, and they and the adults are more able to relax and enjoy their family. Formation of a "parenting coalition" (Visher & Visher, 1989) can occur when all the adults who are directly involved with the same children appreciate the special attributes and skills that each has to offer to the children. Sharing parental responsibility allows the adults to have more time for themselves than is possible when children are in the household on a full-time basis, and it gives the children an opportunity for more diverse interpersonal experiences.

As a rule it takes time for this type of cooperation to be worked out. The couple relationship needs to have developed so that both partners feel secure in their relationship, and parents and stepparents need the security that comes from recognizing how important they are to their children and stepchildren. Then it becomes possible to view the other household in neutral terms rather than as a threat of more loss of the children. Some remarriage families become friendly with each other and come together fairly frequently. However, this is not the usual situation and certainly is not a necessary foundation for working together. Whatever the amount of contact, successful stepfamilies feel independent of the other household, and at the same time they feel connected through the children. For many it is a "business relationship" that allows the households to work together in matters connected with the children. This is invaluable when family events take place—holidays, graduations, weddings—as these important times can then be pleasant and fulfilling moments for all.

THERAPEUTIC IMPLICATIONS

Many stepfamilies need education and support to assist them in their journey together. Educational groups and mutual help groups are forming around the country in answer to this need. In addition, organizations have been formed to meet the need for an ongoing education and/or support network for stepfamilies.[1]

An increasing number of individuals in stepfamilies are also seeking professional help. Although the basic therapeutic skills used with stepfamilies are the same as with other families, there are a few specific guidelines that make a great deal of difference when working with individuals in step-families, either singly, in different subgroup combinations, or as a family unit (Visher & Visher, 1988):

1. It is difficult but extremely important to overcome the emotional concept of the "ideal" American family, so that there is no futile attempt to fit a stepfamily into a nuclear family mold.

2. It is helpful to assess stepfamilies differently from first-marriage families. Because of cultural and structural characteristics producing added external stress, individuals in stepfamilies may seem to be more emotionally upset. However, unlike similar behavioral characteristics of individuals living in nuclear families, these behaviors in stepfamily members may simply indicate a need for support and validation of their experience rather than medication and in-depth therapy. They need help to increase self-esteem and the ability to make productive choices. As they begin to experience a sense of mastery, the chaos tends to be controlled. Deeper couple or individual issues may emerge if they are in need of attention. In most cases, child behavior problems improve dramatically as remarried family tasks are accomplished.

3. In a study of successful stepfamily therapy, Elion (1990) found that the most important therapeutic interventions were: validation, education, reduction of helplessness, and the strengthening of the couple relationship.

4. Together with the new couple, it may be important at times to include ex-spouses, grandparents, or other significant adults in the therapeutic process. The focus of the meeting needs to be clearly stated ahead of time: it should be limited to issues involving the children and not serve as an attempt to resolve former spousal relationships. Such meetings occur most frequently in regard to custody and visitation questions. Meetings need to include stepparents to validate their position and to solidify the remarriage family unit.

5. Countertransference, both positive and negative, can be particularly difficult to deal with in stepfamily situations, where the therapist's feelings

---

[1]Stepfamily Association of America, Inc., 215 Centennial Mall South, Lincoln, NE 68508, is a national organization with a variety of services for stepfamilies.

may be strong. For this reason, consultation or the use of cotherapists can be extremely valuable.

SUMMARY

As society changes, new patterns may evolve. However, at the present time we have discussed characteristics of stepfamilies that have been validated by clinical and empirical observation. Stepfamilies are families emerging out of hope. Being a remarried parent or a stepparent is different from being a parent in a first-marriage family, and growing up in a stepfamily can be more complicated than growing up in a biological family. Successful stepfamilies accept and understand these differences and allow themselves the necessary time to accomplish the tasks that lead to successful integration. They understand that their transitional difficulties are predictable and are not related to personal inadequacies and that there are actions they can take that can lead to happiness and satisfaction for all the members of the family unit. They also understand that the task they have set themselves is challenging, but not impossible, and that "second chances" may ultimately work for everyone.

REFERENCES

Anderson, J. Z., & White, G. D. (1986). An empirical investigation of interaction and relationship patterns in functional and dysfunctional nuclear families and stepfamilies. *Family Process, 25*, 407–422.

Becker, G. W., Landes, E. M., & Michael, R. T. (1977). An economic analysis of marital instability. *Journal of Political Economy, 85*, 1141–1187.

Bernstein, A. C. (1989). *Yours, mine and ours: How families change when remarried parents have a child together.* New York: Scribners.

Bohannan, P., & Yahraes, H. (1979). Stepfathers as parents. In E. Corfman (Ed.), *Families today: A research sampler on families and children* (pp. 347–362). Washington, DC: U.S. Government Printing Office.

Bumpass, L., Sweet, J., & Martin, T. C. (1990). Changing patterns of remarriage. *Journal of Marriage and the Family, 52(3)*, 747–756.

Cherlin, A. (1978). Remarriage as an incomplete institution. *American Journal of Sociology, 84(3)*, 634–650.

Chollak, H. (1989). *Stepfamily adaptability and cohesion: A normative study.* Ann Arbor, MI: University Microfilms.

Clingempeel, W. G., Brand, E., & Segal, S. (1987). A multi-level, multi-variable developmental perspective for future research on stepfamilies. In K. Pasley & M. Ihinger-Tallman (Eds.), *Remarriage and stepparenting: Current research and theory* (pp. 65–93). New York: Guilford Press.

Clingempeel, W. G., Ievoli, R., & Brand, E. (1984). Structural complexity and the quality of stepfather–stepchild relationships. *Family Process, 23*, 547–560.

Coleman, M., & Ganong, L. (1987). The cultural stereotyping of stepfamilies. In K. Pasley & M. Ihinger-Tallman (Eds.), *Remarriage and stepparenting: Current research and theory* (pp. 19–41). New York: Guilford Press.

Crosbie-Burnett, M. (1984). The centrality of the steprelationship: A challenge to family theory and practice. *Family Relations, 33,* 439–463.

Elion, D. (1990). *Therapy with remarriage families with children: Positive interventions from the client perspective.* Unpublished master's thesis, University of Wisconsin-Stout.

Furstenburg, F. F. (1987). The new extended family: The experience of parents and children after remarriage. In K. Pasley & M. Ihinger-Tallman (Eds.), *Remarriage and stepparenting: Current research and theory* (pp. 42–64). New York: Guilford Press.

Glick, P. C. (1991, October). Address to Annual Conference, Stepfamily Association of America, Lincoln, NE.

Glick, P. C., & Lin, S. (1986). Recent changes in divorce and remarriage. *Journal of Marriage and the Family, 48,* 737–747.

Hetherington, E. M. (1989). Coping with family transitions: Winners, losers, and survivors. Meetings of the Society for Research in Child Development. *Child Development, 60(1),* 1–14.

Hetherington, E. M., Cox, M., & Cox, R. (1985). Long-term effects of divorce and remarriage on the adjustment of children. *Journal of the American Academy of Child Psychiatry, 24(5),* 518–530.

Jacobson, D. S. (1987). Family type, visiting patterns, and children's behavior in the stepfamily: A linked family system. In K. Pasley & M. Ihinger-Tallman (Eds.), *Remarriage and stepparenting: Current research and theory* (pp. 257–272). New York: Guilford Press.

Kelley, P. (1993). *Developing healthy step families: 20 families tell their stories.* Binghamton, NY: Haworth Press.

Landau-Stanton, J. K. (1985). Adolescents, families and cultural transition: A treatment model. In M. P. Mirkin & S. Koman (Eds.), *Handbook of adolescent and family therapy* (pp. 363–381). New York: Gardner Press.

McCarthy, J. (1978). A comparison of the probability of dissolution of first and second marriages. *Demography 15,* 345–360.

McGoldrick, M., Anderson, C., & Walsh, F. (Eds.). (1989). *Women in families.* New York: W. W. Norton.

McGoldrick, M., & Carter, B. (1989). Forming a remarried family. In B. Carter & M. McGoldrick (Eds.), *The changing family life cycle* (pp. 402–426). Boston: Allyn & Bacon.

Mills, D. M. (1984). A model for stepfamily development. *Family Relations, 33,* 365–372.

Papernow, P. (1993). *Becoming a stepfamily: Patterns of development in remarried families.* San Francisco: Jossey-Bass.

Pasley, K. (1987). Family boundary ambiguity: Perceptions of adult remarried family members. In K. Pasley & M. Ihinger-Tallman (Eds.), *Remarriage and stepparenting: Current research and theory* (pp. 206–224). New York: Guilford Press.

Santrock, J. W., & Sitterle, K. A. (1987). Parent–child relationships in stepmother families. In K. Pasley & M. Ihinger-Talman (Eds.), *Remarriage and stepparenting: Current research and theory* (pp. 273–302). New York: Guilford Press.

Santrock, J. W., Sitterle, K. A., & Warshak, R. A. (1988). Parent–child relationships in stepfather families. In P. Bronstein & C. P. Cowan (Eds.), *Fatherhood today: Men's changing role in the family.* New York: John Wiley & Sons.

Stern, P. (1978). Stepfather families: Integration around child discipline. *Issues in Mental Health Nursing, 1(2),* 50–56.

Visher, E., & Visher, J. (1979). *Stepfamilies: A guide to working with stepparents and stepchildren.* New York: Brunner/Mazel. (Also in paperback as *Stepfamilies: Myths and realities.* Secaucus, NJ: Citadel Press.)

Visher, E., & Visher, J. (1988). *Old loyalties, new ties: Therapeutic strategies with stepfamilies.* New York: Brunner/Mazel.

Visher, E., & Visher, J. (1989). Parenting coalitions after remarriage: Dynamics and therapeutic guidelines. *Family Relations, 38,* 65–70.

Visher, E., & Visher, J. (1990). Dynamics of successful stepfamilies. *Journal of Divorce and Remarriage, 14,* 3–12.

Walsh, F. (1991). Promoting healthy functioning in divorced and remarried families. In A. Gurman & D. Kniskern (Eds.), *Handbook of family therapy* (2nd ed.). New York: Brunner/Mazel

Walsh, F., & McGoldrick, M. (Eds.). (1991). *Living beyond loss: Death in the family.* New York: W. W. Norton.

White, L. K., & Booth, A. (1985). The quality and stability of remarriages: The role of stepchildren. *American Sociological Review, 50,* 689–698.

Whiteside, M. F. (1982). Remarriage: A family developmental process. *Journal of Marital and Family Therapy, 8,* 59–68.

Whiteside, M. F. (1988). Creation of family identity through ritual performance in early remarriage. In E. Imber-Black, J. Roberts, & R. A. Whiting (Eds.), *Rituals in families and family therapy.* New York: W. W. Norton.

CHAPTER 9

NORMAL PROCESSES
IN ADOPTIVE FAMILIES

Sherry Anderson,
Maria Piantanida,
and Carol Anderson

Adoptive parents must come to grips with the fact that
the biological chain that links one generation to the
next, from the past to the future, will have a missing
link, and that it will be the psychological relationship
that will give continuity to the family history.—*Sorosky*

WHY A CHAPTER ON ADOPTION?

Adoptive families have many of the same experiences and processes as other
families. When the adults face the transition to parenthood, they must adjust
their relationship to make room for children, take on parental roles, and
realign themselves within their extended families. As their children grow,
adoptive parents nurture their children, teach them values and behaviors
that will enable them to make the transition from family to the larger worlds
of school and community. When these children reach adolescence, the adoptive family system must accommodate their growing needs for individuality and autonomy, just as any other family system. Like most caring mothers
and fathers, adoptive parents strive to launch their children into happy and
productive adulthood. Given all of these similarities, one might conclude
that adoptive families do not warrant special attention in the literature of
family systems.

This conclusion has been challenged by a growing awareness of the differences and complexities inherent in both the process of adoption and the families created in this way. These differences and complexities arise to a great extent from the experiences of loss upon which adoptive families are built (Brodzinsky & Schecter, 1990; Brodzinsky, Schecter, & Henig, 1992; Delaney, 1991; Fahlberg, 1990, 1991; Grabe, 1990; Jewett, 1978; Kadushin & Martin, 1988; Kirk, 1981, 1984; Melina, 1986; Tansey, 1988). These experiences impact and alter the way in which family members attribute meaning to normative events, create their family structure, and respond to life-cycle transitions. Understanding adoptive processes, then, is crucial to understanding and working with adopted individuals and their families.

FRAMEWORK FOR UNDERSTANDING ADOPTION

Adoptive Parents

Adults come to adoption for a variety of reasons along a continuum from *traditional* on one end to *preferential* at the other (Feigelman & Silverman, 1979; Kadushin & Martin, 1988). According to Kadushin and Martin, the former are typically infertile, white couples who want to adopt a healthy, same-race newborn and ". . . are interested in substituting the adopted child for an infant they cannot have biologically" (p. 542).

During the first half of the 20th century, it was common for such adoptive couples and the professionals who worked with them to see the placement of a child as a discrete event that, when completed, could and should be pushed as far into the background as possible so that the family could "get on with a normal life." A host of commonly accepted adoption practices reinforced this approach—for example, efforts to match the physical, ethnic, and religious characteristics of infant and parents; changing the child's birth certificate; sealing records to assure anonymity; keeping the "secret" of the adoption from the child. These practices were meant to protect the family and child from feeling "different" and to avoid the stigma of out-of-wedlock birth. Such measures obscured the differences between adoptive families and the prevailing ideal of the self-sufficient, intact, nuclear family.

The consequences of this "let's pretend" mentality were generally not acknowledged until the early 1960s, when H. David Kirk (1981, 1984) published a theory of adoptive kinship based on a series of studies spanning two decades and involving well over a thousand couples who had turned to adoption because of infertility. Kirk used the term, role handicap, to describe the situation faced by couples who, having grown up with a cultural expectation of marriage and childbearing, suddenly find themselves with few models to help them in coping with their infertility. Kirk discovered two fundamentally different patterns by which couples coped with the feelings of alienation associated with their role handicap—either *acknowledgment* or *rejection* of their difference from parents who can conceive. Kirk theorized that the more acutely deprived a couple feels because of their infertility, the more likely they are to use rejection-of-difference as a coping mechanism once they adopt a child. Unresolved feelings about their infertility work to intensify the couple's need to deny or reject difference within their own family and between adoptive and biological families. Sameness or uniformity is often seen as (1) the criteria for acceptance and belonging within the family, (2) the basis for family stability, and (3) the outcome of successful parenting. Kirk concluded:

> Adoptive parental coping activities of the type of "acknowledgment-of-difference" are conducive to good communication and thus to order and dynamic stability in adoptive families. Coping activities of the type of "rejection-of-difference" on the other hand can be expected to make for poor communication with subsequent disruptive results for the adoptive relationship. (1984, pp. 98–99)

Coinciding with the dissemination of Kirk's research, preferential adoption was becoming more prevalent (Piasecki, 1987). Individuals with this orientation see adoption as a life-style choice and tend to accept and value difference. Interestingly enough, this attitude of openness and comfort with adoption has been a long-standing tradition within the African-American community. Historically, both one- and two-parent families cared for children within the extended family or the community, with or without the formality of a legally finalized adoption (Boyd-Franklin, 1989).[1]

Despite the diversity of adults who fall under the umbrella of preferential adopters (Kadushin & Martin, 1988; Groze & Rosenthal, 1991), the circumstances leading to adoption minimize either the possibility of or concerns about secrecy and difference. Preferential adopters may already have one or more biological children, be past their child-bearing years, or may simply have elected to add to their family by adoption for a variety of personal or humanitarian reasons. Some adopt out of a deep sense of caring and moral or religious duty. Others may be members of a helping profession who believe their clinical expertise will facilitate the task of parenting a child with a physical, cognitive, or emotional disability. Many other preferential adopters are couples in their 30s or 40s who have married late and/or delayed child bearing.

Since the mid-1970s, when many social and legal barriers to single-parent adoption began to disintegrate, a growing number of unmarried women and

---

[1]More recently, the cultural norm of informal adoption within the African-American community has not kept pace with the number of black children who need homes. Since the early 1980s, there has been a growing awareness of the need to recruit actively in the black community for prospective parents and to adapt white social service agency procedures and requirements to meet the needs of those prospective parents.

men have joined the ranks of preferential adopters (Feigelman & Silverman, 1977; Marindin, 1987; Prowler, 1991). For these individuals, being single is not a transitional life stage, but rather a life style, within which the desire to parent becomes an important goal. Because single parenthood has become both more prevalent and more acceptable for women in our society, several options are open to them—for example, donor insemination, insemination by a partner willing to relinquish claims on the child, or adoption. For single men, however, the options are limited to adoption unless they want to become involved in the increasingly controversial and problematic process of surrogate pregnancy. Single, white adults who do not meet the eligibility criteria for healthy infant adoption may turn to special needs or international adoption.

Preferential and traditional patterns in adoption are the two extremes of a continuum, with most adoptive parents falling somewhere in the midrange. Nevertheless, their basic orientation toward adoption profoundly influences the reasons why they adopt, the type of child they are willing to adopt, and their expectations for family life and their own role as parents.

Adopted Children

Just as adults come to adoption from different life circumstances, so too, do children. When adoption was seen primarily as a service for infertile, white couples, it was generally assumed that placements could be found only for healthy, same-race newborns. Once children reached the age of 24 months, they were assumed to be unadoptable. Over the past 25–30 years, several social forces have altered these assumptions.

Perhaps the most powerful of these were changing norms regarding female sexuality, and the concomitant acceptance of birth control, abortion, and a single woman's right to keep and parent her child. As a result, fewer healthy, white newborns were available for adoption at a time when the incidence of infertility among white couples was rising (Menning, 1977; Salzer, 1986). These trends forced many traditional adopters to pursue alternatives. Some adopted healthy Asian or Latin American infants (who were often seen as exotic), or African-American, Latino, or Native American children from the United States (Berlin, 1978; O'Rourke, & Hubbell, 1990; Small, 1984; Tizard, 1991). Others adopted "older" children (e.g., 2–5 years old), or children with mild disabilities (e.g., cleft palate, club foot, correctable heart defects, blindness, deafness).

As adoption professionals recognized these changes, they began to reassess assumptions about the types of children who were placeable (Chambers, 1970; Triseliotis, 1991). This reassessment was supported in the mid-1970s by a growing awareness of child abuse and neglect and the enactment of protective services legislation at the state and federal levels. The Congressional report *No Place to Call Home: Discarded Children in America* (Select

Committee, 1990) estimates that nearly 500,000 children are currently in out-of-home placements, and, if current trends continue, this number is likely to rise to 840,000 by 1995. In 1985, adoption was the goal for approximately 36,000 children in foster care (Select Committee on Children, 1990, pp. 5–9). Thus, despite the persistent interest in healthy infant adoption, far more families are needed for these "unrooted" (Sonne, 1980), "system" (Grabe, 1990) children. Included under a designation of special needs adoption are:

- Children of color, regardless of age or health status,[2]
- White children over the age of 8,
- A sibling group who must be placed together in the same home, and/or
- Children with moderate to severe cognitive, emotional, and/or physical disabilities.

Of growing concern among adoption professionals and parents are the older children who come under the purview of protective services because of abuse and neglect. Many of these children languish for years in a legal limbo, enduring numerous placements in foster homes or residential institutions as efforts are made to rehabilitate their birth parents and reunify the family. In 1985, for example, 39% of children in foster care had been in placement for over 2 years (Select Committee on Children, 1990). Prolonged tenure in the child welfare system and multiple moves among multiple care-givers often result in distorted ideas about family relationships (Delaney, 1991).

The most difficult children to place are those special-needs children with profound cognitive and/or physical disabilities resulting from genetic, prenatal, or traumatic factors. Many of these children have multiple handicaps. For example, an examination of 92 children placed by an adoption agency that specializes in finding families for children with developmental disabilities revealed 90% had some degree of mental retardation, 12% had a physical disability, 4% had autism. More outstanding is the fact that 90% of these children had been abused or neglected, a finding consistent with recent research indicating that children with disabilities have a higher vulnerability for abuse and neglect (Ammerman, Lubetsky, Hersen, & Van Hasselt, 1988). A less obvious and often overlooked aspect of parenting children with developmental disabilities is the fact that these children carry the same emotional wounds from abuse, neglect, separation, and loss as other children with special needs. Many parents report that the cognitive and/or physical

[2]For African-American children, racial attitudes as well as practices embedded in the child welfare system have affected their need for home and family. As a result, black children come into public care in greater proportion than do white children, at earlier ages, and stay for longer times (Select Committee on Children, 1990). For this reason, African-American children of any age have been designated as "special needs."

disability is often easier to manage than the severe emotional disabilities that accompany most of these children (S. Maczka, personal communication, February 1992). Despite these difficulties, however, progress is being made in finding permanent families for many of these children (Leof, undated). Glidden (1989) suggests that parents adopting children with developmental disabilities report a high rate of satisfaction, often "deriving considerable pleasure and self-respect" from their successes.

For many special-needs children, impermanence and uncertainty are a way of life. Using Olson's (Olson & Laver, 1989) circumplex model of family systems, both Duehn (1990) and Mahoney (1990) point out that such children often come from chaotically disengaged, chronically dysfunctional, multiproblem birth families in which recurring physical, sexual, mental, and/or emotional abuse are common. Such a family history leaves these children with an impaired capacity for attachment and intimacy, expressed by rage, mistrust, little comprehension of cause and effect, and stunted conscience development. As might be expected, these children typically experience some combination of cognitive, emotional, physical, and social developmental delays. Concomitantly, they tend to exhibit problematic behaviors in more than one area of their lives—for example, family, school, peer relationships. The trauma experienced by these children prior to adoption give rise to a host of previously unrecognized parenting and family issues (Barth & Berry, 1988; Braden, 1981; Derdeyn, 1979; Grabe, 1990; Katz, 1977, 1986; Reitz & Watson, 1992).

The preceding comments suggest a continuum of children being placed for adoption. At one end of the continuum is the proverbial healthy newborn. These idealized children of adoption are often seen by our society as fortunate, having been spared a life of deprivation, insecurity, and suffering by early placement with a loving, committed family. This rosy image tends to gloss over the fact that even these relatively nontraumatic adoptions are based on the most profound loss that any child can experience—the loss of those parents who gave them life. Even individuals adopted as infants often report a feeling of loss—and a need to grieve this loss—at adolescence, young adulthood or when other significant losses occur. Over the past 30 years, our understanding of parent–child attachment (Bowlby, 1970; Ainsworth, 1979; Main, 1973) and child development (Mahler, 1973) has illuminated the tremendous and lasting impact of separation and loss on children. Although research on the life-stage transitions and developmental issues for adults adopted as infants is still limited, an increasing body of anecdotal information suggests that for some, issues of loss, belonging, and identity can persist and reverberate throughout an adoptee's life, particularly as they affect life-cycle transitions involving separation (Crook, 1986; Powledge, 1982; Brodzinsky & Schecter, 1990; Brodzinsky et al., 1992; Fahlberg, 1990, 1991; Jewett, 1978, 1982; Rosenberg, 1992). At the opposite end of the continuum are children whose physical, cognitive, and/or emotional disabilities are so profound, that their capacity to attach to and live within a normal family is severely impaired (Cline, 1992; Delaney, 1991).

Configurations of Adoptive Families

By juxtaposing the continuum of adoptable children with the continuum of adult orientations toward adoption, it is possible to conceptualize four different configurations of adoptive families (Figure 9.1).

Families represented by the upper-left quadrant tend to be infertile couples who adopt healthy, same-race infants. Families falling in the upper-right quadrant are those who would prefer to adopt a healthy, same-race infant but cannot afford the time and/or money to pursue this option. Being somewhat accepting of difference, these adults enter into arrangements (e.g., transracial adoption, adoption of children with mild disabilities) that place special demands on the family. When adults who were willing to adopt a child with special needs are matched with a basically healthy, fairly young child, a preferential–traditional family is formed. Preferential–special needs families are formed when adults choose to parent children with more extreme disabilities.

A note of caution—many families enter into more than one type of adoption. For example, some couples may first adopt a healthy infant and subsequently adopt an older child with special needs. Thus, these family configurations are meant to illustrate the diversity and complexity of adoptive families. They are in no way meant to negate the uniqueness of each family, or to be used as precise, diagnostic categories.

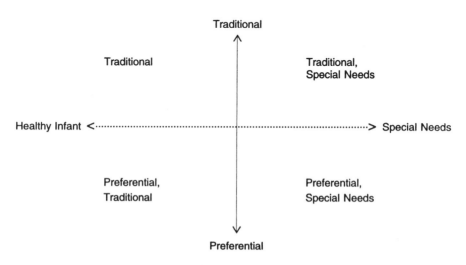

FIGURE 9.1. Configurations of adoptive families.

NORMAL PROCESSES IN ADOPTIVE FAMILIES

Reaching the Decision to Adopt

Carter & McGoldrick (1988) suggest that on average the birth of a couple's first child occurs about 1–2 years into the marriage, although recent trends suggest that many two-career couples are postponing childbearing (Menning, 1977). For infertile couples, however, the "married but childless" stage can last for well over 10 years. A cycle of seeking help, hoping for a solution, and experiencing disappointment can replay for years, until the couple finally acknowledges that conception and childbirth are not possible for them. Coming to this realization precipitates the most fundamental process that is normal for and distinctive of traditional adopters—that is, mourning their infertility. Working through the mourning process and reaching resolution are crucial precursors to the second normal process—that is, deciding whether parenting is still a goal and whether adoption is a different, but acceptable, method of achieving the goal (LePere, 1988).

Without adequately resolving the pain, guilt, and anger associated with infertility, couples can bring to adoption an inner, and probably unspoken, belief that adoption is a poor second best (Small, 1987). Unfortunately, a number of factors can short circuit the process of mourning. The couple themselves may be so distraught and desperate after years of frustration and disappointment that they leap too quickly to the idea of adoption. It is not uncommon for agencies to receive a telephone call, typically from the wife, saying, "We just learned from the doctor that we can't have children. We want to adopt."

The task of mourning can also be diverted if only one spouse is assumed to be infertile, if one spouse is dramatically more invested in becoming a parent, or if the style with which two spouses cope with their sense of disappointment is markedly different. Some difference between spouses in the pace of mourning, finding resolution, and consideration of adoption is inevitable, with partners often feeling "out of sync" with one another. These differences, however, can place a great deal of strain on the marriage. Over time, infertility tests and procedures also tend to impact negatively on the couple's sexual satisfaction, further straining their relationship. Kirk (1984) discovered that women experience their infertility more intensely and more negatively than men, probably because of the value and emphasis placed on motherhood for and by women. Nevertheless, many men are also committed to having children, and many experience infertility as a threat to their manhood and thus have their own feelings and conflicts to resolve.

Fortunately, resources are now available to help couples deal with their infertility. RESOLVE, an organization founded in 1973 to support and counsel infertile couples, now has active chapters throughout the United States (Menning, 1977). At least some fertility specialists have specially trained staff who offer support throughout the emotionally draining series of fertility tests and treatment. As adoption professionals have become aware of the emotional impact of infertility and the importance of mourning, they have become far more skilled in counseling couples during preplacement preparation.

As is the case with traditional adopters, those who decide to pursue special-needs adoption must come to grips with their motivations and expectations. Two variations of this decision-making process are worth mentioning. First are couples who have feelings of regret over earlier life choices (e.g., commitment to a career, postponement of marriage) that have now resulted in limiting their options for building a family. Second are individuals who choose to pursue single-parent adoption and who must face the fact that they are not married and for the foreseeable future are not going to be married. Within this context, individuals must then decide whether parenthood is a goal they value and, if so, make additional decisions about how to fulfill this goal. Once single persons reach the decision to adopt, they, like their married counterparts, must learn about the realities of adoption and the adoption process. If this stage is discouraging for couples, it can be even more so for single adopters, because of persisting prejudices:

> When single individuals seek to adopt a child, workers are concerned about their personal motives. Male applicants, in particular, have been scrutinized for possible sexual interest in children. The impact on the child of living with a single parent is also of concern to the worker . . . Finally, the adoption worker assesses the single parent's ability to handle the added responsibility of caring for a child with the more limited resources than are available in the two-parent family. (Kadushin & Martin, 1988, p. 551)

It is ironic that adopters seen as having the most limited resources are often matched with children who have greater disabilities and therefore greater needs. This pattern seems to be based on the assumption that less than ideal (single) candidates will have to "settle" for a problem child if they want any child at all. It appears to matter little that some of these pairings are almost inevitably destined for major trouble.

Pursuing Adoption

Once the decision to adopt a child is made, adults begin the most obvious process—that is, the adoption process itself, which encompasses a series of subphases:

1. *Exploration*—adoption is seriously considered, information is gathered, agencies are identified and contacted.
2. *Acceptance*—an agency accepts the individual or couple as a client. This in itself is a major milestone and is often preceded by a period of 3–5 years on a waiting list. For African-American families this phase is much shorter.

3. *Preparation*—most agencies now require prospective parents to complete an educational process focusing on issues and dynamics inherent in adoptive families.
4. *Waiting*—all preadoptive requirements have been met, and the individual or couple is waiting to be matched with a specific child. Although a great sense of relief and hope accompanies this stage, the uncertainty and lack of control may reactivate anxiety.
5. *Placement*—the individual or couple receives physical custody of the child and brings him or her home.
6. *Postplacement*—the child is living in the adoptive home, but the adoption has not been finalized by a court of law.
7. *Legal Finalization*—the adoption is made permanent by formal decree of the courts.

Unfortunately, the adoption process sounds much calmer and smoother in abstraction than it is in reality. Having already lost their biological dream child that "should have been," individuals or couples learn during the exploration phase that they may have to wait years for a newborn, or they may face the devastating realization that they do not meet the age, financial, or other eligibility criteria for infant adoption. This precipitates another round of grief, anger, and feelings of helplessness. These feelings are intensified as prospective adopters realize that total strangers wield the power to place or withhold a child and that the life experience that others take for granted is for them to be a painful, and seemingly unending, obstacle course.

Even for preferential adopters, the process of pursuing adoption is demanding and fraught with anxiety. Often well-intentioned, but fairly naive, prospective adopters must assimilate the harsh realities of special-needs adoption—the overwhelming number of children who need families as well as the severity of their problems. Preferential adopters often have second thoughts as they gather information. They may wonder whether they have the financial resources or personal stamina to parent children who will need intensive care, perhaps for a life time. They may also question the impact of a new child with problems on other children in the family.

Claiming and Entitlement to Parent

As couples achieve their goal and make the transition to parenthood, the adjustment is likely to be more intense, because of the prolonged childless phase of marriage as well as the increasing amount of emotional energy invested in becoming parents. Although it is not unusual or abnormal for new parents to feel twinges of annoyance over the restrictions imposed by their new responsibilities, some adoptive parents experience excessive shame or guilt about such feelings since they had worked so long and hard to have a child. A potentially more problematic reaction to inevitable irritating or negative child behaviors is the fantasy, "If I had a baby of my own, I wouldn't be feeling like this." Or, "A child of my own wouldn't act like this." Such responses to a normal process of adjustment in families with young children point to two interconnected processes that are distinctive and normative in adoptive families—claiming and entitlement to parent.

In adoption, social and legal contracts establish the parent/child relationship that is a given in biological families. "Claiming" is the process through which the parents commit themselves emotionally to the new child and see him or her as a full and equal member of the family. In recent years, adoptive parents and professionals have been creating customs and rituals for celebrating the child's arrival in the family (Jewett, 1992; Whiting, 1988). Despite the tremendous strides that have been made to destigmatize adoption, the claiming process can be impeded by a host of fears that are fueled by the parents' sense of vulnerability—for example, fear that birth parents will suddenly reappear and try to reclaim the child, fear that the adoption agency will remove the child, and fear the child will eventually reject them in favor of their birth parents.

As with other processes in adoptive families, the issue of claiming periodically recycles, especially when children do not match the idealized fantasies of their parents. Whether the cause is a genetic disorder, prenatal exposure to drugs, an undiagnosed medical condition, malnutrition, failure to thrive, or a host of other possibilities, parental disappointments can develop into a serious problem for both parents and child. When the discrepancy between fantasy and reality begins to surface, parents who are able to acknowledge difference are more likely to readjust their expectations, thereby restabilizing the family. Conversely, families may "get stuck" if parents are more extreme in their rejection of difference, have unresolved grief, or feel inadequate because of their child's needs and limitations.

It is not unusual for a family to experience a crisis in the claiming process when the child's curiosity about his or her biological family and assertions of difference are seen as betrayal and rejection of the adoptive family. In some cases, normal adolescent defiance and acting-out can reawaken fears of the child's genetic endowment—the latent "bad seed"—and threaten the family's stability.

Another process, closely related to claiming, is entitlement to parent (Ward, 1981). Our society automatically and unconditionally sanctions the rights and authority of biological parents. Even in situations where birth parents abuse and neglect their children, the legal system is often reluctant to sever this natural bond. Although the legal process of adoption gives parents full and equal rights over their children, some may have difficulty internalizing these rights. This can occur if infertile couples unconsciously believe they are unworthy of parenthood. Other parents are so grateful to have a child, they can nurture without difficulty but have difficulty providing the discipline so necessary for a child's development and a family's sanity.

Forging a Sense of Family

In cases of older-child adoption, families must deal with the other side of the claiming issue—that is, helping the child to develop a sense of belonging and attachment within the new family. Often older children view themselves as having lost their "real" family and find it difficult to accept their new parents. Resistance to nurturing can be further exacerbated if parents attempt to move too quickly or intrusively into the child's emotional world. The more temporary placements the child has experienced, the more difficult this process of attaching will be. Older system children are likely to resist nurturing, because their world view is colored by mistrust, low self-esteem, learned helplessness, and conflicted loyalties toward multiple caretakers. For families who adopt preadolescents or adolescents, a distinctive twist in attachment issues arises from the mismatch of developmental processes. The goal of the family formation process is to establish a sense of closeness, belonging, and identification. Developmentally, however, the adolescent is, or feels he or she should be striving for independence and the assertion of individuality. Finding ways to simultaneously allow the adolescent to save face, act independent, and yet get the nurturance and sense of belonging that are so badly needed requires creative parenting strategies.

Parents must also work to establish their authority to set and enforce family rules. This enforcement often precedes the nurturing parents would much prefer to provide; however, it is only when children feel safe and secure within the rules that they are able to genuinely accept the love their new parents offer. With system children, who have little regard for adult authority, discipline can become a struggle for power and control. From the child's perspective, surrender to adult authority entails surrendering a lifetime of survival strategies and accepting vulnerability. From the adults' perspective, this surrender is often seen as the necessary prerequisite for healing and attachment. The tension between nurturing and discipline, the struggle for power and control, can continue for years.

Good preplacement casework with both the child and the parents can help to deescalate the intensity of the power and control struggles. Giving the child a voice in the placement process can restore some sense of control and strengthen his or her commitment to the new family. Providing the child's complete family history to the adoptive family can help members respond to the child's questions and thus minimize fantasy and confusion about "how I got here." Helping parents master techniques for dealing with oppositional behavior can help them avoid needless confrontations (Wilson & Sturgeon, 1992), but even skilled and knowledgable parents occasionally experience the frequent rebuffs and emotional distancing of these children as rejection.

Thus, when children move from the child welfare system into an adoptive home, it is expected and normal for an intense and protracted process of family formation to occur (Delaney, 1991; Elbow, 1986; Katz, 1977, 1986; Pinderhughes & Rosenberg, 1990). Further, it is expected and normal that the process will entail a clash of diametrically opposed belief systems. On the one hand are the parents (and any biological or previously adopted children in the family) with their belief in family, trusting relationships, internalized values, and conscience. On the other hand is the child with his or her need to reenact familiar patterns established in the chaotic systems of previously experienced history (Ward & Lewko, 1988; Delaney, 1991). The more disturbed the child, and the more unstable the prior living arrangements, the more intense will be the challenge to the parents' assumptions, values, and expectations.

Inherent in the family formation process are a number of developmental issues common to all families with young children. In a special-needs adoptive family, issues that normally span a 6- or 7-year period must be dealt with simultaneously and in a compressed period of time. In addition, the issues must be worked out with a child who is chronologically older than his or her psychosocial development. These disparities that can exist in the child's development have caused these children to lose the innocence of youth and to become far more "streetwise" than older children or even their parents. At the same time, they may be completely unaware of very basic aspects of childhood, like the ability to play. School-age children may have been promoted from one grade to the next with large gaps in their knowledge.

Another fundamental family formation process that comes into play is the delineation of generational and relationship boundaries. An estimated 80% of all children who are in the foster care system have experienced sexual abuse. In addition, a number of these children have assumed a parental role, because of the dysfunctional nature of their birth families. Establishing appropriate generational boundaries is often complicated by these past violations of healthy boundaries, as well as by the child's well-honed skills in playing adults against each other. Creating dissension between parents is one of the ways in which the children are able to maintain a sense of control, gain power in the family, and avoid consequences for violating family rules.[3] Boundaries between the parental and child subsystems must be clear and consistently maintained. The boundary around the spousal subsystem must be strong enough for the husband and wife to present a unified front to the child, at least most of the time. If there are other children in the family, they must also be kept safe, and maintaining parental control of the family system is vital to this process.

---

[3]Interestingly enough, this is one of the ways in which a single-parent household has a distinct advantage in special-needs adoption since opportunities for triangulation are not readily available. It would not be surprising, however, for the child to seek out an adult outside the family (e.g., caseworker, teacher, therapist) to play the role of the missing parent figure.

For parents, the emotional intensity of these issues is fueled by uncertainty about how long to "hang in" hoping for a break through. Often it is impossible to determine the child's capacity for attachment before placement (Fahlberg, 1991; Donley, 1978; Watson & Bourguinnone, 1987; Brodzinsky & Schechter, 1990). It is not unusual for the records of the child's history to be fragmented and incomplete, making it difficult to determine the full nature and scope of the child's problems. Often these children have spent so much time in temporary foster care, group homes, residential treatment centers, or other institutional settings that they feel much more comfortable and appear to function much better within environments where there are few expectations for intimacy, trust, responsibility, and attachment. Only when they are finally placed in an adoptive home with expectations for permanence and bonding is it possible to discover the child's capacity to fit into and live with a family.

Once parents begin to live with their child's problems on a daily basis, the reality often proves to be more difficult than they had ever expected—so difficult, in fact, that the placement may be in jeopardy. When troubles such as these occur, families with a traditional orientation may be less likely to seek mental health services. They may rely instead on more traditional avenues (e.g., boarding school) to place distance between themselves and the child who is not meeting their expectations. If they do seek mental health services, they may insist on a more traditional therapy in which the "defective" child is fixed, and they may deny the influence of any issues related to family functioning or loss.

On some occasions it is deemed appropriate for an adoptive parent–child relationship to be terminated. This disruption can occur before or after legal finalization of the adoption. It is important that all parties—parents, child, caseworker, and mental health professionals—have a part in the communication concerning how and why this must occur. Openness will help everyone manage rekindled feelings of failure, anger, loss, and abandonment that accompany this decision.

Ironically, one signal that may indicate a child is effectively forming an attachment may appear, on the surface, to be just another set of problems. Giannotta (1982) found that older children may begin to exhibit regressive behaviors as they settle into the adoptive placement. Although this can be alarming to the parents, it is often a good sign. By regressing, the child creates an opportunity for reparenting. Parents can support their child's need for basic nurturing by creating opportunities such as playing with a baby or toddler and their toys. They may also encourage fantasy play by latency age children featuring themes that are more appropriate to younger children. Participation in a parent support group can give the parents a space in which they can describe their child and their mixed feelings about the immature play that may provoke criticism or judgments from adults who are unaware of the child's developmental needs.

Telling

Telling is another fundamental and distinctive process in adoptive families. When the results of Kirk's research first began to filter through the adoption community, adoptive parents equated "telling" with announcing—an unpleasant, but apparently necessary, task to be gotten through. In time, however, parents and professionals came to understand that telling is actually an ongoing process that establishes the family's sense of comfort and openness in talking about adoption. Initially, the process of telling includes deciding when to inform the child of his or her adopted status and finding age-appropriate ways to explain what adoption means. Adoption-appropriate "birth" announcements and baby books have helped families to develop positive ways of explaining the child's entrance into the family. In recent years a host of fiction and nonfiction books have been published to help parents explain to their children what it means to be adopted and to normalize the feelings associated with adoption.

In mixed-race families, the fact of adoption is more visible, which lends a different twist to telling as parents and children must develop strategies for dealing with the rude and intrusive behaviors of others, even total strangers, who casually approach ethnically and/or racially mixed, adoptive families and ask questions or make comments such as:

- Couldn't you have children of your own?
- What happened to your child's real family?
- Why would you want to take on somebody else's problems?
- Where is he from?
- Oh, I really admire you for taking on this problem!

In families of mixed races and cultures, telling must be expanded to help children maintain a sense of contact with their own ethnic heritage. Many families find it useful to mark the child's day of arrival from his or her own country (calling these anniversaries "airplane days"); others make albums that include memorabilia, photographs, and a story about the child's country of origin.

Lingering stereotypes about adopted children also complicate the process of telling, especially as children enter school. Donley (1978) coined the term "cover story" to describe a socially appropriate response to intrusive questions about the circumstances of adoption. Developing and teaching the child the cover story without activating feelings of shame or secrecy is a part of the telling process. So too, is helping the child develop both a sense of privacy and an ability to make wise decisions about what to share and with whom it is safe to do so.

As children mature and ask more pointed questions that touch on sensitive issues, parents may find it more difficult to maintain an aura of openness and comfort. They may struggle with how to respond appropriately to their child's pain, questions about past trauma, and disclosures of sexual abuse. Providing accurate information in ways that neither sugar-coat the truth nor denigrate the child's birth parents is important. For years, one stock answer to the question, "Why didn't they keep me?" was "They loved you so much, they gave you away so you could have a good home." Children, with their egocentric, concrete thinking, can translate this into a fear of being sent away by the adoptive parents who end the story with "and we love you very much." Portraying the birth parents as "the bad guys" can also backfire, making it more difficult for latency-age children to integrate disparate information and form a more balanced and realistic self-concept. More health-promoting responses can be given when parents convey the message that adoption is a process that solves adult problems—for example, "Your birth mom was not ready to be a mom to any child, so she made a plan to find you an adoptive mom and dad who were ready."

In families where discussing loss or difference is taboo, adoptees may struggle silently and privately with these complex issues. For others, a variety of problematic behaviors can emerge—for example, acting-out, regression, rejecting the adoptive family as a means of "beating them to the punch," or self-destructive behaviors such as substance abuse, promiscuity, or suicide. Whenever such behaviors occur, adoptive parents face one of the most pervasive processes unique to adoption: the intertwining of the child's troublesome behaviors with fears of abandonment and the pain of separation and loss. Adoptive parents must walk a fine line of responding to the behaviors per se and responding to recycling fears of abandonment and recurring pain of separation and loss (Piantanida & Anderson, 1990). It is crucial that they continue to set limits, which provide the security the child needs, even when they know the behaviors are symptoms of loss, which then must be discussed.

Even when families freely discuss adoption, such openness is not without difficulty as well. In particular, the process of telling has been further complicated by the emerging trends of open adoption and legal-risk placements. At present, there is no standardized definition of open adoption and arrangements can vary from an exchange of letters and pictures at the time of placement to ongoing involvement of the birth family in the adopted child's life (Andrews, 1978; Arms, 1988; Borgman, 1982; Gritter, 1989; Demick & Wapner, 1988; McRoy, Grotevant, & White, 1988; Silber & Dorner, 1989; Triseliotis, 1991). A distinctive, yet normal, process for these families involves clarifying the extent of openness and the nature of the relationships among birth and adoptive family members. When members of the birth family have ongoing involvement in the child's life, it is incumbent on all parties to work constantly to make these complex and unusual relationships understandable to the child.

In a legal-risk placement (Lee & Hull, 1983), there is some possibility that the rights of the birth parents will not be terminated, and the child could be reunified with his or her biological family. This legal uncertainty can persist for months, even years, leaving adoptive parents with the task of claiming the child as their own, while knowing that they may lose him or her. Outsiders to the adoption process may wonder why anyone would enter into such an ambiguous arrangement. Again, it is important to keep in mind that many adopters have a strong desire to parent an infant. Agreeing to become foster parents for an infant who is likely (but not certain) to be freed for adoption is one way to accomplish their goal.

Supporting the Struggle for Identity

At adolescence, the adoptee's questions about belonging and identity often surface with greater intensity, thereby complicating the family's task of "increasing flexibility of family boundaries to include children's independence" (Carter & McGoldrick, 1988, p. 176). This increase in flexibility of family boundaries is almost always more complicated for adoptive families. It is often at this stage that children want and need more information about their biological family. Even those placed as newborns ponder questions such as:

- Who am I and how did I get here?
- If someone else could give me away, will these people do the same?
- Who is my family, really? Where and to whom do I belong?
- Who looks like me? Are there other people like me?
- Do I have brothers and sisters out there somewhere?

One key to solving the puzzle of the adopted adolescent's identity lies in understanding the circumstances surrounding both the birth and placement for adoption. Thus, adolescents are likely to ask more pointed questions, perhaps expressed as interest in search and reunion with their birth parents. Even secure adoptive parents can have feelings and worries about the adolescent's desire to find his or her "real" parent(s), making this a possible time of turmoil for both generations.

Transracial and/or transcultural adoption raises special issues that had not been fully recognized by early adopters. From the parents' perspective, one of the most basic, and often unanticipated, issues to be dealt with is the redefinition of the family's ethnic and/or racial identity within the community (Ladner, 1978; van Gulden-Wicker, 1984). Often the full force of this change in perceived ethnic and/or racial status emerges when adoptees reach adolescence and begin to mature physically. Parents need strategies for protecting themselves or their children from racial prejudice, sexual stereotypes, and social biases that are activated by interracial dating.

Other problems arise from the children's need for and right to their racial, ethnic, and cultural heritage. In the early years of transracial placements, African-American, Native American, and Asian children were placed in white families with little consideration for the child's sense of identity and social belonging. Accompanying the growing awareness of the children's needs was a growing appreciation of the difficulty of instilling racial or ethnic pride and transmitting a cultural heritage that is different from one's own (Koh, 1988; McRoy, Zurcher, Landerdale, & Anderson, 1984; Pahz, 1988; Simon & Alstein, 1977). In 1972 the National Association of Black Social Workers issued a policy statement opposing this practice on the grounds that it denies children their ethnic identity and ill equips them to cope with racism in our society. Similarly, the Indian Child Welfare Act (1978) legislated the placement process for Native American children, giving priority to same-race families and limiting placements in white families.

The developmental impact of adoption continues as adolescents move into young adulthood. Abandonment, separation and loss issues, as well as issues of identity and belonging, tend to recur and complicate family-life transitions such as leaving home, marriage, birth of a child, and death of adoptive parents (Brodzinsky and Schechter, 1992; Downes, 1982). For example, it is a natural developmental step for families to encourage young adult adoptees to leave home and establish themselves as independent adults. Adopted young adults share the same concerns of their emancipating peers. Some of these normal concerns may be more intense; and there is likely to be an added layer of highly charged unspoken questions, including:

- Can I survive on my own?
- Will my family still be there?
- Who is my "real" (definition: birth) family?
- Where is my "real" (definition: birth) family?
- What will my children be like?

A common response to these concerns in adulthood is a renewed interest in searching for the birth family. Unlike adolescents, adult adoptees are more likely to succeed in locating and contacting members of their birth family. These reunions have a variety of outcomes, welcome and unwelcome. Interestingly enough, it is often connections with birth siblings that endure and deepen after the initial contact.

IMPLICATIONS FOR PROFESSIONAL PRACTICE

General Considerations

Throughout our discussion of adoption, we have stressed several points that form a backdrop to any therapeutic encounter with adoptive families. First and foremost, old stereotypes and assumptions about who adopts and why must give way to a greater appreciation for the variety and complexity of adoptive family configurations. Second, clinicians must recognize the importance and prevalence of two themes that permeate adoptive families—i.e., loss and control. All members of the adoptive family are likely to have a greater sensitivity to events or behaviors that impact on the integrity of the family unit—no matter how expected or normal these events might be. Even welcome and positive changes such as children leaving for college, marriages, or the birth of a new child may reactivate deepseated feelings of loss.

Although control issues are inherent in all family systems, they can be particularly charged in adoptive families. For parents, much of the adoption process is beyond their control. From consultations on infertility to sharing their innermost feelings about parenthood with caseworkers, these families have had to allow their boundaries to be permeable in ways most adults have not even considered. Although parents may have learned the importance and necessity of such flexibility, therapists must recognize the emotional aftermath of having to allow so many incursions into what others preserve as a "haven in a heartless world." For children who have lost their birth parents through no fault of their own and whose fate has been decided by strangers (e.g., social workers, judges, therapists), issues of control are paramount. We flag these sensitivities of adoptive families, not to imply abnormality or pathology, but rather to highlight some of the fundamental issues that are likely to surface periodically and bring members of the adoptive family to the therapist's doorstep. In addition, clinicians who themselves know they are especially vulnerable to the dynamics of loss and control may benefit from arranging supervision or periodic consultation on these cases to avoid under- or overreactions driven by their own unfinished business.

Working with Individuals and Couples Considering Adoption

Adoption is a big step, described by some as going on a blind date for life. It is a decision that will affect not only the lives of parents and child, but also the entire extended family system, as divergent destinies become irrevocably intertwined. This decision, best made after considerable thought and discussion, is typically reached without consulting a mental health professional. Nevertheless, there are two ways in which therapists may become involved in the preplacement process.

Increasingly, adoption professionals are including therapists as presenters, or even co-leaders, of adoption preparation classes. Given such an opportunity, therapists can be most helpful by encouraging prospective parents to carefully examine the possible ramifications of adoption—for example, reactions to infertility, whether or not the dream child has been mourned, differential desires to adopt between spouses, the relentlessness of parenting (especially single parenting), the infant's unknown genetic "credentials," and the ramifications of taking a child of another race or culture, or a child who has been neglected or abused. Helping parents to see mental health services as a source of support, rather than a sign of weakness and inadequacy, is another important goal for these early interactions.

Another opportunity for involvement during preplacement occurs when clinicians have been working with a child who is in foster care or residential placement. In such cases, the therapist may join a team of professionals to evaluate the suitability of a potential placement; that therapist may also be asked to support the entire family's adjustment during postplacement. Therapists who are accustomed to working exclusively with the child or the parents may have difficulty redefining the client as the family system, rather than any particular member. Some therapists respond by referring the child and his or her new parents to a new clinician, who can start "fresh" with the whole family. Because separation and loss are such highly charged issues for special-needs adoptees, this solution to the "client loyalty" issue can result in a major setback for the child and a lost opportunity to facilitate the restabilization of the family's equilibrium.

Working with Adoptive Families

It is likely that helping professionals will encounter adoptive families as they experience a developmental crisis. Often families present in one of two modes. Some are intently focused on the fact of adoption, "blaming" it for all aspects of the family's distress. Others tend to gloss over the adoptive dimension of the family and focus exclusively on the child's problematic behaviors—e.g., disruptive behavior, acting-out, depression, school problems, or child-management issues. Because this latter mode is so prevalent, clinicians may not even be aware of the high percentage of adopted children on their caseloads. Unless adoptees are asking questions about their biological parents, many clinicians will simply note adoption as a fact of the family's social history with no attempt to address it in the treatment plan or in the process of therapy. Such an approach handicaps treatment, since the therapist is, in essence, trying to do therapy with the equivalent of a large, but not discussable, "elephant" in the middle of the office.

For this reason, it is essential that therapists begin by taking a complete history of placement issues in the family. This includes:

1. The extent to which the parents' issues of infertility have been dealt with and resolved.
2. Communication within the family—not just from the parents' perspective but from the child's—about (a) the fact and circumstances of adoption, (b) the child's biological family and other significant families/caregivers in the child's life, and (c) the child's exposure to inappropriate sexual activity.
3. A placement history of the child—that is, determine the nature and extent of separation and loss experienced by the child and the likelihood that the child has had an opportunity to mourn these losses.
4. The adoptive parents' understanding and explanation of the birth parent's decision to place the child.

There is growing recognition among clinicians who work with adoptive families that a family therapy approach is crucial. Within the context of family therapy, it is often necessary to work on several levels, at different times helping parents to establish firm generational boundaries, or to reorder their relationships with their own families of origin, or to work through unresolved losses, or to manage specific behavioral problems. Simultaneously, it may be necessary to meet separately to help children resolve issues of loss and come to terms with past histories of abuse. Family sessions can be helpful to make sure communication is maintained, secrets are managed within the system, and trust is built. Successfully combining these interventions necessitates a reconceptualization of the issue of patient confidentiality. Otherwise, the potential for the child triangulating the parents and therapists escalates.

Regardless of the specific treatment goals dictated by the specific problems at hand, it is important to:

1. Affirm the adoptee's right to integrate his or her biological and adoptive heritages into his or her evolving identity.
2. Assess the child's capacity for attachment and intimacy as well as help the adoptive parents develop realistic expectations and learn ways to encourage the attachment process.
3. Recognize that although the child may present for a particular problem, a range of issues may need to be addressed;
4. Recognize, affirm, and support the health of the family while working with the disturbed child; this may necessitate a psychoeducational intervention with parents and psychotherapy with child;
5. Recognize the therapist's potential for precipitating triangulation. The therapist's fantasy that he or she can fix the child more effectively than the parent may result in undermining parental authority and bonding within the family. Supporting the family's right and power to be the primary healer is essential.
6. Recognize that there are issues specific to adoptive families with children of color that should be made discernible and assessed for their impact on other family decisions.

Working with Issues of Loss and Attachment

With adopted children, acting-out behaviors are often related to unresolved rage and grief, fears of abandonment, and other threats to survival and self-esteem. There are different views about how and when these underlying issues should be addressed. Some believe they should be first on the agenda, since they permeate the child's view of himself, the world, and the meaning of family. Others believe that the issues should be contained as much as possible. Recognizing that catharsis alone is not particularly helpful, healing strategies include validating the child's feelings, helping him or her express these in socially acceptable ways, and consistently protecting all family members from the child's anger. Adoption and mental health professionals have found the process of creating a lifebook with the child to be an extremely effective intervention (Aust, 1981; Backhaus, 1984; Harrison, Campbell, & Chumbley, 1987; Piantanida & Anderson, 1990b). The lifebook creates a concrete, visual record that helps the child answer some very basic questions about history and identity. Affirming the child's past allows for continuity and connection with present and future experiences. Most importantly, when the process of creating a lifebook includes the expression, acknowledgment, and exploration of feelings, the child is better able to make sense of his or her life experience. Lifebook work often requires collaboration among therapist, caseworker, and parents.

It may also be necessary to modify the structure of the therapy session—in order to allow enough time to bring a session to closure. Since the child's rage often stems from unresolved abandonment issues, to arbitrarily terminate a session may exacerbate the problem. Sometimes sessions can be allowed to continue until an issue has reached some resolution. If this is not feasible, it is good for the therapist to keep track of time carefully, and warn the child and/or family when the session is drawing to a close. Stressing the importance of the topic being addressed and respectfully noting that it will be placed at the top of the agenda for the next session serve to mitigate some of the negative effects of premature closure.

Because the placement of severely disturbed children in adoptive homes is a fairly recent phenomenon, we are only now beginning to understand the potential and the limitations of these placements. Likewise, our understanding of effective treatment modalities is still emerging and requires far more careful research. There are, however, several centers and a professional association where clinicians specialize in the treatment of children whose capacity for attachment is extremely impaired. Efforts to disseminate the work of these centers and to add to the knowledge base being generated through clinical casework are essential.

Siblings: Adoptive and Biological

Adoption can create some special issues for the sibling subsystem within families. When taking the family's psychosocial history, particular attention should be given to identifying various sibling configurations. Possibilities include:

- Blending birth and adopted siblings
- Blending a number of biologically unrelated children in one adoptive family
- Placing biological siblings in one adoptive home
- Separating biological siblings and placing them in different adoptive families

- Separating biological siblings, placing some for adoption and leaving some with the birth family

Adoptive families may need the support of helping professionals as they deal with a variety of sibling issues. Biological children may wonder about their parents' motivation for adopting—secretly pondering "Wasn't I enough?" or "Wasn't I good enough?" Tension is likely to occur when adoptees need excessive reassurance and biological siblings fear they are being displaced or neglected. As unrelated children enter the family system, fundamental rules about communication, family roles, and boundaries must be renegotiated. A particularly complicated boundary issue has to do with sexual roles both within the sibling subsystem and between the parent/child subsystems. Normal sibling rivalries can be exacerbated as children from different families must readjust their roles within the family structure. The intensity of these family formation issues can make the families more vulnerable to dysfunctional solutions such as scapegoating.

When biological siblings are placed in different adoptive homes, another set of boundary issues arises. Contrary to past practice, adoptive families are now advised to help their children maintain contact with biological siblings. This gives new meaning to the concept of extended family, as different systems are linked through the biological ties of their children. The advantages the children reap through the maintenance of these contacts are worth the time and trouble it takes to make the arrangements. In particular, it decreases the probability of polarized views of biological and adoptive families and thus also any unspoken pressures to choose between conflicting loyalties.

Community Resources and Advocacy

Although it is impossible to deal exhaustively with all facets of normal processes in adoptive families, we have tried in this chapter to highlight some of the most common, distinctive, and expected dynamics. No matter how conscientiously adults prepare for adoptive parenthood, how thoroughly caseworkers prepare children, and how expertly therapists support the formation of families, countless variations on these fundamental processes will arise. Therefore, one of the most productive processes in which families can engage is participation in adoptive parent support groups. Fortunately, such groups now exist in many cities, and they offer a level of on-going self-help and peer education that extends beyond the formal intervention of professionals. Clinicians who are familiar with the resources available in their community can utilize them as an integral part of their treatment plans. In addition, professionals who are willing to forge collaborative relationships with these groups can do much to enhance their own understanding of the processes and dynamics inherent in adoption as well as contribute to the learning of adoptive parents and their children.

CONCLUSION

As growing numbers of children with more severe problems enter the child welfare system, we as a society must find creative ways in which to meet their needs for permanence. Given the severity of their problems, at least some of these children "may be placeable, but not parentable" (Van Gulden-Wicker, 1990). Yet, to whatever extent possible, these children benefit from the on-going involvement of caring adults. As a society, we need to expand our concepts and metaphors of "family."

Considering all this, it is important for parents and professionals to know that adoption can and does work. Parents, in particular, need to hear that their commitment and investment in their children's welfare do make a difference. They need affirmation from family, friends, professionals and society at large that they have done a good job, a job that many others were unwilling to take on. In recent years, there has been growing a rhetoric of concern about the welfare of our nation's children. These families, particularly those who have taken society's damaged and discarded children into their homes and hearts, have translated the rhetoric into the most personal level of commitment and action. They deserve our gratitude, our respect, and most importantly, our understanding.

REFERENCES

Ainsworth, M. S. (1979). Infant–mother attachment. *American Psychologist, 34*(10), 932–937.

Ammerman, R., Lubetsky, M. J., Hersen, M., & Van Hasselt, V. B. (1988). Maltreatment of children and adolescents with multiple handicaps: Five case examples. *Journal of the Multihandicapped Person, 1*(2), 129–139.

Andrews, R. G. (1978). Adoption: Legal resolution or legal fraud? *Family Process, 17*, 313–328.

Arms, S. (1988). *To love and let go.* New York: Alfred A. Knopf.

Aust, P. H. (1981). Using the life story book in treatment of children in placement. *Child Welfare, 60*(8), 535–560.

Backhaus, K. A. (1984). Life books: Tool for working with children in placement. *Social Work, 29*, 551–554.

Barth, R. P., & Berry M. (1988). *Adoption disruption: Rates, risks and response.* New York: Aldine de Gruyter.

Berlin, I. N. (1978). Anglo adoptions of native Americans: Repercussions in adolescence. *American Academy of Child Psychiatry, 17*(2), 387–388.

Borgman, R. (1982). The consequences of open and closed adoption for older children. *Child Welfare, 61*(4), 217–226.

Bowlby, J. (1970). *Attachment: Loss.* New York: Basic Books.

Boyd-Franklin, N. (1989). *Black families in therapy.* New York: Guilford Press.

Braden, J. A. (1981). Adopting the abused child: Love is not enough. *Social Casework, 62*(6), 362–367.

Brodzinsky, D., & Schechter, M. (1990). *The psychology of adoption.* New York: Oxford University Press.

Brodzinsky, D. M., Schechter, M. D., & Henig, R. M. (1992). *Being adopted: The life-long search for self.* New York: Doubleday.

Bulter, I. C. (1989). Adopted children, adoptive families: Recognizing differences. In L. Combrinck-Graham (Ed.), *Children in family contexts: Perspectives on treatment* (pp. 161–186). New York: Guilford Press.

Carter, B., & McGoldrick, M. (Eds.) (1988). *The changing family life cycle: A framework for family therapy.* New York: Gardner Press.

Chambers, D. E. (1970). Willingness to adopt atypical children. *Child Welfare, 69*(5), 275–279.

Cline, F. (1992). *Hope for high risk and rage filled children.* Evergreen, CO: Ec Publications.

Crook, M. (1986). *The face in the mirror.* Toronto: NC Press.

Delaney, R. J. (1991). *Fostering changes: Treating attachment-disordered foster children.* Fort Collins, CO: Walter J. Corbett.

Demick, J., & Wapner, S. (1988). Open and closed adoption: A developmental conceptualization. *Family Process, 27,* 229–249.

Derdeyn, A. P. (1979). Adoption and the ownership of children. *Child Psychiatry and Human Development, 9*(4), 215–226.

Donley, K. S. (1978). *The cover story: Helping children explain their placement.* New York: New York Spaulding for Children.

Donley, L. (1986). Post placement service analysis. In P. Grabe (Ed.). *Adoption resources for mental health professionals.* New Brunswick, NJ: Transaction Publishers.

Downes, C. (1982). How endings are experienced in time limited family placement of difficult adolescents. *Journal of Adolescence, 1*(5), 379–394.

Duehn, W. (1990, March). *Beyond sexual abuse: The healing power of adoptive and foster families.* Paper presented at Three Rivers Adoption Council, Pittsburgh, PA.

Elbow, M. (1986). From caregiving to parenting: Family formation with adopted older children. *Social Work, 31,* 366–370.

Fahlberg, V. I. (1990). *Residential treatment—A tapestry of many therapies.* Indianapolis: Perspectives Press.

Fahlberg, V. I. (1991). *A child's journey through placement.* Indianapolis: Perspectives Press.

Feigelman, W., & Silverman, A. R. (1977). Single parent adoptions. *Social Casework, 58*(7), 418–425.

Feigelman, W., & Silverman, A. R. (1979). Preferential adoption: A new mode of family formation. *Social Casework, 60*(5), 296–305.

Giannotta, V. M. (1982). The postplacement process in older child adoption. *Dissertation Abstracts International, 49,* 14-A (University Microfilms No. 88-08250).

Glidden, L. (1989). *Parents for children—Children for parents: The adoption alternative.* In M. Begab (Series Ed.), *Monographs of the American Association on Mental Retardation,* 11. Washington DC: American Association on Mental Retardation.

Grabe, P. (Ed.). (1990). *Adoption resources for mental health professionals.* New Brunswick, NJ: Transaction Press.

Gritter, J. L. (Ed.). (1989). *Adoption without fear.* San Antonio: Corona.

Groze, V., & Rosenthal, J. A. (1991). A structural analysis of families adopting special-needs children. *Families in Society: The Journal of Contemporary Human Services*, 78(8), 469–482.

Harrison, J., Campbell, E., & Chumbley, P. (1987). *Making history: A social worker's guide to lifebooks*. Frankfurt: Kentucky Cabinet for Human Services, Department of Social Services.

Indian Child Welfare Act. Public Law 95-608 United States Department of Health and Human Services (1982), pp. 66.

Jewett, C. L. (1978). *Adopting the older child*. Boston: The Harvard Common Press.

Jewett, C. L. (1982). *Helping children cope with separation and loss*. Boston: The Harvard Common Press.

Kadushin, A., & Martin, J. A. (1988). Substitute care: Adoption. In A. Kadushin & J. A. Martin (Eds.), *Child welfare services* (4th ed., pp. 533–668). New York: Macmillan.

Katz, L. (1977). Older child adoptive placements: A time of family crisis. *Child Welfare*, 55(3), 165–171.

Katz, L. (1986). Parental stress and factors for success in older-child adoption. *Child Welfare*, 65(6), 569–578.

Kirk, H. D. (1981). *Adoptive kinship, A modern institution in need of reform*. Toronto: Butterworths.

Kirk, H. D. (1984). *Shared fate: A theory and method of adoptive relationships* (2nd ed.). Port Angeles, WA: Ben-Simon Publications.

Koh, F. M. (1988). *Oriental children in American homes* (rev. ed.). Minneapolis: East West Press.

Ladner, J. (1977). *Mixed families—adopting across racial boundaries*. Garden City, NJ: Doubleday.

Lee, R. E., & Hull, R. K. (1983). Legal, casework, and ethical issues in "risk adoption." *Children*, 62(5), 450–454.

Leof, J. (undated). *Adopting children with developmental disabilities*. Washington, DC: National Adoption Information Clearinghouse.

LePere, D. (1988). Vulnerability to crisis during the life cycle of the adoptive family. In *Infertility and adoption: A guide for social work practice* (pp. 73–85). Binghamton, NY: Haworth Press.

Mahler, M. (1973, January). *Symbiosis and individuation: The psychological birth of the child*. Fifteenth Sophia Miniss Lecture to the San Francisco Psychiatric Institute, Mount Zion Hospital and Medical Center.

Mahoney, J. (1990, January). *Post adoption stress disorder: The hidden contract in adoption*. Paper presented at Three Rivers Adoption Council, Pittsburgh.

Main, M. (1973). *Play, exploration and competence as related to child–adult attachment*. Unpublished doctoral dissertation, Johns Hopkins University.

Marindin, H. (Ed.). (1987). *The handbook for single adoptive parents*. Chevy Chase, MD: Committee for Single Adoptive Parents.

McRoy, R. G., Grotevant, H. D., & White, K. L. (1988). *Openness in adoption: New practices, new issues*. New York: Praeger.

McRoy, R. G., Zurcher, L. A., Lauderdale, M. L., & Anderson, R. E. (1984). The identity of transracial adoptees. *Social Casework: The Journal of Contemporary Social Work*, 65(1), 34–37.

Melina, L. R. (1986). *Raising adopted children: A manual for adoptive parents*. New York: Harper & Row.

Menning, B. (1977). *Infertility: A guide for the childless couple.* Englewood Cliffs, NJ: Prentice-Hall.

National Association of Black Social Workers. *The New York Times*, April 12, 1972.

Olson, D. H., & Laver, Y. (1989). Family systems and family stress: A family life cycle perspective. In K. Kreppner & R. M. Lerner (Eds.), *Family systems and lifespan development* (pp. 165–195). Hillsdale, NJ: Lawrence Erlbaum Associates.

O'Rourke, L., & Hubbell, R. (1990). *Intercountry adoption.* Washington, DC: National Adoption Information Clearinghouse.

Pahz, J. A. (1988). *Adopting from Latin America, an agency perspective.* Springfield, IL: Charles C. Thomas.

Piantanida, M., & Anderson, S. (1990a). *The fine line of adoptive parenting: A resource guide for adoptive parents.* Pittsburgh: Three Rivers Adoption Council.

Piantanida, M., & Anderson, S. (1990b). *Creating and using lifebooks: A guide for adoptive parents.* Pittsburgh: Three Rivers Adoption Council.

Piasecki, M. (1987). *Who adopts special needs children?* Washington, DC: National Adoption Center.

Pinderhughes, E. E., & Rosenberg, K. F. (1990). Family-bonding with high risk placements: A therapy model that promotes the process of becoming a family. In L. Glidden, (Ed.), *Formed families: Adoption of children with handicaps* (pp. 209–230). Binghamton, NY: Haworth Press.

Powledge, F. (1982). *So you're adopted.* New York: Charles Scribner's Sons.

Prowler, M. (1991). *Single parent adoption: What you need to know.* Washington, DC: National Adoption Information Clearinghouse.

Reitz, M., & Watson, K. (1992). *Adoption and the family system: Strategies and treatment.* New York: Guilford Press.

Rosenberg, E. B. (1992). *The adoption life cycle: The children and their families through the years.* New York: Free Press.

Salzer, L. P. (1986). *Infertility: How couples can cope.* Boston: G. K. Hall & Co.

Select Committee on Children, Youth, and Families, U.S. House of Representatives. (1990). *No place to call home: Discarded children in America* (DDHS Publication No. 101-395). Washington, DC: U.S. Government Printing Office.

Silber, K., & Dorner, P. (1989). *Children of open adoption.* San Antonio, Corona.

Simon, R., & Alstein, H. (1977). *Transracial adoption.* New York: John Wiley.

Small, J. W. (1984). The crisis in adoption. *International Journal of Social Psychiatry, 30*(1–2), 129–142.

Small, J. W. (1987). Working with adoptive families. *Public Welfare, 37*(3), 33–41.

Sonne, J. C. (1980). A family system perspective on custody and adoption. *International Journal of Family Therapy, 2*(3), 176–192.

Sorosky, A. (1992). Somebody else's baby. *Readings: Journal of Reviews and Commentary in Mental Health, 7*(4), 10–13.

Tansey, B. J. (Ed.). (1988). *Exploring adoptive family life, The collected adoption papers of H. David Kirk.* Port Angeles, WA: Ben-Simon Publishers.

Tizard, B. (1991). Intercountry adoption: A review of the evidence. *Journal of Child Psychology and Psychiatry, 32*(5), 743–756.

Triseliotis, J. (1991). Perception of permanence: Adoption and fostering. *Journal of Social Policy, 15*(4), 6–15.

Van Gulden-Wicker, H. (1990). *Can I love this child? Can this child love me?* Paper presented for the North American Council on Adoptable Children annual conference, Washington, DC.

Ward, M. (1981). Parental bonding in older child adoptions. *Child Welfare, 60*(1), 24–34.

Ward, M., & Lewko, J. H. (1988). Problems experienced by adolescents already in families that adopt older children. *Adolescence, 23*(89), 221–228.

Watson, K., & Bourguignon, J. (1987). *After adoption.* Springfield: Illinois Department of Children and Family Services.

Whiting, R. (1988). Therapeutic rituals with families with adopted members. In E. Imber-Black, J. Roberts, & R. Whiting (Eds.), *Rituals in families and family therapy* (pp. 211–229). New York: W. W. Norton & Co.

Wilson, J., & Sturgeon, V. (1992). *A cast of thousands: Preparing children for placement.* Presented for Three Rivers Adoption Council training conference, Pittsburgh.

LESBIAN AND
GAY FAMILIES

Joan Laird

INTRODUCTION

Some readers may be surprised to discover a chapter on gay and lesbian families[1] in a volume entitled *Normal Family Processes*. Only recently has there been any acknowledgment, in professional or popular literature or in the media, that lesbians and gay men live in family forms. It is quite a leap from that point to conceive of such families as possibly "normal." Indeed, 10 years ago, in the first edition of this book, neither the word "gay" nor "lesbian" is mentioned in the index, and "homosexuality" receives peripheral mention in one or two chapters.[2] At the end of the last chapter of that volume, however, Harevan comments:

> Much anxiety has . . . been expressed over the increase in the proportion of couples living together unmarried, over homosexual partners or parents, and over a whole variety of alternative family forms and life styles. What we are

[1]In this chapter I use the term "gay family" and "lesbian family" to refer to same-sex couples and to families with children headed by a lesbian or gay couple or solo parent. I am indebted to Robert-Jay Green for pointing out that some of the families I refer to in this chapter are composed of both gay and/or lesbian and heterosexual members and, strictly speaking, deserve some new terminology such as "mixed gay/straight" or "dual-orientation" families.

[2]The terms "gay," "lesbian," and "homosexuality" have different meanings in sociocultural discourse and to the individuals and communities who are using these terms. For many, the term "homosexual" identifies a person exclusively with his or her sexual preference and, historically, has been used pejoratively. "Gay," a term more identified with notions of pride and with a culture or subculture, generally refers to males but is sometimes used more generically to refer to both gay men and lesbians. In this chapter, I rarely use the term homosexual, preferring the terms "gay men" and "lesbians." Occasionally, for shorthand purposes, I will use the term "gay" to refer to both males and females.

witnessing in all these varieties of life styles are not necessarily new inventions. Many different forms have been in existence all along, but they have been less visible. The more recent forms of alternative life styles have now become a part of the official fiber of society, because they are now being tolerated much more than in the past. In short, what we are witnessing is not a fragmentation of traditional family patterns, but, rather, the emergence of a pluralism in family ways. (1982, pp. 462–463)

Some 10 years later, it is clear that lesbian and gay families are here to stay and that they are an important part of that pluralist society Harevan envisions. But "normality," an idea located in the eye of the beholder, is quite another issue and one that will be returned to many times in this chapter as we consider the position in society today of gay and lesbian families.

Goffman (1963) defined normality as the absence of stigma. If we adopt this view of normality, since gay men and lesbians constitute one of the most if not the most stigmatized groups in this society, we cannot consider such individuals "normal," whether or not they live in formations that resemble or may be defined as American families. If we approach from another direction and study whether or not these "families" seem to carry out successfully what have traditionally been conceptualized as family functions in this society, we may find these families as normal or abnormal as any other type of family.

The notions of "gay" or "lesbian" and that of "family" have, for the most part, been mutually exclusive concepts in public discourse. This failure to allow into public consciousness a definition of family that might refer to same-sex couples living alone or with children and/or other adults, of gay people as parents, may account in part for the striking lack of attention to this family form in social science research, in the clinical literature, and, particularly, for our purposes here, in the family therapy field. Only in recent years have the injustices, the sins of commission perpetrated against gays and lesbians in the name of psychoanalytic and medicobiological theory, been confronted; it may now be time to address the sins of omission in the family field. For, with some notable exceptions,[3] family therapy theorists and practitioners have acted as if lesbian and gay families did not exist. In one sense this silence in the family field is part of a larger silence that ignores many other family forms as well. In spite of the fact that the traditional family has become only one of a virtual plurality of family forms in this society, it has remained the model for the creation of practice theory and method. In another sense, the

---

[3]These include Crawford (1987, 1988), Goodrich et al. (1988), Krestan (1988), Krestan and Bepko (1980), Roth (1989), and Roth and Murphy (1986). See, also, the recent special issue of *The Family Therapy Networker* on gay and lesbian concerns (January/February, 1991). Interestingly, the first article I am aware of in the mainstream family therapy literature (Osman, 1972) was entitled "My Stepfather Is a She." Not only does the title reflect the lack of any language to define lesbian family relationships, but the solution to the case presented is also interesting; the therapist recommends out-of-home placement as a solution to the "acting-out" child's difficulties.

particular invisibility of lesbian and gay families in the family field undoubtedly reflects the pervasive context of homophobia from which family therapists are not exempt.

Family theorists would do well to heed the lesbian and gay family, for
it can teach us important things about other families, about gender relationships, about parenting, about adaptation to tensions in this society, and especially about strength and resilience. For in spite of the pervasive and profound stigmatization of gay life, gay men and lesbians are building stable
and satisfying couple relationships and forming families that seem to be doing
at least as well as other kinds of families in carrying out their sociologically
defined family roles and tasks.

However, the fact that these families are in many ways so invisible, the
fact that they have flourished in an atmosphere of silence and secrecy, makes
it more difficult to study and describe them in the same ways that other
families, such as families with schizophrenic members or ethnic or single-
parent or postdivorce families, have been studied and described. There have
been a very small number of studies of gay male and lesbian couples, of
lesbian mothers, and of the children of lesbian mothers. Most of these studies are quantitative in nature, frequently using personality or self-assessment
measures, exploring one or more characteristics of the couples or individuals of interest, and/or comparing this population to other populations. There
are even fewer studies of gay fathers.

Other sources, clinical case reports (e.g., Crawford, 1987, 1988;
Goodrich, Rampage, Ellman, & Halstead, 1988; Krestan, 1988; Krestan &
Bepko, 1980; Laird, 1988, 1989; Roth, 1989; Roth & Murphy, 1986), journal-
istic accounts (e.g., Miller, 1989), oral histories and indigenous accounts (e.g.,
Hall Carpenter Archives, 1989a, 1989b), culture and kinship studies (e.g.,
Herdt, 1992; Weston, 1991), and qualitative parts of larger survey studies
(e.g., Blumstein & Schwartz, 1983) take us inside the everyday lives of gay
and lesbian families, giving us brief glimpses. However, to my knowledge,
there are no ethnographic studies of gay and lesbian family life in this society, that is, wholistic studies that might give us a fuller sense of the complexity and richness of everyday life in these families.

There has been considerable interest, over a long period of time and
particularly in the psychological literature, in studying gay men and lesbians as individuals. More recently, lesbians and gay men seem to be attract-
ing more attention from sociologists, anthropologists, historians, and in interdisciplinary gender studies. Although these sources have not yet told us
very much about *families*, they do tell us something about the historical and
sociocultural milieus in which gay families have existed and do exist today;
thus, they form starting point and context for any examination of gay and
lesbian family life.

This chapter is organized using a time–space diagram (see Figure 10.1)
that also served as the organizing conception for an earlier work (Hartman
& Laird, 1983). Beginning with an ecological view, I look first at the social
and cultural contexts, then and now, in which gays and lesbians have been

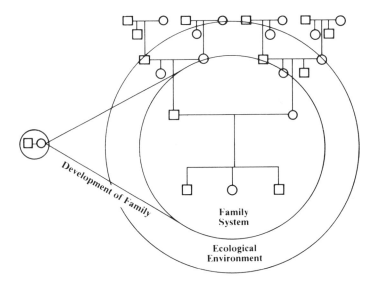

FIGURE 10.1. The family in space and time. (Source: *Family-centered social work practice*, by Ann Hartman and Joan Laird [p.113]. Copyright © 1983 by The Free Press a Division of Macmillan, Inc. Reproduced with the permission of the publisher.)

and are defined by others and by themselves. Several questions implicit in this discussion of context or space are raised but cannot be fully addressed here. Is there such a thing as gay culture? Lesbian culture? Subcultures? If so, how is this culture(s) different from the larger melange of values, norms, meanings, beliefs, and practices that make up what we think of as United States culture? How and in what ways do lesbians and gays construct their identities and their families differently from people who define themselves and are defined by others as straight? What, if anything, is essential about being gay or lesbian? Is it a matter of "being" at all? Is there such a thing as the lesbian or gay "community?" If so, what are the implications of "community" and "social network" for lesbian and gay families?

Second, gay and lesbian families, like all families, must be viewed intergenerationally; each partner, child, and other family member is influenced by and must come to terms with the specific history and culture of his or her own family of origin in its sociocultural context. Each new family must determine how it will fit on the family tree and how it will negotiate family-of-origin issues. This can be particularly difficult and complex when neither legal nor biological relationships, prevailing determinants of family relatedness, constitute necessary norms for gay or lesbian coupling or parenthood. How do lesbian and gay families, often rejected by their families of origin, deal with this rejection?

Third, the family life cycle of the lesbian or gay family must be explored. "Stage" theories have been central in the last two decades of study of individual gay and lesbian identity and development. Some researchers have turned their attention to the life cycle of the gay couple and, most recently, to the family life cycle of the lesbian family. Is the life-cycle model useful, and what are the limitations of this metaphor for describing the life course of gay and lesbian families?

I then move inside the lesbian and gay family, using some of the dimensions and metaphors that have been of interest to family theorists. What can we say at present about family structure and process, and about how these families are doing? Do such family theory concepts as boundary, enmeshment or fusion, cohesion, symmetry and asymmetry, and so on have relevance for understanding families headed by same-sex partners? What are the limitations of such conceptions in understanding lesbian and gay families? What can these families teach us about heterosexual families, about gender identity and relationships? About courage under fire? About resilience? Do such families have special strengths? Do they have unique kinds of problems?

The chapter concludes with a brief commentary on what I see as current research priorities.

Finally, something should be said about my own aims and context, for the writer is part of the written, the researcher part of the researched (Geertz, 1988; Ricoeur, 1979). We, I believe, are part of the texts we produce and are ourselves recast in the process. First, I try, in this chapter, to pivot the center, that is, to start from the standpoint of the gay and lesbian experience itself. Most studies of "minorities," including many done by gay or lesbian researchers, start from a majority perspective (usually white, middle-class, male), comparing and searching for "difference," measuring the population of interest against some accepted norm and describing how it is different, exotic, or deviant. Here, to coin an anthropological phrase, whenever possible I look for "the native's point of view" (Geertz, 1979). Secondly, it is important to note that it is never accurate to talk about "gays" or "lesbians" as if they were a monolithic group with a common experience or point of view. Lesbians and gays come in all shades of color and types of faith; they are Republicans and Democrats, anarchists and revolutionaries. Their experiences, like those of all individuals and groups, are mediated by race, class, sex, age, and other sociocultural categories. They fight among themselves and with others about political correctness and the question of culture, and at times they look at their own racism, sexism, heterosexism, and homophobia.[4]

---

[4]For readers who may be unfamiliar with the terms heterosexism and homophobia, the following definitions may be helpful. Falco (1991) defines *heterosexism* as "the assumption that heterosexuality is in any way better than homosexuality" (p. 7), and Rich (1980), in her now classic article on "compulsory heterosexuality," argues that heterosexuality is a powerful political institution of patriarchy in which it is assumed that heterosexuality is the preference for most human beings. *Homophobia* has been defined by Weinberg (1972) as "the dread

SOCIOCULTURAL CONTEXT

Homosexuality: Essential or Constructed Identity and Behavior?

Homosexuality traditionally has been viewed both as an essential and more or less permanent part of individual being and identity and, at the same time, as aberration or deviance from the norm. Social definitions of homosexuality, which have characterized it as everything from sin and perversion to mental illness, contributed to a history in which homosexuals in many societies through the centuries have faced severe social sanctions, including burning, hanging, beheading, institutionalization, castration, clitoridectomy, lobotomy, electroshock treatment and, during the Nazi regime, concentration camps and death by starvation and excecution (D'Emilio, 1983; Faderman, 1981). Today, in spite of the fact that many researchers believe gays "come out" to a much more tolerant society, it is clear that they continue to face social approbation, isolation, and public humiliation. Their relationships lack legal sanction, and they are not afforded many social protections heterosexual people take for granted; their families face threats of dissolution through child removal, their families of origin may disown them, and some are subjected to violence (Comstock, 1991).

Until very recently the central mission of researchers from across the social science, medical, and mental health disciplines was to locate the "causes" of homosexuality; its sources were "discovered" in faulty chromosomes, genes, or hormonal imbalances; in arrested psychosexual development (often, in turn, "caused" by insufficient mothering and/or the weak father–dominant mother constellation) for males, in feminine role identity and for females in masculine protest and role identity; and as an extension of autoeroticism.[5] Currently, there is renewed interst in brain research on biological causation, which has important legal and political ramifications. If homosexuality is seen as biologically or genetically caused, homosexuals may be considered a protected class under the United States Constitution. However, if homosexuality is seen by the courts as voluntary, it is a practice less clearly protected under the law.

In sociological and anthropological studies, deviance and labeling theory prevailed (e.g., Becker, 1973). The latter kinds of studies were valuable in exploring the social functions of labeling and its impact on stigmatized individuals. Nevertheless, most scholars have assumed not only that hetero-

---

of being in close quarters with homosexuals" (quoted in Forstein, 1988, p. 33) and by Falco (1991) as "the fear of gayness said to be at the root of the denial of civil and economic rights to gays" (p. 7). Also, see Forstein (1988), who sees homophobia as an internalization of negative and violent attitudes toward homosexuality, for an elaboration of its psychological and social ramifications.

[5]Browning (1984) offers an interesting review of some of the major theories concerning the "causes" of homosexuality.

sexuality is the norm for human sexual behavior, but that sexual behavior is largely an individual matter, only peripherally relevant to the functioning of the larger group. Even past students of other cultures, taking their Western biases with them, have assumed that homosexuality was deviant in all cultures.

Blackwood (1985) argues that anthropologists of the past have taken an "essentialist" position, accepting Western biases that define homosexuality as unnatural and dysfunctional and failing to note the culturally specific meanings and values attached to homosexual behavior in various societies throughout the world, a perspective affirmed in Greenberg's (1988) comprehensive cross-cultural review. In her view, homosexual behavior is culturally constructed and can only be understood by investigating the complex interactions of cultural and social factors in any society. She maintains that closer study indicates that in many traditional societies, homosexuality practices are accepted and indeed integral to the society. As Ross and Rapp (1981) phrase it:

> Sexuality's biological base is always experienced culturally, through a translation. The bare biological facts of sexuality do not speak for themselves; they must be expressed socially. Sex feels individual, or at least private, but those feelings always incorporate the roles, definitions, symbols and meanings of the worlds in which they are constructed. (p. 51)

Sexuality, in their view, is conditioned, constrained, and socially defined by kinship and family system, sexual regulations, and definitions of communities and national and world systems.

Richardson (1987) reviews more recent studies that support the notion that homosexuality is a cultural "invention," that sexual identities and behaviors are socially constructed. Foucault (1979), for example, maintained that the notion of the "homosexual" as a type of person rather than a type of behavior that might be engaged in by people with varying personal and social identities is largely a 20th-century development. Several contemporary studies (e.g., Bell & Weinberg, 1978; Ponse, 1978; Weinberg, 1978) have failed to find any relationship between particular patterns of sexual behavior and particular sexual identities. What these studies indicate are crucial are the particular meanings individuals ascribe to their sexual feelings and activities, which in turn depend on the situation and on the significance of sexual orientation in particular historical, social, and cultural contexts (Richardson, 1987). Dank (1971), Plummer (1975), Troiden (1979), and Weinberg (1978) are among those who suggest that sexual identities are socially constructed and who recommend that we need to elaborate the complex social and cognitive processes by which individuals in particular contexts come to assume and interpret particular sexual selves. Other researchers (e.g., Blumstein & Schwartz, 1983; Pattison & Pattison, 1980; Ponse, 1978) have concluded that sexual orientation is not a permanent characteristic.

Some people do not "come out" until their twilight years, whereas others may redefine their sexual identities several times over the life course. The early Kinsey studies (Kinsey, Pomeroy, & Martin, 1948; Kinsey, Pomeroy, Martin, & Gebbhard, 1953) demonstrated that many people who had homosexual experiences did not define themselves as homosexual, whereas many others changed their preferences one or more times over their lifetimes.

From a narrative/constructionist point of view, once persons of whatever age find themselves attracted sexually to members of the same sex or who engage in sexual relations with members of their own sex, they begin to seek understanding and to give meaning to these experiences. Some would argue the experiences or events have no meanings until they are named or given language. In some times and places, only the language of doubt, mystery, silence, and secrecy is available to stigmatized individuals and families, which most commentators believe has been psychologically handicapping for many, if not most, gay and lesbian individuals and has influenced, as I discuss later, a preoccupation with the notion of "fusion" in lesbian relationships. In any case, once the label "gay" or "lesbian" or "homosexual" is attached to such experiences, individuals recast their pasts to make sense of current feelings, thoughts, and behaviors. Thus, the typical adolescent "crush" of a young girl for her female teacher may become reconstructed in adulthood as an early lesbian attraction or a single incident of same-sex sexual experimentation on the part of a teenage boy as evidence of the young man's early bent toward homosexuality. Whether or not we believe that homosexuality is an "essential" part of being, or a personal narrative that can only be understood in historical and sociocultural context, it is the case that many of those who identify themselves as lesbian or gay see homosexuality as a core, fundamental, or essential part of their being, "who they really are." For many it is not a matter of choice, or of political belief and action; for some it becomes a matter of "accepting" and coming to terms with the inevitable, of developing strategies for managing one's own stigmatized identity (de Monteflores, 1986). As Richardson (1987) points out, "as members of a stigmatized and oppressed group in society, homosexuals very often experience their identity as one they fought hard for and as one in need of protection" (p. 8).

What virtually every researcher sympathetic to and affirming of gay and lesbian identity and behavior seems to agree upon is the pervasiveness of societal homophobia and its impact on individual psychological and familial functioning. However, it is clear that gays and lesbians in and out of various social groupings are as diverse in their individual adaptations and cultural performances as heterosexuals. Although certain patterns of cultural or subcultural expression may be observed (e.g., the bar culture among some gay men) and certain patterns of stress and adaptation traced, not only do individuals and families experience and cope with societal homophobia differently, but there is increasing evidence that time and space are crucial variables in the making of the American gay or lesbian. In the next section

I examine the question of "culture" and ask whether there is something that can be identified as gay culture. What does gay culture look like? How is it like or different from, how does it interact with, the larger culture?

Gay Culture and Subculture: Coming Out to What?

Gilbert Herdt (1992), an anthropologist, argues persuasively for "the existence of a gay *cultural system*, with a distinct identity and distinct institutions and social supports in particular times and places" (p. 3). Furthermore, neither Herdt (1992) nor Weston (1991), in her study of gay and lesbian families, sees gay culture as existing in bounded communities or as subcultures in larger urban environments, but rather as an important force in the remaking of the larger American culture. Herdt believes that gay culture will be a major battleground for social change in America into the 21st century, whereas Weston argues that gay and lesbian notions of family and kinship are already having profound effects on the larger society's construction of these categories.

One of the pervasive themes in the last two decades of research, the search for "causes" having been largely abandoned, has been the "coming out" process. The making of homosexual identity, which has usually been conceptualized as a series of stages (a theme I will return to) has been studied primarily as an individual process. Herdt, in his critique of this body of research, believes that more important and neglected questions are: (1) What does a gay man (or lesbian) come out *to*?, and (2) What does a gay man (or lesbian) come out *to be*? In his view, being gay signifies identity and role, familiar notions, but more than that a "distinctive system of rules, norms, attitudes . . . and beliefs from which the culture of gay men is made, a culture that sustains the social relations of same-sex desire" (p. 5). For Herdt, "homosexual" and "gay" are distinct cultural systems and life-course trajectories that must be distinguished from each other. Identifying as "homosexual" is "not the same thing as living one's life openly as a gay person and a member of the gay community. . . ." (p. 7). Gay, in his view, can no longer be seen as merely a sexual matter, or a life style, or an enclave. The Gay Liberation Movement and the gradual rise of cultural symbols and institutions (music and music festivals, bookstores, local and national newspapers and periodicals, films, plays, community and social groups, centers for gay adolescents, social networks, the Gay Pride Day March, and so on) signal the rise not only of a sense of *communitas*, or of *Gemeinschaft*, but also of a larger national culture, or *Gesellschaft*. Interestingly, AIDS has had an important role in welding together gay men and lesbians into a common cause, part of the crystallization of "a new moral order of gay prosocial attitudes and political activism across the country" (p. 11). These and other changes are making possible a meaningful and rich cultural life to come out to, a life course for the lesbian and gay man, and presumably for the lesbian and gay family as well, that will be quite different from the possibilities just a generation ago (Faderman, 1991).

Not only will coming out experiences be characterized by great diversity depending on what individuals are coming out *to*, then, but Herdt points out that researchers have overlooked the question of how the individual's identity and life course evolve after reaching some level of acceptance or resolution of gay identity. He argues that adolescents currently coming out "have the unprecedented opportunity to integrate their homoerotic desires with other components of their developing identities, including social roles, life style choices, and transitions into gay cultural communities" (p. 19). Similarly, gay and lesbian couples and families may have very different experiences depending on such factors as the culture and availability of gay and lesbian communities, on their ethnic and family-of-origin ties and loyalties, and on their social-class positions.

If Herdt and others argue that a vital and influential national gay culture is taking shape, it is also clear that there is tremendous diversity in its more local translations. Geography, nature of the larger community (and, if it exists, the local lesbian or gay community), class, ethnicity, gender, religious belief, and other social forces influence the availability of gay cultural symbols and models as well as how individuals enact their cultural beliefs and values.

Gay families, like heterosexuals, vary tremendously in how they live and story their lives. For example, Lynch (1992), in his study of "nonghetto" gays, found that suburban homosexuals were more circumspect, more fearful of exposure, anticipated more intolerance and discrimination, and had fewer homosexual relations, less homosexual sex, and less social involvement with homosexuals and more social involvements with heterosexuals than their urban counterparts. Although the same-sex behaviors of black men and women have rarely been studied (the overwhelming profile of the subject in most research has been the young, white, well-educated, middle-class male), there seems to be widespread agreement that there are even stronger antihomosexual attitudes in the black than in the white community. Peterson (1992) finds no distinct gay culture in the black community and suggests that many black men experience racism and prejudice not only from the larger society but also in the white, gay community. Oppressed ethnic minorities confront troubling conflict between their ethnic loyalties and their sexual orientations; to endorse gay identity may mean to betray ethnic identity. Carrier (1992) argues that gay liberation in the United States has been a middle-class Anglo phenomenon, "a social movement organized and run by middle-class Anglo-American males" (p. 202). His research suggests that ethnic minority gay males who do join the mainstream gay world are generally highly acculturated Latino, black, and Asian-American males.[6]

[6]For an exception to this view, see Morales (1989).

One other issue should be addressed here. Researcher after researcher has argued that gay and lesbian individuals and families have no role models, no guidelines or social prescriptions for how to live their lives. It seems to me two assumptions are implicit in this stance. The first is that gays and lesbians somehow cast off or eschew American culture or are *different* cultural beings from heterosexuals. In my view, to take this stance is to make what Hare-Mustin (1987) terms the "alpha error," that is, in this case to exaggerate the differences between lesbians and gays and their heterosexual counterparts. Gay male and lesbian researchers here seem to assign to sexual identity and behavior what Goffman (1963) and Fein and Nuehring (1981) have called "master-status," that is, all of life comes to be defined by one's status as "homosexual." Gay men and lesbians are for the most part raised in families headed by opposite-sex parents, where they are taught to be males and females and to embrace American cultural values as well as the norms and beliefs in their particular families and ethnic groups, what might be called "family culture." Their families of origin and the families they form must deal with all of the same issues any family must deal with, as is so powerfully documented in the Blumstein and Schwartz (1983) study of American couples.

Although gay culture is frequently contrasted to American "heterosexual" culture, to adopt gay symbols, to join gay organizations, to identify to self and others as gay is not to abandon American culture. Heterosexuals do not "own" American culture, and gay families, like other families, crosscut all social classes, ethnic and religious groups, and political affiliations, mixing gay symbols with many of the same symbols important to most American families. Lesbian and gay couples are rejecting the more traditional notions of gender roles learned in their families of origin, but carry on other family traditions, relational patterns, parenting models, and values about morality or politics or career choices. Like many heterosexual American couples these days, gay and lesbian families are searching for new ways to make families work, to share home and career responsibilities, and are questioning traditional ways of handling money, sex, and power. If lesbian couples are said to be in the midst of a "baby boom" and are organizing their families around child-rearing, many heterosexual couples today are choosing *not* to have children. In other words, "choice" rather than "tradition" has become the clarion call for both straights and gays, and heterosexual couples too, perhaps as a response to American geographic mobility, have formed extended families and social support networks based on friendship and common interests. Lukes and Land (1990) argue, and I agree, that the concept of "biculturality" offers a more useful construction in thinking about gay and lesbian culture than "difference."

A Comment on "Community"

The notion of gay or lesbian "community" is as broad and diverse as that of gay "family." As Krieger (1982), writing about the relationships between lesbian identity and community, points out, some gay communities are geographically specific, such as San Francisco's Castro district, some exist within institutions, such as the gays and lesbians in a graduate school of social work, and some exist only in spirit. Others are primarily ideological or social. Some lesbian and gay couples and families live in (and contrary to conventional wisdom are quite contented and well-functioning in) cultural milieus that are almost entirely heterosexual and afford little access to the symbols and organizations of gay community. The latter may be, for some, an assimilationist choice. At the other extreme, some lesbian and gay families may choose to locate in areas with very strong lesbian or gay communities, adopting a more separatist strategy and socializing almost exclusively with other gays and lesbians. Krieger argues that, at times, lesbian (and presumably gay male) communities can threaten as well as affirm individual identity. Like all communities, groups, and families, they can provide a haven from a hostile or unaccepting outside world, or they can constrain individuality.

Furthermore, gay and lesbian communities are just as diverse as other kinds of communities; it is crucial that we not assume, from experience with one community, that we understand gay or lesbian "culture" or "norms" for all such communities or that all gays or lesbians in a particular community are similarly enculturated to what seem to be local gay or lesbian cultural norms.[7] Again, there are important differences among communities as well as families, mediated by class, gender, ethnicity, historical experience, and other sociocultural variables. As clinicians, it is essential that we understand overarching cultural themes for gays and lesbians, the particular community context in which our clients live, as well as their relationships with that community.

Many students of gay and lesbian life have argued that the lack of accessible gay and lesbian models in the larger culture in general and in local communities in particular casts gay individuals and families adrift without any stars or charts to follow. Many lesbians and gays, however, are actively involved in their communities and move easily back and forth between their gay networks and extended kinship groups and the larger community. In one sense, gay and lesbian families may be more free to choose from the best of both the straight and gay worlds, innovating in those areas where neither community practices nor family traditions meet their visions.

The gay and lesbian movement, like the black pride movement, at times has had an investment itself in highlighting and maintaining "difference," and has gone through several different phases in defining "political correct-

---

[7]In addition to the collection of ethnographic studies in Herdt (1992), there are a number of studies of diverse gay and lesbian communities. These include Ponse (1978) and Warren (1974). Gibbs and Bennett (1980) examine class and race differences within the lesbian community, whereas Barnhart (1975) focuses on the tension between the demands of the lesbian couple relationship and the demands of the community.

ness." In the early days of the modern women's movement, radical lesbian feminists tended to see forming families with children and even coupling as imitations of oppressive, patriarchal, heterosexual marriage. Lesbian single mothers or couples with children found themselves unwelcome in certain gay communities and even now, in the midst of the lesbian baby boom, children and particularly male children in some communities are prohibited from attending lesbian gatherings. Whatever the political pulls and community pressures, it is likely that, for many gay and lesbian people, gay culture is only one of many resources, albeit an important one, for anchoring one's identity and for seeking cultural guidance.

Defining the Same-Sex Family

Up to this point, what we mean by gay or lesbian "family" has not been defined, a task central to any discussion of family yet one as amorphous and complex as determining the meaning of "heterosexual" or "homosexual." Definitions of "family," it is argued here, are political and ideological, created and recreated in social discourse and shaped in social relations of power. Particular definitions gradually assume the strength of conventionality. In the United States, as mentioned above, common definitions of "family" have been built on symbols of law and nature, legal marriage, and blood relatedness. Weston (1991) points out that even when anthropologists and other social scientists study the fictive kin relationships of urban blacks in the United States, they describe these relationships as "just as real" as blood ties, an argument that "takes blood relationships as point of departure" and privileges "a particular symbolic system rather than describing an empirically verifiable universe" (p. 106). However, in recent decades some theorists have argued for broader definitions of family that encompass ideas of "household," a notion incorporated in Mary Richmond's (1930) idea that a family consisted of "all who share a common table."

Such broader, less restrictive, definitions imply that what constitutes a family is a moveable feast, on the one hand shaped by codifications in law or religion and on the other by groups of individuals who share particular kinds of commitments and roles. Definitions of gay and lesbian families defy cultural assumptions about the meaning of "family," cross over family definitions organized by blood and legality and, in blood terms, make for a genealogical nightmare. They are families formed from lovers, friends, biological and adopted children, blood relatives, stepchildren, and even ex-lovers, families that do not necessarily share a common household. In fact, in some lesbian communities, the boundaries between family, kinship, and community become quite diffuse. Although it's been said, "You can't pick your relatives," in fact that is exactly what gay families, in devising a new system of kinship, do. They "choose" their families, retaining the familiar symbol of blood and combining it with symbols of love and choice. It is important to recognize, as Weston (1991) points out, that there is no uniform or normative definition for "gay family" any more than there is for "American family." Further, there is no normative structure for the gay or lesbian family. These families, like all families, come in many sizes and shapes. Some consist of couples without children and others of groups of adults, some of whom may be lovers. Families with children may be headed by a single parent, a same-sex couple, or a multiple-parent–extended-family arrangement. Some lesbian families incorporate biological or, for want of a better word, "fictive" fathers. They are rich and poor, black and white, Jewish and Gentile, Italian and Armenian; except for the fact that one or more members are lesbian or gay, these families cross cut the same social categories as other families.

In spite of the fact that gay and lesbian families constitute a significant percentage of American families, the gay family has been virtually invisible in the family therapy field. This invisibility undoubtedly reflects a society-wide reluctance to link the construct of "gayness" with that of "family," for the same-sex family, more than any other form, challenges fundamental patriarchal notions of family and gender relationships. Such notions assume the primacy of heterosexual coupling.

Family therapists, in their research, theoretical, and practice writing, with some important exceptions, have usually unquestioningly incorporated prevailing cultural conceptions of family grounded in metaphors of blood and law. To unpack the first of these notions, that of blood, in this society and in western culture we have largely assumed that it is biological relatedness that is at the heart of family formation. This idea, and I stress that it is an idea, a definitional process and not a "reality," makes procreation the heart of family life. Conceptions of the family life course, for example, have typically been child-centered, beginning with legal marriage and following the course of children's growth and separation through various stages. In traditional family life-cycle conceptions, family constellations that do not begin in legal marriage, are not headed by heterosexual couples, and/or do not produce children are seen as "other," as "nontraditional," "alternate," or "deviant," exceptional, and marginal to what is considered "normal" family form. The prevailing biological metaphor leads to the notion that any family not blood-related is "fictive" or substitute, a family-like alternative to the "real" thing, which has been, of course, the male-headed, nuclear family with its 2.4 children. Weston (1991) points out, however, that the notion of fictive kin has lost credibility in this age of symbolic anthropology, attention to the ideas of text and narrative in literary criticism, and Continental philosophy. All kinship, she suggests, is in some sense fictional—"that is, meaningfully constituted rather than 'out there' in a positivist sense" (p. 105). Genes and blood, then, are merely symbols "implicated in one culturally specific way of demarcating and calculating relationships" (p. 105).

The notion of biological family in the family field has been strengthened by structural and functional notions about how families should be organized, what their central roles and tasks are, and how they should be carried out. These templates are organized by age and sex. Central to structural conceptions of family are normative notions concerning hierarchy, internal and external boundaries, and degrees of separateness and connectedness. It is not my purpose here to elaborate on these much-researched familiar conceptions except to note that the feminist critique in family therapy has stimulated a reexamination of our assumptions about family structure and process, bringing history, the cultural context, and the politics of gender and heterosexual relationships into the theoretical and definitional arena.[8] However, most feminist family therapists have sorely neglected the lesbian experience and the lesbian family, mirroring the early dichotomizing in the women's movement.

The current phenomenon of same-sex couples choosing and forming families, pioneering and innovating family forms in which legal marriage and heterosexual partnering and, in many cases, procreation, are not the organizing metaphors, like feminism offers a rich resource for reexamining and perhaps reshaping family therapy assumptions about family and kinship. These families are generating new ideas not only about the formation and structure of families but also about how couples and families may operate, as they pioneer new ways to conceptualize and practice parenting, couple relationships, and role and task divisions. With their relatively fluid boundaries and varied memberships, their patterns of nonhierarchical decision making, their innovative divisions of labor, and the relative weight given to friendship as well as blood relatedness, such families offer further challenge to dominant notions of family structure and function and present an opportunity for mental health professionals to assess the limitations in current definitions of family and kinship.

THE FAMILY OVER TIME

How then, if many of these families are not bound by legal marriage or organized by biological procreation and parenting, are we to understand them in intergenerational terms? What is the meaning of "family of origin" and how important are blood relationships?

Up until 15 to 20 years ago, the family of origin was of great interest in studies of the "etiology" of homosexuality. Martin (1984) suggests that the fact that we think we need to account for homosexuality, that it is not simply accepted as a given, means that is is seen as a failure of heterosexuality. Reviewing the research literature on gays and lesbians between 1967 and 1974, Morin (1977) found that 30% of the research studies focused on "cause,"

[8]See, for example, Goldner (1985, 1988); Goodrich et al. (1988); Hare-Mustin (1978, 1987); Lerner (1988); Luepnitz (1988); McGoldrick, Anderson, and Walsh (1989); and Walters, Carter, Papp, and Silverstein (1988).

thus implying a search for cure. But Bell, Weinberg, & Hammersmith (1981), among others, argue that studies on nonpatient populations have failed to find any significant links between family constellation and the development of a particular sexual orientation. This does not of course mitigate the fact that generations of parents of gays have felt they have failed in some fundamental way in relation to the gay child.

The biological metaphor has dominated family therapy theory, particularly in Bowen (1978) intergenerational or "family of origin" theory, where blood-origin relationships imply great power throughout the life course. The blood in Bowen theory is thick and sticky. Individual and family problems are attributed to lack of sufficient differentiation, and therapy focuses on becoming "unstuck" or at least less stuck in the undifferentiated family ego mass. Bowen's central concepts of "differentiation" and "fusion" were derived from biology. There is little room in this conception for considering more fluid notions of family organized by choice and constructed in various ways, for such families by their very construction question the primacy of the biological metaphor.

A second assumption predominant in our culture and implicit in family theory has to do not only with the power but the importance of the blood family. It is assumed that people *need* families, and they particularly need their families of origin. Loyalty and cohesiveness are fostered through this discourse; blood families are seen as crucial to survival for the child and retain their emotional power over the adult. Individuals without families, particularly women, are still viewed with some pity in this culture—the old maid or the lonely widow, the "dyke" who wasn't attractive enough to catch a man. As an individual, it is believed one must come to terms with the family of origin, if only to rid oneself of troubling emotional baggage, and the newly joined couple must renegotiate relationships and boundaries with both families of origin (Bowen, 1978; Carter & McGoldrick, 1980, 1988; Hartman & Laird, 1983). Many gays and lesbians, even those living with partners for many years, are still defined as single by their families, their families of choice unrecognized in a homophobic silence that serves to obliterate the competition for the loyalty of the son or daughter.

Certainly the now famous case of Sharon Kowalski, the disabled Minnesota woman whose life partner, Karen Thompson, was denied guardianship and even the right to visit Sharon, while Sharon herself was denied adequate rehabilitation or any voice in decision making about her own life, provides a powerful commentary on how this society views both the blood family and the lesbian family. Sharon's father was awarded guardianship and the right to make all decisions concerning Sharon's care. Griscom (1992) argues that the case illustrates multiple modes of oppression, including ableism, heterosexism, and sexism. At one point Thompson was denied visitation because a psychologist testified that (because she was lesbian) she might sexually abuse Sharon! Thompson recently won guardianship rights and Sharon won the right to choose to live again with Karen, after Karen, in a 9-year battle in the courts, took her plight to the national press and enlisted the help of many national organizations.

But how important is the family of origin to the gay or lesbian individual or family? The clinical and indigenous literature on relationships between gays and lesbians and their families of origin is replete with stories of harsh and rejecting family-of-origin responses to their children's gay sexual orientation and choice of relationships and, indeed, in a 1973 study, Saghir and Robins found that 48% of parents responded to their child's disclosure with anger, condemnation, shame, disbelief, or alienation. Chafetz, Sampson, Beck, and West (1974) found that only half of the lesbians they studied had "come out" to family members; the other half feared disapproval and rejection. Many gays have been "disowned," whereas others have had to make serious personal compromises and relational sacrifices in order to maintain their contact with parents, siblings, and other family of origin members.

Although the situation has undoubtedly improved with the trend toward greater openness and "outing," many still choose to keep their sexual identity secret from the family of origin, whereas others make a tacit agreement not to talk about it, to keep that part of their lives entirely separate. This conspiracy of denial, many believe, may preserve family harmony and maintain connection, but it dilutes the intimacy and undermines authenticity in family relationships. In some cases it may allow the family of origin to emotionally tyrannize its adult offspring and may exact heavy costs to the psychological well being and personal integrity of the gay child. We might note here that in recent work several students of lesbian development (e.g., Krestan, 1988; Murphy, 1989; Rosen, 1990; Zitter, 1987) have expressed the notion that it is mother who is most often at the heart of the conflict, because of the importance of the mother–daughter relationship in a woman's development. Zitter (1987), for example, suggests that when a heterosexual daughter marries she replaces her father in the original family triangle, but the lesbian daughter symbolically replaces her mother. The mother, she believes, may feel rejected and competitive. Many parents respond to their male and female children's self-disclosure of homosexuality with feelings of shame, guilt, and self-blame. But mothers in particular, Krestan (1988) believes, tend to react with hurt and self-recrimination at the self-disclosure of their children, since they are given more responsibility for their well being. Furthermore, mothers may be more frightened for their daughters, since they generally have been "taught to believe that a woman cannot be happy or safe or secure without a man" (p. 122). Whereas fathers sometimes are less threatened by or competitive with their daughters' female partners than they would be in the case of the male rival, they may be more shamed by and contemptuous of what they perceive as their sons' abandonment of norms for masculinity. For the gay male, it is usually the father who is less accepting than the mother, who is not replaced as the central woman in her son's life.

Just as "coming out" to self and others is seen as essential to the development of a coherent sense of self, of self-esteem, and of healthy homosexuality, so "coming out" to family has also been seen as essential to the gay family member's identity development and to the integrity of the gay couple's relationship.[9] Much of the "coming out" literature contains the essentialist notion that there is a closeted, "real" homosexual self whom the individual must come to recognize and accept. Interestingly, the bisexual is often defined as someone who has not accepted his or her real, homosexual self, even though his or her heterosexual experiences may be emotionally and sexually satisfying and may predominate. Such assumptions mirror the tendency in the United States to define someone as black who may have very little "black blood" in his or her ancestry.

Brown (1989), a family clinician, suggests that the family is often the *last* group to whom gay men and lesbians come out because the fear of rejection, sometimes based on the person's own internalized homophobia, is so great. She also points out that, unlike the case of ethnic minorities, where it is in the family that ethnic bonds are celebrated and strengthened, gay bonds do not link the family, and gay culture is typically not shared or celebrated within the family of origin. Two of the ways families pass on and maintain their traditions and values and socialize their young are through family story and ritual. Imber-Black (1988), Laird (1988, 1989), Roth (1989), and Slater and Mencher (1991) are among those who have pointed out that many of our most important cultural rituals and celebrations are not easily available to gays and lesbians, and frequently the creative rituals they devise are not enacted in conjunction with families of origin or in contexts of societal recognition and support. Laird (1989) has argued that women's narratives and the narrative genres available to women in general and lesbians in particular are constrained in patriarchal societies and in the patriarchal family. Thus it seems important to ask what place gays and lesbians and *their* new couple and family experiences occupy in the ongoing ritual life, folklore, and mythology of the extended family. Do their cultural experiences become part of the larger biological family folklore? Or does the gay/lesbian branch break off the family tree?

Much has been written in the psychoanalytic psychotherapy literature about the problems of fusion or "merger" and the evils of mutual overdependence in the lesbian couple, problems that are believed to lead to increasing couple conflict, sexual dysfunction, and a host of other individual and couple ills. Merger problems are attributed to familial and societal homophobia as well as to the fact that the lesbian couple is comprised of

---

[9]Berger (1990), Berzon (1979), Kleinberg (1986), and Myers (1982) are just a few of the many authors who have discussed various aspects of the coming-out process. Most are concerned with the effects on the psychological adjustment and self-esteem of the gay or lesbian individual of coming out or not coming out, but Herdt (1992) is more interested in the cultural meanings of the coming-out rite of passage.

two women, both of whom have been socialized to be caring, nurturing, giving, self-sacrificing, and sensitive to feelings. Further, women are said to flourish in connectedness rather than in separateness, in mutual dependence rather than in autonomy.[10] In lesbian couples, it is argued, each may be hypersensitive to the feelings of the other and insufficiently attuned to her own feelings and needs. Krestan and Bepko (1980) argue that social and family-of-origin homophobia can lead to a rigidifying of lesbian couple boundaries and potential isolation, making inordinate demands on the lesbian couple relationship for emotional and other kinds of satisfaction and increasing the risk of problematic levels of fusion. (The theme of fusion pervades the clinical literature on lesbians and will be explored in more detail in the next section of this chapter.) Brown (1989) outlines a number of strategies for juggling the family and closet relationship, such as maintaining rigid emotional and/or geographic distance, cooperating in tacit agreements not to speak of gay matters, and coming out to some family members and not others, thus triangling or participating in problematic coalitions.

The few family therapists who have written of gay and lesbian matters tend to agree that it is extremely important to help their gay and lesbian clients "come out" to their families of origin. Krestan (1988), for example, writing of lesbian daughters and their mothers, believes that the daughter who pretends to be something she is not denies her own freedom of expression and invests her energies in maintaining secrecy, thus compromising her personal integrity. She points out that, on the one hand, to disclose is to invite vulnerability to discrimination, cutoff, and invasions of privacy, whereas to be secretive is to deprive oneself of family caring and resources and to reinforce the idea that gayness is wrong, thus discounting oneself. Krestan quotes Rita Mae Brown, who said "We are as sick as we are secret," affirming a notion common in family theory that secrecy is destructive to the integrity of the self and the family.

It is important to note, however, that although secrecy can be handicapping it can also be highly adaptive and useful. Ponse (1978), for example, argues for the importance of secrecy to the very existence and cohesiveness of many lesbian communities, whereas Laird (1993) maintains that secrecy for lesbians can serve the important purposes of fostering a common language and traditions and a sense of "we-ness" or specialness; secrecy, used by resistance movements everywhere, helps combat oppression.

It is not clear that we "need" our families of origin to function well, or that emotional cutoff from families dooms us to loneliness and isolation, haunted by invisible loyalties and stuck in the undifferentiated family ego

---

[10]This has become a familiar theme in women's studies and feminist research. Among many others, several researchers associated with the Stone Center for Developmental Services and Studies at Wellesley College are building on the work of Chodorow (1978), Gilligan (1982), Miller (1976), and others, developing "self-in-relation" theory. See, for example, Jordan (1984), Kaplan (1984), Miller (1988), and Surrey (1985).

mass. Whereas the family of origin is an important part of the context surrounding gays and lesbians and is important in understanding individual, couple, and family dynamics, it should be pointed out that we know very little about the ways that gay and lesbian offspring who do defy their families' proscriptions and do incur rejection forge their lives apart from their families. Can the friendship networks and innovative kinship systems many gays and lesbians build offer a context for, not only "familiness," but continued personal and familial growth? Kurdek (1988), based on his study of the perceived social supports of gay and lesbian couples, concludes that partners and friends, not family-of-origin members, are the primary providers of support for most gays and lesbians. Friends, he suggests, can easily fill the vacancies created by absent family members, a conclusion supported by Levy's (1989) research. Kurdek and Schmitt (1987) also found that the frequency of support from family members was not related to the psychological adjustment of the gay or lesbian. In Savin-Williams' (1989) study of 317 gay and lesbian youths, a lesbian was more comfortable with her sexual orientation if her parents accepted her homosexuality, but these variables did not predict her level of self-esteem. Among the gay males, parental acceptance predicted the gay youth's comfort with his sexual orientation only if the parents were perceived as important components of his self-worth. Family rifts and emotional cutoffs occur for many reasons. As Friedman (1988) points out, the family's rejection of a child's choice of partner or spouse for reasons of religion or ethnicity can camouflage efforts to keep a son or daughter closely bound. Homosexuality offers a convenient excuse for demanding such loyalty.

In a study not yet completed, my own ethnographic interviews with a nonclinical sample of 19 lesbians of widely varying ages suggest that lesbians develop any number of creative strategies for dealing with homophobic and rejecting families without necessarily sacrificing their own integrity. Some lesbians very consciously choose to allow a certain level of family denial; they accept it, dislike it, but do not let it or family emotional distance dominate their lives. There is reason to believe that, for many, the process of constructing a lesbian identity and facing the adversities of family outrage and community homophobia can be enriching and strengthening, for many if not all of the women I have interviewed seem to be "exceptional" in their families of origin. Perhaps to take the path less traveled can widen one's intellectual and emotional horizons, as those who have studied resilience have learned. The following illustrations point to adaptations characterized by strength and resilience:

> Lucille, now 29 and pursuing a career in college administration, is the second youngest in a large, Italian-American family of 10 children. She was "disowned" by her family when at 18 she chose to live in a lesbian relationship with Maggie, a high school friend. Although Lucille's very traditional

family believe the role of daughters is to marry, have children, leave college to the sons, and live close by, Lucille, with the help and support of Maggie, left home, went on to save money, collect scholarships, and eventually to graduate from a prestigious midwestern college. She was given several major awards at commencement, an event her parents shared but, in her view, could not fully understand or appreciate. Lucille believes that her choice of lesbianism made it possible for her to separate from a very fusing family that could tolerate little departure from family traditions and insisted on total loyalty; for her, lesbianism was a liberating choice. Maggie is still not allowed in Lucille's family's home for family holidays or celebrations, although Lucille is welcome at Maggie's family home. Although the lack of family-of-origin acceptance is an issue that injects stress and conflict into the relationship, these young women have worked hard to define their own family ritual life and to develop boundaries around their chosen family.

Ellen, a 26-year-old lesbian who is part of the maintenance crew for an apartment complex, was twice hospitalized at 18 for, she believes, her lesbian leanings and her drug and alcohol abuse. She is the youngest of the 13 children born to either her mother or father and the only one born to her parents' marriage. She describes her rural family as poor and working class, old Yankees with some English, Irish, Scottish, and American Indian ancestors. No one in her family approves of her sexual orientation. Fiercely political and feminist, she values her independence both from the politics of her family as well as from some of the demands of "political correctness" in the local lesbian community. Ellen is still quite close to her family of origin, where she does not talk much about her lesbian life. She hopes to develop a relationship of commitment in the near future. Ellen, interestingly, who indicates that her entire family is alcoholic, is the only member of her family who is "dry," an achievement of which she is very proud. She attends AA regularly and hopes to be the first member of her family to attend college.

Lila, a 44-year-old woman who has a serious chronic illness and who weaves and cleans houses for a living, lives alone in a rural area with a strong lesbian community. Her primary and longest-term love and sexual relationships have been with men; she has never lived in a long-term relationship with a woman. Lila chose to be lesbian because "I am a woman-identified woman who wants to share my life with other women." With only an elderly, ill mother left from her immediate family of origin, Lila describes her network of lesbian friends, who helped her build her tiny and charming house a year ago, as her family. This is a family that has developed its own important ritual and celebratory culture. Lila's mother accepts Lila's lesbian identity, attributing it to a medication Lila was given when she was ill as a child. This "causal" explanation, of course, frees her mother from guilt or self-recrimination.

Sally and Pat, 47 and 36 years of age respectively, have been together for 12 years and live in the same community as Lila. Being lesbian, for these two women, goes beyond sexual and emotional commitment to a shared political ideology and a commitment to an ecologically sound, nonmaterialistic way of life. For them, as for Lila, the boundaries between "family" and "community," the personal and the political, strongly overlap. Sally and Pat describe how this family/community helps its members in times of illness and other kinds of adversity and how they join together in political and socially useful projects. Both women remain connected with their families of origin but the relationships seem somewhat circumscribed, clouded by the unspoken "L" word. Whereas Sally's mother is more warm and accepting, Pat feels that her parents are knowledgable about the relationship but not fully accepting. Pat believes that they still think of her as "single." She wishes for more intimacy and authenticity in her relationship with her parents, but isn't certain how much their emotional distancing has to do with her lesbianism and how much is simply part of their connectedness style.

Although none of the 19 women interviewed to date is completely cut off from family of origin, and some indeed enjoy close and accepting relationships with their parents and siblings, several wish their families were more accepting and even proud of their lesbian choices. But these women, without exception, have constructed narratives to explain their relationships and uses of language with their blood families that are not self-shaming or self-blaming. They believe they have made good choices and regret their families cannot be more joyful about their lives.

Several expressed a sense of loss, a loss of childhood fantasies about family life, of shared rituals, of appropriate status in the family. Loss is a pervasive theme in families of origin as well, and even the most accepting of families must face various hurdles of its own. Several students of gay and lesbian families have noted that the family must mourn multiple losses when their children declare a gay orientation (e.g., Sanders, 1993). These include mourning the loss of some of the dreams and expectations they may have had for their children and themselves, based on the assumed heterosexuality of their children, such as a long-held wish for a daughter-in-law or grandchildren. Their stories about their gay children must be stringently edited in a homophobic world, and difficult decisions made about how to explain that man standing next to their son in the family photo album. Ordinary kinship language will not suffice.

Many gays and lesbians who have children from former heterosexual partnerships, or lesbians who choose to have biological children with a known or unknown donor or to adopt, have found that the lure of the grandchildren often helps to soften family homophobia, linking family of blood and family of choice. Some families who have shunned their child's lover "come around" when a child is born to their own daughter or even the partner. In some cases, the nonbiological grandparents maintain close relationships with the grandchildren even after a lesbian couple has separated.

Families of origin also live in a sociocultural context in which homophobia is pervasive. Not only must they face their own confusion and homophobia, but many feel responsible, blaming themselves for their child's sexual identity. Some may feel somehow contaminated by the offspring's homosexuality. Families worry about their own fit with socially constructed notions of normality; having a gay or lesbian child raises the specter of abnormality or family pathology. Families of origin do not have the same kind of "alternative" cultures or extended support networks that many gays and lesbians can turn to in times of stress; they often have no one with whom they can share their confusion and hurt. Indeed, some families may be actively shunned by others, a particularly painful experience for parents of HIV-infected gay men who may find themselves ostracized from the very communities whose support they desparately need. As Walker (1991) points out, "Isolation, secrecy, stigma, and discrimination further compound and intensify family difficulties" (p. 4) at a time when extensive assistance is needed. In her view it is essential for both gay person and family to convert a narrative of shame about HIV-infection into one of pride "to counterbalance society's stigmatizing account" (p. 9) and to allow the family to reach out for the support it needs.

The Family Life Cycle

Stage and life-cycle theories, central in individual developmental theory, have their analogues in family therapy research and writing (e.g., Carter & McGoldrick, 1980, 1988) and have also been central in gay and lesbian studies. The "coming out" process (the evolution of an individual's gay identity), the stages of couple development, the stages families learning they have a gay child go through and, most recently, the lesbian family life cycle have all been scrutinized using a "stage" conception.

Minton and McDonald (1984) conceptualize "coming out" as "a lifespanning developmental process that eventually leads to personal acceptance of a positive gay self-image and a coherent personal identity" (p. 91). Their model posits a three-stage process in which the individual moves from: (1) an egocentric interpretation of homoerotic feelings to (2) an internalization of the normative, conventional assumptions about homosexuality to (3) a postconventional phase in which societal norms are critically evaluated, and the positive gay identity is achieved and managed. In the final stage of Troiden's (1979) four-stage model, commitment is achieved, whereas Henken and O'Dowd (1977), in their final stage, link identity consolidation with public identification of one's sexual identity. Cass's (1979, 1984) six-stage model moves from identity confusion, through identity comparison, identity tolerance, identity acceptance, and identity pride to a final stage she labels identity synthesis.

In McWhirter and Mattison's (1984) six-stage model of gay male couple development, which spans a period of 20 years and beyond, the gay couple moves from a blending/merging phase high in limerance, through nesting, maintaining (reappearance of the individual, dealing with conflict, establishing traditions), building (collaborating, increasing productivity, establishing independence), releasing (trusting, merging of money), to a final stage of renewing (achieving security, shifting perspectives, restoring the partnership, and remembering) (Cabaj, 1988; McWhirter & Mattison, 1984). Each stage, as in Eriksonian theory, has its developmental tasks and risks.

DeVine (1984) offers, based on clinical experience, a five-stage developmental model to explain the systemic changes families undergo as they try to cope with their children's homosexual preferences. He argues that the family experiences a crisis that destabilizes its equilibrium. In the first three stages, which he labels subliminal awareness, impact, and adjustment, the family attempts to maintain some level of homeostasis. In the last two stages the family moves toward resolution and integration, meaning that it changes its structure to accomodate the life-cycle movements of the focal member. Outcomes depend on, he believes, the degree of family cohesion, the nature of its regulative structure, and particular family themes.

Most recently Slater and Mencher (1991) have applied family life-cycle notions to what they term the "lesbian family life cycle." Pointing out that Carter and McGoldrick's conception of the family life cycle is child-centered and occurs in a context of social validation and support, they argue that the lesbian life cycle is typically and traditionally not child-centered and not affirmed in the larger society. Although they believe that lesbian family life experience may parallel heterosexual experiences in some ways, they see the lesbian family as largely bereft of useful role models, a situation that can at times lead to greater flexibility, liberating the couple from more rigid models, but one that introduces more uncertainty and complexity into role negotiation.

Just as gay and lesbian family life-cycle models are beginning to make their way into the family therapy literature, stage models in general and gay and lesbian life-cycle models in particular are coming under increasing criticism. Sophie (1986), for example, examined six theories of lesbian identity development through repeated interviews with 14 women currently undergoing change with respect to their sexual orientation. She found some support for a general stage theory but also marked discrepancies, concluding that the process of lesbian identity development is highly sensitive to the social/historical context.

Historian Lillian Faderman (1984/1985) argues that Minton and McDonald's (1983/1984) three-stage model of progression toward homosexual identity does not generally fit lesbian experience. She believes that the process for women who came out through the radical feminist movement occurred in reverse order; coming out is highly influenced by historical circumstance. Women came to view heterosexuality as detrimental to their freedom, often assuming a lesbian identity before they had had a lesbian sexual experience. In their discussion of the "coming out" of gay and lesbian youth today, anthropologist Andrew Boxer and psychologist Bertram Cohler (1989) question the validity of developmental research in general. Most such research, they argue, relies on respondents' recollections of their childhood and adolescence, leading to a "developmental psychology of the remembered past" (p. 316). Much of the research, they argue, fails to account for significant changes in personality and adjustment from childhood to adulthood, the discontinuities and changes that characterize the lives of many gay and lesbian adults, and the changing social contexts that "dramatically affect the lives of persons within a specific generation or age-linked cohort" (p. 319). The identity "gay" itself appears to represent a relatively new and unique cultural category in history (Herdt, 1992, pp. 1–28). Boxer and Cohler believe that the issues of vulnerability and resistance, that is, the capacity of gay and lesbian youth to remain resilient when confronted by adverse circumstances, are crucial to understanding the life course. Predictive approaches must

> be complemented by a narrative or interpretive approach that is concerned with the manner in which persons experience and interpret or "make sense" of these life changes. Little is known of the manner in which persons create a narrative that renders adversity coherent in terms of experienced life history, or the manner in which presently constructed meanings of life changes may be altered in order to maintain a sense of personal integration. . . . For some persons, the experience of adverse life events may be used as an explanation for the failure to realize personal goals. For others, this misfortune becomes the impetus for increased effort in order to attain these goals. (1989, pp. 319–320)

Longitudinal studies show lives are not as ordered and predictable over time as we have assumed. Age, Boxer and Cohler argue, without cultural and historical knowledge, is an "empty" variable in the study of lives.

Taking a somewhat different slant but also clearly influenced by postmodern thinking, Weinberg (1984) critiques what he sees as the biological and moral underpinnings of developmental models for understanding homosexual identity formation. Included in his critique is his own earlier work (Weinberg, 1978). For Weinberg, whereas biological models are used to foster more credibility for psychoanalytic thinking and sociocultural models,

> stages are not necessarily experienced in ways researchers (and even their respondents) claim. They are not invariant; they have no clearly discernible beginning or end; and they are culture bound. In the social sciences, they are merely heuristic devices, developed solely to organize reflections and data. (p. 78)

Slater and Mencher (1991), in their thinking about the lesbian family life cycle, make an argument similar to that of Carter and McGoldrick (1980,

1988) and Combrinck-Graham (1985), namely that families will oscillate between periods of greater cohesion (connectedness, centripetality) and periods when individual differentiation is paramount (autonomy, independence, centrifugality). Even though they acknowledge they are using the term "cycle" broadly, they believe that lesbian family life progresses through a series of stages that can be normatively mapped and that they hope to delineate through study of lesbian families.

As mentioned earlier, many students of gay and lesbian life, straights and gays alike, have tended to stress differences at the expense of similarities between gay, lesbian, and heterosexual family life. For example, Zitter (1987), writing of the special issues lesbians experience in coming out to their mothers, says:

> Sociologically, lesbians are in the unusual position of belonging to a culture in which their parents do not belong, and indeed find repugnant. . . . Lesbians, however, grow up without the role modeling and mentoring that most people take for granted. For a mother to discover . . . that her daughter belongs to a different culture evokes a powerful "not me" response that can cause her to react as if her daughter were practically a Martian. (p. 185)

Similarly, Slater and Mencher (1991) argue that "for the young lesbian, her adult life is often such a departure from the family life of her childhood that her training is rendered inapplicable to her adult experience" (p. 375). Furthermore, "even lesbian families with children cannot predict a replication of their life cycle in the next generation, since their children may not themselves form lesbian families" (p. 381).

Not only does Zitter's statement contain the assumption that gays and lesbians (who may come out at any age, even at 65) suddenly, somehow, have had a different growing up than they thought they had, one with no role modeling or mentoring, but such positions belie the complexity and richness of family culture. As families, we hand down much more than a particular family structure or heterosexist role divisions. Has the heritage of the traditional heterosexual couple been lost when a child chooses a gay or lesbian family, any more than when a heterosexual adult child chooses to remain single or becomes divorced or adopts children? Or when their heterosexual children experiment with new and more flexible family role divisions, or balances of home and work lives? Must we either be identical to our parents or repudiate all of their teachings? It is far more likely that gays and lesbians, like everyone else, adopt, reject, and emerge with some blend of the life patterns and values of their blood families. A gay man may not choose to form his most intimate relationship with someone just like Mom but, on the other hand, he may choose someone sensitive, flexible, and resilient, like his mother, and assertive, socially conscious, and risk-taking, like his father. And, if he has children, he may consider these important qualities to hand down the generations.

Stage research in pursuit of the normative gay and lesbian experience tends to be generated by a search for "difference" rather than diversity, using normative models based on research with nongay populations and organizing gay and lesbian experience along the lines the researcher expected to find in the first place. Although such models can contribute to our knowledge of gay and lesbian family culture, it is important to point out that there are enormous differences in the social, historical, and community contexts in which gays have formed and are forming families, gays come out at widely varying ages over the life span, and there are also wide variations in family pattern, form, and membership. It is challenging to even map who is inside and who is outside in some lesbian families, for example. More useful, in my view, will be a search for the unique narratives such families construct to give meaning to their lives, longitudinal studies that capture changes over time as the social context changes, descriptions of the varied and complex ways they go about family life, and especially the strategies they develop to cope with homophobia. It is important to *begin* with the gay and lesbian experience, in all of its many variations.

INSIDE THE FAMILY

The Lesbian Couple—The Gay Couple

Lesbians and gays, contrary to popular myth, are as likely to live in couple relationships as heterosexuals. In the late 1940s, Kinsey and his colleagues (Kinsey et al., 1948) found that 71% of gay men between the ages of 36 and 45 were living with a partner, while more recently Bell and Weinberg (1978) discovered that 82% of the lesbians in their sample were currently living with a partner. What is more remarkable, given the lack of legal sanction or social recognition, is the stability and longevity in gay and lesbian couple relationships.

Lesbian and gay families are, in most respects, like all families. They must negotiate their relationships with the larger community and their families of origin, forging social networks and establishing boundaries between themselves and the outside world, as well as negotiating relationships and roles, developing problem-solving strategies, mediating conflicts, and marking boundaries inside the family. They must decide who will do what, when, where, and how in order to meet the particular needs of the family as a whole and of individual family members, whose interests at times may conflict or compete. Like all families, they face possibilities for conflict over divisions of labor, the use of money, space, and time, their sexual and intimate relationships, issues of closeness and distance, dominance and subordination, child-rearing ideologies, and so on.

However, these families differ from others in at least two important ways. First, the families are headed, usually, by same-sex couples, although some are headed by single gay or lesbian parents and others by multiple parenting figures; some may include close friends who are not sexually involved with each other, grandparents, and biological or nonbiological children. Same-sex couples with children from former marriages resemble and encounter many of the same special issues as stepfamilies, whereas families headed by gay single parents face the same shortage of labor problems as most single parent families do. Second, these families function in a world that may not recognize or accept their family commitment and definition, a pervasive issue in their daily lives. Many such couples or families are stigmatized; in Goffman's (1963) terms they must manage a "spoiled identity."

A number of researchers in the last decade or so have been studying same-sex couples, comparing them to heterosexual and/or cohabiting couples along a number of relationship dimensions. Such research, presumably, can shed light not only on what same-sex "marriage" is like but, as Blumstein and Schwartz (1983), Kurdek and Schmitt (1987), and others have pointed out, can highlight the effects of gender on relationship quality.

The most comprehensive research project on American couples was carried out by Philip Blumstein and Pepper Schwartz (1983), who studied heterosexual married, heterosexual cohabiting, gay male, and lesbian couples along the dimensions of money, sex, and power. Using both quantitative and qualitative data (over 12,000 returned questionnaires, as well as intensive interviews with 300 couples), they investigated the relational complexities in these marital and nonmarital family forms. It is not possible to report their rich and useful findings here except to say that there are striking similarities across family forms. What *American Couples* achieves is a close and comprehensive look at how gender and sexual orientation affect the ways couples choose to live their lives, the kinds of rewards they encounter, problems they confront, and problem-solving strategies they adopt. Blumstein and Schwartz conclude, as we might suspect, that there are many issues in coupling where gender "sameness" can be valuable and other areas where it can generate problems. Nowhere is this clearer than in role and task distribution. For example, whereas the "heterosexual model for marriage offers stability and certainty, it inhibits change, innovation, and *choice* regarding roles and tasks" (p. 324). Furthermore, whereas the heterosexual model offers efficiency in terms of role allocation, Blumstein and Schwartz conclude it is contingent upon the male being the dominant partner, a contingency now being challenged by many women. Same-sex couples on the other hand, whereas they do not struggle with assumed inequality based on sex difference, lack clear traditions or guidelines for role and task decision making. In one sense, each couple must create its culture anew.

The fact that heterosexual marriage is "institutionalized" means that it offers rules, standards, and practices, as well as social sanctions for continuance. The rules, argue Blumstein and Schwartz, help to "keep people together and help to make an orderly exit if the relationship ends" (1983, p. 318). Gay male and lesbian culture or subcultures contain no such clear prescriptions except perhaps a common emphasis on egalitarianism, and there are no external supports or sanctions for stability. Gay male culture, for example, has been organized around singlehood and sexual marketability, not stable coupling and family making, and in lesbian culture it is sometimes the friendship network or "community" that is promoted over the notion of family. In our complex and change-oriented society, with its emphasis on individual fulfillment, these family forms, I believe, contain their own special strengths and face their own particular challenges in making their families stable and viable.

Two of the many issues of interest concerning lesbian and gay coupling merit some discussion here, however, since they tend to dominate the mythology, clinical reporting and, to some extent, the lesbian and gay research coming from both the psychodynamic and family systems traditions. The first is the issue of fusion in lesbian couples, and the second is the issue of monogamy or sexual promiscuity in the gay male world.

Fusion in the Lesbian Couple

Clinicians have tended to agree that "fusion," defined by Burch (1982, 1986, 1987) as a state of psychic unity in which ego boundaries are crossed and two individuals experience a sense of oneness and by Karpel as a "state of embeddedness in, of undifferentiation within the relational context" (1976, p. 67), is *the* predominant relational quality in lesbian relationships. Although most would also agree that merger or fusion is an important part of sexual and emotional intimacy, it is also marked as the primary cause of tension and conflict. Clinicians, however, differ on what they see as the root causes of fusion. Krestan and Bepko (1980), in their pioneering paper in the family literature, hypothesized that lesbian couples, because the larger society both stigmatizes the relationship and fails to respect couple boundaries, "tend to rigidify those boundaries further and to turn in on themselves, adopting what has been described as a 'two against a threatening world' posture" (p. 278). They also introduce the notion that, because women have been socialized to deny self, neither partner in a lesbian couple "has had much practice at self-definition and autonomy in a relational context" (p. 284). Fusion, in turn, is blamed for diminishing sexual interest, many other relationship difficulties, and the major cause of relationship termination. Burch (1982, 1986, 1987), Elise (1986), and Lindenbaum (1985) link fusion to preoedipal gender differences in the intrapsychic process of separation–individuation and in early female socialization, whereas Henderson (1984) points to the greater mutual identification of two people of the same sex. Elise, in fact, argues that women's sex-role socialization is *the* fundamental issue since, if the Krestan and Bepko hypothesis concerning societal homophobia were correct, she reasons, gay male relationships would also be characterized by fusion, and they are not.

Zacks, Green, and Marrow (1988), in their comparison of lesbian and heterosexual couples using Olson's Circumplex Model, found that lesbian couples reported significantly highter levels of cohesion, adaptability, and satisfaction than did heterosexual couples. They conclude that:

> exceptionally high levels of cohesion and adaptability may help lesbian couples function more successfully in a predominantly heterosexual world. Further, women's socialization may predispose female couples to form more cohesive and adaptable relationships than heterosexual couples. (p. 471)

Their results lead them to argue for the cultural relativity of family norms for studies of lesbian and other kinds of minority population couples. Burch points out that the idea of merger is a concept, a metaphor, not an empirical reality. Women, she argues, are viewed in the light of a cultural bias that values separateness and autonomy; thus the emotional intensity of female–female relationships can be misunderstood or interpreted pathologically when in fact it may be normative for female couples. Goodrich et al. (1988), in their chapter on "The Lesbian Couple," also point out that the concept of fusion is highly gendered, arguing that lesbian couples intend a different relational vision, one based not on power politics, but on intimacy, mutuality, interdependence, and equality. This is a theme that Mencher (1990) develops at some length. She takes the argument a step further, grounding the notion of fusion in contemporary self-in-relation theories of women's development and relational capacities and casting a more positive, strength-oriented light on the meaning of fusion in lesbian relationships. As she points out, the very qualities that are pathologized are often seen by lesbians themselves as relational advantages. The intense intimacy typical in lesbian relationships can create "the trust and safety which foster self-actualization and risk taking, [promoting] a sense of security and faith in the relationship . . ." (1990, p. 4).

Mencher rightly points out that there is a tendency to pathologize women's relational ways, based on male heterosexual norms. To the best of my knowledge, there is no definitive research on fusion levels in lesbian couples, and no clear notion of what levels of fusion or differentiation may be normative for couples in general or lesbian couples in particular. Notions about woman–woman relational problems and their levels of sexual desire are penetrated by a social discourse that uses male norms for both sexuality and relationship to evaluate women's lives.

What we probably can say with some assurance is that those aspects of emotional intensity in lesbian couple relationships that lead to trouble (wherever their roots are planted—in adaptation to social homophobia and discrimination, in early socialization, or in norms for woman-to-woman relationships) are far more remarked in the clinical literature than those aspects that make for couple harmony and resilience and individual strength and growth. Another problem is the popular tendency to present autonomy and intimacy, or differentiation and fusion, as polar opposites. As Peplau, Cochran, Rook, and Padesky (1978) point out, "it is possible for individuals to be oriented toward both ideals" (p. 25). The majority in their study of a diverse sample of 127 lesbians evaluated their relationship as both extremely close and egalitarian, as well as personally satisfying. Attachment and autonomy are both important and, moreover, they co-exist in lesbian couples. Blumstein and Schwartz (1983) conclude that lesbians were "the vanguard in changing women's roles in the 1980s" (p. 329). Like most women, they value companionship, and they want their relationships at the center of their lives. But they do not wish either to dominate or to be dependent or subordinate; they want their partners to share domestic life and work and to succeed in the outside world of work as well. However,

> lesbians are in a double bind: On the one hand they want a great deal of attention and communication from a partner. On the other hand they do not want a partner who is so relationship-centered that she has no ambition or attachment to work. Lesbians want an intense home life, but they also want a strong, ambitious, and independent partner. . . . The lesbians are trying to carve out a new female role. This is an exceptionally difficult challenge and it is a testimony to their persistence that so many of their relationships do thrive. We think that one reason some are successful is because lesbians still retain women's desire for closeness and nurturance. (pp. 328–329)

Gay Male Couples and Monogamy

If the spectre of fusion and myths about women's sexuality haunt the thinking on lesbian relationships, the gay couple is tainted by social images that portray gay males as promiscuous, flamboyant, bar-hopping clones, with coupleness itself an anomaly. Several researchers have attempted to move beyond the stereotypes, examining more closely what the relationships and sexual behaviors of gay male couples are like. For example, McWhirter and Mattison (1984), who studied 156 couples from the San Diego area, concluded that "openness" in terms of extra-couple relationships seemed to enhance couple longevity, since all of the couples together longer than 5 years had open relationships. Harry (1984), studying a large sample of gay men (774) in Chicago, found similar patterns. Bell and Weinberg (1978), who compared closed and open couples from San Francisco, found that closed couples were more "happy" than open couples, whereas open couples tended to be more exclusively homosexual, to do more worrying in relation to their cruising, to report somewhat higher levels of sexual activity, and to have more regret about their homosexuality. Peplau and Cochran (1981) found no differences, between open and closed couples together 3 years or longer, in intimacy, satisfaction, security, or commitment, and Kurdek and Schmitt (1985), who compared gay men in monogamous and nonmonogamous relationships, found more longevity in open relationships but no differences in psychological adjustment.

Ideas like promiscuity or monogamy are concepts that are highly value-laden. What is important, Blumstein and Schwartz (1983) point out, is what these concepts mean to the couples themselves. For some couples, an extra-couple sexual encounter or affair may feel like the ultimate betrayal; for others it may be interpreted as an experience that has little to do with and does not contaminate the couple relationship. Their research indicates that women, whether in heterosexual marriage, cohabiting, or same-sex couples, have fewer outside partners than men. Thirty-three percent of the hetero-sexual men in their sample had been nonmonogamous since the beginning of the relationship and 82% of the gay males, compared to 26% of cohabit-ing women, 21% of married women, and 28% of lesbians. Whereas lesbians had been slightly less monogamous than female cohabitors or marrieds, they had had fewer outside partners than any of the other groups, their affairs often a one-time event or single affair. Gay men, Blumstein and Schwartz report, do commonly have sex with strangers; sex with strangers, or what they call the "trick mentality," has been a social institution within the gay male world for a long time. Tricking allows men to have sex without emo-tional involvement, one reason, in their opinion, that gay male couples can tolerate very high rates of nonmonogamy without serious threat to the rela-tionship. Interestingly, heterosexual married men are far more promiscu-ous than their wives, whereas heterosexual women resemble lesbian women in their intolerance for disloyalty to the relationship; thus monogamy seems to be more related to gender socialization than to sexual orientation. Out-side sex in the gay male couple is not related to gay men's overall happiness or commitment to the relationship.

At the time of the Blumstein and Schwartz study, AIDS was just com-ing to more widespead public attention. They predicted in 1983 that AIDS would lead gay males to reduce tricking behavior and, indeed, current com-mentators (e.g., Forstein, 1986; Herdt, 1992) are pointing out that AIDS has and is shaping a trend toward more sexual exclusivity and more stability in gay male couple relatonships.

Children of Lesbian and Gay Parents

In addition to study of the mental health and social adjustment of gays com-pared to heterosexuals and the relationship qualities of lesbian and gay couples compared to other couples, the last two decades have also brought a substantial number of studies devoted to the psychological growth and social adjustment of children of gay parents. Patterson (1992), in a compre-hensive review of this research, suggests that this trend has been motivated by several factors. These include: (1) The need on the part of gays and les-bians considering parenthood to understand the issues and challenges they may face, (2) the concerns of social scientists with how such families and their children cope with oppression, (3) the impact of this nontraditional family form on psychosocial development, and (4) the provision of more accurate information to a legal system that has operated largely on prejudice and mythology in custody situations and in addressing questions concerning the rights of gay and lesbian parents and their children.

The estimates of how many children live with lesbian or gay parents fluctuate as widely as the estimates for gay and lesbian people, since sexual orientation has been such a necessary and well-kept secret nationally. Patterson (1992) reports that the estimates of lesbian mothers range from 1 to 5 million, whereas those of gay fathers fluctuate from 1 to 3 million. The number of children of such parents is believed to range from 6 to 14 million. Large-scale surveys from the 1970s (Bell & Weinberg, 1978; Saghir & Robins, 1973) estimated that some 10% of gay men and 20% of lesbians were parents. There is reason to believe, with greater openness, with changes in the politics of family in the lesbian community, with an apparent growth in the numbers of lesbian couples choosing to bear children (a phenomenon some are calling the "lesbian baby boom,") that these figures have increased in the last decade, particularly in the case of lesbians.

Although there have always been gay male and lesbian parents, until recently most children of gay parents were born in the context of heterosexual marriages that later ended in divorce. The gay or lesbian parent may have full custody, shared custody, or visitation rights or may, in fact, have been denied any rights in relation to her or his children, solely on the basis of sexual orientation. The gay parent may be single or in a couple relationship in which one or both life partners have brought children from their heterosexual marriages into the newly formed family. Today many more lesbian couples are consciously choosing to have biological children through known or unknown donor insemination, and in some instances both partners may choose to bear children (Pies, 1985, 1990; van Gelder, 1988). Some gay men have served as sperm donors, co-parenting with the mother or with a gay male partner. Although no state, to my knowledge, sanctions adoption by a gay or lesbian couple, in many couples one partner has adopted or become a foster parent either by mispresenting or keeping invisible his or her sexual orientation (Ricketts & Achtenberg, 1989). In many instances, caseworkers and others, desperate for good homes for so-called hard-to-place children, look the other way and purposely do not ask. Whereas these are pragmatic strategies, such practices do little to help dispel the various social myths concerning parenting by gays. Furthermore, the co-parent not only lacks legal rights in relation to the child but is rendered invisible. Other couples avoid adoption establishment channels in the United States, seeking children from other countries, where infants are available with few questions asked.

If the question of "normality" is a difficult and controversial or even a useful one in thinking about families headed by opposite-sex parents, it becomes even more complex when applied to families headed by same-sex parents. Since such families have barely been recognized in this society, there are no social or popular visions about what is normative behavior for such families and very little "normal family" research. As mentioned earlier, several writers have argued that there are no "role models" for such families, implying that they must in some sense invent themselves, a position I believe exaggerates the differences between these families and others.

One theme that dominates the literature, whether clinical, research, or the stories of gays and lesbians themselves, is that children of these relationships are raised in a world where they will likely face social discrimination and perhaps even ridicule and isolation. Crawford (1987) is among those who have called attention to the problem of language, to the fact that there are no socially approved terms that define the couple relationship or name the role of the co-parent. Not only do children not have an accepted or comfortable language to describe their families, but they are sometimes, because of external threats from exhusbands, exwives, grandparents, and others, enjoined from talking about their families at all. Adolescents, often insecure about their own only partially resolved sexual identities, are particularly vulnerable to peer pressure and harassment in social climates in which "faggot" is the ultimate putdown for the male and "dyke" for the female. Children may be embarrassed to bring their friends to their homes or to have to explain that other woman who comes to Parent's Night at the school or visits them in the hospital. And school or other important community figures in the lives of chidren may project their own homophobic fears onto the children, offering them little support or understanding.

Interestingly, in spite of the special difficulties children in gay families face, to date the research suggests that the peer and other social relationships of children of lesbian and gay parents do not differ significantly from those of any children [see Patterson (1992) for a review of this research]. Furthermore, in spite of myths about lesbian manhating and separatism, there is evidence to suggest that lesbian mothers are more concerned than single heterosexual mothers that their children have opportunities for male role models and good relationships with adult men. Kirkpatrick, Smith, and Roy (1981) found that lesbian mothers had more adult male family friends and included male relatives more often in their children's activities, whereas Golombok, Spencer, and Rutter (1983), working with a sample that included 37 lesbian and 38 heterosexual mothers, found that children of lesbian mothers were far more likely to have contact with their fathers than the children of heterosexual mothers.

Many social myths and concerns about what will happen to children in gay families influence lawmakers, and a number of studies have sought clearer information about how such children fare. Topics of interest to researchers include gender identity, sex-role behavior, sexual orientation, various personality dimensions, behavioral and emotional problems, self-concept, moral judgment, and intelligence of children of gay and lesbian parents.

One of the most prevalent myths is that children of gay parents will themselves grow up gay; another that daughters will be more masculine and sons more feminine than "normal" children. A number of researchers (Bozett, 1981, 1987, 1989; Golombok et al., 1983; Hoeffer, 1981; Huggins, 1989; Kirkpatrick et al., 1981; Miller, 1979; Paul, 1986; and Rees, 1979) have concluded that the sexual orientations/preferences of children of gay or lesbian parents do not differ from those whose parents are heterosexual. This makes sense since it is equally clear that most homosexual adults were themselves reared in heterosexual families. Neither homosexual nor heterosexual orientation of parents predicts the sexual orientation of their children. Neither do children of lesbian mothers differ in terms of gender role identity. The findings of Green (1978), Green, Mandel, Hotvedt, Gray, and Smith (1986) and Kirkpatrick et al. (1981), who used projective tests as well as various interview procedures, suggest that gender identity development among 5- to 14-year-old children of lesbian mothers proceeds along normal developmental lines. Rees (1979), using the Bem Sex Role Inventory in comparing 12 10- to 20-year-old children of lesbian mothers to a similar sample of children of heterosexual mothers, found no significant differences in sex role or gender identity. In fact, the children of lesbian mothers reported greater psychological femininity. Neither Golombok et al. (1983) nor Green et al. (1986) found any differences between the children of lesbian and heterosexual mothers in sex-role behavior. Patterson (1992) states that "although studies have assessed over 300 offspring of gay or lesbian parents in 12 different samples, no evidence has been found for significant disturbances of any kind in the development of sexual identity among these individuals" (pp. 25–26). In her view, prevailing fears that children of gay and lesbian parents will have sexual identity problems are groundless. She concludes:

> The picture of lesbian mothers' children which emerges from results of existing research is thus one of general engagement in social life with peers, with fathers, and with mothers' adult friends—both male and female, both heterosexual and homosexual. Insofar as one can tell from the existing research literature, then, fears about children of lesbians and gay men being sexually abused by adults, ostracized by peers, or isolated in single-sex homosexual communities are unfounded. (1992, p. 34)

Of great interest is the fact that children of gay and lesbian parents appear to grow and thrive as well as children in heterosexual families, *in spite of* the prejudice and discrimination that can and does surround them. Although many of the myths concerning the evil effects of the parent's homosexuality on his or her children still infect the legal system, a generation of research has failed to demonstrate that gays or lesbians are any less fit to parent than their heterosexual counterparts. Furthermore, a substantial number of studies on the psychological and social development of children of lesbian and gay parents have failed to produce any evidence that children of lesbian or gay parents are harmed or compromised or even differ from, in any significant ways along a host of psychosocial developmental measures, children raised in heterosexual families.

It should be noted that most of the research to date focuses on the children of white, middle-class, formerly married lesbians. A few studies examine children from the heterosexual relationships of gay men (Barrett & Robinson, 1990; Bozett, 1981, 1987, 1989; Miller, 1979; Paul, 1986), and to date only a few studies have examined children born to women in the context of lesbian relationships (McCandlish, 1987; Patterson, 1991; Steckel, 1985, 1987). Whereas some studies focus exclusively on the children of gay or lesbian parents, as Patterson (1992) points out, much of the research assumes that children living in families headed by formerly married lesbian mothers are best compared to children of divorced, heterosexual mothers. Some of this research is compromised by the fact that in many cases lesbian mothers were living with co-parenting life partners who may have played significant parenting roles and were important sources of attachment and identity for children but were invisible to the researchers, as were noncustodial fathers of children being raised by single heterosexual mothers.

In fact, children raised by lesbian parents may have some advantages. For example, some researchers have found that children of lesbian parents tend to be more flexible and tolerant than other children, and one small sample study (Steckel, 1985, 1987) found that children of heterosexual parents saw themselves as more agressive and were seen by their teachers and parents as more domineering and negativistic than children of lesbian parents. Teachers and parents saw children of lesbian parents as more affectionate and responsive, and the children saw themselves as more lovable than children of heterosexual parents. In a study that included gay fathers, lesbian mothers, heterosexual single fathers, and heterosexual single mothers (Harris & Turner, 1985/1986), gay parents reported few social problems for their children. Many of the homosexual parents felt that their children had developed considerable tolerance and empathy for others, and an openness to various viewpoints. Keating (1991) also found, in her study of a small sample of young adult children of lesbian mothers, that her informants saw themselves as more tolerant of and knowledgable about varying world views and lifestyles than their peers from heterosexual families.

A number of important questions remain unanswered. For instance, whereas much is made of the fusion in lesbian relationships, might there not be beneficial effects for children being raised in families that are not structured along patriarchal lines, in which there generally are no rigid, sex-linked role divisions that circumscribe the potentials for male or female children, a family in which both parents may have been socialized to be nurturing and emotionally expressive? Interestingly, if lesbian couples do indeed experience more fusion in their relationships, more intense intimacy and togetherness, perhaps the emotional needs of the couple are more likely to be met in the relationship rather than through the children. Do children of lesbian parents do better with lovingness, connectedness, and intimacy but perhaps worse with anger, competition, and conflict than children from heterosexual families?

What are the gender development issues for children when both parents have been socialized to be men? So far there is very little data, since few gay male couples have full custody of children or are allowed to adopt or foster children. Will children raised by gay male couples have more opportunities to form close relationships to fathers/men who may be more flexible and nurturing than many heterosexual fathers? Will they have more or less difficulty with emotional expressiveness and intimacy, given there is no woman in the household? Will they be more or less comfortable with issues of competition and conflict? These and many other questions await further research.

A Note on Family Theory

Are family theory concepts such as differentiation, fusion, cohesion, or triangling useful in the study of gay and lesbian families? The feminist critique has taught us that many of these concepts are "gendered" and that they have biased "normative" implications growing out of patriarchal cultural traditions. Goodrich et al. (1988), for example, questioned whether the notion of "triangle" had the same meanings when applied to the more fluid definitions of family and of monogamy she and her colleagues believed they discovered in their clinical case study of a lesbian couple and their small social network. The authors rightly critique such concepts as fusion and triangling in terms of their universal meanings in understanding all families. However, in the process they imply that lesbian couples may have a different culture and a different set of rules for monogamous behavior, an implication that does not fit with current research data (see, e.g., Blumstein & Schwartz, 1983).

My own sense is that family theory concepts are as useful or as limited and problematic in studying lesbian and gay families as they are in studying any families. They are concepts that grow out of particular cultural constructions and may or may not be particularly relevant to any one family's own narratives, to their understandings of their own experiences, or to their kinship patterns. We need to always be sensitive to the cultural, sexist, heterosexist and other biases in whatever templates we use and with whatever families we are studying. In terms of gay and lesbian life, we are a long way from understanding whether there is something we can call gay culture and what it looks like, and what "normative patterns" for gay and lesbian family and kinship may be. Furthermore, in this postmodern era, perhaps concepts that lead us to search for the essential parts of kinship and culture and make assumptions about normality are not the most useful tools we might employ for family research.

CONCLUSION

Lesbian and gay families are both like and different from other families, and there is tremendous diversity among them. Much of the clinical and research literature to date has stressed the differences rather than the similarities between gay/lesbian and heterosexual families and, at the same time, has emphasized the commonalities rather than the diversity among lesbian and gay families. Certainly much of the work from the late 1960s to the present time has been extremely valuable in correcting a clinical and research discourse that mirrored the larger social discourse, one which stressed deviance and pathology. This tradition of research was oriented toward a search for "cause" and thus for "cure." Since the late 1960s, the effort has been primarily one of demonstrating that gays, lesbians, their children, and their families are as "normal" and as "healthy" as everyone else and, when they are not, attributing the problems to the noxious homophobic environment.

In this sense, however, it is a deficit literature, a defensive stance. It is not a literature that points to the amazing levels of resilience of these individuals, couples, and their children, to their creativity and to their pioneering efforts to fashion families that may, more than many families caught in the war between the sexes, offer contexts that are facilitating for individual growth and gender flexibility. "Gay pride" hasn't caught up with the research and clinical family literature. The current body of feminist theory and research and the growing body of interesting and rich work on African-American culture offer meaningful contrasts to the predominant deficit perspective in gay and lesbian studies. It takes time, as scholars from other oppressed groups have learned, to move from a reactive to a more proactive stance. "Pride," of course, brings its own set of complexities. It also can mean exaggerating difference and uniqueness, political separatism, and the heightening of "essentialist" notions, another force keeping gay and lesbian studies out of the postmodern era.

My effort in this chapter has been to try to counter some of the prevailing myths about gay and lesbian families and to point wherever possible to strengths. This is not to argue for an idealized notion of the gay and lesbian family or to gloss over the many problems such families face, including relatively high rates of alcoholism. Nor does the model of same-sex coupleness protect these families from internal violence or from the kinds of social stresses all families today face. But the fact that these families do have special strengths and do well in spite of a context of oppression suggests we all need to know more about their secrets to success. How do they overcome the lack of socially sanctioned language and ritual, the lack of other social and legal sanctions, the fact that they cannot story their lives as openly as other people, that they need at times to be guarded and secretive?

Part of the reason we do not know as much as we might has to do with the fact, in my view, that as students and as researchers we have started from the standpoint of majority culture and have attempted to measure deviation/difference, which fails to get us "inside" the lives and meanings of those we study. We have, too often, started with templates of structure, process, and developmental stage, as well as narrow defintions of family and of kinship, using them to map the data. Experience that does not fit these maps fails to be named or included. We have rarely listened to the unfettered voices of those we study. It reminds me of the "male" problem in anthropology. Generations of anthropologists, Margaret Mead and a few others notwithstanding, had little access to, and seemingly little interest in, the women of the world. What little they knew about their lives, they learned from the tribal leaders and the women's husbands. We know now that the women, had they been asked, would have told a different story.

Researchers, on the other hand, have been handicapped by the secrecy and invisibility that characterizes gay and lesbian life. It has been next to impossible to obtain random or representative samples. Another problem is that, as in much social science and particularly in psychological research, the great majority of work has centered on white, middle-class, well-educated, often male populations, usually from large urban areas where there are known gay communities and thus a pool of informants. We know very little about lesbians and gays of color and how they fare in their ethnic communities and in the white gay or lesbian worlds, about lesbians and gays who are less well educated or financially secure, about those who live in largely heterosexual suburbia or in small towns and rural areas.

In my view, what this field needs more than any other kind of study at this stage are detailed, wholistic accounts of the daily lives of gay and lesbian families, studies that might reveal the complexity, the richness, the diversity of their lives. We need studies that are done in many different kinds of contexts and that include lesbians and gays in all of their own diversities. We need studies that center around their narratives, their meanings and beliefs, studies that bracket prior theories, rather than those that tend to produce what it is we thought we would see in the first place. We need an Oscar Lewis, or better yet, many of them. We should look to the rich and deeply descriptive, interpretive contributions researchers like Oscar Lewis (1963, 1965) and Jules Henry (1965) made to the study of the family for methodological ideas. Interestingly, Lewis attracted a great deal of criticism because he confused the effects of oppression and of poverty with "culture." Similarly, much of what looks like "culture" to students of gay and lesbian life has much more to do with societal homophobia and some of it has to do with conscious and adaptive mockery of conservative cultural prescriptions around sexual behavior and object choice.

Family and kinship, as we have become aware, are much more complex cultural categories than any of the early leaders in the family therapy movement or the family social scientists of the time might have envisioned. What is more, the meanings of family and of kinship keep shifting and are reconstructed in social discourse, to meet the needs of a changing world. Lesbian and gay families are taking an active and creative role in that reconstruction. As we approach the turn of the century, it would be helpful for the world of family theory and practice to know more about what they are doing and how they are doing it.

ACKNOWLEDGMENTS

I would like to thank Robert-Jay Green and Ann Hartman for their thoughtful comments and suggestions on an earlier draft of this chapter and Froma Walsh for her careful editing.

REFERENCES

Barnhart, E. (1975). Friends and lovers in a lesbian counterculture community. In N. Glazer-Malbin (Ed.), *Old family/new family* (pp. 90–115). New York: Van Nostrand.

Barrett, R. L., & Robinson, B. E. (1990). *Gay fathers*. Lexington, MA: Lexington Books.

Becker, H. S. (1973). *Outsiders: Studies in the sociology of deviance* (rev. ed.). New York: Free Press.

Bell, A. P., & Weinberg, M. S. (1978). *Homosexualities: A study of diversity among men and women*. New York: Simon & Schuster.

Bell, A. P., Weinberg, M. S., & Hammersmith, S. K. (1981). *Sexual preference*. Bloomington: Indiana University Press.

Berger, R. (1990). Passing: Impact on the quality of same-sex couple relationships. *Social Work, 35*(4), 328–332.

Berzon, B. (1979). Telling your family you're gay. In B. Berzon & R. Leighton (Eds.), *Positively gay* (pp. 88–100). Millbrae, CA: Celestial Arts.

Blackwood, E. (1985). Breaking the mirror: The construction of lesbianism and the anthropological discourse on homosexuality. *Journal of Homosexuality, 11*(3/4), 1–17.

Blumstein, P., & Schwartz, P. (1983). *American couples: Money, work, sex*. New York: William Morrow.

Bowen, M. (1978). *Family therapy in clinical practice*. New York: Jason Aronson.

Boxer, A. M., & Cohler, B. J. (1989). The life course of gay and lesbian youth: An immodest proposal for the study of lives. *Journal of Homosexuality, 17*(3/4), 315–355.

Bozett, F. W. (1981). Gay fathers: Evolution of the gay father identity. *American Journal of Orthopsychiatry, 51*, 552–559.

Bozett, F. W. (1987). Children of gay fathers. In F. W. Bozett (Ed.), *Gay and lesbian parents* (pp. 39–57). New York: Praeger.

Bozett, F. W. (1989). Gay fathers: A review of the literature. In F. W. Bozett (Ed.), *Homosexuality and the family* (pp. 137–162). New York: Harrington Park Press.

Brown, L. (1989). Lesbians, gay men, and their families: Common clinical issues. *Journal of Gay and Lesbian Psychotherapy, 1*(1), 65–77.

Browning, C. (1984). Changing theories of lesbianism: Challenging the stereotypes. In T. Darty & S. Potter (Eds.), *Women-identified women*. Palo Alto, CA: Mayfield Publishing Co.

Burch, B. (1982). Psychological merger in lesbian couples: A joint ego psychological and systems approach. *Family Therapy, 9*(3), 201–277.

Burch, B. (1986). Psychotherapy and the dynamics of merger in lesbian couples. In T. S. Stein & C. J. Cohen (Eds.), *Contemporary perspectives on psychotherapy with lesbians and gay men* (pp. 57–71). New York: Plenum Press.

Burch, B. (1987). Barriers to intimacy: Conflicts over power, dependence, and nurturing in lesbian relationships. In Boston Lesbian Psychologies Collective (Eds.), *Lesbian psychologies: Explorations and challenges* (pp. 126–141). Urbana: University of Illinois Press.

Cabaj, R. (1988). Gay and lesbian couples: Lessons on human intimacy. *Psychiatric Annals, 18*(1), 21–25.

Carrier, J. (1992). Miguel: Sexual life history of a gay Mexican American. In G. Herdt (Ed.), *Gay culture in America: Essays from the field* (pp. 202–224). Boston: Beacon Press.

Carter, B., & McGoldrick, M. (Eds.). (1980). *The family life cycle.* New York: Gardner.

Carter, B., & McGoldrick, M. (Eds.). (1988). *The changing family life cycle.* New York: Gardner.

Cass, V. (1979). Homosexual identity formation: A theoretical model. *Journal of Homosexuality, 4*(3), 219–237.

Cass, V. (1984). Homosexual identity formation: Testing a theoretical model. *Journal of Sex Research, 20*(2), 143–167.

Chafetz, J. S., Sampson, P., Beck, P., & West, J. (1974). A study of homosexual women. *Social Work, 19,* 714–723.

Chodorow, N. (1978). *The reproduction of mothering.* Berkeley: University of California Press.

Combrinck-Graham, L. (1985). A developmental model for family systems. *Family Process, 24,* 139–150.

Comstock, G. D. (1991). *Violence against lesbians and gay men.* New York: Columbia University Press.

Crawford, S. (1987). Lesbian families: Psychosocial stress and the family-building process. In Boston Lesbian Psychologies Collective (Eds.), *Lesbian psychologies: Explorations and challenges* (pp. 195–214). Urbana: University of Illinois Press.

Crawford, S. (1988). Cultural context as a factor in the expansion of therapeutic conversation with lesbian families. *Journal of Strategic and Systemic Therapies, 7*(3), 2–10.

Dank, B. M. (1971). Coming out in the gay world. *Psychiatry, 34,* 180–197.

D'Emilio, J. (1983). *Sexual politics, sexual communities: The making of a homosexual minority in the United States, 1940–1970.* Chicago: University of Chicago Press.

de Monteflores, C. (1986). Notes on the management of difference. In T. S. Stein & C. J. Cohen (Eds.), *Contemporary perspectives on psychotherapy with lesbians and gay men* (pp. 73–101). New York: Plenum Press.

DeVine, J. L. (1984). A systemic inspection of affectional preference orientation and the family of origin. *Journal of Social Work and Human Sexuality, 2,* 9–17.

Elise, D. (1986). Lesbian couples: The implications of sex differences in separation–individuation. *Psychotherapy, 23*(2), 305–310.

Faderman, L. (1981). *Surpassing the love of men: Romantic friendship and love between women from the Renaissance to the present.* New York: William Morrow.

Faderman, L. (1984/1985). The new "gay" lesbians. *Journal of Homosexuality, 10*(3/4), 85–95.

Faderman, L. (1991). *Odd girls and twilight lovers: A history of lesbian life in twentieth-century America*. New York: Columbia University Press.

Falco, C. (1991). *Psychotherapy with lesbian clients: Theory into practice*. New York: Brunner/Mazel.

The Family Therapy Networker (Vol. 15, January/February, 1991). Special issue on gay and lesbian issues.

Fein, S. B., & Neuhring, E. M. (1981). Intrapsychic effects of stigma: A process of breakdown and reconstruction of social reality. *Journal of Homosexuality, 7*(1), 3–13.

Forstein, M. (1986). Psychodynamic psychotherapy with gay male couples. In T. Stein & C. Cohen (Eds.), *Contemporary perspectives on psychotherapy with lesbians and gay men* (pp. 103–137). New York: Plenum Press.

Forstein, M. (1988). Homophobia: An overview. *Psychiatric Annals, 18*(1), 33–36.

Foucault, M. (1979). *The history of sexuality*. London: Allen Lane.

Friedman, E. H. (1988). Systems and ceremonies: A family view of rites of passage. In B. Carter & M. McGoldrick (Eds.), *The changing family life cycle* (pp. 119–147). New York: Gardner Press.

Geertz, C. (1979). From the native's point of view: On the nature of anthropological understanding. In P. Rabinow & W. M. Sullivan (Eds.), *Interpretive social science: A reader* (pp. 225–241). Berkeley: University of California Press.

Geertz, C. (1988). *Works and lives: The anthropologist as author*. Stanford: Stanford University Press.

Gibbs, J., & Bennett, S. (1980). *Top ranking: A collection of articles on racism and classism in the lesbian community*. New York: February 3rd Press.

Gilligan, C. (1982). *In a different voice: Psychological theory and women's development*. Cambridge: Harvard University Press.

Goffman, E. (1963). *Stigma: Notes on the management of spoiled identity*. Englewood Cliffs, NJ: Prentice-Hall.

Goldner, V. (1985). Feminism and family therapy. *Family Process, 24*, 31–47.

Goldner, V. (1988). Generation and gender: Normative and covert hierarchies. *Family Process, 27*, 17–31.

Golombok, S., Spencer, A., & Rutter, M. (1983). Children in lesbian and single-parent households: Psychosexual and psychiatric appraisal. *Journal of Child Psychology and Psychiatry, 24*, 551–572.

Goodrich, T. J., Rampage, C., Ellman, B., & Halstead, K. (1988). *Feminist family therapy: A casebook*. New York: Norton.

Green, R. (1978). Sexual identity of 37 children raised by homosexual or transsexual parents. *American Journal of Psychiatry, 135*, 692–697.

Green, R., Mandel, J. B., Hotvedt, M. E., Gray, J., & Smith, L. (1986). Lesbian mothers and their children: A comparison with solo parent heterosexual mothers and their children. *Archives of Sexual Behavior, 15*(2), 167–183.

Greenberg, D. F. (1988). *The construction of homosexuality*. Chicago: University of Chicago Press.

Griscom, J. (1992). The case of Sharon Kowalski and Karen Thompson: Ableism, heterosexism, and sexism. In P. S. Rothenberg (Ed.). *Race, class, and gender in the United States: An integrated study*. New York: St. Martin's Press.

Hall Carpenter Archives. Lesbian Oral History Group. (1989a). *Inventing ourselves: Lesbian life stories*. London: Routledge.

Hall Carpenter Archives. Gay Men's Oral History Group. (1989b). *Walking after midnight: Gay men's life stories*. London: Routledge.

Hare-Mustin, R. (1978). A feminist approach to family therapy. *Family Process, 17*(4), 181–194.

Hare-Mustin, R. (1987). The problem of gender in family therapy theory. *Family Process, 26*, 15–33.

Hareven, T. K. (1982). American families in transition: Historical perspectives on change. In F. Walsh (Ed.), *Normal family processes* (1st ed., pp. 446–466). New York: Guilford Press.

Harris, M. B., & Turner, P. H. (1985 / 1986). Gay and lesbian parents. *Journal of Homosexuality, 12*, 101–113.

Harry, J. (1984). *Gay couples*. New York: Praeger.

Hartman, A., & Laird, J. (1983). *Family-centered social work practice*. New York: The Free Press.

Hencken, J. D., & O'Dowd, W. T. (1977). Coming out as an aspect of identity formation. *Gay Academic Union Journal: Gay Saber, 1*, 18–26.

Henderson, A. F. (1984). Homosexuality in the college years: Developmental differences between men and women. *Journal of the American College Health Association, 32*, 216–219.

Henry, J. (1965). *Pathways to madness*. New York: Vintage Books.

Herdt, G. (1992). *Gay culture in America: Essays from the field*. Boston: Beacon Press.

Hoeffer, B. (1981). Children's acquisition of sex-role behavior in lesbian-mother families. *American Journal of Orthopsychiatry, 5*, 536–544.

Huggins, S. (1989). A comparative study of self-esteem of adolescent children of divorced lesbian mothers and divorced heterosexual mothers. In F. W. Bozett (Ed.), *Homosexuality and the family* (pp. 123–135). New York: Harrington Park Press.

Imber-Black, I. (1988). Idiosyncratic life cycle transitions and therapeutic rituals. In B. Carter & M. McGoldrick (Eds.), *The changing family life cycle* (pp. 149–163). New York: Gardner Press.

Jordan, J. (1984). *Empathy and self-boundaries. Work in progress, No. 16*. Wellesley, MA: Stone Center Working Paper Series.

Kaplan, A. (1984). *The "self-in-relation": Implications for depression in women. Work in progress, No. 14*. Wellesley, MA: Stone Center Working Paper Series.

Karpel, M. (1976). Individuation: From fusion to dialogue. *Family Process, 15*, 65–82.

Keating, C. T. (1991). *Legacies: An exploratory study of young adult children of lesbians*. Unpublished master's thesis, Smith College School for Social Work, Northampton, MA.

Kinsey, A. C., Pomeroy, W. B., & Martin, C. E. (1948). *Sexual behavior in the human male*. Philadelphia: W. B. Saunders.

Kinsey, A. C., Pomeroy, W. B., Martin, C. E., & Gebbhard, P.H. (1953). *Sexual behavior in the human female*. Philadelphia: W. B. Saunders.

Kirkpatrick, M., Smith, C., & Roy, R. (1981). Lesbian mothers and their children: A comparative survey. *American Journal of Orthopsychiatry, 5*, 545–551.

Kleinberg, L. (1986). *Coming home to self, going home to parents: Lesbian identity disclosure. Work in Progress, No. 24*. Wellesley, MA: Stone Center Working Paper Series.

Krestan, J. (1988). Lesbian daughters and lesbian mothers: The crisis of disclosure from a family systems perspective. *Journal of Psychotherapy and the Family, 3*(4), 113–130.

Krestan, J., & Bepko, C. S. (1980). The problem of fusion in the lesbian relationship. *Family Process, 19*(3), 277–289.

Krieger, S. (1982). Lesbian identity and community: Recent social science literature. *Signs, 8*(1), 91–108.

Kurdek, L. A. (1988). Perceived social support in gays and lesbians in cohabiting relationships. *Journal of Personality and Social Psychology, 54*(3), 504–509.

Kurdek, L. A. (1988). Perceived social support in gays and lesbians in cohabiting relationships. *Journal of Personality and Social Psychology, 54*(3), 504–509.

Kurdek, L. A., & Schmitt, J. P. (1985). Relationship quality of gay men in closed or open relationships. *Journal of Homosexuality, 12*(2), 85–99.

Kurdek, L. A., & Schmitt, J. P. (1987). Perceived emotional support from family and friends in members of homosexual, married, and heterosexual cohabiting couples. *Journal of Homosexuality, 14*(3/4), 57–68.

Laird, J. (1988). Women and ritual: In E. Imber-Black, J. Roberts, & R. Whiting (Eds.), *Rituals in families and family therapy* (pp. 331–362). New York: Norton.

Laird, J. (1989). Women and stories: Restorying women's self-constructions. In M. McGoldrick, C. M. Anderson, & F. Walsh (Eds.), *Women in families: A framework for family therapy* (pp. 427–450). New York: Norton.

Laird, J. (1993). Women's secrets—women's silences. In E. Imber-Black (Ed.), *Secrets in families and family therapy*. New York: W. W. Norton.

Lerner, H. G. (1988). *Women in therapy*. Northvale, NJ: Jason Aronson.

Levy, E. (1989). Lesbian motherhood: Identity and social support. *Affilia, 4*(4), 40–53.

Lewis, O. (1963). *Children of Sanchez: Autobiography of an American family*. New York: Vintage Books.

Lewis, O. (1965). *La Vida; A Puerto Rican family in the culture of poverty—San Juan and New York*. New York: Random House.

Lindenbaum, J. P. (1985). The shattering of an illusion: The problem of competition in lesbian relationships. *Feminist Studies, 11*(1), 85–103.

Luepnitz, D. A. (1988). The family interpreted: Feminist theory in clinical practice. New York: Basic Books.

Lukes, C. A., & Land, H. (1990). Biculturality and homosexuality. *Social Work, 35*, 155–161.

Lynch, F.R. (1992). Nonghetto gays: An ethnography of suburban homosexuals. In G. Herdt (Ed.), *Gay culture in American: Essays from the field* (pp. 165–201). Boston: Beacon Press.

Martin, A. D. (1984). The perennial Cannanites: The sin of homosexuality. *Et Cetera, 41*, 340–361.

McCandlish, B. (1987). Against all odds: Lesbian mother family dynamics. In F. Bozett (Ed.), *Gay and lesbian parents* (pp. 23–38). New York: Praeger.

McGoldrick, M., Anderson, C. M., & Walsh, F. (Eds.). (1989). *Women in families: A framework for family therapy*. New York: W. W. Norton.

McWhirter, D. P., & Mattison, A. M. (1984). *The male couple: How relationships develop*. Englewood Cliffs, NJ: Prentice-Hall.

Mencher, J. (1990). *Intimacy in lesbian relationships: A critical re-examination of fusion. Work in progress, No. 42*. Wellesley, MA: Stone Center Working Paper Series.

Miller, J.B. (1976). *Toward a new psychology of women*. Boston: Beacon Press.

Miller, J. B. (1979). Gay fathers and their children. *The Family Coordinator, 28,* 544–552.

Miller, J. B. (1988). *Connections, disconnections, and violations. Work in progress, No. 33.* Wellesley, MA: Stone Center Working Paper Series.

Miller, N. (1989). *In search of gay America.* New York: Harper & Row.

Minton, H. L., & McDonald, G. J. (1983/1984). Homosexual identity formation as a developmental process. *Journal of Homosexuality, 9*(2/3), 65–77.

Morales, E. S. (1989). Ethnic minority families and minority gays and lesbians. *Marriage and Family Review, 14,* 217–239.

Morin, S. F. (1977). Heterosexual bias in psychological research on lesbianism and male homosexuality. *American Psychologist, 32,* 629–637.

Murphy, B. (1989). Lesbians and their parents: The effects of perceived parental attitudes on the couple. *Journal of Counseling and Development, 68*(1), 46–51.

Myers, M. F. (1982). Counseling the parents of young homosexual male patients. *Journal of Homosexuality, 7,* 131–144.

Osman, S. (1972). My stepfather is a she. *Family Process, 11,* 209–218.

Patterson, C. J. (1991). *Children of the lesbian baby boom: Behavioral adjustment, self-concepts, and sex-role identity.* Unpublished paper, Department of Psychology, University of Virginia, Charlottesville, VA.

Patterson, C. J. (1992). Children of lesbian and gay parents. *Child Development, 63,* 1025–1043.

Pattison, E. M., & Pattison, M. L. (1980). "Ex-gays": Religiously mediated changes in homosexuals. *American Journal of Psychiatry, 137,* 1553–1562.

Paul, J. P. (1986). *Growing up with a gay, lesbian, or bisexual parent: An exploratory study of experiences and perceptions.* Unpublished doctoral dissertation, University of California, Berkeley.

Peplau, L. A., & Cochrane, S. (1981). Value orientations in the intimate relationships of gay men. *Journal of Homosexuality, 6*(3), 1–19.

Peplau, L. A., Cochran, S., Rook, K., & Padesky, C. (1978). Loving women: Attachment and autonomy in lesbian relationships. *Journal of Social Issues, 34,* 7–27.

Peterson, J. L. (1992). Black men and their same-sex desires and behaviors. In G. Herdt (Ed.), *Gay culture in America: Essays from the field* (pp. 147–164). Boston: Beacon Press.

Pies, C. (1985). *Considering parenthood.* San Francisco: Spinsters/Aunt Lute.

Pies, C. (1990). Lesbians and the choice to parents. In F. W. Bozett & M. B. Sussman (Eds.), *Homosexuality and family relations* (pp. 137–154). New York: Harrington Park Press.

Plummer, K. (1975). *Sexual stigma: An interactionist account.* London: Routledge & Kegan Paul.

Ponse, B. (1978). *Identities in the lesbian world: The social construction of self.* Westport, CT: Greenwood.

Rees, R. L. (1979). *A comparison of children of lesbian and single heterosexual mothers on three measures of socialization.* Unpublished doctoral dissertation, California School of Professional Psychology, Berkeley, CA.

Riceour, P. (1979). The model of the text: Meaningful action considered as a text. In P. Rabinow and W. M. Sullivan (Eds.), *Interpretive social science: A reader* (pp. 73–101). Berkeley: University of California Press.

Rich, A. (1980). Compulsory heterosexuality and lesbian existence. In C. R. Stimpson & E. S. Person (Eds.), *Women—sex and sexuality* (pp. 62–91). Chicago: University of Chicago Press.

Richardson, D. (1987). Recent challenges to traditional assumptions about homosexuality: Some implications for practice. *Journal of Homosexuality, 13*(4), 1–12.

Richmond, M. (1930). *The long view*. New York: Russell Sage Foundation.

Ricketts, W., & Achtenberg, R. (1989). Adoption and foster parenting for lesbians and gay men: Creating new traditions. *Marriage and Family Review, 14*(3/4), 83–118.

Rosen, W. B. (1990). *Self-in-relation development in lesbians and the mother–daughter relationship*. Unpublished doctoral dissertation, Smith College School for Social Work, Northampton, MA.

Ross, E., & Rapp, R. (1981). Sex and society: A research note from social history and anthropology. *Comparative Studies in Society and History, 23*, 51–72.

Roth, S. (1989). Psychotherapy with lesbian couples: Individual issues, female socialization, and the social context. In M. McGoldrick, C. Anderson, & F. Walsh (Eds.), *Women in families* (pp. 286–307). New York: W. W. Norton.

Roth, S., & Murphy, B. C. (1986). Therapeutic work with lesbian clients: A systemic therapy view. In M. Ault-Riche & J. C. Hansen (Eds.), *Women and family therapy* (pp. 78–89). Rockville, MD: Aspen Systems Corp.

Saghir, M. T., and Robins, E. (1973). *Male and female homosexuality: A comprehensive investigation*. Baltimore: Williams and Wilkins.

Sanders, G. (1993). The love that dares not speak its name: From secrecy to openness in gay and lesbian affiliations. In E. Imber-Black (Ed.), *Secrets in families and family therapy* (pp. 215–242). New York: Norton.

Savin-Williams, R. C. (1989). Parental influences on the self-esteem of gay and lesbian youths: A reflected appraisals model. *Journal of Homosexuality, 15*, 93–109.

Slater, S., & Mencher, J. (1991). The lesbian family life cycle: A contextual approach. *American Journal of Orthopsychiatry, 61*, 372–382.

Sophie, J. (1985/1986). A critical examination of stage theories of lesbian identity development. *Journal of Homosexuality, 12*(2), 39–51.

Steckel, A. (1985). *Separation-individuation in children of lesbian and heterosexual couples*. Unpublished doctoral dissertation, The Wright Institute Graduate School, Berkeley, CA.

Steckel, A. (1987). Psychosocial development of children of lesbian mothers. In F. W. Bozett (Ed.), *Gay and lesbian parents* (pp. 75–85). New York: Praeger.

Surrey, J. (1985). *Self-in-relation: A theory of women's development. Work in progress, No. 13*. Wellesley, MA: Stone Center Working Paper Series.

Troiden, R. R. (1979). Becoming homosexual: A model for gay identity acquisition. *Psychiatry, 42*, 362–373.

van Gelder, L. (1988). Gay gothic. *Plain Brown Rapper, 2*, 5–12.

Walker, G. (1991). *In the midst of winter: Systemic therapy with families, couples, and individuals with AIDS infection*. New York: W. W. Norton.

Walters, M., Carter, B., Papp, P., & Silverstein, O. (1988). *The invisible web: Gender patterns in family relationships*. New York: Guilford Press.

Warren, C. A. B. (1974). *Identity and community in the gay world*. New York: John Wiley & Sons.

Weinberg, G. (1972). *Society and the healthy homosexual*. New York: St. Martin's Press.

Weinberg, T. (1978). On "doing" and "being" gay: Sexual behavior and homosexual male self-identity. *Journal of Homosexuality, 4*, 143–156,

Weinberg, T. (1984). Biology, ideology, and the reification of developmental stages in the study of homosexual identities. *Journal of Homosexuality, 10*(3/4), 77–84.

Weston, K. (1991). *Families we choose: Lesbians, gays, kinship.* New York: Columbia University Press.

Zacks, E., Green, R-J., & Marrow, J. (1988). Comparing lesbian and heterosexual couples on the circumplex model: An initial investigation. *Family Process, 27,* 471–484.

Zitter, S. (1987). Coming out to Mom: Theoretical aspects of the mother–daughter process. In Boston Lesbian Psychologies Collective (Eds.), *Lesbian psychologies: Explorations and challenges* (pp. 177–194). Urbana, IL: University of Illinois Press.

PART IV

Normal Family Processes in Social and Developmental Contexts

CHAPTER 11

ETHNICITY, CULTURAL DIVERSITY, AND NORMALITY

Monica McGoldrick

You yourself are the embodied continuance
Of those who did not live into your time
And others will be (and are) your immortality on earth.
—*Jorge Luis Borges*

INTRODUCTION

There is a complex web of connections that cushions us as we move through life: family, community, and culture. Even though it is said we are moving toward becoming a global community, we are still very much embedded in our local context. Families do not develop their rules, beliefs, and rituals in a vacuum. What you think, how you act, even your language, are all transmitted through the family from the wider cultural context. This context includes the culture in which you live, and those from which your ancestors have come. This context is influenced not only by the class, religion, and geographic background of your family, but also by its ethnicity and by the cultural experiences its members have had. No two families share exactly the same cultural roots. Thus the family in which you were born comprises strands of all the cultural roots of which it is comprised. Understanding a family's cultural roots is essential to understanding its members' lives, and the development of the particular individual as well.

Understanding our cultural experiences involves being able to explore both similarities and differences. It was "discovered" in the fall of 1991 that all people of the earth descend from a common mother who lived about 200,000 years ago in central Africa. Whether or not this specific connection exists, our connections to each other are not actually too remote in the whole scheme of things. But the profound differences that divide us culturally must be acknowledged. Dealing with the subject of cultural diversity is a matter of balance between validating the differences among us and appreciating the forces of our common humanity. The goal of cultural diversity is for people to be in harmony with their heritage and future—not in a struggle to recapture some mythical past of cultural harmony or to ignore and avoid their history. Those of us who were born white and sufficiently like the dominant norm of the society probably grew up believing we were the norm and that "ethnicity" referred to others who were different from us. We were "regular." We thought culture referred to people on the periphery, and there was a lot of pressure in the dominant society for such a view. Now we are facing the realization that "normal" is never more than a point of view, and we never have more than a working hypothesis. African-Americans and other so called "minorities" have always had an edge in the awareness of this fact. For the rest of us, understanding concepts of normality and health from this perspective is a new endeavor.

What it requires is that we develop an open social system with flexible, but workable, boundaries—so people can define themselves by the groupings they are connected with by heritage and culture and go beyond labels such as "minorities" "Blacks," "Hispanics" or "Americans." Our very language reflects the bias embedded in our society's dominant beliefs. The term Hispanic, for example, refers to Taino Indians, Cubans of Spanish origin, Chinese who settled in Puerto Rico, families from Africa whose ancestors were brought over as slaves, and Jews who came to Argentina in the 1930s, whose ancestors had been in Europe for over a thousand years. The term "minority" peripheralizes groups whose heritage is different from the dominant groups. The term "Black" obliterates the ancestral heritage of Americans of African heritage altogether and defines people only by their color. And the fact that there is no term "United Statesan" to describe people of the United States but only the inaccurate "American," which makes invisible Canadians, Mexicans, and other Americans is a serious handicap to our even discussing these issues.

Culture itself is not a monologue, but a dialogue. No matter what your family background is, it is multicultural. All marriages are to a degree intermarriages. While it is always true that we are a product of our context, the multiple parts of our cultural heritage often do not fit easily into any description. As the narrator says in *The Crown of Columbus* (Erdrich & Dorris, 1992):

I belong to the lost tribe of mixed bloods, that hodgepodge amalgam of hue and cry that defies easy placement. When the DNA of my various ancestors—Irish and Coeur d"Alene and Spanish and Navajo and God knows what else—combined to form me, the result was not some genteel undecipherable puree that comes from a Cuisinart. You know what they say on the side of the Bisquick box, under instructions for pancakes? Mix with fork. Leave lumps. That was me. There are advantages to not being this or that. You have a million stories, one for every occasion, and in a way they're all lies and in another way they're all true. . . . (pp. 166–167)

If we look carefully enough, all of us are a hodge-podge. Part of the issue about culture and cultural identity is to be able to go beyond the dominant values and explore the complexity of culture and cultural identity, not without values and judgments about what is adaptive, healthy, or "normal," but without accepting unquestioningly our society's definitions of these culturally determined values, so that people can stand in all their complexity and multifacetedness, not having to suppress parts of themselves in order to "pass" for normal according to someone else's arbitrary standards.

The concept of "home" is crucial to our sense of personal and cultural identity. As one commentator put it:

Home is an English word virtually impossible to translate. . . . No translation catches the associations, the mixture of memory and longing, . . . the aroma of inclusiveness, of freedom from wariness, that cling to the word home. . . . Home is a concept, not a place, it is a state of mind where self-definition starts; it is origins—the mix of time and place and smell and weather wherein one first realizes one is an original, perhaps like others, especially those one loves, but discrete, distinct, not to be copied. Home . . . remains in the mind as a place where reunion, if it were ever to occur, would happen. . . . [It] is the goal—rarely glimpsed, almost never attained—of all the heroes descended from Odysseus. All literary romance derives from the Odyssey and is about rejoining. . . . It is about restoration of the right relations among things—and going home is where that restoration occurs, because that is where it matters most. . . . Everyone has a "hometown" back there, at least back in time, where stability or at least its image remains alive. . . . To go home may be impossible but it is often a driving necessity, or at least a compelling dream. . . . To attempt to go home is to go the long way around, to stray and separate in the hope of finding completeness in reunion, freedom in reintegration with those left behind. (Giamatti, 1989, p. 254)

Home is about having a sense of being at peace with who we are. All of us are immigrants, always moving between the traditions of our ancestors and the worlds we inhabit ourselves and with our partners, friends, and children. Probably no one ever has such a complete sense of connection to culture that there is no sense of disjunction ever, and for most of us finding out who we are culturally means putting together a unique internal combination of cultural identities. Maya Angelou went to live in Africa, hoping in some way to be home, and found there that who she was could not be encompassed by that part of her heritage, even though it was an important one.

> If the heart of Africa still remained illusive, my search for it had brought me closer to understanding myself and other human beings. The ache for home lives in all of us, the safe place where we can go as we are and not be questioned. It impels mighty ambitions and dangerous capers . . . Hoping that by doing these things home will find us acceptable or, failing that, that we will forget our awful yearning for it. (Angelou, 1986, p. 54)

I myself first went to Ireland, the country of my ancestors, when I was 32 and experienced a sense of having "come home." But home to what? I had never been there before. My family had never spoken of our heritage. The notion of culture is almost a mystical sense of connection with all the threads of which our human community is woven. Understanding people in cultural context means having a concept of normality that encompasses everyone together in a context that connects us all. Paul Robeson, one of the most magnificent geniuses of our century or probably any other, wrote in describing one of his brothers who did not live up the the father's expectations and eventually became involved in drugs and crime before dying an untimely death.

> He won no honors in classroom, pulpit or platform. Yet I remember him with love. Restless, rebellious, scoffing at conventions, defiant of the white man's law. I've known many Negroes like Reed. I see them every day. Blindly, in their own reckless manner, they seek a way out for themselves; alone, they pound with their fists and fury against walls that only the shoulders of many can topple . . . When . . . everything will be different . . . the fiery ones like Reed will be able to live out their lives in peace and no one will have cause to frown upon them. (Robeson, 1958, p. 16)

Robeson was aware that only if we acknowledge the connections that actually exist among all of us can we find ways to be healthy. There is a beautiful moment in *Raisin in the Sun*, when the mother reminds her daughter of this point after the daughter says she's giving up on her brother:

> You've written his epitaph too—like the rest of the world? Well, who gave you the privilege? . . . When you start measuring somebody, measure him right, child, measure him right. You make sure you've taken into account the hills and valleys he's come through before he got to wherever he is. (Hansberry, 1958, p. 145)

We are all a part of all that we have been—our families, our cultures, no matter how our society may propagate the myth that we are not all connected in both our history and our fate.

Cultural Differences, Norms, and Stereotypes

While the stereotyping of groups has often reinforced prejudices, there is no way to discuss cultures without generalizing about their patterns. The alternative of pretending we do not notice these patterns mystifies and disqualifies our experience. This perpetuates negative stereotyping. Only if we allow ourselves to air our assumptions can we open ourselves to new information about cultures. In our work we have taken the risk of trying to articulate typical differences among groups in order to sensitize clinicians to the range of values held by different people. Of course, each family must be dealt with as unique, and the characterizations made about particular groups are meant to broaden our framework, not to constrict it. They are intended to put more questions on the table and help us develop perspective on the values of our own backgrounds and assumptions that we have taken for granted.

Ethnicity patterns our thinking, feeling, and behavior in both obvious and subtle ways, although generally operating outside our awareness. It plays a major role in determining what we eat, how we work, how we relate, how we celebrate holidays and rituals, and how we feel about life, death, and illness. Our very definitions of human development are culturally based. Eastern cultures, for example, tend to define the person as a social being and to define development by the growth in the human capacity for empathy and connection. By contrast, many Western cultures begin with the individual as a psychological being and define development as growth in the human capacity for differentiation. African-Americans have a communal sense of identity: "We are, therefore I am," which contrasts deeply with the dominant culture's individualistic: "I think, therefore I am."

Family therapists have recognized that individual behavior is mediated through family rules and patterns, but while we have failed to appreciate that these rules are not idiosyncratic to a particular family, but are generally rooted in cultural norms.

The United States has had the greatest ethnic diversity of any nation in history, but until recently public discussion of differences among American ethnic groups has been virtually taboo. We have talked about the melting pot and blinded ourselves to our country's inherent diversity. Ethnicity should be of particular interest to family therapists, because cultural norms and values prescribe the "rules" by which families operate, including how family members identify, define, and attempt to solve their problems, and how they seek help. Studying culture gives one great respect for differences in groups' attitudes toward many of our core values. Let us consider the value of "talk" for example. The dominant value in the therapy world is that talk is good for you—it heals you. Therapy has even been referred to as "the talking cure." But let us consider the value different cultures place on talk. In Jewish culture for important historical reasons, articulating one's experience may be as important as the experience itself. Cognitive clarity about the many levels of one's experience is extremely highly valued. Verbal communication—clarifying and sharing one's ideas and perceptions—is valued as a way of finding meaning in life. Given the anti-semitic context in which Jews have lived for so long, where their rights and experiences were so often obliterated, it is not surprising that they came to place so much importance on analysing, understanding, and bearing witness to what has happened.

In WASP culture, on the other hand, words are used only as needed to accomplish one's goals. Words are valued primarily for their efficiency—their utilitarian, pragmatic value. As the son says in the movie *Ordinary People* regarding his brother's death: "What's the point of talking about it. It doesn't change anything." In Chinese culture, families may communicate many important issues through food rather than through words. They do not by any means accept the dominant American idea of "laying your cards out on the table." Italians communicate with food, emotional intensity, and words—but words are used primarily for drama—to convey the emotional intensity of the experience, not for pragmatic, logical purposes. The Irish, who are perhaps the greatest poets in the world, use words to buffer experience—they use poetry or humor of language to somehow make reality more tolerable—not to tell the truth as WASPs do, but perhaps to cover up the truth or to embellish it. The Irish have raised poetry, mystification, double meanings, humorous indirection, and ambiguity to a science, in part, perhaps, because their history of oppression led them to realize that telling the truth could be dangerous to their lives.

In Sioux Indian culture there is yet a different attitude toward communication. Talking is actually proscribed in certain family relationships! One colleague, married for many years to a Sioux, has virtually never exchanged a word with her father-in-law, and yet, she has an experience of deep intimacy with him. Such a relationship is almost inconceivable in our digital, pragmatic world. The reduced emphasis on verbal expression seems to free up Native American families for other kinds of experience—of each other, of nature, and of the spiritual.

Groups differ also regarding their attitudes toward spirituality. The dominant WASP and also Jewish value is very pragmatic and "reality" oriented. Other cultures—Hispanic, for instance, move in a very fluid way between dreams and the everyday world. Even to call the latter "reality" expresses a bias of the dominant group in our society toward the pragmatic and disqualifies the validity of other modes of experience.

We believe that therapists who appreciate the cultural relativity of family life are in a position to intervene more effectively and that a therapist's own ethnicity influences the helping process. Furthermore, our therapeutic models are themselves reflections of the cultures in which they developed. A pilot study of family therapists we did a few years ago (McGoldrick & Rohrbaugh, 1987) suggests that ethnic stereotypes are maintained in the minds of family therapists even after they are generations removed from their cultural roots.

Defining Ethnicity

Ethnicity refers to a concept of a group's "peoplehood" based on a combination of race, religion, and cultural history, whether or not members realize their commonalties with one another. It describes a commonality transmitted by the family over generations and reinforced by the surrounding community. But ethnicity is more than race, religion, national and geographic origin, which is not to minimize the significance of race or the profound problems of racism. It encompasses those who are united by their common ancestry or history. It involves a many-layered sense of group identification—of shared values and understandings that fulfill a deep psychological need for identity and historical continuity.

The consciousness of ethnic identity varies greatly within groups and from one group to another. Families vary in attitude toward their ethnicity from clannishness—regressively holding on to past traditions, and fearing any change in cultural norms, on the one hand—to total denial of their ethnicity or its relevance on the other. Those who have experienced the stigma of prejudice and racism may attempt to "pass"—a notion which develops meaning in a context in which one group's characteristics are valued over another's. In groups that have experienced prejudice and discrimination, such as Jews and African-Americans, family members may absorb the prejudices of the larger society and become conflicted or negative about their own cultural identity. Family members may even turn against each other, reflecting prejudices in the outside world, with some trying to "pass," and others resenting them for doing so. Those who are close enough in appearance to the characteristics of the dominant groups, may experience a sense of choice about whether to identify with their own ethnic group or with the dominant group, whereas others, because of their skin color or other physical characteristics, have no choice. The intense conflicts that such issues embody are reflected in group members' attempts through plastic surgery or other processes to change their physical appearance to be more like the dominant "valued" characteristics. Other examples would include in Jewish culture one person saying to another, "You are betraying the Jews," or, in African-American culture one person accusing another of being "an oreo," meaning that he or she has "sold out" to the dominant culture.

Families that are not of the dominant culture are always under pressure to give up their values and conform to the norms of the more powerful group. Family members will differ over time from each other and even in their own behavior on the extent of their willingness to try to "pass" or accomodate to survive or get along in this society. It is important to view conflicts family members have with each other over the level of accomodation they are willing to tolerate as a reflection of the pressure they are all under from outside, and not just as family conflict.

Ethnicity intersects with class, religion, politics, geography, the length of time since a group's migration, the historical cohort, and the degree of discrimination the group has experienced. Generally speaking, people tend to move closer to the dominant value system the longer they remain in the United States and the more they move up in social class. People in different geographic locations evolve new cultural norms. Religion also modifies or reinforces certain cultural values. Families that remain within an ethnic neighborhood, who work and socialize with members of their group, and whose religion reinforces ethnic values, are likely to maintain their ethnicity longer than those who live in heterogeneous settings and have no social reinforcers of their cultural traditions. Another important factor which needs exploration is the impact of political oppression on a group's historical traditions, such as the impact of Communism on Russia, East Germany, or China. The degree of ethnic intermarriage in the family also plays a role in cultural patterns (McGoldrick & Preto, 1984). Nevertheless, there is burgeoning evidence that ethnic values and identifications are retained for many generations after immigration, even after conscious awareness of one's ethnicity is lost, and that they play a significant role in family patterns throughout the life cycle. Second-, third-, and even fourth-generation Americans differ from the dominant culture in values, behavior, and life cycle patterns (McGoldrick, Pearce, & Giordano, 1982).

Ethnicity and Mental Health

Although human behavior results from the interplay of intrapsychic, interpersonal, familial, socioeconomic, and cultural forces, the mental health field has paid greatest attention to the intrapsychic influences—the personality factors that shape life experiences and behavior. The study of cultural influences on the emotional functioning of human beings has been left primarily to cultural anthropologists. And even they have preferred to explore these influences in distant and fragile non-Western cultures, rather than exploring the great diversity among Americans of assumptions about illness and health, normality and pathology. Andrew Greeley, commenting on this tendency, has said:

> I suspect that the historians of the future will be astonished that . . . [we] could stand in the midst of such an astonishing social phenomenon and take it so much for granted that . . . [we] would not bother to study it. They will find it especially astonishing in light of the fact that ethnic differences, even in the second half of the twentieth century, proved far more important than differences in philosophy or economic system. Men who would not die for a premise or a dogma or a division of labor would more or less cheerfully die for a difference rooted in ethnic origins. (1969, p. 5)

When mental health professionals have considered culture, they have been more absorbed in making international, cross-cultural comparisons than in studying the ethnic groups in our own culture. Our therapeutic models are generally presented as if they were culture-free, rather than the reflection of the cultural assumptions out of which they arise. Only recently are we beginning to consider ethnic differences in therapists or in client families when developing therapeutic models (McGoldrick et al., 1982) and to examine the underlying cultural assumptions of our models.

Ethnicity and the Family

Ethnicity is deeply tied to the family, through which it is transmitted. As Billingsley has described the link between ethnicity and family which has enabled African-Americans to survive in a hostile environment for more than 300 years:

> Ethnicity and family life are two concepts which . . . go hand in hand. They are so intertwined that it is very difficult indeed to observe the one or even to reflect it seriously without coming to grips with the other. So when we think of Italians and certain other Southern Europeans, we think of large families; we think of the English and certain Northern Europeans in compact nuclear families. When we think of Black families we think of strong extended families, and when we think of Chinese families we must encompass whole communities. (Billingsley, 1976)

It seems so natural that an interest in families should lead to an interest in ethnicity, that it is remarkable this area has so long been ignored in family therapy. Although a few family therapists have recognized the importance of culture, the major models of family therapy make little reference to ethnic differences in the application of their methods. Minuchin, Montalvo, and their co-workers (1967) focused on multiproblem, inner-city families and developed specific techniques to deal with poor African American and Hispanic families. Whereas the other major models (e.g., Bowen, Haley, MRI strategic, Milan systemic, constructivist, and the various communications models), emphasize the importance of the family context, they do not make explicit reference to the cultural context within which the family is embedded, and which largely determines its values. Almost nothing has been written about the cultural fit between the model and the group for whom it is used. Consider the recent work of Tom Anderson in Sweden, which is meant to be so respectful of the client's culture that the therapist tries not to intrude at all with interventions but merely observes and reflects back to the family what he or she observes. This approach could be experienced as highly threatening and intrusive by a family from a culture that is uncomfortable with such an ambiguous, nondirective relationship to an outsider or a helper. Many therapists say they respect culture in general, but they oppose discussion of particular cultural characteristics. This offers us a paradox. We are supposed to be sensitive to culture, yet if we cannot discuss culture-specific value differences, we cannot learn about the particular beliefs of cultural groups different from our own, since we are warned not to categorize in this way.

Many have opposed discussion of particular cultural patterns as offering too rigid a model for clinicians. They prefer instead to go from the particular—the unique or idiosyncratic to the global. Although the intention of such a perspective is positive (not to limit our thinking with stereotypes), in real life this is impractical. It leads to a lack of attention to culture, when therapists must treat each client's story as unique.

In fact, a family's culture will determine whether its members will even define a symptom as a problem and what symptoms develop in which cultural contexts, bringing into question the usefulness of the present diagnostic nomenclature. In addition, a patient's "illness" (the experience of being ill) is very different from the course of his or her physiological disease and is strongly influenced by cultural beliefs (McGoldrick, 1982a; Rolland, Chapter 15, this volume). And, naturally, seeking help depends greatly on one's attitude toward the "helper." For example, Italians tend to rely primarily on the family and turn to an outsider for help only as a last resort (Gambino, 1974; Rotunno & McGoldrick, 1982; Zborowski, 1969; Zola, 1966). African-Americans have long mistrusted the help they can receive from traditional middle-class institutions (Hines & Boyd-Franklin, 1982; Billingsley, 1988; McAdoo, 1977; Boyd-Franklin, 1989) and Puerto Ricans (Garcia-Preto, 1982) and Chinese (Kleinman, 1975) are more likely to somatize when they are under stress and to seek medical rather than mental health services. For both cultural groups, the mind/body split of the dominant culture in the United States is alien. Norwegians, too, often convert emotional tension into physical symptoms, which are more acceptable in their culture than the overt expression of emotional suffering. As a result, they are more likely to seek out the help of a surgeon than a psychotherapist (Midelfort & Midelfort, 1982). Likewise, Iranians often view medication and vitamins as a necessary part of treating symptoms, regardless of their origin (Jalali, 1982). Thus, a substantial percentage of potential patients experience troubles and cures somatically and strongly doubt the value of psychotherapy. Jews, on the other hand tend to be the most sophisticated of all groups on psychological matters and are the only ones willing to psychologize even physical symptoms.

Almost all of us have multiple belief systems to which we turn when in need of help. We use not only the official medical or psychotherapeutic system, but also religion, self-help groups, alcohol, yoga, acupuncture, chiropractors, and especially if we reside in California, crystals and special foods. We utilize remedies our mothers taught us and those suggested by our friends.

These differences can lead to important misunderstandings in therapy. A group whose characteristic response to illness is too different from the dominant culture is likely to be labeled "abnormal." For example, one researcher found that doctors frequently labeled their Italian patients as having psychiatric problems, although there was no evidence that psychosocial problems occurred more frequently among them (Zola, 1963). And Zborowski (1969) in his classic study, found that Italian and Jewish patients complained much more than Irish or WASP patients, who considered complaining to be "bad form." Differences in style of interaction may also be misinterpreted. A high level of interaction is expected in Jewish, Italian, and Greek families, but WASPs, Irish and Scandinavian families have much less intense interactions and are more likely to deal with problems by distancing. Obviously, therapists need to take these potential differences into account in making an assessment, considering carefully the biases of their own perspective and particular values of their clients.

For the most part, the ethnic differences that have been described in the family therapy literature embody common cultural stereotypes. For example, Jewish families are seen as valuing education, success, family connections, encouragement of children, democratic principles, verbal expression, shared suffering, guilt, and eating. WASPs are seen as generally valuing control, personal responsibility, independence, individuality, stoicism, keeping up appearances, and moderation in everything. By contrast, Italian-American families generally are described as valuing the family more than the individual; food is a major source of emotional as well as physical nourishment; traditional male/female roles are strong, and loyalty flows through personal relationships. African-Americans are seen as valuing an informal kinship network and spiritual values. Their strength to survive is a powerful resource, and they tend to have more flexibility in family roles than many other groups. In Hispanic cultures, family togetherness and respect, especially for one's elders are valued concepts. People are valued more for their character than for their level of success alone. They also hold onto traditional notions of a woman's role as virgin and sacrificial sainted mother who tolerates her husbands adventures and absence with forbearance (Garcia-Preto, 1982). Chinese families value respect for elders, family togetherness, harmony and interdependence in relationships, respect for one's place in the line of generations, ancestor worship, saving face, and food as an emotional and spiritual expression. For Asian Indians, purity, sacrifice, passivity and a spiritual orientation are core values and death is seen as just one more phase in a life cycle that includes many rebirths.

It would require many volumes to consider any single ethnic group in depth. Most groups are themselves combinations of a multitude of cultural groups. Puerto Rican culture, for example, is a product of many diverse influences, including Spanish, African, and Caribbean Indian. Many factors influence the extent to which traditional ethnic patterns will surface in any particular family:

1. The reasons for immigration—what the family was seeking and what it was leaving behind (religious or political persecution, poverty, wish for adventure, etc.).
2. The length of time since immigration and the impact of generational acculturation conflict on the family.

3. The family's place of residence—whether or not the family lives or has lived in an ethnic neighborhood.
4. The order of migration—whether one family member migrated alone or whether a large portion of the family, community, or nation came together.
5. The socioeconomic status, education, and upward mobility of family members.
6. The political and religious ties to the ethnic group.
7. The languages spoken by family members.
8. The extent of family intermarriage with or connection to other ethnic groups.
9. The family members' attitudes toward the ethnic group and its values.

All families in this country have experienced the complex stresses of immigration and migration; these may be "buried" or forgotten, but they subtly continue to influence a family's outlook. Also, under the pressure of accommodating to the new situation, many immigrant groups have been forced to abandon much of their ethnic heritage and thus have lost a part of their identity. The effects of this cutting off on the family may be all the more powerful for being hidden.

If the first generation is older at the time of immigration, or lives in an ethnic neighborhood in this country, its conflicts of acculturation may be postponed. The next generation, particularly in adolescence, is likely to reject the "ethnic" values of their parents and to strive to become "Americanized." The third or fourth generations are usually freer to reclaim aspects of their identities that were sacrificed in the previous generations because of the need to assimilate. To understand ethnic norms, one must maintain a developmental perspective on both variations in family life cycle patterns and the impact that immigration has on families over succeeding generations (Falicov, 1980; McGoldrick, 1989; Sluzki, 1979).

The extensive geographical and class mobility in American culture, although often cutting individuals off from their ethnic heritage, increases their contact with different ethnic groups. The high rate of interethnic marriage means that many Americans will learn about ethnic differences from marriage partners. But, at best, most Americans probably come to understand well only three or four groups in the course of a lifetime. Obviously, no therapist can become an expert on all ethnic groups. Again, what is essential for clinicians is to develop an attitude of openness to cultural variability and to the relativity of their own values.

I offer here short sketches of a few ethnic groups to suggest the flavor of the complex differences among ethnic groups. Rather than being comprehensive, these characterizations are meant to suggest the range of questions for a clinician to keep in mind. The particular insights offered on each group are presented as useful hypotheses, rather than "true truths." The point is to highlight differences so details are as specific as possible, since that gives more reality to the material, and helps clinicians think of this own and their clients' experiences in everyday terms. For a more comprehensive examination of seventeen different American ethnic groups, the reader is referred to *Ethnicity and Family Therapy* (McGoldrick et al., 1982; McGoldrick & Giordano, in press).

IRISH FAMILIES

There are about 16 million Americans of Irish Catholic background, many of whose families have now been in the United States for more than four generations. The culture of this group has remained relatively homogeneous over almost 2,000 years. Irish Catholics began to immigrate in large numbers in the 1840s primarily because of the potato famine and oppressive conditions in Ireland. Irish Protestants, who are a separate group, have been migrating here since before the American Revolution. For historical, economic and political reasons, they generally do not think of themselves as Irish, have the lowest rate of endogamous marriage of any American ethnic group, and have tended to disavow a cultural identity (Fallows, 1979).

The Irish tend to assume that anything that goes wrong is the result of their sins. Their basic belief is that problems are a private matter between themselves and God, and they are therefore, unlikely to seek or expect any help when they have trouble). If they do seek help, the Irish are apt to view therapy as similar to Catholic confession—an occasion in which to tell their "sins" and receive a "penance." They are embarrassed to have to come to therapy and usually only do so at the suggestion of a third party, for example, a school, doctor, or court.

Although the Irish are not very likely to see psychotherapy as a solution to their problems they have had extremely high rates of psychosis and addiction, primarily alcoholism (Malzberg, 1973; Rabkin & Struening, 1976; Roberts & Myers, 1954). While the Irish have, perhaps, the most highly developed skill with words of any culture, they may be at a loss to describe their own inner feelings, whether of love, sadness, or anger. They have more phrases for the use of words to color reality than any other ethnic group: the gift of gabb, blarney, hooey, malarky, palaver, shenanigans, to name just a few. For the many centuries that they lived under the control of the British, clear speech could have meant their death but they have come to place high value on complex, even convoluted, mystification and double entendre in their language. African-Americans have a similarly rich and colorful language, which also evolved as a way to cope with an alien dominant culture. Language and poetry have always been highly valued by the Irish and closely associated with their love of dreaming. Perhaps it is no wonder that they placed so much emphasis on fantasy. For so many centuries the Irish existed under wretched circumstances, and they used their words to enrich a dismal reality. The poet was always the most highly valued member of their culture, in ancient times the only members of society who could travel freely about the country, and even today writers are the only members of Irish society exempted from taxes.

Humor is the greatest resource of the Irish for dealing with life's problems, and wit and satire have long been their most powerful means of attack. Hostility and resentments could (and still can) only be dealt with indirectly in the family through sarcasm or innuendo. As a result, feelings often build up until, finally, family members silently cut one another off. Hostility is only permitted against the out-group and then only for a just and moral cause, such as religion or politics. These values create many difficulties for a therapist trying to understand Irish family patterns. As is reflected in the mystifying character of much Irish literature, the most important things are usually left unspoken or referred to only by allusion. Within the family, feelings are often so hidden that it is hard for anyone to know exactly what is going on. The Irish have been shown to have a much greater tolerance for nonrealistic thinking than other groups do. In contrast to WASPs and Jews, for example, who value the pursuit of truth, clarification of feelings does not necessarily make the Irish feel better. Thus, therapy aimed at opening up family feelings will often be unsuccessful. As a general rule, structured therapy, focused specifically on the presenting problem, will be the least threatening and most helpful to Irish clients. Suggestions for opening communication that also preserve the boundaries of individual privacy, such as Bowen therapy, will be preferable to therapy that brings the entire family drama into the therapy session. The strategic techniques of the Palo Alto and the Milan groups would also be helpful, since they emphasize change without forcing clients to spell out all their feelings or make changes in front of the therapist.

Characteristically, the Irish mother has played a strong central role in the family. She has been seen as morally superior to her husband, who was traditionally a more shadowy figure, who generally found his companionship in the pub (Diner, 1983). She ran things in the home and socialized through the Church. Children were raised to be respectful and well-behaved. Discipline was traditionally strict and enforced with threats such as "It's a mortal sin; you'll go to hell." Parents tend not to praise their children for fear of giving them a "swelled head." It is considered important to keep up appearances and not to "make a scene."

The authority of the Roman Catholic Church was the major unifier for the Irish, to such an extent that the Church came before the family (Italians have had the opposite priorities). Irish Catholics have traditionally viewed most things moralistically, following the rules of the Church without question. This, of course, has changed in recent years, but the underlying rigidity often remains. It is important in working with the Irish to understand how they feel about religion, since the values of the Church have strong bearing on their problems. Even those who have left the Church may have intense feelings about religious issues.

Extended family relationships among the Irish are often not close, in contrast to Jewish, Italian, Black, and Greek families, although families may get together for "duty visits" on holidays and act jovial and "clannish." Family members tend not to rely on one another as a source of support, and if they have a problem they may even see it as an added burden and embarrassment, if the family finds out. The sense of emotional isolation in Irish relationships is frequently a factor in symptom development and has important implications for therapy. For example, whereas large family sessions that draw on the resources of the whole family may be supportive for some groups, for the Irish they may raise the anxiety to a toxic level, leading to denial and embarrassed humor to deal with their sense of humiliation. It is often more fruitful to meet with smaller subgroups of the family, at least in the initial stages of opening up family communication.

For Irish families death is generally considered the most significant life cycle transition and family members will go to great lengths not to miss a wake or a funeral. Like Black families in the South who often went to great expense to have a band play and to have flowers and singing and other accompaniments for their funerals, the Irish often delayed a funeral for days so that all family members could get there. They spare no expense for drink and arrangements, even if they have very little money. Such customs undoubtedly relate to their belief that life in this world is generally full of suffering and death brings release to a better afterworld.

Unlike Black families who openly grieve at their funerals, the Irish are much more likely to get drunk, tell stories and jokes, and relate to the wake as a kind of party, with little or no overt expression of grief. Traditionally wakes were often far merrier than weddings. There is an old Irish saying, "Sing a song at a wake, and shed a tear when a child is born." (For more specific discussion of the Irish and other groups handling of loss, see McGoldrick et al., 1991.)

Trying to talk the Irish out of their sense of guilt and need to suffer is a futile effort. Unlike Jews, for whom the very experience of sharing suffering is meaningful, the Irish believe in suffering alone. Certain strategies may help them limit their guilt and suffering, such as prescribing it within restricted time intervals (McGoldrick, 1982; McGoldrick & Pearce, 1981). But they are unlikely to give up suffering altogether. In fact, to do so would make them feel vulnerable, because they believe that sooner or later they will have to pay for their sins.

The therapist working with an Irish family must be content with limited changes. The Irish may not wish to move beyond the initial presenting problem, and it is important for the therapist not to pressure them into further work. Attempting to get spouses to deal with marital issues after a child-focused problem has been solved, for example, will probably make them feel guilty and incompetent (McGoldrick et al. 1989; McGoldrick et al. 1990). It is better to reinforce the changes that the family members do make and to let them return for therapy later at their own initiative. Even if the therapist perceives that there are emotional blocks in the family that are still causing pain, it is important not to push the matter. Because of the lack of immediate feedback about therapeutic progress from the family, the therapist may be surprised to learn that their Irish families have continued therapeutic work on their own. Their deep sense of personal responsibility is, in fact, their greatest personal resource in therapy. They often do continue efforts started in therapy, though they may not openly admit either fault or the resolve to remedy it.

JEWISH FAMILIES

There are about 5.5 million Jews living in the United States (half of the world's Jewish population). Of these, 35% live in New York City, and another 45% live in nine other major American cities (Goren, 1980). The following comments refer primarily to American Jews whose ancestors had spent the past several generations in Eastern Europe, the largest Jewish group in this country. Obviously German Jews, Sephardic Jews, and other Jewish groups have different characteristics, influenced by the centuries of Jewish migration and settlement in various countries before they came to the United States.

Jewish families have a very strong family orientation and will accept a family definition of their problems more readily than many other groups. Marriage and children play a central role in Jewish family life. As Zborowski and Herzog (1952) have stated in their classic study of East European Jews:

> Marriage is both the climax and the threshold. From birth on, every step is directed with an eye to the *"Khupa"* (marriage canopy), and if that goal is missed, life itself seems to be lost. Once attained, however, marriage is merely the background for the great goal, the great achievement, the great gratification: children. (p. 290)

Parents in Jewish families tend to have democratic relationships with their children and less rigid generational boundaries than most other groups (Herz & Rosen, 1982). They place high value on verbal explanations and reasoning in child rearing. For a non-Jewish therapist, the parents' desire to reason out issues may seem unnecessary, but within a Jewish context it is extremely important. Analytic thinking and cognitive clarity are extremely highly valued in Jewish culture. Parents take great pride in their children's verbal skill, intelligence, and ability to think things out logically.

Jewish families are more likely than all other ethnic groups to seek and be receptive to psychotherapy in almost any form. They value talk, insight, and the recognition of complex levels of meaning. They value the gaining of wisdom, and have a long tradition of consulting with a wise person, or several wise people, while always remaining the final judge of the opinions they hear. This contrasts markedly with, for example, the Irish, for whom the priest was supposed to be the final judge. The development of psychotherapy has been strongly influenced by these Jewish values. Because history and tradition are highly valued in Jewish culture, intergenerational approaches make good psychological sense to them, unless they have become cut off from their culture or their family. The first problem in therapy may come when the patient questions the therapist's credentials. Although the therapist may perceive this as confrontation or criticism, it may instead reflect the high value Jews place on education and success, as well as their need to be sure they are receiving the best care.

Jewish verbal skill and willingness to talk about troubles and feelings are important assets, but these too can lead to problems (Herz & Rosen, 1982; Zuk, 1978). Families may get so preoccupied with the need to analyze and understand their experience that at times they become immobilized. Jewish patients frequently wish to appear intellectual and psychologically aware, which may make their articulation a difficulty as well as a strength in therapy. The need to appear insightful, interesting, and successful, can in the extreme make them unable to stop analysing their experience or do anything without being preoccupied with what they are accomplishing. The solutions offered by traditional therapy at times compound these problems. Therapists may need to find such ways around the tendency to talk or analyze, as structural techniques or those of strategic therapy. However, therapists should be warned against applying solutions that might seem simplistic. Jewish clients will generally prefer more complex, sophisticated interventions. Behavior modification techniques, for example, might be very useful, but may be viewed as superficial, covering up the "real" underlying problem, which, they fear, will resurface elsewhere.

The Jewish tradition of valuing education and learning has a history dating back millenia and has produced an unprecedented culture in artistic and intellectual achievements. Jews generally lived in situations of oppression and were not allowed to own land or have the right to property, and thus it was natural that they came to value those strengths that could not be taken from them but that could be transferred from one context to another, if they were forced to flee from their homes.

Jewish families generally show much more concern for their children's emotional, intellectual, and physical well-being throughout all stages of their development than do other groups. The non-Jewish therapist may fail to appreciate the meaning of Jewish concern for children's success and upward mobility. Raising successful children is a major responsibility of the parents, particularly the mother. Underachievement or more serious problems are often felt to reflect not only on the family, but also on the ethnic group as a whole. Parents are expected to make great sacrifices for their children, and when children grow up they are expected to repay their parents in "naches," a special pleasure one gets only from the success and happiness of one's children. Non-Jewish therapists may be puzzled by the extent of parental upset when their children do not provide them with such rewards. An obvious contrasting value can be seen in WASPs, who raise their children to be independent and to leave home. Whereas WASPs expect their children to be productive and a credit to the family, they do not expect to "kvell" or experience personal pleasure in their children's accomplishments.

Jewish mothers, at times a harshly stereotyped group, reflect many positive aspects of Jewish culture. Mothers have been the ones primarily responsible for the education and development of children. Their success in this realm is overwhelming, as generations of successful Jewish doctors, lawyers, artists, businessmen, and other professionals attest. But until recently they were unable to fulfill their dreams for themselves directly. Their intensity was turned primarily toward their children. The recent opportunities for women to succeed have offered a chance for Jewish women, who had already internalized the values of success and education, to flourish in their own right. Their success reveals the potential that until now has been invested in Jewish children, especially male children.

Jewish families show strong concern for the ebb and flow of life at all stages. This is indicated by the importance they place on life-cycle rituals, which reflects their awareness of the complexity of the transitions at all phases of life. For example, Jewish mourning rituals have several phases. The burial occurs as soon as possible after the death, if possible, within 24 hours, followed by a week of "sitting shiva," when friends and extended family come to share in the mourning. After a year has passed, family members again gather for the "unveiling," which marks the end of the mourning period, although yearly prayers are still said after this. The emphasis placed on the bar mitzvah, which marks the transition of children into adulthood, reflects the value of the transition to serious adult learning and work experiences in Jewish culture. It is important for the therapist to recognize the underlying power of these transitions for Jewish families and to help them to refocus their energies on the important underlying values if they get stuck on the more superficial aspects of the rituals (Friedman, 1980).

Another issue that may be particularly misunderstood by non-Jewish therapists is the meaning of suffering in Jewish families. Sharing suffering may be an expression of loyalty to those who have suffered in the past. It is part of their heritage, to be experienced and shared rather than overcome. The legacy of centuries of anti-Semitism and threatened annihilation have created a history of suffering and loss and an ever-present threat of renewed suffering. In this context Jewish people have developed a comfort in open sharing of suffering experience with kin. This attitude contrasts sharply with that of the Irish, who have responded to their own history of oppression with a very different response. They believe they should suffer alone and in silence. African-Americans, a group with a history of extreme oppression, tend neither to suffer alone nor to share their discussion of their suffering, but to transform it through music, prayer, and spiritual transformation of their common experiences into an emphasis on hoped for deliverance in the future. All these groups contrast with WASPs who, as the dominant group have not surprisingly evolved the belief that suffering is to be overcome by personal fortitude, hard work, and good intentions.

Conflicts and hostility are generally expressed directly in Jewish families. In fact, a therapist from a more restrained culture may be uncomfortable with the intensity of Jewish criticism and verbal aggression (Herz & Rosen, 1982). Conflicts or cutoffs with the extended family often occur over money or loyalty and may at times be extremely bitter. A child's marriage to a non-Jew may precipitate a cutoff or even the parents sitting *shiva* for that child, as if he or she, by marrying out of the religion had died. Preservation of the Jewish heritage (not necessarily religious practices) is often felt to be fundamental to their sense of identity. Intermarriage, which is occurring with increasing frequency, especially among Jewish males, creates a great sadness and pain for parents. There is considerable pressure for Jews to identify with the group, and if family members reject their cultural background, it may create devastation for others in the family. These problems are naturally more prominent in the Northeast than elsewhere in the United States, where the percentage of Jews is much larger and the cultural patterns less pronounced (Sanua, 1978).

Jewish families have a number of strengths that are important in therapy. One is their humor—their ability to make fun of their own situation—which offers a release and perspective on themselves and their foibles. Generally, they also have an openness to new ideas and new ways (they are foremost among American ethnic groups in their willingness to explore new ideas). Further strengths are their belief in philanthropy and good works for the benefit of others and the esteem for family and extended family relationships. Although Jews may at times be caught up in deeply ambivalent attitudes about their own ethnicity, their cultural ties are a profound part of their heritage and their identity, perhaps more so than for other groups. This may be because they experience their 4,000-year history of living in the diaspora as foreigners in other cultures, always under the threat of expulsion or persecution, as a continuous life in exile. Bringing them back in touch with their cultural roots may be a particularly rich experience for them.

ITALIAN-AMERICAN FAMILIES

Poverty and hopes of a better life led to large-scale Italian immigration to the United States in the late 19th and early 20th centuries. By now they are the fifth largest American ethnic group. Since southern Italians compose by far the largest population of Italian-Americans (80%), the comments here will be limited to this group. Northern Italians are a more industrialized and different group culturally (Nelli, 1980)

Although all cultures value the family, Italians give it higher priority than other groups do. (For more details on Italian families and therapy see

Rotunno & McGoldrick, 1982.) Family life is their primary orientation. It is seen as one's greatest resource and protection against all troubles. For this reason, family intervention would seem to be the treatment of choice. But Italians tend to distrust outsiders. Thus, gaining acceptance with the family is the first hurdle in dealing with Italians. The therapist must not take their mistrust personally. Everyone outside the family is mistrusted until they prove themselves loyal—and loyalty to the family is everything to an Italian.

The basic difficulties for Italian families relate to differentiation and/or separation from the family. The family provides such an intense and wide network of support that developing away from it is a major problem. This tendency is in direct contrast to core values of the dominant culture in the United States, which emphasizes independence, individualism, and personal achievement over affiliation.

Anyone who tries to break the close bonds of an Italian family collides with Italian cultural norms. Therapy with Italian families involves not so much helping them deal with any particular emotional issue as facilitating the renegotiation of system boundaries, which tend to rigidify, with the holding of insiders (family members) in, and outsiders (everyone else) out. Within the family context itself, all emotions are viewed as understandable. Italians do not have the problem with "disallowed" feelings that some cultural groups such as the Irish do, although there are clear values for right and wrong behavior, based primarily on how such behavior affects the family.

Historically, the family in Italy became the anchor amidst the constant flux of foreigners, changing governments, and natural disasters (floods, volcanos, and famines). Through the centuries, Italians have learned to define themselves not by association with Italy, but by their association with their families first and by their immediate neighbors, or *paisani*, second. Allegiance to the family has come to surpass all other loyalties, and separation from the family is tantamount to spiritual death. Education and occupation are seen as secondary to the security, affection, and sense of relatedness the family has to offer.

Italians have learned to take maximum advantage of the present. They have a tremendous ability for intense enjoyment and experience in eating, celebrating, fighting, and loving. They take great pleasure in festivals and fiestas. Church rituals have always been prized for their pageantry, spectacle, and value in fostering family celebrations and rites of passage.

The relatively low utilization of mental health facilities by Italians reflects their tendency to turn first to the family for support. Although the enmeshment of Italian families certainly creates difficulties and conflicts for them, it also provides much that family members from less supportive cultural environments lack. They have one of the strongest informal community networks of any ethnic group, and are less likely to leave the neighborhood in order to get ahead. When they do break away, it is often very stressful for both the individuals involved and their families. When cut off from the family, Italians are much more likely to become symptomatic. For example, a study of Italian-American patients in Boston revealed that rates of schizophrenia and manic-depressive disorders varied inversely with the number of Italians living in their particular neighborhood (Mintz & Schwartz, 1976).

There is virtually no such thing as a separate nuclear family unit in Italian culture. *La famiglia* includes, first, all blood relatives and all relatives by marriage. Beyond this come the *comparaggio* or godparents, an important kinship network established in conjunction with rites of passage, and then the *gumbares* (old friends and neighbors). Close and intense contacts are maintained with a wide circle of family and friends. It is not unusual for adults to maintain daily contact with their siblings and parents throughout their lives. Even if they move apart, frequent telephone calls maintain close ties.

It is essential in working with Italian-American families to learn the whereabouts of and level of contact with members of the extended family. Usually they are in the same neighborhood, if not on the same block, or even in the same building. This contrasts sharply with habits of WASPs, who raise their children to be independent and self-sufficient above all else, and who think themselves failures if their children do no leave home on schedule. Italians raise their children to be mutually supportive and to contribute to the family. Separation from the family is not expected.

The mutual support and complementarity of roles between husband and wife relate to their obligations to the entire family of at least three generations and not to marital intimacy. The father tends to be the undisputed head of the Italian household, and he is often authoritarian and rigid in his rule setting and guidelines for behavior. A kind of benevolent despot, he usually takes his responsibility to provide for his family very seriously. Any situation that erodes his authority is likely to have a pronounced negative impact on the Italian father. Since it is in the nature of adolescents to question parental authority, the adolescence of his children may be particularly difficult for him.

The Italian mother, on the other hand, is the heart of the home (Gambino, 1974). Although yielding authority to the father, she traditionally assumes total control of the effective realm of the family. She is the family's emotional sustenance. Her life centers on domestic activities, and she is expected to receive her primary pleasure from nurturing and servicing her family. Her personal needs are expected to take second place to those of her husband. In exchange, she is offered protection and security from all outside pressure or threat. This pattern is not usually perceived as a problem by either partner, although to an outsider it appears to reinforce an extreme degree of dependence. The mother in an Italian family may, for example, not drive or even go out alone, but this may not be labeled a problem by her or her husband or children, who take driving her around for granted.

There is marked role differentiation between sons and daughters in Italian families. Although both are permitted to leave home when they marry, sons are given considerably greater latitude prior to marriage. A bit of acting out is expected, even subtly encouraged, as a measure of manliness. Proficiency in the sexual domain is important, not only to fulfill the masculine image, but also to exemplify a sense of mastery in interpersonal relations, which is a core Italian value. Although social skills are considered important for females as well, their behavior is subject to closer scrutiny by their fathers and brothers. They are much more restricted socially; in particular, they are taught to eschew personal achievement in favor of respect and service to their parents, their husbands, and their children. Traditionally, Italian males have been trained to be understated in their emotional reactions. But within the family they may at times be impulsive, loud, volatile, or even violent without sanction from others. This has nothing to do with embarrassment about expressing feelings, as it does with WASP or Irish males. Rather, it reflects the historical need to protect oneself against dangerous exposure to outsiders. Women, on the other hand, are allowed to express their emotions freely, but are kept out of "men's business."

Italians tend to dramatize their experiences. Similarly, they may exaggerate their symptoms (Zborowski, 1969; Zola, 1966) and are characteristically colorful and dramatic in their talk. Their expressiveness may be overpowering to a therapist from a more restrained culture, in which, for example, powerful expressions of hostility would be interpreted literally. For Italians, words give expression to the emotion of the moment and are not taken so seriously. Another difficulty for a non-Italian therapist may be the way to deal with family "secrets." Whereas Italian families may appear to talk openly and engagingly, even in the initial contact, sharing real family secrets is an entirely different matter. The existence of the secret may be puzzling to the therapist, since otherwise the family seems to talk openly about all kinds of issues, including sex, death, hostility, and/or antisocial behavior. Often the content of the secret in itself is not important. Secrets may seem to be aimed more at marking and preserving the boundaries of the system—clarifying who is inside and who is not. Therapists must deal delicately with secrets, remembering the sense of betrayal families will feel if their boundaries are crossed.

Therapists may also be frustrated by the Italian family's demand for immediate solutions. If a therapist operates on the assumption that change occurs through long evaluation and discussion of problems, Italian families will be exceedingly difficult to help. If, on the other hand, the therapist focuses on mobilizing the family's own natural supports (as noted, this is the preferred Italian solution) and does not try to replace this orientation with one that stresses the therapy as primary, there is a much better chance of constructive intervention.

AFRICAN-AMERICAN FAMILIES

About 12% of Americans in the United States are of African background (Holt, 1980). It would be a serious mistake to think of them as an ethnic group like any other or to assume their problems could be solved like those of other ethnic groups. However degrading the life conditions of early white immigrant groups, they were not brought here as slaves. The combination of the slavery experience and racism, which focuses most intensely on Blacks, has put them at an extreme disadvantage in this society. The ongoing impact of institutionalized racism and discrimination is a continuing and pervasive aspect of the lives of all Black families and cannot be overestimated when one is treating them therapeutically. Even without leaving their homes— just by turning on the radio or television—Black Americans are exposed daily to the continuing pernicious effects of racism.

We cannot understand the inner context of a Black family without looking at the context of the larger system: less access to medical care, housing, education, employment, political power, and a general sense of powerlessness and of not belonging to the larger society. All these will have their impact on African-American families, even across class lines. They influence how parents raise their children—knowing they will be exposed to hatred and discrimination. It influences how women respond to men—with awareness that whatever sexism they experience in their relationships, they are always cognizant of the particularly destructive ways that racism is directed against Black males.

Much has been written about the characteristics of Black family structure and the socioeconomic forces behind these family patterns. Much useless debate has been generated about the "pathological" nature of Black families. Many whites, ignoring racism, have subtly or more directly accused African-Americans of creating their own dysfunction. African-Americans, not surprisingly, have tried to compensate with positive counter-descriptions, but more recently they have recognized that they must speak out about both the positive and the negative—in spite of fears of misperception of the information by white society. The escalation of devastation that is occcurring to the poor in Black communities must be addressed. The imbalance in the statistics for Black families in poverty are overwhelming. Whereas 8% of white families live below the poverty line, the percentage for Black families is 29%. Whereas among the elderly 8% of white men live below the poverty line, 32% of elderly Black men and 42% of elderly Black women live in poverty. Seventy percent of children of Black single parents are being raised in poverty. Over 50% of all Black students are in school in the 12 largest inner city districts, where they have virtually no chance of being prepared to succeed in our society (Hale-Benson, 1986; Glick, 1988; McAdoo, 1988; Billingsley, 1988).

Religion has been the major formal institution in our society available to Blacks for support. It is both a social and a personal resource. It has been a major source of status and community support for Black families. Most African-Americans will turn to religion as a solution to their problems before they think of therapy. It is always important to check out the role that religion plays in the family's life, as it may be a powerful spiritual and emotional resource.

In spite of the severe disadvantages of Black families in our culture, they may be closer to accomplishing flexibility in male-female roles and relationships that many families have been striving for in recent years (Gluck et al., 1980). There appears to be more role flexibility between Black spouses. There are also indications that Black fathers may take a bigger part in house keeping, child-rearing activities, and the nurturing of children, than white fathers (Allen, 1978; Axelson, 1970; Kunkell & Kennard, 1971; Lewis, 1975). Although sex appears to be less a source of marital tension than with many other groups, couples may play out the combined effects of patriarchy and racism because they cannot successfully deal with these issues outside their homes. Since slave times, Black men have often been forced to be invisible. In slave birth records only the mother and the master were mentioned, and even today, it may be adaptive for a Black man to remain invisible to white institutions. His abuse of his wife may reflect his total powerlessness in the wider world and her contempt or disparagement of him may reflect her internalization of the larger culture's negative image of Black men. Much more research needs to be done on both the positive and negative aspects of couple relationships as well as on many other aspects of Black family life that differ from the patterns of other groups.

Black families have traditionally lived much more embedded in a wide network of extended kin and community, a pattern which appears rooted in both African traditions of strong community and in their slave history, which systematically broke up biological families and forced Blacks to turn to a wider network for support.

Black families develop strong kinship networks that serve as their major resource in times of trouble. Among lower-class African-Americans, economic factors often militate against the establishment and maintenance of nuclear family units. These stresses make Blacks more vulnerable to illness and death than whites are (e.g. Black males have a mortality rate twice that of white males). Extended households provide the most stable and enduring form of family unit for any family under stress. Kinship networks, including both family and close friends, share resources, household tasks, and housing, in a system characterized by mutual obligation (Stack, 1974; Hines & Boyd-Franklin, 1982; Boyd-Franklin, 1989).

The numbers of Black families headed by women are increasing to about the same proportions as two-parent families. Like the Irish, women in Black families tend to be strong and independent, and their sphere of activity often goes beyond the home to work situations and community activities. Given the economic and social pressures on their families and the special pressure of racism frequently directed against Black men, women have generally been employed outside the home to help support the family.

We are currently experiencing an epidemic number of Black teen parents, who generally do not marry and often leave their children to be cared for by their mothers. Abortion seems less common in Black communities and formal adoption was never really an option for parents who could not raise their children themselves, as it was for whites. Instead African-Americans have tended to rely on family and friends for necessary support for children, who were always viewed as an important resource in the Black community. As the grandmother puts it in *Raisin in the Sun*:

> It seems like God didn't see fit to give the Black folks much in this world except dreams. But he did give us children—to make those dreams seem worth while. (Hansberry, 1958, p. 65)

Black families consider children extremely important. Other adults often readily assume childcare responsiblilites, if a mother cannot handle them. Extended kin generally take a more active role in the socialization of Black children than is true with white children. Black families tend to deemphasize sex differences in their socializaiton of children.

Disciplining of children is often strict and direct, a pragmatic practice necessary for survival—sometimes misjudged by therapists not familiar with Black culture. Because they rarely have the support of larger social structures, Black families have great difficulty protecting their children against prejudice, crime, or drugs. No Black family, regardless of class is very removed from the poverty and loss that are so much the accompaniment of centuries of prejudice, mistreatment and disadvantage. When Black adolescents rebel, they are much more likely than whites are to associate with peers who are engaged in serious antisocial behavior. They have fewer nondangerous options for acting-out adolescent rebellion, and their families have very few societal supports to protect them from antisocial influences. African-American families do not have the same cushion or safety net that families in the dominant culture have to protect them against adversity. They are unlikely to find protection in the law or in our social institutions that are supposed to protect those in need—the school system, the healthcare system, the job market. As Elaine Pinderhughes describes it, families may push their children hard because failure will be so much more devastating than it is for other groups (Pinderhughes, 1992).

In therapy, it is essential for the therapist to take into account the realistic pressures on Black families, especially Black youths, even when their families have many financial resources. It appears that children are especially vulnerable in about 4th or 5th grade, in adolescence, and in young adulthood—all times when their inability to achieve the American Dream put them at great risk for taking a disastrous downward turn. When social pressures have led to underorganization of the family (Aponte, 1976; Hines, 1989), children often either prematurely take on adult roles or fail to develop the discipline necessary for adult functioning. In such situations, "talking" therapy is unlikely to be effective or acceptable for Black families. Structural therapy to strengthen family organization and add to its flexibility is probably the most effective model.

Initially, African-Americans are likely to view therapy within the context of other traditional dealings with white institutions, which have basically never served their needs; a healthy mistrust or even paranoia can be taken for granted (Cobbs, 1968). In the early stages of therapy, they may keep their distance, participate in the meetings with some reluctance, and offer minimal information. Their lack of response could look like the characteristic inarticulateness of the Irish in therapy, who are uncomfortable, embarrassed, and guilt-ridden about their feelings. However, African-Americans are quite different from the Irish emotionally. They are likely to be realistic, emotionally aware, and comfortable with the full range of their feelings (Sanua, 1960). Their withholding or reticence has more to do with the specific context of therapy than with discomfort about their feelings or about communication in general.

Initially, the therapist needs to help the family deal with whatever has brought the family to therapy and promote positive links with any resources or institutions that are, or should be, involved with the family. Beyond this, strengthening the family's sense of ethnic identity and connectedness may be a crucial part of therapy. It has been shown that having a positive sense of their cultural identity is even more important for African-Americans than for white families, for obvious reasons. Genograms can be an important resource for the therapist to help contextualize the family. However, because of the painful legacy in most African-American family backgrounds and their need for secrecy in most contexts, the therapist should be sensitive to timing in asking families to discuss their history. They should be taken only after trust with the family has been developed. Understanding and supporting the family's network may be extremely important in fostering their ability to mobilize resources and feel supported. Their strength in having been able to survive is one of their most remarkable resources and should be highlighted and built on to help them overcome the countervailing "victim system," a psychological disempowerment, which is a common outgrowth of their painful history of discrimination (Pinderhughes, 1982).

CONCLUSION

I have tried to articulate different possibilities and patterns of a variety of groups, and how these make psychological sense within each context. I have perhaps exaggerated the patterns for particular groups, hoping to clarify different world views to raise consciousness about the multiple possibilities in a society where the dominant values have passed for truth and normality (McGoldrick, 1982b). What we have found is that ethnic patterns are retained much longer than we consciously realize, even though they are, of course, modified by complex socioeconomic forces, ethnic intermarriage, geographic mobility, and the rapidly changing patterns of the family life cycle. The result is that there is less continuity than ever before between the demands on current families and the patterns of past generations. Thus it is easy to lose all sense of connection with what has come before in your family, and this can be a serious loss. Although we have the technology in tapes, film, photographs and video for transmission of much more of the culture from one generation to the other than ever, families often spend much more time watching television than sharing the family and group stories that have for centuries been a primary wellspring of group and personal identity. We are living a great deal longer than human beings ever lived before, so we have much more potential for connecting with other generations of our family, and at the same time, as a culture we have become so geographically mobile there is often a great deal of disconnection.

But as we are moving toward a recognition of cultural diversity, I am concerned about what seems to be a romanticizing of culture. Even as we learn to appreciate cultural differences and the limitations of any one perspective, it makes no sense to say that just because a culture proclaims a certain value or belief that it is sacrosanct. We must not move away from responsibility for the complex ethical stance required of us in our clinical work. All cultural practices are not equally ethical. Every intervention we make is political. We must not use notions of neutrality or deconstruction to shy away from committing ourselves to the values we believe in. We must have the courage of our convictions, even while realizing that we can never be too sure that the way we see things is the "correct" way. Unfortunately, as it is now, violence is presented in our culture as entertainment. Abusive relationships are the subjects of sitcoms. Many religions still preach: "Spare the rod and spoil the child," which passes violence on from generation to generation. We need to transform our world by redrawing the map and rewriting the rules and values. As Riane Eisler has expressed it in her call for a new world order:

> The issue is not and never has been Arab versus Jew, American versus Iraqi, Lithuanian versus Russian, white against Black—or man against woman. Rather, the problem is a way of structuring interpersonal and international relations based on domination, violence, and conquest that today threatens our very survival. (p.10)

REFERENCES

Allen, W. R. (1978). Black family research in the United States: A review, assessment and extension. *Journal of Comparative Family Studies, 9,* 166–188.

Angelou, M. (1986). *All God's children need traveling shoes.* New York: Vintage.

Aponte, H. J. (1976). Underorganization in the poor family. In P. J. Guerin (Ed.), *Family therapy.* New York: Gardner Press.

Axelson, L. J. (1970). The working wife: Differences in perception among Negro and white males. *Journal of Marriage and the Family, 32,* 457–464.

Billingsley, A. (1976, January). *The family and cultural pluralism.* Address at Baltimore Conference on Ethnicity and Social Welfare. New York: Institute on Pluralism and Group Identity.

Billingsley, A. (1988). *Black families in white America.* New York: Simon & Schuster.

Boyd-Franklin, N. (1989). *Black families in therapy: A multisystems approach.* New York: Guilford Press.

Diner, H. R. (1983). *Erin's daughters in America.* Baltimore: Johns Hopkins University Press.

Eisler, R. (1988). The chalice and the blade. New York: Harper & Row

Erdrich, Louise, Dorris, Michael. (1992). *The Crown of Columbus.* New York: Harper & Row.

Falicov, C. (1980). Cultural variations in the family life cycle. In E. A. Carter & M. McGoldrick (Eds.), *The family life cycle: A framework for family therapy.* New York: Gardner Press.

Fallows, M. A. (1979). *Irish Americans: Identity and assimilation.* Englewood Cliffs, N.J.: Prentice-Hall.

Friedman, E. (1980). Systems and ceremonies. In E. A. Carter & M. McGoldrick (Eds.), *The family life cycle: A framework for family therapy.* New York: Gardner Press.

Gambino, R. (1974). *Blood of my blood: The dilemma of Italian-Americans.* New York: Doubleday.

Garcia-Preto, N. (1982). Puerto Rican families. In M. McGoldrick, J. K. Pearce, & J. Giordano (Eds.). *Ethnicity and family therapy.* New York: Guilford Press.

Garcia-Preto, N. (1990). Hispanic mothers. *Journal of Feminist Family Therapy, 2*(2), 15–22.

Giamatti, A. B. (1989). *Take time for paradise. Americans and their games.* New York: Summit.

Glick, P. C. (1988). Demographic pictures of Black families. In H. P. McAdoo (Ed.), (1988). *Black families.* (2nd ed.). Newbury Park, CA: Sage Publications.

Gluck, N. R., Dannefer, E., & Milea, K. (1980). Women in families. In E. A. Carter & M. McGoldrick (Eds.), *The family life cycle: A framework for family therapy.* New York: Gardner Press.

Goren, A. (1980). Jews. In S. Thernstrom (Ed.), *Harvard encyclopedia of American ethnic groups.* Cambridge: Harvard University Press.

Greeley, A. (1969). *Why can't they be like us?* New York: Institute of Human Relations Press.

Hale-Benson, J. E. (1986). *Black children: Their roots, culture and learning styles: Rev. Ed.* Baltimore: Johns Hopkins University Press.

Hansberry, L. (1958). *Raisin in the sun.* New York: Penguin.

Herz, F., & Rosen, E. (1982). Jewish families. In M. McGoldrick, J. K. Pearce, & J. Giordano (Eds.). *Ethnicity and family therapy.* New York: Guilford Press.

Hines, P. (1989). The family life cycle of poor Black families. In B. Carter & M. McGoldrick, (Eds.), *The changing family life cycle.* Boston: Allyn & Bacon.

Hines, P. (1990). African–American mothers. *Journal of Feminist Family Therapy, 2*(2), 23–32.

Hines, P., & Boyd-Franklin, N. (1982). African-American families. In M. McGoldrick, J. K. Pearce, & J. Giordano (Eds.). *Ethnicity and family therapy.* New York: Guilford Press.

Hines, P., Garcia-Preto, N., McGoldrick, M., Almeida, R., & Weltman, S. (1992). Intergenerational relationships across cultures. *Families in Society, 73*(6), whole volume.

Jalali, B. (1982). Iranian families. In M. McGoldrick, J. K. Pearce, & J. Giordano (Eds.), *Ethnicity and family therapy.* New York: Guilford Press.

Kiev, A. (1972). *Transcultural psychiatry.* New York: Free Press.

Kleinman, A. M. (1975). Explanatory models in health care relationships. In *Health of the family (National Council for International Health Symposium).* Washington DC National Council for International Health.

Kunkell, P., & Kennard, S. (1971). *Spout Spring: A Black community.* Chicago: Rand McNally.

Lewis, D. (1975). The black family: Socialization and sex roles. *Phylon, 26,* 221–237.

McAdoo, H. (1977). Family therapy in the Black Community. *American Journal of Orthopsychiatry, 47,* 75–79.

McAdoo, H. P. (Ed.). (1988). *Black families* (2nd ed.) Newbury Park, CA: Sage Publications.

McGoldrick, M. (1982a). Irish Americans. In M. McGoldrick, J. K. Pearce, & J. Giordano (Eds.), *Ethnicity and family therapy.* New York: Guilford Press.

McGoldrick, M. (1982b) Ethnicity and family therapy: An overview. In M. McGoldrick, J. K. Pearce, & J. Giordano (Eds.), *Ethnicity and family therapy.* New York: Guilford Press.

McGoldrick, M., Almeida, Hines, P. M., Garcia-Preto, N., Rosen, E., & Lee, E. (1991). Mourning in different cultures. In F. Walsh & M. McGoldrick (Eds.), *Living beyond loss.* New York: Norton.

McGoldrick, M., Braverman, L., Garcia-Preto, N., Hines, P. M., Almeida, R., Schmidt, M., Taylor, J., Koslosky, M., Theresa G., & Lee, E. (1990). Ethnicity and mothers. *Journal of Feminist Family Therapy, 2*(2), 1–70.

McGoldrick, M., & Garcia-Preto, N. (1984). Ethnic intermarriage. *Family Process. 23*(3), 347–362.

McGoldrick, M., Garcia-Preto, N., Hines, P. M., & Lee, E. (1988). Ethnicity and women. In M. McGoldrick, C. Anderson, & F. Walsh (Eds.), *Women in families.* New York: Norton.

McGoldrick, M., Giordano, J., & Pearce, J. K. (1981). Family therapy with Irish Americans. *Family Process, 20.*

McGoldrick, M., Pearce, J. K., & Giordano, J. (Eds.) (1982). *Ethnicity and family therapy.* New York: Guilford Press.

McGoldrick, M., & Giordano, J. (Eds.) (in press). *Ethnicity and family therapy* (2nd ed.). New York: Guilford Press.

McGoldrick, M., & Rohrbaugh, M. (1987). Researching ethnic stereotypes. *Family Process, 26*(1), 89–99.

Malzberg, B. (1963). Mental disease among the Irish-born and native white of Irish parentage in New York State, 1949–1951. *Mental Hygiene, 47,* 284–295.

Midelfort, C. F. & Midelfort, H. C. (1982). Scandinavian families. In M. McGoldrick, J. K. Pearce, & J. Giordano (Eds.), *Ethnicity and family therapy.* New York: Guilford.

Mintz, N., & Schwartz, D. Urban ecology and psychosis: Community factors in the incidence of schizophrenia and manic depression among Italians in Greater Boston. *International Journal of Social Psychiatry, 10,* 101–118.

Myerhoff, B. (1978). *Number our days.* New York: Simon & Schuster.

Nelli, H. S. (1980). Italians. In S. Thernstrom (Ed.), *Harvard encyclopedia of American ethnic groups*. Cambridge: Harvard University Press, 1980.

Pinderhughes, E. (1982). Afro-Americans and the victim system. In M. McGoldrick, J. K. Pearce, & J. Giordano (Eds.), *Ethnicity and family therapy*. New York: Guilford.

Rabkin, J., & Struening, E. (1976). *Ethnicity, social class and mental illness in New York City*. New York: Institute on Pluralism and Group Identity, 1976.

Roberts, B., & Myers, J. K. (1954). Religion national origin, immigration and mental illness. *American Journal of Psychiatry, 110,* 759–764.

Robeson, P. (1958). *Here I stand*. Boston: Beacon Press.

Rotunno, M., & McGoldrick, M.(1982) Italian families. In M. McGoldrick, J. K. Pearce, & J. Giordano (Eds.), *Ethnicity and family therapy*. New York: Guilford.

Sluzki, C. (1979). Migration and family conflict. *Family Process, 18,* 379–390.

Stack, C. (1974). *All our kin: strategies for survival in a Black community*. New York: Harper & Row, 1974.

Stoeckle, J. Zola, I. K., & Davidson, G. (1964). The quality and significance of psychological distress in medical patients. *Journal of Chronic Disease, 17,* 959–970.

Zborowski, M. (1969). *People in pain*. San Francisco: Jossey-Bass.

Zborowski, M. (1972). *Life is with people*. New York: Schocken Books.

Zborowski, M., & Herzog, E. (1952). *Life is with people*. New York: Schocken Books.

Zola, I. K. (1963). Problems of communications, diagnosis and patient care: The interplay of patient, physician and clinic organization. *Journal of Medical Education, 38,* 829–838.

Zola, I. K. (1966). Culture and symptoms: An analysis of patients' presenting complaints. *American Sociological Review, 5,* 141–155.

Zuk, G. H. (1978). A therapist's perspective on Jewish family values. *Journal of Marriage and Family Counseling, 4,* 101–111.

RACE, CLASS, AND POVERTY

Nancy Boyd-Franklin

IN ORDER TO EVALUATE WHAT is "normal" in the development of any family, clinicians must explore the larger social context in which the family lives. Race and class are two of the most complex and emotionally loaded issues in this country. And for poor, inner-city, African-American families, the day-to-day realities of racism, discrimination, classism, poverty, homelessness, violence, crime, and drugs create forces that continually threaten the family's survival. Many clinicians who have no framework with which to view these complicated interrelationships become overwhelmed. The purpose of this chapter is to provide a framework that will be helpful in understanding and working with these families.

The first part of the chapter explores the complexity of these issues for African-American families in this country. The second part explores the issues that race, class, and poverty raise for family therapists.

Two cautions are in order. First, discussing race, class, and poverty in one chapter necessitates a less thorough treatment of each than warranted. A second caveat is that race, class, and poverty are not monolithic constructs that apply unilaterally. Race, for example, has many different levels of meaning for African-American individuals and families in the United States. Class as an issue is equally complex and not merely a socioeconomic distinction. For many African-Americans, class or socioeconomic level does not foreordain value system: For example, a family classified as "poor" because of income may have "middle-class" values. Also, a "culture of poverty"—coping mechanisms necessary for survival "on the streets"—may exist in families. Finally, the societal realities of racism, oppression, and classism contribute to perpetuate the "victim system" (Pinderhughes, 1982) that many African-American families experience.

RACISM AND OPPRESSION

It is important to explore the societal context of life for African-American families. Historically, they share a common African heritage as well as the degradation of slavery in the United States. In order for Americans of European ancestry to have justified slavery, persons of African-American descent had to be viewed as subhuman. Thus, for African-Americans, skin color became a "mark of oppression." This oppression of slavery—and later segregation and discrimination—contributed to create a sense of rage that persists to this day in many African-Americans.

Slavery created a legacy for white people as well. Grier and Cobbs (1968) have indicated that the consequences of slavery were as evident in the children of slavemasters as they were in the children of slaves. Race continues to be an extremely conflicted issue for many white Americans. For some, the subject elicits emotions of guilt, rage, or fear. The increasing numbers of bias-related incidents in this country reveal that these old wounds remain an indelible part of the American psyche (Grier & Cobbs, 1968).

THE ISSUE OF RACE

For African-Americans, the concept of race has many levels of meaning. On the one hand, it identifies those of African ancestry and implies a shared origin. Often it applies to shared physical characteristics such as skin color, hair texture, and appearance. However, African-Americans as a race present in many different skin colors, and appearances because individuals may have various mixtures of ancestry including Native American and European.

Pinderhughes (1989) has shown that as "over time, race has acquired a social meaning . . . via the mechanism of stereotyping. . . . status assignment based on skin color identity has evolved into complex social structures that promote a power differential between Whites and various people of color" (p. 71). Hopps (1982) has stated that "although many forms of exclusion and discrimination exist in this country, none is so deeply rooted, persistent or intractable as that based on color" (Hopps, 1982, p. 3).

For this reason, many African-American families' perceptions of the world—including self-identity, racial pride, child rearing, educational and school-related experiences, job or employment opportunities or lack of them, financial security or the lack of it, as well as treatment in interpersonal encounters and male–female relationships—are screened through the lens of the racial experience (Boyd-Franklin, 1989; Grier & Cobbs, 1968).

IMPACT OF RACE ON CHILD REARING

Many African-American parents, aware of the degrading messages their children receive from society, particularly through the school systems, make a conscious effort to instill a sense of racial pride and strong positive identity in their children. A further difficulty in childrearing for African-Americans is combating pervasive negative images, particularly in the media.

Thus, within such a context, "normal family development" requires many African-American parents to educate their children in the realities of racism and discrimination and prepare them for the negative messages they will encounter. African-American parents whom I have interviewed have frequently stated that they feel they have to be more "vigilant" in order to raise an African-American child today. However, parents must walk a fine line between giving children the tools with which to understand racism so they do not internalize the process and instilling in their children a belief that they can achieve despite the odds and overcome racism without becoming consumed with rage and bitterness. This is a complex task and a difficult developmental journey for a family or an individual to navigate.

RACISM, THE INVISIBILITY SYNDROME, AND GENDER ISSUES

There are many levels of complications of racism that African-Americans must contend with in the process of "normal family development." The legacy of slavery and oppression has contributed to create a fear in American society of African-American males that begins at a very early age. A.J. Franklin (1992) has referred to an "invisibility factor," a paradoxical process by which the high skin-color visibility of African-American men causes society to view them with fear and, as a consequence, to treat them as if they are "invisible."

African-American male children who may begin school being perceived as "cute" by teachers, at a very young age (7, 8, or 9) are viewed as a threat. Kunjufu (1985) in his book *Countering the Conspiracy to Destroy Black Boys* discusses the "fourth grade failure syndrome" in which teachers (and therapists) become intimidated by African-American male children and begin to label these children as aggressive, hyperactive, and as failures.

African-American families are thus in a double-bind, particularly when rearing male children. Although racism clearly exists for both male and female African-American children, society tends to be more punitive toward and restrictive of male children. Raising sons to be assertive risks that society will see them as aggressive, the consequences of which have many levels of impact, including labeling within the school system, high drop-out and unemployment rates, overrepresentation in the prison system, and, most tragically, early death on the streets.

CLASS

Social class is extremely complicated in the United States, particularly when coupled with issues of race. Many African-American families find that their experience of class distinctions within their own communities are very different from the class categories applied in the broader American society. For example, there are many poor and working-class African-American families who are considered "middle class" within their own communities because of their values, aspirations, and expectations for their children. On the other hand, class status is very precarious for many African-Americans. In times of economic recession, African-Americans are particularly vulnerable to layoffs as they often fall victim to "last hired, first fired" policies.

THE "CLASS NOT RACE" MYTH

There has long been a tendency in the social sciences as well as in the mental health field to minimize the importance of race and to focus more on class variables. A prominent sociologist William Julius Wilson in his book *The Declining Significance of Race* (1980), has argued that whereas race and racism were factors in the past in creating the poverty of African-Americans, the opportunities of the late 1960s and 1970s made middle-class status available to many African-Americans.

However, Wilson incorrectly concludes that because there now exists an African-American middle class, class has replaced race as the salient distinction, with the vast numbers of African-American families who are trapped in the vicious cycle of poverty constituting an "underclass." Although he later modified his views, Wilson (1987), in his initial work *The Truly Disadvantaged*, has had a major impact on public policy.

Wilson's theory is far too simplistic in dismissing the complex interplay of variables such as race, class, and poverty. Other researchers, Thomas and Hughes (1986) and Boyd-Franklin (1989) have argued that there is a "continuing significance of race" that must be explored in assessing the normal family processes of these families. It is important to acknowledge class and race together with oppressive poverty in working with inner-city, African-American families.

POVERTY AND THE "VICTIM SYSTEM"

Although, as discussed above, numbers of African-Americans have benefited from job and educational opportunities, multigenerational poverty remains mired in many African-American communities. These families are faced with drug and alcohol abuse, gangs, crime, homelessness or increasingly dangerous public housing, violence and death, teenage pregnancy, high unemployment, high school dropout rates, poor educational systems, and ongoing issues with the police and the justice system. They see little in terms of options for their children, and many feel trapped, which leads to what Pinderhughes (1982) has termed as "the victim system":

A victim system is a circular feedback process which . . . threatens self-esteem and reinforces problematic responses in communities, families and individuals. The feedback works as follows: Barriers to opportunity and education limit the chance for achievement, employment, and attainment of skills. This limitation can, in turn, lead to poverty or stress in relationships, which interferes with adequate performance of family roles. (p. 109)

Many of these individuals feel trapped, disempowered, and a growing rage, as the Los Angeles riots in May 1992 have demonstrated. As the recession of the late 1980s has intensified, economic conditions for these families have worsened; many live in fear for themselves and for their children.

Adolescence begins early within poor, inner-city communities when, at a very young age, children are faced with choices related to sexuality, household responsibility, drugs, and alcohol use. Random violence, particularly drug-related violence, has become a major concern for poor, inner-city families. Parents struggle with helpless feelings about preventing "the streets" from taking over their children. This sense of futility and disempowerment is a potent issue for many poor, African-American families.

CHRONIC POSTTRAUMATIC STRESS DISORDER

Inner-city children and families frequently experience chronic trauma and stress. Children and adults living in housing projects or housing shelters often report intense fear in walking through darkened halls, or past deserted buildings, and crack houses. It is not unusual for children to have to walk through a "needle park" to get to school, or to climb over crack vials and discarded syringes in the playground. Many are acquainted from an early age with violence in their homes in the form of child abuse, sexual abuse, drug overdose, and AIDS. Children often begin to exhibit behavior problems after witnessing traumatic events, such as violent deaths in their communities. In addition to acting-out behaviors manifested in oppositional or conduct disorders, one often sees anxiety or depressive symptoms. However, the classic features of posttraumatic stress disorder—nightmares, flashbacks of the traumatic event, generalized fear and anxiety, and fears of entering areas where traumatic events occurred—are often overlooked by clinicians.

RACE AND POVERTY

Although there are significant numbers of poor families in this country who are not African-American and who have lived for generations in poverty, as discussed above poor African-Americans experience a dual oppression based on race and class. Although members of other ethnic groups have attained upward mobility within one or two generations of immigrating to the United

States, chronic unemployment and high drop-out rates for African-American youth (particularly men, aged 15–25) have affected the views that many families have of their options.

RACISM AND POVERTY, ANGER, AND RAGE

The combination of discrimination and oppression augmented by racism and poverty have produced a fierce anger in many African-Americans, which Grier and Cobbs (1968) have called "Black Rage." This was demonstrated by the riots during 1965 and 1968 in major cities across this country. The government responded to this rage with the "Great Society" and the "War on Poverty" programs of the late 1960s. However, the shortfall in funding and commitment doomed most of these initiatives. Affirmative action programs in the 1970s led to educational and job opportunities for a greater (but still relatively small) number of African-Americans.

Gains against racism and discrimination were threatened and in some cases undone during the conservative Reagan and Bush Administrations of the 1980s and 1990s. While wealthy white Americans became wealthier, other segments of society found their prospects diminished, and poor African-Americans felt even more trapped by racism and poverty. Middle-class, educated African-Americans who encountered a "glass ceiling" when anticipating promotions in their professions were rudely reminded of the existence of an institutionalized racism in this country. Bias-related incidents in cities and on college campuses increased. Many African-Americans began to experience a "white backlash" from those who felt their own opportunities threatened, and the "blaming the victim" philosophy of an earlier era has since returned.

For African-American families trapped in poverty and assaulted by unemployment, high drop-out rates, drugs, violence, crime, and homelessness (at times the result of urban gentrification), anger and rage have been growing for decades.

Jesse Jackson, in a television interview about the tragic riots of Los Angeles following the acquittal of four white police officers in the beating of Rodney King, an African-American man, stated that "desperate people do desperate things." It is this desperation that one so often senses when working in poor, African-American communities.

Often rage is turned on those living in the community, as can be seen in increasing rates of "black on black" crime. It can be acted out through conduct-disordered or delinquent behavior, or in the family by stealing, child abuse, or domestic violence. Finally, rage can be internalized and manifest as depression, or drug or alcohol abuse.

Both African-American and white service providers must be aware that anger and rage may be directed against them. This anger and rage frequently paralyzes well-meaning clinicians who work in these communities. Training programs must address this issue and prepare clinicians for it by helping them learn not to personalize it and by teaching them effective strategies for joining and building trust with these families.

ATTITUDES OF MENTAL HEALTH WORKERS TOWARD POOR, AFRICAN-AMERICAN FAMILIES

There are those in the mental health field who see poor African-Americans as "unmotivated" or "lazy," "disorganized," "deprived," or "disadvantaged," which gives rise to a tendency by clinicians to "blame the victim" and dismiss these individuals as untreatable.

Treatment models often offer a limited focus on "individuals" or "families" without considering their social context. Mental health workers who enter inner-city communities may thus be overwhelmed and ill-equipped to cope with the realities of poverty, for example, homelessness, teenage pregnancy, unemployment, crime, appalling living conditions, hunger, poor health care, and maltreatment of the poor by public agencies such as schools, police, and juvenile justice and court systems. As a consequence, mental health workers and family therapists may find themselves mirroring the lack of empowerment that these families feel.

RESPONSES OF POOR AFRICAN-AMERICAN FAMILIES TO MENTAL HEALTH SERVICES

For many families, poverty leads to a greater likelihood of intrusion by outside agencies: The intrusiveness of the welfare department into the homes of poor families is legend. Often inner-city families live with the fear of the removal of their children by child protective agencies. Because Aid to Dependent Children may be withheld if a man is contributing to the support of a family, this policy sets a disincentive for couples to marry when pregnancy occurs. Women, moreover, may be motivated to claim they head "single parent" households and men to remain peripheral to their families, a factor that contributes significantly to the "invisibility" of African-American men (Franklin, 1992).

The legacy of intrusion by social and child protective services, police, legal, and criminal justice systems into poor, African-American communities has resulted in a "healthy cultural paranoia" or suspicion (Grier & Cobbs, 1968). Although "healthy cultural paranoia" is evident in other poor families, it is far more intense when one adds the variable of racism. This "healthy cultural paranoia" encompasses "helping institutions" and "helping professions" as well. Thus, schools and teachers, social service agencies and social workers, mental health clinics, and therapists of all disciplines, hospitals, and medical, nursing, and other health care professionals are faced with families who are suspicious of their efforts. Service providers who are unaware of the legacy of racism and classism may personalize this initial rejection and feel that these families do not want their services or cannot be treated, which as discussed above, perpetuates the process of "blaming the victim."

Another complication is that many African-American families, particularly those living in the inner-city, are not self-referred and thus may feel coerced to enter treatment. There is also a very widely held stigma in this community that therapy is "for crazy, sick, or weak people" or for "white folks." In addition, because of "healthy cultural paranoia" resulting in part from the intrusiveness of the welfare department, poor, African-American families may tell their children that family business is "nobody's business but our own," and may caution against "airing the dirty laundry outside the family." Therefore, mental health service providers may find it necessary to first address these issues and establish trust with families before any intervention can take place (Boyd-Franklin, 1989).

STRENGTHS AND SURVIVAL SKILLS

Many social scientists and service providers have tended to focus on the deficiencies in inner-city, African-American families. Viewing families through a deficit lens blinds one to their inherent strengths and survival skills. It is extremely important that public-policy and clinical-training programs focus on strengths, as these are what must be mobilized to produce change.

The first strength is an extensive kinship network comprised of "blood" and "nonblood" family members (Hill, 1972; Stack, 1974; Boyd-Franklin, 1989; Billingsley, 1968) who help these families survive by providing support, encouragement, and "reciprocity" in terms of sharing goods, money, and services (Stack, 1974). This network might include older relatives such as great-grandparents, grandmothers, grandfathers, aunts, uncles, cousins, older brothers and sisters, all of whom may participate in childrearing, and "nonblood relatives" such as godparents, babysitters, neighbors, friends, church family members, ministers, ministers' wives, and so forth.

As it is "normal" for African-American families to be connected to such a network, those families who come to the attention of mental health services may have become isolated or disconnected from their traditional support network. Families may become disconnected as the key "switchboard" family members of the older generation begin to die. These are often the family members who kept the family together through Thanksgiving and Christmas dinners, special holidays, family reunions, and "family news" such as births, deaths, and marriages. Also, family members who engage in substance abuse may have become "cut off" from their family network because their stealing from the family in order to support a drug habit has given rise to much anger. Additionally, a "cut off" may occur when a family member becomes homeless as a result of being "burnt out" or evicted. In some inner-city areas, entire neighborhoods have been dispossessed through arson or efforts of gentrification.

Establishing trust is frequently difficult at first, particularly if the therapist is of a different race, class, or culture. However, once trust has been established after a number of contacts, families are often more willing to share vital information, their genograms, family trees, or "real family" networks.

The task for therapists is often to search for persons who represent "islands of strength" within the family. Unfortunately, these family members often do not come in to agencies or clinics. Therefore, in order to identify and or meet the individuals who really hold the power in African-American families, the worker may have to obtain the family's permission to go out to the home. It is not unusual for poor African-American mothers to present at mental health centers as overwhelmed single parents with their children.

In traditional clinical settings, the distress presented by such women has been overpathologized by locating the source of their problems in their own character disorders and misapplication of such diagnoses as "borderline." It is crucial to appreciate the context of their sense of being overwhelmed or their disorganization and lack of resources to manage realistically overwhelming situations. It is crucial that therapists not accept first impressions but familiarize themselves with the formal and informal networks to which the family may be connected. For families who are "cut-off" from these support systems, a part of the therapy must focus on helping them either to work through and resolve their issues with their families of origin and reconnect or on helping them to form new support networks within their communities. Such methodology might prove particularly empowering for some poor families who experience a sense of isolation and fear within their own communities.

RELIGION, SPIRITUALITY, AND OTHER SURVIVAL SKILLS

Many poor, African-American families have gained strength from their spiritual and/or religious orientation. Particularly for the older generation, this translates into church membership and a feeling of community or connectedness to a "church family" (Boyd-Franklin, 1989). Many poor families have used this church family to provide role models and supports with childrearing. For families who feel the constant battle to "save their children from the streets," churches often provide an alternative network for friends, junior choir, after school and summer activities, babysitting, and male and female adult role models who have achieved stature and distinction including the minister, minister's wife, deacons, deaconesses, elders, and trustee boards. These role models are very visible and very active.

Many younger African-American families in inner-city areas have either rebelled against this support system or have become disconnected. It is essential that we learn from the functional, poor families in African-American communities who identify these supports for themselves and their children. It is important that service providers be aware of the "church families" and be acquainted with the ministers in African-American communities as these individuals have a great deal of power and influence and can sometimes provide help and support for a family who is homeless, for a mother who is struggling to raise her children alone and who is searching for after-school activities, or for a chronically mentally ill adult who has become "cut off" from his or her extended family after the death of the main caregiver.

It is also important to note a distinction between "spirituality" and "religious orientation" in African-Americans. Family members who may not have a "church home" or be formal members of a church community, may still have a deep, abiding "spirituality." In the Afrocentric tradition and view of the world, the "psyche" and the "spirit" are one. Therefore, this is often a strength and a survival mechanism for African-American families that can be tapped, particularly in times of death and dying, illness, loss, and bereavement. Thus, family members may not go to church but they may "pray to the Lord" when times are hard.

LOVE OF CHILDREN: ANOTHER LOOK AT EXTENDED FAMILY CHILD-REARING PRACTICE

Therapists working with African-American, inner-city families may find themselves making judgments about values regarding child rearing. Because of the harshness of their lives, and the skills necessary for survival in a racist society, African-American families may have adopted the child-rearing posture known as "spare the rod, spoil the child." It is important for clinicians to recognize that this concept of discipline is often a "normal family value" for these families. Despite what may be seen by therapists as abusive treatment of children, this often masks underlying feelings of love and concern, which may cause these families to fear for their children's well being, particularly that of their male children. Reframes with these families that focus on concepts such as "you love him (or her) so much that you are trying to teach him right and protect him from harm," are very powerful. Once this respect has been given, parental family members will be more able to hear "but I have the sense that all of your efforts do not seem to be working."

Some families preach this "tough" philosophy but are very inconsistent in their parenting. Once the underlying love has been recognized, these parents can hear the need for consistency. Another variable related to consistency has to do with extended family involvement in childrearing. As discussed above, researchers have documented the concepts of "multiple mothering or fathering," which is often shared by grandmothers, grandfathers, aunts, uncles, cousins, older brothers and sisters, and "non blood relatives" such as ministers, church family members, neighbors, friends, and babysitters (Stack, 1974; Boyd-Franklin, 1989; Hines & Boyd-Franklin, 1982; Hill, 1972; Billingsley, 1968). These supports often provide aid and strength to burdened parents, however, the negotiation of these relationships can be complex, and inconsistencies in parenting may develop because so many individuals are involved. In family assessments, practitioners need to go beyond household to identify important kin. Alas, overvaluing of the "nuclear family" in the dominant culture may blind workers to the rich multigenerational ties. The clinician's task in working with such families is to open communication between the "parental" figures and reach consensus on boundaries, rules, and disciplinary practices.

SINGLE-PARENT FAMILIES

There is a tendency in the social science literature to treat single-parent families as if they represent a homogeneous group. In fact, there are many different kinds of single-parent families whose circumstances vary according to family functioning, capabilities of the mother, socioeconomic and income level, employment, and degree of extended family support.

In an earlier work (Boyd-Franklin, 1989), service workers are cautioned about the tendency to automatically mislabel all single-parent families as dysfunctional. *The fact of single parenthood does not automatically make a family "dysfunctional"* (Boyd Franklin, 1989). Lindblad, Goldberg, and Dukes (1985) and Lindblad-Goldberg, Dukes, and Lasley (1988) compared functional and dysfunctional low-income, African-American single-parent families living in Philadelphia. The functional families predictably had clear boundaries and role responsibilities. They were not isolated but drew readily on the support of their extended family kinship network.

In addition to this aspect, there are also differences in the way in which families became single parents. There are increasing numbers of African-American single parents who become single through divorce, separation, or death (a trend that mirrors a similar pattern in American society as a whole) (Boyd-Franklin, 1989). Also, there are a number of women in their 30s and 40s who become single parents by choice as they become older and are concerned about being childless. Although the above trends are important, the largest number of African-American single parents initially attain that status through unwed, teenage pregnancy.

TEENAGE PREGNANCY

One of the most complicated phenomena in African-American communities is the issue of teenage pregnancy. There has been an ongoing tendency in social science literature to "blame the victim" and label these young women as irresponsible. This phenomenon must be viewed within the context of poverty, unemployment, racism, and the general sense of hopelessness that frequently pervades inner-city urban communities. For many young women living in these areas, having a child becomes a "rite of passage" to womanhood. Unemployment and lack of opportunity affect both young women and men in inner-city African-American neighborhoods. Wilson (1987) has clearly shown that when men had jobs or believed they had prospects as breadwinner/provider, they were significantly more likely to marry. Unfortunately, the realities of a declining economy and the results of racism and discrimination leave them with few options. For some African-American men who feel disenfranchised in this way, having a child becomes a way to demonstrate one's manhood. Because of the sense of lack of a future, immediate pleasure and the potency involved in creating a life become a part of a more present-oriented way of life. Once a child is born, if the mother is too young to be employed, the child is placed on Aid to Dependent Children (welfare). This system further reinforces the exclusion or "invisibility" of the man by penalizing a family's financial support if he is present. Generally, because females become pregnant as young as 13, 14, or 15, there are older women in the family who are actively involved in childcare. This creates complex family and parenting dynamics.

MULTIGENERATIONAL ISSUES

For many of these young women, single parenthood and teenage pregnancy constitute multigenerational family patterns—both the mother and the grandmother in the family also became pregnant during their adolescent years. Often, as a daughter approaches puberty, there is increased anxiety within the family system. Families react in a variety of ways; the most common are: (1) to become overly rigid, restrictive, and punitive with the child in an attempt to protect the child from pregnancy; and (2) overwhelmed with this multigenerational family transmission process (Bowen, 1976) to "throw up their hands," leaving the child with the responsibility of raising herself. These adolescents often appear very much out of control, and parents often feel helpless to make a difference. It is paradoxical that either of the above responses will be likely to cause the girl to, in fact, carry out the family script of multigenerational teenage pregnancy.

EMPOWERMENT

For reasons already discussed, such as racism, classism, poverty, and "the victim system," many inner-city African-American families feel disenfranchised and powerless. Therefore, a key factor in any treatment approach must focus on empowerment (Solomon, 1976; Boyd-Franklin, 1989). This concept of empowerment is multifaceted, consisting of both the empowerment of the "executive" or parental system in the family (Minuchin, 1974) and the empowerment of families to intervene in the multisystems that intrude on their lives.

The deceptively simple concept of the Structural Family Therapy School, which encourages clinicians to put parental figures in charge of their children, is a very powerful approach (Minuchin, 1974; Aponte, 1976). When these families feel that they are "losing their children to the streets," it is very empowering to pull extended family members together to fight back and "take their children back from the streets."

Empowerment through Multiple Family Groups

As discussed, isolation from traditional cultural, family, and community supports is not a part of the "normal family processes" for poor African-American families. Therefore, the homeless who have been evicted or victims of arson may have been forced to relocate to a new area. Their very isolation serves to exacerbate mental health problems. One approach that is extremely empowering to family members as well as the clinicians who work with them is the process of multiple family groups whereby a family isolated from support systems is brought together in a group with other families in their community who are experiencing similar problems. Together they become a support system for each other and often form relationships that continue beyond the life of the group.

African-American families traditionally search out and create these supports on moving to a new community. However, because of the fear of violence, crime, and drugs, many inner-city African-American families today find themselves isolated, virtually held hostage within their own homes and apartments. Therefore, it is truly empowering to introduce these families to one another and bring them together around their common concerns for their children as the enhanced sense of community destigmatizes common dilemmas. It is both comforting and personally empowering to know that one is not alone and that there exists support for change. An example of such a support situation would be for families to be able to go together to discuss with the principal at their children's school their concerns related to drugs, crime, and so forth.

Empowerment through a Multisystems Model

Treatment must take into consideration the fact that, as discussed above, poor, inner-city, African-American families cope with the intrusiveness of many organizations, such as agencies, schools, hospitals, police, courts, juvenile justice systems, welfare, child protective services, housing, and mental health services on a daily basis (Boyd-Franklin, 1989). Empowerment within this context requires identifying the various agencies or institutions that effect a family's life. An eco map (Hartmann & Laird, 1983; Boyd-

Franklin, 1989) can be helpful in diagramming these systems. The family members can then be empowered to intervene in these systems by use of the following: (1) calling meetings of various agencies that have the power to make decisions for their families; (2) writing letters, and getting letters from therapists, doctors, and so forth in support of their families; (3) obtaining a therapist's support to be empowered to ask for conferences with supervisors of resistant workers.

The key here is that clinicians must resist the urge to do all of the work themselves. Family members must be empowered to take charge of these issues.

Empowerment of Clinicians

Training programs in all disciplines in the mental health field have not been effective in adequately preparing clinicians for working with poor African-American families. Well-meaning, eager clinicians may be unprepared for the racial tension, anger, and "healthy cultural paranoia" that they encounter. They also may well be overwhelmed by the realities of poverty, or they may be unprepared to cope with the myriad of multisystems levels and agencies that are factors in these families' lives. There are also difficulties in outreach, as families may not have phones or may live in dangerous neighborhoods. Practitioners may find it helpful to work through natural community bases in schools, churches, and health care clinics.

The process of training clinicians to work effectively with families who are dealing with racism, classism, and poverty is also one of empowerment. It is not surprising that this process must begin by helping therapists to look at themselves—at their own values, upbringing, and attitudes about race, class, and poverty. There are now a number of excellent training tools available. Pinderhughes (1989) in her book *Understanding Race, Ethnicity and Power* describes in detail a training program designed to help therapists explore these issues. Aponte (1985) has long been a pioneer in helping therapists explore their own use of self with these families. His training program at Hannemann Hospital in Philadelphia is a model of such an approach.

In *Black Families in Therapy: A Multisystems Approach* (Boyd-Franklin, 1989), a chapter is devoted to therapist's use of self with relevant countertransference issues for African-American patients and white clinicians. The last chapter explores the role of training and supervision in the process of empowering clinicians.

The Multisystems Model (Boyd-Franklin, 1989) addresses and helps prepare clinicians to deal more effectively with the complex issues of race, culture, class, and poverty. It also helps them to look at African-American families within the context of their history and culture and to recognize the strengths that can be utilized to produce empowerment.

Work with African-American inner-city families requires a therapist who is prepared to be "active" and committed to activating families toward their own empowerment. Not surprisingly, it also requires supervisors who are also committed to being "on the front lines" with their trainees and empowering them to look at the complex and difficult questions of race, class, poverty, and our own values and responses to these issues. Beyond didactic teaching, however, this model produces empowerment by focusing on the process of supervision and line training as an opportunity to develop the "person of the therapist" (Aponte, 1985). It is only through a very personal process that therapists can be trained to recognize the complex issues discussed in this chapter, be true to themselves, and allow their own humanity to be communicated to the families with whom they work.

Empowerment through Social Policy Intervention

The era of the 1980s has represented an avoidance of the issues facing poor, inner-city African-American families. The Los Angeles riots in 1992 were a tragic cry of anger and pain by a community that feels trapped and desperate. Those in the mental health field including family therapists, social workers, psychologists, and psychiatrists must unite to put these key issues back on the national agenda.

Strong social policy programs must address this issue of empowerment of families and communities by incentives that encourage self-determination. These programs should provide housing to counteract homelessness, better and more responsive educational systems, and work incentives.

CHANGE IN SOCIETAL ATTITUDES THAT FOSTER RACISM, CLASSISM, AND POVERTY

Ultimately, mental health providers must accept a personal sense of social responsibility for changing those attitudes that foster racism, classism, and poverty. The first step is honestly acknowledging the existence of these phenomena and their complex interplay. On a microcosm level, we can begin with ourselves and the families with whom we work. Many mental health clinicians, however, like the families they serve, become overwhelmed when asked to move to a "macro" level. If these issues are ever to be resolved fully in this country, we must be willing to speak out and advocate for change in our own agencies and clinics, communities, and local, state, and national government.

REFERENCES

Aponte, H. (1976). Underorganization in the poor family. In P. J. Guerin (Ed.), *Family therapy: Theory and practice*. New York: Gardner Press.

Aponte, H. (1985). The negotiation of values in therapy. *Family Process, 24*(3), 323–338.

Billingsley, A. (1968). *Black families in white America*. Englewood Cliffs, NJ: Prentice-Hall.

Bowen, M. (1976). Theory in the practice of psychotherapy. In P. J. Guerin (Ed.), *Family therapy: Theory and practice*. New York: Gardner Press.

Boyd-Franklin, N. (1989). *Black families in therapy: A multisystems approach*. New York: Guilford Press.

Franklin, A. J. (1992). Therapy with African-American men. *Families in Society: The Journal of Contemporary Human Services, 73*(6), 350–355.

Grier, W., & Cobbs, P. (1968). *Black rage*. New York: Basic Books.

Hartman, A., & Laird, J. (1983). *Family centered social work practice*. New York: The Free Press.

Hill, R. (1972). *The strengths of black families*. New York: Emerson-Hall.

Hines, P. M., & Boyd-Franklin, N. (1982). Black families. In M. McGoldrick, J. K. Pearce, & J. Giordano (Eds.), *Ethnicity and family therapy* (pp. 84–107). New York: Guilford Press.

Hopps, J. (1982). Oppression based on color [editorial]. *Social Work, 27*(1), 3–5.

Kunjufu, J. (1985). *Countering the conspiracy to destroy black boys* (Vol. 1). Chicago: African-American Images.

Lindblad-Goldberg, M., & Dukes, J. (1985). Social support in black, low-income, single-parent families: Normative and dysfunctional patterns. *American Journal of Orthopsychiatry, 55*, 42–58.

Lindblad-Goldberg, M., Dukes, J., & Lasley, J. (1988). Stress in black, low-income, single-parent families: Normative and dysfunctional patterns. *American Journal of Orthopsychiatry, 58*(1), 104–120.

Minuchin, S. (1974). *Families and family therapy*. Cambridge, MA: Harvard University Press.

Pinderhughes, E. (1982). Afro-American families and the victim system. In M. McGoldrick, J. K. Pearce, & J. Giordano (Eds.), *Ethnicity and family therapy* (pp. 108–122). New York: Guilford Press.

Pinderhughes, E. (1989). *Understanding race, ethnicity and power: The key to efficacy in clinical practice*. New York: The Free Press.

Solomon, B. (1976). *Black empowerment: Social work in oppressed communities*. New York: Columbia University Press.

Stack, C. (1974). *All our kin: Strategies for survival in a black community*. New York: Prentice-Hall.

Thomas, M., & Hughes, M. (1986). The continuing significance of race: A study of race, class and quality of life in America, 1972–1985. *American Sociological Review, 51*, 830–841.

Wilson, W. (1980). *The declining significance of race* (2nd ed.). Chicago: The University of Chicago Press.

Wilson, W. (1987). *The truly disadvantaged: The inner city, the underclass and public policy*. Chicago: The University of Chicago Press.

CHAPTER 13

CHANGING
GENDER NORMS

Barbara Ellman and
Morris Taggart

A son in all sorts of trouble finally seeks out his father for advice during a particularly bad crisis. But when he finds his father wearing an apron while washing dishes in the kitchen, the son recoils in disgust.[1]

The parents of an 18-year-old girl describe their fear that their daughter will be an old maid because she is so terribly bright and independent. They decide that the mother will have a "talk with her."[2]

INTRODUCTION

We suspect that the exhibits above have a quaint, if not bizarre, ring to them, especially for those who have no direct experience of living in the United States during the 1950s. Their inclusion at the beginning of this chapter reminds us that gender norms are hardly forever, no matter how eternal they seem to be at the apex of their influence. Only recently, however, has this lack of permanence been recognized as, not the result of shortcomings in our ability to discern *true* femininity and masculinity, but rather our com-

[1]This is actually a scene from the film *Rebel Without a Cause*, and used as an example of 1950s concerns about "weak fathers" by Pleck (1987).
[2]Similarly, the television programs of the 1950s abounded in warnings about girls and women who were "too smart" to be considered attractive by men.

ing to see that gender itself is socially constructed: historically, politically, and economically. Consequently, there is no attempt in this chapter to provide a compendium of current gender norms complete with predictions as to those that will still be around 5 years from now. Instead, we try to establish gender, particularly in the form of "gender relations," as an indispensable category in exploring, understanding, and even changing, human experience and behavior.

We acknowledge that gender norms, as we have come to understand them in predominantly white American culture, have been changing in the last 30 years with unprecedented speed and reach. At the same time we recognize the need for more radical change as we continue to challenge ourselves and our cultural presuppositions about gender and other far-reaching cultural distinctions. We interweave both meanings of the term *changing*. Therefore, our title, "Changing Gender Norms," is about what is and what still needs to be.

Talking about gender reminds us of other categories of difference, such as race, ethnicity, and class that punctuate our discourse and our lives (Hooks, 1990). Our emphasis on gender is not to say that it is more important than these others, but that an analysis of gender—its presence in every aspect of our lives—is indispensable to understanding who we are and hope to become. There are some problems here. In attempting to talk about gender we tend to universalize, as if gender means the same thing cross-culturally. It does not (McGoldrick, Garcia-Preto, Hines, & Lee, 1989; Webb-Watson, 1991). There is a tendency to treat the subject out of its historical context, and yet it is this particular historical moment that has given weight to the concept of gender (Nicholson, 1990).

We are mindful of our biases. Our own clinical work is principally with white, middle-class to upper-middle-class, educated heterosexual couples. However, since this is the population most directly challenging gender norms in their family and work life, we have access to the issues as they effect and are worked out in these families. Finally, the overwhelming majority of membership in both the Women's Movement as well as the neophyte Men's Movement is white, educated, and middle class.

THE IMPORTANCE OF POWER AND THE EMERGENCE OF GENDER STUDIES

Nothing has transformed our view of what are "normal family processes" more than the changes that have come about in how we think about gender. Initiated by the feminist critique, appreciation for the importance of gender has spawned a rich body of interdisciplinary studies that has challenged all the traditional academic and practical disciplines. Feminist theory now plays a critical role in fields as diverse as physics, biology, law, philosophy, and literary studies. Nowhere has its challenge been greater than in the social sciences—anthropology, political science, history, sociology, and psychology—and their clinical applications (psychotherapy, social work, and family therapy).

Traditionally, gender has not been considered problematic. "Becoming a woman" or "becoming a man" has been understood as a *natural* process grounded firmly in biology and in the *essential* masculine and feminine attributes that God-given biological differences have been assumed to entail. If culture played a role, it was primarily to protect, then to give shape to, what was already given in nature. Social science's exploration of gender in the years after World War II scarcely challenged this view, doing little more than provide a scientific gloss to conventional language and beliefs. Instead of speaking of a "woman's place," there was now the more scientific-sounding "female role."

In this "sex-role" model as it came to be called, there was always a measure of ambivalence about the distinction between *descriptive* norms (the characteristics men and women are perceived as having) and *sociocultural* norms (the characteristics a society prescribes for women and men). Empirical researchers tended to insist that their concern was always the former, but, since sex roles are operationalized by the latter, empirical research reflects the manifestations of sociocultural norms (Thompson & Pleck, 1987). Thus, gender norms are actually the culture's list of prescriptions and proscriptions considered appropriate to that sex, and individuals are assessed as properly "feminine" or "masculine" in terms of their attitude toward, and degree of compliance with, these social expectations.

The family has been the primary arena for the socialization of each generation toward their gender-specific roles and behaviors by treating boys and girls differently, holding different expectations, and employing different social pressures toward them (Goodrich, Rampage, Ellman, & Halstead, 1988). Father, mother, sister, and brother predictably play the same roles and functions in each household. The ideology of the "normal family" demands its enactment and reenactment: father as head of household; mother as caretaker. Additionally, women, in their role as mothers, are charged with executing the particular gender demands required by the culture and are the ones blamed when children do not behave in their assigned gender roles.

The deficiencies of sex-role theory are now so apparent that we forget that this paradigm dominated the social sciences for decades after World War II. Its earliest critics were feminists (Ellmann, 1968; Friedan, 1963) who were quick to discern the theory's functions in maintaining social control by pathologizing women's attempts to question the roles assigned them (Broverman, Broverman, Clarkson, Rosencrantz, & Vogel, 1970). The endorsement, indeed promotion, of "female roles" by social science "served to give a spurious modernity to the old conservatism" (Rowbotham, 1973, pp. 6–7). More recently, Kimmel (1987b) has pointed to the crucial distinction that the sex-role paradigm is based on *traits* associated with "female" and "male" roles rather than their *enactments* in real life. This, he argues, leads to traits being idealized and "essentialized" as either masculine or feminine without the slightest reference to how women and men actually behave. Thus masculinity is associated a priori with traits implying autonomy and authority, and femininity is associated with those suggesting dependency and passivity.

Sex-role theory's essentialist descriptions of femininity and masculinity obscure that these are *relational* constructs. By "relational," we mean that "female" and "male" are constructed such that the definition of one can only be understood in light of the other. This brings us to the most serious defect in the sex-role paradigm—its failure to recognize that gender relations are based on power. "Not only do men as a group exert power over women as a group, but the socially derived definitions of masculinity and femininity reproduce those power relations" (Kimmel, 1987b, pp. 12–13). Thus, the power differential between women and men is institutionalized by the culture and finds expression in the everyday relations of men and women. It is in the everyday life of the family "that women's oppression and men's power are enacted most plainly and personally" (Goodrich, 1991, p. 11). Consequently, it is in the discourse on family and family relations that an understanding of power and most specifically power differential must be included. Without an analysis of power, issues of inequity in decision making through wife battering and incest are never confronted (Avis, 1991). Romanticized notions of family life as a safe haven deny the all too common reality of abuse and violence. Clinical interventions with families and couples must begin with an active inquiry around how power is specifically allocated and experienced in order to make inequities visible and create the possibility of change.

It does not follow however that, since male and female roles are socioculturally defined and mediated, they are easily changed. Despite having noted at the beginning of the chapter that some elements of what is considered appropriate behavior can change appreciably within a generation, there are many more aspects of "male" and "female" roles that are far less malleable. Some (Paglia, 1990) have taken this to support the view that sex differences are primarily biological and that there is truth in sexual stereotypes. Such arguments seriously underestimate the power of the sociohistorical discourse to define not only behavior and its relationship to gender but how we think about behavior and its relationship to gender.

The feminist refusal to accept the definition of female that was reflected in sex-role theory gave the feminist movement its distinctive character in the 1960s and 1970s. This was a time in which it became absolutely essential that women leave the conversation with men and speak with each other. This experience was vital to women because for the first time they could experience themselves with a different mirror than the ones that men in their relationships with women had shown them. They began to articulate a set of common themes that in their separation from each other and reliance on men had eluded them.

One powerful theme for women was that of femininity itself. Women began to understand that femininity is a demand that always demands more. "It must constantly reassure its audience by a willing demonstration of difference, even when one does not exist in nature, or it must seize and embrace a natural variation and compose a rhapsodic symphony upon the notes. . . . To fail at the feminine difference is to appear not to care about men, and to risk the loss of their attention and approval" (Brownmiller, 1984, p. 15). Why else would women risk their health as well as their lives with experimental breast implants, if the breast were not the embodiment of their sex and sexuality, and painfully for many, their self-esteem (Hilts, 1992). They understood that, in this culture, when women disliked their bodies, it was difficult for them to like themselves. Women realized they had been taught that to be insufficiently feminine was a failure of core sexual identity and a demonstration of how little a woman cared for herself. They began to be aware how powerful the requirement of femininity was and how essential the need to challenge it. For these women a confidence born of shared identity with a voice and definition began to replace the damning objectification of woman as the Other (Beauvoir, 1974). A flurry of activity took place that produced women's history, women's literature, women's music, and feminist criticism. In turn, the larger culture was also enriched by the introduction of what had been buried under the dominant one.

As a byproduct, the study of gender involving both women *and* men, began in the early 1980s in such disciplines as history, anthropology, philosophy, psychology, and natural science. Fields involving family studies, particularly family therapy, came late to an appreciation of the feminist critique, and the shift toward an interest in gender as involving men as well as women is not as advanced as in, say, literary studies (Boone and Cadden, 1990; Jardine and Smith, 1987) or natural science (Harding, 1986; Keller, 1985). Thus, when feminist criticism in family therapy is directed toward men, it tends to deal with them as if they were *outside* the topic of gender altogether, for example, as "sexist" or "patriarchal." Ironically, this recapitulates an important patriarchal theme: that it is women (and gay men) who have "gender," whereas heterosexual men's view of themselves and the world represent the unproblematic norm against which others are judged and found wanting. Within the dominant culture it has seemed natural at times to question whether women as a class are qualified to own property, vote, aspire to a profession, or political office. But few have wondered if it is proper for men to become priests or presidents unless they happen to be gay, black, or have some other impediment to "real" manhood.

Not insisting that *men's* lives too are *gendered* encourages men's invisibility to themselves and, for men, reduces the feminist critique to something merely to be defended against. This allows men to be content with their self-definition as a negative identity, as not-female (Chodorow, 1978; Seidler, 1989; Thompson & Pleck, 1987). The challenge here is for men to abandon their absurd genderless and transhistorical status as "the measure of all things" and move on to explore critically how "masculinity" shapes and directs their lives. However, the structure of masculinity prohibits this kind of self-reflection by men. As Schwenger (1989, p. 110) puts it, for a man "to think about masculinity is to become less masculine oneself. . . . Self-consciousness is a crack in the wholeness of his nature." To hear a father justifying his participation in childcare as "helping out the wife" is to see the prohibition at work.

Men's reluctance to tell other men their self-doubts and fears while expecting their wives to know and give comfort is an example of how the culture of masculinity works. In turn, of course, femininity requires that the wife carry out his expectation graciously, that is, without discussion, so that his vulnerability remains concealed. Masculinity keeps him appearing strong and needless. Femininity keeps her powerless, yet responsible to respond. The husband, whose dissatisfactions with the relationship depend entirely on his wife's articulation of the problems in effect avoids asking himself what *he* wants. Leaving to the woman the work necessary to stay connected, he remains invisible to himself and avoids the possible discovery that masculinity is problematic for him also.

To explore the meaning of "masculinity" is a far more radical challenge to a man than having to respond to the charge of being sexist, especially when the latter can simply be denied or agreed to with relative impunity. Implicit in men's study of themselves as gendered *is* to "make their own oppressive structures (ideological, social, psychological) *present* for critique . . ." (Boone, 1990, pp. 23–24). Men can begin to take initiatives in critically assessing their family roles and relationships. Rather than accept, for example, their traditional position on the periphery of the family as "natural," men might explore the costs of marginality to *themselves* as well as to their wives and children. How does a man's role as provider affect his sense of self, his health, his well-being, and his relations within the family? If masculinity requires of a man a certain impenetrability, lack of awareness of bodily sensation, indifference to his affective processes, obtuseness about the role of desire in his life, what are the consequences of all this for him? For his partner? For his children? For his relationships with other men and the community at large?

Men's resolve to explore their own pain depends on their willingness to give up cherished habits in relation to gender difference. As they struggle to change, can men any longer hold on to their difference from women as signifying more than just difference?

VIVE LA DIFFÉRENCE?

How we think about difference will make all the difference. Do we approach the world the way the geneticist Barbara McClintock suggests: that an understanding of nature comes to rest with difference? Commenting on McClintock's views, Keller states that:

... difference constitutes a principle for ordering the world radically unlike the principle of division of dichotomization (subject–object, mind–matter, feeling–reason, disorder–law). Whereas these oppositions are directed toward a cosmic unity typically excluding or devouring one of the pair, toward a unified, all-encompassing law, respect for difference remains content with multiplicity as an end in itself. (Keller, 1985, p. 163)

We attach hierarchical value to our claim of difference; valuing one forces us to devalue the other. In relationships, our sense of completion appears contingent on finding our different and essential Other, with two incomplete and different halves making a whole. Men, the dominant group, use difference as a way to project onto women all that is unacceptable in themselves; namely, dependency, emotionality, subjectivity. Women, the subordinate group, are left experiencing differences between themselves and men as meaning that they are somehow "wrong," inferior, less worthy. Gender relations have been about valuing the male over the female; men claiming objectivity and rationality as their own but needing the female as the embodiment of emotions.

The fears and aspirations one holds about the future of relationships (and the world) are a consequence of how one thinks about difference. Although several other essential themes would also influence how one thinks about the future of heterosexual relations, (e.g., power, love, intimacy, sex) the issue of how one understands and experiences difference holds primacy. Can we tolerate differences without dividing them into categories of good and bad, hierarchies connoting greater and lesser power and value? Whereas, division splits off connection and inflicts distance, "the recognition of difference provides a starting point for relatedness" (Keller, 1985, p. 163). There is no comparable equivalent where one group is contrasted with another in which difference is in and of itself so highly valued. Nowhere except in the comparison of genders is difference itself held as a sine qua non of the comparison.

To speak of heterosexual couples is to speak about difference as the absolutely indispensable category of description. It has been argued that it is heterosexuality, whether described as "compulsory" (Rich, 1980) or "contractual" (Wittig, 1992) that characterizes "a hegemonic discursive/epistemic model of gender intelligibility that assumes that for bodies to cohere and make sense there must be a stable sex expressed through a stable gender (masculine expresses male, feminine expresses female) that is oppositionally and hierarchically defined through the compulsory practice of heterosexuality" (Butler, 1990, p. 151).

For these theorists, gender is derivative of heterosexuality. They view heterosexuality as a cultural demand that necessitates opposing, and therefore gendered, individuals. Gender comes on the scene as the requirement (as well as the necessary acquirement) of the social construction, not simply of difference, but of dichotomization. Gender identity becomes the primary dichotomizing category among human beings, wherein what one is said to have, the other cannot. Consequently, heterosexual couples find themselves expecting and often demanding that their partner exhibit qualities that they themselves are not permitted. For example, women often desire men for their rationality and authority; whereas men often desire women for their emotionality and dependency. Except in very circumscribed ways in their relationship to each other, women are not permitted to exhibit rationality and authority, and men are not permitted to exhibit emotionality and dependency. When men and women do exhibit these behaviors, they risk serious disjunction to their sense of self and their desirability, since gender norms plays such an important part in shaping who we are and what makes us attractive.

For heterosexuals, differences between men and women have been the essential ingredient explaining attraction and need as well as repulsion and fear. What is it about the way the relationship between men and women is constructed that locates their experiences, feelings, and behaviors in gender? If gender is understood as being a socially constructed category, then gender itself is normative—a prescriptive, indoctrinating, idealizing category. However isn't it redundant to speak of gender norms? Isn't gender the norm? Hasn't human behavior in all its diversity been forced into dichotomized categorizes as male or female, masculine or feminine, manly or womanly?

In families, husbands and wives are responsible for demonstrating prescribed gender roles and behaviors so their sons and daughters will be able to demonstrate appropriate gender behavior. These roles have, until the appearance of the feminist critique, been viewed as *complementary*, a system of balance suggesting how behaviors, roles, or emotions of each person induce the other into behaviors, roles, or emotions that complement the other.

> The need to maintain complementarity or balance in the family is used as a reason to assign roles to women that complement the roles chosen by men. In this way, women perform those tasks that men prefer not to do, for example, housework and child care, and do not compete in those areas that men select as their domains, namely achievement, work, finances, and the like. (Walters, Carter, Papp, & Silverstein, 1988, p. 23)

Human capacities have been divided up, split off from each other, and relegated as if they were the natural and rightful property of one gender, not the other. This division is not natural and accidental, nor is the booty equal (cf. Goldner, 1991; Hare-Mustin, 1991; Walsh, 1989). Who could possibly argue that household tasks (the traditional and on-going domain of women) are equivalent in value and esteem to the rewards of career—money, authority, and power (the traditional and on-going domain of men)? Yet, this obvious disparity in power and value is rarely confronted in family life because it so perfectly mirrors the disparity between men and women in the culture. "Father as the 'head' of the family supports the notion of 'father' as head of the country, leader of the people, and recognized authority in the world. Mother as the 'caretaker' of the family supports the stereotype of woman as nurturer, harmonizer, peacekeeper of the world" (Goodrich et al., 1988, p. 6). Masculinity and femininity are cultural constructs rooted in a caste system in which femininity is relegated all that is less valued by the dominant culture. The feminist position argues that this is accomplished by the cultural hegemony that the male position has had in our society. Miller describes it as follows:

> A dominant group, inevitably, has the greatest influence in determining a culture's overall outlook—its philosophy, morality, social theory, even its science. The dominant group, thus, legitimizes the unequal relationship and incorporates it into society's guiding concepts. The social outlook, then, obscures the true nature of this relationship—that is, the very existence of inequality. The culture explains the events that take place in terms of other premises, premises that are inevitably false, such as racial or sexual inferiority. (Miller, 1986, p. 8)

NO DIFFERENCE/ALL THE DIFFERENCE

Feminist psychological theorists have responded to the issue of gender difference in primarily two ways. The first approach has been to deemphasize differences between men and women. These theorists are located in the liberal or modern tradition of individual capacities and rights. They employ empirical research to show that women's capacities are not demonstratively different than those of men, thereby paving the way for women's equality via similarity. This work is best exemplified by Maccoby and Jacklin in their study, *The Psychology of Sex Differences* (Maccoby & Jacklin, 1974). The second approach, represented by Chodorow (1978), Miller (1986), the Stone Center's "Works in Progress" (Jordan, Kaplan, Miller, Stiver, & Surrey, 1991), and Gilligan (1982) not only reaffirms gender differences but valorizes the female.

The first position, that of minimizing difference, has unquestionably contributed to improving the status of women by demonstrating similarities with men. Maccoby and Jacklin are most often cited by feminists as researchers proving the corrective stance of equality between men and women. Although acknowledging the contribution that this kind of research has made in facilitating correcting perceptions about women's ability as compared to that of men, Hare-Mustin and Marecek (1990, p. 44) caution us that: "Arguing for no differences between women and men. . . . draws attention away from women's special needs and from differences in power and resources between women and men." As marriage and family therapists, we know that treating the couple as if they were equal partners leads us to ignore the reality of unequal power and economic resources and has us participating in maintaining the status quo. Family therapy, traditionally sensitive to the function of generational issues, needs to be informed by the recognition that gender is often the determining variable in how heterosexual couples and families go about their daily lives (Goldner, 1989; Goodrich et al., 1988; Walsh & Scheinkman, 1989; Walters et al., 1988).

The second approach, with its emphasis on difference in its contemporary feminist cast, highlights the female as essentially a relational being. The slim volume that set off a stream of other feminist writers highlighting difference (e.g., Belenky, Clinchy, Goldberger, & Tarule, 1986) is Jean Baker Miller's (1986) *Toward a New Psychology of Women*. Miller persuasively claims that connection and relatedness, assigned to women and forever judged in Western societies as demonstrating weakness and dependency, are strength and competency. Miller takes every characteristic attributed to the female (vulnerability, dependency, caregiving) and demonstrates not only its essential worth and its inherent goodness, but she makes a strong case for men as well as women to embrace these "female" qualities for their own good as well as the world's. The distinctive language of Jean Baker Miller and others at Wellesley's Stone Center honors women as "relational selves" in contrast to men's positioning of themselves as autonomous selves. They see women's contribution as holding more promise for a qualitatively better life. Their contribution to women's self-esteem has been enormous. Women, who had felt apologetic, ashamed, and subordinate to men in virtually every way were helped to feel that their way of perceiving and being in the world was not only honorable but potentially healing.

The danger inherent in such theories, (Chodorow, 1978; Gilligan, 1982; Miller, 1986), is that they can be exploited to "emphasize the essential nature of men and women rather than the social context that shapes them" (Hare-Mustin, 1991, p. 70). Although, the "feminine" attributes are reframed as highly preferable, the discourse about gender—as dichotomous, oppositional, and ultimately hierarchical—is basically unchanged.

Even where psychology addresses "categories" rather than "essential natures," interrelationships between categories have been overlooked. For example, Block (1976, p. 297) points out that Maccoby and Jacklin's concentration on sex differences in the performance of tasks ignores the interrelationships between intellectual performance and personality characteristics, thereby leaving out an important gender difference. It is in the area of motivation that these interrelationships become critical. Girls' achievement motivation brings out the importance of this point. Girls have been shown to be conflicted between their need to be close or connected (a need that does not appear to be as great in boys) and their need to achieve. Another researcher claims that even at younger ages when girls' achievement is the same or higher than boys', "it appears that female achievement behavior . . . is motivated by a desire for love rather than mastery" (Holmstrom, 1986, p. 54).

Additionally, the empirical evidence supports what we've observed for years, that with increasing age girls seem to compromise personal success for what appears to be a more highly valued desire for connection and love

(Gilligan, Lyons, & Hanmer, 1990). How we understand difference proves particularly revelatory. Is this a particular manifestation of the essential and immutable difference between men and women where men are intrinsically motivated by mastery and women by love? Is this an example of a relational and contextual difference, whereby men are taught to aspire for mastery and women are taught to aspire for love? Is this an indication of how women, the subordinate class, must concern themselves with connection in order to survive and prosper in a social environment that makes it difficult for them to master much of anything?

The complexity of human thought, feeling, and behavior cannot be reduced to simple categories, particularly the dichotomizing category of gender. Too often gender difference has obscured other, perhaps more salient, differences. Holstrom (1986) reports, one piece of research shows that black males and white females, different biologically but with similar social handicaps, are similar in their fear of success, conformity, and perceptual judgment. She describes another study demonstrating that Protestant, Jewish, and Catholic women experience significant differences in menstrual discomfort.

Psychological discourse, whether emphasizing difference or minimizing difference, has tended to be ahistorical, essentialistic, and universalistic. In their comparisons of boys and girls, or men and women, ethnicity, class, race, region of the world, and recognition of the particular moment in social history have too often been ignored. Finally, the researchers' goal of documenting the differences between the genders uncritically accepts the social categories that shape their inquiry as if they were dealing with categories belonging to science. And science itself is not free from social constructions. ". . . The feminist challenges reveal that the questions that are asked—and, even more significantly, those that are not asked—are at least as determinative of the adequacy of our total picture as are any answers that we can discover" (Harding, 1987, p. 7).

CREATION OF THE MYTHIC FEMININE AND MASCULINE

An "answer" that has emerged recently is the idealization of "the feminine," looked upon as the necessary panacea to our ailing, wounded culture. Woman as cultural healer is not a new role for women. Sufficiently outside the sphere of power, Woman has often been called upon to heal wounds, nurture broken souls, revive crushed spirits. The spiritual hunger of the 80s and 90s and its attendant goddess literature have exalted the feminine as that which will save our own lost soul as well as our planet. This literature selects out what certain theorists find admirable about women and asserts these as the predominant characteristics of being female, locating the quality "inside" the female sex.

A related phenomena for men is the rise of the men's movement as personified by Robert Bly, poet and lecturer, who encourages men to find themselves through a relationship (a distinctly "feminine" path) with a male mentor, who is not merely a mentor but a "Mother–Man" (Bly & Moyers, 1989). He describes the relationship as mutually enhancing—whereby the younger man honors the elder for his years and his wisdom, and the elder, the Mother–Man, actively admires the younger for traits, talents, and aspirations that the elder encourages him to manifest in the world. This is a very different story than Oedipus. Singularly missing is the Biological Mother. She is replaced by the Mother–Man who does not compete, ward off, or feel threatened by the younger one, but wants what every Mother wants— what is best for his son. The male appropriation of the feminine may be somewhat of an acknowledgment to women, however "leaving the mother" —the necessary step in the boy's journey toward finding himself—does little to change either attitudes toward women, the view of the self as autonomous, or the dichotimization of gender. In effect, Bly is appropriating "the good mother" in the Mother–Man and "the bad mother" in the biological one who must be left.

Another form of appropriation are the accoutrements of the men's movement taken, ironically, from the very people that the white man attempted to destroy, the American Indian (Mander, 1991). This movement, so overwhelmingly comprised of white, educated, middle-class men drumming and passing the talking stick, earnestly seeks to find something good, something healing, in something male. As with women in relation to the goddess material, such approaches may indeed help men recover a sense of honor and wholeness, but they do little to change the oppressive structures that inevitably advantage them. The cultures of women and Native Americans, both subordinated by white male culture, are borrowed from in an attempt to construct a new mythic masculinity. Significantly, these appropriations rarely express any identification with the social needs or the political aspirations of either Native Americans or women and do little to assist men in coming to terms with the problem of masculinity.

What is it about being white, middle class, heterosexual in the America of the 1990s that has us, women *and* men, turning toward myths, goddesses, and tribal rituals? What are we trying to correct, change, or challenge about ourselves that seems so connected to our gender?

CHALLENGING GENDER

There is growing awareness of the gross exaggeration of gender in our culture. What function has traditional gender served, or simply, gender itself served? In whose interest? How does it function? Who and what suffers as a consequence? What exactly are we changing when we consider changing this norm called gender? Are we the agents of change? The subjects? The objects?

Gender, the dichotomizing category, to the extent that it has served anyone, has served white men in access to resources and power. It has functioned by virtue of white male dominance over our theories, institutions, language, social structure, and values. It has been maintained by the unchallenged belief in the natural superiority of men (over the inherent inferiority of women) and their unwillingness to relinquish control. Men and women suffer as a consequence by not being able to fully develop their human capacities and by becoming almost caricatures to each other. But, as it has been persuasively argued for over two generations in the struggle for equality, women suffer greater harm than men. Women are the ones restricted, held back from positions of power and influence, they are the ones made dependent so that survival takes prominence over aspiration, and women are the all too common victims of male violence: sexual harassment, rape, battering, and incest.

Humor has been used as a way to deflect from the seriousness of "the war between the sexes." The audience's (men and women) responsive laughter to "wife" jokes in the 1950s and 1960s and to "PMS–bitch" jokes in the 90s make us feel that we are in on something we all understand—that there is a familiar, cultural bond between us. (The fact that wives and women are the predominant butt of the joke serves to highlight the intentional derision.) This is precisely what is so compelling about exaggerated gender difference. It gives us the feeling that we have an immutable connection to the natural order of things. It gives us comfort in knowing our place. It may limit us as individuals and as a culture, indeed create caricatures of us all, yet we cleave to it as if it were life itself. It unites the men around their self-righteous and disingenuous question: "Why can't a woman be more like a man?" (Lerner & Loewe, 1956). It bonds women ever closer in sisterhood against a common enemy in search of empathy and empowerment. And all the while, amidst the anger and despair, we hold on to the stranglehold of gender.

To add to our own perversity, we neutralize gender by speaking and acting as if power plays no part. We speak of love between a man and a woman as transcending power differences. Yet, power and the balance of power run throughout a love relationship. The psychoanalyst Ethel Person, in her impressive analysis of love, power, and gender, summarizes it well:

> By and large there is a gender difference in the techniques of control that each sex favors, though these are by no means invariable. Woman often exerts her control through either a dependent or caretaking modality. As the submissive one, eager to do her lover's bidding, she manifests her moral superiority, and manipulates by eliciting guilt in the beloved. She ensnares and manipulates the beloved through her submission and her high moral standards, through her self sacrifice and faithfulness. . . . Man, on the other hand, generally opts for dominance, coercing and manipulating more directly by physical or verbal abuse,

economic, social, or other kinds of sanction. These differences reflect both gender socialization and a real difference in the power positions of men and women in our society. (1989, pp. 178–179)

In the last decade, couples and families have been challenged to confront the power differences between men and women. The two factors most responsible for the public challenge have been the women's movement (including the burgeoning prochoice agenda, equal pay, sexual harassment, violence against women, women's health issues) and the economic necessity of two-paycheck families. The combination of the women's movement and economic necessity makes, possibly for the first time, a majority of women working outside the home a permanent reality. In time, women's presence at work will not only transform her, but work itself will be transformed. It has been working-*women*, after all, who have raised the issues of family leave, flex time, and child care.

What had once been a mysterious male domain, the world of work, is no longer quite so mysterious. And with that comes an inevitable demystification of men. All the qualities that had once been the exclusive property of men—recognition, competition, acknowledgment, financial reward, and status are now possible for women to experience and evaluate for themselves. In fact, as the last decade has brought more women into competitive work and fields traditionally blocked from them, their relationship to men has changed. The motivation of finding a man who will be a good provider has begun to be superseded by wanting a man who will be a good partner.

What happens when a heterosexual couple purposefully lessens the grip of exaggerated gender and confronts power differences directly? What challenges meet them both in their relationship and as individuals that are not confronted within the borders of traditional/exaggerated gender?

We need to ask questions of the couple with an eye on the prevailing reality of gender-based expectations, behaviors, and responsibilities as they are played out. Questions proposed by Goodrich et al. (1988, pp. 24–25) serve as points of analysis as the therapist works with couples and families:

- How does gender affect the allocation of labor, power, and rewards in this family?
- How do the stereotypes and the consequent allocations of labor, power, and rewards interact with the presenting problem?
- What do the family members believe about male and female labor that distributes labor in the specific manner that it does and prevents its distribution in some other way? (This question refers to parenting and nurturing functions, as well as household chores, financial control, and breadwinning.)
- What do family members believe about male and female power that distributes power the way that it does and prevents its distribution some other way?

- What do family members believe about male and female desires, worth, values, and entitlement that makes rewards be distributed the way they are and prevents their distribution some other way?

This perspective clearly takes the position that gender plays an all too vital role in the daily existence of family life to be ignored or minimized by therapists who might like to believe that difference (particularly regarding power) is minimal, complementary, or irrelevant.

Case Study: Mark and Donna

This is the second marriage for both Mark and Donna. Their conversation is filled with words of intent, boundary setting, language of perspective, labeling of feelings, and assuring the other of nonblame. They are both highly inspired by the notion that caring is a mutual responsibility.

Donna is in a position of management with an appreciable amount of responsibility. Mark has a technical position without a college degree. Donna's salary is higher and her professional responsibilities are greater than Mark's. Donna does considerably more domestic tasks than Mark (caring for the children, cooking, cleaning, etc.). She has been confused about her right to bring these issues up and fearful about overwhelming Mark.

In therapy she is confirmed on both counts. The therapist tells Donna that her confusion about what is "right" to want regarding domestic responsibility is not only about her particular family history but the particular transitional moment between men and women today. Her fear of overwhelming Mark is confirmed by Mark's highly defensive and reactive response that he "can't ever do enough." Donna becomes upset and confused that her complaint has hurt Mark, causing him to feel inadequate, and she starts to back off. The therapist encourages Donna to face her wishes honestly as well as the effect of Mark's response on her thoughts and feelings. She is surprised to discover that beyond her confusion is tremendous despair about this aspect of their relationship. She wishes that she had never raised the complaint, since it feels irreconcilable. Her solution is to just "do more" herself rather than make Mark upset and create a conflict.

The therapist acknowledges Donna's dilemma. She is then told that it is a loss to her and the children that Mark does not participate more in the daily patterns of family life. She is reassured that it is apparent that she has no interest in hurting her husband. She is also encouraged not to feel responsible for Mark's reaction and assured that her raising the issue of greater participation on Mark's part is an acknowledgment of an inequity that must be addressed. For his part, Mark is encouraged to face his fears and sense of being overwhelmed and begin confronting his notion of masculinity that seems to suggest some kind of entitlement on his part. With the therapist's help, he is able to delineate the stressors in his life: a possible corporate lay-off, going back to college, and lack of male support. After Mark is able to express his feelings on each of these issues and receive Donna's honest empathy, the couple is directed to return to the unresolved issue of inequity of domestic tasks in their family. The couple's near derailment of the inequity issue is an illustration of women's overresponsibility for the relationship and for men's feelings and men's inexperience with working through feelings and staying through a negotiation as an equal.

Case Study: Suzanne and James

Suzanne and James are also in their second marriages. They are in their late 40s, with grown children. In the first session, they each presented absolute failure on their partner's part to live up to their expected gender roles. James described Suzanne as woefully inadequate as a supportive and nurturing wife, whereas Suzanne described James as failing her in not allowing her to be free of economic responsibility by providing sufficiently for both of them.

By the second session, fearing that the marriage was about to end, James proposed that he would be the sole provider for the couple's financial well-being in exchange for Suzanne's support of his emotional well-being. By the third session, Suzanne recognized that this was inherently a dangerous deal for her to agree to; servicing anothers' emotional well-being has no boundaries. James recognized that if he followed through on his proposal he would never know why Suzanne chose to stay with him beyond her need for financial security. By the fourth session they began to look at what they needed to address in themselves. Suzanne decided to move out (the only way she could be less reactive) while continuing in couple therapy. She commited to becoming more financially responsible and began job interviews. Once Suzanne moved out, James commited to becoming responsible for his own emotional well-being for the first time in his life: he joined a men's group and began letting his friends and adult sons support him emotionally.

James and Suzanne are not sure whether they will now stay together. Without the gender ideals and accompanying expectations they projected on each other (he supports financially, she supports emotionally), it is not clear what they really think and feel about each other. It will take some time for them to know. In the meantime, however, they are learning more about themselves and are able to be more interested and curious about the other than they ever were when gender dominated.

Husbands, by virtue of their manhood, are presumed to be rational, objective, independent, and dominant. Wives, by virtue of their womanhood, are presumed to be emotional, subjective, dependent, and subordinate. These presumptions not only obscure and deny the possibility of each finding his or her unique voice, proclivity, and task, but the range of permissible forms that a marital relationship or a family may properly assume is restricted. Immutable gender norms may indeed construct the family as a "natural" coherent structure, but only at the cost of much pain and confusion for countless families and family members who experience themselves as failures in their prescribed gender identities.

MEN AND FEELINGS

As they came into the therapist's office it was clear that both spouses were upset. The husband launched into an appeal for the male therapist to support him in what was, to him, a perfectly reasonable judgment. "It is obvious that she shouldn't go out of the house alone at night; the city is a jungle at the best of times, and after 9:00 it is doubly so. She doesn't realize how dangerous it is, how foolish she is to take such unnecessary risks." The wife then expressed her resentment at what she described was her husband's patronizing attitude and attempts to control her. "I'm sick of you talking down to me as if I were an irresponsible child who can't take care of herself. How dare you judge my reasons for doing anything as unnecessary!"

The argument continued along predictable lines for most of the session. He accused her of being too sensitive and of hearing criticism where none was intended. She complained of his total and long-standing lack of interest in what was important to her. He wonders why they cannot talk about their differences in reasonable tones. She marvels at his ability to discern what is best for everyone around him but never even seems to know what movie *he* wants to see.

The excerpt captures only too well the generic conversation between women and men in recent years, and highlights how differently men and women converse (Tannen, 1990). Whereas the wife appears to value her feelings as a source of information about a situation and a basis for behavior, her husband seems oblivious not only to her feelings but to his own as well. Rather than state what he would like, the man speaks as if he were the representative of some essential state of affairs or general truth. When the woman resents (what she attributes to him as) his attempts to control her, he is bewildered by her attribution and may fall back on some stereotype about how emotional women are.

"Why can't he share what he's feeling?" is the universal grievance of women about male partners, colleagues, and friends. And men's response is an equally frustrated "I don't ever know what she wants; and when I think I do, it's never enough!"

There was a time, prior to the feminist critique, when an interaction such as that above would have led almost automatically to a therapeutic effort designed to deal with the wife's "excess" of emotions and neediness. The idea that the husband's apparent lack of emotion could be a contribution to the conflict would have seemed very strange. Feminist contributions to psychotherapy make it easier to understand how a man's not being in touch with his feelings, and his consequent inability to ask clearly for what he wants, helps maintain the communicational impasse (McGoldrick, 1989; Walsh, 1989; Walters et al., 1988).

The man in this case was able eventually to *feel* what he was feeling and communicate it: "When you go out alone in the evenings, I fear for your safety. If something were to happen to you, I would blame myself because, for whatever reason, I feel responsible for protecting you. In addition, especially when you don't come home till bedtime, I get afraid that you might be seeing another man." He discovered that, painful and risky though this way of stating his concerns were, his partner was now more willing to discuss them.

The apparent success of this kind of clinical intervention might lead us to conclude that men's relationship to their feelings is best thought of in purely psychological terms—as a personal deficit or some failure of socialization to be handled through psychotherapy or some other form of broadly therapeutic instruction. Such approaches tend to locate men's difficulties (as well as their cures) within individuals, never quite challenging the cultural demands that shape men's sense of themselves, and certainly never confronting the culture itself as a masculinist construction (Taggart, 1992). Male authors of books on psychotherapy with men (cf. Meth & Pasick, 1990; Osherson, 1992) thus far are less likely to explore the social and cultural origins of masculinity than are their female counterparts (cf. Bograd, 1991).

MAKING MASCULINITY VISIBLE

Men's estrangement from their feelings is only one aspect of a deep cultural inheritance affecting men, yet, still largely invisible. The challenge is to be able to comprehend the dominant images and guiding metaphors of masculinity in ways that make visible its social and historical formation. There is a sense in which masculinity is "the great unsaid" (Rutherford & Chapman, 1988, p. 11). The vast majority of news reports, articles, and essays addressing sex and gender talk about women, gays, and lesbians, as if heterosexual males had neither sex nor gender! Thus, the standard by which all sexuality is judged, white, heterosexual masculinity, *itself* stands outside the realm of judgment. Thus, "heterosexual men have inherited a language which [sic] can define the lives and sexualities of others, but fails us when we have to deal with our own heterosexuality and masculine identities" (Rutherford and Chapman, 1988, p. 22).[3]

What is called for is something over and above becoming more sensitive to the social expectations placed on men by the culture and seeking to ameliorate their consequences through psychotherapy. It is, rather, to come

---

[3]We can see here that the "negative identity" aspect of masculinity is not only a matter of what happens in the young boy as part of his socialization. Just as the boy defines himself as *not* female, so the discourse on masculinity defines it as *not* (black, gay, female, lesbian, etc.).

to grips with the realization that the very components with which we image masculinity—history, language, concepts, categories of behavior, experience, and so forth—are themselves gendered in ways that we have not yet imagined, and that making masculinity more visible will require men ". . . to get down to serious work. And . . . that involves struggle and pain" (Jardine, 1987, p. 60).

The paths by which feminism has, over the past three decades, helped women to understand their lives as gendered provide markers to men as they set out on similar journeys. As Kimmel (1987b) points out, changes in how masculinity gets constructed are often historically responsive to changes in femininity. Social changes reverberate to alter the family's structure and especially its relation to economy and society. This in turn creates shifts in gender relations as women begin to move from domestic to public spheres and construct an ideology to account for such movement. As women thus define themselves differently, given that the two are relational constructions, the definition of masculinity is necessarily called into question. But no matter how one punctuates social changes of this kind, it is men's work on themselves that will be crucial in the reconstruction of men's lives.

Important beginnings of this work have already appeared (Abbot, 1987; Absher, 1990; Bly, 1990; Boone & Cadden, 1990; Chapman & Rutherford, 1988; Gerzon, 1982; Jardine & Smith, 1987; Kaufman, 1987; Keen, 1991; Kimmel, 1987a; Kimmel, 1990; Meth & Pasick, 1990; Nelson, 1988; Osherson, 1992; Segal, 1990; Seidler, 1989, 1991; Stoltenberg, 1989; Taggart, 1985, 1989). We stand at the very beginning of what hopefully will be a radical change in men's relationship to what defines them as men and consequently, how they relate to women and children. Only the barest outlines of the task have appeared thus far.

Where the task will take men is unclear. However, it is useful as we consider the evolution of masculinity to keep in mind the connection between the emergent identification of masculinity with a particular conception of Reason as both ideas coevolve as anchors of the 17th century Enlightenment (Seidler, 1989). Seidler explores how the overwhelming commitment to the Enlightenment's conception of Reason has shaped men's experience of themselves and their world. Men's power and their propensity to impersonalize and universalize their own particular experience have made the fact of men's gendered subjectivity invisible. This is demonstrated daily by men, typically out of touch with their own needs, but speaking for others while presenting themselves as the neutral voice of reason. Furthermore, the culture of rationalism defines freedom as the exercise of rational choice unhampered by emotions and desire. Thus, autonomy becomes the *absence* of connectedness, reason the *negation* of desire. Seidler traces how men's denial of their emotional selves legitimates a culture of self-denial and self-rejection in which it is hard for men to ask for what they need to nourish themselves. It is at this point that the cultural imperative laid on women to nourish men emotionally emerges. This is *not* a request by a man who knows what he needs and asks for it. It appears as an imperative for the woman because it is deemed to be in her nature to nourish and in his to expect it from her. Perhaps this is another aspect of men bypassing the whole notion of need altogether by taking what they want *as their due* in a world they dominate.

The cultural legacy that has come down from the Enlightenment, though still vigorous, is increasingly being challenged by postmodernist critiques.[4] Our inherited conceptions of masculinity are part and parcel of the modern world, and as modernity itself comes into question, so masculinity has to revision itself in radical new terms.

CHANGES IN FAMILY LIFE

As men begin to envision and live their lives differently, we can expect the changes to reverberate through their marital and family relationships. We should expect that reactions to the changes will be mixed. Some women will feel relief when husbands, accustomed to relying solely on them for emotional support, enter nurturing relationships with other men. Other women may feel deprived of the only role that is truly theirs in relation to their husbands.

It is well known that complementary gender roles, and the separate spheres they presume, act to obscure conflict in a marriage (Walters et al., 1988). Even when the change from a complementary to a symmetrical pattern comes about by mutual agreement, conflict between partners will often escalate. The woman who has always wanted her husband to be more involved in childcare now finds herself having to resolve parenting differences with him. Similarly, the man who has fervently wished that his wife be more involved in the family's long-term financial planning now has to justify his investment strategies to someone who has ideas of her own.

Most challenging are the changes that bring family members directly up against a society still organized along rigid gender lines. It is one thing for parents to encourage a seven-year-old boy to follow up his interest in ballet by taking dance lessons. It is quite another for them to prepare him (and themselves) to cope with the inevitable cruelty of peers and the questions of adults. Rigidity is often expressed institutionally. Flex time and family leave for working mothers are still controversial ideas even when political rhetoric extols the family. Extending such options to fathers, lesbian co-mothers, or gay co-fathers meets progressively stiffer resistance the more the parenting unit differs from that of the "traditional" family.

Working couples often have difficulty negotiating how to balance work and childcare responsibilities. After the birth of their baby, a young profes-

---

[4]For an introduction to postmodernism's possible relationships to social science, see Rosenau (1992).

sional couple had arranged excellent live-in help, leaving only the evenings and weekends for them to be directly involved in childcare. The father resented that his position in the family's economy meant that he worked much longer hours than his wife, thus cutting into his parenting time. When he suggested cutting back at work to spend more time with the baby, his wife was doubly upset. Not only was her already limited time with the baby threatened by his proposal, but the additional expense of a baby and live-in help suggested to her that he needed to spend *more* time at work, not less. To make things worse, the father's business partners were critical of his shift in energy from work toward his family. Business, and the acquisitive culture that values material success above everything, make it difficult for families to put changing values into practice.

Transitions with respect to values are difficult. As patterns shift, traditional and nontraditional roles may be combined in complex and confusing ways. The social and economic challenges associated with social change are often unprecedented. Another professional couple resolved similar issues by each working half-time and sharing childcare and domestic tasks equally. Their decision to settle for a lower economic standard of living seemed to them to be the best way to shape the family's structure in ways that pleased them both. This couple clearly valued active involvement as a family over the broader culture's definition of success—increased professional responsibilities, larger house, and more possessions.

Such remedies, even the problems that evoke them, are restricted to families with the economic resources to consider them in the first place. Most families cannot afford live-in (nor much of any) help, nor can they reduce their incomes even marginally and survive. The emergence of new options for men will mean very little to these families unless the new versions of what it means to be a man are accompanied by a new politics. Issues such as childcare, flex time, family leave, health care, reproductive rights, economic and social justice are *not* the exclusive province of women. Unless men join women in securing a truly pro-family social and economic environment in this society, other changes will count for little.

RAISING GENDER

In order to change, or more radically challenge, gender we need to change how we raise our children. However, the solution is not as simple as it might have initially appeared when books like Selma Greenberg's *Right from the Start: A Guide to Nonsexist Child Rearing* (Greenberg, 1978) first appeared. In fact, even as she set out to inform parents how they could change their stereotypic behavior toward their boy and girl children, Greenberg recognized that it was "simplistic and unhelpful to discuss mothering and fathering as if women and men's relation to each other, to the world, and to their children are the same. It is nonproductive to write about equal child-caring independent of the inequality that exists in two-parent families because one is female and one is male" (Greenberg, 1978, p. 10). She pointed out that our efforts would be misdirected if we attempted to speak of parenting before we spoke of two equal people in a relationship of equality.

Ten years later we learn from Arlie Hochschild's (1989) study, aptly named *The Second Shift*, that women who work outside the home come home in the evening to yet another job, whereas their husbands continue to view the domestic sphere as still primarily hers. She found that, on the average, women work an additional month every year because of the second shift's demands. Her interviews with the men and women (well distributed across class and ideological differences) found that over half the working mothers had tried in various ways to alter the pattern of domestic responsibilities, since they were the ones who bore "the weight of the contradiction between traditional ideology and modern circumstances" (Hochschild, 1989, p. 194). These women had to assume the additional task of changing the division of labor. "If women lived in a culture that presumed active fatherhood, they wouldn't need to devise personal strategies to bring it about" (Hochschild, 1989, p. 194).

We are not yet at the point of "presumed active fatherhood." Although there are individual men who are active fathers, the social context has changed very little regarding making father's involvement a given. Men who are deeply aware of their wish to be actively involved with their children must manage the predominant culture's interpretation that they are probably not very serious about their work. (Similarly, women with children who work have been relegated to what has been pejoratively called "the mommy track.") No matter how in vogue it might be for a man to give dissertations on the joy of fatherhood, his and other men's judgment of him are still based on that part of him remaining on the periphery. In our society, salaried employment and advancement in the workplace are valued over domestic (family) responsibility and participation. Men's identity and self-esteem have traditionally been tied to job performance, financial success, and status. Parenting and homemaking have been designated women's work and consequently devalued.

The dichotomization of work and family hurts women too. Working mothers, (the vast majority who work because of economic necessity) often report feeling tremendous guilt about not being home more with their children. But, guilt is only one aspect of the situation. The more poignant facet is the sadness and pain that some women describe as they have to manage the loss of a part of themselves, the part that they have been conditioned toward desiring all their lives—Motherhood (Braverman, 1989). Adrienne Rich (1976) may be correct that Motherhood as an institution may itself be a historical and cultural construct shaped out of industrialization and patriarchy, having little to do with the actual and natural experience women have of being mothers. But working mothers today who are white and middle to upper-middle class (black mothers have always had to work) are caught between the popular culture they were raised on (television shows like "Donna Reed," "Leave It to Beaver," "Father Knows Best"), their experience of their own mothers, and their feminist-informed critique. The syndicated political cartoonist Gary Trudeau portrayed the gender difference brilliantly. The new mother shares her upset about feeling that she is not doing enough for her child, asking her spouse if he, too, ever feels this way. In one cartoon frame he lays out the truth of the gender difference in contemporary parenting: "No matter what I do it will always be more than my father did, and no matter what you do it will always be less than your mother."

Are the other institutions that raise and shape our children doing any better regarding gender? How are our schools doing in expanding what little boys and girls can feel, think, and become? School texts below college level remain woefully inadequate in reporting women's contributions. In fields such as the sciences, where women's contribution has been sparse, texts do not educate children to understand the reasons for women's near absence. Recently, the American Association of University Women (Editorial, 1992) released a study ("How Schools Shortchange Girls") documenting how girls and boys are treated differently in the classroom. It notes that, although girls and boys enter school with equal abilities, girls' performance declines steadily from the earliest grades all the way through to the end of high school. The research noted a pattern in which girls receive consistently less encouragement than boys. When, for example, boys call out answers in class (which they do eight times more often than girls), teachers are apt to respond supportively. On the other hand, when girls call out answers, teachers are likely to instruct them to raise their hands if they wish to speak. Compared with boys, girls are not encouraged to take advanced courses in math and science. Furthermore, girls will encounter few positive female role models in textbooks and other instructional media over the course of their schooling. The report concludes that schools actually interfere with girls' educational advancement.

And what of the the popular media? These have shaped and invaded our images of gender and male–female relationships. Precisely at this time in history, when women are demonstrating their abilities in fields traditionally closed off to them, the media, particularly film, have depicted independent, competent women as treacherous, murderous, and malevolent. The timing is hardly coincidental in that, with the infusion of women in more positions of power, there should appear this cautionary subtext in film: Beware! Women are not just interested in equality (Faludi, 1991).

Saturday-morning cartoon shows are still dominated by heroic males, animal or human, accompanied by adoring, secondary female characters. The weekly television sit-coms, current in their inclusion of contemporary male–female challenges and social issues (working mothers, gender-sensitive boyfriends, little girls who aspire to greatness) continue to promote the traditional male–female paradigm in most of their scripts. Girls and women are still required to devote slavish attention to their looks and their ability to "catch the guy." A New York Times article (Carter, 1991) reports a media representative admitting that the underrepresentation of girls as the central character in children's television programming is clearly because girls will watch shows that have a boy as the protagonist, but boys will not watch shows with girls in the lead. Finally, media images of women as sex objects, victims of violence, and co-participants in their own subordination are still more often the rule than the exception.

Children will only be free of gender bias and domination in homes where their mother and father actively demonstrate mutual respect, have equal responsibility for domestic tasks as well as care-giving, openly discuss gender issues, find texts (stories, books, articles) that challenge gender outright, and can tolerate and support their children in thinking, feeling, or behaving outside traditional gender roles. This will not be easy. Social pressure comes down very hard on children, especially adolescents, who do not conform to stereotypic gender behavior. Parents and children will need supportive peers, teachers, counselors, as well as balanced media representations, if the family is to be encouraged in its goal of gender-neutral child rearing.

This is a transitional time regarding gender. Many of us no longer feel comfortable with what has shaped us as men and women. At the same time, what is familiar is powerful, and gender habits die hard. Will we be willing to challenge culturally prescribed beliefs and behavior? Will we be tolerant of our own and others' awkwardness as we change? To inspire and facilitate us on our journey we take some liberty with the epilogue that ends Evelyn Fox Keller's *Reflections on Gender and Science*:

> My vision of a gender-free . . . [society] is not a juxtaposition or complementarity of male and female perspectives, nor is it the substitution of one form of parochiality for another. Rather, it is premised on a transformation of the very categories of male and female, and correspondingly, of mind and nature.
>
> A healthy . . . [culture] is one that allows for the productive survival of diverse conceptions of mind and nature, and of correspondingly diverse strategies.
>
> To know . . . history . . . is to recognize the mortality of any claim to universal truth. Every past vision of . . . truth . . . has proved in time to be more limited than its adherents claimed. The survival of productive difference . . . requires that we put all claims for intellectual hegemony in their proper place— that we understand that such claims are, by their very nature, political rather than scientific. (Keller, 1985, pp. 178–179)

REFERENCES

Abbot, F. (Ed.). (1987). *New men, new minds: Breaking male tradition*. Freedom, CA: The Crossing Press.

Absher, T. (1990). *Men and the goddess*. Rochester, VT: Park St. Press.

Avis, J. M. (1991). Power politics in therapy with women. In T. J. Goodrich (Ed.), *Women and power: Perspectives for family therapy* (pp. 183–200). New York: W. W. Norton & Co.

Beauvoir, S. de. (1974). *The second sex.* New York: Vintage Books.

Belenky, M. F., Clinchy, B. M., Goldberger, N. R., & Tarule, J. M. (1986). *Women's way of knowing: The development of self, voice, and mind.* New York: Basic Books.

Block, J. (1976). Issues, problems and pitfalls in assessing sex differences: A critical review of *The Psychology of Sex Differences. Merrill-Palmer Quarterly, 22,* 283–308.

Bly, R. (1990). *Iron John: A book about men.* Reading, MA: Addison-Wesley.

Bly, R., & Moyers, B. (1989). *A gathering of men.* Public Broadcasting System (television program).

Bograd, M. (Ed.). (1991). *Feminist approaches for men in family therapy.* New York: Harrington Park Press.

Boone, J. A. (1990). Of me(n) and feminism: Who(se) is the sex that writes? In J. A. Boone & M. Cadden (Eds.), *Engendering men: The question of male feminist criticism* (pp. 11–25). New York: Routledge.

Boone, J. A., & Cadden, M. (Eds.). (1990). *Engendering men: The question of male feminist criticism.* New York: Routledge.

Braverman, L. (1989). Beyond the myth of motherhood. In M. McGoldrick, C. M. Anderson, & F. Walsh (Eds.), *Women in families: A framework for family therapy* (pp. 227–243). New York: W. W. Norton & Co.

Broverman, I. K., Broverman, D. M., Clarkson, F. E., Rosencrantz, P. S., & Vogel, S. R. (1970). Sex role stereotypes and clinical judgements of mental health. *Journal of Consulting and Clinical Psychology, 34,* 1–7.

Brownmiller, S. (1984). *Femininity.* New York: Fawcett Columbine.

Butler, J. (1990). *Gender trouble: Feminism and the subversion of identity.* London: Routledge, Chapman & Hall.

Carter, B. (1991, May 1). Children's T.V., where boys are king. *The New York Times,* p. 1.

Chapman, R., & Rutherford, J. (Eds.). (1988). *Male order: Unwrapping masculinity.* London: Lawrence & Wishart.

Chodorow, N. (1978). *The reproduction of mothering.* Berkeley, CA: University of California Press.

Editorial. (1992, February 19). Gender bias in U.S. education. Boston: *Christian Science Monitor,* p. 20.

Ellmann, M. (1968). *Thinking about women.* New York: Harcourt Brace Jovanovich.

Faludi, S. (1991). *Backlash: The undeclared war against American women.* New York: Crown.

Friedan, B. (1963). *The feminine mystique.* New York: Norton.

Gerzon, M. (1982). *A choice of heroes.* Boston: Houghton Mifflin.

Gilligan, C. (1982). *In a different voice: Psychological theory and women's development.* Cambridge, MA: Harvard University Press.

Gilligan, C., Lyons, N. P., & Hanmer, T. J. (Eds.). (1990). *Making connections: The relationship worlds of adolescent girls at Emma Willard School.* New Haven, CT: Harvard University Press.

Goldner, V. (1989). Generation and gender: Normative and covert hierarchies. In M. McGoldrick, C. M. Anderson, & F. Walsh (Eds.), *Women in families: A framework for family therapy* (pp. 42–60). New York: W. W. Norton & Co.

Goldner, V. (1991). Sex, power, and gender: A feminist analysis of the politics of passion. In T. J. Goodrich (Ed.), *Women and power: Perspectives for family therapy* (pp. 86–106). New York: W. W. Norton & Co.

Goodrich, T. J. (1991). Women, power, and family therapy: What's wrong with this picture? In T. J. Goodrich (Ed.), *Women and power: Perspectives for family therapy* (pp. 3–35). New York: W. W. Norton & Co.

Goodrich, T. J., Rampage, C., Ellman, B., & Halstead, K. (1988). *Feminist family therapy: A casebook.* New York: W. W. Norton & Co.

Greenberg, S. (1978). *Right from the start: A guide to nonsexist child rearing.* Boston: Houghton Mifflin.

Harding, S. (1986). *The science question in feminism.* Ithaca, NY: Cornell University.

Harding, S. (1987). Introduction: Is there a feminist method? In S. Harding (Ed.), *Feminism and methodology* (pp. 1–14). Bloomington, IN: Indiana University Press.

Hare-Mustin, R. T. (1991). Sex, lies, and headaches: The problem is power. In T. J. Goodrich (Ed.), *Women and power: Perspectives for family therapy* (pp. 63–85). New York: W. W. Norton & Co.

Hare-Mustin, R. T., & Marecek, J. (1990). *Making a difference: Psychology and the construction of gender.* New Haven, CT: Yale University Press.

Hilts, P. J. (1992, February 18). Panel to consider what rules should control gel implants. *The New York Times,* p. D10.

Hochschild, A. (1989). *The second shift.* New York: Avon Books.

Holstrom, N. (1986). Do women have a distinct nature. In M. Pearsall (Ed.), *Women and values: Readings in recent feminist philosophy* (pp. 51–61). Sacramento, CA: Wadsworth Publishing Co.

Hooks, B. (1990). *Yearning: Race, gender, and cultural politics.* Boston: South End Press.

Jardine, A. (1987). Men in feminism: Odor do uomo or compagnons de route? In A. Jardine & P. Smith (Eds.), *Men in feminism* (pp. 54–61). New York: Routledge.

Jardine, A., & Smith, P. (Eds.). (1987). *Men in feminism.* New York: Routledge.

Jordan, J., Kaplan, A., Miller, J., Stiver, I., & Surrey, J. (1991). *Women's growth in connection.* New York: Guilford Press.

Kaufman, M. (Ed.). (1987). *Beyond patriarchy.* New York: Oxford University Press.

Keen, S. (1991). *Fire in the belly: On being a man.* New York: Bantam Books.

Keller, E. F. (1985). *Reflections on gender and science.* New Haven: Yale University.

Kimmel, M. S. (Ed.). (1987a). *Changing men: New directions in research on men and masculinity.* Newbury Park, CA: Sage.

Kimmel, M. S. (1987b). Rethinking "masculinity": New directions in research. In M. S. Kimmel (Ed.), *Changing men: New directions in research on men and masculinity* (pp. 9–24). Newbury Park, CA: Sage.

Kimmel, M. S. (Ed.). (1990). *Men confront pornography.* New York: Crown Publishers.

Lerner, A. J., & Loewe, F. (1956). *My fair lady.* New York: Chappell.

Maccoby, E., & Jacklin, C. N. (1974). *The psychology of sex differences.* Stanford, CA: Stanford University Press.

Mander, J. (1991). What you don't know about Indians. *Utne Reader,* (48), Nov./Dec., 1991, 67–74.

McGoldrick, M. (1989). For love or money. In T. J. Goodrich (Ed.), *Women and power: Perspectives for family therapy.* (pp. 239–244). New York: W. W. Norton & Co.

McGoldrick, M., Garcia-Preto, N., Hines, P. M. & Lee, E. (1989). Ethnicity and women. In M. McGoldrick, C. M. Anderson and F. Walsh (Eds.), *Women in families: A framework for family therapy* (pp. 169–199). New York: W. W. Norton & Co.

Meth, R. L., & Pasick, R. S. (1990). *Men in therapy: The challenge of change.* New York: Guilford Press.

Miller, J. B. (1986). *Toward a new psychology of women* (2nd ed.). Boston: Beacon Press.

Nelson, J. B. (1988). *The intimate connection: Male sexuality, male spirituality*. Philadelphia: Westminster Press.

Nicholson, L. (1990). *Feminism/postmodernism*. New York: Routledge, Chapman & Hall.

Osherson, S. (1992). *Wrestling with love: How men struggle with intimacy with women, children, parents, and each other*. New York: Fawcett Columbine.

Paglia, C. (1990). *Sexual personae*. New Haven, CT: Yale University Press.

Person, E. S. (1989). *Dreams of love and fateful encounters: The power of romantic passion*. New York: Penguin Books.

Pleck, J. H. (1987). American fathering in historical perceptive. In M.S. Kimmel (Ed.), *Changing men: New directions on research on men and masculinity* (pp. 83–97). Newbury, CA: Sage.

Rich, A. (1976). *Of woman born*. New York: Norton.

Rich, A. (1980). Compulsory heterosexuality and lesbian existence. *Signs, 5*(4), 631–660.

Rosenau, P. (1992). *Post-modernism and the social sciences: Insights, inroads, and intrusions*. Princeton, NJ: Princeton University Press.

Rowbotham, S. (1973). *Women's consciousness, man's world*. New York: Penguin Books.

Rutherford, J., & Chapman, R. (1988). The forward march of men halted. In R. Chapman & J. Rutherford (Eds.), *Male order: Unwrapping masculinity* (pp. 9–18). London: Lawrence & Wishart.

Schwenger, P. (1989). The masculine mode. In E. Showalter (Ed.), *Speaking of gender* (pp. 101–112). New York: Routledge.

Segal, L. (1990). *Slow motion: Changing masculinities, changing men*. New Brunswick, NJ: Rutgers University Press.

Seidler, V. J. (1989). *Rediscovering masculinity: Reason, language and sexuality*. London: Routledge.

Seidler, V. J. (1991). *Recreating sexual politics: Men, feminism and politics*. London and New York: Routledge.

Stoltenberg, J. (1989). *Refusing to be a man: Essays on sex and justice*. New York: Penguin.

Taggart, M. (1985). The feminist critique in epistemological perspective: Questions of context in family therapy. *Journal of Marital and Family Therapy, 11*, 113–126.

Taggart, M. (1989). Epistemological equality as the fulfillment of family therapy. *Journal of Feminist Family Therapy, 1*, 85–110.

Taggart, M. (1992). Review of Meth & Pasick's Men in Therapy. *Journal of Feminist Family Therapy, 4*, 96–99.

Tannen, D. (1990). *You just don't understand: Women and men in conversation*. New York: William Morrow & Company.

Thompson, E. H., & Pleck, J. H. (1987). The structure of male role norms. In M. S. Kimmel (Ed.), *Changing men: New directions in research on men and masculinity* (pp. 25–36). Newbury Park, CA: Sage.

Walsh, F. (1989). Reconsidering gender in the marital quid pro quo. In M. McGoldrick, C. M. Anderson, & F. Walsh (Ed.), *Women in families: A framework for family therapy* (pp. 267–285). New York: W. W. Norton & Co.

Walsh, F., & Scheinkman, M. (1989). (Fe)male: The hidden gender dimension in models of family therapy. In M. McGoldrick, C. M. Anderson, & F. Walsh (Eds.), *Women in families: A framework for family therapy* (pp. 16–41). New York: W. W. Norton & Co.

Walters, M., Carter, B., Papp, P., & Silverstein, O. (1988). *The invisible web: Gender patterns in family relationships*. New York: Guilford Press.

Webb-Watson, L. (1991). The sociology of power. In T. J. Goodrich (Ed.), *Women and power: Perspectives for family therapy* (pp. 48–60). New York: W. W. Norton & Co.

Wittig, M. (1992). *The straight mind*. Boston: Beacon Press.

THE CHANGING FAMILY LIFE CYCLE
A Perspective on Normalcy

Monica McGoldrick,
Marsha Heiman,
and Betty Carter

INTRODUCTION

We are born into families. Our first relationships, our first group, our first experience of the world is with and through our families. We develop, grow, and hopefully, die in the context of our families. Embedded within the larger sociopolitical culture, the individual life cycle takes shape as it moves and evolves within the matrix of the family life cycle. Our problems are framed by the formative course of our family's past, the present tasks it is trying to master, and the future to which it aspires. Thus the family life cycle is the natural context within which to frame individual identity and development.

Until recently, therapists have paid little attention to the family life cycle and its impact on human development (Carter & McGoldrick, 1989). Even now most psychological theories relate at most to the nuclear family, ignoring the multigenerational context of family connections that pattern our lives. But our dramatically changing family patterns, which in this day and age can assume many varied configurations over the life span, are forcing us to take a broader view of both development and normalcy. It is becoming increasingly difficult to determine what family life cycle patterns are "normal," causing great stress for family members, who have few consensually validated models to guide the passages they must negotiate.

Just as the texture of life has become a more complicated fabric, so too must our therapeutic models change to reflect this complexity, appreciating both the context around the individual as a shaping environment and the evolutionary factor of time on human development. From a family life cycle perspective, symptoms and dysfunction are examined within a systemic context and in relation to "normal" functioning over time. From this perspective, therapeutic interventions aim at helping to reestablish the family's developmental momentum so that it can proceed forward to foster the uniqueness of each member's development.

THE FAMILY AS A SYSTEM MOVING THROUGH TIME

Families comprise those who have a shared history and a shared future. They encompass the entire emotional system of at least three, and frequently now four generations, held together by blood, legal, and/or historical ties. Relationships with parents, siblings (McGoldrick, 1989d; Cicirelli, 1982, 1985), and other family members go through stages as they move along the life cycle. Boundaries shift, psychological distance among members changes, and roles within and between subsystems are constantly being redefined.

As a system moving through time, the family has basically different properties from all other systems. Unlike all other organizations, families incorporate new members only by birth, adoption (formal or informal), or marriage, and members can leave only by death, if then. No other system is subject to these constraints. A business organization can fire members it views as dysfunctional, or conversely, members can resign if the organization is not to their liking. In families, on the other hand, the pressures of membership with no exit available can, in the extreme, lead to psychosis. In nonfamily systems, the roles and functions of the group are carried out in a more or less stable way, by replacement of those who leave for any reason, or else the system dissolves and people move on to other structures. Although families also have roles and functions, their main value is in the relationships, which are irreplaceable. If a parent leaves or dies, another person can be brought in to fill a parenting function, but this person can never replace the parent in his or her personal emotional aspects. Even in situations of a divorcing couple without children, the bonds linger, so that it is difficult to hear of an ex-spouse death without being shaken.

Despite the current dominant American pattern of nuclear families living on their own and often at a great geographical distance from extended family members, they are still emotional subsystems, reacting to the past, present, and anticipated future relationships within the larger three-generational system. The freedom of choice for the modern family also carries with it many liabilities. The options and decisions to be made are endless and can be confusing: whom to marry, where to live, how many children to bear, how to conduct relationships within the nuclear and extended family, and how to allocate family tasks. As Hess and Waring have observed,

> As we move from the family of obligatory ties to one of voluntary bonds, relationships outside the nuclear unit (as well as those inside it) . . . lose whatever normative certainty or consistency governed them at earlier times. For example, sibling relationships today are almost completely voluntary, subject to disruption through occupational and geographic mobility, as indeed might be said of marriage itself. (1984, p. 303)

The family of days gone by when the extended family reigned supreme, however, should not be romanticized as a time when mutual respect and satisfaction existed between the generations. The traditional, stable, multi-generational extended family of yore was supported by sexism, classism, and racism. In this traditional patriarchal structure of families, respect for parents and obligations to care for elders were based on their control of the resources, reinforced by religious and secular sanctions against those who did not go along with the ideas of the dominant group. Now with the increasing ability of younger family members to determine their own fate in marriage, work, and economic security, the power of elders to demand filial piety is reduced. As women are demanding lives of their own, where before their roles were limited primarily to the caretaking of others, our social institutions are not shifting to fit with these changing needs. Instead of evolving values of shared caretaking, our social institutions still operate on notions of individualism of the pioneering frontier, and those most vulnerable—the poor, the young, the old, the infirm—suffer the consequence.

What we need is not a return to a rigid inequitable three-generational patriarchal family, but rather, to recognize our connectedness in life—regardless of the particular family structure—with those who went before us and those who follow after. At the same time, it is important to appreciate that many problems are caused when changes at the societal level lag behind those at the family level, and therefore, fail to validate and support changes in family structure.

In our times people often act as though they can choose membership and responsibility in a family. In fact, there is very little choice about whom we are related to in the complex web of family ties. Children, for example, have no choice about being born into a system. Nor do parents have a choice, once children are born, as to the existence of the responsibilities of parenthood, even if they neglect these responsibilities. Obviously family members frequently behave as if this were not so, distancing or cutting each other off because of conflicts or because they claim to have "nothing in common." No family relationships except marriage are entered into by choice. Even in the case of marriage, the freedom to marry whomever one wishes, which is a rather recent option, may be less freely made than people think (McGoldrick, 1988a). Whereas partners can choose not to continue a marriage relationship, they remain co-parents of their children. When family members act as though family relationships were optional, they do so to the detriment of their own sense of identity and the richness of their emotional and social context.

Earlier work on the life cycle (e.g., Erikson, 1963, 1968; Levinson, 1978) has rarely taken into account this complex multigenerational perspective, perhaps because there is no unifying multigenerational task such as can be described for individual development or parenting tasks. But the tremendous life-shaping impact of one generation on those following is hard to overestimate. For one thing, three or four generations of a family must accommodate to life cycle transitions simultaneously. While one generation is moving toward older age, the next is contending with the empty nest, the third with young adulthood, forming careers and intimate relationships and having children, and the fourth with being inducted into the system. Events at one level have a powerful effect on relationships at each other level in the intermingling of the generations. Painful experiences such as illness and death are particularly difficult for families to integrate and are among the many family experiences that may have a long-range impact on future generations.

There is growing evidence that life cycle events and stressors have a continuing impact on family development over a long period of time. Hadley, Jacob, Milliones, Caplan, and Spitz (1974) found that symptom onset was strongly related to the developmental crises of adding and losing family members. Walsh (1978) and McGoldrick (1977) both found that a significant life cycle event (death of a grandparent), when closely related in time to another life cycle event (birth of a child), correlated with symptom development at a much later transition in the family life cycle (the launching of the next generation). It is probably our own limited time perspective that inhibits our noticing these long-range patterns. Research is rarely carried out over periods of more than a few years, and thus longitudinal connections can easily get lost. The longitudinal research that has been done indicates clearly the impact of early family relationships on later symptom development and life experience (e.g., Thomas & Duszynski, 1974; Valliant, 1977). From this perspective, tracking family patterns through the life cycle over several generations, focusing especially on nodal events and transition points in family development provides a more encompassing and complete picture of both family and individual dysfunction in the present moment (Bowen, 1978).

UNDERSTANDING THE LIFE CYCLE: THE INDIVIDUAL, THE FAMILY, THE CULTURE

To understand how individuals evolve, we must examine their lives within the context of both the family and the culture, with its inherent set of past and present properties, which change over time (Carter & McGoldrick, 1989;

McGoldrick, 1989b). Each system: individual, family, and culture can be represented schematically (see Figure 14.1) along two time dimensions: one of which is historical (the vertical axis) and one of which is developmental and unfolding (the horizontal axis). For the individual, the vertical axis includes the biological heritage and intricate programming of behaviors with one's given temperament and genetic make-up. The horizontal axis relates to the individual's emotional, cognitive, and physical development over the life span. Each individual begins with a genetic endowment—a set of characteristics within which behavior is guided, shaped, and changed. From birth, for example, some children are more quiet and observant, whereas others are more active, expressive, and involved. Over time, these inherent qualities can become either crystallized into rigid behaviors or elaborated into broader and more flexible repertoires. Certain individual stages may be more difficult to master depending on the person's innate characteristics and the influence of the environment.

At the family level (Carter, 1978), the vertical axis includes the family history, the patterns of relating and functioning that are transmitted down the generations, primarily through the mechanism of emotional triangling

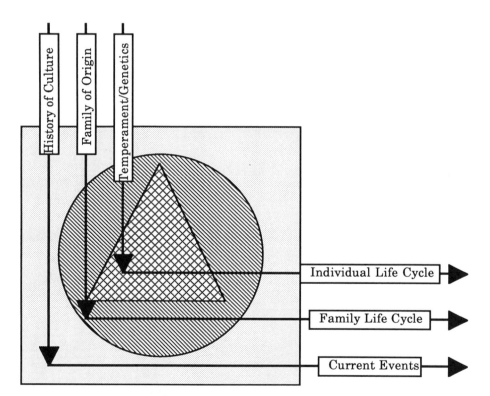

FIGURE 14.1. Systemic model of human development: the individual, the family, and the culture. (Copyright Marsha Heiman, 1993.)

(Bowen, 1978). It includes all the family attitudes, taboos, expectations, labels, and loaded issues with which we grow up. These aspects of our lives are the hand we are dealt. What we do with them is the question. The horizontal flow at a family level describes the family as it moves through time, coping with the changes and transitions of the family life cycle. This includes both the predictable developmental stresses and those unpredictable events, "the slings and arrows of outrageous fortune," that may disrupt the life cycle, e.g., untimely death, birth of a handicapped child, chronic illness, job loss. At each stage of the life cycle, the family memberships must rebalance and redefine themselves, realigning relationships.

At a cultural level the vertical axis includes the culture's history, the archetypes, patterns, and beliefs that have been passed on through the generations. A group's history and in particular the legacy of trauma in its history (e.g., the holocaust on the Jews and the Germans, slavery on African-Americans, the Civil War on Southern WASPs) will have its impact on families and individuals as they go through life. The horizontal axis relates to current events as they impact the family and the individual at a given time. One cannot ignore the impact of the cultural, economic, and political context on families at different phases of the life cycle at each point in their history. For example, there are huge and escalating discrepancies in social and economic circumstances among families in our culture. At present, the top 10% of the population have 57% of the net wealth of the country, whereas the bottom 50% of the population have 4.5% of the total net worth. We have reached the point where most families require the income of two parents to be able to support a middle-class existence (Thurow, 1987). Such economic patterns clearly impact on how families today organize themselves.

As families move along, stress is often greatest at transition points from one stage to another in the developmental process. Symptoms appear most often when transition points cannot be negotiated adequately or there is an interruption or dislocation in the unfolding family life cycle. Given enough stress on the horizontal, developmental axis, any individual family will appear extremely dysfunctional. Even a small horizontal stress, if the vertical axis of past historical givens is full of intense and unresolved stress, will create a great disruption.

The anxiety engendered on the vertical and horizontal axes where they converge, as well as the interaction of the various systems and how they work together to support or impede one another, are the key determinants of how well the family will manage its transitions through life. It becomes imperative, therefore, to assess not only the dimensions of the current life-cycle stress but also their connections to family themes, triangles, and labels coming down the family tree (Carter, 1978) and through the wider culture over time. Although all change is to some extent stressful, when the current developmental stress intersects with historical stress, there is a quantum leap in anxiety in the system. If, to give a global example, one's parents were basically pleased to be parents and handled the job without too much anxiety, then the birth of the first child will produce just the normal stress of a system expanding its boundaries. If, on the other hand, parenting was a cause celebre of some kind in the family of origin, and has not been dealt with, then the transition to parenthood may produce heightened anxiety for the couple. Even without any outstanding family-of-origin issues, the inclusion of a child could potentially tax a system, if there is a mismatch between the child's temperament and the parents'. Or if a child is conceived in a time of great political upheaval, forcing a family to leave its roots and culture and migrate to another country, then the child's birth may carry with it unresolved issues.

LIFE CYCLE STAGES

The stages of the life cycle are by no means universal breakdowns. The notion of childhood has been described as the invention of 18th-century Western society and adolescence as the invention of the 19th century (Aries, 1962), related to the cultural, economic, and political contexts of those eras. The notion of young adulthood as an independent phase could easily be argued to be the invention of the 20th century. The phases of the empty nest and older age are also developments primarily of this century, brought about by the smaller number of children and the longer life span in our era. Given the present rates of divorce and remarriage, the 21st century may become known for developing the norm of serial marriage as part of the life cycle process. Developmental psychology however, has tended to take an ahistorical approach to the life cycle. In all other cultures and historical eras, the breakdown of life cycle stages has differed from our current definitions in terms of timing, importance, and the roles expected. To add to this complexity, cohorts born and living through different periods vary in fertility, mortality, acceptable gender roles, migration patterns, education, needs, resources, and attitudes toward family and aging.

Cultural factors also play a major role in how families go through the life cycle. Not only do cultural groups vary greatly in their breakdown of life cycle stages and definitions of the tasks at each stage, but it is clear that even several generations after immigration, the family life cycle patterns of groups differ markedly (McGoldrick, 1988b; Woehrer, 1982; Gelfand & Kutzik, 1979; Lieberman, 1974; Falicov, 1980, 1988). One must also recognize the strain that the vastly accelerated rate of change puts on families today, whether the changes themselves are for the better or for the worse.

Families characteristically lack time perspective when they are having problems. Overwhelmed and immobilized by their immediate feelings, they tend generally to magnify the present moment, or they become stuck in the past or even fixed on a moment in the future that they long for or dread. They lose the awareness that life means perpetual motion from the past and into the future with a continual transformation of familial relationships. As the sense of motion becomes lost or distorted, therapy involves restoring a sense of life as a continual process from and toward.

WOMEN'S AND MEN'S LIFE CYCLES

Previously "human development" and theories of the life cycle referred to male development. Female development was seen only from an androcentric perspective and involved learning to become an adaptive helpmate. Women have always played a central role in families, but the idea that they have a life cycle apart from their roles as wife and mother is relatively new. They went from being daughter to wife to mother, their status being defined by the male in the relationship and their role by their position in the family life cycle. Rarely has it been accepted that they had a right to a life for themselves.

Although there has always been a "his" and "hers" version of development, until recently (McGoldrick, 1989c; Miller, 1976; Gilligan, 1982; Dinnerstein, 1976) only the former was ever described in the literature. Most male theoreticians, such as Freud, Kohlberg, Erikson, and Piaget, tended to ignore female development or subsume it under male development, which was taken as the standard for mature functioning (Notman, Klein, Jorden, & Zilbach, 1971; Broverman, Vogel, Broverman, Clarkson, & Rosenkrantz, 1972; Tavris, 1992). Separation, differentiation, and autonomy have been considered the primary values for male development, with values of caring and attachment, interdependence, relationship, and attention to context being primary in female development. Whereas men have defined themselves in terms of their work and career, women have tended to define themselves in the context of human relationships and to judge themselves in terms of their ability to care. As Gilligan has described women's place in man's life cycle, it has been that of:

> nurturer, caretaker, and helpmate, the weaver of those networks of relationships on which she in turn relies. But while [sic] women have thus taken care of men, men have, in their theories of psychological development, as in their economic arrangements, tended to assume or devalue that care. (1982, p. 17)

Healthy development requires finding an optimal balance between connectedness and separateness, belonging and individuation, accommodation and differentiation. The major theories of human development, however, have generally equated maturity with autonomy. Concern about relationships has been seen as a lack of complete development in women and a weakness or "softness" in men, rather than a human strength. The studies of Broverman and her colleagues on sex-role stereotypes (1970, 1972) have made eminently clear the biases in our cultural attitudes that equate "healthy adulthood" with "maleness," represented by the capacity for autonomous thinking, rationality, clear decision making, and responsible action. At the same time the qualities our culture has defined as necessary for feminine identity, such as warmth, expressiveness, and caring for others have been devalued. There is social pressure for men to repress or reject their feminine aspects. For women there is a classic double bind. Females are criticized if they have adopted too many masculine traits (e.g., she wears the pants in the family) and yet feminine qualities are never given the same appreciation or value as masculine ones.

In general, developmental theories have failed to describe the progression of relationships toward a maturity of interdependence. Human identity is inextricably bound up in one's relationship with others, and the notion of complete autonomy is a fiction. Human beings cannot exist in isolation, and the most important aspects of human experience are relational. Though most developmental texts recognize the importance of individuation, the reality of continuing connection is lost or relegated to the background. Perhaps this is why there is almost no discussion in developmental literature of the importance of children in redefining one's adult identity (Daniels & Weingarten, 1983).

Erikson's (1963) 8 stages of development suggest that human connectedness is part of the first stage, trust versus mistrust, which covers the first year of life, but this aspect does not appear again until stage 6, intimacy versus isolation. All the other stages described by Erikson leading to adulthood involve individual rather than relational issues: autonomy versus shame and doubt; initiative versus guilt; industry versus inferiority; identity versus role confusion. Identity is defined as having a sense of self *apart from*, not *in relation to* one's family. In addition, from age 1 to 20, those characteristics that refer to interpersonal issues: doubt, shame, guilt, inferiority, and role confusion, (all of which are associated with female characteristics), signify failure, rather than being the important part of a healthy identity that they are. Do we not need these qualities to deal with others realistically? Total emphasis on autonomy, initiative, industry, and a sense of self apart from one's family create a seriously imbalanced human being. Given this idealization of healthy development, it is not surprising that men have difficulty with intimacy and with acknowledging their vulnerability, doubt, and imperfection. In our view, all stages of the life cycle have both individual and interpersonal aspects, and the failure to appreciate this has led to seriously skewed human development.

SIBLINGS AND THE LIFE CYCLE

Sibling relationships are the longest we have in life, and, though often ignored by the culture, they are among the most important resources we have (Cicirelli, 1985; McGoldrick, 1989d; Bank & Kahn, 1982; Kahn & Lewis, 1989).

Even when the life cycle has been discussed in the literature, there is almost no discussion of the adult relationships of siblings. Yet especially in later life, sibling relationships are often a primary source of well-being. According to one important longitudinal study of successful, well-educated men (the Harvard classes of 1938–1944), the single best predictor of emotional health at age 65 was having had a close relationship with one's sibling in young adulthood—more predictive than childhood closeness to parents, emotional problems in childhood, or parental divorce—more predictive even than having had a successful marriage or career (Valliant, 1977). A critical point for siblings comes after the last parent dies, when for the first time their relationships become a matter of choice. Fostering such connectedness throughout the life cycle is an important factor in cushioning families against the stresses of life.

DEFINING NORMAL IN A CHANGING WORLD

The recent changes in life-cycle patterns and patterns of family organization and structure make the task of defining the "normal" family life cycle especially difficult. Since 1980 childbearing has fallen below replacement levels, as many women are electing not to have children or to postpone childbearing in order to pursue career aspirations. In general women are marrying later and less often and are having fewer children (Glick, 1984). Many more women are concentrating on jobs and education. For the first time more women than men are now enrolled in college (Bianchi & Spain, 1986). In fact, the high achievement of mothers is even more predictive of the high achievement of both their sons and daughters than is the high achievement of fathers (Losoff, 1974; Padan, 1965).

Furthermore, over half of all women 45–64 are in the labor force, and most of these are working full time. With the increasing life span, the caregivers themselves are elderly and struggling with declining functioning. Thus today's middle-aged women are caught in a "dependency squeeze" between their parents and their children, being left with the responsibility for both generations (Lang & Brodey, 1983). As women have moved into the work force through necessity and choice, they now are often faced with role strain and role overload, since the gender-role expectations that women place caring for others before their own needs continues to exist. Furthermore, because of their greater emotional involvement in the lives of those around them, women are exposed to higher rates of change and instability in their lives than men (Dohrenwend, 1973; Vernoff, Douvan, & Kulka, 1981).

Men, on the other hand, are having to struggle with their identities because the stable ground of what they expected in life is being shaken by the women in their lives. They are forced to deal with the rebellion of women against traditional expectations that they will take care of men. Increasingly men themselves are becoming aware of the emptiness of their lives as prescribed by our society (Valliant, 1977; Taffel, 1991).

As difficult as traditional patterns may be for many women, changing the status quo is extremely painful for them. Even as women are rebelling against having responsibility for making family relationships, holidays, and celebrations happen, they typically feel guilty for not continuing to do what they have grown up to expect they will do. When no one else moves in to fill the gap, they feel that family solidarity is breaking down, and that it is their fault. The guilt emanating from less-than-perfect motherhood and less-than-perfect career performance are real because it is not possible to "have it all" when jobs are still structured for men whose wives take care of the details of life, and homes and schools are still structured for women whose total responsibility is running their families.

The rigid structure of the workplace carries a cost for men too, keeping them peripheral to family life. If they want to spend time with their families or to care for those in need, it may jeopardize their security and status in the work system. In most work situations, there is no such thing as taking time off to attend a child's school play or take one's mother to the doctor. Especially at midlife, men often have a sense of their family having passed them by while they were preoccupied with their progress at work. They may realize only as their children are leaving that they wished for more family connection (Valliant, 1977; Levinson, 1978).

The laws that regulate social services to support families are determined primarily by men and do not support the women who bear the burden of family responsibilities but lack the power to manage these responsibilities. The failure of our society to provide public services to families will most likely exacerbate intergenerational conflicts, turning family members against each other (Hess, 1985). The record of male lawmakers on legislation in support of family caretaking is abysmal. This is a critical issue for families in our time—affecting most profoundly the poor, the young, the infirm, the aged, who are mostly women, and the caretakers of all these groups, who are women. In hidden ways this hurts the very men who determine the laws by making it practically impossible for them to develop intimate relationships as they move through the life cycle. Certainly if your prescribed social role throughout life proscribes you from giving priority to the everyday needs of your family—if you cannot be there when they are young, sick, dying, or just to play, it is virtually impossible to become intimate with anyone.

The differential role of men and women in the larger context is illustrated by the fact that in the American work place women still make an average of 71 cents to every dollar a man earns for the same job. Economic independence for women, which has profound implications for traditional family structures, and has always been a hallmark for successful males, appears crucial for women's protection in the face of abuse (Aguirre, 1985), divorce (Weitzman, 1985; Faludi, 1991), and old age (Hess, 1985). We must restructure home and work so that women who have children can earn fair and decent wages and have a voice in the decision-making mainstream of society and so that men can have meaningful relationships with their children.

Being part of a family and the breaking up of a family have profoundly different implications for men and women. As Jessie Bernard (1982) has described it, "his" marriage is very different, and a great deal more satisfying than "her" marriage. Although men remain ambivalent about getting married, fearing "ensnarement," it is women who become more symptomatic and prone to stress in the married state on virtually every indicator. Research strongly suggests that married women have more symptoms than married men or unmarried women (Brodsky & Hare-Mustin, 1980; Baruch, Barnett, & Rivers, 1983; Bernard, 1982; Avis, 1985). They experience more depression and more marital dissatisfaction. Women in traditional marital relationships have poorer physical health, lower self-esteem, less autonomy, poorer marital adjustment than women in more equal relationships (Avis, 1985). Conversely, men who are separated or divorced have greater stress, higher rates of psychiatric hospitalization, and higher mortality rates than divorced or separated women (Bloom, White, & Asher, 1979). Men are the only family members who become more symptomatic when women's lives improve through paid work (Tavris, 1992; Faludi, 1991).

The traditional household is fast becoming a relic of the past. Only 29% of households consist of couples with children under 18, compared to 44% in 1960, and since at least half of those mothers work, fewer than 7% of households fit into the traditional ideal of working father and stay-at-home mother with children (Friedan, 1985; Hewlett, 1985). Whereas the number of couple households has been decreasing, the number of single-parent households (mostly headed by women) has more than doubled since 1970 (Rawlings, 1983). For the increasing number of teenaged unmarried mothers, their mothers, aunts, and sisters often have responsibility for the children. The teen fathers are rarely included as part of the picture, and other male family members frequently have no primary role in the family's development.

We are marrying later and less often, having fewer children, and divorcing more. An ever increasing percentage of the population are living together without marrying (3% of couples at any one point in time), and a rapidly increasing number are having children without marrying. At present 6% of households include gay or lesbian couples, whose life cycle patterns are typically made invisible in traditional life cycle descriptions. Present estimates are that 12% of young women will never marry, three times the percentage for their parents' generation; 15% will never have children; 50% will end their marriages in divorce; and 20% will have two divorces. Women with the most education and income are the most likely to divorce and least likely to remarry, in contrast to men, the most wealthy and well-educated of whom are the most likely to stay married or to remarry quickly. After divorce, men have an ever larger pool of marriageable spouses to choose from, because they prefer and can attract younger women. For first marriages, the average wife is three years younger than her husband. For second marriages the wife is on the average 6 years younger than her husband. It is women who are likely to move down to the poverty level if the couple divorces, having a severe drop in income after divorce, whereas men's available income tends to rise. The majority of people who live alone are women, and they tend to be widowed and/or divorced elderly.

Presently 75% of the poor are women or children, mostly living in one-parent households. The increasing feminization of poverty means that by the year 2000 the poor will be primarily women and children. The poor are also constrained by their lack of access to resources, resulting in a much shortened and impoverished life cycle (Hines, 1988; Fulmer, 1989). They become inordinately vulnerable to health problems, early death, and all the other disadvantages that the lack of educational and work opportunities forces on them.

An enormous number of families in our culture do not go through the "normal" phases at the "normal" times. If one adds to this the number of families that experience the death of a member before old age and those that have a chronically ill, handicapped, or chemically abusing family member and those who are chronically unemployed, which dramatically alters their life cycle pattern, the number of "normal" families is even smaller. Another major factor affecting all families at one time or another is migration. The average American moves once every 4 years, and the break in cultural and family continuity created by migration, especially from one country to another, affects family life cycle patterns for several generations. Given the enormous number of Americans who have immigrated within the past two generations, the percentage of families falling into traditional definitions of "normal" is diminished still further.

Even though the traditional paradigm of the family life cycle describes the real life of ever fewer families, it remains to a large extent the ideal against which most families compare themselves. It is imperative that therapists recognize the extent of change and variations in the norms that are now widespread and that they help families to stop comparing their particular structure and life cycle course with that of the white, middle-class traditional families of the 1950s. For although relationship patterns and family themes may continue to sound familiar, the structure, ages, stages, and form of American families have changed radically.

It is time to give up attachments to the old ideals and to put a more positive conceptual frame around what is: two paycheck marriages; permanent "single-parent" households; unmarried couples and remarried couples; single-parent adoptions; and women of all ages alone. It is past time to stop thinking of transitional crises as permanent traumas and to drop from our vocabulary words and phrases that link us to the norms and prejudices of the past: "children of divorce," "broken homes," and "out-of-wedlock" children.

If the ideas of life cycle norms are applied too rigidly, they lead to an anxiety that deviating from the norms is pathological. The opposite pitfall, overemphasizing the uniqueness of the "brave new world" faced by each new generation, can create a sense of historical discontinuity, devaluing the role of parenthood and the relationship between the generations. Our aim is to provide a view of the life cycle in terms of intergenerational connectedness in the family (Hill, 1970), for this is one of our greatest resources. This is not meant to oversimplify the complexity of life's transitions or to encourage stereotyping by promoting classifications of "normality" that constrict our view of human life but, rather, to expand clinicians' views of family problems and strengths.

Our classification of family life cycle stages of American middle-class families in the last decade of the 20th century highlights our view that the central underlying processes to be negotiated are the expansion, contraction, and realignment of the relationship system to support the entry, exit, and development of family members in a functional way. Generally speaking, major life cycle transitions require a fundamental change in the system itself, rather than just incremental changes or rearrangements of the system, which are going on continually throughout life.

BETWEEN FAMILIES: YOUNG ADULTHOOD

Unlike traditional sociological depictions of the family life cycle as commencing at marriage and ending with the death of one spouse, we begin the family life cycle at the stage of "young adulthood." The primary task for this period is for young adults to come to terms with their family of origin—a powerful shaper of reality, influencing who, when, how, and whether they will marry and how they will carry out all succeeding stages of the family life cycle. Adequate completion of this stage requires that the young adult separate from the family of origin without cutting off or fleeing reactively to a substitute emotional refuge. This phase is a cornerstone. It is a time to formulate personal life goals and to become a "self" before joining with another to form a new family subsystem. The more adequately young adults can differentiate themselves from the emotional program of the family of origin at this phase, the fewer vertical stressors will follow them through their new family life cycle. This is the chance for them to sort out emotionally what they will take along from the family of origin, what they will leave behind and what they will create for themselves.

Young adulthood has, until recent decades, been a phase for men only. Women passed from their families of origin to their families of procreation, with no space in between to be independent. For men this phase has tended to emphasize their development of a career, whereas for women, career has almost always taken a back seat to the search for a husband. Women are frequently confronted with a clash between the two roles, family and social pressure conflicting with career demands. The more women focus on career, the less viable are their marital options, in contrast to the situation for men, where education and career success enhance their likelihood of marriage. Daughters who make full use of young adulthood for personal development tend to take greater distance from their families of origin than do sons, probably because there is less family acceptance of women's individual development.

Problems at this phase usually center on either young adults or their parents not recognizing the need for a shift to a less hierarchical form of relating, based on their now all being adults. Trouble in changing status may take the form of parents encouraging the dependence of their young adult children or angrily dismissing the adult child from the family for his or her differences. Young adults may remain in an overly dependent position, unable to leave home or rebel, breaking away in a pseudoindependent cutoff from their parents and families. Whereas for women the problems at this stage more often focus on short-circuiting their definition of themselves in favor of finding a mate, men more often have difficulty committing themselves in relationships, forming instead an incomplete identity focused around work.

Young adults who cut off their parents do so reactively and are in fact still emotionally bound to, rather than independent of, their family's "program." Cutoffs never resolve emotional relationships. The shift toward adult-to-adult status requires a mutually respectful and personal form of relating, in which young adults can appreciate parents as they are, needing neither to make them into what they are not, nor to blame them for what they could not be. Neither do young adults need to comply with parental expectations and wishes at their own expense. Therapy at this phase most often involves coaching young adults to reengage with their parents in a new way that accomplishes the shifting of their status in the system. When parents are the ones seeking help, therapy usually involves helping them to recognize the new status of their adult children and to relate to them as such. Family members often get stuck in a "more of the same" struggle, where the harder they try the worse it gets, whether in prolonged dependence or reactive cutoff. Therapy focuses on helping them make the necessary change in their basic way of relating. Only when the generations can shift their status relations and reconnect in a new way can the family move on developmentally. An increasing problem at this phase is the prolonged dependency that our technological society requires in order to prepare young adults for the work world, long after they would traditionally have been launched, and long after they have usually begun having intimate couple relationships. This creates a difficult situation for both parents and children who will have difficulty establishing appropriate boundaries, since it is almost impossible to be emotionally independent when you are still financially dependent and in the socially ambiguous status of student.

Working with families at this phase of the life cycle is particularly rewarding because of the new options that are opened when young adults are able to move toward new life patterns. At this stage, young men can be encouraged to develop themselves emotionally and expressively, exploring their connections with family and others. For men who have had few male role models or minimal relationships with their fathers, this is a time to reconnect. Because men's socialization so often does not facilitate their learning to have intimacy even in friendship, this period can be a keystone also for them in being proactive about the kind of friendships they want to nurture in life. It is important to help men make connections with other men in and outside their families, without having to forsake their mothers or devalue women. Interventions directed at helping young people reevaluate the gender roles of their parents and grandparents so they do not replicate previous relationships of inequality or dysfunction may be especially valuable at this crucial formative phase. For women, it is important to outline all the unrecognized work that their mothers and grandmothers did to raise their families and keep a household going in order to emphasize their courage, abilities, hard work, and strengths as role models for positive identification, since women are typically hidden from history (herstory!). In general, both men and women can be helped to draw strength from each of their parents.

THE JOINING OF FAMILIES IN MARRIAGE: THE YOUNG COUPLE

The changing role of women, the frequent marriage of partners from widely different cultural backgrounds, and the increasing physical distances between family members are placing a much greater burden on couples to define their relationship for themselves than was true in traditional and precedent-bound family structures (McGoldrick, 1989a). Although any two family systems always have different patterns and expectations, in our present culture, couples are less bound by family traditions and freer than ever before to develop male–female relationships unlike those they experienced in their families of origin. Marriage tends to be misunderstood as a joining of two individuals. It really represents the changing of two entire systems as well as an overlapping of systems to develop a third subsystem. For women it tends to bring a turning back to their parents for more connection, whereas men may increase their separation from their families of origin, seeing the marital relationship as replacing the family of origin (White, 1986). As the saying goes: "My son is my son 'til he takes a wife, but my daughter's my daughter all the days of my life." In fact a daughter is also a daughter-in-law for the rest of her life, since through marriage she typically gains responsibility for the connectedness with her husband's family as well.

Several recent researchers have found a continuing difference in the values of men and women about their marriages (Sternberg, 1984; White, 1986). Although during courtship men may spend "intimate" time with women, after marriage they tend to spend less and less time talking to their wives, often considering doing chores around the house an adequate demonstration of caring and feeling mystified about what women mean about wanting more intimacy (Sternberg, 1984). Men are much more likely to separate sexual interactions from intimacy, or to see the two as the same thing, whereas for women emotional closeness tends to be a precursor to sexual desire.

Achieving a successful transition to couplehood may be an extraordinarily difficult proposition in our time, when we are only beginning a transformation of male/female relationships in the direction (hopefully) of partnership, educationally, occupationally, and in emotional connectedness (Eisler, 1987). Couples can be helped to change the traditional rituals around marriage to symbolize the move toward nonsexist relationships. New rituals that allow both partners to represent their symbolic movement from their parents to their partners (rather than just the woman from her father) can potentially provide couples with the opportunity to redefine traditional family relationships in a way that may make their future marital accommodation more equitable.

The transition to marriage is an important time for helping young couples look beyond the stereotypes that have been so problematic for family development. Patterns that are established at this phase in the life cycle may have great importance later on. Prior to the wedding day, many couples resist looking at the fallacies of their myths about marriage (Walsh, 1989a; Carter, 1992), and as a result, they often do not appear for therapy until after the marriage when the problems surface. Even then, in the early years of marriage, it is a lot easier to change patterns than later when they have become entrenched.

The failure to renegotiate family status with the family of origin may lead to marital failure. Nevertheless, it appears that couples are very unlikely to present with extended family problems as the stated issue. Problems reflecting the inability to shift family status are usually indicated by defective boundaries around the new subsystem. In-laws may be too intrusive, and the new couple may be afraid to set limits, or the couple may have difficulty forming adequate connections with the extended systems, cutting themselves off in a tight twosome. At times the inability to formalize a marriage indicates that the partners are still too enmeshed in their own families to define a new system and accept the implications of this realignment. It is useful in such situations to help the system to move to a new definition of itself rather than to get lost in the details of incremental shifts the couple may be struggling over (sex, money, time, etc.).

FAMILIES WITH YOUNG CHILDREN

With the transition to parenthood, the family becomes a threesome, which makes it a permanent system for the first time. If a childless spouse leaves, there is no system left, but if one person leaves the new triad of couple and child, the system itself survives. Thus, symbolically and in reality this transition is a key one in the family life cycle.

The shift to this stage of the family life cycle requires that adults now move up a generation and become caretakers to the younger generation. Typical problems that occur when parents cannot make this shift are struggles with each other about taking responsibility, or refusal or inability to behave as parents to their children. Often parents find themselves unable to set limits and exert the required authority, or they lack the patience to allow their children to express themselves as they develop. Many parents with children who present clinically at this phase are somehow not accepting the generation boundary between themselves and their children. They may complain that their 4-year-old is "impossible to control." Or, on the other hand, they may expect their children to behave more like adults, reflecting too strong a generational boundary or barrier. In these cases, child-centered problems can be addressed by helping parents gain a view of themselves as part of a new generational level with specific responsibilities and tasks in relation to the next level of the family.

In other families, childhood symptoms may be more a function of the temperamental qualities and developmental needs of the child. Children who are temperamentally difficult create more discomfort for parents and decrease marital and family functioning, making parenting more of a problem (Sheeber & Johnson, 1992). The way in which the child's behavior "resonates" within the family, therefore, becomes a critical factor (Combrinck-Graham, 1989). The family as a shaping environment can either maximize or inhibit growth (Kernberg & Chazan, 1991). They can strengthen positive behaviors, rechannel negative ones, and encourage new patterns, or they can block future adaptations. Sometimes well-meaning solutions to childhood issues can become problems in themselves. For example, shy children may be reinforced in their reluctance to communicate by parents who talk for them. In situations like this, it is important to assess the family's life cycle patterns in relation to individual developmental needs to see whether the family's overfunctioning is a matter of well-meaning ignorance about the child's special developmental needs or a function of the inability to make a life cycle transition in relation to their child's growing need for independence.

The developmental phases children go through in terms of their emotional, physical, cognitive, social, and neurological development must be considered in relation to the family's resources and responsiveness. Gender differences clearly exist. However, it is difficult to determine which behavioral differences between males and females are based strictly on biology, since socialization impacts so powerfully and so early. The major difference in early childhood is that girls develop language skills earlier, and boys tend to be more active. Studies of newborns, however, show that parents tend to encourage more physical activity in boys and more dependency in girls (Lewis & Weintraub, 1974; Maccoby & Jacklin, 1974; Romer, 1981). Research also indicates that parents talk and look more at girls and engage in more rough play with boys. It appears that girls tend already in their childhood play to be more sensitive to relationships and to avoid competition. Already by age three, boys are more oriented to males, to peers, and to nonfamily members, whereas girls are more oriented to females, to family members, and to adults (Lewis et al., 1984). Thus boys may be directed away from the home as early as preschool age, whereas girls are being socialized toward family relationships.

For the modern two-paycheck family with small children, a central struggle during this stage of the life cycle is the disposition of childcare responsibilities and chores. The pressure of trying to find adequate childcare, when there is no satisfactory social provision for this need produces serious consequences: two full-time jobs may fall on the woman; the family may live in conflict and chaos; childcare arrangements may be less than optimal; recreation and vacations may be sharply curtailed to pay for childcare; or the woman may give up her career to stay home or work only part-time. The major research on the transition to parenthood indicates that it is accompanied by a general decrease in marital satisfaction, a reversion to more traditional sex roles even by dual-career couples, who previously had a more equitable relationship, and a lowering of self-esteem for women (Cowen & Cowen, 1985). Even when fathers do participate more actively in relating to children, it is mothers, including career mothers, who bear the major responsibility for overseeing that children's needs are met.

For mothers who do not work, there is not only the pressure of 24-hour-a-day parenting, but the impact of the devaluing of this role by the culture, which says, "You just stay at home." In such families women often feel extremely stressed by their lives and yet guilty for asking a husband to "help," since he brings in the money, which means he has the lion's share of the power in the family (Blumstein & Schwartz, 1983).

In general, the traditional family has often not only encouraged but even required dysfunctional patterns, such as the overresponsibility of mothers for their children and the complementary underresponsibility or disengagement of fathers (Avis, 1985). Society reinforced by developmental literature and psychoanalytic models has focused exclusively on mothers, giving extraordinary importance to the mother–child relationship in the earliest years of life, to the exclusion of other relationships in the family or to later phases (Lewis, Feiring, & Kotsonis, 1984; Braverman, 1989; McGoldrick, 1991). Kagan (1984) has recently drawn our attention to the mythology involved in our assumptions about the importance of infancy and early childhood in determining the rest of human life. The fantasy that mothers are all powerful has resulted in a psychological determinism that blames mothers for whatever goes wrong and also expects that they should be perfect, all giving, and all knowing (Chodorow & Contratto, 1982). The same models that stress the supreme importance of the mother–child bond also view human development as a primarily painful process in which eventually mothers and children are adversaries. Even the recent men's movement (Bly,

1990), which seeks to expand men's options to include more loving and nurturing behaviors is based on the premise that men need to reject their mothers and go in search of their fathers in order to find themselves and be truly liberated.

We urge a different perspective on human development, which views child development and this early stage in the life cycle in the richness of its entire context of multigenerational family relationships, as well as within its social and cultural context. It is not the rejection of mothers that must occur for a child's complete identity and development, but rather a shift within society, which must be made to value, support, and reinforce the active inclusion of fathers and other extended family.

Recently there has been an increase of husbands and wives sharing in childbirth classes and in the delivery. This cultural change has now afforded men with the opportunity to begin the bonding process earlier, cementing the transition to a new group of three, as fathers feel an intimate and useful part of the birthing experience. However, there is still virtually no preparation of men for the much more complicated and longer lasting tasks of childrearing. This is an important area for intervention when working with families at this life cycle stage. Fathers rarely have any experience with small children, so they need to learn these skills. Often this requires time alone, since if they are in the presence of their wives, it is extremely difficult for husbands to take primary responsibility for a child and for wives to give up the responsibility. Mothers may need assistance in allowing fathers and children to flounder, giving them the opportunity to construct and discover their relationship.

At this transition in the family's emerging development, grandparents must shift to a back seat from which they can allow their children to be the central parental authorities, while forming a new type of caring relationship with their grandchildren. For many adults this is a particularly gratifying transition, which offers intimacy without all the responsibilities that parenting requires. It is not unusual to find grandfathers developing a closer relationship with their grandchildren than they had with their own children, thereby opening the system to new relationships for everyone. Furthermore, extended family members can play a crucial role in easing the entrance into parenthood, passing on knowledge and providing emotional support to parents, who feel inexperienced in their new roles.

In treatment with families at this phase of life, it is important to explore boundaries and roles within the nuclear family and between the generations. How the system operates is an important variable in understanding the creation and maintenance of childhood problems. The need for careful history taking, which examines both individual child development and the family's developmental history is imperative. Areas of childhood assessment include problems around conception, pregnancy and delivery; temperamental qualities of the infant; achievement of developmental milestones; and the onset and development of the problem. One must carefully track the child's symptoms, inquiring about changes or stresses within the system that may relate to the problems; adjustment of all family members to the birth of the symptomatic child and to the evolution of symptoms; additional problems with other children; organization of the family; and the impact of family-of-origin issues—who the child resembles, similar problems in the extended family, and how such problems have been or might have been dealt with by others.

A major treatment goal is helping adults become comfortable and effective in their new status as parents and in the new accommodations that must be made within the marital relationship and with other family members. As Daniels and Weingarten (1983) have described: "Parenthood is a powerful generator of development. It gives us an opportunity to refine and express who we are, to learn what we can be, to become someone different." Inquiring about household responsibilities as well as the handling of finances and the specifics of childrearing and childcare help illuminate the major stresses on the family and ineffective solutions. Issues of gender and the impact of sex-role functioning cannot be ignored, for they weigh heavily. Clearly men who do not develop intimate relationship with their children as they grow up will have difficulty changing the pattern later. It is also helpful to convey an awareness of what women have been doing in the family, since their role is most often treated as less important than that of their husbands. Typical questions might be:

- Do both parents usually go to children's school plays and sports events?
- How are your children changing your perspective on the meaning of your life?
- Does the father get to spend time alone with each child? (It is almost impossible to develop intimacy if he does not.) And is the time spent fairly equally divided among the daughters and sons?
- How are domestic responsibilities divided?
- How is money handled and by whom?
- What are each parent's hopes and expectations for each child in adulthood?
- How does each parent manage childhood problems?

Developing and building appropriate boundaries, clarifying family norms and values so as to provide predictable structures that are consistent, warm, empathic, and supportive without being too overdetermined or rigid as to exclude individuality are critical for everyone's well-being during this new phase of the family's formation.

FAMILIES WITH ADOLESCENTS

Although many have broken down the stages of families with young children into different phases, in our view the shifts are incremental. Adolescence, however, ushers in a new era, because it marks a new definition of the children within the family and of the parents' roles in relation to their children. Families with adolescents must establish qualitatively different boundaries than families with younger children, a job made more difficult in our times by the lack of built-in rituals to facilitate this transition and by the lack of community supports to provide continuity of structure as adolescents emerge out of their families. The boundaries must now be permeable. Parents can no longer maintain complete authority. Adolescents can and do open the family to a whole array of new values as they bring friends and new ideals into the family arena. Families that become derailed at this stage may be rather closed to new values and threatened by them, frequently stuck in an earlier view of their children. Differences can arise as the adolescent shifts priorities, focusing more on the peer group. For these families a common complaint is that the teenager is spending more time with friends and "doesn't care about the family." Parents may try to control every aspect of their children's lives at a time when, developmentally this is impossible to do successfully. Either the adolescent withdraws from the appropriate involvements for this developmental stage, or the parents become increasingly frustrated with what they perceive as their own impotence. For this phase the old adage is particularly apt for parents: "May I have the ability to accept the things I cannot change, the strength to change the things I can, and the wisdom to know the difference."

It puts special strains on parents to be able to manage the necessary flexible boundaries that allow adolescents to move in and be dependent at times when they cannot handle things alone and to move out and experiment with increasing degrees of independence when they are ready. This is also a time when adolescents begin to establish their own independent relationships with the extended family. It requires special adjustments between parents and grandparents to allow and foster these new patterns.

For some reason, during certain phases in development including preschool and adolescence, children seem to hold rigidly to sex-role stereotypes—even more so than their parents or teachers. It is important not to reinforce this stereotyping, but instead to encourage girls to develop their own opinions, values, aspirations and interests, while discouraging them from developing such competitive cliques that shun other girls. Likewise, boys need to be encouraged to communicate and express feelings and discouraged from teasing, bullying, or devaluing of girls or anyone who is vulnerable. In keeping with social norms of our culture, during the adolescent years girls often confuse identity with intimacy, defining themselves through relationships with others. It is also a time when the antifemale bias of the culture hits girls hardest, and they tend to have a drop in their self-esteem, to give up on their dreams for themselves, and for their development to slow down or become arrested in comparison to boys (Gilligan, 1989). It is important to raise questions about such norms, since they put girls into an impossible bind—you are only healthy if you define your identity not through your self but through your mate.

At the same time, boys need help in understanding relationships, particularly in differentiating intimacy from sexuality. For boys, the pressure to attract girls sexually, to be both achievement- and sports-oriented, can leave those who are not adept with lower self-esteem. Boys must be given permission to be vulnerable and provided with the avenues and the means to ask for help. Boys' inability to express themselves leaves them at higher risk for acting in more aggressive ways, using risk taking and abusive behaviors with drugs, cars, and sex as ways to deal with their feelings.

Although conventional gender values are at an all time high during adolescence, it is also during this phase that crucial life-shaping decisions are made. Facts about adult life such as about bias in the work force, the feminization of poverty, racism, responsible sexuality, etc., can be conveyed to adolescents to help them make more informed choices regarding their education and relationships.

During adolescence, daughters are particularly torn between identification with their mothers and with their fathers. A particular problem may be distancing between mothers and sons as both respond to the pernicious messages from the culture about the negative results of mother/son bonding. Incidentally, rebellion against parents is only one way, and not the most common, for adolescents to evolve an identity. Most teenagers of both sexes remain close to and admiring of their parents and experience a minimum of conflict and rebellion (Offer & Sabshin, 1984; Tavris, 1992). Fathers may need help to overcome their inhibitions in relating to both sons and daughters emotionally.

Commonly, the father–daughter relationship may be problematic in adolescence. Fathers often become awkward about relating to their daughters as they approach adolescence, fearing their budding sexuality. Given the frequently limited masculine repertoire for handling closeness, they may sexualize the relationship or they may withdraw, even becoming irritated or angry as a way of maintaining the distance they feel is necessary. They may need encouragement to engage actively with their daughters rather than avoid them. They may interact more easily with sons, where shared activities such as sports allow companionship without too many pressures for intimate relating. The unavailability of fathers for their daughters may lead daughters to develop an image of the male as a romantic stranger, an unrealistic image that cannot be met when they reach adult life whereas the unavailability of fathers for their sons may leave sons confused about their identity and questioning of their masculinity.

Therapy at this phase involves helping families make the appropriate transformation of their view of themselves to allow for the increasing independence of the new generation, while maintaining appropriate boundaries and structure to foster continued family development. Since adolescents are in transition from childhood to adult status, their behavior is often unpredictable, variable, and ever changing. Families are often confused by adolescents, who one moment are provocative, testing all limits of authority and in the next are childlike and dependent. As adolescents switch from childish to adult behavior, parents are continually confused and kept off guard. It is hard to know when to set firm limits and when to go easy. A common parental mistake is to view adolescent children as if they were equals in judgment and responsibility. This can lead to the mistaken idea, for example, that if the adolescent, in an obnoxious mood, says, "I want nothing to do with you," the parent engages the adolescent at a teenage level: "Well, if that's what you want." It is indeed difficult to field the impulsive back and forth motion of adolescents between dependence and independence, so much so that some have jokingly referred to this life cycle phase as a diagnosis in itself—one that usually remits in about 7 years!

Clinically, when working with adolescents and their families, it is important to ask questions about the roles each one is asked to play in the family. What are the chores and responsibilities of boys and of girls? Are sons encouraged to develop social skills or are parents focused primarily on their achievement and sports performance? Are daughters encouraged to have high academic aspirations? Are both sexes given equal responsibility and encouragement in dealing with education, athletics, aspirations for the future, extended family relationships, buying gifts, writing, calling, or caring for relatives? Do both sexes buy and clean their own clothes? Are daughters encouraged to learn about money, science, and other traditionally "masculine" subjects? Are boys taught to nurture? Are boys encouraged to express their feelings?

We also need to help families find more positive ways of defining for their daughters the changes of the menstrual and reproductive cycle, so that they do not see themselves as "unclean" or "impure." For so long, if sex was even discussed in the family, mothers have taught their daughters that menstruation was "the curse," whereas sons were taught about their bodily changes as positive, powerful, and fulfilling aspects of their manhood. Boys need to be taught to take responsibility for their sexual behavior and not to view relationships as "conquests," conducting respectful relationships emotionally and sexually. Teenage pregnancy is still viewed as the girl's responsibility. She should learn to say "no." Instead we must teach adolescents that their sexual behavior is the responsibility of both sexes, with consequences for both.

Given the intense biological, physical, and cognitive changes that are occurring during this time, in combination with the search for one's identity and the inherent confusion around negotiating and regulating boundaries and emotional distance between one's family and the outside world, adolescents are extremely vulnerable for developing symptoms. Serious problems such as teenage pregnancy, alcohol and drug abuse, suicide attempts, delinquency, depression, and psychosis may emerge, forcing the family to seek treatment. For some families, adolescent problems are a continuation of earlier emotional and developmental issues, which have never been adequately resolved but now have intensified to a point of being unmanageable and dangerous. For others, the difficulties may be more transient, reflective of the struggle in making the transition to this stage of life and successfully accomplishing the developmental tasks of the period. Symptoms may also be a signal for other dysfunctions within the family, such as alcoholism, marital problems, or abuse, for which the adolescent becomes the lightening rod. When treating adolescent problems, therapists need to stay attuned to the larger perspective, exploring the impact of the family and outside systems to have a full appreciation for the meaning and function of symptoms.

The central event in the marital relationship at this phase is usually the "midlife crisis" of one or both spouses, with an exploration of personal, career, and marital satisfactions and dissatisfactions. This is especially important because parents of adolescents tend to have the lowest marital satisfaction. There is usually an intense renegotiaton of the marriage and sometimes a decision to divorce. An exclusive focus on parent–adolescent complaints by either the family or the therapist may mask an affair or a secretly pondered divorce, or it may prevent the marital problems from coming to the surface. This is not to say that common adolescent symptoms should not be carefully assessed and treated seriously.

FAMILIES AT MIDLIFE:
LAUNCHING CHILDREN AND MOVING ON

This is the newest and longest phase in the family life cycle, and for these reasons it is in many ways the most problematic of all phases. In the past most families were occupied with raising their children for their entire active adult lives until old age. Now, because of the low birth rate and the long life span of most adults, parents launch their children almost 20 years before retirement and must then find other life activities. The difficulties of this transition can lead families to hold onto their children or can lead to parental feelings of emptiness and depression, particularly for women who have focused their main energies on their children and who now feel unprepared for a new career in the work world. However, research suggests that the notion of women's depression at the "empty nest" is generally much more apparent than real (Block, Davidson, & Grambs, 1981).

The most significant aspect of this phase is that it is marked by the greatest number of exits and entries of family members. It begins with the launching of grown children and proceeds with the entry of their spouses and children. It is a time when older parents are often becoming ill or dying. This, in conjunction with the difficulties of finding meaningful new life activities, may make it a particularly stressful period. Parents must deal with the change in their own status as they make room for the next generation and prepare to move up to position of grandparents. They must also forge a different type of relationship with their own parents, who may become dependent, giving them (particularly women) considerable caretaking responsibilities. This can also be a liberating time, in that finances may be easier than during the primary years of family responsibilities, and there is the potential for moving into new and unexplored areas—travel, hobbies, new careers. For some families this stage is seen as a time of fruition and completion and as a second opportunity to consolidate or expand by exploring new avenues and new roles. For others it leads to disruption, a sense of emptiness and overwhelming loss, depression, and general disintegration. The phase necessitates a restructuring of the marital relationship now that parenting responsibilities are no longer required.

Because of the changing economics of our era, there are also many families in which launching is postponed for financial reasons. The younger generation cannot find ways to support themselves, and there is a kind of in and out process with the older generation. They may live together for varying periods or even permanently in order to manage a better standard of living, or because of the needs of one or both generations for sharing resources—whether due to aging parents' need for support or for reasons that the next generation cannot afford a down payment for a new home and must share living space and resources with parents.

There is a tendency for men and women to be going in opposite directions psychologically as their children move out into their own lives. Men, perhaps realizing that they have missed most of the intimacy of their children's development, may begin to seek a closeness they have missed (Levinson, 1978). Women, after years of focusing on caring for others, begin to feel enthusiastic about developing their own lives—careers, friendships outside the family, and other activities. Typically they are grateful and energized by recapturing free time and exploring new options for themselves. Women are not nearly as sorry to see the childrearing era end as has been assumed.

The self-esteem and the confidence that comes from work have always been known to men, at least men of the middle classes. In midlife they often discover intimacy and relationships. For women in traditional families, however, this may be a time of special stress, since they often feel very much behind in the skills needed to deal with the outside world. Just when their children no longer need them and they are beginning to be defined by the male world as too old to be desirable, they must venture outward. The initial steps are usually the hardest. Once they have begun to move in this arena, however, many women experience a new confidence and pleasure in their independence—no longer having to put everyone else's needs first. Because of the social and management skills they have generally developed in the previous life cycle phases, women are remarkably resourceful in building a social network. Their lifelong skills in adapting to new situations also serve them in good stead. But the world of work still does not recognize their efforts in a way commensurate with their contribution. And women have typically not been socialized to expect or demand the recognition they deserve.

The divergence of interests for men and women, as well as the shift in focus of energies required at this phase, can create marital tensions, often leading to divorce. The emotional limitations of work and achievement may lead men to do important soul searching at this phase. They may be feeling the lack of intimacy in their marriages and with their children, now that they have come to realize the limitations in what their work lives can give them. They may hope that starting over will give them a new chance to "do it better." If they do divorce, they typically miss the caretaking functions provided by their wives and remarry rather quickly, usually to a younger woman. For women who divorce at this phase, the likelihood of remarriage is quite slim. In part this is because of the skew in availability of partners, and in part it appears to result from the older women's being less willing to "settle," particularly for a traditional marriage, which would mean a return to extensive caretaking.

It is at this time also that women typically experience menopause. This transition has generally been viewed negatively as a time of physical and psychological distress as women move toward old age. On the contrary, for many women it is a turning point that frees them sexually from worries about pregnancy and marks a new stabilization in their energies for pursuit of work and the social arena.

Therapy at this phase is often aimed at helping family members redefine their lives and relationships, along with expanding and broadening their options, many of which may be different from those of the family in which they were raised. They need to envision new pathways for their lives, which their parents very possibly did not experience. There is also the difficult negotiation required when parents cannot launch their children, who return periodically to the nest, because of the complex and difficult economics of our times and society. This may create a situation of multiple expansions and contractions of the boundaries of the system as children and aging relatives may return to the nest and then leave again.

THE FAMILY IN LATER LIFE

As Walsh (1989b) has pointed out, few of the visions of old age offered by our culture can provide us with positive images for healthy later-life adjustment within a family or social context. Pessimistic views of later life prevail. The current myths are that most elderly people have no families; that those who do, have little relationship with them and are usually set aside in institutions; or that all family interactions with older family members are minimal. On the contrary, the vast majority of adults over 65 do not live alone but with other family members. Over 80% live within an hour of at least one child (Walsh, 1989b).

Another myth about the elderly is that they are sick, senile, and feeble, and can best be handled in nursing homes or hospitals. Only 4% of the elderly live in institutions (Streib, 1972), and the average age at admission is 80. There are indications that if others did not foster their dependence or ignore them as functional family members, even this degree of dependence would be less.

Among the tasks of families in later life are adjustments to retirement, which not only may create the obvious vacuum for the retiring person, but may put a special strain on a marriage that until then has been balanced in different spheres. Men who have defined themselves totally in terms of work and career achievement may have an especially hard time now, feeling stripped of their primary identity and role. A crisis can ensue for those who have an enforced or mandatory retirement. Financial insecurity and dependence are also special difficulties, particularly for family members who value managing for themselves. And while loss of friends and relatives is a common stress at this phase, the loss of a spouse is the most difficult adjustment, with its problems of reorganizing one's entire life alone after many years as a couple and fewer relationships to help replace the loss. Grandparenthood can, however, offer a new lease on life, and opportunities for special close relationships that can offset changes that are inevitable as one faces issues of older age and mortality.

Trouble in making the status changes required for this phase of life are reflected in older family members' refusal to relinquish some of their power, as when a grandfather refuses to turn over the company or make plans for his succession. The inability to shift status is reflected also when older adults give up and become totally dependent on the next generation, or when the next generation does not accept the lessening powers or treats them as totally incompetent or irrelevant. The evidence suggests that men and women respond very differently to their roles in aging, and this too must be carefully assessed (Hesse-Biber & Williamson, 1984).

Even when members of the older generation are quite enfeebled, there is not really a reversal of roles between one generation and the next, because parents always have a great many years of extra experience and remain models to the next generations for the phases of life ahead. Nevertheless, because older age is totally devalued in our culture, family members of the middle generation often do not know how to make the appropriate shift in relational status with their parents and feel great discomfort about having to care for an incapacitated parent, who was formerly a source of strength and inspiration or authority and intimidation.

Clinically it is rare that older family members seek help for themselves, although they do suffer from many psychological problems, primary among which is depression. They are more likely to consult physicians for somatic complaints that may be contextually based. Often it is members of the next generation who seek help, and even they do not usually define their problem as relating to an elderly parent. It is often only through careful history taking that one learns of an aging grandparent just about to move in or be taken to a nursing home, only to discover that the relationship issues around the shift have been left submerged and unresolved in the family. Helping family members recognize the status changes and the need for resolving their relationships in a new balance can become critical to the family's well-being now and later.

The final phase of life might be considered "for women only," since women tend to live longer, and, unlike men, are rarely paired with younger partners, making the statistics for this life cycle phase extremely imbalanced (Congressional Caucus for Women's Issues, 1984):

- Six out of 10 Americans over 65, and seven out of 10 over 85, are women.
- Seventeen percent of American women over 65 have incomes below the poverty line, as opposed to 10% of men.
- Almost half the older women have median incomes of less than $5,000, as opposed to one in five men.
- More than 80% of elderly female householders live alone, and one quarter of them live in poverty.

The increasing proportion of very old women over the next years presages a number of problems. As Hess and Soldo (1984) put it:

> The incomes of women, lower throughout worklife than those of men, remain so in old age. In addition, since the great majority of very old women are widows, and widows typically live alone, their poverty rates increase with advancing age. It becomes ever more difficult to obtain and maintain suitable housing, particularly that which is supportive of declining functional capacity. (p. 2)

Since women are the primary caretakers of other women, these problems will affect at least two generations of women, who will be increasingly stressed as time goes along. Those women who need the care and those who give it, are statistically the poorest and have the least legislative power in our society. The immediate cause of nursing home admission is more likely to be the depletion of family resources than a deterioration in the health of the older relative (Hess & Soldo, 1984). As mentioned earlier, legislators have given little consideration to services that support family caregivers.

As therapists we can counter this imbalance by redefining the dilemmas of both the elderly and their caretakers as serious, significant issues. An important general aim of therapy now becomes the rebalancing of skewed caretaking patterns between spouses, not only in relation to children, but also in dealing with the third generation. Unresolved issues from earlier times are likely to be reactivated as elderly parents become more dependent. Therapy also can assist families in coming to terms with elderly parents in ways that maintain everyone's dignity.

DIVORCE, SINGLE-PARENTING, AND REMARRIAGE

Although the statistical majority of American middle and upper classes still go through the traditional family life cycle stages as outlined above, the largest variation from the norm consists of families in which divorce has occurred. With the divorce rate currently at 50% and the rate of redivorce at 61% (Glick, 1984), divorce in the American family is close to the point at which it will occur in the majority of families and will thus be thought of more and more as a normative event. We have found it useful to conceptualize divorce as an interruption or dislocation of the traditional family life cycle, which produces the kind of profound disequilibrium that is associated throughout the entire family life cycle with shifts, gains, and losses in family membership (McGoldrick & Carter, 1989). As in other life cycle phases, there are crucial shifts in relationship status and important emotional tasks that must be completed by the members of divorcing families in order for them to proceed developmentally. As in other phases, emotional issues not resolved at this phase will be carried along as hindrances in future relationships.

Therefore, families in which divorce occurs must go through one or two additional phases of the family life cycle in order to restabilize and go forward developmentally at a more complex level. Seventy-five percent of men go on to remarry. Of women who divorce, at least 35% do not remarry. These families go through one additional phase and can restabilize permanently as postdivorce families. The other 65% of women who divorce will remarry, and these families can be said to require negotiation of two additional phases of the family life cycle before permanent restabilization. Our concept of the divorce and postdivorce family emotional process can be visualized as a roller-coaster graph, with peaks of emotional tension at all transition points:

- At the time of the decision to separate or divorce;
- When this decision is announced to family and friends;
- When money and custody/visitation arrangements are discussed;
- When the physical separation takes place;
- When the actual legal divorce takes place;
- When separated spouses or ex-spouses have contact about money or children;
- As each child graduates, marries, has children, or becomes ill;
- As each spouse is remarried, moves, becomes ill, or dies.

These emotional pressure peaks are found in all divorcing families— not necessarily in the above order—and many of them take place over and over again, for months or years. The emotions released during the process of divorce relate primarily to the work of emotional divorce—that is, the retrieval of self from the marriage. Each partner must retrieve the hopes, dreams, plans, and expectations that were invested in this spouse and in this marriage. This requires mourning what is lost and dealing with hurt, anger, blame, guilt, shame, and loss in oneself, in the spouse, in the children, and in the extended family.

Clinical work aims to minimize the tremendous tendency toward cutoff of many relationships after a divorce. It is important to help divorcing spouses continue to relate as cooperative parents and permit maximum feasible contact between children and parents and extended family. Our experience supports that of others (Hetherington, Cox, & Cox, 1977; Ahrons, 1981), who have found that it takes a minimum of 2 years and a great deal of effort after divorce for a family to readjust to its new structure and proceed to the next life cycle stage, which may or may not include remarriage, since many families restabilize satisfactorily without a recoupling. Families in which the emotional issues of divorce are not adequately resolved can remain stuck emotionally for years, if not for generations.

The family emotional process at the transition to remarriage consists of struggling with fears about investment in a new marriage and a new family; dealing with hostile or upset reactions of the children, the extended families, and the ex-spouse; struggling with the ambiguity of the new family structure, roles, and relationships; rearousal of intense parental guilt and concerns about the welfare of children; and rearousal of the old attachment to ex-spouse (negative or positive).

Our society offers stepfamilies a choice of two conceptual models, neither of which work: families that act like the intact family next door, glorified in situation comedies on television, and the wicked stepparents of fairy tales. A first clinical step is to validate for remarried families the lack of social support and clarity in the paradigms of family they are offered. They are then challenged to give up the old model of the intact first family, which has no "dangling ends," and reinvent themselves in a new family form with permeable, albeit workable, boundaries, ones that permit shifting household membership, shared responsibility for all children and grandchildren, and open lines of communication between all sets of parents and children and extended family.

In our experience the residue of an angry and vengeful divorce can block stepfamily integration for years or forever. The rearousal of the old emotional attachment to an ex-spouse, which characteristically surfaces at the time of remarriage and at subsequent life cycle transitions of children, is usually not understood as a predictable process and therefore leads to denial, misinterpretation, cutoff, and assorted difficulties. As in the case of adjustment to a new family structure after divorce, stepfamily integration seems also to require a minimum of 2 or 3 years before a workable new structure permits family members to move on emotionally.

The special dilemmas of women in our culture are most evident in divorce and remarriage (see also Carter & McGoldrick, 1989). Our society's arrangements regarding divorce are rapidly pushing more and more women and their children below the poverty level. With the recent trend toward joint custody following divorce, many complex issues are raised. Until very recently in human history, women never received custody after a divorce. They had no legal rights at all; these belonged to their husbands, as did their children. Gradually we moved toward a system in which custody always went to mothers, unless there was strong countervailing reason. Now many people are moving toward some form of joint custody. Many feminist groups oppose this as not in the best interests of women arguing that in joint custody, women continue to have ultimate responsibility for their children anyway, while lacking adequate financial support and earning powers, and moreover relinquishing some of the little control they had when sole custody was in effect.

In our view joint custody is an extremely important concept for both men *and* women, but even more so for children. The difficulties are that for men, who may have had little practice in childcare during the marriage, it is hard to learn to share real responsibility for the children after the divorce. Men, and their employers, tend to view their work responsibilities as primary and childcare as secondary. Thus if a child is sick or either parent will be away, it is usually the mother who will have to make special arrangements. And yet, because they are working, mothers now lose the opportunity to be with their children fulltime. In the shifting of roles required by joint physical custody following divorce there is a positive value: It allows the mother some time to herself, particularly when the husband has overnight contacts with his children and involves the father in basic childcare responsibilities such as clothing, brushing teeth, and delivering children to school. This increases the likelihood of a father's developing genuine, ongoing intimacy with his children, rather than remaining in a Sunday-father role. Yet most recent research suggests caution in working out joint physical custody arrangements that do not overburden the child in shuttling back and forth between two parttime households and settling in at home in neither. Furthermore, joint custody is likely to be detrimental to children if parents cannot cooperate in parenting without serious conflict (see Hetherington, Chapter 7, this volume). Current research clearly documents the importance for children of having reliable ongoing contact with both parents, and the fact that it is insufficient, especially for young children, to see their fathers only every other weekend (Kelly, 1988).

It is important clinically not to ignore fathers even if they are not active in the household or in the family picture. At the same time one should not invalidate the mother by assuming that the father must be involved in the current situation. Family therapists have all too often disqualified women alone by assuming that children could only be handled if the father were brought in to control and manage the situation. It is advisable to enter a family system of a single-parent household through the custodial parent, usually the mother, and to move only through respect for her responsibility and power toward engagement of the noncustodial father.

The custodial mother in a remarried family typically has the major responsibility for juggling her children's needs, those of her new husband, and those of his children, who visit at times. In addition, it is usually she who will have to manage arrangements for her children's ongoing contact with their own father and the extended family. Meanwhile, the father may be less cooperative now that his ex-wife is remarried or less available if he has a new family. Finally, the custodial mother must find a way to integrate her own personal needs and her own work—a very complex and burdensome set of demands. Custodial fathers, on the other hand, may feel isolated, since they remain in the minority. Those fathers will need support to overcome societal stereotypes that the women will be the primary caregiver.

Remarried families offer a number of particularly trying situations. Most difficult of all family positions is probably the role of stepparent, particularly stepmother. Given our culture's high expectations of motherhood, the woman who is brought in to replace a "lost" mother enters a situation fraught with high expectations that even a saint could not achieve. Women's tendency to take responsibility for family relationships, to believe that what goes wrong is their fault and that if they just try hard enough things will work out are major problems for them in remarried families. In general, being a stepparent carries with it built-in structural ambiguities, loyalty conflicts, guilt, and membership problems. One of the major interventions is to remove from the stepparent the burden of guilt for not being able to accomplish the impossible—taking over the parenting for children who are not their own. Our general guidelines involve putting the biological and adoptive parent, not the stepparent, in charge of the children, however difficult that may be for a father who works full-time and who feels he has no experience with "mothering," or for a mother who wants a strong father to love and discipline the children.

LIMITATIONS OF THIS MODEL

Most descriptions of the typical family life cycle, including our own, fail to convey the considerable effects of culture, ethnicity, race, and religion on all aspects of how, when, and in what way a family makes its transitions from phase to phase. Although we may ignore these variables for theoretical clarity and focus on our commonalties, a clinician working with real families in the real world cannot afford to ignore them. The definition of "family," as well as the timing of life cycle phases and the importance of different transitions, vary depending on a family's cultural background. It is essential for clinicians to consider how ethnicity and a culture's past and present intersect with the life cycle and to encourage families to take active responsibility for carrying out the rituals of their ethnic or religious groups to mark each phase. It is also extremely important for us as clinicians to help families develop rituals that correspond to the actual transitions of their lives, including those transitions that the culture has not validated, such as in the life cycle patterns of the gay community or the multiproblem poor.

The adaptation of multiproblem poor families to a stark political, social, and economic context has produced a family life cycle pattern that varies significantly from the middle-class paradigm so often and so erroneously used to conceptualize their situation. Hines (1989) has offered a thought-provoking breakdown of the family life cycle of the poor into three phases: the "unattached young adult" (who may actually be 11 or 12 years old), who is virtually on his or her own, unaccountable to and unprotected by adults; the single parent, her children, her mother, and perhaps other siblings and their children—a phase that occupies most of the life span and commonly includes three- and four-generation households; and the phase of middle and later life, where women, typically grandmothers, who may often be no older than 35 or 40, are not only involved in a central childrearing role in middle and later life, but are actively in charge of the generations below.

NEW VISIONS FOR OUR CHANGING TIMES

The patriarchal system that has characterized our culture has impoverished both women and men. We look forward to new images and metaphors that reflect the changing life cycle and where both men and women will be free to develop themselves equally inside and outside of the family.

We hope that family therapy can become a force that fosters adaptive changes in human development to allow more latitude for both men and women in their ways of relating to their mates and peers, in their intergenerational connectedness, and in their stance toward work and community. So far the family therapy field has failed to address the gender differences for male and female therapists of different life cycle stages in working with different family members. The little evidence we have so far suggests that there are significant differences in how women therapists, especially young women therapists, are related to in therapy by men and women in families (Warburton, Newberry, & Alexander, 1988) and in the way they perceive themselves and their work (Woodward et al., 1981). We hope that more research will be done in this area.

We do not believe that the relational and the emotionally expressive aspect of development is intrinsic to women. We see the romanticization of "feminine" values as inaccurate and unhelpful to families (Hare-Mustin, 1989). It is also not enough for women to adopt the "male" values of the dominant culture and to devalue what have been traditionally "female" values.

We aim toward a theory of family and individual development where both instrumental and relational aspects of each individual will be fostered. The dichotomy between the "emotional expressiveness" and "instrumental" spheres, and the devaluation and relegation of the former to women, have been very costly to all family members, men and women alike. We believe that it is the socialization of women that reinforces their "intuitive" and "nurturant" qualities and that men could be raised to be equally sensitive if our patterns of education were changed to include this as a desired value. The "feminine" perspective has been so devalued that it needs to be highlighted, as Miller (1976), Gilligan (1982), Friedan (1985), Belenky, Clinchy, Goldberger, & Tarule (1986), Tavris (1992), and others have been doing. Our world needs to appreciate both perspectives and to move toward a society in which men and women have both abilities: to function autonomously and to be intimate. Basic to this change is the notion that nurturing would not be the province only of women and that work and money would not be primarily a male-controlled sphere. We wonder how much richer the patterning of both sexes would be if men and women participated actively in childrearing. It is hoped that both men and women will be able to develop their potential without regard for the constraints of gender stereotyping that have been so constricting on human experience until now. Traditional marriage and family patterns are no longer working, contributing to the enormous stress and dissatisfaction of all family members with family life in our times. In our view it will only be when we have worked out a new equilibrium not based on the patriarchal family hierarchy that these patterns will change.

In conclusion we urge therapists to consider the powerful and preventive implications of family life cycle celebration (Imber Black & Roberts, 1992; Friedman, 1989): those religious or secular rituals designed by families in every culture to ease the passage of its members from one status to the next. All relationships in a family seem to unlock during the time just before and after such events, and it is often possible to shift patterns with less effort during these intense periods than could ordinarily be expended in years of struggle.

REFERENCES

Aguirre, B. E. (1985). Why do they return? Abused wives in shelters. *Social Work, 30*(3), 350–354.

Ahrons, C. (1981). The continuing coparental relationship between divorced spouses. *American Journal of Orthopsychiatry, 51*, 315–328.

Aries, P. (1962). *Centuries of childhood: A social history of family life.* New York: Vintage.

Avis, J. M. (1985). The politics of functional family therapy: A feminist critique. *Journal of Marital and Family Therapy, 11*(2), 127–138.

Bank, S., & Kahn, M. (1982). *The sibling bond.* New York: Basic Books.

Baruch, G., Barnett, R., & Rivers, C. (1983). *Lifeprints: New patterns of love and work for today's women.* New York: New American Library.

Belenky, M. F., Clinchy, B. M., Goldberger, N. R., & Tarule, J. M. (1986). *Women's ways of knowing.* New York: Basic Books.

Bernard, J. (1982). *The future of marriage*. New Haven, CT: Yale University Press.

Bianchi, S. M., & Spain, D. (1986). *American women in transition*. New York: Russell Sage.

Block, M. R., Davidson, J. L., & Grambs, J. D. (1981). *Women over forty: Visions and realities*. New York: Springer.

Bloom, B., White, S., & Asher, S. (1979). Marital disruption as a stressful life event. In G. L. Moles (Ed.), *Divorce and separation*. New York: Basic Books.

Blumstein, P., & Schwartz, P. (1983). *American couples: Money, work, sex*. New York: William Morrow.

Bly, R. (1990). *Iron John*. Reading, MA: Addison-Wesley.

Bowen, M. (1978). *Family therapy in clinical practice*. New York: Jason Aronson.

Braverman, L. (1989). Beyond the myth of motherhood. In M. McGoldrick, C. Anderson, & F. Walsh (Eds.), *Women in families*. New York: Norton.

Brodsky, A. M., & Hare-Mustin, R. T. (Eds.). (1980). *Women and psychotherapy*. New York: Guilford Press.

Broverman, I. K., Broverman, D. M., Clarkson, F. E., Rosenkrantz, P., & Vogel, S. R. (1970). Sex-role stereotypes and clinical judgments of mental health. *Journal of Consulting Psychology, 43*, 1–7.

Broverman, I. K., Vogel, S. R., Broverman, D. M., Clarkson, F. E., & Rosenkrantz, P. S. (1972). Sex-role stereotypes: A current appraisal. *Journal of Social Issues, 28*(2), 59–78.

Carter, B. (1992). *Myths of marriage*. Presentation, Maastrict, Holland, May 21.

Carter, B., & McGoldrick, M. (1989). Overview: The changing family life cycle—a framework for family therapy. In B. Carter & M. McGoldrick (Eds.), *The changing family life cycle*. Boston: Allyn & Bacon.

Carter, E. A. (1978). The transgenerational scripts and nuclear family stress: Theory and clinical implications. In R. R. Sager (Ed.), *Georgetown family symposium* (Vol. 3, 1975–76). Washington, DC: Georgetown University.

Chodorow, N., & Contratto, S. (1982). The fantasy of the perfect mother. In B. Throne (Ed.), *Rethinking the family: Some feminist questions*. New York: Longman.

Cicirelli, V. G. (1982). Sibling influence through the life span. In M. E. Lamb & B. Sutton-Smith (Eds.), *Sibling relationships: Their nature and significance across the lifespan*. Hillsdale, NJ: Lawrence Erlbaum Associates.

Cicirelli, V. G. (1985). Sibling relationships throughout the life cycle. In L. L'Abate (Ed.), *The handbook of family psychology and therapy*. Homewood, IL: Dorsey Press.

Combrinck-Graham, L. (1989). *Children in family contexts*. New York: Guilford Press.

Congressional Caucus for Women's Issues. (1984, September 23). *The New York Times*, p. 38.

Cowen, C. P., & Cowen, H. (1985). Transitions to parenthood: His, hers, and theirs. *Journal of Family Issues, 6*(4), 451–481.

Daniels, P., & Weingarten, K. (1983). *Sooner or later: The timing of parenthood in adult lives*. New York: Norton.

Dinnerstein, D. (1976). *The mermaid and the minotaur*. New York: Harper & Row.

Dohrenwend, B. S. (1973). Social status and stressful life events. *Journal of Personality and Social Psychiatry, 28*, 225–235.

Eisler, R. (1987). *The chalice and the blade*. New York: Harper & Row.

Erikson, E. (1963). *Childhood and society* (2nd ed.). New York: Norton.

Erikson, E. (1968). *Identity: Youth in crisis*. New York: Norton.

Falicov, C. (1980). The life cycle of Mexican American families. In B. Carter & M. McGoldrick (Eds.), *The family life cycle*. New York: Gardner.

Falicov, C. (Ed.). (1988). *Family transitions: Continuity and change in the family life cycle*. New York: Guilford Press.

Faludi, S. (1991). *Backlash: The undeclared war against American women*. New York: Crown.

Freidman, E. H. (1989). Systems and ceremonies. In B. Carter & M. McGoldrick. (Eds.), *The changing family life cycle*. Boston: Allyn & Bacon.

Friedan, B. (1985). How to get the women's movement moving again. *New York Times Magazine*, Nov. 3.

Fulmer, R. (1989). Lower income and professional familes: A comparison of structure and life cycle process. In B. Carter & M. McGoldrick (Eds.), *The changing family life cycle*. Boston: Allyn & Bacon.

Gelfand, D. E., & Kutzik, A. J. (Eds.). (1979). *Ethnicity and aging*. New York: Springer.

Gilligan, C. (1982). *In a different voice*. Cambridge, MA: Harvard University Press.

Gilligan, C., Lyons, N. P., & Hammer, T. J. (1989). *Making connections: The relational worlds of adolescent girls at Emma Willard School*. Cambridge: Harvard University Press.

Glick, P. (1984). How American marriages are changing. *American Demographics*. January.

Hadley, T., Jacob, T., Milliones, J., Caplan, J., & Spitz, D. (1974). The relationship between family developmental crises and the appearance of symptoms in a family member. *Family Process, 13*, 207–214.

Hare-Mustin, R. (1989). The problem of gender in family therapy theory. In M. McGoldrick, C. Anderson, & F. Walsh (Eds.) *Women in families*. New York: Norton.

Hess, B. B. (1985). Aging policies and old women: The hidden agenda. In A. S. Rossi (Ed.), *Gender and the life course*. New York: Aldine.

Hess, B. B., & Soldo, B. J. (1984, August). *The old and the very old: A new frontier of age and family policy*. Paper presented at Annual Meeting of the American Sociological Society, San Antonio.

Hess, B. B., & Waring, J. M. (1984). Changing patterns of aging and family bonds in later life. *The Family Coordinator, 27*(4), 303–314.

Hesse-Biber, S., & Williamson, J. (1984). Resource theory and power in families: Life cycle considerations. *Family Process, 23*(2), 261–278.

Hetherington, E. M., Cox, M., & Cox, R. (1977). The aftermath of divorce. In J. J. Stevens, Jr., & M. Matthews (Eds.). *Mother–child, father–child relations*. Washington, DC: National Association for the Education of Young Children.

Hewlett, S. A. (1985). *A lesser life*. New York: Morrow.

Hill, R. (1970). *Family development in three generations*. Cambridge, MA: Schenkman.

Hines, P. (1989). The life cycle of poor black families. In B. Carter & M. McGoldrick. (Eds.), *The changing family life cycle*. Boston: Allyn & Bacon.

Imber Black, E., & Roberts, J. (1992). *Rituals*. New York: Harper & Row.

Kagan, J. (1984). *The nature of the child*. New York: Basic Books.

Kahn, M., & Lewis, K. (1989). *Siblings in therapy: Life span and clinical issues*. New York: Norton.

Kelly, J. C. (1988). Longer term adjustment in children of divorce: Converging findings and implications for practice. *Journal of Family Psychology, 1*(2).

Kernberg, P., & Chazan, S. (1991). *Children with conduct disorders*. New York: Basic Books.

Lang, A. M., & Brody, E. M. (1983). Characteristics of middle-aged daughters and help to their elderly mothers. *Journal of Marriage and the Family, 45*, 193–202.

Levinson, D. (1978). *The seasons of a man's life*. New York: Knopf.

Lewis, M., Feiring, C., & Kotsonis, M. (1984). The social network of the young child. In M. Lewis (Ed.), *Beyond the dyad: The genesis of behavior series* (Vol. 4). New York: Plenum Press.

Lewis, M., & Weintraub, M. (1974). Sex of parent × sex of child: Socioemotional development. In R. D. Friedman, R. M. Richart, & R. C. Vandewiele (Eds.), *Sex differences in behavior*. New York: Wiley.

Lieberman, M. (1974, October). *Adaptational patterns in middle aged and elderly: The role of ethnicity*. Paper presented at the Gerontological Society Conference, Portland, OR.

Losoff, M. M. (1974). Fathers and autonomy in women. In R. B. Kundsin (Ed.), *Women and success: The anatomy of achievement*. New York: William Morrow.

Maccoby, E. E., & Jacklin, C. N. (1974). *The psychology of sex differences*. Stanford, CA: Stanford University Press.

McGoldrick, M. (1977). *Some data on death and cancer in schizophrenic families*. Paper presented at Georgetown Presymposium. Washington, DC.

McGoldrick, M. (1989a). The joining of families through marriage: The couple. In B. Carter & M. McGoldrick (Eds.), *The changing family life cycle*. Boston: Allyn & Bacon.

McGoldrick, M. (1989b). Women and the family life cycle. In B. Carter & M. McGoldrick (Eds.), *The changing family life cycle*. Boston: Allyn & Bacon.

McGoldrick, M. (1989c). Ethnicity and the family life cycle. In B. Carter & M. McGoldrick (Eds.), *The changing family life cycle*. Boston: Allyn & Bacon.

McGoldrick, M. (1989d). Sisters. In M. McGoldrick, C. Anderson, & F. Walsh (Eds.), *Women in families*. New York: Norton.

McGoldrick, M. (1991). Gender, class, and culture. *Smith College School for Social Work Journal, IX*(2), Commencement Address.

McGoldrick, M., & Carter, B. (1989). Forming a remarried family. In B. Carter & M. McGoldrick (Eds.), *The changing family life cycle*. Boston: Allyn & Bacon.

Miller, J. B. (1976). *Toward a new psychology of women*. Boston: Beacon.

Notman, M., Klein, R., Jordan, J., & Zilbach, J. (1991). Women's unique developmental issues across the life cycle. In A. Tasman & S. Goldfinger (Eds.), *Review of psychiatry*, (Vol. 10). Washington, DC: American Psychiatric Press.

Offer, D., & Sabshin, M. (1984). Adolescence. In D. Offer & M. Sabshin (Eds.), *Normality and the life cycle*. New York: Basic Books

Padan, D. (1965). *Intergenerational mobility of women: A two-step process of status mobility in a context of a value conflict*. Tel Aviv: Tel Aviv University.

Rawlings, S. W. (1983). *Household and family characteristics: March 1982. Current Population Reports, Series P 20 (381)*. Washington, DC: U.S. Bureau of the Census.

Romer, N. (1981). *The sex-role cycle: Socialization from infancy to old age*. New York: McGraw-Hill.

Sheeber, L., & Johnson, J. (1992). Child temperament, maternal adjustment, and changes in family life style. *American Journal of Orthopsychiatry, 63*, 178–186.

Sternberg, D. (1984). The nature of love. *Journal of Personality and Social Psychology, 47*(2), 312–329.

Streib, G. (1972). Older families and their troubles: Familial and social responses. *The Family Coordinator, 21,* 5–19.

Taffel, R. (1991). Why is daddy so grumpy? In T. J. Goodrich (Ed.), *Women and power.* New York: Norton.

Tavris, C. (1992). *The mismeasure of women.* New York: Simon & Schuster.

Thomas, C. G., & Duszynski, D. R. (1974). Closeness to parents and the family constellation in a prospective study of five disease states: Suicide, mental illness, malignant tumor, hypertension, and coronary heart disease. *The Johns Hopkins Medical Journal, 134,* 251–270.

Thurow, L. (1987). The surge in inequality. *Scientific American, 256*(5), 30–37.

Valliant, G. E. (1977). *Adaptation to life.* Boston: Little, Brown.

Vernoff, J., Douvan, E., & Kulka, R. (1981). *The inner American: A self portrait from 1957 to 1976.* New York: Basic Books.

Walsh, F. (1978). Concurrent grandparent death and the birth of a schizophrenic offspring: An intriguing finding. *Family Process, 17,* 457–463.

Walsh., F. (1989a). Reconsidering gender in the marital quid pro quo. In M. McGoldrick, C. Anderson, & F. Walsh (Eds.), *Women in families.* New York: Norton.

Walsh, F. (1989b). The family in later life. In B. Carter & M. McGoldrick (Eds.), *The changing family life cycle,* Boston: Allyn & Bacon.

Warburton, J., Newberry, A., & Alexander, J. (1988). Women as therapists, trainers, and supervisors. In M. McGoldrick, C. Anderson, & F. Walsh (Eds.), *Women in families.* New York: Norton.

Weitzman, L. (1985). *The divorce revolution.* New York: The Free Press.

Woehrer, C. E. (1982). The influence of ethnic families on intergenerational relationships and later life transitions. *Annals of the American Academy of Psychological and Social Science, 464,* 65–78.

Woodward, C. A., Santa-Barbara, J., Streiner, D. L., Goodman, J. T., Levin, S., & Epstein, N. B. (1981). Client, treatment, and therapist variables related to outcome in brief, systems-oriented family therapy. *Family Process, 20,* 189–197.

CHAPTER 15

MASTERING FAMILY CHALLENGES IN SERIOUS ILLNESS AND DISABILITY

John S. Rolland

INTRODUCTION: A NORMATIVE SYSTEMIC HEALTH PARADIGM

Illness, disability, and death are universal experiences in families. The real question is not "if" we will face these issues, but when in our lives, what kind of condition, how serious, and for how long. With major advances in medical technology, people are living much longer with conditions they used to die from. Cancer, heart disease, diabetes, and now AIDS are just a few examples. Many children with chronic conditions that were previously fatal or necessitated institutional life are now reaching adulthood, and, with the help of new policies, they are assimilating into mainstream adult life. This means that ever-growing numbers of families are both living with chronic disorders over an increasingly long time span, and they are coping with more chronic conditions often simultaneously.

The extension of later life has heightened the strain on sons and daughters who must contend with divided loyalties and a complex juggle between caretaking for aging parents, childrearing, and financial provider demands— and they must do this in a society where families are geographically dispersed and health care is exorbitant and inadequate.

Given these changes, how can we best describe the normative challenges of serious illness and optimal family coping and adaptation? We are advancing past stereotypic definitions of "the family" and the view of normal family life as "problem-free" to recognize that all families are challenged by adversity. In the same way, when serious illness strikes, we need to move beyond an outdated, rigid, and often romanticized version of coping.

This chapter provides a normative, preventive model for psychoeducation, assessment, and intervention with families facing chronic and life-threatening conditions (Rolland 1984, 1987a, 1987b, 1990, 1991, in press). This model offers a more useful systemic view of healthy family adaptation to serious illness as a developmental process over time in relation to the complexities and diversity of contemporary family life, modern medicine, and existing flawed models of health-care delivery and access to care. First, before describing the model, some basic constructs are useful.

As a first step to constructing a normative model, we need to redefine the unit of care in terms of the family or caregiving system as distinct from the ill individual (McDaniel, Hepworth, & Doherty, 1992). An effective biopsychosocial model, defined in systems terms, needs to encompass all those affected psychosocially rather than to focus narrowly on the patient receiving health care. By using a broad definition of family as the cornerstone of the caregiving system, we can describe a model of successful coping and adaptation based on family system strengths.

Second, we need to describe the complex mutual interactions between illness, ill member, and family within a normative framework. There is a vast literature describing the impact of chronic disorders on individuals and families. However, the impact of individual and family dynamics on disease has historically been defined as psychosomatic processes and almost invariably in pathological terms. The definition of a condition as "psychosomatic" is a shameful label associated with a number of pejorative cultural meanings that imply characterological or family weakness.

An alternative framework would describe psychosomatic in more holistic, interactive, and normative terms. All illnesses can be viewed as having a psychosomatic interplay, where the relative influence of the biological and psychosocial varies over a range of disorders and phases of an illness. From this perspective, a psychosomatic interplay provides an opportunity for psychosocial factors, not just biomedical interventions, to be important influences in the healing process.

We need to transform traditional theories about mind–body relationship into one of individual and social-system–body. The fundamental idea of a biopsychosocial interaction remains an uncomfortable paradigm within the traditional medical model. In part, resistance to changing the biomedical paradigm stems from a reluctance to broaden the net of influences on biological processes to include nonbiological systemic factors, as one health expert put it, beyond the boundary of the skin. Acknowledgment of this interaction is difficult in the context of extraordinary technological advances, where the primary objective of medicine has been to perfect a biological/technical mastery over disease. Resistence to a systemic framework is heightened by the pathological skew of "psychosomatic" literature, considering the family only in cases of severe dysfunction. The idea that systems dynamics and human interactions beyond the patient can influence his or her physical state affirms the importance of the "social" in the biopsychosocial model.

Family research in the arena of chronic illness, like studies of the individual, has tended to emphasize pathological family dynamics that are associated with poor disease course or treatment compliance (Campbell, 1986). This leads to paradigms that emphasize illness-based family systems and psychosomatic families. By defining pathological systems at one end of a continuum, we do not clarify what constitutes healthy family coping and adaptation to illness.

At the other end of the continuum, especially in the popular literature, there has been a focus on the exceptional patient (Siegel, 1986; Simonton, Mathews-Simonton, & Sparks, 1980). Numerous personal accounts highlight the superstar patient or family. Although these provide a refreshing relief from descriptions of pathological patients and families, they often err toward superhuman epic descriptions that leave the average family without a reference point. The average family is vulnerable to double jeopardy. Its members can feel pathological either by noting any similarities with severely dysfunctional families or by not measuring up to the exceptional one. This leaves families with a view of healthy adaptation that is rarely achieved and perpetuates self-judgments about performance that are infused with blame, shame, and guilt. The inspirations of the exceptional and the warning signs of dysfunction need to be grounded by descriptions of the typical experience. Only recently have investigators shifted attention toward the efficacy of social support and a range of family dynamics that enhance coping and adaptation. This has led to a beginning literature examining the impact of individual and family strengths on the quality of life for all family members and on disease course and outcome.

Finally, definitions of what constitutes normal families are integral to defining healthy caregiving systems. The myth that normal families are "problem-free" (Walsh, 1983) must be replaced by the recognition that all families confront adversity. What distinguishes a well-functioning family must be viewed in relation to the family's ability to cope effectively with the life challenges its members face. Outdated, rigid, gender-based models of the family invariably define a narrow range of acceptable roles and strategies for coping with illness and disability. Traditional models of patient and caregiver roles shackle families in the face of the protracted strains of illness and threatened loss. A rich and broad multigenerational definition of family, that evolves over the life cycle (Carter & McGoldrick, 1988), is essential to constructing a normative model.

By viewing the family as the unit of care, where a broad range of family forms and biopsychosocial interactions are normative, we can develop a model that uses as its central reference point, the idea of goodness of fit between family style and the psychosocial demands of different disorders over time. From this perspective, for example, high versus low family cohesion is not viewed as inherently healthy or unhealthy. Rather, the organizing principle becomes relative: What degree of family cohesion will work optimally with this illness now, and how might that change in future phases of the condition?

In situations of chronic disorders, a basic task for families is to create a meaning for the illness situation that preserves their sense of competency and mastery. At the extremes, competing ideologies can leave families with a choice between a biological explanation or one of personal responsibility (bad things happen to bad people). Families desperately need reassurance that they are handling the illness normally (bad things do happen to good people). These needs often occur in the context of a vague or nonexistant psychosocial roadmap. Many families, particularly with "off-time" disorders find themselves in unfamiliar territory and without guides. This highlights the need for a preventive, psychoeducational approach that helps families anticipate normative illness-related developmental tasks over time in a fashion that maximizes a sense of control and mastery.

In order to create a normative context for their experience with chronic disorders, families need the following foundation. First, they need a psychosocial understanding of the condition in systems terms. This means learning the expected pattern of practical and affective demands of a disorder over the life course of the condition. This includes a time frame for disease-related developmental tasks associated with different phases of the unfolding disorder. Second, families need to understand themselves as a functional unit in systems terms. Third, they need an appreciation of individual and family life cycles to facilitate their incorporation of changing developmental demands for the family unit and individual members in relation to the demands of a chronic disorder. Finally, families need to understand the beliefs that guide the type of caregiving system they construct. This includes guiding principles that define roles, rules of communication, definitions of success or mastery, and fit with the beliefs of the health care providers. Family understanding in these areas facilitates a more holistic integration of the disorder and the family as a functional family–health/illness system evolving over time.

FAMILY SYSTEMS HEALTH MODEL

A normative, preventive model has been developed for psychoeducation, assessment, and intervention with families facing chronic and life-threatening disorders (Rolland 1984, 1987a, 1987b, 1990, 1991, in press). This model is based on the concept of a systemic interaction between an illness and family that evolves over time. The goodness of "fit" between the psychosocial demands of the disorder and the family style of functioning and resources is a prime determinant of successful versus dysfunctional coping and adaptation. The model distinguishes three dimensions: (1) psychosocial "types" of disorders, (2) major phases in their natural history, and (3) key family-system variables (Figure 15.1). A scheme of the systemic interaction between illness and family might look like the diagram in Figure 15.2. Family variables given particular emphasis include: (1) the family and individual life cycles, particularly in relation to the time phases of a disorder, (2) multigenerational legacies related to illness and loss, and (3) belief systems.

Psychosocial Types of Illness

The standard disease classification is based on purely biological criteria that are clustered in ways to establish a medical diagnosis and treatment plan, rather than the psychosocial demands on patients and their families. I have proposed a different classification scheme that provides a better link between the biological and psychosocial worlds, and thereby, clarifies the relationship between chronic illness and the family (Rolland, 1984, 1987a). The goal of this typology is to define meaningful and useful categories with similar psychosocial demands for a wide array of chronic illnesses affecting individuals across the life span.

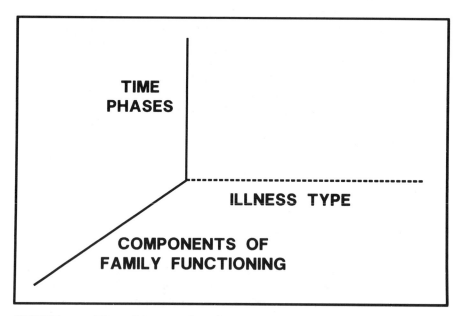

FIGURE 15.1. Three-dimensional model representing the relationship between illness type, time phases, and family functioning. (From Rolland, 1987a, with permission.)

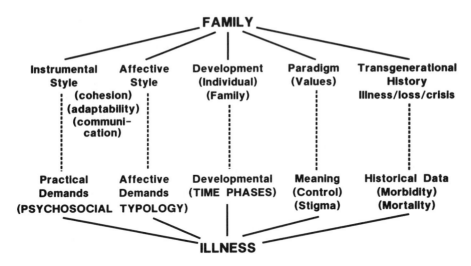

FIGURE 15.2. Interface of chronic illness and the family. (From Rolland, 1987c, with permission.)

Onset

Illnesses can be divided into those that have either an acute onset, such as strokes, or gradual onset, such as Alzheimer's disease. For acute-onset illnesses, affective and practical changes are compressed into a short time, requiring of the family more rapid mobilization of crisis-management skills. Families able to tolerate highly charged emotional situations, exchange roles flexibly, problem-solve efficiently, and utilize outside resources will have an advantage in managing acute-onset conditions.

Course

The course of chronic diseases can take three general forms: progressive, constant, or relapsing/episodic. With a *progressive* disease such as Alzheimer's disease, the family is faced with a perpetually symptomatic family member, where disability worsens in a stepwise or gradual way. The family must live with the prospect of continual role change and adaptation as the disease progresses. Increasing strain on family caretakers is caused by exhaustion, with few periods of relief from demands of the illness, and by new caretaking tasks over time.

With a *constant*-course illness the occurence of an initial event is followed by a stable biological course. A single heart attack or spinal-cord injury are examples. Typically, after an initial period of recovery, the chronic phase is characterized by some clearcut deficit or limitation. The family is faced with a semipermanent change that is stable and predictable over a considerable time span. The potential for family exhaustion exists without the strain of new role demands over time.

Relapsing- or *episodic-*course illnesses, such as disk problems and asthma, are distinguished by the alternation of stable low-symptom periods with periods of flare-up or exacerbation. Families are strained by both the frequency of transitions between crisis and noncrisis and the ongoing uncertainty of *when* a recurrence will occur. This requires family flexibility to alternate between two forms of family organization. The wide psychological discrepancy between periods of normalcy versus flare-up is a particularly taxing feature unique to relapsing diseases.

Outcome

The extent to which a chronic illness leads to death or shortens one's life span has profound psychosocial impact. The most crucial factor is the *initial expectation* of whether a disease is likely to cause death. On one end of the continuum are illnesses that do not typically affect the life span, such as disk disease or arthritis. At the other extreme are illnesses that are clearly progressive and fatal such as metastatic cancer or AIDS. An intermediate, more unpredictable category includes both illnesses that shorten the life span, such as heart disease, and those with the possibility of sudden death, such as hemophilia. A major difference between these kinds of outcome is the degree to which the family experiences anticipatory loss and its pervasive effects on family life (Davies, Quinlan, McKegney, & Kimball, 1973; Derogatis, Abeloff, & Melisartos, 1979; Schmale & Iker, 1971; Rolland, 1990; Simonton et al., 1980).

Incapacitation

Disability can involve impairment of cognition (e.g., Alzheimer's disease), sensation (e.g., blindness), movement (e.g., stroke with paralysis), stamina (e.g., heart disease), disfigurement (e.g., mastectomy), and conditions associated with social stigma (e.g., AIDS). The extent, kind, and timing of incapacitation imply sharp differences in the degree of family stress. For instance, the combined cognitive and motor deficits caused by a stroke necessitate greater family role reallocation than for a spinal-cord injury where cognitive abilities are unaffected. For some illnesses, like stroke, disability is often worst at the beginning. For progressive diseases, like Alzheimer's disease, disability looms as an increasing problem in later phases of the illness, allowing a family more time to prepare for anticipated changes and an opportunity for the ill member to participate in disease-related family planning.

By combining the kinds of onset, course, outcome, and incapacitation into a grid format, we generate a typology that clusters illnesses according to similarities and differences in patterns that pose differing psychosocial demands (Table 15.1).

TABLE 15.1. Categorization of Chronic Disorders by Psychosocial Type

		Incapacitating		Nonincapacitating	
		Acute	Gradual	Acute	Gradual
Progressive	F A T A L		Lung cancer CNS metastases AIDS Bone marrow failure Amyotrophic lateral sclerosis	Acute leukemia Pancreatic cancer Metastatic breast cancer Malignant melanoma Lung cancer Liver cancer, etc.	Cystic fibrosis*
Relapsing				Cancers in remission	
Progressive	POSSIBLY SHORTENED LIFE SPAN		Emphysema Alzheimer's disease Multi-infarct dementia Multiple sclerosis (late) Chronic alcoholism Huntington's chorea Scleroderma		Juvenile diabetes* Malignant hypertension Insulin-dependent adult-onset diabetes
Relapsing	FATAL LIFE	Angina	Early multiple sclerosis Episodic alcoholism	Sickle cell disease* Hemophilia*	Systemic lupus erythemastosus*
Constant	SPAN	Stroke Moderate/severe myocardial infarction	PKU and other inborn errors of metabolism	Mild myocardial infarction Cardiac arrhythmia	Hemodialysis-treated renal failure Hodgkin's disease
Progressive	N O N F A T A L		Parkinson's disease Rheumatoid arthritis Osteoarthritis		Non-insulin-dependent adult-onset diabetes
Relapsing		Lumbosacral disk disease		Kidney stones Gout Migraine Seasonal allergy Asthma Epilepsy	Peptic ulcer Ulcerative colitis Chronic bronchitis Other inflammatory bowel diseases Psoriasis
Constant		Congenital malformations Spinal cord injury Acute blindness Acute deafness Survived severe trauma and burns Posthypoxic syndrome	Nonprogressive mental retardation Cerebral palsy	Benign arrhythmia Congenital heart disease	Malabsorption syndromes Hyper/hypothroidism Pernicious anemia Controlled hypertension Controlled glaucoma

*Early.

Excerpted from Rolland (1984), with permission.

The *predictability* of an illness, and the degree of uncertainty about the specific way or rate at which it unfolds, overlays all other variables. For illnesses with highly unpredictable courses, such as multiple sclerosis, family coping and adaptation, especially future planning, are hindered by anticipatory anxiety and ambiguity about what they will actually encounter. Families able to put long-term uncertainty into perspective are best prepared to avoid the risks of exhaustion and dysfunction.

Time Phases of Illness

Too often discussions of "coping with cancer," "managing disability," or "dealing with life-threatening illness" approach illness as a static state and fail to appreciate the dynamic unfolding of illness processes over time. The concept of time phases provides a way for clinicians and families to think longitudinally and to understand chronic illness as an ongoing process with normative landmarks, transitions, and changing demands. Each phase of an illness poses its own psychosocial demands and developmental tasks that require significantly different strengths, attitudes, or changes from a family. The core psychosocial themes in the natural history of chronic disease can be described in three major phases: crisis, chronic, and terminal (Figure 15.3).

The *crisis* phase includes any symptomatic period before diagnosis and the initial period of readjustment after a diagnosis and initial treatment plan. This period holds a number of key tasks for the ill member and family. Moos (1984) describes certain universal, practical illness-related tasks, including: (1) learning to cope with any symptoms or disability; (2) adapting to the hospital environment and any treatment procedures and; (3) establishing and maintaining workable relationships with the health care team. Also, there are critical tasks of a more general, existential nature. The family needs to: (1) create a meaning for the illness that maximizes a sense of mastery and competency; (2) grieve for the loss of "life before illness"; (3) gradually accept the illness as permanent while maintaining a sense of continuity between their past and future; (4) pull together to cope with the immediate crisis and; (5) in the face of uncertainty, develop flexibility toward future goals.

During this initial crisis period, health professionals have enormous influence over a family's sense of competence and the methods devised to accomplish these developmental tasks. Initial meetings and advice given at the time of diagnosis can be thought of as a "Framing Event." Because families are so vulnerable at this point, clinicians need to be extremely sensitive in their interactions with family members. They need to be aware of messages conveyed by their behavior with the family. Who is included or excluded (e.g., patient) from a discussion can be interpreted by the family as a message of how a family should plan their communication for the duration of the illness. This "Framing Event" has a powerful influence on

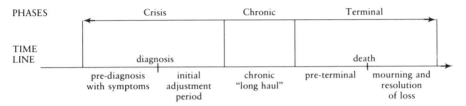

FIGURE 15.3. Timeline and phases of illness. (From Rolland, 1984, with permission.)

families deciding what is normal. For instance, a clinician may meet with family members separately from the patient to give them information about the illness diagnosis and prognosis. At this vulnerable moment, the family may assume they are being instructed implicitly to exclude the patient in any discussion of the illness. Clinicians also need to be careful not to undercut a family's attempt to sustain a sense of competence by implicitly blaming the patient or the family for an illness (e.g., delay in seeking an appointment, negligence by parents, poor health habits) or by distancing themselves from the family.

The *chronic* phase, whether long or short, is the time span between the initial diagnosis/readjustment and the third phase when issues of death and terminal illness predominate. This era can be marked by constancy, progression, or episodic change. It has been referred to as "the long haul," or "day-to-day living with chronic illness" phase. Often the patient and family have come to grips psychologically and organizationally with permanent changes and have devised an ongoing modus operandi. The ability of the family to maintain the semblance of a normal life with a chronic illness and heightened uncertainty is a key task of this period. If the illness is fatal, this is a time of "living in limbo." For certain highly debilitating but not clearly fatal illnesses, such as a massive stroke or dementia, the family can feel saddled with an exhausting problem "without end." Paradoxically, a family may feel its only hope to resume a "normal" life can be realized after the death of their ill member. The maintenance of maximum autonomy for *all* family members in the face of protracted adversity helps offset these trapped, helpless feelings.

For long-term disorders, customary patterns of intimacy for couples become skewed by discrepancies between the ill member and the well spouse/caretaker. As one young husband lamented about his wife's cancer, "It was hard enough 2 years ago to absorb that, even if Ann was cured, her radiation treatment would make pregnancy impossible. Now, I find it unbearable that her continued slow, losing battle with cancer makes it impossible to go for our dreams like other couples our age." Normative ambivalence and escape fantasies often remain underground and contribute to "survivor guilt." Psychoeducational family interventions that normalize such emotions related to threatened loss can help prevent destructive cycles of blame, shame, and guilt.

In the *terminal* phase of an illness, the inevitability of death becomes apparent and dominates family life. Now the family must cope with issues of separation, death, mourning, and resumption of "normal" family life beyond the loss (Walsh & McGoldrick, 1991). Families that adapt best to this phase are able to shift their view of mastery from controlling the illness to a successful process of "letting go." Optimal coping involves emotional openness as well as dealing with the myriad of practical tasks at hand. This includes seeing this phase as an opportunity to share precious time together to acknowledge the impending loss, to deal with unfinished business, and to say goodbyes. If they have not decided beforehand, the patient and key family members need to decide about such things as: a living will, the extent of medical heroics desired, preferences about dying at home, in the hospital, or at hospice, and wishes about a funeral and memorial service.

Critical *transition periods* link the three time phases. Transitions in the illness life cycle are times when families reevaluate the appropriateness of their previous life structure in the face of new illness-related developmental demands. Unfinished business from the previous phase can complicate or block movement through the transitions. Families can become permanently frozen in an adaptive structure that has outlived its utility (Penn, 1983). For example, the usefulness of pulling together in the crisis phase can become maladaptive and stifling for all family members in the chronic phase.

The interaction of the time phases and typology of illness provides a framework for a normative psychosocial developmental model for chronic disease that resembles models for human development. The time phases (crisis, chronic, and terminal) can be considered broad developmental periods in the natural history of chronic disease. Each period has certain basic tasks independent of the type of illness. Each "type" of illness has specific supplementary tasks.

Clinical Implications

This model provides a framework for assessment and clinical intervention with a family facing a chronic or life-threatening illness. It facilitates a grasp of chronic illness and disability in psychosocial terms. Attention to features of onset, course, outcome, and incapacitation provides markers that focus clinical assessment and intervention with a family. For instance, acute-onset illnesses demand high levels of adaptability, problem solving, role reallocation, and balanced cohesion. In such circumstances, helping families to maximize flexibility enables them to adapt more successfully.

An illness timeline delineates psychosocial developmental stages of an illness, each phase with its own unique developmental tasks. It is important for families to address normative phase-related tasks in sequence to optimize successful adaptation over the long haul of a chronic disorder. There-fore, attention to time allows the clinician to assess family strengths and vulnerabilities in relation to the present and future phases of the illness.

The model clarifies treatment planning. First, goal setting is guided by awareness of the components of family functioning most relevant to par-ticular types or phases of an illness. Sharing this information with the family and deciding on specific goals provides a better sense of control and realis-tic hope to the family. This process empowers families in their journey of living with a chronic disorder. Also, this knowledge educates the family about warning signs that should alert them to call at appropriate times for brief, goal-oriented treatment.

The framework is useful for timing family psychosocial checkups to coincide with key transition points in the illness life cycle. Preventively ori-ented psychoeducational or support groups for patients and their families (Gonzales, Steinglass, & Reiss, 1989) can be designed to deal with different types of conditions (e.g., progressive, life-threatening, relapsing). Also, brief psychoeducational "modules," timed for critical phases of particular "types" of diseases, enable families to digest manageable portions of a long-term coping process. Modules can be tailored to particular phases of the illness life cycle and to family coping skills necessary to confront disease-related demands. This provides a cost-effective preventive service that also can iden-tify high-risk families.

FAMILY ASSESSMENT

As chronic illnesses become incorporated into the family system and all its processes, family coping is influenced by illness-oriented family dynamics that concern belief systems and the dimension of time.

Transgenerational History of Illness, Loss, and Crisis

A family's present behavior, and therefore its response to illness, cannot be adequately comprehended apart from its history (Boszormenyi-Nagy & Spark, 1973; Bowen, 1978; Byng-Hall, 1988; Carter & McGoldrick, 1988; Framo, 1976; McGoldrick & Walsh, 1983). Systems-oriented clinicians can use historical questioning and construct a genogram and timeline (McGold-rick & Gerson, 1985) to track key events and transitions to gain an under-standing of a family's organizational shifts and coping strategies *as a system* in response to past stressors, and more specifically, to past illnesses. Such inquiry may help explain and predict the family's current style of coping and adaptation. For families facing a chronic disorder, a multigenerational assessment helps clarify areas of strength and vulnerability. Also, it identi-fies high-risk families burdened by past unresolved issues and dysfunctional patterns who cannot absorb the challenges presented by a serious condition.

A historical systemic perspective focuses on how a family organized around past stressors and tracks the evolution of family adaptation over time. Patterns of coping, replications, discontinuities, shifts in relationships (i.e., alliances, triangles, cutoffs), and sense of competence are noted. These patterns are transmitted across generations as family pride, myths, taboos, catastrophic expectations, and belief systems (McGoldrick & Walsh 1983).

A chronic-illness-oriented genogram focuses on how a family organized as an evolving system specifically around previous illnesses and unexpected crises in the current and previous generations. A central goal is to bring to light areas of consensus and "learned differences" (Penn, 1983) that are sources of cohesion and conflict.

Whereas a family may have certain standard ways of coping with any illness, there may be critical differences in their style and success in adaptation to different "types" of diseases. It is important to track prior family illnesses for areas of perceived competence, failures, or inexperience. Inquiry about different types of illness (e.g., life-threatening vs. non-life-threatening) may find, for instance, that a family dealt successfully with non-life-threatening illnesses but reeled under the weight of metastatic cancer. Such a family might be well-equipped to deal with less severe conditions, but it might be particularly vulnerable if another life-threatening illness were to occur. A different family may only have had experience with non-life-threatening illnesses and need psychoeducation to successfully cope with the uncertainties particular to life-threatening diseases. Such inquiry clarifies areas of strength and vulnerability for a family facing a particular type of illness.

Tracking a family's coping capabilities in the crisis, chronic, and terminal phases of previous chronic illnesses highlights legacies of strength as well as complication in adaptation related to different points in the "illness life cycle." One man grew up with a partially disabled father with heart disease and witnessed his parents successfully renegotiate traditional gender-defined roles when his mother went to work while his father assumed household responsibilities. This man, now with heart disease himself, has a positive legacy about gender roles from his family of origin that facilitates a flexible response in his own crisis. Another family with a member with chronic kidney failure functioned very well in handling the practicalities of home dialysis. However, in the terminal phase, their limitations around affective expression left a legacy of unresolved grief. Tracking prior illness experiences in terms of phases helps clinicians see both the strengths and vulnerabilities in a family, thereby counteracting the assignment of dysfunctional labels that emphasize the difficult periods. Clinicians need to ask specifically for *positive* family-of-origin experiences with illness and loss that can be used as models to adapt to the current situation.

The family's history of coping with crises in general, especially unanticipated ones, should be explored. Illnesses with acute onset (i.e., heart attack), sudden disability (e.g., stroke), or rapid relapse (i.e., diabetic insulin reaction, disk disease) demand rapid reorganization and crisis mobilization skills. Other illnesses place a continual high demand for family stamina (i.e., spinal-cord injury, rheumatoid arthritis). The family history of coping with moderate to severe ongoing stressors is a good predictor of adjustment.

For any significant illness in either adult's family of origin, a clinician should try to get a picture of how those families organized to handle the range of disease-related affective and practical tasks. Also, it is important to find out what role each played in handling emotional or practical tasks and whether they emerged with a strong sense of competence or failure. Such information can help to anticipate areas of conflict and consensus and similar patterns of adaptation. Hidden strengths, not just unresolved issues, related to illness and loss can remain dormant in a marriage, and suddenly reemerge when triggered by a chronic illness in the current family unit.

The reenactment of previous system configurations around illness can occur largely as an unconscious, automatic process (Byng-Hall, 1988). Whether adaptive or dysfunctional, complementarity can emerge de novo specifically within the context of a chronic disease. Typically, the role chosen represents a repetition or opposite of a role played by themselves or the same-sex parent.

Many families facing chronic disease have not had dysfunctional multigenerational family patterns of adaptation. Yet, any family may falter in the face of multiple superimposed disease and nondisease stressors that impact in a relatively short time. With progressive, incapacitating diseases or the concurrence of illnesses in several family members, a pragmatic approach that focuses on expanded or creative use of supports and resources outside the family is most productive.

Interface of the Illness, Individual, and Family Life Cycles

A life-cycle lens provides a powerful way to construct a normative framework for serious illness. To place the unfolding of chronic disease into a developmental context, it is crucial to understand the intertwining of three evolutionary threads: the illness, individual, and family life cycles. The psychosocial typology and phases of illness framework facilitate this goal by describing the psychosocial pattern of any illness in longitudinal terms.

The life cycle is a central concept for both family and individual development. Life cycle means there is a basic sequence and unfolding of the life course within which individual, family, or illness uniqueness occurs. Illness, individual, and family development have in common the notion of phases (each with its own developmental tasks) and are marked by the alternation of life structure-building/maintaining and life structure-changing (transitional) periods linking developmental phases (Levinson, 1978). The primary goal of a structure-building/maintaining period is to form a life structure and enrich life within it based on the key choices an individual/family made during the preceding transition period. Transition periods are potentially the most vulnerable because previous individual, family, and illness life structures are reappraised in the face of new developmental tasks that may require major, discontinuous change rather than minor alterations (Hoffman, 1988).

The concepts of centrifugal and centripetal family styles are useful in integrating illness, individual, and family development (Beavers 1982; Beavers & Voeller, 1983). Combrinck-Graham (1985) describes a family life-spiral model, envisioning a three-generational family system oscillating over time between periods of higher (centripetal) and lower (centrifugal) family cohesion. These periods coincide with shifts between family developmental tasks that require intense bonding or high cohesion, as in early childrearing, and tasks that emphasize personal identity and autonomy, as in adolescence. In life-cycle terms, centripetal and centrifugal periods suggest a fit between family developmental tasks and the relative need for family members to direct their energies inside the family and work together to accomplish those tasks. During a centripetal period, both the individual member's and family unit's life structure emphasize internal family life. External boundaries around the family are tightened, whereas personal boundaries between members are somewhat diffused to enhance family teamwork. In the transition to a centrifugal period, the family life structure shifts to accomodate goals that emphasize individual family members' life outside the family.

Several key life-cycle concepts provide a foundation for understanding the experience of chronic disorders. The life cycle contains alternating transition and life-structure building/maintaining periods. Further, particular periods can be characterized as either centripetal or centrifugal in nature as diagrammed in Figure 15.4.

The notion of centripetal and centrifugal modes is useful in linking the illness life cycle to those of the individual and family. In general, serious disorders exert a centripetal pull on the family system. Analogous to the addition of a new family member, the occurrence of chronic illness sets in motion a centripetal family process of socialization to illness. Symptoms, loss of function, the demands of shifting or acquiring new illness-related roles, and the fear of loss through death all require a family to refocus inward. This centripetal pull of the disorder causes different normative strains depending on timing with the family's and family members' stages of development.

The degree of centripetal/centrifugal pull varies enormously in different types and phases of illness. The tendency for a disease to pull a family inward increases with the level of incapacitation or risk of progression and death. Progressive diseases over time are inherently more centripetal than constant course illnesses. The ongoing addition of new demands as an illness progresses keeps a family's energy focused inward, often impeding or halting the natural life-cycle evolution of other members. After a modus operandi has been forged, a constant-course disease (without severe incapacitation) permits a family to get back on track developmentally. Relapsing illnesses alternate between periods of drawing a family inward and

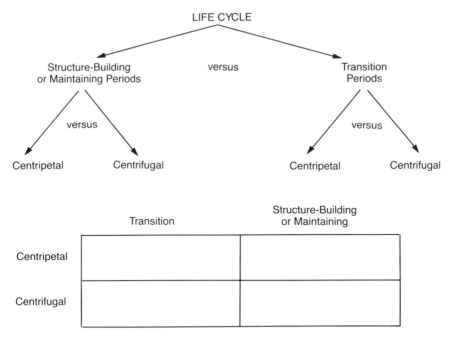

FIGURE 15.4. Periods in the family and individual life cycles. (From Rolland, 1987a, with permission.)

periods of release from the immediate demands of disease. However, the on-call state of preparedness dictated by many such illnesses keeps part of the family focus in a centripetal mode despite asymptomatic periods, hindering the natural flow between phases of the family life cycle.

One way to think about the phases of illness is that they represent to the family a progression from a centripetal crisis phase to a more centrifugal chronic phase. The terminal phase, if it occurs, forces most families back into a more inward mode. Optimally, families adapt their so-called "illness life structure," to accomodate each illness phase's inherent centripetal/centrifugal nature.

If illness onset coincides with a centrifugal period in the family's development, it can derail the family from its natural momentum. Illness or disability in a young adult may require a heightened dependency and return to the family of origin for disease-related caretaking. The autonomy and individuation of parents and child are diminished, and separate interests and priorities are relinquished or put on hold. Family dynamics as well as disease severity will influence whether the family's reversion to a centripetal life structure is a temporary detour within their general movement outward or a permanent reversal.

When the inward pull of disease onset coincides with a centripetal period in the family life cycle (e.g., early childrearing), it can foster a prolongation of this period. The research of Minuchin, Rosman, and Baker (1978) (Minchin et al., 1975) with "psychosomatic" families has documented the risk to vulnerable families dealing with childhood disorders becoming permanently enmeshed and developmentally stuck. On the other hand, in situations of chronic disorders, there is a risk of labeling enmeshment during which the normative lengthening of developmental phases for child and family is disregarded. Often, families coping with a chronically ill child are tentative about giving more autonomy not because of inherent family dysfunction, but, rather, because of chronic anticipation of further loss coupled with a lack of preventive psychoeducation from professionals.

In situations of serious disorders, definitions concerning normative family structure need to be reconsidered. Enmeshment with blurred generational boundaries is touted as the hallmark of family dysfunction. Yet, the very real demands on older children and adolescents to assume adult functions, in the interest of family survival, need to be distinguished from rigid pathological descriptions of "parentified" children (Beavers, Hampson, Hulgus, & Beavers, 1986).

For instance, when a parent develops a serious disorder during a centripetal, child-rearing phase of development, a family's ability to stay on course is most severely taxed. The impact is twofold: A "new" family burden is added as a parent is "lost," analogous to becoming a single-parent family with an added child. To meet simultaneous child-rearing and caretaking needs, an older child or grandparent may need to assume parental responsibilities. These forms of family adaptation are appropriate, if structural realignments are flexible, shared and sensitive to competing age-related developmental needs.

The onset of a serious disorder forces a family into a transition in which one of the family's main tasks is to accommodate the anticipation of further loss and possibly untimely death. When illness onset coincides with a transition in the individual or family life cycle, issues related to previous, current, and anticipated loss will tend to be magnified. Transition periods are often characterized by upheaval, rethinking of prior commitments, and openness to change. As a result, those times hold a greater risk for the illness to become unnecessarily embedded or inappropriately ignored in planning for the next developmental phase. During a transition period, the very process of loosening prior commitments creates a context for emergence of family rules regarding loyalty through sacrifice and caretaking. These "vulnerable" nodal points provide opportunities for clinicians to help family members clarify and resolve divided and competing loyalty demands.

Illness onset that coincides with a life structure-building/maintaining period in individual or family development presents a different challenge. These periods are characterized by the living out of choices made during the preceding transition period. Relative to transition periods, family members try to protect their own and the family unit's current life structure. Milder conditions may require some revision of individual/family life structure but not a radical restructuring that would necessitate a return to a transitional phase of development. A severe chronic illness will force families into a more complete transition at a time when individual/family inertia is to preserve the momentum of a stable period. To successfully navigate this kind of crisis, family adaptability requires the ability to transform the entire life structure to a prolonged transitional state.

From a systems viewpoint, at the time of diagnosis, it is important to know the phase of the family life cycle, and the stage of individual development of all family members, not just the ill member. Chronic disease in one family member can profoundly affect developmental goals of another member. For instance, a disabled infant can be a serious roadblock to parents' preconceived ideas about mastery of childrearing, or a life-threatening illness in a young adult can interfere with the spouse's readiness to become a parent. Also, family members frequently do not adapt equally to chronic illness. Each member's ability to adapt and the rate at which he or she does so is related to the individual's own developmental stage and role in the family (Ireys & Burr, 1984). Family members in tune with each other's developmental processes, while promoting flexiblity and alternative means to satisfy developmental needs, maximize successful long-term adaptation.

The timing of chronic illness in the life cycle can be normative (e.g., expectable in relation to chronological and social time) or nonnormative (e.g., "off-time"). Coping with chronic illness and death are considered normally anticipated tasks in late adulthood, whereas their occurrence earlier is "out of phase" and developmentally more disruptive (Herz, 1988; Neugarten, 1976). As untimely events, chronic diseases can severely disrupt the usual sense of continuity and rhythm of the life cycle. The timing of an unexpected event, like a chronic illness, will shape the form of adaptation and influence subsequent development (Levinson, 1978).

Chronic diseases that occur for adults in the child-rearing period can be most challenging because of their potential impact on family financial and child-rearing responsibilities (Herz, 1988). The actual impact will depend on the "type" of illness and pre-illness family roles. Families governed by flexible gender-defined roles about financial provider and caretaker of children will tend to have a better adjustment.

The notion of "out of phase" illnesses can be conceptualized in a more refined way that highlights patterns of strain related to time. First, since diseases have a centripetal influence on most families, they can be more disruptive to families in a centrifugal phase of development. The period of transition generated by the onset of a serious illness is particularly "out of phase" if it coincides with a life structure-building/maintaining period in the individual or family's life cycle. Third, if the particular illness is progressive, relapsing, increasingly incapacitating, and/or life-threatening, then the unfolding phases of the disease will be punctuated by numerous transitions. Under these conditions a family will need to more frequently alter their illness life structure to accommodate shifting and increasing demands of the disease.

This level of demand and uncertainty keeps the illness in the forefront of a family's consciousness, constantly impinging on their attempts to get back "in phase" developmentally. Finally, the transition from the crisis to the chronic phase of the illness life cycle is often the key juncture where the intensity of the family's socialization to living with chronic disease can often be relaxed. In this sense, it offers a "window of opportunity" for the family to recover its developmental course.

In the face of chronic disorders, an overarching goal is for a family to deal with the developmental demands presented by the illness without family members sacrificing their own or the family's development as a system over time. It is important to determine whose life plans were cancelled, postponed, or altered and when plans put on hold and future developmental issues will be addressed. In this way, clinicians can anticipate life-cycle nodal points related to "autonomy within" versus "subjugation to" the condition. Family members can be helped to strike a healthier balance with life plans that resolve feelings of guilt, overresponsibility, and hopelessness and find family and external resources to enhance freedom, both to pursue personal goals and provide needed care for the ill member.

HEALTH/ILLNESS BELIEF SYSTEM

Each of us individually and as part of our family and other systems develops a belief system, or philosophy that shapes our patterns of behavior toward the common challenges of life (Kluckhohn, 1960). Beliefs provide coherence to family life, facilitating continuity between past, present, and future and a way to approach new and ambiguous situations such as serious illness. At a practical level, belief systems serve as a cognitive map guiding decisions and action.

Reiss (1981) has shown that families as a unit develop paradigms for how the world operates. One component of the family's overall construction of reality is a set of health/illness beliefs that influence how they interpret illness events and guide their health-seeking behavior (Rolland, 1987b). Although individual family members can hold different beliefs, the values held by the family unit may be the most significant.

At the time of a medical diagnosis, a primary developmental challenge for a family is to create a meaning for the illness that preserves a sense of competency and mastery in the context of partial loss, possible further physical decline, and/or death. Since, serious illness is often experienced as a betrayal of our fundamental trust in our bodies and belief in our invulnerability and immortality (Kleinman, 1988), the creation of an empowering narrative can be a formidable task. Family health beliefs help us grapple with these existential dilemmas of our fear of death, attempts to sustain our denial of death, and attempts to reassert control over unjust suffering and untimely death.

In the initial crisis phase, it is essential for clinicians to inquire about key family beliefs that shape the family's narrative and coping strategies. This includes tracking beliefs about: (1) normality; (2) mind–body relationship, control, and mastery; (3) meanings attached by a family, ethnic group, religion or the wider culture to symptoms (e.g., chronic pain), types of illnesses (e.g., life-threatening), or specific diseases (e.g., AIDS); (4) assumptions about what caused an illness and what will influence it's course and outcome; (5) multigenerational factors that have shaped a family's health beliefs and; (6) anticipated nodal points in the illness, individual, and family life cycles when health beliefs will be strained or need to shift. Second, a clinician needs to assess the fit of health beliefs within the family and its various subsystems (e.g., spouse, parental, extended family) as well as between the family and health care system and wider culture.

Beliefs about Normality

A family's beliefs about what is normal or abnormal and the importance members place on conformity and excellence in relation to the average family have far-reaching implications in the context of protracted adversity such as a chronic disorder. Family values that allow having a "problem" without self-denigration have a distinct advantage in utilizing outside help and maintaining a positive identity in the face of chronic illness. If seeking help is defined as weak and shameful, the process undercuts this kind of resilience. Essentially, in situations of chronic disorders where problems are to be expected and the use of professionals and outside resources are necessary, a belief that pathologizes this normative process adds insult to injury.

Two excellent questions to elicit these beliefs are, "How do you think other *normal, average,* families would deal with a similar situation to yours?" And, "How would a *healthy* family cope with your situation?" Families with strong beliefs in high achievement and perfectionism are prone to apply standards in a situation of illness where the *kind* of control they are accustomed to is impossible. Particularly with "off-time" conditions that occur early in the life cycle, there are additional pressures to keep up with normative socially expectable developmental milestones of age-peers or other young couples. The fact that life-cycle goals may take longer or need revision requires a flexible belief about what is normal and healthy. To effectively sustain hope, particularly in situations of long-term adversity, demands an ability to embrace a flexible definition of normality.

Successful coping and adaptation are enhanced when a family believes in a biopsychosocial frame for illness that normalizes a psychosomatic interaction. This highlights the importance of the initial "framing event" and whether professionals actively normalize a psychosomatic interplay, thereby helping to undercut pathologizing family and cultural beliefs. This promotes a positive attitude toward the potential role of psychosocial factors in influencing disease course and the quality of life. Rather than a shameful liability, a family can approach a psychosomatic interplay as an opportunity to make a difference and increase their sense of control.

The Family's Sense of Mastery over an Illness

It is critical to determine how a family defines mastery or control in general and how they transpose that belief to situations of illness. Mastery is similar to the concept of health locus of control (Lefcourt, 1982; Dohrenwend & Dohrenwend, 1981), which can be defined as the belief about influence over the course/outcome of an illness. It is vital to distinguish whether a family's beliefs are based on the premise of internal control, external control by chance, or external control by powerful others (Levenson, 1973, 1974, 1975).

An internal locus of control orientation entails a belief that an individual/family can affect the outcome of a situation. In illness, such families believe they are directly responsible for their health and have the power to recover from illness (Wallston, Walston, & Kaplan, 1976; Walston & Walston, 1978).

An external orientation entails a belief that outcomes are noncontingent upon the individual's or family's behavior. Families that view illness in terms of chance believe that when illness occurs it's a matter of luck and that fate determines recovery. Those who see health control as in the hands of powerful others view health professionals, God, or sometimes "powerful" family members as exerting control over their bodies and illness course.

A family may adhere to a different set of beliefs about control when dealing with biological versus other day-to-day problems. Therefore, it is important both to assess a family's basic value system and beliefs about control for illnesses in general, chronic and life-threatening illness, and finally the specific disease facing the family. For instance, regardless of the actual severity or prognosis in a particular case, cancer may be equated with "death" or "no control" because of medical statistics, cultural myth, or prior family history. On the other hand, families may have enabling stories about a member or friend who in spite of cancer and a shortened lifespan lived a "full" life centered on effectively prioritizing the quality of relationships and goals. Clinicians can highlight these positive narratives as a means to help families counteract cultural beliefs that focus exclusively on control of biology as defining success.

A family's beliefs about mastery strongly affect the nature of its relationship to an illness and to the health care system. Beliefs about control predict certain health behaviors, particularly treatment compliance, and suggest the family's preferences about participation in their family member's treatment and healing process. Families that view disease course/outcome as a matter of chance tend to establish marginal relationships with health professionals largely because their belief system minimizes the importance of their own or the professional's impact on a disease process. Just as any psychotherapeutic relationship depends on a shared belief system about what is therapeutic, a workable accommodation among the patient, family, and health care team in terms of these fundamental values is essential. Families that feel misunderstood by health professionals are often reacting to a lack of joining at this basic value level. Too often their healthy need to participate was ignored or preempted by a professional needing unilateral control.

The goodness of fit between family beliefs about mastery can vary dependent on the time phase of the condition. For some disorders, the crisis phase involves protracted care outside the family's direct control. This may be stressful for a family that prefers to tackle its own problems without outside control and "interference." The patient's return home may increase the workload but allow members to reassert more fully their competence and leadership. In contrast, a family guided more by a preference for external control by experts can expect greater difficulty when their family member returns home. Recognition of such normative differences in belief about control can guide an effective psychosocial treatment plan tailored to each family's needs and affirming rather than disrespecting their core values.

In the terminal phase of an illness, a family may feel least in control of the biological course of the disease and the decision-making regarding the overall care of their ill member. Families with a strong need to sustain their centrality may need to assert themselves more vigorously with health providers. Effective decision making regarding the extent of heroic medical efforts or whether a patient will die at home, an institution, or hospice requires a family/provider relationship that respects the family's basic beliefs.

In situations of illness and disability, we must be cautious about judging the relative usefulness of positive illusions or minimization versus direct confrontation with and acceptance of painful realities. Often both are needed, and the skilled clinician must thread the needle supporting both the usefulness of exaggerated hope and the need for treatment to control the illness or a new complication. There is greater incentive for a family to confront denial of an illness or its severity when there is hope that preventive action or medical treatment can affect the outcome. Yet, to cope with an arduous, uncertain course, families often need simultaneously to acknowledge the condition itself, while minimizing treatment risks or the likelihood of a poor outcome.

Most of us cannot tolerate an unrelenting encounter with stark reality. There is a need for mental and physical respite. Taylor (1989) has described the normal, healthy need for positive illusion and its importance in successful coping and adaptation. The healthy use of minimization or selective focus on the positive, timely uses of humor should be distinguished from the concept of denial, regarded as pathological.

Family Beliefs about the Cause of an Illness

A family's beliefs about the cause of an illness need to be assessed separately from its beliefs about what can affect the outcome. The context within which an illness occurs is a very powerful organizer and mirror of a family's belief system. With limits of current medical knowledge, tremendous uncertainties persist about the relative importance of a myriad of biopsychosocial factors leaving individuals and families to make highly idiosyncratic attributions about what caused an illness. If every family member is asked for his or her explanation about what caused the illness, responses will reflect a combination of medical information and family mythology. Negative myths might include punishment for prior misdeeds (e.g., an affair), blame of a particular family member ("Your drinking made me sick"), a sense of injustice ("Why am I being punished, I have been a good person"), genetics (e.g., cancer runs on one side of the family), negligence by the patient (e.g., careless driving) or by parents (e.g., sudden infant death syndrome), or simply bad luck.

Optimal family narratives respect the limits of scientific knowledge, affirm basic competency, and promote the flexible use of multiple biological and psychosocial healing strategies. In contrast, causal attributions that invoke blame, shame, or guilt are particularly important to uncover. Such beliefs make it extremely difficult for a family to establish functional coping and adaptation to an illness. In the context of a life-threatening illness, a blamed family member is implicitly, if not explicitly, held accountable for murder if the patient dies. Decisions about treatment then become confounded and filled with tension. A mother who feels blamed by her husband for their son's leukemia may be less able to stop a low-probability experimental treatment than the angry, blaming husband. A husband who believes his drinking caused his wife's coronary and subsequent death may increase self-destructive drinking in his profound guilt.

Belief System Adaptability

It is difficult to characterize an "ideal" family health belief about mastery or control. A major thesis of systems-oriented medicine is that there is always an interplay between disease and other system levels. Yet, illnesses and the course of disease may vary considerably in responsiveness to psychosocial factors. Distinctions need to be made between a family's beliefs about their overall participation in a long-term disease process, their beliefs about their ability to control the biological unfolding of an illness, and the flexibility with which a family can apply these beliefs. An optimal expression of family competence or mastery depends on their grasp of these distinctions.

A family's belief in their participation in the total illness process can be thought of as independent from whether a disease is stable, improving, or in a terminal phase. Sometimes, mastery and the attempt to control biological process coincide, as when a family tailors its behavior to help maintain the health of a member with cancer in remission. This might include changes in family roles, communication, diet, exercise, and balance between work and recreation. Optimally, when an ill family member loses remission, as the family enters the terminal phase of the illness, participation as an expression of mastery is transformed to a successful process of letting go.

Families with flexible belief systems are more likely to experience death with a sense of competency rather than profound failure. The death of a patient, whose long, debilitating illness has heavily burdened others, can bring relief as well as sadness to family members. Since relief over death goes against societal conventions, it can trigger massive guilt reactions that may be expressed through such symptoms as depression and negative family interactions. Clinicians need to help family members minimize guilt and defensiveness, to accept the naturalness of ambivalent feeling they may have about the death.

Thus, flexibility both within the family and the health professional system is the key variable in optimal family functioning. Rather than linking mastery in a rigid, circumscribed way with biological outcome (survival or recovery) as the sole determinant of success, families can define control in a more "holistic" sense with involvement and participation in the overall process as the main criteria defining success. This is analogous to the distinction between curing "the disease" and "healing the system." Healing the system may influence the course/outcome of an illness, but disease outcome is not necessary for a family to feel successful. This flexible view of mastery permits the quality of relations within the family or between the family and health professional to become more central to criteria of success. The health provider's competence becomes valued from both a technical and caregiving perspective (Reiss, 1989) that is not linked only to the biological course of the disorder.

Ethnic, Religious, and Cultural Beliefs

Ethnicity, race, and religion strongly influence family beliefs concerning health and illness (McGoldrick, Pearce, & Giordano, 1982; Zborowski, 1969). Significant ethnic differences regarding health beliefs typically emerge at the time of a major health crisis. Cultural norms vary in such areas as: the definition of the appropriate "sick role" for the patient; the kind and degree of open communication about the disease; who should be included in the illness caretaking system (e.g., extended family, friends, professionals); who is the primary caretaker (almost always wife/mother/daughter/daughter-in-law); and the kind of rituals viewed as normative at different stages of an illness (e.g., hospital bedside vigils, healing, and funeral rituals).

Health professionals need to become familiar with belief systems of various ethnic, racial, and religious groups in their community, particularly as these translate into different illness behavioral patterns. For instance, it is customary for Italians and Jews to describe physical symptoms freely and in detail, whereas individuals from Irish or White Anglo-Saxon Protestant descent tend to minimize or conceal ailments. Clinicians need to be mindful of the cultural differences between themselves, the patient, and the family as a necessary step to forging a workable alliance that can endure a long-term illness. Disregarding these issues can lead families to wall themselves off from health providers and available community resources—a major cause of noncompliance and treatment failure. Sometimes, professionals may need the flexibility to suspend their need to prevail, especially in relation to family/cultural beliefs that proscribe certain standard forms of medical care (e.g., blood products for Jehovah's Witness). This requires an acceptance that the patient, not the physician, retains final responsibility for decisions about his or her body.

Family and Family-Provider Health Belief Fit

It is a common, but unfortunate, error to regard "the family" as a monolithic unit that feels, thinks, believes, and behaves as an undifferentiated whole. Clinicians should inquire both about the level of agreement and tolerance for differences among family members' beliefs and between the family and health care system. Is the family rule: "We must agree on all/some values," or are diversity and different viewpoints acceptable? How much do they feel the need to stay in sync with prevailing cultural or societal beliefs, or family tradition.

In general, family beliefs that balance the need for consensus with diversity and innovation are optimal and maximize permissible options. If consensus is the rule, then individual differentiation implies disloyalty and deviance. If the guiding principle is "We can hold different viewpoints," then diversity is allowed. This is adaptive because it facilitates the bringing to the family novel and creative forms of problem solving that may be needed in a situation of protracted adversity, such as serious illness.

To assess the fit between the family and health care team, the same questions concerning beliefs asked of families are relevant to the medical team:

1. What is their attitude about their own and the family's ability to influence the course/outcome of the disease?
2. How does the health team see the balance between theirs versus the family's participation in the treatment and control of the disease?
3. If basic differences in beliefs about control exist, how can these differences be reconciled?

Because of the tendency of most health facilities to disempower individuals and thereby foster dependence, utmost sensitivity to family values is needed to create a therapeutic system. Many breakdowns in relationships between "noncompliant" or marginal patients and their providers can be traced to natural disagreements at this basic level that were not addressed.

Normative differences among family members' health beliefs may emerge into destructive conflicts during a health crisis, as in the following case:

When Stavros H., a first-generation Greek-American, became ill with heart disease, his mother kept a 24-hour bedside vigil in his hospital room, so she could tend to her son at any hour. His wife, Dana, from an Anglo-Saxon family, greatly resented the "intrusive behavior" of her mother-in-law, who in turn criticized Dana's emotional "coldness" and relative lack of concern. Stavros felt caught between his warring mother and wife and complained of increased symptoms.

In such situations, clinicians need to sort out normative cultural differences from pathological enmeshment. In this case, all concerned behaved according to their own cultural norms. In Greek culture, it is normal to maintain close ties to one's family of origin after marriage and expected that a mother would tend to her son in a health crisis. A son would be disloyal not to allow his mother that role. This sharply differs with Anglo-Saxon traditions of the wife. Each side pathologizes the other, creating a conflictual triangle with the patient caught in the middle. In such situations, the clinician who affirms normative multicultural differences promotes a transformation of process from blaming or pathologizing to one of accommodating different equally legitimate cultures.

It is common for differences in beliefs or attitudes between family members to erupt at major treatment or illness transition points. For instance, in situations of severe disability or terminal illness, one member may want the patient to return home, whereas another prefers long-term hospitalization or transfer to an extended care facility. Since the chief task of patient caretaking is usually assigned to the wife/mother, she is the one most apt to bear the chief burdens in this regard. A family able to anticipate the collision of gender-based beliefs about caregiving with the potential overwhelming demands of home-based care for a dying family member and flexibly modify its rules would avert the risk of family caretaker overload, resentment, and deteriorating family relationships.

The murky boundary between the chronic and terminal phase highlights the potential for professionals beliefs to collide with those of the family. Physicians can feel bound to a technological imperative that requires them to exhaust *all* possibilities at their disposal, regardless of the odds of success. Families may not know how to interpret continued lifesaving efforts, assuming real hope where virtually none exists. Health care professionals and institutions can collude in a pervasive societal wish to deny death as a natural process truly beyond technological control (Becker, 1973). Endless treatment can represent the medical team's inability to separate a general value placed on controlling diseases from their beliefs about participation (separate from cure) in a patient's total care.

Because community resources and services are so valuable, clinicians should assess how family health beliefs influence their overall health behavior within a community (Mechanic, 1978; Kleinman, 1975). Has a family's prior experience with such resources been affirming or alienating? Families need health care professionals to provide adequate information about potential outside sources and linkage when helpful.

CONCLUSION

In the face of the risks and burdens of a serious chronic disorder, the "healthiest" families are able to harness that experience to improve the quality of life. Families need to achieve a healthy balance between accepting limits and promoting autonomy. For illnesses with long-range risks, families can maintain mastery in the face of uncertainty by enhancing the following capacities: acknowledge the possibility of loss, sustain hope, build flexibility into family life-cycle planning that conserves and adjusts major goals and helps circumvent the forces of uncertainty. The systemic model described here, which integrates the psychosocial demands of disorders over time with individual and family life cycles and belief systems, provides a foundation for such a normative perspective.

A serious illness or brush with death provides an opportunity to confront catastrophic fears about loss. This can lead to family members developing a better appreciation and perspective on life that results in clearer priorities and closer relationships. Seizing opportunities can replace procrastination for the "right moment" or passive waiting for the dreaded moment. Serious illness, by emphasizing life's fragility and preciousness, provides families with an opportunity to heal unresolved issues and develop more immediate, caring relationships. For illnesses in a more advanced stage, clinicians should help families emphasize quality of life by defining goals that are attainable more immediately and that enrich their everyday lives.

Recent writings (Imber-Black, Roberts, & Whiting, 1988; Imber-Black, 1991) in the family therapy field have underscored the lack of rituals for many families dealing with chronic and life-threatening disorders. Heightened uncertainty and loss increase awareness that each family gathering and ritual may be the last together. Clinicians can help families dealing with serious illness by promoting the timely creation and use of rituals of celebration and inclusion. A family reunion can invigorate a family and serve to coalesce its healing energies to support the ill member and key caretakers. In the context of a serious illness, traditional celebrations offer an opportunity to affirm, strengthen, and repair *all* family relationships.

Finally, clinicians need to consider their own experiences and feelings about illness and loss. Awareness and ease with our own multigenerational and family history with illness and loss, our health beliefs, and our current life-cycle passage will enhance our ability to work effectively with families facing serious illness.

REFERENCES

Beavers, J., Hampson, R. B., Hulgus, Y. F., & Beavers, W. R. (1986). Coping in families with a retarded child. *Family Process, 25*, 365–378.

Beavers, W. R. (1982). Healthy, midrange, and severely dysfunctional families. In F. Walsh, (Ed.), *Normal family processes* (pp. 45–66). New York: Guilford Press.

Beavers, W. R., & Voeller, M. M. (1983). Family models: Comparing and contrasting the Olson Circumplex Model with the Beavers Systems Model. *Family Process, 22*, 85–98.

Becker, E. (1973). *The denial of death.* New York: Free Press.

Boszormenyi-Nagy, I., & Spark, G. (1973). *Invisibile loyalties.* New York: Harper & Row.

Bowen, M. (1978). Theory in the practice of psychotherapy. In *Family therapy in clinical practice.* New York: Jason Aronson.

Byng-Hall, J. (1988). Scripts and legends in families and family therapy. *Family Process, 22*, 167–181.

Campbell, T. L. (1986). Family's impact on health: A critical review. *Family Systems Medicine, 4*, 135–328.

Carter, E. A., & McGoldrick, M. (Eds.). (1988). *The changing family life cycle: A framework for family therapy* (2nd ed.). New York: Gardner Press.

Combrinck-Graham, L. (1985). A developmental model for family systems. *Family Process, 24*(2), 139–150.

Davies, R. K., Quinlan, D. M., McKegney, P., & Kimball, C. P. (1973). Organic factors and psychological adjustment in advanced cancer patients. *Psychosomatic Medicine, 35*, 464–471.

Derogatis, L. R., Abeloff, M. D., & Melisartos, N. (1979). Psychological coping mechanisms and survival time in metastatic breast cancer. *Journal of the American Medical Association, 242*, 1504–1508.

Dohrenwend, B. S., & Dohrenwend, B. P. (Eds.). (1981). *Stressful life events and their contexts.* New York: Prodist.

Framo, J. (1976). Family of origin as therapeutic resource for adults in marital and family therapy. *Family Process, 15*, 193–210.

Gonzales, S., Steinglass, P., & Reiss, D. (1989). Putting the illness in its place: Discussion groups for families with chronic medical illness. *Family Process, 28*, 69–87.

Herz, F. (1988). The impact of death and serious illness on the family life cycle. In E. A. Carter & M. McGoldrick (Eds.), *The changing family life cycle: A framework for family therapy* (2nd ed.). New York: Gardner Press.

Hoffman, L. (1988). The life cycle and discontinuous change. In E. A. Carter & M. McGoldrick (Eds.), *The changing family life cycle: A framework for family therapy* (2nd ed.). New York: Gardner Press.

Imber-Black, E. (1991). Rituals and the healing process. In F. Walsh & M. McGoldrick (Eds.), *Living beyond loss: Death in the family.* New York: W. W. Norton.

Imber-Black, E., Roberts, J., & Whiting, R. (Eds.). (1988). *Rituals in families and family therapy.* New York: W. W. Norton.

Ireys, H. T., & Burr, C. K. (1984). Apart and a part: Family issues for young adults with chronic illness and disability. In M. G. Eisenberg, L. C. Sutkin, & M. A. Jansen (Eds.), *Chronic illness and disability through the life span: Effects on self and family*. New York: Springer Publishing.

Kleinman, A. M. (1975). Explanatory models in health care relationships. In *Health of the family (National Council for International Health Symposium)*. Washington, DC: National Council for International Health.

Kleinman, A. M. (1988). *The illness narratives: Suffering healing and the human condition*. New York: Basic Books.

Kluckhohn, F. R. (1960). Variations in the basic values of family systems. In N. W. Bell & E. F. Vogel (Eds.), *A modern introduction to the family* (pp. 304–315). Glencoe, IL: The Free Press.

Lefcourt, H. M. (1982). *Locus of control* (2nd ed.). Hillsdale, NJ: Lawrence Erlbaum Associates.

Levenson, H. (1973). Multidimensional locus of control in psychiatric patients. *Journal of Consulting and Clinical Psychology, 41*, 397–404.

Levenson, H. (1974). Activism and powerful others: Distinctions within the concept of internal–external control. *Journal of Personality Assessment, 38*, 377–383.

Levenson, H. (1975). Multidimensional locus of control in prison inmates. *Journal of Applied Social Psychology, 5*, 342–347.

Levinson, D. J. (1978). *The seasons of a man's life*. New York: Knopf.

McDaniel, S. H., Hepworth, J., & Doherty, W. J. (1992). *Medical Family Therapy*. New York: Basic Books.

McGoldrick, M., & Gerson, R. (1985). *Genograms in family assessment*. New York: Norton.

McGoldrick, M., Pearce, J. K., & Giordano, J. (Eds.). (1982). *Ethnicity and family therapy*. New York: Guilford Press.

McGoldrick, M., & Walsh, F. (1983). A systemic view of family history and loss. In M. Aronson & L. Wolberg (Eds.), *Group and family therapy*. New York: Brunner/Mazel.

Mechanic, D. (1978). *Medical sociology* (2nd ed.). New York: Free Press.

Minuchin, S., Baker, L., Rosman, B., Liebman, R., Milman, L., & Todd, T. (1975). A conceptual model of psychosomatic illness in children: Family organization and family therapy. *Archives of General Psychiatry, 32*, 1031–1038.

Minuchin, S., Rosman, B. L., & Baker, L. (1978). *Psychosomatic families*. Cambridge, MA: Harvard University Press.

Moos, R. H. (Ed.). (1984). *Coping with physical illness: Vol. 2. New perspectives*. New York: Plenum Press.

Neugarten, B. (1976). Adaptation and the life cycle. *The Counselling Psychologist, 6*(1), 16–20.

Penn, P. (1983). Coalitions and binding interactions in families with chronic illness, *Family Systems Medicine, 1*(2), 16–25.

Reiss, D. (1981). *The family's construction of reality*. Cambridge, MA: Harvard University Press.

Reiss, D. (1989). The family and medical team in chronic illness: A transactional and developmental perspective. In C. N. Ramsey, Jr. (Ed.), *Family systems in family medicine*. New York: Guilford Press.

Rolland, J. S. (1984). Toward a psychosocial typology of chronic and life-threatening illness. *Family Systems Medicine, 2*(3), 245–263.

Rolland, J. S. (1987a). Chronic illness and the life cycle: A conceptual framework. *Family Process, 26*(2), 203–221.

Rolland, J. S. (1987b). Family illness paradigms: Evolution and significance. *Family Systems Medicine, 5*(4), 467–486.

Rolland, J. S. (1987c). Family systems and chronic illness: A typological model. *Journal of Psychotherapy and the Family, 3*(3), 143–168.

Rolland, J. S. (1990). Anticipatory loss: A family systems developmental framework. *Family Process, 29*(3), 229–244.

Rolland, J. S. (1991). The impact of illness on families. In R. E. Rakel (Ed.), *Textbook of family practice* (4th ed.). Philadelphia: W. B. Saunders.

Rolland, J. S. (in press). *Helping families with chronic and life-threatening disorders*. New York: Basic Books.

Schmale, A. H., & Iker, H. (1971). Hopelessness as a predictor of cervical cancer. *Social Science in Medicine, 5*, 95–100.

Siegel, B. S. (1986). *Love, medicine and miracles*. New York: Harper & Row.

Simonton, C. O., Mathews-Simonton, S., & Sparks, T. F. (1980). Psychological intervention in the treatment of cancer. *Psychosomatics, 21*(3), 226–233.

Taylor, S. (1989). *Positive illusions: Creative self-deception and the healthy mind*. New York: Basic Books.

Wallston, B. S., Wallston, K. A., Kaplan, G. D., & Maides, S. A. (1976). Development and validation of the Health Locus of Control (HLC) Scale. *Journal of Consulting and Clinical Psychology, 44*, 580–585.

Wallston, K. A., & Wallston, B. S. (1978). Development of the Multidimensional Health Locus of Control (MHLC) Scales. *Health Education Monographs, 6*(2), 160–170.

Walsh, F. (1983). Normal family ideologies: Myths and realities. In C. Falicov (Ed.), *Cultural dimensions in family therapy*. Rockville, MD: Aspen.

Walsh, F., & McGoldrick, M. (Eds.). (1991). *Living beyond loss: Death in the family*. New York: W. W. Norton.

Zborowski, M. (1969). *People in pain*. San Francisco: Jossey-Bass.

CHAPTER 16

CHALLENGES FOR FAMILY POLICY

Ann Hartman

FAMILY POLICY HAS BEEN ONE of the most complex and contentious fields of debate in the American public arena, partly because ownership of the very definition of "family" is continuously a hot political issue, one that taps into fundamental American cultural values. Some have claimed the field of family policy doesn't exist, some say it does but shouldn't, whereas still others argue for a clear and coherent national family policy.

To embark on an examination of family policy is to be cast adrift in a sea of conflicting and strongly held moral and value positions. It is understandable that this should be the case. Public policy has enormous power to reward and to punish, to encourage and prohibit, to shape behavior, and to exert control. When this power and intimate, private, human relationship systems meet, the clash can be great. It is perhaps at that intersection that family policy comes into being, implicitly if not explicitly.

In this chapter, I attempt to navigate the stormy sea of controversy surrounding family policy. After exploring definitions, I place family policy in its historical and sociopolitical contexts. In the process, some of the major policy areas and enactments that may be included under the rubric of family policy are examined, and the goals and assumptions embedded in these policies explored and critiqued. The chapter ends with some recommendations about family policy taking into consideration today's political realities as well as possibilities for the future.

DEFINING FAMILY POLICY

Public policy is that body of laws, regulations, statutes, executive orders, and programs that emanate from various branches and levels of government.

It includes economic, military, social, and myriad other areas of policy about which the collective government takes a position or formulates an action. The sources of public policy are many, including the Constitution, the Supreme Court as well as all of the other federal, state, and local courts, the various law-making bodies on every level, and the executive and administrative offices of federal, state, and local governments. Public policy intentions and values are expressed not simply by virtue of legislative enactment but through the extent to which laws and regulations are actually implemented by the officials charged with this responsibility.

Public policy includes those social policies that pertain particularly to the ordering of social relationships and the meeting of social need. Obviously, social policies, as attempts to respond to people's needs for security and well-being, are inexorably related to economic policies. In fact, all areas of government action have some direct or indirect impact on social well-being, social structures, and the quality of life.

Although family policy is very much a part of public discourse, defining it is extremely difficult. Some writers have taken the position that there is no family policy in this country (Bane, 1980), and the argument may be made that there is no comprehensive and coherent body of policies directly and specifically focused on the family. On the other hand, if the family policy arena is seen as encompassing all those policies that have an impact on the family, then it is clear that we have many family policies. Many if not most of our public acts and decisions on every level of government implicitly, if not explicitly, affect the family.

It is perhaps more useful, if not more accurate, to define family policy as Aldous and Dumon (1990) do, as "objectives concerning family well-being and specific measures taken by governmental bodies to achieve them" (p. 1137). First, this definition clearly raises the most troublesome and currently unresolvable problems about family policy. What are the objectives for family well-being? Who is to determine what those objectives may be? How can consensus be reached? Second, any definition surfaces a great deal of confusion and conflict around definitions of the family, as various groups jockey for position in their claims to speak for the American family. Defining the family is a problem that has haunted discussions about family policy from the beginning and, in fact, was the point upon which the 1980 White House Conference on Families foundered.

In this chapter, I take yet another position on defining family policy. Although we do not have a coherent and consistent family policy, governmental bodies promulgate all sorts of policies that are very directly related to the welfare of the family and to the shape and direction of family life. These policies may have the objective of enhancing the well-being of the family, but they also may include other more subtle agendas. The meanings of family expressed in such policies are often heavily value-laden, allowing the definitions of those in power to influence the social discourse concerning what families should be like, fostering support for some forms of families but not others, and legislating family behavior. I consider "family policy" to encompass all those policies that affect families.

It must be remembered that the national public discussion of family policy started on the campaign trail with Jimmy Carter who, speaking in New Hampshire before his first primary, bemoaned the state of the American family. He promised to make the welfare of the family a central goal of his domestic policy, but it was clear that the family he wanted to support and indeed to recreate was the quickly disappearing family of the 1950s. Conservatives were quick to pick up this theme and to adopt the goal of saving the family, which meant a return to the traditional "Father Knows Best" image of family. Other forms of family, such as the sole-parent family, the cohabiting family, or the family headed by same-sex parents, and so on, were to be defined as examples of family breakdown.

This discussion leads us to what are perhaps the most crucial issues in any consideration of family policy, issues that I will call here "meta" policies. Meta policies are overarching assumptions that shape and direct more specific policies, or what we might think of as policies about family policies. Three such meta policies are of particular interest here: the definition of the family, conceptions of the family–state relationship, and views of the relative merit of familism versus individualism.

The public or approved definition of the family is central to all family policy.

Defining the Family

Once the family is defined, policies that reward and support families will be directed at groups that meet that definition, and all intimate domestic systems that do not meet prevailing criteria will be disadvantaged. The advantages and rights connected to being legally defined as "family" are many; the fact that many kinds of domestic partnerships and fictive kinship systems found, for example, among certain racial and ethnic populations, fall outside of those definitions clearly raises the constitutional issue of "equal treatment under the law."

It is in the definition of the family that value issues are most dramatically apparent. As Poverny and Finch phrase it:

> The state monopolizes access to marital status, thus imposing traditional definitions of the family on those who desire legal recognition of their relationship. Unfortunately, traditional assumptions that underpin policies and programs devoted to family life do not adequately account for the various family life styles found today. (1988, p. 116)

There are, of course, various definitions of the family encoded in law, judicial opinion, and administrative regulations. For example, the United States Bureau of the Census (1988) currently defines the family as a group of two persons or more related by birth, marriage, or adoption and residing together. All other household units are considered nonfamily (Poverny & Finch, 1988).

Although this definition rules out many who would define themselves as a family, it is probably the broadest of existing public policy definitions and the one most commonly accepted. However, public policy goes beyond simple definitions of family and of kinship, specifying within this broader definition which relationships are preferred or privileged. An amazing example of this privileging may be found in the Supreme Court's unaccountable decision in *Levy v. Louisiana* (1968) to permit illegitimate as well as legitimate children to recover for the wrongful death of their mother; however, in another case, the Court permitted states to limit the out-of-wedlock child's right to inherit from her father [*Lalli v. Lalli*, 439U.S.259 (1978) as discussed in Clark, 1982]. Adoption laws and policies provide another example. Laws in most states privilege the parent–child relationship constituted through adoption over the biological relationship, sealing adoption records and making it illegal to give either adoptees or birth parents identifying information.

Policies not only define and privilege certain kinds of relationships, they also serve to reward or punish certain family forms. For example, informal adoption or fostering by members of a family's fictive kinship network are often not honored, thus separating children from important family ties. The discriminatory treatment of particular family forms is demonstrated in the welfare enactments that continuously punish female-headed, single-parent families. Some of the questions asked by researchers in studies on the outcomes of improved benefits to AFDC recipients clearly express the core value issue at stake. Did more generous public assistance payments mean that more women left their husbands? The results of these studies are equivocal, but even liberals rush to reassure that more generous payments do not really increase the rate of separation. The implicit concern that women should remain in their marriages, no matter how abusive the husbands or how miserable the wife, is clear. Daniel Patrick Moynihan (1990), long a commentator on the American family, states quite flatly that family policy should encourage the maintenance of the two-parent family. The subtle agendas of various socioeconomic programs to shape families will be explored in more detail below.

Exclusionary and privileged definitions of the family, however, are being challenged on several fronts. For example, many adoptees and birth parents are pressing for open adoption records. An active, and at times successful, challenge to families determined by legal marriage and blood relationship is coming from lesbian and gay families. Comprising 10% of the population, gay and lesbian domestic partnerships have, until recently, been totally unrecognized and unprotected. Courts have taken action in a variety of cases concerning death and other employee benefits, co-parent adoption, bereavement leave, the protection of a rent-controlled home on the death of a partner, visitation rights, and so on.

All of these cases turn around a key issue: Do same-sex domestic partners have the same rights as married heterosexual partners? The response to this question varies from court to court and case to case. For example, in the groundbreaking case, *Braschi v. Stahl Associates* (1989), New York State's highest court found in favor of the long-time partner of a man who had died in regard to the companion's ability to retain a lease on the rent-controlled apartment they had shared. As leases are only transferable to cohabiting family members, the court, in making this historic decision, stated that the government's proper definition of "family" should not "rest on fictitious legal distinctions or genetic history, but instead [sic] should find its foundation in the reality of family life" (Lambda, 1992, p. 5). The opinion in this case set forth the following criteria for determining family status: (1) The degree of emotional commitment and interdependence (this includes such notions as that of an interwoven social life, visibly maintaining each other as a couple/family, thinking of each other as a couple/family, and visiting each other's families of origin); (2) financial interdependence; (3) cohabitation; (4) longevity; and (5) exclusivity of relationship (State of New York Court of Appeals, July 6, 1989, #108). In another decision, a lower court in New York City upheld gay and lesbian partners' rights to challenge the denial of spousal insurance and health care benefits by the New York City Board of Education (Lambda, 1991c). Many firms and institutions are currently considering including domestic partners in benefit packages. This is a crucial issue for all families as fringe benefits often account for close to 40% of workers' compensation packages (Lambda, 1992, p. 5).

Several municipal governments have enacted and some states are considering domestic partner legislation and/or registration. Although domestic partner registration is a long way from legal marriage of same-sex partners, it is a public recognition of the fact of commitment.

The above situations constitute pioneering exceptions and are, in fact, so rare that they are newsworthy. Much more common are the continued oppressive and discriminatory laws and policies that exclude millions of Americans from the benefits of "familiness" and go even further to punish and destroy certain kinds of family bonds. This has been particularly true in situations where children are involved. In many courts and localities, lesbian mothers still have a difficult time obtaining and maintaining custody of their children (Achtenberg, 1985). The rights of co-parents have rarely been recognized. Typical was a recent Wisconsin Supreme Court decision in which custody, visitation, and enforcement of a co-parent contract were denied a lesbian co-parent on the basis that if the court "were to allow custody to persons 'who stood in the place of parents,' the door would be open for multiple parties to claim custody of children based on that status" (Lambda, 1991b, p. 14).

The tragic and widely publicized case of Sharon Kowalski and Karen Thompson demonstrates most dramatically the lack of protection available to couples in domestic partnership. In 1983, Sharon Kowalski, 27, who had lived in a committed relationship with 36-year-old Karen Thompson for almost 4 years, was in a head-on car collision with a drunk driver and suffered a severe brain stem injury, losing both her mobility and the ability to speak. Karen Thompson, after working very successfully with Sharon in her rehabilitation program, was forbidden any further contact with Sharon by Sharon's parents after they were awarded sole custody of their daughter. The parents placed Sharon in a minimum care facility where she was isolated from Karen and from former friends. Her condition markedly deteriorated. Karen has been fighting in the Minnesota courts ever since to gain the right to visit Sharon, to intervene in her medical situation, and to move her to the home they shared, as Sharon has requested. The parents finally withdrew from the situation but not before Sharon suffered irreversible damage from years of isolation and depression. This case has become a cause celebre and an example of legalized heterosexism, ableism, and sexism (Griscom, 1992). It has served as a warning to domestic partners to do everything they can to legally protect their relationships.

Despite the fact that there has been some movement toward the expansion of the definition of the family, meta family policy for the most part assumes that families are formed by birth, marriage, or legal adoption. As long as this is the case, family policies will be discriminatory, excluding a sizeable percentage of American families. This de facto kind of discrimination is not accidental; it protects certain kinds of interests and reflects a strong resistance on the part of certain segments of our society against the acceptance of a broader definition of the family. Sole-parent, female-headed families and lesbian families are, after all, ultimately a challenge to patriarchy. Those who support exclusionary or privileging family definitions believe that to include nontraditional or alternative family forms in social provisions on behalf of families, even the single-parent family, is to encourage the development of such families and thus the breakdown of American family values. It is because family definitions are so deeply involved in value and moral issues that many oppose the development of a national family policy. For example, as early as 1979, Barbaro warned that "the United States can not deal with an issue so emotionally charged as family life in a comprehensive manner and could not do so without violating civil liberties or discriminating against non-conventional families" (1979, p. 455). Nonetheless, the meta issue of the family definition remains a crucial one. It is important to ask of any family policy, what definition does this policy imply and how does it effect family definition? Who is included in the benefits provided through this policy, who is excluded, and how are the excluded disadvantaged?

The Family–State Relationship

The second meta policy concerns the extent to which, and under what circumstances, the state should intrude upon family life. The family–state relationship is clearly crucial to family policy considerations; thus we need to examine those transactions that occur at the boundary between the family and the state and the nature of the state's excursions across that boundary in order to explicate that relationship.

These boundary definitions and decisions are again value-based. Several cherished American beliefs give direction to the family–state relationship. Paramount is the view, a clarion call of patriarchy, that "a man's home is his castle." This powerful metaphor implies that the family should be surrounded by impenetrable walls; within the walls of the family, man/husband/father is king.

Slowly, over the years, the state has put limits on family inviolability, particularly in regard to the protection of children. The state may, and frequently does, enter and even dismember families on behalf of abused or neglected children. However, the state has been less ready to intervene in the marital relationship. For example, the landmark decision that strengthened the boundary between the family and the state, *Griswald v. Connecticut* (1968), protected a couple's privacy and began the protection of reproductive rights by establishing that it was unconstitutional for a state to make the possession or use of contraceptives by married couples a criminal offense. This crucial decision was followed by *Roe v. Wade*, in which it was determined that it was unconstitutional for a state to intervene in the matter of abortion during the first trimester.

The state has also been reluctant to intervene in the marital relationship to protect abused and battered wives. People on both the political right and the left hold inconsistent views on the matter of the state's intrusion into family life. Those on the right generally favor intruding into family life through the prohibition of abortion and the sharp curtailment of reproductive rights. Rightists also tend to favor prayer in the schools, a situation that fosters particular beliefs but also one in which the state intrudes upon the family's socialization role. On the other hand, rightists would limit the state's power to intervene to protect women in situations of domestic violence. Many of those on the left take equally inconsistent positions, generally favoring reproductive rights, the separation of religion and the state, but supporting the entry of the state into the family to protect women and children.

The state intervenes in the family not only to foster social order and to control behavior, but also to meet social need. Moroney, who has studied family–state relationships in England and the United States, writes:

> The structure of the welfare state has been shaped by a number of beliefs concerning the responsibilities which [sic] families are expected to carry for the care of the socially dependent and a set of conditions under which this responsibility is to be shared or taken over by society. (1980, p. 1)

We have witnessed, in the past 20 years, a major shift in the pattern of sharing between the state and the family. Deinstitutionalization in health and mental health care and permanency planning and family preservation in child-welfare programs have all been efforts to meet the needs of dependent populations in the "least restrictive environment." The family is usually considered the most favorable and least restrictive environment. These trends in service provision, strongly supported by liberals and most health care and social welfare professionals, have shifted more responsibility for the care of dependent populations to the family. Unfortunately, this shift occurred concurrently with sharp cuts in a variety of supports for the family and in the context of a worsening economic situation that now usually requires two paid workers to maintain a family. Women, who traditionally provided domestic care, are now in the work place and suffering considerable conflict between their jobs and what have been traditionally defined as their caretaking responsibilities. What began as a progressive movement toward deinstitutionalization and family-centered services has too often led to the state's withdrawal from the task of caring for the dependent. In today's society, the family and the caretakers in the family, usually women, must do more with less.

Finally, it must be added in terms of the state's intrusion in family life that autonomy and privacy are clearly tied to class. There is a long tradition in this country that makes it not only permissible but desirable for the state to enter a family's life if that family requires financial aid. There is also a long tradition that such aid should be contingent and structured in such a way as to manipulate the family's behavior and to "rehabilitate."

A third meta policy concerns the conflict between individualism and familism. Although the value assumptions underlying policy in regard to this conflict are rarely stated, they are implicit. Feminists have been particularly concerned about this issue, as public policy has frequently reinforced the control of women by men (Miller,1990) and because the welfare of women has often been sacrificed to the welfare of the family (Ehrenreich, 1988). The conflict emerges most dramatically around the shaping of programs for battered women and the extent to which the programs are focussed on the maintenance of the marriage or on the development of opportunities for women, economic support, job training, childcare, and housing that open up options for women and make it possible for them to separate from their husbands and live independently (Davis & Hagen, 1992). These and other issues have caused feminists to be wary of strongly family-centered social policies as they fear that such policies, in the guise of supporting the family, actually support the oppression and control of women by men (Ehrenreich, 1988).

Another example of conflict between individualism and familism is found in the contentious discussions around parental rights versus children's rights (Clark, 1982). Parental rights are supported, and the privacy of minors invaded through the laws that require parents to be notified or even to give permission before a minor can have an abortion (*H.L. v. Matheson*, 101 SCT. 1164, 1981). Although the Supreme Court has tempered this ruling by insisting that such laws contain a judicial by-pass, that is, that adolescents may obtain a confidential court ruling on abortion without the parents' involvement, there have continued to be efforts, into the 1990s supported by the Bush administration, to strike this down (Aldous & Dumon, 1990).

A recent case in Florida in which a minor child sued his family in order to be freed for adoption so that he could be adopted by his foster family raises the parent versus children's rights issue to a new level. The fact that the judge decided in favor of the youngster and his foster parents establishes a new precedent and one that could have enormous implications for family and child-welfare policy. If the child's biological mother were truly unable to provide him with a home now or in the future, the child's cause should have been brought to the attention of the courts by the welfare system. Either the child-welfare system was not fulfilling its function of protecting and providing for permanent care, or the mother has been unjustly deprived of her parental rights.

In summary, in exploring family policy, it is necessary to consider the fundamental value-based assumptions that underlie and shape that policy. Of particular importance are views about the definition of the family, the nature of the family–state relationship, and the relative importance of family or individual welfare and rights. In evaluating any social policy affecting the family, we must ask how is the family defined, how is the family–state relationship characterized, and what is the balance between the promotion of individual and family well-being.

A BRIEF HISTORY OF FAMILY POLICY— THE LAST 25 YEARS

It is hard to believe that the first term of Richard Nixon's presidency was a period of major social reform. Nixon was a conservative, but he was also an astute politician and, particularly during his first term (1968–1972), was sensitive to the continuing impetus for social change still echoing from the 1960s. In fact "the greatest extensions of the modern welfare system were enacted under the conservative presidency of Richard Nixon with bipartisan congressional support, dwarfing in size and scope the initiatives of Lyndon Johnson's Great Society" (Levitan & Johnson, 1984). During the Nixon years, there was an extensive expansion of the food stamp program, indexing of social security, development of affirmative action policies, and the establishment of the Occupational Safety and Health Administration (OSHA). Further, policies were enacted that led to the desegregation of virtually all Southern schools, and progressive legislation was passed including the Comprehensive Employment and Training Act (CETA), the community Development Block Grants Program, The Rehabilitation Act of 1973, and two key family policy measures, the addition of family-planning programs to the Public Health Act and the passage of the Child Abuse Prevention Act of 1973.

Further, advised by Daniel Moynihan, Nixon attempted a major overhaul of the welfare system through the establishment of a Family Assistance

Plan that would provide a nationwide guaranteed income for all families, generous work incentives, day care for young children, and the creation of a large number of public service jobs. Caught in the crossfire between liberals who felt these measures didn't go far enough and conservatives who felt these measures went too far, the FAP was defeated in 1972.

Interestingly enough, Old Age Assistance, Aid to the Blind, and Aid to the Disabled were federalized by creating the far less stigmatizing and more generous Supplementary Security Income Program. With the adoption of SSI, Aid to Families with Dependent Children (AFDC) remained as "the welfare mess" and its recipients, primarily women and children, were even more stigmatized (Miller, (1990).

Nixon was hostile to service programs of all kinds, and one reason why he was supportive of the FAP was that he was promised that it would make possible a massive reduction in the number of social workers in the social welfare system. His antipathy to service programs was illustrated by his veto of child development legislation that was intended to respond to the changing situation of American families and the increasing move of mothers into the work force by providing a number of free and low cost services to American families, including day care and expanded preschool programs. Adopting the language of the right wing of the Republican Party, which, in some matters, becomes the staunch defender of the boundaries around the family, he charged that the legislation "would destroy the institution of the family, which [sic] should be retained in its rightful position as the keystone of American civilization . . . [and] would commit the vast moral authority of [institutional] child rearing as against the family centered approach" (Jansson, 1988, p. 189). Clearly illustrated here is the power of the government to shape and regulate family life.

Conservative Gerald Ford's contribution to family policy was to preside over a stalemate between the liberals and conservatives over the future of the welfare state and the frequent use of the veto to halt any social programs generated by the Democratic majorities in both houses.

Although Carter began his campaign and entered the White House with the support of the American family at the center of his political rhetoric, his 4-year term saw few successes in the development of programs or the passage of legislation that would really make a difference for American families. The family Carter wanted to preserve and support was the family of the 1950s, and his basic conservatism led him to vacillate on measures that would lend support to new families emerging in the 1970s, such as day care, services to families headed by teenagers, and the extension of federal subsidies to shelters for battered women. Furthermore, in the area of family policy, Carter was bitterly opposed to abortion and supported legislation that prohibited the use of federal Medicaid funds for abortion, with the result that federally funded abortions declined from 275,000 in 1976 to 1,250 in 1978 (Jansson, 1988).

Perhaps the most important legacy of Carter's concern about the family was the passage, at the very end of his term, of the Adoption Assistance and Child Welfare Reform Act of 1980. This act, extending the notion of least restrictive environment, translated the permanency planning movement into national child-welfare policy, taking a strong position that every child should be in a family; first, his or her own or, if that is impossible, an adoptive home. The legislation, although never adequately funded, survived the Reagan administration, and redefined good child-welfare practice as focused on the welfare of the child but family-centered in its convictions and its practice prescriptions. This bill laid the foundation for a revolutionary change in adoption practice, home-based services to families, and the current Family Preservation initiative.

The conservative drift, which began in Nixon's second term and continued almost unabated through the Ford and Carter administrations, found its full expression in the presidency of Ronald Reagan, who set about from his first day in office to systematically dismantle the welfare state and to revolutionize American economic policy. The results have been devastating for all but the wealthiest American families.

Reagan's administration may be characterized by three main goals or objectives. First, a major goal was to sharply reduce spending on social welfare and social programs and to shift responsibility for meeting human need to the states, localities, and to the family. A second goal was to institute the principles of supply-side economics, the famous or infamous "trickle down" theory. The position was that taxes should be cut at the higher personal income levels and for corporations to make available a larger pool of investment capital. It was assumed that this capital would then be invested in business and industry, thereby promoting economic growth, creating more jobs, and improving the tax base which would make up for the sharp reduction in federal income. Reagan's third objective was to construct a massive military machine.

By August of his first term, the Omnibus Budget Reconciliation Act (OBRA) and massive tax cuts for corporations and upper-income individuals had been passed. In no time, 57 federal programs were eliminated or folded into block grants, and total expenditures for social programs were sharply cut.

Reagan's particular targets were the means-tested programs and AFDC. Once again, the security program most important to American families was under fire. Not only did the levels of support for families steadily erode throughout Reagan's years in office but eligibility levels were lowered and work incentives eliminated, which forced many women, working at low-paying jobs, to quit work and return to full welfare support. Thus OBRA had an important role in what came to be called the "feminization of poverty." The discriminatory treatment of those on AFDC is illustrated by the fact that by 1988, the average monthly payment per person on AFDC was $126.52, whereas the monthly benefit for a person on SSI was $259.43 (Miller, 1990). Once again we see the old tradition of distinguishing between the "worthy" and the "unworthy" poor. The worthy are considered to be in need "through no fault of their own" and thus deserving of better treatment.

What were the outcomes of Reagan's economic, social, and military strategies? First, supply-side economics did not work as predicted, and, with reduced tax income and increased military spending, by the end of his first term, Reagan had accumulated a budget deficit that surpassed the deficits of all of the previous presidents combined (Jansson, 1988).

At the same time, the gap between the rich and the poor was greater than it had ever been since such records had been kept and greater than in any other industrialized nation. The family policy implications of economic and income security policies are clear when we learn that, by the end of Reagan's presidency, the average income of the 10% of families at the bottom of the income ladder was $3,504, down 18% from 1977, whereas the average income of the top 10% was $166,000, up 16.5% for the same period. Particularly shocking is the fact that the income of the top 1% increased 49.8% to $404,566 (Phillips, 1990), whereas the average income of working AFDC families declined from 101% to 81% of the poverty level (Aponte, 1987). "The critical concentration of wealth in the United States was developing at the higher level—decamillionaires, centimillionaires, half billionaires, and billionaires. Garden variety American millionaires [were] so commonplace that there were 1.5 million of them by 1989 (Phillips, 1990). The weight of the tax burden fell proportionately much more heavily on people in the lower-income brackets, exacerbating the situation. During the 1980s, poor families paid 16.1% of their income in federal taxes, whereas the wealthiest families were taxed 10.6% (Greenstein & Leonard, 1990).

At the same time, the increasingly vocal "moral majority" had hopes that Reagan would support the Family Protection Act, their agenda for moral reform. The Family Protection Act includes a series of propositions of great importance to the American family, including prayer in the schools, tax exemptions for families with children in private schools, and an end to abortion rights. Reagan, however, although giving lip service support to these views, was too astute a politician to take a stand on issues that cut so close to the bone for most Americans. These issues have been featured in the 1992 Presidential Campaign in which George Bush, misjudging the American electorate, embraced the right wing of the Republican Party.

FAMILY POLICY: THE 1990s AND BEYOND

The recent civil violence in Los Angeles and the threat of violence and unrest in other urban areas is a message that this nation is in crisis. The steady disinvestment in the welfare of the American people, the abandonment of the cities, massive unemployment, and the transfer of income up the economic ladder has created conditions that are destroying millions of American families and children and jeopardizing the future of the nation. The Bush administration, sometimes referred to as the third Reagan term, continued this disinvestment despite President Bush's campaign promises to build a "kinder, gentler nation" and his espoused commitment to education. Any effort to halt the flow of resources up the economic scale have been met with overwhelming resistance as those in power, in government, in business and industry, and in higher levels of the military, have profited and continue to profit under Reagan–Bush policies.

For real economic and social change to take place, those who have garnered the resources of this enormously wealthy country will have to return some portion to the rest of the American people. We are, in Lincoln's words, a house divided against itself, a nation divided by the enormous chasm between the rich and the poor. In between is the shrinking middle class, usually with both parents in the work force, struggling to maintain a home, educate their children, provide health and day care, and keep from slipping into poverty. Although poverty cuts across racial lines, the unrelenting impact of institutionalized racism in this country has meant that a large proportion of those most deprived and oppressed are people of color (Wilson, 1989) and that many families of color who have moved into the middle class are at risk of losing their hard won position. For example, the average median income of the households of black college graduates is less than two thirds of the income of white families on the same educational level (Abramovitz, 1991).

Evidence of the continued disinvestment in the welfare of our citizenry under the Bush administration abounds. We are the only industrialized nation with neither family allowances nor a national health care system. The continued deterioration of the inner city, the growing population of homeless people, the steady decrease in the funding of Title XX, the major source of federal support of social programs (down 55% in real dollars since 1977), and cut backs in Medicare, Medicaid, and AFDC benefits all illustrate this disinvestment. By the end of the 1980s, 20% of all white children, 40% of Hispanic children, and half of all African-American children were living in poverty (Greenstein, 1989). "Since the era of the New Deal, most Americans have come to expect government to cushion low wages, to lessen poverty, to provide social services. And from the 1935 Social Security Act to the demise of the Great Society in the mid 1970s, the Federal Government did just that" (Abramovitz, 1991). However, during the Reagan and Bush administrations, an historical reversal has taken place. "For the first time since the New Deal, the government has ceased acting as a buffer against the vicissitudes of capitalism. The government has responded to the polarization of income by not responding, in effect leaving rich and poor to fend for themselves (Passell, 1989).

As President Clinton assumes office, American families are in trouble, not only families in poverty but working- and middle-class families as well. The new administration must begin its work in the context of national neglect and governmental paralysis, as well as a climate of hopelessness, alienation, and violence. Clinton's promises and the outcome of the election have kindled hopes and raised expectations, but these hopes and expectations can be realized only if strong, positive action is taken to change the direction and the priorities of the nation.

Concerning the welfare of families, the key arenas for action include economic security, the family's relation to the world of work, day care, health care, and family planning.

I now turn to these core areas of family policy, explore the current situation, and suggest possible goals and strategies for the future.

Economic Security

Economic security is the bed rock upon which all family policy rests. In fact, some believe that if true economic security were guaranteed to all Americans through a strong economy, nondiscriminatory employment practices, education and job training, a universal nonstigmatizing income support plan, and a national health plan, little other family policy would be required as individuals and families in all their different forms could meet their needs through the purchase of resources and services.

We are a long way from providing all Americans with such security and thus must turn to an examination of the patchwork of programs that provide a modicum of security, at least for some people in need. As discussed earlier, fairly adequate nonstigmatizing programs are available through SSI for the aging, the blind, and the disabled. Although often inadequately funded and administered in a fashion that discourages rather than encourages their use, this system of entitlement is in place and, if expanded, properly funded, and administered, could offer economic security for these populations.

AFDC, the only categorical program that was not moved to SSI, continues to be the most stigmatized, the most criticized social welfare program, the program that has become synonymous with "welfare." It is also the program most crucial to the well-being of American families in poverty.

After years of acrimonious debate about the need to "do something about welfare" and months of negotiation and compromise, the Family Support Act of 1988 (FSA) was passed, heralded as a major reform of the welfare system. The key to the consensus wrought in the Congress between the neoliberals who wanted to separate themselves from a generous and universal economic security system and the neoconservatives who challenged any but an extremely limited and contingent support program was the focus of the 1988 Act on the achievement of parental responsibility and self-sufficiency (Kohlert, 1989). After years of disincentives to work that were increasingly a part of AFDC, the heart of the new program is the effort to put mothers to work and to force absent parents to contribute to the support of their children. Interestingly, even social workers, who have historically been opposed to mandatory work programs, have supported the bill in what has been called "the latest surrender in the War on Poverty" (Nichols-Casebolt & McClure, 1989).

A major provision of FSA is the Job Opportunities and Basic Skills Training Program (JOBS). By October, 1990, all states were required to institute a JOBS program to ensure that "needy families with children obtain education, training, and employment to help them avoid long term [sic] dependency" (Hagen, 1992). States are required to offer basic and remedial education, job readiness activities, high school or high school equivalency programs, English proficiency, and a range of job development and search services and community work experience.

In a significant departure from the national policy concerning families that has been in place since early in the century when mothers' pensions were enacted to keep mothers at home with their young children, mothers of children 3 years or older are required to participate in the JOBS programs. States may even include mothers of children as young as 1 year in the requirement. Mothers under 20 who have not completed high school are required to participate in an educational program no matter how young their children are. The above requirements are contingent on the availability of childcare, a formidable barrier. Policy around day care will be discussed later in this chapter.

Perhaps the most useful portion of the bill, the portion that truly represents a reform, is that on transitional benefits. It has long been known that the immediate withdrawal of support upon employment has been a powerful disincentive to obtaining and keeping a job. The FSA supports the transition to work through the provision of childcare and medical benefits for up to 12 months after the recipient becomes ineligible for AFDC through employment.

How can we assess the value, the possibilities, and the potential outcomes of the jobs program? Certainly, if states are genuinely interested in helping women move out of poverty into meaningful careers that pay enough to support a family, the structure and some federal support are available. To realize the stated goals of the program, however, states will have to make a considerable investment. Most states are unlikely to do so. The history of previous welfare-to-work programs does not encourage optimism as these initiatives, with the possible exception of a few of the heavily funded demonstration programs, have actually moved few families out of poverty. What they have done is place some women into low-paying jobs that may take them off of the welfare roles, usually temporarily, but retains them in poverty (Miller, 1989). It takes extended training and education to enable welfare recipients to qualify for jobs that will pay enough to support a family above the poverty level. The new law requires states to demonstrate that a substantial number of recipients have been moved into the work force or lose their funding. This requirement will have the effect of promoting brief job readiness training and job search rather than the slower, more costly, but more meaningful preparation for better jobs.

The success of the program depends on the willingness of all to take it seriously and really invest but also on the state of the economy and of the labor market. The current recession and continuing high rates of unemployment are not encouraging in terms of the placement of welfare recipients in jobs that will support a family.

There are predictions that there will be an expansion in the labor market, but an analysis of trends indicates that these positions will be low-level, dead-end, service jobs that will not support a family above the poverty line (Miller, 1989). In fact, 30% of the jobs in the current labor market will not raise a family of three out of poverty (Hagen, 1992).

One may well ask, in examining the provisions of JOBS, what kind of work are welfare recipients going to be prepared to do? What kind of skills will be taught? Will job training and work experience really move these millions out of poverty? Is the federal government and are the states really ready to finance the kind of education that would enable people to compete and to support a family in a postindustrial society? Unless there is a substantial improvement in the economy and the labor market and unless the new administration can stimulate an extensive investment in the program on the federal and state levels, it is likely that this widely heralded JOBS program will turn out to be the latest in a series of efforts to force poor women, many of whom are of color, into low-paying service jobs that offer neither economic security nor a future. Once more, those in power are "regulating the lives of women" (Abramovitz, 1988) and assuring an available pool of cheap labor, which, according to some analysts, has been the function of welfare policy since the time of the English Poor Laws (Piven & Cloward, 1971).

The second major portion of the 1988 welfare reform act establishes a more extensive system to enforce mandatory support by absent parents, most frequently the father. It is well known that the economic situation of men improves following divorce, whereas the situation of women, who usually have primary custody of the minor children, markedly deteriorates (Garfinkel & McLanahan, 1986). In a remarkable intrusion by the state into the lives of individuals and families, beginning in 1994, automatic wage withholding will become universal for all court-ordered support (Hagen, 1992). Whether this really makes a difference for working- and middle-class families depends on the adequacy of the support formulae devised and the resolution of marked inequities across the states. Further, of particular significance for low-income custodial parents and their children is whether states will adopt the very innovative program piloted in Wisconsin that supplements low child-support payments to a guaranteed minimum.

Without such supplementation, poor custodial parents and their families are unlikely to be benefited by vigorous child support strategies. Unrealistic efforts to obtain child support from noncustodial parents who are marginal earners may well alienate them, drive them into hiding, and disrupt both their and the extended family's relationship with the children.

The value assumptions expressed in the Welfare Reform Act of 1988 are clearly rooted in traditional American conservatism: the work ethic, the importance of individual and familial responsibility, independence, and individualism. Embracing these values and expectations without establishing genuine opportunities for their achievement once again dooms poor American families to failure, to rejection and criticism, alienation and anomie. The welfare reform bill has created an illusion that action is being taken to solve the problem of poverty and long-term dependency. On the contrary, the program is poorly funded, shifts responsibility to the states, which are already struggling with mammoth budget deficits, and announces the aim of moving recipients off welfare through job training and placement at a time when there are over 7 million unemployed workers and over 5.5 million people engaged in part-time work because they could not find full-time jobs, as well as several million who are working at full-time jobs but are not earning enough to escape poverty (Stoetz & Karger, 1990).

Piecemeal, means-tested, inadequate, and stigmatized income-support programs, and work programs that do little more than manipulate the pool of cheap labor, will not provide American families with economic security. The future of American families rests on the development of a strong economy and on the more equitable redistribution of profits from that economy. It depends on reducing the gap between the rich and the poor. It depends on opening up the opportunity structure and making it possible for people to obtain real education and training and enter the work force to do meaningful and profitable work. The economic security of American families depends on some form of universal guaranteed minimum income through children or family allowances or a negative income tax. Other far less-well-endowed industrialized countries have managed to offer all families economic security. Why can't we?

Work and the Family

A major social revolution has gathered momentum in recent decades that has totally changed the participation of American families in the work force. In 1940, families in which the husband and not the wife was in the labor force accounted for nearly seven out of 10 American families. By 1988, this "typical" family accounted for only 20.9% of American families. There is now no modal family, as the remaining 79% of American families are diverse in their relationship to the world of work. The most common is the dual-worker family, which represents 41% of American families. The remainder includes families maintained by women with no spouse present (16.8%), by men with no spouse present (4.2%), and married-couple families in which neither husband nor wife is in the labor force (13.3%). The biggest changes have been the influx of married and single women with children into the work force and the increase of two-worker families. In 1940, in only 9% of families were both husband and wife in the work force compared to 41% in 1988 (Hayghe, 1990). The percentage of all women participating in paid employment out of the home grew from 26% in 1940 to 57% in 1989 (Wiatrowski, 1990).

Women go out to work for two reasons, the primary one being economic necessity. As the real value of wages has deteriorated over the last two decades, it frequently takes two incomes to maintain a family. Secondly, many women want to go to work to acquire and use knowledge and skills, to be participating actors in the world outside the home, to earn an income that decreases their dependency on others, to establish a social place and a network of friends and colleagues.

This major change in American family life has significant family-policy implications. However, neither governmental policy nor employers have kept abreast of this major revolution nor made the adjustments required by such a fundamental change in our socioeconomic system. Employers and governmental bodies are, for the most part, continuing to operate as if only fathers are at work and mothers are at home providing full-time care to children, elders, and other dependent family members (Levitan & Gallo, 1990). This is causing considerable strain for working people, caught between the demands of family and job. And, not only do workers and their families suffer, but employers are faced with high rates of absenteeism and turnover and with worried and distracted employees who are unable to function at an optimal level. "As long as the two basic elements of human activity—family and work—are in conflict, our society is in serious trouble. This conflict . . . can be resolved only through public policy initiative" (Akabas, 1990, p. 366).

Some firms have learned how expensive chronic work–family conflict is for their operation and have become more sensitive to family needs, establishing some positive initiatives to reduce this conflict such as information and referral services, employee assistance programs, family-leave guarantees, childcare, and elder-care support. The military, the nation's largest single employer (if civilian employees are included), is becoming sensitive to family needs. In an extensive study on retention, they found that it was necessary "to make career military service more attractive to families and more supportive to family life in order to retain experienced personnel" (Ortiz & Bassoff, 1987, p. 57).

In recent decades, benefit packages, including employer-provided and government-managed provisions, have become an increasingly important part of compensation, until they now may represent 30% of worker's actual pay. For the most part, they continue to be based on the family of former times, the father in the work place and the mother at home with children. This means that such benefits tend to be inadequate or redundant and to disadvantage many (Wiatrowski, 1990). For example, if both marital partners are working in situations that include family health benefits as part of compensation, either their coverage is unnecessarily duplicated or one of them elects not to be covered by their employer and receives less real compensation than his or her fellow employees. Further, the limited definition of the family generally used in the distribution of benefits discriminates against families that fall outside the definition, as discussed earlier in this chapter.

Some employers, responding to the growing diversity in family forms and work lives, are offering "cafeteria-style" benefit plans that allot workers a certain amount of money for benefits, thus giving them the opportunity to choose among a number of options and to create individualized packages that meet their families' needs.

Although some employers are moving to more flexibility in family benefits, another trend detrimental to families' economic situations has been developing in both government- and employee-provided benefits. As the cost of benefits has escalated, employers and the government are attempting to shift more and more of the burden, particularly of medical care, to employees by requiring co-payments and increased deductibles. They are also moving to decrease costs by turning to managed health care, limiting eligibility, and reducing retirement benefits. The government's initiative to tax Social Security benefits, to limit Medicare, and to sharply increase Social Security taxes exemplifies the government's efforts to limit benefits and reduce costs.

Although a few firms are moving to be more responsive to families, it is likely that a restructuring of the world of work to become supportive to families will have to come through some sort of governmental intervention, either through mandatory regulations or through the use of tax breaks, an old and very effective federal strategy, to manipulate companies' behavior.

Currently, there is little optimism that such changes will take place until we have a major shift in governmental philosophy or until American business and industry learns what most other modern industrialized countries have known for a long time, that secure, unstressed, and supported workers are productive workers.

A rather minimalist but nonetheless important venture into the regulation of business and industry toward the end of supporting the family was the Family Leave Act of 1990, passed by both houses of Congress but vetoed by President Bush. An even more limited bill has been passed and was again vetoed. This bill, the Family and Medical Leave Act of 1991, gives workers up to 12 weeks of unpaid, job-protected leave for a serious illness, birth, or adoption of a child, or a serious illness of a parent or spouse. The measure exempts companies with fewer than 50 workers and also the 10% of the workers in the highest salary range. It is highly likely that with the change in administration, mandatory family leave will soon be a reality. However, such a bill, as welcome as it would be, also demonstrates how enacted family policy that uses a narrow definition of the family discriminates against those in alternate family forms. Family leave benefits will not be available to unmarried domestic partners, children not related by birth or adoption, or for the care of ill and aging fictive kin.

Other initiatives that could begin to reduce the gap between the world of work and the family are job sharing, flex time, facilitation of part-time employment rather than discrimination against these workers in relation to benefits and promotion, pay equity, support for elder care and childcare, family-centered employee assistance programs, and career support that allows women to interrupt their careers to have a family without being penalized. Tax breaks for firms that would institute family-sensitive policies and programs would encourage business and industry to move in this direction and to learn that they, as well as their workers and their workers' families, benefit from such changes.

Finally, unpaid work in the home continues to be unrecognized economically in the benefit and Social Security structure. Although clearly an option that has gathered little support, some concerned about the economic situation of women have proposed tax credits for homemakers and displaced homemakers (Schroeder, 1989).

As the nation's attention is turned to domestic policy, it can be hoped that work–family relationships will receive attention.

Childcare Policy

Intimately related to the world of work, the influx of women into the work force, and the increasing number of dual worker families and of women supporting children alone is the issue of childcare. The lack of available and quality childcare has been a growing problem. Until recently, the federal government's primary initiative in relation to childcare has been Head Start and Dependent Care Tax Credit. Head Start is not really focused on the provision of childcare for working parents but rather is a developmental and educational program focused on the needs of children. It is generally a part-time program and does not provide coverage for a working parent.

Dependent tax credit benefits only those who pay income taxes and therefore advantages middle- and upper-income families, offering no relief to the families most in need. Studies have shown that childcare for one child in families with incomes below $15,000 often consumes as much as 23% of the family's income. Throughout the 1970s and 1980s, Dependent Tax Credit was increased but not childcare programs targeted for low-income parents (Consortium of Family Organizations, 1992).

Finally, the federal government did act, primarily out of the growing conviction that parents should support their children by participating in the work force. A federal childcare package was passed as a part of the Omnibus Budget Reconciliation Act of 1990. This package included the Child Care and Dependent Block Grant (CCDBG), an expansion of childcare funds through Title IV-A as a part of the JOBS program of the Family Support Act. The CCDBG authorizes funds to the states without a required match to be used to supplement existing support for childcare. Seventy-five percent of the funds are to be used for the provision and improvement of the quality of childcare for eligible families. The Act calls for financial participation by the families based on a sliding fee scale. Families are eligible if their income is less than 75% of the state median income and if the parents are working or enrolled in job training or an educational program.

The remaining 25% of the funds are to be spent for early childhood developmental programs and for before- and after-school services. An aspect of the Act that has particular relevance to family policy is the focus on parental choice, achieved through the use of vouchers with which the parents pay for care and providers collect from the state. Also important is the fact that eligible childcare providers may include friends, relatives, and neighbors. Although some sort of registration and compliance with state health and safety regulations are required, the implementing regulations of the bill state that if such regulations limit parental choice, federal funds will be withheld. The government's concern is that regulations or complicated registration and payment procedures will reduce the use of informal care. For day care centers and formal family day care, the Act does not include requirements for staff/child ratios, group size limits, or minimum staff qualifications. It is clear that a major concern of the federal government is the availability of childcare. With the priority placed on the expansion and availability of childcare, concern develops concerning the quality of care. The assumption of the current bill is that protecting parental choice will promote quality as parents select care for their children in a free market with many options. The law also states that the parent shall have unlimited access to the child when in the care of the provider. It is the assumption that parents can identify and will choose the best care for their children with little to aid them in making choices or in monitoring their children's care.

Various constraints on the parent's ability to make a choice that will ensure quality of care will, however, exist, as will the availability of quality care, the cost and availability of transportation, and the parent's ability to gain the knowledge required to make the best choice.

Although increased federal support for childcare is to be welcomed, the emphasis on availability and the underlying motive that relates, not to the welfare of children, but to getting parents into the work force, does provoke concern. With the pressure states are under to achieve required participation rates of parents in the JOBS program, the emphasis will be on the utilization of their childcare funds to expand the quantity of childcare available rather than on the establishment of developmental and enriching programs.

Childcare has been referred to as a "women's issue." It is, in truth, a child-welfare and family-policy issue. Several questions fundamental to the development of sound family policy around childcare remain. What are the effects of the various models of care on children? We need more research on the outcomes for children of various kinds of care. For example, a major research project has been jointly developed by the Rockefeller Foundation and the Department of Health and Human Services to investigate the effects over time of enrollment in educationally enriched care settings versus standard settings for children whose mothers are on public assistance and are enrolled in job training programs. The current plan calls for following the children for 15 years (Cherlin, 1989).

Further, in the new JOBS program discussed earlier in this chapter, states may require mothers of 1-year-old children to enter the work force. What are the long-term effects of this on these very young children?

A second unresolved issue revolves around the cost of good childcare. Policy planners have not seemed to have faced the fact that good group care for children is very expensive. Estimates of the costs per child of high-quality, center-based care that meets the accreditation standards of the National Association of Education for Young Children are $5,267. More common are centers with annual salaries as low as $12,000 for teachers, and staff ratios of 6 to 1 for infants, 12 to 1 for 3-year-olds, and 20 to 1 for school-age children. The cost for such care is estimated at $2,937. This is the average cost reported by parents in surveys (Cherlin, 1989). The high staff to child ratios would hardly indicate individualized care.

Health Care Policy

Another crucial family-policy issue concerns the delivery of health care to families, an issue high on President Clinton's agenda. Our health care system has been trapped in our inability as a nation to come to terms with the major meta policy issue in health care delivery. Americans have been unable to "discuss and decide whether basic health care is a social good that is intrinsically related to individual liberty, independence, and equal opportunity and, therefore, a collective obligation or a private good to be left as an individual responsibility" (H. Shapiro, unpublished manuscript). We are clear that people have a right to life, at least when no exotic intervention is required to maintain it, but apparently we are not clear about whether they have a right to health.

We are spending an enormous amount of our nation's resources on health care; 12% of our gross national product—50% more than the average of all other industrial countries. In 1990, we spent more than $2,000 per person compared to $1,000 among our industrial competitors. The rise in health care costs has been twice the rate of inflation over the last decade. But with this considerable investment of resources and our highly-skilled and well-equipped medical system, by most measures, the overall health status of Americans lags behind that of many others. Among the nations of the world, the United States ranks 12th in life expectancy, 19th in infant mortality, 21st in deaths of children under 5, and 29th in the percentage of low-birth-weight babies. Our low immunization rates are a national disgrace (Children's Defense Fund, 1990).

Our health care system had been shaped by the changing policy positions of national leadership concerning the collective obligation to provide care. Until the Reagan presidency, the federal government had moved steadily toward assuming more and more responsibility for the health of the nation, particularly for the most vulnerable populations. Medicare, Medicaid, maternal and child health programs developed and flourished. Hopes were high for some sort of national health plan, and in the 1970s, such plans were brought to the Congress although none survived.

In the past decade, however, this trend toward increased governmental responsibility has been reversed. Although some say that we have no national health policy, the policies of the Reagan–Bush administrations have been clear and implicit. During these administrations, there has been a steady reduction in the federal government's involvement and expenditure in health care. Programs have been widely and deeply cut, and the responsibility for the financing of care has been steadily shifted to the patient, the family, and to localities. Cost containment measures, such as DRG's, have limited hospital stays and shifted the burden of care to families at the same time that the programs that might support families in providing care have been reduced or eliminated.

Our national health care policy has also supported the drift toward privatization and toward an increasingly market driven health care system. This Social Darwinian view of the distribution of health care services leads quite dramatically to the survival, not necessarily of the fittest, but of those with the greatest power and command of resources and those with the most extensive and generous insurance coverage.

The combination of privatization and competition has led to the development of for-profit medical facilities that can cream off the well-insured, high-fee patients, leaving the voluntary hospital and particularly the public, city, and county hospitals to care for those without resources and often those who are the sickest. This competition and neglect has promoted a two- or three-track health care system based on ability to pay.

The state of our health care system is of vital concern to all families, and most currently agree that the system is urgently in need of reform. In order to bring about such reform in the health care system, three major and interrelated issues must be resolved; access, cost, and the nature and definition of health care, which has, primarily, been defined as sickness care.

Because Americans have not considered health care a universal entitlement or right and have largely left it to the individual to achieve, millions of Americans are without access to any care at all. Thirty-seven million Americans have no public or private health insurance. This is a 38% increase since 1977 (NASW, 1991). Many more are under-insured. Private insurance companies are increasing exclusions, deductions, and co-payments, and shifting more of the cost burden to the consumer. Courts have been upholding employers' rights to limit coverage in cases of serious illness (Employers Winning, 1992). In most states, insurers have the right to test and refuse anyone who is HIV-positive, and some have even tried to refuse coverage to people based on occupation or zip code (Lambda, 1991a).

To even begin to make sure that all Americans have access to basic health care, we must affirm that basic health care is a right, and cost should be shared. This fundamental assumption must then be operationalized through a national health plan that assures access for all. A number of plans are currently under consideration by the Congress, and President Clinton has promised to give top priority to a national health care plan. The National Association of Social Workers has developed and is promoting a national health care scheme that proposes a federally administered single-payer system (S. 2817, The National Health Care Act of 1992), but it is very unlikely that any single payer program will pass. We must act on access to health care. The human costs and the costs to families and to our nation of uncared-for people, children without immunization, of undiagnosed and untreated illness, of people suffering mental and emotional pain without care cannot continue to be tolerated.

Second, the cost of health care is sapping our national resources, even though a large number of Americans are under-served. As access is expanded, what of the parallel expansion of cost? As we make basic health care more available to all, we must face the fact that this cannot mean that every person gets availability to every service. This raises the controversial issue of the rationing of health care. Many vociferously oppose rationing on moral and ethical grounds, but we are rationing health care now, on the basis of the ability to pay. Somehow we must face the fact that heroic efforts to forestall death in extreme situations "reduces resources available for other forms of life saving and life enhancing measures" (Silverman, 1992). We must face these difficult, ethical decisions.

An adequate National Health plan must include a means for establishing priorities. The resolution of access and priority issues will inevitably alter the nature and definition of health care in the United States. It is hoped that priorities will focus on family well-being, and on universally available preventive, health maintenance, and basic care.

Family-Planning Policy

Although family-planning policy should extend far beyond the issue of abortion, the attention of Americans has been focused on abortion almost exclusively.

This most contentious and conflictual area raises issues with deeply held moral, ethical, and political significance. Embedded in the reproductive rights controversy are conflicting convictions about when life begins, the fetus' "right to life" versus the mother's right to control her own body, and parental rights versus the teenager's right to privacy. Also, central in the ideological struggle are views about the role of women, about women's obligations in marriage and parenthood versus a woman's right to control her own destiny, to be free of enforced parenthood. It is not surprising that these issues, so intensely important to people, have spawned a violent and bitter struggle that remains unsolved, a struggle that has eclipsed other equally important but less controversial areas of policy related to family planning.

The abortion issue is not a new one on the American scene, and it is important to note that there was no question of its legality until the 1850s when the newly organized American Medical Association as a part of its goal of legitimizing the medical profession began campaigning to forbid the performing of abortions by nonmedical practitioners. By the turn of the century, all states had antiabortion legislation on the books, although the laws were not always enforced (Mohr, 1978).

The struggle around contraception also resulted in the prohibition of the sale of contraceptive devices so that reproductive behavior became widely controlled, condemning couples to obligatory parenthood or considerable constriction of their sexual life.

In the last 25 years, we have witnessed dramatic pendulum swings in national policy on family planning and reproductive rights. The trend to limit the states' interference in the reproductive lives of people began with the Supreme Court decision in 1965 in the case of *Griswold v. Connecticut*, which ruled that a statute that made it a criminal offense for a married couple to possess or use contraceptives was unconstitutional. This was followed, in 1973, by *Roe v. Wade*, which made it unconstitutional for state law to prohibit a woman from terminating a pregnancy in the first trimester. Both of these decisions were based on the Bill of Rights and on the Fourteenth Amendment, which supports the right to privacy of individuals in personal matters.

It must be remembered that such a position guarantees noninterference but does not guarantee self-determination. Social supports and resources are required for true self-determination. *Roe v. Wade* really won women the right to be left alone. Subsequent legislation has reinforced this. For example in *Harris v. McRae* (1980), the Supreme Court upheld the right of Congress and State legislatures to refuse to pay for abortions for poor women, and in *Rust v. Sullivan* (1991) the Court upheld the right of the government to even refuse support for abortion counseling, information, or referral. This famous gag rule prohibited any discussion of abortion by staff of medical facilities receiving any federal funds (with the exception of physicians).

The current situation means that those with information, access, and resources may achieve reproductive choice. Reproductive choice has become a privilege of the economically secure and enormously burdensome or unattainable for those with limited resources.

Not only the poor, but also teenagers face constraints in their attempts to terminate a pregnancy. In many states, minors are required to obtain parental consent. The Supreme Court has ruled that such laws are constitutional but must include a judicial by-pass, that is, that the Court may give permission without parental notification.

Roe v. Wade was a highly controversial decision and demonstrates that social policy enactments can lead but cannot get too far from the sentiments of large groups of the American people without generating backlash. Across the nation, states are passing laws and policies that constrain and limit access to abortion. Support has been withdrawn from other less controversial means of enhancing reproductive self-determination. Funds have been cut for all aspects of family planning and research on contraception. The nation's ambivalence in the area of reproduction, family planning, and women's wish to be freed from compulsory motherhood is evident. American family policy in this area lags far behind the programs, entitlements, and supports available in most other industrialized nations.

The legal right to have an abortion, which, with the change in federal leadership, will probably continue to be protected, is not an isolated issue. It should be a fail-safe protection but only one part of an integrated and available group of services that pertain to the conception, birth, and rearing of children. Such services should include extensive reproductive health education available to all, free and universally available contraceptive information and devices, and the investment of public funds in research to discover improved contraceptive methods for men as well as women. Universally available prenatal care should be included, along with universal health benefits that include maternity, family care, and parental leave with job security guarantees.

Family policy in the area of reproduction has been dominated by the abortion issue. The right to privacy that has been the guiding principle of the nation's family-planning policy, should not be interpreted as the right to be left alone, even to be abandoned.

THE FUTURE

Every third decade, our nation has embarked on a period of social change. In these periods, the progressive era, the 1930s, and the 1960s, efforts were made to construct social programs that would meet social need, enhance the quality of life of the American people and offer protection or relief from the impact of changes in the economic system and from life events or natural catastrophies.

It is hoped that the 1990's may be yet another period of social invention and of concern for social welfare and social justice. During the past 12 years we have witnessed the dismantling of the programs developed in the 1960s and early 1970s and even an attack on the programs created as a part of the New Deal in the 1930s, programs we have long taken for granted. We have even reached back to question the wisdom of those participants in the first White House Conference on Children that established mother's pensions so that women would be able to stay home and care for their young children.

As we move toward the year 2000, we again have the opportunity to attend to the welfare of the American people under an administration that is ready to focus on domestic issues. The task of social reform, however, may be even more difficult than in the past. Now we must not only move forward in new and creative ways, we must also rebuild essential social programs that were neglected or destroyed by years of indifference and hostility.

Second, it will cost a great deal of money to repair our social fabric, and not only are we saddled with an insupportable national debt and ongoing deficit, but the norms of the nation about sharing the cost of a healthy and socially responsible government have changed. The slogan "no new taxes," coined by Bush, has become accepted as a right and a guarantee by the American people. There must be major income and resource redistribution through tax and economic reform that will shrink the enormous gap between the rich and the poor.

Finally, new solutions for the enhancement of human well being must be developed in a period of enormous social change. The growing diversity in our society in terms of race, ethnicity, family structure, and life-style choices demands flexible and adaptable programs that are sensitive to the various needs and goals of our diverse society.

Political rhetoric about the family may well now recede, but social programs and reforms will have their effect on families and will often be targeted to support the family unit. Clearly action is needed in the key areas reviewed in this chapter, economic security, the world of work, childcare, health care, and family planning. As these issues are addressed, it is essential to be sensitive to the family policy significance and to the assumptions implicit in the initiatives proposed, assumptions about the definition of the family, the relationship between the state and the family, and the balance maintained between the, at times, competing interests of the individual family members and the family unit.

The challenge of creating a just and caring society is enormous, but if our nation is to survive on into the 21st century, there is no other option.

REFERENCES

Abramovitz, M. (1988). *Regulating the lives of women*. Boston: South End Press.

Abramovitz, M. (1991). Social policy in disarray: The beleaguered American family. *Families in Society, 72*(8), 483–495.

Achtenberg, R. (1985). *Sexual orientation and the law*. New York: Clark Boardman.

Akabas, S. H. (1990). Reconciling the demands of work with the needs of families. *Families in Society, 71*(6), 366–371.

Aldous, J., & Dumon, W. (1990). Family policy in the 1980s: Controversy and consensus. *Journal of Marriage and the Family, 52*, 1136–1151.

Aponte, R. (1987). Urban poverty: A state-of-the-art review of the literature. In W. J. Hudson (Ed.), *The truly disadvantaged: The inner city, the lower class and public policy* (pp. 165–187). Chicago: University of Chicago Press.

Bane, M. J. (1980). Toward a description and evaluation of United States family policy. In J. Aldous & W. Dumon with K. Johnson (Eds.), *The politics and pro-*

grams of family policy (pp. 155–191). Notre Dame, IN: University of Notre Dame and Leuven University Press.

Barbaro, F. (1979). The case against family policy. Social Work, 24, 455–457.

Braschi v. Stahl Associates. (1989). New York Court of Appeals, July 6, 1989, #108.

Cherlin, A. (1989). Child care and the family support act: Policy issues. Washington, DC: Foundation for Child Development Research Forum, November 9–10, unpublished.

Children's Defense Fund (1990). S.O.S. America: A children's defense budget. Washington, DC: Author.

Clark, H. (1982). The Supreme Court faces the family. Children Today, 11(6), 18–22.

Consortium of Family Organizations Family Policy Report (1992). The child care and development block grant program: A family impact assessment, 2(1) 1–10. Washington, DC: Author.

Davis, L.V., & Hagen, J. L. (1992). The problem of wife abuse: The interrelatinship of social policy and social work practice. Social Work, 37(1), 15–20.

Ehrenreich, B. (1988). The family is not an ideal slogan for the left. The Democratic Left, 16(3), 7.

Employers winning right to cut back medical insurance. (1992, March 29). The New York Times, p. 1.

Garfinkel, I., & McLanahan, S. S. (1986). Single mothers and their children. Washington, DC: Urban Institute.

Greenstein, R. (1989). Increased poverty and growing inequality: What the 101st Congress can do. Washington, DC: Center on Budget and Policy Priorities.

Greenstein, R., & Leonard, P. (1990). The Bush administration budget: Rhetoric and reality. Washington, DC: Center on Budget and Policy Priorities.

Griscom, J. L. (1992). The case of Sharon Kowalski and Karen Thompson: Ableism, heterosexism, and sexism. In P.S. Rothenberg (Ed.), Race, class and gender in the United States: An integrated study. New York: St. Martin's Press.

Griswold v. Connecticut. (1965). 381 U.S. 479, 486.

Hagen, J. (1992). Women, work, and welfare: Is there a role for social work? Social Work, 37(1), 9–14.

Harris v. McRae. (1980). 448 U.S. 297.

Hayghe, H. V. (1990). Family members in the work force. Monthly Labor Review, 113, 14–19.

H.L. v. Matheson. (1981). 450 U.S. 398.

Jansson, B. S. (1988). The reluctant welfare state. Belmont, CA: Wadsworth.

Kohlert, N. (1989). Welfare reform: An historic consensus. Social Work, 34(4), 303–306.

Lalli v. Lalli. (1978). 439 U.S. 259.

Lambda. (1991a). Access to health care: A Lambda priority. Lambda Update, 8(2), 1–27.

Lambda. (1991b). Docket update. Lambda Update, 8(2), 10–19.

Lambda. (1991c). Gay teachers association v. New York Board of Education. Lambda Update. 8(2), 5.

Lambda. (1992). Domestic partnership: Issues and legislation. New York: Lambda Legal Defense and Education Fund, Inc.

Levitan, S. A., & Gallo, F. (1990). Work and family: The impact of legislation. Monthly Labor Review, 113, 34–40.

Levitan, S., & Johnson, C. (1984). *Beyond the safety net: Reviving the promise of opportunity in America.* Cambridge, MA: Ballinger.

Levy v. Louisiana. (1968). 391 U.S. 68.

Miller, D. (1989). Poor women and work programs: Back to the future. *Affilia, 4*(1), 9–22.

Miller, D. D. (1990). *Women and social welfare: A feminist analysis.* New York: Praeger.

Mohr, J. (1978). *Abortion in America: The origins and evolution of national policy, 1800–1900.* New York: Oxford University Press.

Moroney, R. (1980). *Families, social services, and social policy: The issue of shared responsibility.* Rockville, MD: National Institute of Mental Health.

Moynihan, D. P. (1990). Toward a post industrial social policy. *Families in Society, 71*(1).

National Association of Social Workers. (1991). *NASW health care fact sheet.* Silver Spring, MD: Author.

Nichols-Casebolt, A. M., & McClure, J. (1989). Social work support for welfare reform, the latest surrender in the war on poverty. *Social Work, 34*(1), 77–80.

Ortiz, E. T., & Bassoff, B. (1987). Military taps, emerging military family service roles for social workers. *Employee Assistance Quarterly, 2*(3), 55–66.

Passell, P. (1989). Forces in society and Reaganism help dig deeper hole for the poor. *New York Times,* July 16, p. A1.

Phillips, K. (1990). *The politics of the rich and the poor.* New York: Random House.

Piven, F. F., & Cloward, R. (1971). *Regulating the poor: The functions of public welfare.* New York: Pantheon.

Poverny, L. M., & Finch, W. A., Jr. (1988, February). Gay and lesbian domestic partnerships: Expanding the definition of the family. *Social Casework, 69* (2), 116–121.

Roe v. Wade. (1973). 410 U.S. 113, 153.

Rust v. Sullivan. (1991). 500 U.S. 114L. Ed 2nd 233, 111 SCT.

Schroeder, P. (1989). Toward a National Family Policy. *American Psychologist,* November, 1410–1413.

Silverman, E. (1992). Hospital bioethics: A beginning knowledge base for the neonatal social worker. *Social Work, 37,* 150–154.

Stoesz, D., & Karger, H. (1990). Welfare reform: From illusion to reality. *Social Work, 35,* 141–147.

Wiatrowski, W. J. (1990). Family related benefits in the workplace. *Monthly Labor Review, 113,* 28–33.

Wilson, W. J. (1989). *The truly disadvantaged: The inner city, the underclass and public policy.* Chicago: University of Chicago Press.

INDEX